Acclaim for Tony Blair's

A JOURNEY

"A political biography of unusual interest. . . . Blair is one of the great politicians of this generation and that makes his candid moments particularly interesting."   —*The Philadelphia Inquirer*

"Well-written and perhaps unintentionally self-revealing. . . . Blair reveals himself through his thrusting political ambition, his rationales for decisions, his preoccupation with public image and his determination to play a prominent role on the world stage." —*The Washington Post Book World*

"Fluently written. . . . Engaging."
    —Michiko Kakutani, *The New York Times*

"Absorbing. . . . Surprisingly candid. . . . A political argument about how to win elections and make social progress." —*The Independent* (London)

"That Blair was a formidable politician can be seen in the glimpses we get of how his mind works. . . . You are left thinking two things: that it would be a blessing if some of today's politicians took note . . . and that, whatever your view of Blair, you still wouldn't want to take him on in an election."   —*The New Yorker*

"Impressive. . . . Intellectually and emotionally engaging. . . . Blair writes well, practices transparency, and on almost every page explains his decisions in detail."   —*The Christian Science Monitor*

"Unique. . . . A political biography of unusual interest."
    —*Los Angeles Times*

"Unusually direct. . . . He is compellingly candid about how scared he was when he first became prime minister." —*The Guardian* (London)

"Compelling. . . . Candid and comprehensive."   —*Tulsa World*

"Blair comes across as likable, if manipulative; capable of dissembling while wonderfully fluent; in short, a brilliant modern politician."
    —*The Boston Globe*

TONY BLAIR
A JOURNEY

Tony Blair became an MP in 1983, leader of the Labour Party in 1994, and was prime minister of the United Kingdom from May 1997 to June 2007. Since leaving office, he has served as the Quartet Representative to the Middle East, representing the U.S., the UN, Russia, and the EU in working with the Palestinians to prepare for statehood as part of the international community's effort to secure peace. In May 2008 he launched the Tony Blair Faith Foundation, which promotes respect and understanding among the major religions. His Africa Governance Initiative works with leaders and their governments on policy delivery and attracting sustainable investment in Rwanda, Sierra Leone, and Liberia. He also works with world leaders to build consensus on an international climate-policy framework.

A JOURNEY

TONY BLAIR

A JOURNEY

My Political Life

VINTAGE BOOKS

A DIVISION OF RANDOM HOUSE, INC.

NEW YORK

The Library of Congress has cataloged the Knopf edition as follows:
Blair, Tony.
A journey: my political life / Tony Blair.—1st ed.
p.   cm.
Includes bibliographical references and index.
1. Blair, Tony.   2. Great Britain—Politics and government—1997–2007.
3. Great Britain—Foreign relations—1997–   4. Prime ministers—Great
Britain—Biography.   5. Labour Party (Great Britain)—Biography.   I. Title.
DA591.B56A3   2010
941.085'9092—dc22
2010028262

Vintage ISBN: 978-0-307-39063-9

www.vintagebooks.com

Printed in the United States of America
10 9 8 7 6 5 4 3 2

To Cherie, Euan, Nicholas, Kathryn and Leo
and my wider family who have shared the journey with me

CONTENTS

ACKNOWLEDGEMENTS

When it was first suggested that I write this book, Bob Barnett, lawyer, friend and negotiator extraordinaire, expertly steered the negotiations that brought me to Random House. It has been a happy partnership ever since. I would like in particular to thank Gail Rebuck, a long-time friend and also, I can now add with pride, my publisher. Gail's passion for this project, and her faith that she would one day receive a completed manuscript, despite indications to the contrary, never wavered.

I would like to pay tribute to the calm professionalism of her team at Random House. My foremost editorial thanks go to Caroline Gascoigne and David Milner, who have lived with this book almost as long as I have and who have been wonderful throughout. Thanks are also due to Susan Sandon, Charlotte Bush and Claire Round; John Swannell for the photo-shoot that produced the front cover; Richard Ogle for the cover design; Fiona Greenway for the picture research; and the rest of the dedicated production team.

In the U.S., Sonny Mehta and Jonathan Segal of Knopf have been enthusiasts for this project from the start—I have found their guidance and advice to be invaluable.

Among my own team it would have been impossible without Catherine Rimmer and Victoria Gould standing over me as I wrote out each word on hundreds of notepads, refusing all phone calls, meetings and other welcome distractions from the creative process. As the publisher's deadline approached, they even took my BlackBerry away from me. My researcher, Anthony Measures, provided facts and research material and tirelessly trawled through thousands of documents. I am grateful to my band of armchair book critics for their insights and editorial advice: Andrew Adonis, David Bradshaw, Alastair Campbell, Matthew Doyle, Peter Hyman, Philip Gould and Jonathan Powell.

There are countless people from my life in politics without whom this journey would never have begun: my agent in Sedgefield, John Burton; his wife, Lily, and the members of the Sedgefield Labour Party, who put their faith in me right back at the beginning and whose loyalty has been steadfast ever since. I owe a huge debt of gratitude to my staff in the early years as Leader of the Opposition and then those in Downing Street; you could never wish for a more loyal and professional group of people—many of whom are mentioned in the book. Of course this book is dedicated to my family. So that tells its own story.

Finally, I would like to thank the people who now work for me in the new chapter of my journey since leaving Downing Street. I am constantly impressed by the enthusiasm and commitment they bring to helping solve some of the issues in the world today, on which I try to work: a greater understanding between the religious faiths; peace in the Middle East; solutions to climate change; and governance in Africa. They know who they are and they should be immensely proud of the work they do.

INTRODUCTION TO THE VINTAGE EDITION

It's almost a year since the hardcover edition of this book was published. So much has happened, not least in the region where I spend so much time—the Middle East. Following the financial crisis, there have also been developments in Europe and the U.S. that merit comment.

This introduction plainly connects to the last chapter of the book, but here I develop an argument only touched on there: the traditional left/right divide of Western politics still dominates much of our political discourse, yet it is an essentially twentieth-century construct that is now not only increasingly redundant, it is an obstruction to new ideas and sound policy.

This is not to say that ideals or values no longer matter—they matter hugely, and the progressive/conservative divide (a more modern version of left/right) still has relevance. What is more, that divide offers a big opportunity for progressive politics since the spirit of the times is meritocratic and modernising. Yet such labels have to be treated with caution. I remain unequivocally on the progressive side of politics, but I am fiscally more conservative, and on markets, liberal. Many conservatives are today socially liberal, in favour of gay rights and passionate advocates of women's equality. A foreign policy of liberal interventionism has its detractors and supporters in both camps.

When it comes to policy, the challenge today is efficacy, not ideology. People want government that works, that is above all effective in making change. To achieve this, governments have to liberate themselves from ideology based on left/right and embrace new ways of thinking that cross the traditional party lines. In pursuit of this objective, I argue that a more relevant political divide for the twenty-first century is "open vs. closed". It defines attitudes to globalisation; to culture and identity; and to change. The open-minded see globalisation as an opportunity; the closed-minded as a threat, a process driven by greed and big business, in which we are helpless pawns. The open-minded are accepting of those of different faiths and cultures; the closed-minded regard them as alien and corrupting. Above all, the open-minded embrace new ideas and change, seeing the potential for advancement; the closed-minded tend to defend the status quo. This divide zigzags across traditional politics. You find those who call themselves progressives and conservatives on both sides of the debates about immigration, free trade and energy, for example.

The twenty-first century will belong to those who by instinct and education are open to the world as it changes, and are prepared to modernise and think anew. This open-minded attitude is not just about the way we view the world; it is intrinsic to whether the West regains its sense of self-confidence and self-belief. There is, at present, and for reasons that are completely comprehensible, an acute pessimism in the West. Any young graduate seeking work can tell you how tough it is. For those without qualifications, jobs are often low paid or highly insecure. Add to this alarm over extremism, anger at what appears to be uncontrolled immigration, and the gathering sense that new powers, notably China, are emerging to take our place, and it is easy to see why this pessimism is so rampant.

It is, however, misguided and unnecessary. We have been through tough times before—actually much tougher—and survived and prospered. It's true new powers are emerging. But ask the immigrants why they prefer our way of life. If these new powers succeed, it will be at least as much by emulation as by difference.

For example, I believe that this century will see Africans seize their destiny in their own hands and triumph over their adversities. The world needs what they have to offer in raw materials, commodities and agriculture. There is a new generation of smart, capable leaders coming to the fore, but whether and how fast they succeed will depend to a significant extent on the degree to which they take the best lessons of governance from us and apply them. They still look to us, and rightly so. And the Middle East? It turns out they do want democracy.

Above all, we are the birthplace of the open-minded. We were the leaders in ideas; and to a large extent we still are. We were the creative ones, the innovators, the radical reformers of the status quo, not just in economics, governance, social progress but in thought, and other disciplines whose ideas define the future. Our problem is not our situation but ourselves. Do we still want to lead the world? Do we still want to be led by leaders capable of harnessing that innate power of creativity?

The world needs our leadership for a very simple reason: while our values may have been nurtured in the West, their appeal and their ownership is vested in humanity. Liberty, justice, the people above the government not the government above the people: these are the values we forged over centuries and they represent the steadfast evolution of human progress.

At present we have this curious jumble of paradoxes and contradictions: the world needs our leadership but we are fearful of leading; our politics is organised according to distinctions of left vs. right that, in their most crude form, the people have long since moved on from; and though the future belongs to the optimistic and open-minded, we are in danger of being defeatist and closed-minded.

What should leaders do? When people ask me about leadership, I can talk about character, temperament and attitude, about "doing the right thing" and having "the right stuff", all of which is important. But sometimes I think that the hardest thing is getting the right answer. This is harder still in an era of uniquely low predictability.

The oddest yet most interesting thing about being an ex-leader is how much I did not know when I was a leader, how much there is to learn about the world and how endlessly fascinating are the processes of change going on within it. I've been to the Middle East twelve times in the last few months and over sixty times since leaving office. I travel regularly to China and of course to the U.S. I have seen for myself that the U.S. is more than New York and Washington, as China is more than Beijing and Shanghai. I've learned about Indonesia and Malaysia, and started to know Mexico, Brazil and Colombia, countries I had barely visited before. I also spend time in Africa.

The relief from the day-to-day pressure of office has given me space to analyse. The memory of what it was really like to lead means that I retain real respect for those who assume the mantle of leadership. I know it is a lot easier to give the advice than to take the decision.

Occasionally I even wonder if I became a leader too young. Of course, nowadays we tend to like our leaders younger. They look better, seem more dynamic, have a positive energy that stimulates in the electorate a positive glow; but in my case judgement and experience have deepened with age. In a curious way, as a younger leader I was better able to articulate the bright, new horizon; but as a more mature leader I was better able to get there. (Though being now two years off sixty as I write this, I suppose I would say that.)

I now feel a huge pulse of urgency about our situation. This is not simply the onset of age or the musings of a global wanderer—indeed I have never felt more adrenalin or energy—it is that the key to our success today is to analyse, understand, and then be part of the way the world is changing. When times are hard, the inclination is to be introspective. But it is in the nature of these times that in order to advance, we have to be global.

The chief characteristic of today's world is the speed of change, driven by technology. When I was growing up, technological advance was often to do with how we made things. It was about how we travelled—by car or plane—and then about how we got the news. In the 1960s and 1970s, we had very standard ways of getting information. There were major news channels that everyone shared. The choices we could make were limited by the technology, and we depended on government for a range of decisions only they could make.

The Internet has changed that world. We have the power in our own hands to communicate, interact and obtain information. The result is transformative. We don't just work differently, we live and think differently. There is the instantaneous transmission not only of news, but of thoughts, moods, opinions and sentiment.

The world is ever more interdependent. OK, that's a cliché now, but what isn't grasped are the consequences of it. Take the financial crisis— significant for many reasons, but perhaps most importantly as the most dramatic demonstration of what it means to live in a truly interdependent global financial market. Those countries most deeply wired into that global market suffered for it. Those who avoided it—very few— could do so both because their banks were far more tightly controlled but also because they lagged behind the rest of the world in financial innovation (characteristics which themselves bring a separate raft of problems associated with them). And crisis did not spread simply as a result of rational analysis, by market participants, of failing financial products; rather, market sentiment gathered pace and rolled into tidal waves of panic, shifting perceptions of both the financial system as well as individual nations' economic stability.

This linkage isn't only financial. Political, cultural and social ideas are also communicated in real time and have global reach and power. The uprisings in the Middle East are partly the product of the new social media's ability to pass information within a country; but also the global reaction to events bouncing back into the national political debate, fuelling and shaping it. All of this is accelerating the pace of change. Leaders are taking decisions against a background of uncertainty and change that both constantly alter that background and constrain enormously what any one country on its own can do to manage the consequences.

Added to all this is the rise of China, and India, and others not far behind. The most elusive thing in any discussion of China is to get your head round its size. We know it's big, has 1.3 billion people, and is now a power; but none of that conveys adequately the immensity of its impact on us. If you shut down the whole of the UK—the fifth largest economy in the world—so that it emitted no greenhouse gas emissions whatsoever, the rise in emissions from the Chinese economy would make up the difference in under two years. We debate, rightly, the third runway at Heathrow, on environmental grounds; China will build seventy new international airports in the next decade. By 2030 there will be 300 commercial airports. The USA has nine, maybe ten cities with a population of over a million, while the EU has around twenty; China has over 160. Think how different Finland is from Greece, or even Germany and Italy, the British and the Spanish. In Western Europe there are great differences of culture, ethnicity and habits. Now think of that multiplied by three. Think of sixty different Chinese ethnic groupings. Think of hundreds of millions of Chinese industrialised in the last twenty years which has produced China's transformation economically and politically. Then think of the same again in the next twenty. You start to get some idea of the scale, complexity and depth of change that China's development is going to bring. Not a single aspect of our lives will be untouched by it. From the environment, to the production of cheap consumer goods we take for granted, to the way the world's commodities are mined and used, China's rise will transform our lives.

India's population is 1.2 billion and rising. Indonesia has three times the number of people as Germany. Brazil and Russia are going to be giants of the world economy. All these nations face serious challenges, of course, but the trend is unmistakable and irreversible: the geopolitics of the twenty-first century will be unlike anything the modern world has seen. Our children in the West will be a generation growing up in a situation where virtually every fixed point of reference that my and my parents' generation knew has changed or is changing. Included in these fixed points of reference is traditional politics—and that is why leadership is so tough.

Of course there are voters who remain absolutely committed to traditional left/right politics—often they make most noise—but there is a swelling crowd of people who don't conform to such politics and who can determine elections. One group are those who focus as much on "cultural" questions as normal left/right politics. The Tea Party in the U.S. is a reaction to what they perceive as the dominance of a liberal elite. In Europe, you have the far right parties like that of Le Pen in France, or the new parties that have popped up in countries such as Sweden, Holland and Finland that we used to think of as having very predictable politics. But the other group are a large, somewhat disenfranchised group of centrist voters who just distrust the simplicity of the left/right labels.

Let us try for a moment to disentangle this. At one level, given the debates in the U.S. such as the programme of cuts in Wisconsin, or in the UK about tuition fees for students, you might think it bizarre to claim left/right battles a thing of the past. Surely these are just that: left vs. right and very much with us. But that is an illusion. That is to focus on the surface noise. Look deeper and actually what has happened in this past half-century is that the left/right distinctions have become blurred. It would be too simplistic to say the left has won the battle over values and the right has won the battle over policy direction, but it is a little like that.

When I was growing up, social justice was a value of the left. Today, conservatives as well as progressives will lay claim to fairness. The argument is over who has the best policy to achieve it. Both groups say they represent "regular" people or "hard-working" families; both identify with enhanced opportunity and social mobility; both are against "elites". The patrician Republican or Tory is in short supply and even shorter demand. Where the right are more traditionally "right" on values—abortion, gay rights, etc.—this tends to be at the base, not amongst voters.

However, on policy, we are in the course of a long steady march to a rebalancing of individual responsibility and choice with the power of the state—on taxes, welfare and public services. At first this was driven by the costs of the state, the widening of the tax base and the sense of the state taking up too much ground. Now there is a fresh driver: a desire to exercise much greater choice and individual preference—the norm in private-sector transactions—in the public sector. And all of it, of course, enhanced by the potential of technology.

What is interesting is how little this march has been arrested by the financial crisis. In 2008, it was commonly believed that the left would gain from a mess thought not just to be "of the market" but begotten by unrestricted market practices. The state was said to be back in fashion. If it was, the fashion quickly passed. European elections and the U.S. midterms saw, if anything, a move rightwards. Even the conservative leaders in Europe today tend to be under threat from parties more to the right or on non-traditional platforms rather than from the conventional left.

Here is the point of fascination: many people voting this way don't regard themselves as going "right" on these issues. They don't view it in partisan terms. They view it practically.

This is not to say that because ideology is discredited, politics has become a game of realpolitik, everything traded and bartered and bargained in a never-ending street haggle. There's an enormous appetite for ideas and ideals. Neither does it mean that people don't want big change. They do. They know they need it and they will vote for it. It's just that they won't buy it from someone who they regard as ideologically motivated. They will pick and choose policy options. They will not conform to neat twentieth-century distinctions because experience has taught them to be wary of such things. None of this means they think small—indeed their irritation with much of what passes for political campaigning is precisely because they believe the thinking is not big enough or broad enough to change lives. They are radical, not ideological. You can call this the radical centre, though that doesn't properly describe it. Such a radicalism is not positioned between traditional left/right but above it.

And here is a strange paradox. The real challenge for leaders is how to change their countries, yet first they have to persuade their own party base, since party organisations have the ability to determine the contenders for leadership; and though the people distrust ideologically driven politics, party activists are even more wedded to them. The party battle then turns into a series of set-piece staged fights, a bit like re-enactments of English or American civil wars. What comes out of it is a form of transactional politics in which the risk is that even if you start with the right answer, it's slowly whittled away into mush. Meanwhile, in the real world, this unstoppable force of change is beating down upon us, demanding something transformative in order to cope with it.

Democracy is supported for two reasons (and by the way supported the world over—no nation that is a democracy has ever chosen willingly to surrender it, and no two democracies have ever gone to war): the first is justice—it is the fairest way to choose a government; the second has been efficiency. Dictatorships, at least over time, tend to inefficiency, corruption and repression.

The challenge of modern democracy is efficacy. Not accountability, transparency or whether it is honest or not, but whether it works to deliver effective change in times that need that radical change. It is here that our traditions weigh us down. We have inherited very binary, polar two-party politics or, even where there are more than two parties, very stratified veins of left and right. What's more, our systems were designed when politics was a "later in life" mission; it is now a career that often starts shortly after university and progresses through a series of political posts until the summit is reached. Checks and balances are there for very good reasons in most constitutional democracies; but in the modern world they often lead not to consensus for change but to sclerosis or minimal change. Above all, over a period of years since the war as the state has grown and public services and welfare systems have developed, there is a vast network of special interests that have every incentive to defend the status quo vigorously, and virtually none to alter it or even adjust it.

Some of these state systems are extraordinarily complex. Reforming them is intellectually, as well as politically, profoundly challenging. To get that right requires great effort and space—political space in which things can be thoroughly explored, iterated and reiterated. The answers matter. They have effects that don't just run into billions of pounds or dollars or euros but affect lives. But without care, even the act of intellectual inquiry is itself demonised.

Politicians—especially when trying to reform complicated systems built up over decades that employ thousands and impact upon millions—require the brains of the best talents. It should be a national enterprise driven by a shared sense of purpose. Creating the means of achieving this is near to impossible the way we do politics right now. Outsiders come in usually from a genuine sense of patriotic endeavour. Their motives are rubbished, their backgrounds scrutinised to the point of obloquy and pretty soon they wonder why on earth they ever got mixed up in it all.

The gene pool going into politics is now frighteningly limited. This is not because there is a reduced desire for public service. It is that too many smart people no longer see it as public service—they're wrong in that, by the way, but that's how a lot of people who otherwise might well be tempted, resist the temptation.

The way modern parliaments work has also changed. I don't mean in terms of procedures and so on—they are all too familiar—but in terms of how they function in practical ways. Very few listen to parliamentary debates any more. Press releases matter more than considered speeches. Getting re-elected, fund-raising, building networks of supporters, can be almost a full-time occupation today. In other words, the time for the real job—which, just to recall, is participating as an elected national political leader in national debates—comes a poor second to the business of staying there.

The way our democracies work in the early twenty-first century is virtually a conspiracy against rational decision-making. In times when the political system needs to roll along because we're doing fine and, frankly, the less done the better—and there are such times—these flaws of modern democratic politics do not matter so much. Today they do.

Now, in saying all this, I've not gone soft. I spent twenty-five years in politics. I know the game; it's competitive and occasionally brutal. It's always been like that. But here's the difference today: these are times in which we need to effect radical change. In this regard Europe and America face the same challenges. In Europe it is absolutely plain that the crisis in the eurozone has merely exposed, not originated, the need for reform. The truth is that welfare and public service systems over the years have grown up to become wholly different from the original conception. To have debates over whether to raise the retirement age by one or two years with generous pension provisions is next to absurd. Life expectancy has dramatically altered, while the birth rate is lower. You simply can't, therefore, have smaller numbers of working-age people supporting larger numbers of the retired. Public services that, when first created, were basic services, which were a momentous advance for a generation that had nothing, are never going to satisfy a generation that in the rest of its life has a vast array of choices, preferences, individualised service and custom, and will expect and demand the same from state services for which they pay their taxes.

I follow the debate about the U.S. deficit with a degree of bewilderment, as befits the foreigner. Some say: isn't it a trifle weird to have such a fierce debate about $30 billion vs. $60 billion vs. $100 billion of cuts to discretionary spending, when the issue is a trillion-dollar budget deficit?

This concern has increased with the ratings agencies now suggesting that the AAA rating of U.S. debt is at risk of downgrade. The European Stability Framework has now been announced, reannounced and again reannounced. On each occasion, the time lag between initial relief and then later disappointment is getting shorter. That is because people know—and in this case, at least, the markets are not behaving irrationally—that the social and economic systems in Europe need fundamental reform and the euro needs an alignment of fiscal and monetary policy.

So I believe there is a systemic political challenge that is about how we mature and modernise our democracies to include not just the form of democracy—voting for the governments—but the substance underpinning it. In a world that is transforming, we cannot govern ourselves with transactional politics, otherwise we will find our Western leadership position not merely assailed—as in a sense it is bound to be—but corroded to the point where the twenty-first century happens on someone else's terms.

This is where we need to rise above partisan politics—which is not as quixotic as it may sound. Look at certain currents in politics right now and you can see a genuine new politics straining at the leash: New Labour, the new Democrats of President Clinton's time and the movement that brought President Obama to power, all consciously reached out beyond their traditional base; there is the coalition government in the UK, and perhaps more interesting the involvement of former Labour ministers in making long-term government policy; President Sarkozy's inclusion of Socialist Party members in his government; the bipartisan efforts of Simpson–Bowles and the six senators on the U.S. deficit. Where political leaders deliberately go outside their own political base, they almost always win public approval. The very fact of overtly embracing bipartisanship would itself create confidence economically as well as politically. It would give people the sense that politics was rising to the challenge.

This is not about enforced coalition through electoral arithmetic. It has, of course, to be a genuine coalition of ideas and open-minded people. The problem with the coalition government in the UK, is the coalition. It is, when you really analyse it, a coalition of people and party organisations born of necessity, not a coalescence of ideas. The most imaginative policy from non-Tory sources has not come from the Liberal Democrats, but from the former Labour (usually New Labour) ministers I mentioned above.

I am talking about an approach that avows a different way of doing politics by preference. Take the debate over the role of government. There is a perfectly sensible case for reshaping and reinventing government today to make it more effective; to take it out of areas of delivery and execution better done by others; to reduce its cost; to make it an agent of strategic change rather than the type of heavy hierarchical structure of the "one size fits all" state of the past. There are a thousand efficiencies anyone used to dealing with private sector reorganisation could make in any government department or service you care to mention.

Putting this argument in terms of some piece of zealotry that assumes the very notion of government is at best a necessary evil, distracts from the core reason for reform: making government work better for people. This then motivates those on the other side of the spectrum to launch their own ideological "crusade" to prevent any such change happening. So parts of the right end up arguing that the state as a concept is wrong; and on parts of the left that even if it's not working effectively, the state has to be defended. The casualty is common sense.

Now, personally, I see changing this politics as very much consistent with the finest traditions of progressive politics. I am still, as the book shows, an ardent advocate of third-way politics. I believe in community, in a society that shares purpose and values and is cohesive, rather than simply a collection of individuals and families striving and struggling on their own. A belief in social justice brought me into politics, and it is still what motivates me. In terms of ends, objectives and values, progressive politics should be well placed to lead this new approach to modern democracy, precisely because its roots are in popular movements of change and progress.

However, I am a third-way progressive because I have always thought that these ideals have been diminished by a refusal to distinguish between values as principles and values applied in the practical world. Values as principles are timeless. Their practical application is very much time-bound; and therefore as times change, so should policy. Instead, progressives have often clung to particular concepts of the state, government, and collective institutions like trade unions whose radical reform has been long since demanded by changing times. Failure to appreciate this is why voters in Europe are preferring conservative governments to make the changes, even though they often distrust their values. Face people with a choice between traditional left and traditional right and there is a traditional outcome: the left loses.

I am impatient with much of progressive politics when it fails to see that values are dynamic; that they guide you as to the why and the where, but not as to the how. How you do it is today's challenge, and that depends on the way the world is now, which is different from how it used to be in a multitude of ways. If we were to apply this approach to the key challenges facing us, what would the correct policies be? I would identify five such challenges:

Reform of Government
Reform of the Economy
Foreign Policy and the Transatlantic Alliance
The Middle East and North Africa
Energy

Reform of Government

This is in two parts: altering the way government works internally; and changing its services, some of which, of course, are delivered at a state or regional level. As for government itself, it should be smaller, more strategic and more focused on policy. I found in office there was a real dearth not of conventional policy advice—we excelled in that—but of new thinking, radical policy ideas. Take the way a large company works today and compare it to a government department. In the company there would be a continuous reassessment, from first principles, of what the company is trying to do and how it is doing it. In particular there would be a relentless focus on system improvement through use of technology; perpetual analysis of the customer base and how its habits and wishes were changing; and a comparative study of what the competition is up to.

Government doesn't much function like that. For example, there is very little work by government—as opposed to think tank—on how other governments have created change, on what the empirical evidence is for certain policies. In Downing Street, I formed a Delivery Unit, Policy Unit and Strategy Unit, staffed largely by outsiders and charged specifically with trying to learn the lessons of change: how others had tried to effect it; to think new thoughts about systemic change; and to distinguish between day-to-day policy management and radical long-term policy. In departments, such an infrastructure was largely absent, yet there were hordes of people dedicated to monitoring and managing and issuing guidelines. Where there were research capabilities, they worked in very conventional ways and rarely did they come up with practical methods of delivering effective results as opposed to sociological essays that had limited value.

What should happen, therefore, is an attempt to create a genuine consensus around long-term reform of the way government works in order, radically, to realign government with the modern world.

In public services and welfare, the changes are much harder to make, since they touch not just entrenched interests but people's lives. Change will therefore necessarily only happen over time. But, again, round the world certain lessons are obvious. Any welfare system that encourages people to be welfare recipients is constructed contrary to purpose. It is better to spend money on equipping people to retrain and find work, than on benefits. The retirement age has to be raised in line with the age to which people are living. Over time, we have to rebalance what the general taxpayer, through the state, contributes to pension provision and how people provide for themselves; and the regulation of the latter has to be sensible and not so burdensome that the costs make it prohibitive for middle-class people.

In social exclusion and help targeted at those at the very bottom of society, we have to be prepared to intervene radically and early. One of the greatest mistakes of social policy is to treat "the poor" or "the disadvantaged" as one homogeneous grouping. They are not. There is all the difference in the world between a family that is poor but functioning as a family, where the child and the parents with the right education and opportunities (to which I shall come) can succeed; and the family that is dysfunctional, where the parent/s has/have drug, alcohol or behavioural problems. No amount of opportunity will offer them a way out until the dysfunction is tackled head-on. Even in the worst neighbourhoods, my experience was that the majority were law-abiding and decent. They were, however, regularly overwhelmed by a small number of totally dysfunctional families operating outside of society's mainstream. They are a special case. They need treating as one. Conventional social work or social policy is utterly hopeless in dealing with them. We can spend billions as a result with little progress.

So, towards the end of my time in government, we began to utilise methods for dealing with severely dysfunctional families that meant a considerable degree of contact and intervention at an early stage. Again, conventional policy will tell you little can be done, except by way of traditional social work, until a crime is committed or abuse is discovered, for example. Yet we know very early which families are at risk. It is very early that intervention is necessary. Or take the inefficiency of adoption laws where there is a long, drawn-out process, full of rules and restrictions, not all of which make sense, while we leave children in the care of parents who will not look after them. The point is we have to conduct the policy inquiry from first principles, not within a system that is itself at fault.

Which brings me to an obsession I had before government and during my time as prime minister: law and order. I remain militant on the subject. This is far more than the usual debate about whether prison "works"—of course it does at one level, since it gets the offenders off the streets—but at another, as rehabilitation figures show, it isn't the answer. I introduced a series of measures as prime minister on organised crime, seizure of assets and antisocial behaviour. All of them altered the normal rules of the criminal justice system, but we needed to go much further. I still think we fail completely to understand the link between crime, especially organised crime, social deprivation and opportunity. Give people a law-abiding environment and a good education, and a large part of the benefit system would become irrelevant.

Again, the point is that the criminal justice and welfare systems have grown up unchanged in a world light years away from the social setting in which they were originally conceived. The question is therefore less a right vs. left one. It is rather: given how society has changed, how do we reorder the systems so that they accomplish their original goals of creating law-abiding communities and providing opportunity to those without it?

Health care would need its own book. Having studied different systems and different attempts to reform them, I have to say one thing at the outset: no system provides the answer and all systems are under strain. However, I would say two things stand out.

First, the benefit of a universal, taxpayer-funded system is access; the benefit of a privately funded system is quality of service and adaptability to the patient's wishes. The question is: can you devise a system that combines the two? In any universal system, the key to change is to introduce centres of competition, to give patient choice and to have measures of accountability that are transparent, with information freely available. Whatever process of commissioning is used, it will only work effectively if patients have power and providers are diverse. This is the only way also to encourage the system to self-reform, which is vital in circumstances where medical technology is routinely changing the nature and extent of treatment and care and also changing the best place to get care which, increasingly, will be in a primary health-care setting. Indeed, I would say the same of mainly privately funded systems: the more competition the better. You need to deal with soaring legal costs. And where, for reasons of access and equity, the state subsidises the health care of the needy, try in so far as is possible not to push their health care into a different system. Rather, help them to be part of the private system everyone else uses.

The other point is to recognise that no country can afford its health-care system without the active participation of its citizens. People know more today, learn about their conditions, self-diagnose, can manage their own conditions and want to do so. We all need to look after ourselves better: eat well, exercise, drink responsibly, don't smoke. There has to be a huge move towards prevention, which needs to become part of how we live. In the book I examine these policy issues in detail by reference to my own travails as prime minister, so necessarily here I am just making general health policy points; but the one large point is: the right answer does not begin with conventional left/right politics, whether in regard to health care or anything else.

Actually, it often starts in school.

Reform of the Economy

Which is also where a sensible long-term economic policy begins. But before that, let me turn to a more immediate economic discussion. I develop this in detail in the last chapter. In summary, the danger, as I see it, is as follows.

The financial crisis is bound to change economic policy. The danger is it regresses it. At the moment, Western policymakers are in this bind. The deficit is bad because it saps confidence in the economy, but cutting the deficit too fast may risk cutting growth, thereby making the deficit worse (since, as government swiftly educates you, the biggest swings in the surplus or deficit of government spending come from levels of growth). Higher interest rates also limit growth since they raise the cost of borrowing, yet rates that are too low may cause inflation. So the macro picture is confused. The key starting point here, though, is to make these judgements those of right vs. wrong, not right vs. left.

Debating whether Keynesian economics should be revived or not is simply distracting. It is clear that we need credible plans for deficit reduction. It is obvious these will only happen over time. Given the propensity of government to spend, a judgement can be made and adjusted over the course of the plan, as can the management of interest rates.

The decisions that will contribute hugely to the success of the macro strategy, however, will be on the micro side, i.e. on tax, spending, regulation, the general business environment, and, above all, jobs. Here the policymakers are in a different sort of bind. The conventional wisdom, at least, of today's politics is that the people are anti-bankers, big business, everyone who "got us into this mess". There is also a genuine and burgeoning reaction against those who earn "too much", against elites, and to put it more fairly and rationally, against inequality, a lack of social mobility and a fear that this generation may be the first in the modern era whose children don't expect to do better than their parents.

At an emotional level I have a huge sympathy for those arguments; but, as ever, the question for the decision-maker, as opposed to the columnist, is what would make the difference, i.e. what works to change this situation? Here, unfortunately, there is a clash between the correct short-term politics and the correct long-term policy. A sensible policy would be: to be cautious on regulation since we need business, including the financial sector, to be vibrant and confident (though as I say later, we should have major reforms on global supervision and coordination); tax reform to reward work and help create jobs; and use the necessary changes in public services and welfare spending to shape the platform for future growth. Above all, education—both investment in it and reform of it—would move centre stage; and education not simply at school or university, but pre-school and in adult life.

In other words, we would use the crisis and the reinforced urgency to change as a result of it, in order to make reforms that, if we analyse our economies from first principles, we should be doing anyway. Instead, the overwhelming urge of politicians, for reasons that are completely understandable, will be to address business under the mantra "this must never happen again" (one of the most commonly used, often futile, and occasionally counterproductive slogans in politics); have more regulation; raise taxes on the wealthy; and try to protect the vulnerable by retaining as much of the existing system of support as possible in straitened times, and cutting back on capital investment in the future.

Let me single out two of these items. Both show how hard it is to make such changes; but also why they are so necessary. "Tax reform" is an easy phrase to utter because stated like that it is essentially anodyne; and as I learned in office, everyone is in favour of reform in general, just not in particular. However, the way our tax systems have evolved—with all sorts of tax breaks, loopholes, assorted special reliefs—means that we have tax systems today that we would never design this way were we able to start from scratch. This is not just a matter of logic but of experience. We have learned what is effective and what isn't. Taxes on jobs reduce jobs. High taxes on income reduce the incentive to work. Indirect taxes on consumption need to be on a rational basis. Complexity employs accountants; it doesn't produce efficiency or growth.

Most people would agree with this. The problem is that each tax break and each special relief has its own interest group. Taking away any one of them causes a mini political storm that can become a major one; but the consequence of not reforming is that we end up with taxes on business—which create the jobs—and on direct income, which limits incentives and, by the way, invariably means the very wealthy can find ways to dodge, while the comfortably off get hit. That is why the only way of doing it is to take it out of a partisan fight between right and left, construct a platform of shared national purpose, and make our system competitive in the new global economy.

The other issue is education. I came to power on a programme of "education, education, education" so I know first hand how hard it is to do it. I believe people will look back, in time, at the state of our education system and be truly appalled that a situation had been allowed to develop whereby, in a world where education defines your life chances, a good 40 to 50 per cent of our children, possibly more, had an inadequate start in life. By the end of ten years in office, we had made the first really important reforms to secondary schools in Academy and self-governing Trust schools; to universities through the introduction of tuition fees; and to early years learning through Sure Start and the "No Child Left Behind" programme. But each step was fraught with opposition and obstruction and we still have a long, long way to go. However, from the UK experience, and that of the U.S., Scandinavia and elsewhere, one thing stands out: the bigger the reforms, the better the results.

Of course we need the investment, which is why when we look at spending on benefits and spending on education, the disparity is so crushing. But it is now clear which reforms work. Schools run by bureaucracies don't; schools with an independent ethos, run by teachers in the interests of parents and pupils, do. Teachers' unions can't have a veto over policy. Where schools know parents have a choice, they improve. Discipline, respect, an environment that encourages application and hard work: these are the obvious things we want for our own children. As I always used to say when beginning an education policy debate in Downing Street: let's start as parents, not policymakers.

The lessons of reform from around the world are now definable. (I set many of them out in later parts of this book.) So we should do them.

The reason for urgency in all this is how the rest of the world will develop. This is something I see so much more clearly now since leaving office. It is fascinating to see those countries at an earlier stage of development. They begin to shape their rudimentary systems of education, health and welfare. I always say to them: learn from what we got wrong; don't assume we would do it this way if we had our time again. By and large that is how they're approaching it. As they grow, they will provide markets for us. They will also be our competitors. But one thing is for sure: we will have to be better, smarter, move up the value chain just to stay afloat, never mind ahead. That is why education is so crucial. Take manufacturing. Those who say we need modern manufacturing, that we need to make things as well as having service companies, are right; and the way to do it is through a focus on education, technology, on higher attainment in engineering, chemistry and science. It is to encourage young people to see a future in manufacturing that is not about assembly lines and blue overalls, but about creativity, ingenuity and innovation. If I had my time over again, I wouldn't be a lawyer, I would go into industry.

The point is that the way the world around us is changing means we just can't afford to stay still. We have to stride out; and our method of politics is holding us back.

Foreign Policy and the Transatlantic Alliance

If we lack confidence about our future at home, we are unlikely to project confidence about our future abroad. If I had any simple message for America and Europe right now, it would be: show strength. I understand completely why it jars to say something that sounds, in a sense, rather primitive and of course can lead to the accusation of arrogance. We have to liberate ourselves from the posture of apology. To be strong is not the same as being arrogant. Being humble is not the same as being passive.

Both America and Europe have got a certain psychological challenge right now. For the U.S. it is partly a desire to retire in order to reflect upon and deal with what appear to be significant internal issues that preoccupy the country. That is why there was no rush to be involved in Libya. Also, the years after 9/11 have taken their toll on the lives of brave and committed servicemen and women, in emotional wear and tear, and also financially. These have been tough years, made tougher by a feeling that despite acting for what America perceived to be the best of motives, American action was disputed, even scorned, and America's reputation was said to have suffered. It is dispiriting to fight the good fight and yet be excoriated for fighting it. This is why the action President Obama authorised, which resulted in the death of Osama bin Laden, is so hugely significant. It shows that, no matter how long it takes, those who kill the innocent in deliberate acts of terrorism will eventually face justice. It showed strength. It showed staying power. It was assertively but not arrogantly executed. This could be a turning point.

I go into all the different policy details and conundrums of America's position in the book. I want to debate here the psychology. One thing I learned in politics is that although it would be great if the crises came sequentially, unfortunately they don't. It would be good if we could deal with the financial crisis in an otherwise calm world; and then having dealt with that, turn our attention to foreign affairs as those waters become choppy, but that's not what happens. They come on their own timetable with their own agenda. And at this moment, the world is a very dangerous place.

Secondly, there is a real risk that a perceived conventional wisdom amongst a certain intellectual elite becomes a policy. Here's the surprising thing: much of the world wants America to be strong, and those that don't, want it weak for bad reasons. An assertive America causes people all sorts of problems, makes them uncomfortable, forces them to do things they would rather not, and can even make them fearful; so does an unassertive America. Take that strong hand off the tiller and, sure, the risk of getting seasick as the vessel carves through the water is reduced; but the risk of drift arrives very quickly and is infinitely more alarming. That is why the action against bin Laden was celebrated even in many parts of the Middle East.

The important thing to realise is that this is not just about the assertion of power but of values. At its best, the U.S. doesn't just stand for liberty, but also for justice, for a world in which people are not only free but equal. How the world develops, with new centres of global power arising and huge challenges of cultural as well as political ideology confronting us, will depend dramatically and fundamentally on how willing America is to stand up for those values.

For Europe, the challenge is strength. This challenge is simple, unadorned, obvious, and desperately insistent. As a result of its economic woes, Europe finds it hard at this moment to act with coherence and strength. Yet the most frustrating thing is not the size of the challenge, but the size of the opportunity. America needs Europe as its partner. The transatlantic alliance is more relevant today, not less. The rise of new powers with different traditions and, more important, different systems of government, means that Europe and America should stand strong together in order to shape the world's development. For that to happen, Europe has to act in unison.

The trouble is that—quite apart from the immediate economic crises—Europe is a collection of proud, independent nations, each with its own views, culture and traditions. So, for example, Germany will approach certain issues very differently from France, however close the ties between the two nations are. What is necessary is to look at Europe in the early twenty-first century in a quite different way from the Europe of the immediate post-war years. Back then, the issue was peace; how to prevent Europe going back to the wars that periodically had defined European history. Since that was the rationale, the cause of European integration was born and it was very straightforward. Europe would be bound together by a set of institutions that over time would acquire more power. The Council would be the place of the leaders of the individual nations, but over time its power would reduce; the Commission would be the powerhouse of integration; the Parliament would be the nascent forum of European democracy. The more integration, the more peace, because the less scope there would be for individual nations to break out and restart old enmities. It is a measure of how fast the world changes today that in the span of less than one lifetime, the very thought of hostility between European nations is now fatuous.

The danger for Europe today is not war; it is weakness. The rationale for Europe is not how to keep the peace between European nations, it is how, together, they project power, influence and strength in a world in which any of them, even the largest, is going to be small in comparison with the new, emergent powers of the East. The purpose of this, of course, is not power or influence per se; it is because the world can be better through Europe having power and influence. Europe has many faults, but it has progressive values, a decent basic adherence to the Judeo-Christian heritage that precisely because of its tumultuous and often terrible history has achieved a considerable measure of humane civilisation today. The world needs Europe to be strong. And for Europe and the U.S. to be together.

Once this new rationale for European unity is understood, it changes profoundly not just the way Europe looks at itself, but the way it needs to work. At present, the debate in Europe is poised precariously between the federalists and the phobes, those who believe in "ever closer integration"; and those who see such a plan as an assault on the nation state. Both positions exclude the majority of European people. People recognise the need for Europe to act coherently but are anxious about a Europe that takes away power from parliaments to which people feel close and gives it to institutions to which they feel little affinity or loyalty.

This polarised debate is the product of the old rationale for Europe. Integration in these terms is seen as institutional integration since the nation state is seen as a symbol of independence that is contrary to the European ideal. It then becomes an objective in itself. The constitutional changes eventually embodied in the Lisbon Treaty were less about what Europe wanted to do, in specific policy terms, than about the mechanisms by which it was governed, and what that symbolised in terms of "European integration". The result is an obsession about institutional integration in itself rather than a debate about what we want to do as Europe, where the institutions should be at the service of the policy, rather than the policy at the service of institutions.

If the debate becomes one about how to project European power, then a quite different agenda arises. This would mean, in certain areas, more integration but for a defined purpose. Europe needs a common defence policy. Why? To increase its leverage and power so that if the U.S. decides not to act, Europe can; or if the U.S. is acting in concert with Europe, the partnership can be on more equal terms. A common energy policy makes sense to reduce cost, improve efficiency and cut energy consumption. The single market will require greater integration but rightly so, for economic growth and to produce jobs. Hence the importance of the single EU patent recently approved by the mechanism of reinforced co-operation, where some countries can act together and others are allowed to opt out. Fighting organised crime and illegal immigration across borders makes sense, so integrate where necessary to do so—but don't fixate on every aspect of immigration law being identical across all countries. It isn't necessary. Most immediately for the health of the single currency, there will need to be greater integration and co-ordination of fiscal policy. If done in order to improve stability and therefore growth, it will be accepted; but not if it's seen as an end in itself to give Europe more power over individual countries.

Focusing on European power, then, gives a different complexion to the discussion of Europe's institutions. The Council needs to work more effectively with strong leadership. The Commission is allowed to do its job as the engine of effective decision-making. The Parliament can be a forum of revision, debate and initiative. But one thing would be abundantly clear. Ask UK voters to name an MEP and I would be surprised if above 10 per cent could do so. The result in other European countries won't be wildly different except where the MEP was at one time a national figure. So the notion of a steady evolution towards a reduced Council and an enhanced Parliament is based on a fundamental diversion from democratic accountability. It won't work. If pushed it will feed scepticism about Europe, if not outright opposition. It is a twentieth-century agenda.

If, instead, Europe concentrates on projecting power—possibly even eventually with a European president directly elected by European people, but presiding still over an alliance of nation states, it can do what the citizens and countries of Europe urgently need, namely ensure that Europe's voice, its interests and its values play their proper part in fashioning the new geopolitical era.

A crucial test of both U.S. and EU strength will come over how events in the Middle East are handled.

The Middle East and North Africa

I said earlier that sometimes the hardest thing in politics is just getting the right answer. Leadership in politics is about answers, i.e. you have to come down on one side or another. There's another thing: inaction is also a decision, with consequences. Indecision simply becomes a different, more passive form of decision-making.

People often say to political leaders: listen! Get advice! Seek views! By and large leaders do so. But here is the problem: when you listen, you hear different voices. Advisers disagree. The views cover a range of disparate options. Then you have to decide.

As these uprisings change the face of the Middle East and North Africa—and as I write, this revolution is nowhere near being over—a leader seeking counsel will get two opposing views, both within his country and outside it. The first view is, in effect: stay out; this is their struggle, they have to do it; learn from Iraq and Afghanistan and realise that to interfere is to make things worse. Besides, we have plenty back here to think about. Let's look after ourselves first, for a change.

It's a beguiling argument. What's more, it may be where the people are. I don't notice much appetite in the U.S. or Europe for activism.

The alternative view is that we have major interests engaged in the region. We have no real option but to be active. The question is: what's the right action?

It won't surprise you to know I favour the second argument. Libya is an interesting test case. Suppose we had done nothing. Gaddafi would have retaken the country and suppressed the revolt with extraordinary vehemence. Many would have died. But the more far-reaching consequence is that within a period of months, we would have supported the removal of a key ally, President Mubarak of Egypt (and you can't rewrite history, he was our ally); and then stood by as Gaddafi (who despite his change on WMD and terrorism could not be considered in the same way) kept power. The damage to the West's reputation, credibility and stature would have been not just massive but potentially irreparable. That's what I mean by saying inaction is also a decision.

But it doesn't stop there. What do we do when Bahrain is in the grip of a Shia/Sunni power struggle? What do we say when Saudi Arabia believes its core interests are threatened and intervenes? Where are we on the removal of the Assad regime in Syria? What do we do if Iran decides to suppress internal dissent and continue to pursue its nuclear weapons ambitions? Do we regard stability in Jordan as a vital interest? And if the peace process between Israel and Palestine is in disarray, do we take the view that the vacuum matters when a short time ago it was in our strategic interest to resolve it? To this list you could add another ten questions, not the least of which is what is happening post-revolution in Egypt particularly, but also in Tunisia.

The point is: we need a Plan. None of these questions is easy to answer. All involve an immensely tricky interplay between interests, values, practical activity and political judgement. Nothing we do will be free from criticism or opposition, our motives in any action will be suspected, and it will be impossible to predict accurately the outcome of any action decided upon. But Europe and America came together over Libya and, though it is difficult and though the way things will turn out is uncertain, it showed leadership; and amongst the criticism, there was also—in the region—relief that leadership was shown. So what is the Plan to guide us through what is happening? I think it consists of the following.

Evolution is better than revolution; but the status quo is not an option. The truth is, it would have been better in Egypt if the regime had laid out a plan for change and steady evolution towards proper democracy some years back. It didn't, and the lesson for all autocratic regimes the world over is: change, or be changed. But where there is the possibility of evolutionary change, we should encourage and support it. This is the case in the Gulf States. Instability there would be damaging not just to our interests but to those countries and their people. Many are already embarking on a path of steady change. We should help them keep to it and support it. None of this means we do not criticise strongly the use of violence against unarmed civilians. Or that if that violence continues, we do not reserve the right then to move to outright opposition to the status quo, as has happened in Libya. But it is more sensible to do so in circumstances where the regime has excluded a path to evolutionary change. Then it is clear: the people have no choice. But if there is a process that can lead to change with stability, we should back that policy. My point is simple: we need to have an active policy, be players and not spectators sitting in the stands, applauding or condemning as we watch. Like it or not, we have to participate.

In Egypt and Tunisia, we should work closely with the new governments to help them navigate their way to genuine democracy. Only they can decide on their future. It is not for us to try to impose—it wouldn't work anyway—but there is a space between imposing and just watching events unfold. We should be very clear, especially in relation to Egypt: democracy is not just about the right to vote a government in and out. It only works if a whole array of other freedoms come with freedom to vote: the rule of law, properly and impartially administered; freedom of expression; free markets; and freedom of religion. We should stand ready to help with aid, debt relief and the muscle of the international financial institutions, but we should also be quietly insistent that such help won't succeed unless proper rules and order are put in place.

Iran should be put under renewed and intense pressure to back off from both its nuclear ambitions and its deliberate attempts to foment instability and terrorism in the region. I am an unashamed advocate of regime change in Tehran. At the least, they should know that we are strong, determined and resolute on pushing back against their influence; and that an Iranian nuclear bomb is a red line for us. The sooner we are explicit about this and expose at every turn what they are doing or trying to do, the better.

We need to lay out a strategy for getting us to Palestinian statehood; and an end to the Israel/Palestine dispute. Of course at one level it is even harder now for Israel. What stability and predictability it had in its neighbours has been replaced by instability and unpredictability. For similar reasons, but with an opposite conclusion, the Palestinian leadership find it hard to go into negotiation with an Israeli partner they don't trust, to make difficult compromises which will be tough to sell, in circumstances where they don't know the regional context into which such compromises will be played.

So the Israeli security concerns are even greater than before, and the Palestinian leadership task—to carry their people with them in a unified politics—is even more challenging. Nevertheless, look at it a different way: precisely for reasons of security, now is a sensible time for Israel to make peace, if those concerns can be addressed, while for the Palestinians, and at least for their moderate leadership, now is the moment when they need the prospect of genuine statehood more than ever.

What is necessary therefore is a strategy that a) sets out a framework for peace, guiding the negotiations to a deal that is fair for the Palestinians on territory and realistic for the Israelis on security; and b) creates the momentum on the ground in support of such a strategy by making real changes in the lives of Palestinians in the West Bank, East Jerusalem and Gaza.

If there has been any bright spot in the last three years, it has been the state-building programme of Prime Minister Fayyad, under President Abbas' leadership. The militia have been replaced by proper police and security forces; the courts and prisons have begun to function; social programmes have been introduced; the environment for doing business has been transformed; the economy has grown and, for the first time in years, in 2011 the need for outside aid has been substantially cut. Even Gaza has seen a significant opening up, despite continuing attacks.

Whatever happens in respect of relations between Fatah and Hamas, this programme must continue.

What works, therefore, is clear. We just need to do much more of it.

I started this part by saying we needed a Plan, with a capital P. Usually I am sceptical about such things. They can end up having grandiose titles and ambitions and very modest impact. In this case, though, I think there is a lot to be said for having something that very clearly denotes that we are taking a "whole region" view; that we are going actively to engage and support evolutionary change; that we will stand up for a platform that delivers greater freedom with stability; that where there have been revolutions, we are ready to assist the new governments if they are moving towards genuine democracy; and that we will not allow those who have a different agenda to gain the upper hand.

In this I also favour being quite specific about our anxieties and concerns. They can be and should be put simply and plainly: that the move to democracy is subverted by Islamist groups whose concept of democracy is alien to what we believe. There is a fear in part of the West that by doing so, we are insensitive. This is an error. Actually many of those within the region want us to be open about this anxiety; because they share it.

What's more, the anxiety is fully justified. The truth is there is another big struggle going on alongside that for democracy and freedom. It is about the nature and the future of Islam in the twenty-first century. The sooner we engage with this openly, the better. It is absolutely at the heart of our future security and stability. It requires a quite different sort of strategy, policy and engagement from that to which we are accustomed. The foundation I began, the Tony Blair Faith Foundation, is no doubt seen as eccentric by those who ask why a former political leader should concern himself with religion. But how different faiths, and therefore different cultures, relate to each other, learn to work and live with each other, will be quite possibly the determinative issue of the twenty-first century. For the reason I gave earlier, this century is unlikely to see a repetition of the clashes of fundamental political ideology which so marked and scarred the twentieth century, but it could easily be a century shaped by clashes of cultural or religious ideology.

Over four billion people in our world today identify themselves as having religious affiliation. Islam is the world's fastest growing religion, though in China, for example, the fastest growing faith is Christianity. In surveys asking people how important religion is to them, the number saying religion is important or very important is around 30 per cent in the UK, roughly the same in the rest of Europe, over 60 per cent in the U.S., and in virtually every country in the Middle East over 90 per cent.

We still have much work to do in getting proper data for religious attitudes worldwide, and it is a big and complex task, but just think for a moment about the gap between the West and the Middle East. Take Britain. Imagine if the figure here was also over 90 per cent. Leave aside whether that would be good or bad, just think how different a country we would be—a different society, a different culture, with a different way of thinking about and looking at the world.

Now let us assume for the purpose of argument (and this isn't a daft assumption) that there are two essential religious types. The first believe their faith is the only true valid faith; that there is no other path to salvation; and that those who don't share that faith are condemned as unbelievers. This is an exclusivist view of faith. We know that type. Then the second are those who believe strongly in their faith, believe in its claims to exclusive truth, but are, nonetheless, open-minded towards those of other faiths, recognising that different people with different histories have different religious experiences and beliefs, even if they don't analyse it closely; but seeing in the best of what each faith has to offer, some commonality of values and principles that guide good living. We know this type too. Of course, many fit some way along the spectrum towards either end, but each faith has identifiable and clear elements that conform to those two types.

In a society where over 90 per cent of people identify religion as important or very important in their lives, isn't it significant to know which type is in the ascendant and what we might do to encourage the group that embraces co-existence? Isn't it vital in our society as well as theirs that children are educated at a young age about different faiths so that at least they know what "the other" really believes? Shouldn't we see interaction between faiths not as a nice gesture but as politically, socially and culturally important? Even if we are not in any way religious, religion matters. In the way the predominantly Muslim nations of the Middle East and North Africa develop, it will matter profoundly. This is not even to mention the circumstances of nations like Pakistan, Somalia, Indonesia and the huge Muslim population of India.

We need a Plan that covers all this, from the economic to the cultural, and we need it fast.

Energy

For reasons both of energy security and climate change, I put this challenge up there with those of the global economy and terrorism. There are still many sceptics on climate change. For all I know they may eventually turn out to be right, but if they're wrong and we have missed the chance to act, or (at least) vastly increased the costs of dealing with it by acting late, a future generation will find it hard to forgive us. As I say, I am no scientist and therefore I feel unqualified to debate whether the changes in weather patterns and the predictions of catastrophe if we allow greenhouse gas emissions to rise without mitigating action are accurate or not; but plenty of those who are qualified say that they are. Even as an unqualified observer, my best guess is that they are right. And this is a judgement we cannot afford to get wrong.

However, today, there is a far more immediate reason to act: energy security. As the cost of oil spirals upwards again, dragging behind it coal and other fossil fuels, and the supplies of energy come often from unstable and uncertain parts of the world, I would rank energy security for many countries as important as defence. Moreover, we are still at a point where a large part of the world, not least hundreds of millions of people in China and India, and almost one billion people in Africa, has yet to industrialise.

Currently China consumes around 10 per cent of worldwide demand for oil. If its GDP per head carries on rising—and follows the path of similar increases in living standards in South Korea and Taiwan, say—the world output will need to double, and China's share of demand will rise from 10 per cent to 50 per cent. And this is just China. If, as people in poorer parts of the world will want and press for, we go from a world today where a majority are still on low incomes to, say, five billion living the energy-rich lifestyles we take for granted, we would have to increase energy productivity by five to ten times while dropping carbon emissions per unit of energy by a similar factor.

Of course it is true we still have large reserves of oil and oil sands, shale oil, coal and other carbon fuels, but the cost of extraction can be high and the environmental consequences are challenging. To base our future on the assumption that such fossil fuels will satisfy our demand for energy (leaving aside the environment for a moment) would be a dangerous gamble.

Now here is where the challenge deepens. There is no way that we are going to meet the challenge by telling people not to consume; or by raising, heavily, taxes on energy. This argument won't work in the U.S. or even the UK. It has no chance whatever in the emerging markets. China and India will industrialise, period. They are not going to be told by wealthy nations that have raised living standards, precisely by industrialisation through the burning and consumption of fossil fuels, that in the interests of the global environment, they now have to hold back.

There is only one way to solve this challenge: science and technology. We have to improve radically, not marginally, energy productivity and carbon energy efficiency. These technologies therefore have to be disruptive—i.e. alter the game entirely. Government can help, not by picking winning technologies, but by setting a framework globally and nationally that can incentivise the development of such technologies.

Partly this will be about reordering subsidies away from the current bias in favour of fossil fuel. These industries are subsidised, worldwide, at present to around \$312 billion, as opposed to \$57 billion for renewables. It will also be to put in place a global framework that gives clear direction to the private sector that governments are united in a desire to reduce carbon emissions and move over time to a low-carbon economy. In this regard, there is a huge danger we make the best the enemy of the good in the negotiations for a successor treaty to Kyoto. Kyoto was a treaty whose purpose was to make a point. Its successor is happening in far more serious times, with governments now anxious to make a policy, not a point. But it has to be realistic and practical, otherwise we're asking leaders to pay a political price they just can't. So I would take the commitments already entered into by national governments which cumulatively mean a big shift in policy; not fixate on precise percentages of carbon reduction by precise dates (which is based on data that is actually less precise than many pretend); focus heavily on areas like deforestation and sharing of technology where steps forward are being taken; and get the treaty agreed and under way.

The signal this would send would itself multiply the efforts in the private sector to develop the game-changing technologies of the future. To those who say such technologies may never come, it's worth analysing the impact of disruptive technologies over the last few decades. In almost every case, people made predictions of the market on assumptions that technology turned on their head. For example, in the 1980s, McKinsey were asked by AT&T to project the market size of mobile phones in the year 2000. The prediction was a market of one million in the U.S. In fact by 2000, there were over 100 million U.S. mobile phones, and of course there are many more today. A whole series of innovations from lithium ion batteries to ultra low-power processors changed a great clunking, heavy box into the pocket-sized phone we use today.

We can do the same in energy. We just need to create a structure that incentivises it. This will mean not only developing entirely new technologies, but also improving existing ones. For example, as a result of Fukushima, many countries will hesitate over nuclear power. In my view, it would be a tragic mistake if we allowed what happened there to close down the potential of nuclear power. Of course, we will have to study the lessons carefully, but we should also be seeing how the technology can be further developed and improved so that risks are minimised and the nuclear waste generated is cut radically. Already there are such technologies in formation. My plea would be not to overreact to what has happened, but to keep the enormous and liberating potential of this technology in being. We will need it.

A number of things stand out from this analysis of issues and challenges. If we compare it with a late twentieth-century analysis, we can see how different it is. Some issues are new—for example the importance of religious and cultural ideology and its link with security. Some are now given hugely accelerated importance—as in energy and its link to the environment. But in a sense this could always be so for every generation.

Notice, however, how little either the agenda or the answers conform to a typical right/left analysis. The values that underpin the solutions are often more identifiably progressive in that they concern the necessity of improving the lives of all citizens not just a few; but the solutions themselves treat individuals as individuals, and recognise that today the freedom not just to elect governments but to choose how to live, is an essential aspiration all people share.

Most challenging of all, though, is the fact that all those solutions require us to change; and to understand that a preparedness to change is an indispensable part of preserving those values and enhancing them in a world so radically different from the world my generation grew up in.

The final message I would convey in this introduction is the possibility, the opportunity, that this change presents to us. I have learned a lot in the different phases of my life. I don't mean policy and decision-making and all of that, which is gone into in detail in the book. I mean about how as a human being you approach life. Whenever I have the chance and the privilege to talk to groups of students even as young as my son Leo is now (eleven), I try to get them to see that people like me—prime minister for ten years—don't come ready-made or predestined. I explain to them that once, believe it or not, I was like they are. I was the same jumble of failed dreams, thwarted hopes, and disappointed expectations along with the achievements. I used to look at successful people and think: I'm not sure I could ever be like that. I know what it's like to lose self-confidence. I know what it's like to fail, come second, to let people down, to let yourself down. Success is a mixture of natural talent, hard work, judgement and, yes, a bit of luck along the way. Not everyone gets to the top; and even those who do, don't always find fulfilment there.

But one thing I have learned: nothing ever comes to those with a negative mind. Nobody achieves without an energy that is essentially positive. Start each day by counting your blessings. There will be plenty of time to contemplate and experience the sad, the depressing, the tragic. Those are emotions any life will have its fill of. But understand life is a gift. If you approach it with that frame of mind, you can always perceive, no matter how dark the time appears to be, some shaft of light, and move towards it.

It's the same for a country. It is the optimistic spirit that gets it going, makes it achieve and shows it that among all the challenges of change, there are fantastic opportunities, and that though change is hard, it can also be exciting and liberating.

I don't think the West should give up on itself or think the twenty-first century will belong to someone else. We may have to share it, but that too can be exciting. All we need is to recover our self-confidence and the self-belief that, although the challenges will be difficult, we have the ability and application to overcome them.

Tony Blair
May 2011

INTRODUCTION

America's burden is that it wants to be loved, but knows it can't be. Love is given to nations with which we sympathise; nations that are victims of tragedy, oppression or even poor governance. Powerful nations aren't loved. They can be admired by their friends, respected by neutrals; they have to be feared by their enemies.

This is especially so of a nation like America that is not only powerful, but aspires to lead. The leadership will be resented, sometimes actively opposed. It will also, however, be expected.

This book, in many ways, is a story about America as well as, evidently, a history of my time as British PM. In it, I describe my relationship with Presidents Bill Clinton and George W. Bush, with whom I worked closely, and also with President Obama, who I never worked with in office but who I work with now in the Middle East.

With Presidents Clinton and Bush, I lived through some turbulent and difficult times. Their consequences resonate today and very often have provided the context for the decisions of the Obama presidency. Though this book covers the period from 1997 to 2007, it has a chapter about 2007–10 and the economic and security challenges that are current. In any event, as the reader will know, events after September 11, 2001, continue to reverberate. It is hard to know how we best navigate where we must go without knowing where we have been and how we got to our present position.

Leadership is personal. People often think of leaders as the repositories of unique knowledge, even thought, who can survey, by reason of their office, things that others cannot. Despite the modern media way, which is to bring leaders down to earth and expose their frailties more rapidly and intrusively than in times gone by, there is still a sense in which the leader, and most particularly the president of the United States, remains on the Olympian heights. Mere mortals are still inspired by a certain awe, at least for the office if not always the human being who occupies it.

Once you know the truth, and as a fellow leader and a British PM you see American presidents close up, you do indeed see the personal side and you no longer look at them as remote office holders but also as human actors in the unfolding dramas of political affairs. This is the best vantage point and a more honest one. But in my case, it has led me to more not less respect for the quality of what America can produce. I will describe each president in a moment—and indeed do in the chapters of this book—but first let me say a word about my own relationship with America.

I came to love America. Frankly, I didn't start that way! Not that I disliked it; but I hadn't visited America, and didn't know many Americans at school or university. My first trip was in 1985, at the age of thirty-two. I was a junior Opposition Treasury spokesman. My view of America had been formed from countless movies and TV shows and the odd interaction with American tourists. I had a touch of that British raised eyebrow at our American cousins. At the time, Britain had an issue over double taxation rules with the U.S. administration. I was in a delegation of Parliamentarians sent to see the then U.S. Treasury Secretary James Baker. I knew nothing much about Jim. Given that glorious ignorance, the senior Conservative members of the delegation—I was the only Labour representative—decided I should be the one who gave the treasury secretary a good tough talking to. "They need to be told," I was confidently informed, "so go give it to them and him [Baker] in particular." Like the diligent lawyer I was, I brushed up on the facts, became an overnight expert on double taxation and was duly thrown into the meeting, the flight over on the Concorde having boosted my sense of my own importance.

I came out of the meeting feeling a little like a boxer who had been told that the fight was fixed and the other guy would go down in the second round, finding he was in the ring with Rocky Marciano and no one had told him about the deal.

Jim was focused, on top of the detail, erudite, answered my points one by one, threw in a few of his own, took my warnings of tough action and exposed them as a series of paper tigers, and sent me out of there reeling and seeing stars. Above all, he was smart. It is important to learn from these lessons. And that's what I learned that day. These Americans can be smart, really, really clever. Homely, folksy, in certain aspects disarmingly simple; but don't let any of that fool you. Underneath all the pop culture, old-fashioned courtesy, Disney, McDonald's and the rest of it, there beats a brain.

In the years that followed, I thought I got to know America better. "Yes, I know America well," I said to someone who asked shortly before I left office in 2007: "I've been many times to D.C., N.Y. and now to L.A." Of course, I didn't know America at all. I had made a tour for a month in 1986 which the U.S. government provided for up-and-coming foreign politicians. I had even seen the Charleston Regatta, and Jerry Lee Lewis play live!

But the reality was that I was woefully ignorant. Only since leaving office have I truly seen some of what America offers, the variety and richness of its peoples, cultures and landscape. During the course of this journey, I have had countless debates and discussions with Americans of every stripe of politics and position in life.

As a result and in a strangely different but deeper way than when PM I have come to love America and what it stands for. Not that there aren't a thousand points of criticism or disagreement. But I have a settled belief that was once intellectual and political and is now emotional, that the essential values it embodies are so much more fundamental to our fortune than even Americans themselves may appreciate. I have also seen more closely the parts of the world where those values are not in place; and I perceive more plainly the difference.

The three presidents I have known themselves represent in a curious way the facets of the American character, both in their diversity and their points of similarity. People often ask me: "Tell me, how was it with Bill Clinton, and then George Bush?" I always reply jokingly: "Here's a real insight: they were very different from each other!"

Bill is an extraordinary mixture of easygoing charm and ferocious intellectual capacity. Probably, in terms of political intuition and certainly in terms of turning such intuition into analysis, he is the most formidable politician I ever met. My theory is that, in a curious way, the blessing of his times is the disadvantage of his legacy. As with any period, the years 1993–2000 were full of events, many of them hugely significant. But the world-changing events—9/11 and the financial crisis—happened in the next presidency.

Bill was actually a brilliant president. He made it at times look easy. He ran a good economy; made big reforms; handled, as I will relate, Kosovo with real leadership. But it is fascinating to speculate how he would have handled later world-changing events. There neither charm nor intellect would have been sufficient. It would have been pure calibre that determined the outcome. I believe he would have had it.

George W. Bush was straightforward and direct. The stupidest misconception was that he was stupid. He also had (has) great intuition. But his intuition was less—as in the case of Bill—about politics and more about what he thought was right or wrong. This wasn't expressed analytically or intellectually. It was just stated. At times—since I was more from the Clinton school—I would find this puzzling, even alarming. I would be at a press conference with him, in the epicentre of those world-changing events, and I would think "George, explain it; don't just say it."

However, over time, and more even in retrospect as events have continued to unfold since I left, I have come to admire the simplicity, the directness, almost the boldness of it, finding in it strength and integrity. Sometimes, in the very process of reasoning, we lose sight of the need for a destination, for finding the way out of the labyrinth to solid ground that stands the test not of a few weeks, months or even a year or two, but of the vastness of the judgement of history.

Into the aftermath of the financial crisis and wars in Iraq and Afghanistan stepped Barack Obama. And as if that weren't enough, he faces the challenges of avoiding a double dip recession and preventing Iran acquiring nuclear weapons capability. As ever, with a new leader, the political character cannot be fully formed or comprehended immediately but happens over time. The personal character, however, is clear: this is a man with steel in every part of him. The expectation was beyond exaggeration. The criticism is now exaggerated. He has remained the same throughout. And believe me, that is hard to do. I achieved that serenity only at the end.

I think I understand what the new president is trying to do. He is less opposed to some of the aims of the previous president than is supposed, or even politically convenient to admit. He is under no illusions as to the scale of the economic or security challenge; and in his own way, every bit as tough. He is trying to shape a different policy to meet these aims, avoiding market excesses in economics and the alienation of America from its allies, potential or actual, in meeting the security challenge.

Being a progressive myself, not a conservative, I entirely empathise with that objective in policy-making. In many ways, this book describes how in trying in my own way to do the same thing I learned some hard lessons. These form the staging posts of my political character on my journey through the ten years of my premiership.

Clinton, Bush, Obama: I can see the difference, I hear you say; what on earth is the similarity? However, at a certain point and that the highest one, they do meet and that point is not about them but about the character of America itself. Leaders come in all shapes and sizes and I have stumbled across the full range in my time. I recall sitting across the table from some leaders, unable to think of anything other than: My God, the poor people of that country. You get the dumb, the cynical, the tedious, the mildly unsuitable, the weird, the products of systems so mad and dysfunctional you find yourself marvelling that the leader is sentient let alone capable. And frankly some weren't sentient. I remember asking rather unkindly when told of one leader's death, "How could they tell?"

Then there are the clever, wise and good ones, the ones you have to admire and like, and here's the thing: there are more of them than you would think.

But the real test of leadership—amongst all the tests of policy, judgement, politics and ability—is whether, in the final analysis, you put the country first. I don't mean that you do something people agree with or even what is objectively right, if there is such a thing in politics. I mean that you are, ultimately, prepared to put what you perceive to be the common good of the nation before your own political self. It is the supreme test. Very few leaders pass it. Each of these presidents does and for a reason not connected simply to them.

Americans can be all that the rest of the world sometimes accuses them of: brash, loud, insular, obsessive and heavy-handed. And no other culture delights as much as the American culture, in countless movies, books and TV shows, in exposing that parody of itself.

But America is great for a reason. It is looked up to, despite all the criticism, for a reason. There is a nobility in the American character that has been developed over the centuries, derived in part no doubt from the frontier spirit, from the waves of migration that form the stock, from the circumstances of independence, from the civil war, from a myriad of historical facts and coincidences. But it is there.

That nobility isn't about being nicer, better or more successful than anyone else. It is a feeling about the country. It is a devotion to the American ideal that at a certain point transcends class, race, religion or upbringing. That ideal is about values: freedom, the rule of law, democracy. It is also about the way you achieve: on merit, by your own efforts and hard work. But it is, most of all, that in striving for and protecting that ideal, you as an individual take second place to the interests of the nation as a whole. It is what makes the country determined to overcome its challenges. It is what makes its soldiers give their lives in sacrifice. It is what brings every variety of American, from the lowest to the highest, to their feet when "The Star-Spangled Banner" is played. Of course the ideal is not always met—that is obvious. But it is always striven for.

The next years will test the American character. America won't be loved in this presidency any more than in previous ones. But America should have confidence. That ideal, which produces the optimism which generates the achievement, is worth all the striving. It is the most precious gift a nation can have. The world is changing. New powers are emerging. But this does not diminish the need for that American ideal. It re-affirms it, renews it, gives it added relevance. There is always one, more prosaic, test of a nation's position: "Are people trying to get into it; or to get out of it?" I think we know the answer to that in America's case; and that ideal is the reason.

A friend of mine whose parents were immigrants, Jews from Europe who came to America in search of safety, told me this story. His parents lived and worked in New York. They were not well off. His father died when he was young. His mother lived on and in time my friend succeeded and became wealthy. He often used to offer his mother the chance to travel outside America. She never did. When eventually she died, they went back to recover the safety box where she kept her jewellery. They found there was another box. There was no key. So they had to drill it open. They wondered what precious jewel was in it. They lifted the lid. There was wrapping and more wrapping and finally an envelope. Intrigued, they opened it. In the envelope were her U.S. citizenship papers. Nothing more. That was the jewel, more precious to her than any other possession. That was what she treasured most. So should America today.

—Tony Blair, July 2010

A JOURNEY

ONE

HIGH EXPECTATIONS

On 2 May 1997, I walked into Downing Street as prime minister for the first time. I had never held office, not even as the most junior of junior ministers. It was my first and only job in government.

The election night of 1 May had passed in a riot of celebration, exhilaration and expectation. History was not so much being made as jumping up and down and dancing. Eighteen years of Conservative government had ended. Labour—New Labour—had won by a landslide. It felt as if a fresh era was beginning. As I walked through the iron gates into Downing Street, and as the crowd—carefully assembled, carefully managed—pressed forward in enthusiasm, despite the setting, the managing and the fatigue of being up all night, I could feel the emotion like a charge. It ran not just through the crowd but through the country. It affected everyone, lifting them up, giving them hope, making them believe all things were possible, that by the very act of election and the spirit surrounding it, the world could be changed.

Everyone except for me, that is. My predominant feeling was fear, and of a sort unlike anything I had felt before, deeper even than the fear I had felt the day I knew I was going to take over the leadership of the Labour Party. Until election night, this fear had been kept in check by the routine, rigour and sheer physical and mental exertion of the campaign. Also, campaigning was familiar emotional as well as political territory. I had a strategy for guiding us from Opposition into government; I adhered to it, and I knew if I did so, I wouldn't fail. I had redefined the Labour Party as New Labour, a changed progressive force in British politics; I had set out an outline programme of sufficient substance to be credible but lacking in the details that would have allowed our opponents to damn it; and I had fashioned a strong but believable attack on the government, and assembled a ferociously effective election-fighting machine.

In order to instil discipline, into the party and even my close team, I was the eternal warrior against complacency. I regularly spoke about how big opinion-poll leads could be lost, how the Tories should never be underestimated, how we had this problem and that challenge. Since we had lost four elections in a row and had never won two consecutive full terms, I was cultivating fairly fertile ground. The party had almost come to believe that it couldn't win, that for some divine or satanic reason, Labour wasn't allowed an election victory no matter what it did. For some, it was like the old football adage: a game played with a round ball, two teams of eleven players, forty-five minutes in each half and the Germans always win.

I thought that was complete baloney. We had lost because we were out of touch with the modern voter in the modern world. The first rule in politics is that there are no rules, at least not in the sense of inevitable defeats or inevitable victories. If you have the right policy and the right strategy, you always have a chance of winning. Without them, you can lose no matter how certain the victory seems.

Pretending that it was all really on a knife-edge helped motivate, galvanise and keep us in line. Though underneath I was very confident, you never know. What's more, I believed the current prime minister John Major was much better than most others thought. He had real appeal as a person. Fortunately, his party had gone off the rails, to a heavy, hard-right position, and over the seemingly interminable time I had spent as Leader of the Opposition—almost three years—I had learned how to play him and his party off against each other.

Major had decided on a long campaign of three months (it's usually less than a month). It was tough, of course, but it wasn't an uncharted landscape and it fitted a pattern. The hope was that we would trip up, I would suddenly lose my head, by some trick of fate or fortune the mood of the public would switch. It was never really going to happen.

Instead, and rather more predictably, the Tories fell apart. Every time Major tried to get them on the front foot, someone in his ranks resigned, said something stupid, got caught in a scandal and frequently all three at once and occasionally the same person. It was like watching a slow-motion suicide or an escape artist who ties concrete blocks to his legs, puts on handcuffs, gets in a lead box, has it sealed and jumps into deep water. You think, how's he going to get out of that?—and then you realise he isn't. Amazing how a political party can go like that, though it is possible to tempt them to it if their opponents are smart enough; and by occupying the centre ground, make them foolishly go off to the side.

So the election campaign was long, enervating—as they always are—full of phoney ups and downs, shock polls and startling happenings, but in the end the result was obvious. The scale of the victory, however, was not clear. I had an inkling. If I had had to bet on it, I would have bet big. On the night of 1 May it became clear just how big. And that was when the fear started to set in.

The actual day of the election had passed uneventfully, as they do. Campaigning stops. You go to vote. I walked out of our constituency home in Trimdon Colliery, an old mining village near Sedgefield in County Durham where I had been MP serving the local constituency for fourteen years. The mine had been a casualty of the closure policy of the 1960s, which had been set out by the National Coal Board and the government to concentrate coal production at the most highly productive mines. I strode to the polling station with Cherie and the children, the ideal family picture, while a horde of snappers took our photograph. Smile, but not exuberantly. Talk, but not with too much animation. Look natural, as if you would naturally walk hand in hand with your wife, in suit trousers, shirt and tie, with your children in tow, to vote in a makeshift wooden polling booth and claim your place in history.

Then back home. I had waited on election day three times before—in 1983, 1987 and 1992—for the defeat I thought would come. I had wondered what it would mean for me, how I would position myself for the next bout of Opposition, how and whether I would ever get the chance to help steer us from the path of defeat. This time, all eyes were focused on me as I travelled the last steps of the path to victory. Anxiety displaces all other emotions. You can't settle. I tried to concentrate on choosing a Cabinet, and phoned Gordon Brown, then Shadow Chief Secretary, and Peter Mandelson, who was in charge of strategy. (The Shadow Cabinet is of course made up of a group of senior MPs who are in Opposition and who "shadow" their equivalents in the ruling government.) John Prescott came up from Hull to talk through the Cabinet. I spoke incessantly to Philip Gould, our chief pollster, and party staff about the prospects of the majority, but all really to pass the time. Even then, the enormity of what was about to happen didn't really sink in.

But it did by the time we got to the count, just after midnight, in the cavernous indoor sports centre at Newton Aycliffe, a town in County Durham in my former constituency of Sedgefield. The exit polls had shown big leads. They might be out a fraction, but there was no way they were going to be that wrong. We were going to win. I was going to be prime minister. During the course of the evening, my psyche shifted as the results came in. Of course the journey's end had always been changing the country, but in the intense struggle to get to the point where that could be achieved, every waking moment had been bent to eliminating the challenges, making sure the vehicle was fit for the voyage, the engine sparking, the passengers either on board or shouting impatiently from behind us, not barring the way ahead. To be sure, we conducted genuine and in-depth discussions to map out how we would navigate the new terrain of government once past the post; but living in the moment, it was the business of Opposition—which we were adept at and had been practising these long years in the wilderness—that dominated our thinking. Our intellectual and rational attention was drawn to the processes of government as the day came nearer, but our emotional core was still directed at getting there.

It was the only business we knew. One or two of the older hands like Jack Cunningham and Margaret Beckett had been very junior ministers in the Callaghan government of 1976–9, but the rest of us were going to come to power as utter novices. Even those older hands knew only a Labour government in its death throes, and the time, temper and spirit of 1997 were as far removed from that of the 1970s as Mars from Earth.

On our side, we had the mood. We had the momentum to sustain it. We had the self-belief that the start of a new adventure often bestows on the ignorant. We had the confidence that in reaching this stage we had swept all before us, conquered with ease, strode out with abandon. Hadn't we fought a great campaign? Hadn't we impaled our enemies on our bayonet, like ripe fruit? Hadn't our strategies, like something derived from destiny, scattered the proud in the imagination of their hearts? Wasn't government just another point on the same journey, a new point maybe, further in its distance, uncertain and unpredictable for us here and now; but could it really be that different? Surely by being bold and acting with confidence, by retaining the same spirit of possibility, the team that had done so brilliantly to get to that point wouldn't forfeit those qualities in the march ahead?

I could see those around me thinking all this. At times I thought the same. On that night, as the probability of being prime minister turned to certainty, I was no longer seeing through the glass darkly, but face to face with the light. And I was scared.

I was afraid because I knew this was not just another stage on the same journey. Now we would enter a new and foreign land. I was afraid because I felt instinctively that its obstacles and challenges were of an altogether different order of complexity and difficulty. I was afraid because, intent as I was on destroying the government, I could see over time that, even when it was in the right, once public opinion had gone sour it didn't seem to matter whether what it did was right or wrong; and that once the mood had turned from the government and embraced us, the mood was merciless in its pursuit, indifferent to anything other than satisfying itself. I was afraid because, at that instant, suddenly I thought of myself no longer as the up-and-coming, the challenger, the prophet, but the owner of the responsibility, the person not explaining why things were wrong but taking the decisions to put them right. Deep down—but fighting its way to the surface—I realised I knew nothing about how tough it really was, nothing about how government really works, most of all nothing about how I personally would react when the mood turned against me, as I knew it would.

Down in London in the HQ at Millbank (the building from which Labour ran its campaign, and a byword for electoral ruthlessness) the partying had begun. In the hall in my County Durham constituency where the votes were being counted, the air was of almost manic excitement. The Labour people naturally were suffused with it, but even the Tories, Lib Dems and assorted others had a sense of history.

There is a strange consequence of the parliamentary system whereby the prime minister is an MP with a constituency in which they stand for election like any other candidate. It is at one level very humbling, for at that moment you are just the constituency candidate, you stand on a platform along with the other candidates as the returning officer reads out the result. Odd, but very democratic and rather good. But of course, since there is so much coverage given to high-profile battles, the constituencies of the prime minister and Leader of the Opposition do not have only the mainstream parties standing, but also countless other candidates seeking publicity for causes (or sometimes just seeking publicity). They had such weird and wonderful names, such as Screwy Driver (Rock 'n' Roll Party), Boney Maronie Steniforth (Monster Raving Loony Party), Jonathan Cockburn (Blair Must Go Party) and Cherri Blairout-Gilham (the Pensioners' Party)! Each party has the right to send some of its people to the count, and there in the hall they were all mingling as I watched the national race on TV upstairs.

Pretty soon, the scale of the victory became clear. This was not a win. It was a landslide. After about two hours, for a time I actually became worried. The moving line at the bottom of the TV screen was showing over a hundred Labour seats. The Tories had just six. I began to think I had done something unconstitutional. I had meant to defeat the Tories and do so handsomely; but what if we had wiped them out? Fortunately, a little later their tally began to mount, but the majority was clearly still going to be historic. People started to relax and have a drink. I remained completely sober. I had work to do. There would be speeches to make; messages to give; tones to get right; comportment to maintain that needed to be consistent with the magnitude of the win.

It was at this point that my emotions began to diverge from those of virtually everyone else around me. As they became more and more buoyed up with the vastness of the victory, I became more and more weighed down by the burden of responsibility that was about to fall on me. I know this sounds completely bizarre but I even became slightly irritated with it all. Couldn't they see what a great big job it was? Did they really think a manifesto written essentially to capture a mood, and whose details were deliberately and necessarily limited, was going to be enough to govern a country?

Someone lurched up to me—the first of many that night—and said, "Isn't it incredible? You are going to be a great prime minister, Tony, you really are," to which I'm afraid I said, "Oh, bugger off." How could he know? How could *I* know?

Around midnight we called David Hill, a very sane and solid individual who was the party press officer down at Millbank, and started to bark at him that the party staff were going over the top in their celebrations, that it looked complacent and they should all calm down. "We are about to win the biggest victory in our history and end eighteen consecutive years of Tory government," he said. "I think it's going to be a little hard to tell them all to look sombre."

I turned my attention to what I was going to say. There would be three speeches: at the count when confirmed as an MP; at the local party meeting in the Labour Club in Trimdon Village, just up the road from my constituency home; and at the Royal Festival Hall in London at around 5 or 6 a.m., where a big event had been planned for the party faithful and the media.

I discussed the content with Alastair Campbell, in charge of communications. He had been like a rock throughout the previous three years. In my experience there are two types of crazy people: those who are just crazy, and who are therefore dangerous; and those whose craziness lends them creativity, strength, ingenuity and verve. Alastair was of the latter sort. The problem with them is that they can be mercurial, difficult and on occasions erupt with damaging consequences. Above all, you must realise you can't tame them; you can reason with them, but the thing that makes them different and brilliant is the same thing that means they don't conform to normal, predictable modes of behaviour. And they are always on the edge. In the later stages, before he left at the end of 2003, Alastair had probably gone over the edge. Like all creative people, he can snap, but for most of the time—especially in those years of Opposition and the first part of government—he was indispensable, irreplaceable, almost an alter ego. Along with Gordon and Peter Mandelson, he carried out with near genius the political concepts of New Labour and was able to give them media expression in a media age. Funnily enough, on policy he was really much more Old Labour. In mood, that night, he reflected mine: he too felt flat, almost anticlimactic. We went over what I would say, and as I withdrew from the euphoria around me we focused on what each of the speeches needed to emphasise: first speech, family; second, party; third, country.

My only real emotion came when I spoke about my dad. As I gave my speech at the count, I saw him there with tears of pride in his eyes. I thought back on his life: a foster-child in Glasgow; his foster-father a rigger in Govan shipyard; his foster-mother a strange mixture of fanatical parent—she refused to give him back to his real mother—and militant socialist; in his youth, secretary of the Glasgow Young Communists; then to the war as a private, ending it as an acting major and Tory, when virtually everyone else made the opposite political journey.

He became an academic, a practising barrister and then an active Conservative. The one safe Tory seat in the north of England was Hexham and for the 1964 election he was a racing certainty to be the candidate. He even had his own slot on local TV. He was bright, charming and ambitious to an unnatural degree. He fitted the mould the Tories were looking for in a changing world: no one could argue class with him. He knew it, had lived it and had learned to escape it.

Then one night that year, after his usual round of meetings, social events and hard work, he suffered a serious stroke and was near to death. He survived, but for three painful years he had to learn to speak again. I remember how my mother helped him, day after day, word after word, agonising sentence after agonising sentence. I remember, too, how our income dropped overnight, some of his friends fell away, and the crushing recognition came that since his speech would never return to normal, his political career was over.

My dad had been formative in my politics. Not because he taught me a vast amount about politics in the sense of instruction in its business (and him being on the opposite side of the political fence to me had given rise to some fairly heated debate, though much less frequently than might have been the case), but as a child I used to listen to his discussions with friends and absorb some of the arguments, hear the passion in their voices, and I obtained a little understanding of politics' intricacies.

I recall the very first time I met any politicians. Bizarrely, they weren't Labour; I think they were Michael Spicer, later a Tory MP, and even—but my memory may play me false—Patrick Jenkin, who went on to serve in Mrs. Thatcher's Cabinet. They came to dinner at our house in High Shincliffe in Durham, the reason, I dimly recall, because Michael—a young Tory prospect at the time—wanted to fight a hopeless seat to cut his teeth, and Dad had influence in the Durham seats.

But none of that defined the principal impact on my political development. What Dad taught me above all else, and did so utterly unconsciously, was why people like him became Tories. He had been poor. He was working class. He aspired to be middle class. He worked hard, made it on his merits, and wanted his children to do even better than him. He thought—as did many others of his generation—that the logical outcome of this striving, born of this attitude, was to be a Tory. Indeed, it was part of the package. You made it; you were a Tory: two sides of the same coin. It became my political ambition to break that connection, and replace it with a different set of options. In Britain you can vote Labour if you are compassionate; you care about those less fortunate than yourself; you believe in society as well as the individual. You can be successful and care; ambitious and compassionate; a meritocrat and a progressive. Moreover, these are not alien sentiments in uneasy coexistence. They are entirely compatible ways of making sure progress happens; and they answer the realistic, not utopian, claims of human nature.

So he affected me deeply, as in another way did my mum. She was as different from my dad as it is possible for two people living together to be. Dad was more like me: motivated, determined, with a hard-focused ambition that, I fear, translates fairly easily into selfishness for both of us. Mum, by contrast, was a decent, lovely, almost saintly woman. She was shy, even a little withdrawn in company. She supported Dad politically as his wife and companion, but, as she used to confide in me occasionally, she was not really a Tory. For some reason—maybe to do with her Irish background—she felt somehow excluded; and she thought that some of the more Tory friends had fallen away when Dad took ill.

She died when I had just turned twenty-two. She had been ill with cancer of the thyroid. Looking back, it was clear she couldn't survive, clear indeed that it was a minor miracle that she survived for the five years after she was first diagnosed.

But the shock of it. There is nothing like losing a parent. I don't mean it's worse than losing a child. It isn't. I don't think anything can be. I mean that it affects you in a unique way, at least if it happens when you're young. Mum's death was shocking because I couldn't contemplate it. As she deteriorated and I was in my last months at Oxford, working hard for the final exams, Dad and my brother Bill kept from me the truth of her condition. I came home at the end of June and Dad picked me up from the station. "Your mother's really very ill," he said.

"I know, but she's not dying, is she?" I said, stating the worst so that he would reassure me, as I stupidly expected.

"Yes, I am afraid she is," he replied. My world turned upside down. I could not imagine it. The person who had brought me up, looked after me, was always there to help and cherish me; the person who loved me without a consideration of my entitlement, without an assessment of my character, without wanting anything from me; the person who simply loved me: she would be gone.

Life was never the same after that. That was when the urgency took hold, the ambition hardened, the recognition grasped that life was finite and had to be lived in that knowledge. I miss her each day of my life.

With all the euphoria and celebration of election night rolling around me like a tidal wave, even with all I had to think of and to do at that momentous time, which was the fulfilment of my ambition, I thought of her and knew that though she would have been unutterably proud, it would not have altered one fraction of her love for me. It was already complete, entire unto itself. And, of course, more real than the transient adulation of 1 May 1997.

Now I saw my dad there in Trimdon, looking at me, realising that all his hopes could be fulfilled in me. As our eyes met, I knew also that we were thinking the same thought: Mum should have been there to see it.

I wrenched my mind away and got back to the business in hand. There were crowds everywhere. The Labour Club in Trimdon was ecstatic. We got a plane down from Teesside airport, and the results were paged in to Alastair as we flew. Big Tory Cabinet members were losing their seats, such as the Defence Secretary Michael Portillo and the Foreign Secretary Malcolm Rifkind. It was a political earthquake. I sat with Cherie, collecting my thoughts for the Festival Hall. She knew what I was thinking and, as ever at times like these, could speak to me in a way no one else could. She told me that she knew it would be very hard, that bad times as well as good lay ahead, that politics begins like this but never ends the same way, that it was a privilege to do it, we had something genuine to offer and we would do it together.

In one of these ridiculous mishaps that happen, we lost our way to the Festival Hall and kept being announced by our campaign theme song "Things Can Only Get Better" to the waiting crowd but, like the von Trapps, never actually appeared onstage. Finally we got there. My mental discipline was total. It was going to be a huge victory, therefore be even more aware of the responsibility. Don't for a moment look as if the whole thing has gone to the party's head. Look like a prime minister, not the guy who's just scored the winning goal at Wembley.

It was not easy. I have come to the conclusion that one of life's more annoying experiences is to be the only sober person at a party. Nothing can alter the fact that you are without drink and they are full of it. They are shouting, weeping and laughing, and you say, "Yes, thank you, it is a very special moment." There are cameras trained on you all the time; snappers snapping; scribblers scribbling. You smile, but you must not enter into the spirit; you embrace, but with a pat on the back; you thank, but with your effusion measured. There were familiar faces from the campaign, friends I knew from years back, people I had never seen before. For them, each greeting was a moment to savour; for me, a moment that had to be treated as a duty before passing on.

I saw Neil Kinnock, the Labour leader who had taught me so much, and the greeting was genuine, the warmth natural and irrepressible. But even with him, I was aware of the nervous gaze of Alastair directing me to the podium, aware that while others could relax, we were still onstage and the audience had to be pleased.

As Opposition leader, you carry great responsibility; to campaign for the top job in any country is onerous. You are the standard-bearer for your politics, your party and the beliefs both hold dear. Anyone who has ever run a campaign to win an election knows how big a task it is. There are a million decisions of organisation, communication, person-nel and policy which have to be taken quickly and effectively. If you can do it well, it is good preparation and a real indication of leadership, but it isn't the same in its impact on you as a person. From the moment the mantle is on your shoulders as prime minister, you understand that the scale, importance and complexity are completely different. They are not at the end of the same spectrum of leadership. You inhabit a new dimension altogether. There is something more: running for the job, you have a team and it feels like a team. Yes, you're the leader, but your collaboration is so close, your intimacy so refined by experience, your interaction so governed by familiarity of an almost telepathic nature, that you feel like a family or a cabal of like-minded conspirators.

As I took the steps up to the podium and tried to push my mind and energy reserves on to the words I was going to say, I finally defined the root of the fear that had been growing all day: I was alone. There would be no more team, no more friendly clique, no more shared emotions among a band of intimates. There would be them; and there would be me. At a certain profound point, they would not be able to touch my life, or me theirs.

I stood on the podium and scanned the crowd. People were stacked up on Waterloo Bridge, massed not just outside the Festival Hall but around the Embankment by the River Thames, cheering, gesturing, waves of emotion reverberating through them. I felt the same impa-tience that I had felt all day, anxious to get the damn celebrating over with and get down to work; most of all, to see what it was really like to govern. But I put on my best face.

Just as I began to speak, the sun made its first appearance and the dawn started to come through with that rather beautiful orange, blue-grey light that heralds a good day. I couldn't resist saying it, though as soon as I did I regretted it: "A new dawn has broken, has it not?" This gave those already stratospheric expectations another and higher orbit. I swiftly tried to take them back to earth, emphasising that we were elected as New Labour and would govern as New Labour. Probably it wouldn't have mattered what I said, but I was already obsessed with the notion that the country might take fright at the mandate it had given us, and believe that we may revert to the Labour Party of old, not the New Labour that we had promised to deliver. I sought to soothe and to settle, conscious that anything that smacked of hubris or arrogance, however faintly, would quickly return to haunt us.

Eventually at about 7 a.m. I went back with Cherie to our home in Islington in north London, now surrounded by people, to grab an hour's sleep before going to the Palace to see the Queen and take the reins of government. It was strange to be back home with everything just as we had left it, knowing that we would sleep here for one or per- haps two nights more, and then leave forever.

The hour's sleep revived me more than I expected. The results were now all in. Our majority of 179 over all the other parties combined was seismic, the largest in British history. Seats we had never won before, like Hove (which we kept even in 2005), had fallen to us. Some had returned to us for the first time since Attlee's landslide of 1945. Places we assumed were true blue and unchangeable were now red: Hastings, Crawley, Worcester, Basildon and Harrow. And by the way, all stayed red through the following two elections.

Shortly after the polls had closed the night before and the exit polls had shown victory, John Major had called me to concede. He had been gracious, but it can't have been easy. He had many strengths, but his weakness was he took personally the fact that I tried so hard to dis- lodge him.

It's a strange thing about politics, but leaders and parties can be absolutely and genuinely outraged at what they perceive to be unfair attacks made on them (I dare say I suffer from this too, though I always fought the feeling), and yet seem completely oblivious to the fairness or otherwise of attacks they make on their opponents. When I look back on how we conducted ourselves as an Opposition, I admire enormously the professionalism but some of the tactics were too opportunistic and too facile. More than that, they sowed seeds that sprouted in ways we did not foresee and with consequences that imperilled us.

My attack on Major had always been political—weak leader, divided party—whereas the Tory attack on me was then, and continued to be, highly personal—liar, cheat, fraud, etc. So it was hard for Major to make the call, but he did and I paid fulsome tribute to him the next day (though I'm not sure that didn't rub salt in the wound).

The other call I had taken was from Bill Clinton. That was great—he was really warm, plainly delighted to have a fellow third-way progressive in power—though I could tell that, as ever, he knew what I was thinking, knew the pitfalls ahead and was gently but clearly getting me ready for the change about to come.

The journey from Richmond Crescent in Islington to Buckingham Palace was extraordinary. People came out of their houses, thronging the route, waving, cheering. There were helicopters whirring overhead filming it live, and as they did so, people knew where we were and came out to greet us. It seemed as if the country had taken the day off. There is a strange unification at moments of great political change. People vote for many reasons. Some people vote for the same party regardless. (I voted Labour in 1983. I didn't really think a Labour victory was the best thing for the country, and I was a Labour candidate!) Hordes of people vote from allegiance or tradition, and when the result is in and it really is the best thing for a nation that needs change, even those who vote against you join in the celebration. It is as if they had two votes: one they cast in the booth, the other they cast in their mind.

As we drove through the gates of Buckingham Palace there were more crowds, frantic to get a sight of the new prime minister. I could tell Cherie was very excited. As ever, I just wanted to get on with it. By now, I was straining at the leash of the convention, tradition and ceremony that delayed the doing.

I was shown into a little antechamber, outside the room where the Queen was. I suddenly became nervous. I knew the basic protocol, but only very vaguely. It is called "kissing hands," the laying on of the Queen's authority to govern. She was head of state. I was *her* prime minister. A tall official with a stick stood by me. "I should tell you one thing, Mr. Blair," he began (note "Mr. Blair" until I had been appointed), "you don't actually kiss the Queen's hands in the ceremony of kissing hands. You brush them gently with your lips."

I confess that floored me. What on earth did he mean? Brush them as in a pair of shoes, or touch them lightly? Still temporarily disconcerted, the door opened and I was ushered in, unfortunately tripping a little on a piece of carpet so that I practically fell upon the Queen's hands, not so much brushing as enveloping them. I recovered sufficiently to find myself sitting opposite her. I had met her before, of course, but this was

different. It was my first audience. There is much to say about the
Queen. At this encounter, I noticed two things: she was quite shy,
strangely so for someone of her experience and position; and at the
same time, direct. I don't mean rude or insensitive, just direct. "You are
my tenth prime minister. The first was Winston. That was before you
were born." We talked for a time, not exactly small talk but general guff
about the government programme, the conversation somewhat stilted.
Then Cherie was brought in to pay her respects, and the Queen relaxed
more as they chatted. (Contrary to popular belief, Cherie always got on
well with her.) Cherie was explaining very practical things we would
need to do with the children and how strange it would be for them to
live in Downing Street, and the Queen was generally clucking sympathetically. I fear I sat there looking a trifle manic, unsure how or when
to end the conversation, focusing on what I would say on the steps of
Downing Street and feeling, through lack of sleep, more than a little
spaced out. The Queen understood it all, of course, and kept the conversation going for just the right length of time; then, by an ever so
slight gesture, she ended it and saw us out.

"This way, Prime Minister," said the tall chap with the stick as he
ushered us down the stairs to the waiting car.

And so to Downing Street. After working the crowd, I got to the
stand-alone pedestal that would serve me on so many occasions over the
coming years. What I said reflected my incessant, gnawing desire to get
away from the congratulatory euphoria—which I knew would mean
little in terms of how we governed—and get down to business. I spoke
of plans and programmes and policies—not a long speech, but clearly
focused on what we would do when I stepped inside that door for the
first time.

But, in truth, it no longer mattered what I said. The mood was the
mood, and I might as well try to thwart it as try to stop an oncoming
truck. The pent-up expectations of a generation were vested in me.
They wanted things to be different, to look, feel, have the attributes of a
new era, and I was the leader of this sentiment. We were like a movement, connected by a single converging interest: to chuck out the old
and usher in the new. They weren't troubled by the dilemmas of policymaking or the savage nature of decision-making. They were raised up
on stilts far above the ugly street on which the real, live business of politics is conducted, and from that height could only see the possibility, the
opportunity, the distant but surely attainable horizon of future dreams.

When Barack Obama fought and won his extraordinary campaign for the presidency in 2008, I could tell exactly what he would have been thinking. At one level, the excitement and energy created by such hope vested in the candidate has the effect of buoying you up, driving you on, giving all that you touch something akin to magic. The country is on a high and you are up there with them.

At another, deeper level, however, you quickly realise that though you are the repository of that hope and have in part been the author of it, it now has a life of its own, a spirit of its own and that spirit is soaring far beyond your control. You want to capture it, tame it and harness it, because its very independence is, you know, leading the public to an impossible sense of expectation.

Expectations of this nature cannot be met. That's what you want to tell people. Often you do tell them. But the spirit can't be too constrained. And when finally it departs, leaving your followers with reality—a reality you have never denied and which you have even sought to bring to their attention—the danger is of disillusion, more painful because of what preceded it.

Anyway, so I felt.

It seemed unreal because it *was* unreal. It was understandable the people should feel like that; understandable that I should want to lead it; understandable that together we became an unstoppable force. But it was, in a profound way, a deception on both our parts—not a deception knowingly organised or originating from bad faith or bad motives, but one born of the hope that achievement and hard choices could somehow be decoupled. A delusion perhaps describes it better; but as the policeman stood aside and the door of 10 Downing Street opened, my election as prime minister felt like a release, the birth of something better than what had been before.

For the poor old staff of Number 10, it was something of a shock, however. As per convention, John Major had walked out only moments before I had come in. There is a tradition that when the new prime minister enters, the staff line up in the corridor that leads to the Cabinet Room and applaud. A couple of the staff vaguely remembered the last Labour government, but they had been young things back then. The vast majority had now just said goodbye to eighteen years of one-party rule.

As I walked down the row of faces, all unfamiliar to me—people who would be companions in the events to come, and many of them friends—some were a little upset at the departure of the old guard, and a few of the women were sniffling or weeping. By the time I reached the end of the line, I was beginning to feel a right heel about the whole thing, coming in and creating all this distress. Needless to say, I got over it.

Then I entered the Cabinet Room. I had never seen it before. It is immediately impressive, both in itself and because of the history made within it. I stopped for a moment and looked around, suddenly struck by the sanctity of it, a thousand images fluttering through my mind, like one of those moving picture-card displays, of Gladstone, Disraeli, Asquith, Lloyd George, Churchill, Attlee, of historic occasions of war and peace, of the Irish and Michael Collins, of representatives of numerous colonies coming through its doors and negotiating independence. This room had seen one of the greatest empires of all time developed, sustained and let go. I thought of the crises and catastrophes, decisions and deliberations, the meetings to discuss the mundane and the fundamental business of governing a nation. All of it had run through this smallish room looking out over the Downing Street garden, with two false pillars marking the end of the table. The table itself is the product of a decision by Macmillan to have it shaped oval so that the prime minister sitting in the centre could see the faces and body language of all the Cabinet, and in particular any little signal of loyalty or dissent. There was the prime minister's chair, the only one with arms to it, either because it should be more grand, or perhaps because the prime minister, above all others, needs more support.

Sitting in the chair next to it, in the otherwise empty room, was the Cabinet Secretary Sir Robin Butler, famous in his own right and immensely experienced, who had worked closely with both Margaret Thatcher and John Major. He indicated to me the prime minister's chair, which I sat down in, relieved to get the weight off my feet after the tumult of the last twenty-four hours.

"So," he said, "now what?" It was a good question. "We have studied the manifesto," he went on, something which rather irrationally disturbed me, "and we are ready to get to work on it for you." (The manifesto is a public document that sets a political party's programme of key legislation.)

In the light of what later became quite a vigorous disagreement about the nature of decision-making in my government and the so-called "sofa" style of it—a phrase the media used to describe our government meetings that took place in addition to Cabinet meetings—I should say that right at the outset I found Robin thoroughly professional, courteous and supportive. He didn't like some of the innovations, but he did his level best to make them work. He was impartial in the best traditions of the British Civil Service, intelligent and deeply committed to the country.

But he was a traditionalist with all the strengths and weaknesses that reverence for tradition implies; and in this, he was thoroughly representative of a large part of the senior Civil Service. Very early on, I could tell that he didn't really approve of the positions of Jonathan Powell as chief of staff, Alastair and, though less so, my old friend and general factotum Anji Hunter. Even though Jonathan had been in the Civil Service, they were all "special advisers," political appointments brought in by the new government. The British system is essentially run by the career Civil Service right up to the most senior levels. Special advisers are few and far between, unlike in the American system, for example, which has thousands. When after a few years in government I accumulated seventy of them, it was considered by some to be a bit of a constitutional outrage.

They are, however, a vital part of modern government. They bring political commitment, which is not necessarily a bad thing (I always used to think such commitment was more frowned upon when originating from the left, but maybe that's paranoia!); they can bring expertise; and properly deployed they interact with and are strengthened by the professional career civil servants, who likewise are improved by interaction with them. In the light of what I am going to say, I should emphasise that many of the civil servants not merely worked well with the special advisers, but enjoyed doing so and genuine friendships were often made.

There was a discussion between Robin and Jonathan about whether Alastair or Jonathan could give instructions to civil servants, which eventually we compromised over. (And incidentally, neither ever had a single complaint made against them from civil servants all the time they were in Downing Street.) I could not believe, and still don't, that my predecessors did not have a de facto chief of staff, but Jonathan was the first openly acknowledged and nominated one. Robin didn't much like all this, and in his mind it became conflated with another issue: how decisions were taken. Here, he had a more solid point. Truthfully, for the first year or so, as we found our feet and grappled with the challenges of governing, we did tend to operate as a pretty tight unit, from which some of the senior civil servants felt excluded.

From our perspective, we were working flat out to deliver an enormous series of commitments to change. We were very quickly appreciating the daunting revelation of the gap between saying and doing. In Opposition, the gap is nothing because "saying" is all you can do; in government, where "doing" is what it's all about, the gap is suddenly revealed as a chasm of bureaucracy, frustration and disappointment. So we tended to work in the first months of government rather as we had when campaigning for office and changing the Labour Party.

However, Robin was only with us for eight months. In time, we broadened out, we learned, we adjusted. Ministers, sympathetic to the changes we were making, came to the fore. The modus operandi shifted. Cabinet and Cabinet committees flourished, and there was a better balance between special advisers and civil servant input.

The allegations of "sofa government" were always, therefore, ludicrously overblown. For a start, leaders have always had inner circles of advisers. What's more, although Robin used to make much of the fact that my predecessors had been sticklers for Cabinet government, keeping to the traditional way of holding all government business within the Cabinet, I found this a trifle inconsistent with my recollection, admittedly from the outside, of Mrs. Thatcher and her Cabinet relations.

There was a more serious point, at the root of which was a disagreement which touches on the way modern government functions. As I shall come to later, the skill set required for making the modern state work effectively is different from that needed in the mid-twentieth century: it is far less to do with conventional policy advice, and far more to do with delivery and project management. The skills are actually quite analogous to those of the private sector. This is true of civil servants. It is also true of politicians. The skills that bring you to the top of the greasy pole in Parliament are not necessarily those that equip you to run a department with a workforce numbered in thousands and a budget numbered in billions.

Moreover, the pace of modern politics and the intrusion of media scrutiny—rightly or wrongly of an entirely different order today than even fifteen or twenty years ago—mean that decisions have to be made, positions taken, strategies worked out and communicated with a speed that is the speed of light compared to the speed of sound.

Of course, none of the above means that decisions should be taken without proper analysis, but it does mean that the old infrastructure of policy papers submitted by civil servants to Cabinet, who then debate and decide with the prime minister as benevolent chairman, is not suitable in responding to the demands of a fast-changing world or an even faster-changing political landscape. Into this infrastructure, the import of special advisers is not a breach in the walls of propriety; it is a perfectly sensible way of enlarging the scope of advice and making government move. As I discovered early on, the problem with the traditional Civil Service was not obstruction, but inertia.

However, all of that was in the future as I sat and contemplated giving this famed British system its instructions. The first command was in conjunction with the Treasury to work on Bank of England independence, to allow the bank to set interest rates, not the government. The day passed in a bit of a daze, principally preoccupied with appointing Cabinet members and ministers. This was a moment of joy for some and anguish for others. The key positions were already allocated, but the Shadow Cabinet was larger than the Cabinet could be. I had to tell three members that though they could be ministers, I could not put them in the Cabinet. Two agreed to take the ministerial positions, one preferred to go on the back benches, where the majority Members of Parliament who are not ministers sit in the House of Commons. Hmm, welcome to the hot seat, I thought, knowing that in the years to come, the members of the ejected, dejected and rejected would only grow.

But in those first hours, days and weeks, the government led a charmed life, as you might expect. The first evening as prime minister I went back to Richmond Crescent to spend my last night there. A couple of days later we ate a Chinese takeaway in Downing Street and my dad came down to be with me, which was lovely for him and made me feel very proud.

I got my first red box—the official briefcase given to all members of the government, where they keep their papers—my first recommendations, my first letters to sign. The team were all finding their feet, making the transition from Opposition assault unit, scaling the walls of the citadel, to sitting in the ruler's palace in charge of all we surveyed. My core staff were an extraordinary group of people, very different in character and outlook, but knitted together like a regiment, imbued with a common purpose and with a camaraderie that had a spirit of steel running through it. I have a few rules about people I work with really closely. Work comes first. No blame culture. Fun, in its proper place, is good. Disloyalty has no place. Look out for each other. Stick together. Respect each other. It helps if you also like each other.

By and large, they did. Jonathan had had initial difficulty settling in to the role of chief of staff in the Leader of the Opposition's office, finding the change from career diplomat to politico tricky. Once settled in, though, he was brilliant. I describe his contribution to the Northern Ireland peace process later, but his main contributions to the office were a knowledge of the Civil Service system, an extraordinary work rate (he has a lightning ability to absorb information), and a politics that was completely and naturally New Labour. He and Anji were the non-party political side of New Labour. They empathised with business, were indelibly middle class in outlook and could have worked in any apolitical outfit with ease; strong supporters of Labour, but not Labour people.

Sally Morgan, the political secretary and later director of political and government relations, was very much a Labour person and could reach the parts of the political firmament others couldn't; but for all that was totally in favour of aspiration and high standards, and, though a formidable organiser, had no truck with Old Labour organisational politics. But she and Alastair, along with Bruce Grocott, my parliamentary private secretary since 1994, could always understand the party point of view. They didn't necessarily agree with it, but they always got it, and therefore were invaluable in advising how to change it.

Right from the beginning I discovered one thing about Alastair: he had a great ability to instil loyalty. His communications team were a mixture of civil servants and special advisers, and within weeks they were welded together into an immensely effective operation. They adored him and he stood by them and inspired them with that odd combination of humour, forthrightness and bravado.

Kate Garvey was the gatekeeper, the custodian of the diary. There is a whole PhD thesis to be written by some smart political student about the importance of scheduling to a modern prime minister or president. To call it being "in charge of the diary" is like calling Lennon and McCartney people who "wrote songs": it is true, but it fails to convey the seminal importance of the product. How time is used is of the essence, and later I describe how it was done for me. Kate was charming and fun, which concealed a very tough streak. She ran the diary with a grip of iron and was quite prepared to squeeze the balls very hard indeed of anyone who interfered, but with a winning smile, of course.

There was Liz Lloyd, who had come to me fresh out of university as a researcher and who then worked her way up until she was deputy chief of staff. She looked like an English rose, was very intellectually able, could be blue stocking or red stocking according to the occasion, but most of all was so transparently honest and fair to everyone that she exerted a calming influence on the madhouse.

There was James Purnell, incredibly bright, invaluable on policy issues and all the time learning the trade of politics for the future career I was anxious for him to have.

There was David Miliband as head of policy, who did look about twelve at the time. David did a masterful job of putting the government programme together, keeping ministers happy even while guiding them, sometimes fairly forcefully, towards a direction other than the one they intended. He was perfect for the first term: really clever, plainly, and with good party politics. More in the same camp as Sally and Alastair, but New Labour nonetheless.

Pat McFadden did party organising, but it was obvious at a very early stage that he had outstanding political gifts and also the intellect to be a first-class minister.

There was Peter Hyman, who had a roving policy and communications brief, always bright, bubbling with new ideas, utterly unafraid to speak his mind and take issue with me or anyone else, but a lovely character who went off to be a teacher (and a very good one).

Tim Allan was an excellent foil for Alastair as his deputy in the press office, and obviously destined for great things (he should have been in politics, but he decided to start a successful business).

Sarah Hunter, the daughter of a friend of the Lord Chancellor Derry Irvine, and Jonathan Pearse both came with me young, from my time as Leader of the Opposition, to help in the office, and fortunately stayed with me until Sarah went off to have children. Both were hard-working and great people to be around. Hilary Coffman, who had served every Labour leader from Michael Foot onwards, was also part of the team and was incredibly experienced and calm; and since she often had to deal with the (frequent) personal issues in the media, she was the recipient of the most horrendous nonsense from all sides as she sought to sift the slender stalks of wheat from the vast accumulation of chaff.

The two who were in a category *sui generis* were Anji and Derry. Anji was my best friend. We had known each other since the age of sixteen when I had tried climbing inside her sleeping bag at a party in the north of Scotland (without success!). She had looked after me at university, turned up in my life again when I was an MP and had been with me ever since. She was sexy and exuberant and used both attributes to devastating effect, but you underestimated her at your peril. She had perhaps the most naturally intuitive political instinct of anyone I ever met, was very, very clever, and could be ruthless beyond any of us, if she felt it necessary to protect me or the project.

Derry, as with Peter Mandelson and Philip Gould, was outside the office but inside the core team. In those early days, the essential thing Derry brought was a rigorous analytical ability that was put at the disposal of anyone who had a problem that required it. As I used to say—because occasionally people would query my reverential and deferential tone with Derry—he has a brain the size of a melon. When he dies, they will put it in a museum. It's the one Dr. Frankenstein should have stolen. He could be politically blind, but intellectually he could see it all and with a clarity and focus that in the ambiguous and often sloppy world of politics was a precious quality, greatly to be prized. If anyone, whether an outsider or from the Civil Service, got intellectually uppity in those early days and became patronising, I would wheel Derry in and watch them quail as he worked on them like some finely tooled industrial moulding machine, stamping and beating down on them till they were bashed into shape and spat out the other end.

Peter Mandelson was my close friend and ally. He was clever, charming and fun, all of those things that make for someone who is wonderful company. He had two attributes that marked him out as an outstanding political *consiglieri*. He could spot where things were going, not just where they were. As Gordon used to say, Peter could tell you not merely what people were thinking today, but what they would think tomorrow. For political strategy, that is pretty invaluable.

The other attribute was his nerve under fire. Where his own feelings were concerned, like all of us he could be deeply emotional; but put him in the front line, in the heat of the political battle, and he was like a Roman phalanx, calm, disciplined and extraordinarily effective. When the enemy was running amok, he would be imperturbable, rallying the troops and often the generals, looking for the point of counter-attack and all the while seeming rather to enjoy himself. Such a quality is very, very rare. And when you find it, you treasure it.

Philip Gould was the final part of the inner team. He was the one with the divining rod. His job was precisely to tell us what it was like in the instant. In that he was typical of a very good pollster. But over time,

I noticed something else: he was actually a great synthesiser of the public mood. He would analyse it, explain it and predict its consequences with an insight that rose above the mundane expression of "they like this" or "they hate that." It would get to where the public might be brought, as well as to where they presently felt comfortable. In this, he became a strategist not a pollster.

He was also critical to the process of my big, set-piece, annual party Conference speech. Every year, for thirteen years, this process produced agony, consternation, madness and creativity in roughly equal proportions amongst my staff and me. I would immerse myself in it for a week beforehand, and there would frequently be fifteen or twenty drafts. Each year I hoped it would be easier. Each year it was as hard as ever. And 2006—the best speech of all in my opinion—was as hard as any.

In 1995, still in Opposition, I decided on the Monday before the Tuesday speech that it was all hopeless, the draft was useless, my brain had finally become scrambled and I would have to resign on grounds of incapacity. I had also agreed to do a photo-opportunity that morning at a school with Kevin Keegan, then manager of Newcastle United (my team). On arriving, I was in such despair that when Kevin said, Let's do a heading session in front of the kids (and mass media), to the complete horror of Alastair and my staff I said, Sure, fine, whatever. By then I was beyond caring. It was, of course a monumental risk as it always is when a political leader plays sport in public. No one expects you to be brilliant, but you can't afford to be absolutely rubbish, otherwise you are plainly not fit to run a nation. This wasn't kicking the ball—quite difficult to mess up completely—but head to head. That's a very easy way to make a total idiot of yourself.

However, I was so beyond it all, and of course Kevin was such a professional and could head the ball back to where I could get it, that we did twenty-nine headers on the go, which was impressive (and probably got more publicity than the speech!).

The worst sporting challenge was some years later when I agreed to play a charity game with Ilie Nastase, Pat Cash and the author and comedian Alistair McGowan at the Queen's Club. Tennis is a game which you can play well, badly or, if too nervous, in a manner in which your arms refuse to obey your brain. I have played in all three styles. I was prime minister, therefore busy. I had never been to Queen's and had not played on grass since university. I arrived feeling casual, then realised my match was straight after the annual Queen's final, in which Tim Henman was playing, in front of a crowd of 6,000. Casual gave way to panic. Panic is the worst mindset in which to play tennis, certain to produce collapse. I was only saved from humiliation by the fact that Tim's final went on longer than expected. Ilie Nastase kindly agreed to knock-up with me. We ended up playing for almost two hours before we got on court. By then I was so warmed up, the panic subsided and I played fine. But I swore not to take the risk again!

Anyway, I digress. Philip's role in my conference speeches was to help me define my message. So into the competing sounds and chaos of the orchestra tuning up would come a strong, clear note of harmony. I can't tell you how many times he rescued the speech and gave it lift and power.

You will see from all of the above that I was rather proud of the team. They were an unusually talented group of people. The thing I liked most about them? They defied category. They were one-offs. Very normal; but not very conventional. Very human; but with that touch of the magic potion that distinguishes those who strive from those who merely toil, those who take life as it comes and those who live life like an adventure. I was lucky indeed to have them with me.

The first hundred days of government were in one sense remarkably productive. We were storming through the announcements, which ultimately added up not just to a change of government, but a change of governing culture.

On 2 May, we announced the abolition of state-funded assistance for private schools, independent of the state system, in order to put the money into better state provision for infants.

On 3 May, we created the new Department for International Development, separating aid from the Foreign Office. It was not popular with the Foreign Office, who thereby lost control of the largest slice of their budget, and some of their objections gained my sympathy over time. Clare Short was the Secretary of State for the new department. Under her leadership, it led the way globally in terms of development policy, and people just queued up to work in it. It resembled a non-governmental organisation (NGO) inside government and this caused significant problems from time to time, but all things considered, I thought it worth it and it gave Britain huge reach into the developing world. Though I can see Alastair's look of disgust as I write this (he couldn't stand her), I did think she had real leadership talent; the trouble was she thought people who disagreed with her were wicked rather than wrong—a common failing of politicians—and when she turned sour, she could be very bitter indeed. But we should be proud of our aid record and she of her part in it.

On 6 May, Gordon announced the independence of the Bank of England.

On 9 May, we reformed Prime Minister's Questions (PMQs), when the prime minister takes questions on current affairs from Members of Parliament in the House of Commons, to make it one weekly half-hour session, not two sessions of fifteen minutes.

On 11 May, we announced compensation for Gulf War veterans.

On 12 May, we announced reforms to the National Lottery to allow the proceeds to go into health and education, and Gordon cut VAT on fuel to 5 per cent to help with heating bills.

On 14 May, we affirmed our commitment to ban tobacco advertising.

On 15 May, we restored trade union rights to Government Communications Headquarters (GCHQ) staff, reversing a Tory decision to deny intelligence workers—even those way down the chain—the right to join a trade union.

On 16 May, bills for referenda on Scottish and Welsh devolution were introduced, giving some central government powers to national administrations in Scotland and Wales, and we announced a seven-point plan to revive the British film industry.

In week four, we banned the production or export of landmines, and moved to a free vote for a ban on handguns, following the massacre in Dunblane in Scotland in which seventeen people were killed. (In a free vote, Members of Parliament are able to vote as they wish and are not directed by their party.)

At the end of May, Defence Secretary George Robertson set up the strategic defence review, and the following week we appointed the head of the Low Pay Commission, which was to be charged with setting Britain's first ever minimum wage.

By the end of week six, we had started to put in place the literacy and numeracy strategy to raise standards of performance for primary-school children in reading, writing and maths.

On 16 June, we signed up to the European Social Chapter. For over a decade this had been a dividing line with the Tories, who thought it would hinder our competitiveness. We thought it was about basic employment rights like paid holidays and was a necessary feature of a just society. I had actually used our support for the Social Chapter to drop our support for the closed shop (the obligation in certain trades to join a designated union). When we signed it, Robin Cook, the Foreign Secretary, announced triumphantly that we had done so, and it was a cause of much jubilation among party members and unions (who by then had forgotten the closed shop).

On 2 July, Gordon gave his first Budget, including a welfare-to-work package funded by a windfall levy on the privatised utilities. Two days later, Derry announced what became our plans for the Human Rights Act, the enactment into UK law of the European Convention on Human Rights. Tessa Jowell, a new minister in charge of public health, set out proposals to tackle health inequality, when people from different classes and regions have varying degrees of access to the best health care. Tackling health inequality was a top priority for our government, focused on narrowing the health gap between disadvantaged groups and communities and the rest of the country. And so it went on, with actions, announcements and aspirations too many to mention.

These were not just changes in policy; they were radical departures in the way Britain was governed, in the constitution and in attitude.

The hundred days ended with the publication of the plan to give London a mayor for the first time in centuries. And on the hundredth day we rested. Or at least I did, fleeing first to Tuscany and then to the south of France in search of the chance to relax after the helter-skelter of the first months.

What sort of leader was I at that point? I had a philosophy that was clear and clearly different from a traditional Labour politician. I was middle class, and my politics were in many ways middle class. My programme was every bit as much geared by the aspirations of the up-and-coming as the anxieties of the down-and-out. Partly for that very reason, and to emphasise to the party that I had not pulled up its roots, my first major domestic speech outside of the House of Commons was on the Aylesbury Housing Estate in south London on 2 June, a deprived estate forgotten in the Tory years. I set out my basic pitch for the mantle of one-nation politics. Very consciously I was setting out my stall as a unifier. I didn't want class war. I didn't like division or discord. I could see how a coalition of the well off and the less well off could establish points of common interest. I had no patience with tribal party politics, with its exaggerated differences, rancorous disputes and irrational prejudices.

The themes underlying the philosophy were also clearly spelt out: welfare as a hand up, not a handout, where welfare is used not just to hand people money but as a first step to encourage them to get back to work where possible; responsibility accompanying opportunity; a desire to reinvent government and get it to work coherently across departments; quality public services available on the basis of need, not wealth; communities free from the pervasive fear of petty crime and antisocial behaviour. Perhaps above all, an emphasis bordering on the religious on what counts to be what works—i.e. free ourselves, left and right, from dogma and get the country moving for the commonweal.

Rereading it now, it's all good stuff. It echoed many of the sentiments of Bill Clinton. Funnily enough, he visited Britain in May 1997 en route to a NATO summit. I brought him into Cabinet, where they were fairly in awe of him. He gave us a great Bill pep talk, using some of our campaign lines (like a real pro he had studied them all) and interweaving them cleverly with his own experience in office. I always remember him saying, "Don't forget: communication is fifty per cent of the battle in the information age. Say it once, say it twice and keep on saying it, and when you've finished, you'll know you've still not said it enough."

I had led the Labour Party to victory. I had reshaped it. I had given it a chance to be a true party of government. All of this took a degree of political skill and courage. And I wasn't such a fool back then to imagine that it wasn't all going to get tougher, sharper and uglier. I knew I was enjoying a honeymoon and I had no illusions about the marriage, even if my other half did. All of this made me fearful, apprehensive and on edge, even though at that time it seemed as if I could do no wrong and no challenge was beyond me.

What was missing? There was a naivety about my belief that merely by adopting an approach based on reason and the abstinence from ideological dogma, hard problems could be solved, complex issues unravelled, divergent positions reconciled. It is true that such an approach was an advantage, necessary even; but by a large distance, insufficient. In fact, such an attitude only bestows an open mind. It doesn't obviate the need for analysis, in-depth examination of policy options, going right down into the bowels of a problem and, there in the messy tangle, trying to solve it. Once you get down from the Olympian heights, where you can breathe freely the air of consensus and shared values and common goals, and you descend into that morass where the problem lies, what do you find? You find it's full of unforeseen difficulties, technical minefields, and above all vested interests that want the solution to remain buried with the problem. These interests—professional, financial, sectoral—do not take kindly to your disturbing them. Very soon, the political opposition that wants you out and themselves in, allies itself to the vested interests. They fight back.

Here's the thing: they don't fight cleanly either. There are you, the leader, full of genuine desire to do good; yes, of course, to be top dog and decision-maker, but nonetheless sincere in your wish to improve the world. You think: we have a disagreement; let's reason it out. I'll hear you; you'll hear me. We may even persuade each other, but if we don't, well, reasonable people can disagree and I know we both accept that ultimately I'm the prime minister and have to decide.

No, it's not like that; not like that at all, in fact. They get after you. They abuse your argument; they misrepresent your motives; they deride your sincerity and your protestations of good faith and the commonweal. For progressive politicians coming into power, that is always the biggest shock. The right get after you, from the off, with a vigour, venom and vitriol that has you reeling. You're appalled by it, offended by it, but most of all surprised by it. Criticisms become accusations. Disagreements become rows. Attempts at change become assaults on your opponents' fundamental liberties. You think you've come to a debating society but suddenly find you're in a cage with a bare-knuckle fighter and a howling mob outside laying bets on how long you'll last.

I had discovered long ago the first lesson of political courage: to think anew. I had then learned the second: to be prepared to lead and to decide. I was now studying the third: how to take the calculated risk. I was going to alienate some people, like it or not. The moment you decide, you divide. However, I would calculate the upset, calibrate it, understand its dimensions, assess its magnitude, ameliorate its consequences. And so I got over the surprise of the onslaught and became used to the derision, began to develop the carapace of near indifference to dispute that is so dangerous in a leader yet so necessary for survival.

Through it all, I was slowly coming to grips with the other dimension of government for which no amount of political courage is sufficient: the technical details of getting the policy right. I could see I might have to choose between what was right and what was politic, but deciding what was right was itself complex and highly contentious. The more I investigated the facts, the closer came the understanding that changing a nation was a whole lot harder than changing a party. The risks inherent in that, and the courage to take them, were of a different order entirely.

I was going to do my best and I was going to do it carefully; but even in those first months, even as it seemed we were masters of the political scene, I could see where the next lesson lay: what happened when you came to the risk that could *not* be calculated? What happened when your opponents were not the usual vested interests, and the noise was not the normal clamour aroused by anyone who tries to change anything, but came from the mainstream voices of mainstream people? What happened if the disagreement was not with the party or a limited section of the public, but with the body of the people?

I was aware I was a very popular leader. It was a bit like a love affair with the public, on both our parts. Like newly-weds, we envisaged ourselves growing together, learning together, falling out from time to time as all couples do, but retaining something profound that made our love real and whole, always there to be retrieved. What happened if we grew apart?

TWO

THE APPRENTICE LEADER

The journey from Opposition to government had taken three years. It sounds a short time. It's not how it feels. Every day drags. Every week a fresh anxiety or event or statement disturbs the careful orchestration of the march from impotence to power. Every month your competitors, or someone in the media simply bored or irritated by your success, looks to sully the brand, cheapen it, ridicule it. Every year there is a new height to be attained so that the momentum is not lost.

Yet I look back on the stories and commentary during those years, and I deride the feelings of difficulty I had at the time. That was tough? It was a stroll, a breeze, a gentle jog towards the finishing line. I reread the notes, remember the calls, run through the meetings, each one of which mattered so much and, in my mind, contributed so much, and I wonder at the simplicity and ease of it all.

What never changed between Opposition and government was the intensity of the focus. Of course, back then, I was learning and reaching new levels at every important juncture; at the time it naturally felt so much harder and challenging.

As a child you first learn about courage and fear in the playground fight, when the bully bullies and you are scared of being hurt. Finally, at some point, you turn and fight. I can still recall the exact moment for me: aged about ten, outside the gates of Durham Choristers School in the beautiful and ancient Cathedral Close where we first lived when we came to the city, with the old SPCK bookshop and the eighteenth-century houses and cottages beside the Norman splendour of the cathedral.

He wasn't even a very big bully. Certainly not a very frightening one. I even remember his name. He had been on at me for weeks. I hated it, and dreaded going into the class where he was, and avoided going wherever he would be. Then, for some reason or no reason, out there by the school gates when he came upon me unexpectedly and started up, I turned on him and told him I would hit him if he didn't stop. He could tell I meant it, because I did and my eyes would have shown it— so he stopped. Silly, isn't it, to recall that tiny moment of character development after all these years.

Later, you learn courage in different situations: the first time onstage, when you wish you had never agreed to do it, you curse your pretensions and lament your ego, and want only to go back into the corner. But somehow you don't; you step out. Going down to London aged eighteen on my own for the first time; spending months alone in Paris, as I did after my Bar exams in 1976; making that call; seeking that meeting; pushing and striving and driving. Each step is fearful, yet each refusal means not only remorse at an opportunity missed, but, worse, despising yourself for not even summoning up the courage to try.

Sometimes I marvelled at the way I did indeed step forward, but more often I was aware of the constant struggle to make the choice to do so. For it is a choice. The alternative option always beckons and does so adorned with good arguments: it's not a propitious moment; it is a risk too far; others are against it; there will be another moment. Often there isn't, however, and in any event, deep down you know the reason: the fear of being out there, exposed, prone to fail. If you never try to succeed, you never have to fail. So why do it?

There are people I've come across who are shorn of such doubt, who have that inner courage to step out instinctively and without forethought, and for whom it is as natural as breathing. Their problem is rather different: mine is about the battle between courage and fear, while theirs is the consequence of being fearless. Fear makes you calculate and calculation can sometimes save you (though over-calculation finishes you off); for those who don't calculate at all but go headlong, the risk can be foolhardy and lead to downfall. But I always admired that temperament, liked its swagger and absence of manipulation.

After leaving Oxford I had joined the Labour Party. Geoff Gallop, who had left the year before me, had decided to join the Australian Labor Party. "It may be a sell-out," he said cheerfully, "but it's the only way we are ever going to make change." His free spirit had finally rebelled against the dogma and blinkers of the far left, and I suspect he was also prodded by the vast Aussie common sense of his wife Bev.

From 1975 to 1983 I toiled away in various parts of the party. But my views began to shift. For a start I was working, and really hard work it was. Through a girlfriend, I got an introduction to the famous Derry Irvine, then only thirty-six and regarded as one of the best and brightest junior counsels at the Bar. And so began that life-changing relationship.

Derry taught me how to think. In intellectual terms, I had only "passed exams" before meeting Derry, and I hadn't a clue how to think. I mean really think—analyse, dissect a problem from first principles, and having deconstructed it, construct a solution.

As my pupil master, an experienced barrister training a new barrister, he was tyrannical but a genius. I used to help write his opinions and do the briefs (what we call pleadings). I remember the first time I wrote an opinion, I gave it to him expecting him to read it, make a comment or two and then bin it, because naturally I thought he would write it himself. He glanced at it, signed it and to my horror told me to tell the clerk to put it out. "Is that wise?" I said, absolutely aghast. I mean—I was only a pupil!

"Well," he said, looking up from his desk, "it's your best work, isn't it?" He was growling and I was terrified. I stammered something about "Well, it was quite difficult and I hope it's OK, but it's my first . . ." etc. He picked it up and literally threw it at me. "I don't want your ramblings, I don't want your half-thoughts. I want your best work, work that you personally will be responsible for. Understand?"

"Yes," I said humbly.

"Then come back to me when you've done it." And he looked back down at his desk. "Go on, bugger off," he said, without even glancing at me.

I returned with a different and better draft. This time, he told me to sit down and went through it, explaining the faults, questioning the arguments, above all drilling down to the answer. This drilling down is a process that fascinated me then, and fascinates me still.

Most people with a tricky problem grasp that it is difficult, and they think about it. Maybe they read up on it, learn what others have said. They think about which of those solutions they find best. They choose one, or they sort of "um and ah" about it and decide it's really all too difficult.

Faced with a legal problem, Derry was like the proverbial dog with a bone. He would gnaw at it, examine it, turn it over, bury it, dig it up, step back and stare at it. But he wouldn't stop or reflect until he had got every bit of meat there was off it, had extracted its essence and mastered it. Above all, he never accepted the conventional analysis just because it was conventional. He went back to first principles, went behind and beneath the conventional, and occasionally—which was his genius—came back with analysis that looked at the problem in an entirely different way. Time and again, I recall a case that looked hopeless when seen conventionally, but was suddenly given hope by being analysed and looked at differently.

He was completely uncompromising when it came to matters of the mind. Woe betide you if you turned up half prepared, casually interested, semi-engaged. If your grammar or spelling was wrong, you missed a typo, you wrote a sentence that was sloppy, there would be an eruption—and Derry in full flow had an armoury of verbal battery that was truly impressive. I was scared of him, admired him and adored him; but most of all, I was grateful to him.

Derry was moderate Labour. He had never trifled with ultra-leftism, despised the false intellectual basis of it and regarded its adherents as dabblers. In this he was like Cherie. She too had been a major influence, not because she was my girlfriend and then wife, or even because we spent a long time discussing politics—we didn't—but because her support for Labour was natural, sensible and born of real-life experience. She too had never had the slightest interest in intellectual or political posturing. Indeed, practically above all of my contemporaries, she stayed in the same spot politically from beginning to end. She watched as those to the left of her moved to the right of her; but, for herself, she remained in the same place. In that sense, she was like my constituency agent John Burton, a party member of my staff who helped me manage the work in my constituency. Over time, I came to see practical, common-sense progressive politics as indispensable to effecting political change, as opposed to talking about it.

For my first four or five years at the Bar, I was devoted to the law. The work was so time-consuming—I worked at least twelve hours a day—that I had little time for political activism, but I was in my local party, first in Earls Court, then Marylebone, then Hackney; I wrote occasional articles for the *New Statesman*, at that time a serious weekly magazine; and through Derry I met John Smith and other Labour figures.

I can't recall the date I first went to Parliament, but I recall the event and its impact on me vividly. Cherie's dad, Tony Booth, was a long-time Labour supporter and, as a soap star and celebrity, knew a lot of Labour MPs. One was Tom Pendry. Tom was a very shrewd, capable guy, committed of course, but he had seen enough to make himself pretty worldly-wise. Labour Party politics following the defeat of 1979 was a bit like revolutionary France at the time of the Thermidorian Reaction, full of infighting, intrigue and bitter recrimination. The MPs were regarded by a large section of the party as sell-out merchants who had "betrayed socialism." They responded as MPs do, with a mixture of courageous defiance, abject capitulation to the mob, and agonised dithering as they worked out which way the tumbril was heading.

Through Tony, Cherie fixed me up to see Tom. I had been toying with the idea of standing for Parliament, but I was unsure. Tom invited us to have a late-night drink in the Commons Bar, since he had to stay in the House to vote. I went in the door at the gate where they queue for PMQs. Security was looser in those days. I went up the steps, and on my left passed Westminster Hall, where Charles I had been tried, where kings, queens and the high-class officials lay in state, and where the damaged but still recognisable statues of knights from ages past were set high up in alcoves along with the banners of ancient battles.

I walked into the cavernous Central Lobby where the public wait to meet their MPs, and I stopped. I was thunderstruck. It just hit me. This was where I wanted to be. It was very odd. Odd because so unlike me, and odd because in later times I was never known as a "House of Commons man." But there and then, I had a complete presentiment: here I was going to be. This was my destiny. This was my political home. I was going to do whatever it took to enter it.

Cherie was rather startled by the effect on me. I was literally pacing up and down the place, drinking in its atmosphere, studying its architecture as if by looking at the building I would discover the secret of how to get there not by invitation, but by right. As I write this now, suddenly I retrieve the feeling from the shelf of old sentiment where it has lain so long, and I miss Parliament. By the time I finished in June 2007, almost thirty years later, I had had enough, I wanted out and away. But now, as I examine my emotions then, I get some of that passion back. The Bar had its attractions—and it was certainly a wealthier place—but to be a Member of Parliament, to be one of the legislators of the land, to walk unhindered through those hallowed corridors and chambers; what excitement, what an adventure, what a sense of arrival at a new and higher level of existence.

Tom thought me a pretty strange bird that evening. We had barely been introduced when I started plying him with questions. How do you get here? What can you do for me? Who do I see? What do I do? How shall I do it? "I didn't realise you were in such a hurry," he said, amused at my behaving like some hyperactive child.

Tom gave me my first union introductions—vital because unions formed the base of Labour support—and invaluable advice about the low ground of Labour politics. From then on, until the Beaconsfield by-election in 1982, when I stood for office but lost, I pursued my goal without relenting. (A by-election takes place in an individual constituency, outside the general election, when a Member of Parliament dies or otherwise steps down.) And then after that by-election, I redoubled in my determination until Sedgefield came to me at the very tail end of the 1979–83 Parliament. When it looked as if all was lost and I had resigned myself to sitting out the 1983 election, I had even decided to abandon the London Bar, move to Newcastle and take Nick Brown's council seat, Nick having been chosen to fight the safe constituency of Newcastle East. The plan was then to take the neighbouring constituency of Wallsend, later to be Steve Byers' seat. In my desperation, I had contacted Dad's old chambers and made enquiries. In the end I never had to do it; but the fact that I would have done it is a measure of my desire.

As for my views on the Labour Party, these were evolving almost as fast as my ambition. I took care not to depart too far from the party mainstream opinion at that time, much to the left of where it had been; but I was nevertheless aware from the beginning that we were in the wrong place. I admired Michael Foot but he was a quixotic choice over Denis Healey.

Cherie had been chosen for the Thanet North constituency, comprising Herne Bay and Margate, a Tory seat she couldn't win. She had been asked to apply and agreed, but she was never really set on being an MP. And as I got more passionate, she saw herself more as a barrister, working at the highest levels of the law. With her qualifications—top first in her degree, top of her year in the Bar exams—she was going to do better than me.

Her adoption as a candidate allowed me another experience that made its impact. Her dad knew Tony Benn well and asked him to speak to her party in Margate. I was deputed to pick him up at his home in Holland Park and drive him down there. By the way, Tony now is something of a national treasure. Back then, for a large part of Tory and middle-ground opinion, he was the devil. I don't mean he was simply disagreed with; he would make people literally choke with rage. He was the most disliked person for most parts of the media—which of course gave him hero status for a large part of the left.

I had never heard him speak before that night. I sat enraptured, absolutely captivated and inspired. I thought: if only I could speak like that. What impressed me was not so much the content—actually I didn't agree with a lot of it—but the power of it, the ability to use words to move people, not simply to persuade but to propel. For days, weeks afterwards, I sat going over it in my mind. Probably to him it was one of half a dozen he did that week and was nothing special, but for me it was a revelation.

First, there was his utter confidence. From the outset, the audience were relaxed and able to listen, because they knew the speaker was in control. When he began and he looked around at them, there was no squeakiness, no uncertainty, no negative energy. It wasn't the absence of nerves. It was the presence of self-belief. He held them, easily and naturally.

Second, he used humour. If someone can make you laugh, you are already in their power. The tension between speaker and audience, there until they get the measure of each other, evaporates.

Third, there was a thread that ran throughout the speech. There was an argument. Sometimes there was digression and the thread was momentarily obscured, but always he returned and the thread was visible once more.

Fourth, the argument was built, not plonked down. Although introduced broadly at the beginning, it was not glimpsed fully until layer upon layer of supporting words built up to it and finally the argument was brought forth. Suddenly all the words were connected, the purpose was made plain and the argument was out there, and you thought only the wilfully obdurate could not see its force and agree with it.

On the way back, we talked about Militant. I wanted to know what he thought about this Trotskyist sect that had infiltrated Labour. I was representing the party in the legal case against them and, having studied them and their methods, I knew there was no dealing with them, other than by expelling them. He didn't agree, and I spotted the fundamental weakness in his position: he was in love with his role as idealist, as standard-bearer, as the man of principle against the unprincipled careerist MPs. He wouldn't confront those who were actually preventing the idealism from ever being put into effect. He was the preacher, not the general. And battles aren't won by preachers.

Eleven years later, I was leader of the Labour Party, just turned forty-one. John Smith, my predecessor, died on 12 May 1994. He had been leader for just two years. He was an outstanding figure: a minister in the last Labour government, a successful QC (a member of the Queen's Counsel, appointed by Her Majesty), a brilliant House of Commons debater, close friend of Derry and of Donald Dewar—a Labour MP who became Secretary of State for Scotland when I became PM—and one of the sanest, smartest and surest people you could ever meet. In a strange way, he had been instrumental in getting me into Parliament in 1983 and therefore becoming leader of the party. When the Beacons-field by-election came up in May 1982 and I thought about going for it, most people advised me against it since it was a no-hoper for Labour. On the contrary, John said, that was the very reason for doing it. No one could blame me, I would get national attention and be in a better position to have a crack at a good seat in the next election. He was right.

After the 1992 defeat, when Neil Kinnock lost for the second time, John was the obvious choice for leader. He did superbly in the after-math of the Exchange Rate Mechanism debacle, when Britain was dumped unceremoniously out of the precursor to monetary union, and by May 1994 had established a solid, though not spectacular, poll lead.

But John had a health problem. In 1988, he had suffered a serious heart attack. He was at that time Shadow Chancellor of the Exchequer. Gordon stood in for him and did magnificently, thus sealing his reputation as the coming man. After several months off, John came back, resumed his place and seemed to have recovered. However, he had, in part, suffered the attack because of his lifestyle. John was quite tubby, and though he was a great hiker, he was also a stupendous toper. He could drink in a way I have never seen before or since. I don't mean he would ever be in drink when he needed to be sober—he was the complete professional—but if there was an Olympic medal for drinking, John would have contended with such superiority that after a few rounds the rest of the field would simply shake their heads and banish themselves from the track.

When he led a delegation to China in the 1980s, of which I was a member, we ended up with some local Chinese bigwigs in Shanghai. It was a jolly evening and a fair amount of whisky, mao-tai and beer was drunk. As the night progressed—punctuated by frequent toasts—things got a little more competitive, and essentially the chief bigwig and John got into a drinking bout. The Chinese guy was holding his drink in great style and was the closest I ever saw to John being outclassed, but I gave it to John on points in the end (I had switched to green tea several hours before), after he got the entire committee up on their feet to link arms and repeatedly sing a rousing if somewhat unintelligible chorus of "Auld Lang Syne."

John delighted in company. He loved going to the smoking room in the House of Commons after the vote, where in those days Tories and Labour would mix quite merrily, and where politics was taken that bit less seriously for a while. It was where F. E. Smith, a lawyer and Tory statesman, and Churchill would sit and talk like the two close friends they were, whatever hard words had been exchanged across the floor of the House (and some were very hard indeed). It's a shame that such friendship is rare today, very rare. John would love to talk, reminisce, relax and wind down. Drink was a relaxant. In this regard, he was like Derry. They would never do it before a big occasion, but the two of them together betokened a monumental session that, if the time was free, could start at lunch and go on well into the night.

Unfortunately, John could take a lot of it. I say unfortunately because it meant there was no cut-off, no circuit breaker, no warning sign and insufficient punishment the day after. For me, past a very limited point I would be ill, fall asleep and for sure be punished severely the next day; but both Derry and John could get up in the morning and joke about feeling under the weather, but actually be perfectly capable of meeting a reasonably challenging day.

Of course, after the heart attack he had to cut back, and did so—he lost weight, and "bagged" over a hundred Munros (Scottish mountains over 3,000 feet high)—but as the stresses of taking the leadership told on him, and as time progressed into 1993 and 1994, I noticed he was again starting to drink more than was wise. He felt like the old John, so he thought he could act like the old John. I should emphasise again that his drinking never interfered with his performance; it was an end-of-the-day thing, a holiday thing, an evening-with-close-friends thing, but his health was more fragile than he knew (or perhaps more accurately wanted to admit) and despite the constant admonitions of Elizabeth, his wife and his love, he found it hard to do without the relaxation and fellowship with which it was associated.

On the evening of 11 May 1994, there was a fund-raiser for the upcoming European elections. All the Shadow Cabinet were assembled at a reasonably smart London hotel, nothing too fancy but more upmarket than Labour was used to, as we looked to consolidate what was back then fairly limited business support.

I was only a spectator, not a speaker, hosting a table and schmoozing as one of the few members of the Shadow Cabinet (our employment spokesman) who could be safely left alone with the business types. I remember John's arrival as he came in with Elizabeth and greeted people. I remember looking into his eyes as we talked and thinking he looked very tired. I remember his speech, which was fine, though without energy. It had a good ending: "The opportunity to serve our country. That is all we ask."

For myself, I longed to get away. I had an early start the next morning, flying to Aberdeen for a campaign stop for the election. My daughter Kathryn was only six and would often wake up in the night, and even Nicky and Euan, though older, couldn't be relied on to sleep right through or not to wake early, especially as the days got lighter. One way or another, my sleep was usually interrupted, therefore the sooner I got home to bed, the better. As soon as I decently could, I stole away and got back to Richmond Crescent.

The next morning I landed at around nine at Aberdeen airport and was picked up to be driven to party HQ for a brief on the day's campaign. On the way in the car, someone from party HQ in London phoned to tell me John had suffered a serious heart attack; no one could be sure if he would live or not.

Moments later, Gordon called, as shocked as I was. We agreed to speak when I got to HQ. Another call came through just after I'd arrived. John was dead. I tried to compose myself. He had been a big part of my life, and I liked him very much. We had spent many times together, working and socialising. I knew what was coming now he was gone: even as people tried to assimilate the news, even as they mourned, even as they reflected about John Smith as a man, as a political leader, as a friend, attention would shift and they would ask the question that is asked every time a leader falls, and immediately a leader falls: who will be the successor?

It was a moment for which, at points consciously but more often unconsciously, I had been preparing. For years—at least up to 1992—I had always assumed Gordon would be leader. I was not only happy with that, I actually rejoiced in it. I didn't want the job. I was high enough to be able to espy its responsibility and its pain. No, if someone else could do it, I would be the supportive and loyal lieutenant. Fine by me. Good by me, in fact.

But by 1992, the Labour Party had lost four general elections in a row. What's more, our vote was stuck around 32 per cent. After thirteen years of Tory government and in the middle of a recession which you could say they had in part "caused," still we hit a 32 per cent ceiling. Why? For some, electoral reform seemed appealing. No matter how well we did in between times, come the election day, the country reverted. That was the tenor of Labour thinking and of much of the commentary.

To me, such defeatism was not so much wrong as absurd. Why on earth should it be so? From early on, even before my election to Parliament in 1983, I had realised the Labour problem was self-made and self-induced. We were not in touch with the modern world. We could basically attract two sorts of people: those who by tradition were Labour, and those who came to a position of support for socialism or social democracy through an intellectual process. Many trade union activists were in the first category; I was a member of the second. Neither group were what I would call "mainstream," and together they did not remotely add up to a constituency large enough to be in a position to win and to govern.

Furthermore, the first category was becoming smaller. The days of the old trade unionists were passing, along with many of the industries that they dominated—coal, steel, shipbuilding, textiles. The new industries—in particular those driven by emerging technologies, and modern service industries—were not attracted by the trade union mixture of industrial agitation and politics. More importantly, neither were those who worked in them. There was something irretrievably old-fashioned about the union meetings, the rules, the culture. Some trade unionists realised this and tried to effect change, but the comfort zone was too big, too enticing, too enveloping for the leadership ever to feel the necessity to change. They could see it was important and occasionally they made steps towards it, as in the development of new union services, but it was not existential. They didn't feel: change or die. There was no general election that pronounced an unalterable and unavoidable verdict; just the steady draining away of members, support and relevance. Unfortunately, they were still powerful and sufficiently relevant within the Labour Party, where the fact that they were courted and feted only added to their comfort.

Also, the nature of the union leaders themselves was changing. The leaders of the early and mid-twentieth century like Ernie Bevin, or Jack Jones later, were titans: working-class men who, through union meetings, colleges and conferences, achieved the education society had denied them, and who were shining examples of self-improvement. In those days, meetings were well attended—hundreds at a branch meeting was not exceptional. They were arenas of debate, often fiercely conducted, of discussion, of decision. They called for qualities of true leadership, of strategy and tactics combined to advance a cause that at the time was both reasonable and essential.

Old miners who had spent a life in the coalfields of the North-East used to tell me of the solemn ritual of such meetings, their significance in the community, their grandeur even, in terms of what they represented to local people. To be the branch official was a major role. To get to be an official was to have your feet on the rungs of achievement. To lead the Durham coalfield, for example, as Sam Watson, the famous leader of the 1950s, did, was to occupy a position of genuine authority. When Attlee was Labour leader and a dubious proposition was put forward, he would say: "Can't be done. Sam Watson wouldn't have it."

But all progressive movements have to beware their own success. The progress they make reinvents the society they work in, and they must in turn reinvent themselves to keep up, otherwise they become hollow echoes from a once loud, strong voice, reverberating still, but to little effect. As their consequence diminishes, so their dwindling adherents become ever more shrill and strident, more solicitous of protecting their own shrinking space rather than understanding that the voice of the times has moved on and they must listen before speaking. It happens in all organisations. It is fatal to those who are never confronted by a reckoning that forces them to face up and get wise. The new leaders of the unions tended to ape the old, but in a context so changed that it became increasingly pointless except in maintaining the morale of those who just wanted to carry on as they were.

When she took on the trade unions, Margaret Thatcher didn't come out of a sealed chamber with a new idea. It already existed: Harold Wilson and Barbara Castle had it with *In Place of Strife*; Edward Heath had it in the Industrial Relations Act of 1971. Both were attempts to bring union power within the purview of normal law. The difference was that by the time she took over, it was clear that an evolutionary attack on trade union privileges had failed and only a revolutionary one would succeed. And she had the character, leadership and intelligence to make it happen.

She was also greatly helped by her opponents. When Arthur Scargill became leader of the miners and the strike of 1984–5 began, it was plain that the choice was between on the one hand a very right-wing prime minister who was nonetheless democratically elected as leader of the nation and also correct about the excesses of union power, and on the other a leftist union leadership that was obviously undemocratic and completely out of touch with the modern world.

As I surveyed the wreckage of the Labour Party in the aftermath of the 1983 election, I knew change had to come about. The trade union base simply could not support a modern political party if it was to be a governing party.

In time I came to another conclusion, concerning the second category of people attracted to the party. The intellectual Fabian way of the Labour Party had deep roots and a venerable history. Its leading lights, often born relatively wealthy but who were indignant about inequality, were remarkable people. Like George Orwell, Hugh Dalton (a Labour politician who held various government positions during and after World War II), Stafford Cripps (a Labour Chancellor in Clement Attlee's government in the mid-twentieth century), and the members of the New Left Book Club and the Haldane Society, they tended to be erudite, committed, passionate and intensely intellectual in approach. Tony Benn was an example. Tony Crosland was another (indeed he had taught Benn at Oxford). As was the case with me, they had their first taste of left politics through university life. In that rather artificial environment, there had been an insight gained into the iniquity of the system; a conversion arising from a realisation that social conditions did indeed beget opportunity or the lack of it; an encounter of ideas that altered their life view. Once so altered, they became staunch advocates of social action and of the party of the trade unions and the working class whose lives had to be liberated from the conditions of poor housing, poor education and poor health care.

It took me a long time to work out what the problem with this second group was: although they cared for people, they didn't "feel" like them. They were like the Georges Duhamel character who says, "I love humanity, it's just human beings I can't stand." I don't mean, incidentally, that they were aloof or unpleasant—they were often charming and fun—but they didn't "get" aspiration. They were almost too altruistic for their own political good. When injustice and inequality were reduced—in part through their efforts—they failed to see what would happen. A person who is poor first needs someone to care about it, and then to act; but when no longer poor, their objective may then become to be well off. In other words, for such a person it is about aspiration, ambition, getting on and going up, making some money, keeping their family in good style, having their children do better than them. My dad's greatest wish was that I be educated privately, and not just at any old private school; he chose Fettes because he thought and had been told it was the best in Scotland.

The problem with the intellectual types was that they didn't quite understand this process; or if they did, rather resented it. In a sense they wanted to celebrate the working class, not make them middle class— but middle class was precisely what your average worker wanted himself or his kids to be. The intellectuals' belief in equality strayed dangerously into the realm of equality of income, not equality of opportunity. The latter was a liberator; the former would quickly become and be seen as a constraint. The impulse of many of those helped by well-meaning intellectuals was essentially meritocratic, not egalitarian—they wanted to be helped onto the ladder, but once on it, they thought ascending it was up to them.

As the 1980s gave way to the 1990s and the defeats kept coming, I became ever more convinced that there were crucial bits of a governing coalition missing for Labour. Where was our business support? Where were our links into the self-employed? Above all, where were the aspirant people, the ones doing well but who wanted to do better; the ones at the bottom who had dreams of the top? The intellectuals were right in saying social conditions determined success in life—but only in part. So did hard work, character, determination, grit, get-up-and-go. Where were those people in our ranks? Nowhere, I concluded.

Even back in 1983, when I still had ideas on nationalisation and defence that would have astounded and drawn derision from the Tony Blair of 1994, I knew we were a party out of its time. But I had to exercise care. I very nearly failed to become a candidate at all in 1983 because my views on modernising the party were so heretical.

However, I couldn't stop the mask slipping from time to time. Straight after the 1983 election, as a new MP, I attended the post-election rally in Spennymoor Town Hall, in my former constituency of Sedgefield. We had lost by a landslide, worse than in 1979, since when there had been a deep recession. The Labour Party had been monumentally rejected.

The rally was entitled "Lessons from Defeat." The blurb on the leaflet advertising it called for the most frank debate. I had been a barrister for near enough eight years and I was used to taking facts, dissecting them, analysing them, reassembling them and drawing conclusions. I was trained to be very rational in my thought processes. So: we had had a thumping great annihilation. Worst ever defeat. What's more, as I knew from personal canvassing, even those who voted for us told me frequently that they had done so *despite* our policies and leadership, not because of them.

From 1979 to 1983, Tony Benn performed the political equivalent of a conjuring trick. He convinced the Labour Party that the real reason we had lost in 1979 to Margaret Thatcher was because Jim Callaghan, the Labour prime minister, had been too right wing. Weird, I know, but true. Thus convinced, Labour moved sharply left and advocated unilateral nuclear disarmament, pulling out of Europe and wholesale nationalisation. It was remarkable, and a huge tribute to his charisma and persuasive power. For a moment, it looked like he might even win the election for deputy leader and thus become the dominant force in the party. His opponent was Denis Healey, the former Labour Chancellor who had had to take the tough measures to sort out the economy after Britain went to the International Monetary Fund for help in 1976. Had Benn won, it would have been a defeat for the whole leadership, and most likely Michael Foot would have been toppled by him shortly afterwards. This was narrowly averted; but in the leftward march, the Labour Party split. A new party was formed in the centre, the Social Democratic Party, which immediately drew large-scale support from moderate Labour voters.

So you might reasonably conclude that the period 1979 to 1983 had been an unmitigated disaster and that something had gone rather seriously wrong. Pretty obvious, I thought.

The meeting's title appeared to indicate people wanted to learn lessons. The platform consisted of me as the local MP, Dennis Skinner as standard-bearer of the far left at the time, and various assorted union people. Only a complete ingénu or total clot—i.e. me—could have thought it was going to be a balanced, frank debate.

Now, I had won my selection as Labour's candidate for the seat over the far left's choice, a man called Les Huckfield. He was a genuinely interesting political phenomenon—and only goes to show the odd effect politics can have on people. In the 1960s he had been Labour's youngest MP; a moderate; a minister; a rising star. However, for reasons everyone assumed were to do with ambition but may have been sincere conviction, he caught the Benn virus and became overnight a fully paid-up ultra-leftist. When his constituency disappeared in the national boundary reorganisation, which had incidentally brought the Sedgefield constituency into being, where I had stood and won, he then toured the country trying to upend sitting MPs in their reselection. By a mixture of means, the doors were always barred and he became a bit like something out of Transylvania wandering from village to village and having the garlic and crosses hung above the doors. But he damn near succeeded in Sedgefield, and only the organising genius of John Burton prevented it. Les Huckfield's defeat shocked and angered him and there were murmurings and rumours from his camp that they would aim to deselect me and get him in on the next reselection contest. So it was all very raw.

Anyway, I'm the local MP in Spennymoor, so I speak first. I get up. I give a logical, rational and, though I say it myself, entirely accurate analysis of why Labour lost and the lessons we should draw. I was as frank as the blurb could possibly have meant.

I really quite warmed to my theme. Labour had lost touch. It had failed to spot how society had changed. I had two lines I was rather proud of: one was about Labour's attitudes being from the era of "black-and-white TV" (most people by 1983 having colour TVs); the other was about the party "simply repeating old adages learned on your grandparents' knees" or some such.

Even I could tell it wasn't exactly going down a storm; but in those days, I had everything written out and didn't have the facility of adjusting mid-speech. Those were my thoughts. I wrote them down. I read them out. I finished to a smattering of applause from the few supporters John had brought along. The rest sat—and I think this is the only time I ever saw such a thing—and folded their arms, in unison, their faces grimacing as if a thousand lemons had been forced down their throats.

Dennis got to his feet. Still in unison, their arms unfolded and their faces began to smirk in eager anticipation. They knew what was coming. I didn't.

In later years, Dennis was one of my best (if somewhat closet) supporters. He didn't agree with any of my policies, but he liked someone who whacked the Tories. Though I'm not sure he would thank me for saying so, he mellowed and became a nicer person. In particular, he used to give me brilliant PMQs advice, pointing out with uncanny accuracy the weaknesses of my Tory opponents, feeding me one-liners and explaining what would rouse the troops behind me. But back then Dennis was your original firebrand. He was also a genius at a particular type of left-wing rally speech. He was in his element, and little new-boy muggins had given him an opening as large as your average open-cast mine (which he didn't much like either, since he had been a miner and to him proper mines were deep underground).

There's nothing quite like being utterly and publicly humiliated for teaching you a lesson. The meeting learned very few lessons (and those the wrong ones) from Labour's defeat. But I learned one big one from Dennis that day.

"So," he began, "your new MP, supposed to be a Labour MP [particular emphasis on word "Labour"], whose experience in Labour politics [again much emphasis on "Labour"] up to now includes [here reading from a piece of paper with extraordinary thespian timing and skill] Durham Choir School [private school much hated by the local proletariat]; Fettes College, Edinburgh—the Eton of Scotland, I'm told [in an aside], not that I'd know [much laughter and applause]; St. John's College, Oxford [said with an especial sneer]; and the Bar [here applause]—and that's not the one you buy a pint in [uproarious outburst of laughter] but one full of lawyers [pantomime hisses]; your new Labour MP thinks our grandparents didn't know what they were talking about; that it's time we disowned them; that now's the moment when we tell them—many of whom never owned so much as a wireless, never mind a black-and-white TV—that they don't belong in Thatcher's Britain [looks of horror on faces of audience]. Well, let me tell you, Anthony Charles Lynton Blair [my full name, rather unfortunately printed several times in the course of the Beaconsfield by-election], my grandparents were poor, it's true; were humble folk, I admit it; were, I dare say, a little old-fashioned in their principles of loyalty and solidarity; but THEY WERE DECENT PEOPLE AND PROUD OF BEING WORKING CLASS." The last words rose to a crescendo accompanied by an eruption of applause, cheers and general favour to a degree that fairly lifted the roof off the place.

After that the speakers got up one by one, and you never heard so many heart-rending tales of the fortitude, heroism and near-divine decency of grandparents. Several opined that they were only alive today through their nan's dedication; others of how entire mining communities had been on the brink of destruction until rescued by some miraculous intervention of grandma or grandad. Without ever quite being explicit, there were dark insinuations that maybe my own grandparentage had been of the landed gentry, possibly even the mine-owning sort whose adages they could only imagine, but were no doubt along the lines of grinding the faces of the poor into the dust.

Just when I thought it couldn't get any worse, it did. The final speaker, after completing his own cover version of the grandparent riff, turned to me and concluded by saying: "I am sorry you don't understand the history or traditions of the people up here; but, comrades and colleagues, here is someone who does . . ." And, at the back of the hall, in walks Les Huckfield. Cue standing ovation.

As I staggered out, with people avoiding eye contact and scurrying past me like I was diseased, my then constituency agent (and a lovely man) George Ferguson and his wife Hannah each put an arm round me. "Don't worry," George said, "you were the only one in there talking any sense and I'm as working class as any of them."

"He's right," said John, "but in future, learn to say it better." I did.

Hannah was a remarkable woman in many ways. As well as bringing up her own children she had foster-parented others, and was as Labour as Labour could be, but she represented a different facet of what was called, patronisingly, "the working class."

Part of Labour's problem was that such a term was a generic description that obscured as much as it illuminated. I concluded that two different strains of thinking brushed up against each other in that phrase which said something important about contemporary Britain. Probably they were always present, but the very social progress Labour had helped bring about had thrust the tension to the surface.

The genus fitted as a description of income, of type of job, and often, though not always by any means, of voting behaviour; but it didn't fit as a description of attitude. One strain dominated the activists of union and party. They held many of the same leftist views as the intellectual wing, but tended to be even more hard line on areas to do with economic policy.

The other strain was represented by people like George and Hannah, who were out and about far more in the non-political world of most ordinary people. They understood aspiration and applauded rather than resented it. They were tough, eye-wateringly so, on law and order. They believed social conditions had to be changed, but they never accepted them as an excuse for criminal behaviour.

Shortly after I became MP and still a little unused to Sedgefield's ways, I spoke at a branch meeting in a village called Tudhoe where Hannah was a branch member. The issue of the death penalty came up. Someone asked me if I supported it in the case of murder. Now, I was used to the politics of Islington, not County Durham. In Islington, such a question was simple. You gave the stock answer; heads nodded; the meeting moved on. Actually, it was one of the few questions to which I could give a generally left-wing answer and so I rather liked being asked it. And I had, so I thought, a rather neat way of putting the answer.

"No, I don't," I responded confidently, "and I will tell you why. If I am not prepared to hang that person myself, I should not ask the state to do it for me." I sat down rather pleased with myself.

"Well, I'd hang them," Hannah piped up.

"Aye, and I'd draw and quarter them too," said another equally benign-looking elderly woman; and she drew much support.

Nowadays, that sentiment on this issue would be much more rare. But the point is: the "working class" were not as homogeneous a group as many politicians assumed, or based their reasoning upon. Labour was largely losing the strain that Hannah represented. So even back then in 1983, though often imperfectly formed, my drift, politically and intellectually, was clear: Labour had to be radically reformed, and not by an adjustment or a shift of a few degrees, but in a manner that changed profoundly its modus operandi, its thinking, its programme and above all its attitudes. How to do it, how fast to do it, which issues to tackle first, which to leave until later—that was all a matter of tactics, but it was obvious society was undergoing a paradigm shift and Labour was not merely failing to heed it, but hiding from it.

By the 1992 election, I had been in the vanguard of the party's steady but slow move to modernisation. I was often out in front—as City spokesman, energy spokesman, in changing fundamental positions on the unions when holding my brief as our employment spokesman—but never so far in front that I was out of sight. I was the most forward, but took some care to remain with the pack and not to become so isolated that I could be picked off. I learned Dennis's lesson well; there is no point in being right about an organisation's failings if you have lost the ability to persuade it of them. You have to speak the language in order to change the terms of the debate conducted in that language, otherwise you may be a fine example of a person who is right, but irrelevant.

I had come to the conclusion that there were two major problems with the change in the Labour Party: the direction was right but the pace was too slow; more seriously, however, and despite my admiration for him, I was uneasy at the way Neil Kinnock was justifying the change.

Although Neil was seminal in bringing Labour to power—he gave strong leadership over eradicating Militants and taking on the Scargill wing of the union movement (named for Arthur Scargill, leader of the Socialist Labour Party), and this leadership allowed John Smith, then me, to make the changes necessary to win—the unspoken argument was this: look, guys, we've lost elections, the electorate won't wear our policies, so I'm sorry, but we're going to have to change them. The message—obviously one more palatable to party members—was: the party needs power, we're just going to have to compromise with the electorate. Now this was better than the famous dictum of the far left—"No compromise with the electorate"—which was printed on their banners as we tried to reform. But it seemed the party and the voters were in two different places, and so the party had to shift against its will. My own feeling, however, was: the voters are right and we should change not because we have to, but because we want to. It may sound a subtle difference, but it is fundamental.

In my view, we needed a complete, top-to-bottom reorientation of our programme and policies. In particular, we needed to separate conceptually a commitment to our values (timeless) from their application (time-bound). So, of course, we should and always would fight for social justice; but in today's world that didn't mean more state control. And on issues like defence and law and order, being tough was not striking a pose but a sensible reaction to the threats of the modern world, whether globally or on our street corners.

I had also tried to raise with John Smith the issue of asking Neil to step aside. Neil had led the Labour Party with enormous courage, saved it from political extinction and created a foundation for government; but he had to fight the 1987 election on a manifesto that wasn't sellable, and for whatever reason, I was convinced the British people were never going to elect him prime minister. The late-twentieth-century political spirit was changing. Parties were still important, but as party loyalties declined in intensity, much more came to rest on the person of the leader. Political analysts and practising politicians love to speculate on this or that voting trend—and very often there is much truth in it—but there is always a tendency to underplay the importance of the leader. To an extent, this is understandable—surely it's the policies that matter, the social movements that dictate outcomes, the events that shape destiny—but past a certain point, people regard left/right distinctions as less emphatic today, they think policies are open to amendment and know that programmes and manifestos can't set out how someone will react to events. Unless policies are defined to a very clear degree and are way off-centre, the character, likeability and personality of the leader are of paramount importance. They can determine the election, and this is now always a major, if not *the* major factor. Simple as that. So if the people didn't take to Neil, and they didn't, and had rejected him already in 1987, they weren't going to elect him in 1992, unless their view of him had changed significantly. It hadn't.

The election in 1992 was John's. We might have won had he been leader, rather than the Shadow Chancellor. But when I hinted to him in 1991 that he should go to Neil and ask him to step aside and said that myself, Gordon and others would back him up, John dismissed the idea. "I will be leader afterwards," he said. And that was that. The trouble was, partly I fear because John knew that afterwards he might be contesting the leadership, his proposed tax rises for those earning £30,000 and above were great for the party faithful but plainly problematic for the public. John was popular and respected, but this tax hike was, as the Tories cleverly exposed, a real ticking bomb underneath Labour's campaign. Once we were beaten, somehow I felt that the next election would not be John's.

In the run-up to the 1992 election I began a conversation with Gordon that was to have far-reaching consequences. I believed we had held back too much after the 1987 defeat, being too timid. It was true that we were now the undisputed leaders of the new generation. When Gordon had been John's substitute, he had shone in taking on Nigel Lawson, former Conservative Chancellor of the Exchequer in Mrs. Thatcher's government, in House of Commons debates. We were getting a medium level of media interest, which was rising in regularity and usually pretty praiseworthy; we had definitely logged on with the elite class interested in politics. But it wasn't yet our generation in charge. We were still on our way up; we weren't in a position to dictate terms. In the core economic team for the 1992 election—John as

Shadow Chancellor, Margaret as Shadow Industry Secretary, Gordon as Shadow Chief Secretary and me in Employment—we were the junior partners and I was the junior of the two of us. So though frustrated and anxious, I again held back.

Besides, I was still learning, thinking, trying to position myself on issues, beating out the basic elements of future political definition. Gordon and I would spend endless hours, days even, in political debate and discussion, iterating and reiterating, defining and refining, until eventually some sort of clarity appeared. The focus was not so much on the nitty-gritty of policy—or at least not always—but on setting the compass, getting the bearings and marshalling the arguments for the direction the party would or should take. We spent months trying to construct a framework for party reform. He had the idea of achieving mass membership by converting trade union levy-payers, union members who also make a contribution to the trade unions' political fund, into full party members. I concentrated more on what would be the right way to broaden the party base, take power out of the hands of unrepresentative activists, and put the union influence within tight constraints.

I had also broached with Gordon the notion that should the defeat be as I thought, he would run for leader and if necessary challenge John. I liked John a great deal but I felt instinctively and very deeply that another defeat, especially one that indicated we never really came close, meant we had to go for radical change. John was a great politician, a thoroughly good man, but he wasn't a radical reformer, neither in style nor in substance.

By 1992 I was almost forty. I had been in Opposition for a decade. The thought of another five years of merely incremental steps towards change in the party that was so obviously needed, filled me with dismay. If the steps were too incremental, we might fail again and I would be fifty before even getting sight of government; and what was the point of politics if not to win power, govern and put into practice the policies you believe in? There was, in addition, a strand of opinion crossing left and right which saw the party becoming increasingly fatalistic about our chances, fearing that the only answer was to change the voting system or, even worse, accept our fate as the perpetual Opposition.

I was convinced that the assumption that John would become leader following a defeat could and should be challenged. Gordon, to be fair, was non-committal. It would be a big ask, and John would feel it a betrayal. Plus Gordon was unmarried, and I told him, frankly, that I thought that was a problem. But I also thought the party would be ready to be excited and uplifted and that an injection of youth and energy would itself reap huge dividends. I saw myself as Shadow Chancellor in such a scenario. John would have been a perfect Foreign Secretary. And he was a big enough man to take it.

I thought it not wrong or disloyal to be prepared to do this. Others may disagree. I felt that the position of leader had to be taken with some elan, not necessarily at the "due" moment, but seized almost, if you will. Buggins' turn—appointments made by rotation, not merit—was an awful system of choosing the leader and actually at odds with every concept of what leadership should be about. Had John moved to replace Neil, it would have been bloody, but in my view he would have succeeded and history would have been very different. That he wouldn't contemplate it told me what his leadership would be like: steady, serious and predictable. It wasn't what the dire nature of our predicament demanded. Anyway, that's how I felt, right or wrong.

When the results were coming through on the night of 9 April 1992, it looked as if a quirk of the constituency system might yield a hung Parliament, and for a brief while I thought my predictions of defeat were wrong; but as the night wore on, it became all too clear. I spoke to Gordon and Peter Mandelson, just becoming the new MP for Hartlepool. I said we have to go for it. Unsurprisingly, Peter was a trifle distracted. Gordon was again non-committal.

As the morning of another defeat dawned, the party was in despair. I wasn't. I felt energised. What can we say? party HQ wailed. Plenty, I thought. The next morning there were bids from all the media outlets for interviews, and when no one wanted them, I took virtually the lot. I explained with the clarity of a man released from political and intellectual prison that the party had lost because we had failed to modernise sufficiently and we now had to do so, not by shades but by bursts of vivid colour. This time it had to be fundamental, clear and unmistakably geared to reuniting us with the people we sought to serve. I dodged the leadership issue easily enough—Neil hadn't yet declared he was standing down—and planted my banner firmly on the terrain of radical change in the party's organisation, programme and policies. Though I didn't know it and it was not why I did it, the thought of me as leader stemmed from that morning. Years afterwards, party members recalled that it was the time they thought: Hmm, maybe he's what we're looking for.

I returned from the studios. I had told Gordon to come to Sedgefield with Nick Brown, who was an MP in nearby Newcastle. He had always been our campaign manager for the election to choose the Shadow Cabinet, and was a kind of informal chief whip to me and Gordon (and indeed later took the role formally in government in 1997).

First, naturally, I pressed on Gordon the idea of him standing for leader. I rehearsed the arguments. He remained non-committal, however. Meanwhile, John had been phoning round just making sure of support. He phoned my home, Myrobella, in Trimdon Colliery in the heart of the constituency. I had offered to speak to John and explain why it should not be John who was leader, but I was nervous. It was a dilemma. If I indicated lack of support for John and Gordon didn't stand, it would destroy my relationship with John as leader. On the other hand, as I picked up the phone in my office at Myrobella to take his call, I still thought I had a chance to persuade Gordon.

At first I hedged. John, who was nothing if not canny, picked up the hesitation. "I should speak to Gordon," I said.

"I've spoken to him," John said. "He's fully on board."

At that point I dared hesitate no further but came on board too. Some months later John told me, innocently, that he and Gordon had come to an agreement well in advance of the election: John would be leader, with Gordon as Shadow Chancellor. Gordon would not stand. I knew in my bones it was a mistake.

There was still the matter of the deputy leader to be decided. This was an elected position but one usually held by a senior Shadow Cabinet member. Roy Hattersley, the then deputy (and Shadow Chancellor up to 1987), had been with Neil throughout the nine years of Neil's leadership. They weren't exactly bosom buddies, but it worked after a fashion. However, in the aftermath of defeat, he would plainly stand down too. In the course of the call with John, he asked me about the deputy leader role. It makes sense with me as leader, he said, to have one of the younger ones as deputy, either you or Gordon. Decide between you, he said. Clearly, he went on, the problem with Gordon would be two Scots. The alternative was Margaret Beckett, a highly capable woman and, all in all, a sound enough choice, despite being of the same generation as John.

After the call I went back into the sitting room to see Gordon and Nick. "John says you're backing him," I said to Gordon.

"It's difficult to say otherwise," he said, reasonably enough, but I felt a little let down.

"He wants to know if either of us should be deputy," I said. I then explained that though Gordon was senior to me, two Scots would be a problem, especially as it was precisely in the south of England that our support was thinnest. Nick said that there was a strong case for either of us, but that the crucial thing was to see who had most support in the Parliamentary Labour Party (PLP), a collective body of Labour Members who organise and manage the party. He agreed to take soundings.

Discussion took place over the next day or so. We met again. Nick said, "The pretty strong consensus in the PLP is that of the two of you, it should be Gordon."

I knew this was not true. It couldn't be. Not even the PLP at its daftest was that daft. The media was full of how Labour was blocked in its traditional heartlands of the North, Wales and Scotland, of how it was doomed if it couldn't break out and win the middle class and the South. In those circumstances, to have a Scot as leader was a risk, although if there were an English deputy, it was a risk that could be taken; but to then add another Scot as deputy? An all-Scottish ticket? With our devolution commitment in Scotland and Wales? It just wouldn't wash. It was nuts.

So, in those two or three days, I learned two things: one was that Gordon had not seized the moment; the second was that he and Nick were working together and their first loyalty was to each other. From that moment, I think I detached a little bit from Gordon; just a fraction, imperceptible to the eye of the observer, unaccompanied by any expressions of distance, or even by any diminishing of affection. It was a detachment small in space, but definitive in consequence. The seed was sown of my future insistence that I should be leader, not him.

John duly became leader. Gordon took the Shadow Chancellor position. John asked me what I wanted. He was surprised at my choice, but I had thought about it long and hard: I chose to be Shadow Home Secretary. It was usually considered a graveyard position for Tory and Labour politicians alike. Tories could never be hard line enough. Sincere, decent (privately liberal) types would go to Tory Party Conference, try to ham it up, curdle the blood, etc., but they always got found out. The Labour problem was the opposite. Their audience expected something more liberal and yet the Labour Home Secretary or Shadow Home Secretary knew the watching public disliked all the liberal stuff. There's one thing I learned in politics: those of extreme views, right or left, can always spot whether someone is a fellow true believer or not. Occasionally, when forced to pander—throw a bit of left-wing meat out (not on anything too important!)—I would give it my best; but you know something? They always spotted that my heart wasn't in it. It's something in the tone, the body language, which the true enthusiast has and the actor lacks.

Anyway, Shadow Home Secretary was not a job with many applicants. I had, however, come to the view that: a) Labour people, certainly our voters, were really anxious about law and order issues and were far more likely to be tough than soft; and b) intellectually, the polarisation of left/right views was simply and clearly wrong. The left blamed social conditions, the right blamed the individual; any halfway normal person could see—or so I thought—it was a combination of the two.

I felt personally very strongly about crime. For years I had thought it was a disgrace which people shouldn't have to put up with and I hated the liberal middle-class attitudes towards it. Usually they weren't the victims, but the poorer people—the very ones we said we represented—were. The hard-pressed public were similarly outraged by crime, and not just the high-end serious offences, murder and robbery and so on, but also low-level antisocial disorder and vandalism. They couldn't be expected to put up with it while waiting for the good society to be created, to endure it patiently until someone decided to remove the hell from their street. Of course, it also stood to reason that the better educated young people were, especially young men in the inner city, the greater their chance of a job and the increased likelihood that they were going to turn out well behaved.

So: fighting crime was a personal cause, it completely fitted a new politics beyond old right and left, and since no Labour person had ever made anything of it (though there had been great reforming liberal Labour Home Secretaries like Chuter Ede and Roy Jenkins), the field was mine to play on. For once I was very confident of what I could do. And I was correct. It solidified my position in the party and the country. It achieved enormous traction. It showed leadership. I took a traditional Labour position, modernised it, made it popular and upended the Tories with it.

Ironically, in the light of what was to happen, Gordon also played an interesting role in helping me formulate what became my catchphrase.

We used to travel to the U.S. from time to time, essentially just to get away and think. For some bizarre reason or other we would stay at the Carlyle Hotel in New York. The Carlyle is as far removed from New Labour as binge drinking is from Methodism. It is an exclusive hotel that had been used by the likes of Cary Grant and Jimmy Stewart. Eartha Kitt would sing in the cafe and Woody Allen would turn up with his clarinet. At that time, people dressed for dinner, the mood was formal, the decor elegant, the ambience a little austere. Not me at all, but funnily enough I grew to like it. The management were discreet, staff were friendly and behind all the upper-class facade, it was well run.

On one occasion in late 1992 we sat there and talked. Though still ruminating on a missed chance after our election defeat, I had begun to concentrate thoroughly on the task in hand and I explained my essential approach: we should of course stress social conditions and be radical in dealing with them, but we also had to be tough on crime itself. We should make this into a Labour issue by combining a traditional and a modern stance.

This is where Gordon, certainly in those days, would show a streak of genius. "You mean 'Tough on crime, tough on the causes of crime,' " he said.

"Yes," I said, stunned by the brilliance of it, "that's exactly what I mean."

And so it became my slogan, but unusually for a slogan, actually encapsulated a philosophical insight. Shortly after returning, I used it in a speech and really never looked back.

Pretty soon, I had the Tories reeling under the onslaught, surprised and somewhat disbelieving that a Labour person could steal "their" issue, but rather admiring of the way it was done. At that time Ken Clarke was Home Secretary. It was not his scene at all. He was liberal and utterly disdainful of his Conservative Party conference (where decisions were made for the year ahead). After enduring months of being well and truly mugged on the issue, John Major sensibly decided to move Ken to the Treasury, where he was in his element, and Michael Howard into the Home Secretary position, for which he was temperamentally absolutely suited. Thereafter on the issue it got harder, since Michael decisively shifted Tory tone and policy to the right and in turn posed some hard tactical choices for me. He was so hard line that there was a risk that if I followed him I would alienate the party, and if I didn't I would alienate the voter. But by then, my reputation was secure.

I had also articulated very clearly the social context for the policy in a way no Tory could easily match after fourteen years of government and with the memories of Thatcherism still fresh. In February 1993, there had been a horrific murder of a two-year-old boy, James Bulger, by two ten-year-olds up in Merseyside, in northwest England. The tragedy became representative of social breakdown. The ten-year-olds were, needless to say, from broken families. The reporting of the murder was laced with descriptions of the life, times and mores of certain groups of young people whose families seemed separated from the mainstream. Very effectively I made it into a symbol of a Tory Britain in which, for all the efficiency that Thatcherism had achieved, the bonds of social and community well-being had been loosed, dangerously so.

I did it sincerely. In a widely publicised speech—really very widely publicised, unusually so for an Opposition politician who was not a party leader—I set out what I thought was wrong.

> The news bulletins of the last week have been like hammer blows struck against the sleeping conscience of the country, urging us to wake up and look unflinchingly at what we see. We hear of crimes so horrific they provoke anger and disbelief in equal proportions. The headlines shock, but what shocks us more is our knowledge that in almost any city, town or village more minor versions of the same events are becoming an almost everyday part of our lives. These are the ugly manifestations of a society that is becoming unworthy of that name.
>
> The historic problem of old socialism was the tendency to subsume the individual, rights, duties and all, within ideas of the "public good," that at its worst came simply to mean the state. The failure of the present right is to believe that the absence of community means the presence of freedom. The task is to retrieve the notion of community from a narrow view of the state and put it to work again for the benefit of us all. A new community with a modern concept of citizenship is well overdue.

Now, I look back and think that though the problem was real, the analysis was faulty and this came to have policy consequences I describe later. However, at the time, politically, there was a big impact on my standing, which rose still further.

I was also pushing the boundaries in another direction. While in my view John Smith was not a true radical, he was intelligent enough and brave enough to realise that the party had to modernise. One part of that process was in the relationship with the unions, which then revolved around the issue of One Member One Vote (OMOV), whereby instead of union national executive committees voting on the candidate for a selection, the members should all have one vote; and there should be a more balanced vote for leader, with MPs having a say.

Today it seems completely unacceptable, ridiculous even, that the unions played such a decisive role in the selection of candidates and leader, but the Labour Party had been born out of the Labour Representation Committee, a late-nineteenth- and early-twentieth-century body whose aim was precisely to get "working men" into Parliament. It was formed, funded and run by the unions, so the roots were inseparably intertwined, with, I'm afraid, very mixed long-term consequences.

John decided to advocate OMOV, and I put myself full square behind the campaign. The unions already had bitter memories of my decision when Shadow Employment Secretary in 1989 to end Labour's support for the "closed shop," so my espousal of this issue alienated me still further from them, but it was putting me way in front as having a clear, unequivocal position on how the party could win. After years in which Labour people were scoffed at and scorned, in which all those feelings of inferiority were resting only a little below the surface, here was someone who seemed confident, able to take it to the Tories, and in tone and style chime with the very voters we knew we needed but who had always proved elusive.

As the months rolled on, my position as an out-and-out moderniser, stepping out and leading, became ever sharper. I felt a growing inner sense of belief, almost of destiny. I felt compelled, clear, certain and above all confident of my arguments, confident that they were right and confident that they could win the country over.

My relationship with Gordon was still very close, but towards the end of 1992 I took another small yet significant pace apart. There had been the usual merry-go-round on distributing rooms for MPs, and for these purposes all MPs were the same, except government ministers who had rooms set aside for them. A set of rooms in Millbank came up. At that time Gordon and I were both in 1 Parliament Street, just opposite Westminster by the bridge. Gordon decided to move to Millbank and asked me to join him. Cherie emphatically told me I shouldn't. Rather to my surprise, Anji said the same. I didn't go. It was no big deal; but it was another indicator.

Gordon was doing well as Shadow Chancellor, hammering the Tories in a responsible and measured way, although he was cautious, as was his wont; and he was a little discredited, though only a very little, by having supported the Exchange Rate Mechanism (ERM), a system to achieve monetary stability throughout Europe, and therefore when that policy fell apart, he was marginally tarnished by it. Later, he came to see this and his strictures on too much public spending as the reason why I was preferred to him, but it wasn't so. The truth is I was out in front taking risks, and this was a time for risk-takers. I spotted that; he didn't.

As 1993 wore on, something changed that was imperceptible to most people. I say imperceptible, but maybe he and I were both wrong on that count. The *Sunday Times*, for example, had had me on their magazine front cover in May 1992 with the line "The Leader Labour Missed." Normally such a thing would have caused jealousy, but partly because no one took it very seriously, it didn't.

Peter Mandelson, by then a close friend and confidant of us both, noticed the difference in me. "You're getting quite the little leader," he teased me one day as we stood at the railings outside my front door in Richmond Crescent. We had just had a meeting and plainly my assertiveness had made its impression.

"By which you mean . . . ?" I enquired.

"Don't get above yourself," he replied. "Gordon is still the one supposed to be the next leader, you know."

"Hmm," I said.

"Hmm." He looked back at me and smiled in that Peterish way. "I'll have to reflect on this conversation."

"I wouldn't worry," I laughed, concerned that, even with him, I had given too much away.

"Oh, but I do," he said, giving me an affectionate pat on the shoulder and getting into his car.

In truth, I didn't know what I thought. I wasn't really analysing, I was just letting my instinct roam. In fact, I feared to stop and think, because I felt with increasing clarity where my instinct was roaming. It was like I was waking each day feeling stronger, more certain. Each encounter with my own party, the other party, the media, the public, would be like another layer of steel bolted on to an already well-fortified casing. I could see the opportunity to take hold of the Labour Party, rework it into an electoral machine capable of winning over the people. I could see it like I suppose someone in business spots the next great opportunity, or an artist suddenly appreciates his own creative genius, or a coach or player knows that their moment for glory is about to come.

It is an extraordinary feeling, in the sense that you feel you can achieve something beyond the ordinary. And you know it. Maybe you won't do it, but you know at that time, in those circumstances, with those conditions, it can be done. Yes, it can be done. I can see it and I can do it.

I was fighting my feelings towards Gordon, which were still of great affection and loyalty, but I also felt the tectonic plates shifting. For ten years, my judgement had been that he should do it and I should be second in command. I liked the notion of counselling, advising, urging, directing behind the scenes, seeing my work flourish. So at that point, no, there was no overbearing desire to move centre stage, although I sensed the change within me and could almost watch my own metamorphosis. I felt on fire, with a passion and a sense of mission. I was straining at the leash, and for the first time in our discussions, I noticed things about him I hadn't fully noticed before, an intellectual caution that was cleverly coated but didn't seem to me to match the strategic necessity of breaking emphatically with our past.

In our first years in Parliament, 1983–5, I had intermittently kept a diary. Rereading the entries now, it is so plain that from the outset Gordon had a tendency to look for a way of reframing the question rather than acknowledging the need for the hard answer. He was brilliant, had far more knowledge of the party than me, with an acute and, even then, well-honed tactical brain; but it operated essentially within familiar and conventional parameters. Within the box he was tremendous, but he didn't venture outside it.

By 1994, I was straying well outside the box in policy and party reform, and I began to realise, with dismay but then soberly, that something was missing. Something he lacked. Something I started to know inside I had.

Of course I had no knowledge that John would die prematurely. Except that, in a strange way, I began to think he might. I don't mean I had a premonition or anything odd like that, but if you had asked me, in some private contest with Providence, to stake my life on whether he would or not, I would have hesitated. I kept dismissing the thought. It kept intruding.

In April 1994, Cherie and I visited Paris. I was giving a speech to INSEAD, the business school at Fontainebleau. It was to be our last weekend of normal life. We left the kids at home. Derry recommended a little hotel near Montmartre. The rooms were tiny but pretty, and the hotel was central. I remember waking up the first morning and then waking Cherie. I said to her: "If John dies, I will be leader, not Gordon. And somehow, I think this will happen. I just think it will." Is that a premonition? Not in a strict sense; but it was strange all the same.

On Saturday afternoon we went to see *Schindler's List*, the Steven

Spielberg movie about the man who rescued Jews from the Nazi concentration camps, saving thousands of lives.

In later life, when I had got to know Spielberg, I told him how the
movie had affected me more than any I had ever seen. Steven, being
actually a rather modest person, probably thought I was exaggerating in
that way theatrical people do, but I wasn't. I was spellbound throughout
the whole three and a quarter hours. We sat through it, missed our dinner and talked about it long into the night.

There was a scene in it I kept coming back to. The commandant,
played by Ralph Fiennes, is in his bedroom arguing with his girlfriend.
He gets up to urinate, they're still arguing and she is mocking him, just
like any girlfriend might do. While in the bathroom, he spies an inmate
of the camp. He takes up his rifle and shoots him. They carry on their
argument. It's her I think of. She didn't shoot anyone; she was a
bystander.

Except she wasn't. There were no bystanders in that situation. You
participate, like it or not. You take sides by inaction as much as by
action. Why were the Nazis able to do these things? Because of people
like him? No, because of people like her.

She was in the next room. She was proximate. The responsibility
seems therefore more proximate too. But what of the situations we
know about, but we are not proximate to? What of the murder distant
from us, the injustice we cannot see, the pain we cannot witness but
which we nonetheless know is out there? We know what is happening,
proximate or not. In that case, we are not bystanders either. If we know
and we fail to act, we are responsible.

A few months later, Rwanda erupted in genocide. We knew. We
failed to act. We were responsible.

Not very practical, is it, as a reaction? The trouble is it's how I feel.
Whether such reactions are wise in someone charged with leading a
country is another matter. But more of that later.

I returned from Paris exhilarated, and again, with this curious sensation of power, of anticipation, of prescience.

Then John did die. As I began the first of my conversations with
Gordon, I was mentally prepared. I felt I had been disingenuous with
him, which in the light of later events was a mistake. Occasionally
between April 1992 and May 1994, he would seek reassurance and I
would give it. Why not? I knew enough of him to know that had I withdrawn that assurance, we would have been doing battle. And what the

hell. Probably it was just a dumb presentiment. Probably it would never happen. Probably John would go on and be prime minister and then who knows what the future would bring.

"We have to talk," I said on that May morning in Aberdeen sitting in the party office, watching people walk by on the street outside, knowing their lives would go on as before and mine was about to change forever.

I had steeled myself. I knew he would press; probably bully; maybe even threaten. But I had crossed over.

"OK, let's talk when you're back down," he said, a slight shift in the timbre of his voice already clear.

I did a brief visit in Aberdeen as planned, to some science and technology company I seem to remember. I gave a short statement to the press outside on John's death, expressing our sense of shock and grief. I caught the plane back down to London as soon as I decently could. I may even have spoken to Gordon again. I can't recall. As I stepped out on to the passenger tunnel at Heathrow, a cameraman was waiting to photograph me. It gave me a jolt. So this is what it's like, I thought.

I went into Parliament. Everyone was in a state of turmoil, genuinely shocked, genuinely sad, but of course the political wheels were turning. I bumped into Mo Mowlam who, as unsentimental as ever (or appearing to be), came straight out with it: "It's got to be you. Do not on any account succumb." Cherie, who had driven me into London from Heathrow, had given me the same message, in even stronger terms. They hadn't needed to tell me. My mind was made up.

As I wandered through the lobby at the side of the House of Commons Chamber, I came across Peter Mandelson. We had spoken briefly on the phone, but in very guarded terms.

"Ah, I was hoping to see you," he said. "Now, let's not run away with all this. Gordon is still the front-runner, still the person with the claim."

As ever with Peter in a situation like this, you could never be quite sure what he was saying; but I was sure what I wanted to say.

"Peter," I said, "you know I love you, but this is mine. I am sure of it. And you must help me to do it."

"I wouldn't be too sure about that," he said. For once, there was no playfulness; and for a moment we stood, looking at each other by the green leather-topped table at the north side of the Aye Lobby.

"Peter," I said, putting a hand on each shoulder, "don't cross me over this. This is mine. I know it and I will take it."

"You can't be certain of that," he replied.

"I understand." I spoke gently this time, the friendship fully back in my voice. "But just remember what I said."

Someone entered the lobby. As if by telepathy, we moved apart and went in different directions.

THREE

NEW LABOUR

Later that night, the nation still shuddering at the loss of John Smith, Mo insisted I come to a meeting where she had assembled what she called "the hard eggs" who would organise for me. They were a varied group of MPs, with some familiar and some surprising faces there—natural supporters but also unnatural ones. They were all from the non-intellectual part of the PLP who had learned politics the hard way, and they were tough, fearless and disciplined. "These are people who are going to work for you," she said. "This is to show you that you have the breadth and depth necessary to win."

I can't even remember the exact time and place of the first meeting with Gordon. It may even be that I broached the critical conversation with him by phone. It was such a whirl of talking, thinking, speculating, and not so much plotting as just trying to figure it all out.

After the meeting, I went back to Richmond Crescent. There was a stack of photographers outside the house. From then on they stayed, in small or large number, ten feet or so from our bedroom window. It was a strange sensation. Even with the heavy curtains pulled, there was a sudden, disconcerting, but also—at that time—somewhat exciting feeling of being on show.

I kept a strong grip on myself, but the anxiety showed. For weeks after John died—and this is the only time it ever happened to me—I would wake in the morning with the hair on the back of my head damp with sweat. What I could control when awake was overpowering in sleep.

Cherie was an incredible strength during those months. She knew her own life was about to change and for her it was equally frightening, in some ways even more so. She, the intellectually gifted barrister and north London woman, was about to collide with the world of the tabloid paper and the unremitting glare of the spotlight. Her working-class background meant that she was well up to mixing and getting on with anyone, but her only previous experience of that type of publicity had been with her father and it had not been happy.

However, that night she cradled me in her arms and soothed me; told me what I needed to be told; strengthened me; made me feel that what I was about to do was right. I had no doubt that I had to go for it, but I needed the reassurance and, above all, the emotional ballast.

In many ways, I am very emotionally self-sufficient; in some ways, too much so. I make emotional commitment because it comes naturally to me. But I fear it also; fear the loss of control and the fact that the consequences of caring can be painful; fear the dependence; perhaps fear learning the lesson, from love that goes wrong, that human nature is frail and unreliable after all.

On that night of 12 May 1994, I needed that love Cherie gave me, selfishly. I devoured it to give me strength, I was an animal following my instinct, knowing I would need every ounce of emotional power and resilience to cope with what lay ahead. I was exhilarated, afraid and determined, in roughly equal quantities.

The fear, however, had a consequence that to this day I cannot be sure was benign or malevolent. I didn't want to fight Gordon in a leadership contest. There was a rational explanation to this: such a fight required us to differentiate, and inevitably he would pitch to the left of me. Indeed, in the next two days, a story duly appeared in *The Times*—possibly put there by Peter, who was still not committing to me but trying to manage the situation between the two of us—which previewed a speech Gordon was going to make to the Welsh Labour Conference in Swansea. It was presented as a checking of the Blair bandwagon, and was also clearly designed to rally union support. A breach between the two main modernisers—and him the Shadow Chancellor to boot—was not a good thing. I would win; but what would be the cost?

If I'm honest, there was another reason I did not want a head-to-head contest: I was scared of the unpleasantness, the possible brutality of it, the sadness, actually, of two friends becoming foes. I can't tell which feeling was predominant—the political calculation or the emotional fear—but the combination made me determined to try to cajole him out, not confront him.

Many times afterwards, and many rounds of pointless speculation later, I still am not sure if it was the right decision. To have defeated him would have been to have mastered him, at least temporarily, but it would not have removed him—in any event we needed him—and it would have soured and weakened the concept of New Labour which was already formed in my mind. However much we would have tried to keep the contest pretty, it would have been ugly. Anyway, my desire was to get him to leave the field voluntarily. Don't get me wrong, I was prepared to fight; but it wasn't my preference.

Of course, Gordon was not the only potential challenger. I tried in my first conversation with John Prescott to get him to see that he too should vacate the contest and simply stand for deputy. It was a friendly talk, but John was adamant he would stand. He perceived rightly that by standing for both, he enhanced his chances of the deputy leadership. By contrast, Margaret Beckett would have been wiser merely opting for deputy. Then, in recognition of the time immediately after John's death when she became leader until the leadership contest took place, she would have been given the consolation of the deputy position. I suppose pride made her unable to accept it, though I have to say that afterwards she was perfectly good towards me. John's willingness to have a contest, and also his wise remark to me that a coronation was a bad idea, put some more fight into me. I then realised I wouldn't and shouldn't just walk into it; I had to go out and win it.

Gordon participating was another thing entirely, and so began a somewhat tortuous series of parlays, in a variety of secret locations, away from the House of Commons and prying eyes. We met at my sister-in-law's round the corner from Richmond Crescent; we met at my friend Nick Ryden's house in Edinburgh; and in the flat owned by the parents of my old girlfriend and first love, Amanda Mackenzie Stuart. It was right that such a dialogue was confidential for obvious reasons, while the outside world was rampant with speculation. It was only a contest to be Leader of the Opposition, of course, but there was a strong sentiment that Labour had good prospects in the next election. There was a genuine buzz of anticipation—"something in the air," in the words of the song. It was a moment in time; a change in generation; a presentiment, maybe, that the outcome would alter not just the party but the country, and not simply via a change of government, but also with a change in the zeitgeist.

It was strung out over several weeks, since there had been an agreement brokered by the National Executive Committee (NEC) that there would be no campaigning for the leadership until the European elections, scheduled for mid-June, were out of the way. There was another reason to be clandestine. Our respective supporters were anxious about what we might agree: his that he would agree to stand down, many of them urging him to fight; mine that I would concede something to him. Every time we met, there was a ripple of anxiety that spread out among the camp followers (already self-identifying fairly robustly) at what concessions either of us may have made. For that reason Anji and Sue Nye, Gordon's close aide, kept the arrangements to themselves. Also by then, paparazzi were in more or less constant pursuit of me. The venues were chosen with care, but I guess it was indicative that they were my friends' homes we were meeting in. I was making the running.

Cherie's sister Lyndsey and her husband Chris were completely safe and solid. Nick was one of my oldest friends, from Fettes; and just a completely reliable, smart and discreet person. And I loved the romance of meeting at Amanda's. You know the first person you ever fall in love with; you know that incredible outpouring of desire, the overwhelming sense of something unique, inexpressible, inexplicable and even at points incomprehensible, but so thrilling, uplifting, your heart pumping and soaring? I was eighteen, in my last year at Fettes. She was the only girl at the school—the first, the experiment, and so chosen because she was the daughter of the chairman of the governors. They were an amazing family. He was Britain's judge at the European Court of Justice, her mother was a charming and delightful diplomat—not professionally, but naturally.

They had four daughters, of whom Amanda was the oldest. I was utterly love-struck. They had a beautiful eighteenth-century stone house in New Town, whose terraces and crescents are architectural masterpieces. Edinburgh is perhaps as beautiful as any city in the world. I knew and adored every street around New Town. I walked it all, then and for years afterwards, finding security, comfort and repose in the familiarity of it, the sense of certainty and self-sufficiency of its design that seemed also to imbue the middle- and upper-class folk of Edinburgh. I wasn't afraid there, and somehow in some slightly odd way, in Amanda's home, surrounded by evidence of her presence, I felt a confidence about the task in hand.

I consciously exerted every last impulse of charm and affection, not just persuading but wooing. Gordon and I had been well-nigh inseparable for over ten years. We were as close as two people ever are in politics. It was not simply a professional relationship, it was a friendship. Later, when things became difficult, then fraught, and finally dangerous, the wrench was all the harder because the intimacy had been so real. It was a political partnership, of course, but it was buttressed, possibly even grounded, in a genuine and sincere liking for each other. Neither of us had met anyone like that before. I found him odd at points, to be sure: the introspection, the intensity, finding him in his flat in Edinburgh on a Saturday morning in his suit trousers and white shirt, surrounded by a veritable avalanche of papers, but certainly, back then, it seemed an endearing eccentricity. He could be kind, generous, concerned, and often not just funny but with a rapier wit as well as intellect. The discussion wasn't just political—there were laughter, exchanges of deep, personal confidences, debates about philosophy, religion, art and the day-to-day trivia that interests and excites us as human beings.

Likewise, I was a new type of person altogether for him. I was very non-political in my view of politics. There was more instinct than analysis; or perhaps more accurately, since I did analyse and reanalyse politics, the starting point was instinct. At first, he taught me things all the time: how to read the games within the Labour Party; the lines not to cross with the unions; how to make a speech; when to shut up as well as when to speak up in an internal party discussion. With just a phrase, he taught me the business of politics in roughly the same way Derry had taught me the business of the Bar.

Over time, he derived from me a different perspective, a normal person's view of politics. The single hardest thing for a practising politician to understand is that most people, most of the time, don't give politics a first thought all day long. Or if they do, it is with a sigh or a harrumph or a raising of the eyebrows, before they go back to worrying about the kids, the parents, the mortgage, the boss, their friends, their weight, their health, sex and rock 'n' roll.

David Blunkett, who was a remarkable example of someone who spent a lifetime in politics but could think like a human being, once told me that even at the height of his fame as Home Secretary, people would approach him and say, "Seen you on telly, what do you do?," or more bizarrely would see him with his guide dog and would know who he was, but would say, "I never knew you were blind."

At points people switch on. Then they—or at least a goodly proportion of them—are focused and listening. These are defining moments.

The trick is to spot them. Missing them is very bad news. To the professional politician, every waking moment is, in part or whole, defining. To them, the landscape of politics is perpetually illuminated, and a light which is often harsh shines on a terrain that bristles with highs and lows of ambition, risk and fulfilment. They are in a constant fret about what may befall them as they navigate it. For most normal people, politics is a distant, occasionally irritating fog. Failure to comprehend this is a fatal flaw in most politicians. It leads them to focus on the small not the big picture. It means they get things out of proportion, it breeds paranoia and it stops them from understanding what really moves and matters.

Our friendship was real and complemented by a political sum that was much more than its individual parts, and it worked; but it meant when the time came and only one of us could go forward, it was always going to be a whole lot more troubling.

Essentially my argument was this: I was the one who could best succeed with the country (the initial polls on the weekend after John's death had shown I was far ahead of every other contender, and in fact John Prescott was ahead of Gordon), but we shared the same agenda, we would work together, and in time he would be an obvious person, if not *the* obvious person, to take over. There was a proviso, however, which later became the subject of much debate and acrimony: just as I would help him to succeed, so he would work properly with me, accepting that while leader, I would lead, so to speak. At that point, it didn't seem much to ask or hard to give, either way. Though there was never a deal in the sense that his standing down was contingent on my agreeing to help him come after me, nonetheless there was an understanding of mutual interest. Had you asked me then what I would do and what might happen, I would have said I would do two terms and then hand over. It seemed right and fair for party and country, not just the two of us. He was then head and shoulders above the others in ability, in weight, in skill.

But, once again, looking back, I was too eager to persuade and too ready to placate. The truth is I couldn't guarantee it; and it was irresponsible to suggest or imply I could. Most of all, it ignored the fact that it is only in government that the character to lead is clear or not. Opposition is a completely different matter. You don't know that at the time, but it is. It's not that there is no requirement to lead in Opposition, but the need is magnified a hundredfold in government. Foibles in Opposition become disabilities in government; weaknesses become terminal;

things that can be glossed over remain like irremovable stains. Similarly, the impact of strengths is multiplied; decisions resonate not just across a party but through the country and even, on occasions, the world; leadership character, if it is there, stands up and stands out.

Neither of us should have tried to predict the future. I was anxious to sort him out and get on with it; he was anxious to extract the maximum at the maximum point of leverage. Anyway, not sensible really all ways round; understandable, but not sensible, with consequences down the line, though I am not sure to this day how much difference doing it another way would have made. The truth is I got the leadership and he wanted it. It was true then, and remained true. Probably it was always fated to be as it was, unless either of us had pressed the nuclear button and decided to wage all-out war to destroy the other. It was always an option for both of us—me sacking him, him resigning and standing against me—but the enormity of the damage of such a course always drew us back from the brink.

The first occasion he actually broached acceptance that he would stand aside and support me was at Amanda's. Up to then, he maintained the fiction that he would fight me for it. I knew he wouldn't, but I knew, too, that protracted discussion was a prerequisite to steer him successfully to the correct conclusion. My worry was not his reason, but his pride.

There was also an interesting and again telling sidebar to the conversation, one that caused much speculation afterwards. He wanted a free rein on economic policy. At one point Peter—who was by then trying to broker things in my favour—even submitted a paper to me that effectively ceded control of economic policy. The paper unfortunately survived; my response, which was for me unusually brusque, didn't. Close interaction, yes. Partnership, yes. Dual leadership, absolutely not. It gave rise to the myth that I was uninterested in economic policy. On the contrary, I was very interested; and though it was always a tug of war and in time a fairly gruelling one, I always kept, at least up to the third term, a very tight harness around me on it, ready to pull back sharply if I needed to.

The conversations were of their nature difficult, but they were not hostile, bitter or even unfriendly. We were like a couple who loved each other, arguing whose career should come first. While there was a lot at stake, there was also a lot underpinning our relationship. There is no doubt, though, that he felt a sense of shock and betrayal. He never expected me to put myself forward. He thought he was the superior politician. He wasn't, by the way, self-conscious of intellectual superiority. Funnily enough, in the years of permanent debate that characterised our friendship up to that point, I was probably more like an analytical lawyer or professor trying to arrange the logic and reason of our positions on policy. He was the master politician. I don't mean he wasn't intellectually more able—he was and is, in the sense of who would have got the best degree—but in framing the intellectual case for what we were doing, I tended to have the idea and he tended then to translate it into practical politics. He was also a brilliant sounding board. He could instantly see the force of a point, give you six new angles on it and occasionally make you see something in a wholly different light. I often compare him to Derry in that way. I would always learn from a discussion and come away mentally refreshed, stimulated and enthusiastic. The conversations were long, but there were very few wasted moments. Our minds moved fast and at that point in sync. When others were present, we felt the pace and power diminish, until, a bit like lovers desperate to get to lovemaking but disturbed by old friends dropping round, we would try to bustle them out, steering them doorwards with a hearty slap on the back. Our friendship was not a sealed box exactly, but the sense of self-containment was strong, sometimes overpowering. Under the pressure of leadership it was not easy, therefore, to open it up to the influences—good, bad or indifferent—of the outside world. But of course this was what was happening.

It was doubly difficult for him. He had an expectation which was now to be snuffed out, to be relit in time possibly, but when, how or in what circumstances, he couldn't know or determine. For my part—and you can believe this or not, I really don't mind—I had been a reluctant convert to leadership. I remember that weekend after John died and being told of the *Sunday Times* poll about to appear, waiting for it with a bit of me still thinking how much easier things would be if it showed Gordon leading, and I would have the excuse to say to friends and supporters, "Well, it's not me after all." But it didn't, and probably if it had, I was too far gone by then. The point is that in so far as it is ever possible to disentangle motives at such a juncture, I did genuinely believe it was best that I took up the leadership. We were, at that point, fifteen years in Opposition and effectively pinned back in our heartlands—the North, Scotland, Wales, the inner city. Though disillusioned with the Tories, Middle England was still anxious and distrustful of us. The situation was crying out for the party to take a revolutionary modernising leap, to break out of those heartlands, to show for the first time that it could win support anywhere, that it could cross the class and employment divides, that it could unite the nation. I was the moderniser, in personality, in language, in time, feel and temperament. Split it anyway you like, the damn thing was obvious in the end.

After the conversation at Amanda's parents' home, where they had moved as the family grew up, we sat in the kitchen looking out over the gardens and scrubland in the small indentation under Dean Bridge, near to where years ago I had done a spell on a voluntary project for the down-and-out in lieu of school corps. We were then simply managing how he could withdraw gracefully.

Later, there was a moment at Nick Ryden's which illustrated the tenor of it all. Nick had just moved into a big old house and was doing the place up. He kindly agreed to go out and leave us alone to talk. After an hour or so Gordon got up to go to the loo. I waited downstairs. Five minutes passed. Then ten. Then fifteen. I was getting a bit alarmed. Suddenly the phone went. As it wasn't my house, I left it. The answerphone clicked in, and Nick's voice asked the caller to leave a message. Suddenly, out of the machine boomed another voice: "Tony, it's Gordon here." Wow, I was really freaked out. What the hell was going on? "I am upstairs in the toilet," he went on, "and I can't get out."

In the building works, the loo door had been replaced but had no handle on the inside yet. Gordon had spent a quarter of an hour on his mobile trying to track down Nick's number. The soundproofing in the house meant that I never heard him. I went up to the loo. "Withdraw from the contest or I'm leaving you in there," I said.

Finally, with Peter's guidance, we made the announcement that he would support me, and did it walking rather self-consciously round New Palace Yard underneath Big Ben. It worked well as a piece of media management. Very quickly, however, it worked less well as a relationship.

The root of the problem was that he thought I could be an empty vessel into which the liquid that was poured was manufactured and processed by him. I was never totally sure, and still am not, whether he really did buy the illusion that I was just a frontman, carefully tutored by Peter and then, in time, Alastair, but incapable on my own. It was of course nonsense; not because I am so good, but because it is utterly impossible for anyone in a position like that to be the product of someone else. It can't happen. There are a thousand decisions, large and small, that only the leader can take. You can't fake body language or manufacture it. No matter how good an actor you are, in the end it's not an act.

It's like when people say to me: "Oh, so-and-so, they don't believe in anything, they're just a good communicator." As a statement about politics, it's close to being an oxymoron, certainly for the top person. At the top, the scrutiny is microscopic. It is soul-penetrating. People see you like they do a person they see every day at work. For a time, maybe, they can be fooled or blinded, but soon, very soon in fact, they form a real judgement. Regardless of whether they agree or disagree with what you are doing, they can tell whether or not you believe in it. If you don't have core beliefs as a politician, real path-finding instincts groomed out of conviction, you will never be a good communicator because—and this may seem corny, but it's true—the best communication comes from the heart. To me, Bill Clinton was a classic example of this. Regularly it would be written that although he was a wondrous communicator, he didn't believe in anything much. It was complete nonsense. It was true he didn't believe in being a traditional Democrat; but he didn't articulate the policy of the traditional Democrat. He was a new Democrat and that's how he spoke and sounded, because that is what he believed. That's why he was so good at communicating it.

Maybe Gordon thought the glass could be filled as he wished, but it was never going to be that way, and inevitably the rancour started to appear. We fell out over whether John Prescott should be deputy or not. I could live with Margaret Beckett in the position but, on balance, thought John gave something to the ticket which she didn't. We fell out over who should run my leadership campaign. I and my people (the distinction was already taking hold) thought it couldn't be Gordon; it was all too incestuous. I had to prepare now for the time when, as leader, I couldn't live in the sealed compartment. He could be the favoured, but not the only. On my side we thought Jack Straw a better fit since he was from neither camp and so broadened my appeal in the PLP, and I had to explain that to Gordon. He resented it deeply.

The leadership campaign itself passed off without incident. Very few union leaders supported me, but their members did, and we won a majority of party members and MPs. A preoccupation throughout was to minimise stray comments that could be damaging or concessions to the left. Slowly I got used to the feeling I was going to become leader.

The sun used to shine in those days. I remember campaigning around the country, the weather hot, occasionally oppressively so. The mood was buoyant. No great breakthroughs at that point, and no particular mishaps, but it was clear I was a very different type of Labour leader. That in itself was generating interest, excitement and support. The Tories were trying to pretend it was all a chimera but, underneath the bravado, they were really worried. They knew if I turned out to possess the genuine article, with the ability to wear it so that it fitted, they were sunk.

After the nomination as leader, with John as deputy, I began to put the team in place. Peter was now fully on board, but his being so estranged him completely from Gordon, who had come to believe—and such thoughts were never alien to his thinking—that Peter had plotted my ascension all the way along. It was untrue, at least to my knowledge—though the thing with Peter is that maybe it was true but he concealed it brilliantly from me! Actually, I am sure it wasn't. Peter always liked to play the Machiavelli figure, but in my experience he is one of the most transparent and open people I know.

In September 1994 we had had an away day at the Chewton Glen Hotel in the New Forest, then later in 1995 we held a second meeting—just the inner circle of me, Peter, Gordon, Alastair, Philip, Anji, Jonathan, Sue—at Fritham Lodge, also in the New Forest, and the home of Jonathan's brother. News of the second meeting caused no end of problems with John Prescott, who was not there. During the course of the day, Gordon privately took Peter aside and asked him to work under his design and tutelage. Peter pointedly said that he worked for the leader. From that moment there was an enmity between them, and neither was a good enemy to have.

I was supremely fixed on getting the right person to do the media. Peter and I considered the candidates—Andy Grice of the *Independent*, Peter MacMahon of the *Scotsman*, Patrick Wintour of the *Guardian*—but though all were good, really good, I wanted a tabloid person, and thought Alastair Campbell would be best. I'm not sure if it was great for him, but it was certainly great for me. I wanted a hard nut and had thought he was good; what I got was a genius. It was a very lucky strike.

Once we decided on Alastair I decided to pursue him immediately with fervour. I can be like that, when determined on an objective. I resolved not to take no for an answer. It was tricky at first. He had sorted his life out since his nervous breakdown and had given up the booze. His partner, Fiona Millar, was dubious about him taking the job, thinking correctly that it would change their lives. He was destined to go far in the media—even then he had star quality—so he would be giving up a lot. He admired and liked Peter, but also feared ending up in competition with him. For all those reasons, he was hard to persuade.

Eventually in mid-August 1994 I just pitched up at his holiday house in the part of France where he went every summer. For reasons completely beyond me, he would stay near to where Neil and Glenys Kinnock and Philip Gould and his wife Gail were also vacationing. Personally, the thought of going on holiday with people active in politics appalled me. You would never get away from it. But he liked it and they all chatted and plotted away happily.

The house was in Flassan in Provence, a *département* studded with those near-perfect little French villages in beautiful countryside. The attempt by the British to reconquer France by peaceful acquisition isn't daft.

I arrived, stayed to dinner, got Neil on board, talked half the night alone with Alastair and did the deal. I gave what assurances I could on Peter. He was already anxious about Gordon's people, but most of all, he wanted to know that I would back him to do what was necessary.

While there, I broached the subject of Clause IV, the core statement of the Labour Party credo in our constitution. After the 1992 defeat, and without discussing it with anyone, not even Gordon, I had formed a clear view that if ever I was leader, the constitution should be rewritten and the old commitments to nationalisation and state control would be dumped.

Clause IV was hallowed text repeated on every occasion by those on the left who wanted no truck with compromise or the fact that modern thinking had left its words intellectually redundant and politically calamitous. Among other things, it called for "the common ownership of the means of production, distribution and exchange." When drafted in 1917 by Sidney Webb, a great Fabian of the party's intellectual wing, the words had actually been an attempt to avoid more Bolshevik language from the further left. Most of all, of course, it reflected prevailing international progressive thought that saw the abolition of private capital as something devoutly to be desired.

What was mainstream leftist thinking in the early twentieth century had become hopelessly unreal, even surreal, in the late-twentieth-century world in which, since 1989, even Russia had embraced the market. But could it be changed? Fortuitously, I had never been pressed on this during the leadership contest. The issue had been raised, but was never pushed to the point where I lost "wiggle room." I had closed it down without closing it off.

Of course, as opponents of the change immediately pointed out once it was announced, it was largely symbolic. No one except the far left ever really believed in Clause IV as it was written. In a sense, that was my point: no one believed in it, yet no one dared remove it. What this symbolised, therefore, was not just something redundant in our constitution, but a refusal to confront reality, to change profoundly, to embrace the modern world wholeheartedly. In other words, this symbol mattered. It was a graven image, an idol. Breaking it would also change the psychology in the party that was damaging and reactionary and which was precisely what had kept us in Opposition for long periods. It had meant that although we were able erratically to do well against the Tories in response to their unpopularity, we could not govern consistently on our own merits. For me, therefore, removing Clause IV was not a gimmick or piece of good PR or a question of drafting; it was vital if Labour was to transform itself.

Progressive parties are always in love with their own emotional impulses. They have a feeling, however, that the electorate may not be of the same mind, so they are prepared to loosen them. Deep down, they wish it weren't so, and hope against hope that maybe one day, in one possibly unique circumstance, the public will share them. It's a delusion. They won't. But, though progressives know that, the longing is acute and the temptation to rebind themselves to such impulses strong. The most basic impulse is to believe that if power is delivered into their hands, they will use it for the benefit of the people; and the more power, the more benefit. Hence the affinity with the state and public sector.

It's not malignly motivated—on the contrary, the impulse is grounded in real and genuine feelings of solidarity—but history should have taught us to mitigate it in two crucial ways. First, the state and public sector can become great big vested interests that can be clumsy with, or even contradict, the public interest. Second, as people become better educated and more prosperous, they don't necessarily want someone else, anyone else, making their choices for them. If this impulse is kept in check—i.e. active but constrained—progressive government can be a fine and liberating alternative to conservative government; but if not, not, as it were.

By advocating public ownership of the entire means of production, distribution and exchange, Clause IV didn't represent a constraint but an invitation to unfettered indulgence. It was not healthy, wise or, unfortunately, meaningless. At a certain level, it meant a lot and the meaning was bad. Changing it was not a superficial thing; it implied a significant, deep and lasting change to the way the party thought, worked and would govern.

Part of the reason that I took so easily—many thought far too easily—to dismantling some of the sacred myths of the Labour ideology, was because of how I came to politics. As a student I had nothing to do with the Oxford Union, wasn't a member of the Labour Club, and took virtually no part—or certainly no very focused part—in student politics. My main political influences at university were two Australians, an Indian and a Ugandan. Each of these four people gave me an insight which stayed with me and shaped my approach to politics. All were of course on the left, but were very different people with very different experiences.

My fellow student Geoff Gallop was the most active politically, and indeed in later life became premier of Western Australia. He was brilliant, with an extraordinary intellect. He taught me all the right terms and phrases of leftist politics at the time, and was a member of the International Marxist Group, one of the numerous sects—this one Trotskyist—that abounded in the 1970s. Needless to say, anyone in the Labour Party was a sell-out. They were also bitter rivals with the Communist Party people, who tended to be far better organisers, with links to trade unions and the occasional normal person. Although Geoff adhered to the framework of the Marxist dialectic, his own spirit and intellectual curiosity refused to let him be imprisoned by it. He was constantly analysing and reanalysing, breaking out with new thinking and fresh insights. He taught me how social conditions formed character; but he also taught me not to be an unthinking disciple of the left.

Peter Thomson reinforced this. He was an Australian Anglican priest, probably the most influential person in my life. He was a mature student in his mid-thirties when we were at Oxford. When he died in January 2010, I wrote this for his funeral:

There are very few people of whom you can say: he changed my life. Peter changed mine. From the first moment I met him—I was having a party in my room in St. John's and had stepped out onto the battlements, swaying a little, and looking down saw Pete looking up, "I'd be careful if I was you, mate"—from that first moment, he shaped my life, gave it meaning and purpose; and set its course.

He was my friend, teacher, mentor and guide. Any good that I have done, he inspired it. Whatever my manifold faults, he made me a better person for knowing him: better, stronger, more loyal, less frail, more thankful for what I have, more hopeful about life's possibilities, more joyful in fulfilling them, more courageous in accepting their limitations.

We often say, of someone's passing, that they will leave a void in my life. Peter's passing leaves no void. His presence fills it still. He was there when I needed him most. He will be there for me always. The light that shone in Peter is too powerful to be diminished by death.

That is how God worked through Peter. He was, after all, the most un-vicar-like of vicars. He and the adorable Helen kept open house for us all, but though much tea was drunk, along with many other things, a vicarage tea party it wasn't. Never have dog collar and manner of speaking been in such blissful disharmony.

But that defined Peter: a curious mixture of the traditionalist and the iconoclast. His Christianity was muscular not limp. He was a doer not a spectator; and a thinker not just a preacher. Those thoughts were bold, groundbreaking and, for our twenty-first-century world, visionary.

I have met many people, famous and successful people, whom the world would call great. I never met a greater man than Peter. I feel him with me now as I write. I will feel him beside me always. I know, even as I mourn his death, that the greatest achievement I could wish for is that at the hour of my death, he would think proudly of me.

All these years later, his influence remains like an insistent reminder that life has to be lived for a purpose. Politically, Pete was on the left, but religion came first. Therefore, so, in a sense, it did for me. Not that the two were separated by him, or me, but the frame within which you see the world is different if religion comes first. Religion starts with values that are born of a view of humankind. Politics starts with an examination of society and the means of changing it. Of course politics is about values; and religion is often about changing society. But you start from a different place.

This is vital in understanding my politics. I begin with an analysis of human beings as my compass; the politics is secondary. Later, when I became sure that the "progressive problem" was an insufficiently clear separation between ends and means, this approach—very much instilled by Peter—was what allowed me to come to that conclusion freely.

Geoff would give me books on politics to read. Peter would give me the philosopher John Macmurray's works, such as *Reason and Emotion* and *Conditions of Freedom*. I developed a theory about the basis of socialism being about "community"—i.e. people owed obligations to each other and were social beings, not only individuals out for themselves—which pushed me down the path of trying to retrieve Labour's true values from the jumble of ideological baggage that was piled on top of them, obscuring their meaning. For me, it was socialism, and wasn't about a particular type of economic organisation, anchored to a particular point in history.

The Indian was a postgraduate student called Anmol Vellani. One day, sitting in his room on the ground floor of the quadrangle at St. John's College, he gave me an insight that stayed with me and had a curious but profound effect on the public sector reform programme of later years. I can still picture the moment.

Anmol, perhaps because of the experience of India, but also because he had more political maturity, was debating with me the new ideas I had received from Geoff. I was trying them out on him, prodding and pushing, hoping to get a better understanding of the new language I was learning to speak. We were talking about capitalism and the state. I was repeating the view that the state had to take over from the interests of capitalism, which only cared about profit—the usual Marxist line!

Anmol shook his head. "It is not as simple as that," he said. "The state, too, can be a vested interest. It's not the same as the public interest, you know, not in practice at least."

"But it should be," I insisted.

"Should be and is are two very different things, my friend," he replied, laughing at my innocence.

The fourth person was Olara Otunnu, a Ugandan. He had been president of the Students' Guild at university in Kampala and had to flee from Idi Amin. St. John's took him in. He was a gifted speaker, really quite brilliant, and a lovely, spiritual human being. I think he regarded the student leftists enthusing about Marxism in the cloisters of privilege at Oxford with a degree of amused detachment. His politics were all about development and the burden of corrupt and appalling government ruining the prospects of the people. He taught me to look beyond the confines of Western student debate and think about the world that was not debating "capitalism versus socialism," but life, hope and health versus death due to the ravages of poverty, conflict and disease.

It was an unusual group of people—diverse, unconventional, free-thinking—who, at a moment when my mind was open, willing and eager to learn, shaped the structure of my thinking for the years to come.

When I was talking through my thoughts on Clause IV with Alastair in France, I could tell he loved the brassiness of it, and by the time I left I could see his mind whirring away on how to sell it. During the course of the conversation I also discovered something I hadn't been a hundred per cent sure of previously: he had clanking great balls. This was someone you would have to pull back, not push forward. In a world dominated by the timid, cautious and the overcalculating, I liked that. He and Peter Mandelson might fight (and my goodness they did, occasionally literally), but in tandem they would be as formidable a political force as could be imagined. Peter would slip into the castle through a secret passageway and, by nimble footwork and sharp and incisive thrusts of the rapier, cleave his way through to the throne room. Meanwhile, Alastair would be a very large oak battering ram destroying the castle gates, and neither boiling pitch nor reinforced doors would keep him out. With the two of them in harness, the battle would be fought with a boldness just short of madness; but it would be won, and, what's more, won in style.

As I often did in those days, I had split the holiday between France and Italy. The first part had been near Toulouse and then we caught a train to Marseilles to see Alastair, and thence to the very north of Liguria where the parents of Tim Allan had a house in the hills near Crespiano. It was one of the last really free-and-easy holidays I had. No one in the village had a clue who I was. There was no protection back then, no security or staff, just us as a family together. Bliss. We would go up to the village restaurant where you just sat at a table with everyone else. The food was simple but the pasta was home-made with great sauces, and for variety, you could go and participate in any number of August fetes, where in surroundings of extraordinary rustic beauty, each old village would put on entertainment in the square, including a wonderfully cooked local meal.

It was possibly the last time when I could travel abroad normally (I was already a marked man in Britain) without a glimmer of recognition from anyone. One night we visited La Gavarina d'Oro restaurant in the village of Podenzana to sample the special local pizza called *panigacci*, only to be turned away since there had been a mix-up in the booking (my poor Italian), and there was no table for us. We dutifully rebooked and went there two nights later. I don't think that ever happened to me again.

While there, I got news of the latest opinion poll, showing we had achieved the highest rating of any political party ever, and had something ridiculous like a thirty-point lead. I didn't set much store by it as those leads can come and go, but it was an indicator that my election as leader had been well received by the public. And that would help me with the party. I was under no illusions. Many, perhaps even a majority, who had voted for me had done so not because they shared my vision for the party, but because they thought I was a winner. For now, that was enough. I would use the public to change the party. Only later did I learn that it was a lot tougher the other way round.

Over the holiday period, I reflected on Clause IV and my thinking hardened. I now knew it had to be the first essential step. On my return, I began to consult close and senior people. My own associates were either already in the loop or easily convinced. Anji was enthusiastic of course, as was Peter. Philip was in favour but reckoned it was a really big thing that would mean serious, possibly terminal damage if it went wrong. But my staff, who shared my vision, were never going to be the problem.

I spoke to Gordon. He advised me that I had to "get Prescott on board." It was good advice; though he was very non-committal on his own account, not anti, but I thought it a trifle ominous that he dodged the direct question of whether he thought it was a good idea. However, he clearly wouldn't oppose it.

I had made up my mind to change the party General Secretary, Larry Whitty. It would be a key position in any party fight. I liked Larry, but our politics were different. I had begun to think that Tom Sawyer would be the ideal choice: a trade union man, but smart, loyal, modernising, and with the reach and authority to help me get things through. This fence had to be leapt at the gallop and there could be no excess baggage weighing us down as we jumped.

John Prescott was indeed critical, as Gordon had said. I knew it had to be approached with care. I saw him at my house, a gentle, reassuring and intimate environment. He was less taken aback than I thought he would be. As wily and perceptive on such matters as ever, he had already worked out that I wasn't going to be an easy ride and that my desire to change the party—and take it not just to government but to a different frame of mind—was real and indivertible. Right at the outset, his basic line had been: I will argue in private although if your mind is made up, I will come with you; or, if I feel so strongly, I will go, but I won't stay and undermine from within. It was not, of course, a pledge of unconditional support; but it was a promise of straight dealing, which was important and, as it transpired, one that was largely kept.

John made it clear that although he thought the project was altogether unwise, he would reflect and consider it. He had a plethora of questions—how, when, replaced with what, drafted by whom, endorsed in what manner—some of which I could answer. I got him to the point where he at least accepted that a debate around what the party really stood for was necessary, and that Clause IV provided the vehicle. He favoured a delay to see how things went with the public—after all, we were so far ahead of the Tories—but I knew in my own mind that it was precisely at this moment, almost for that reason, that we had to act. We had to show that even with this lead in the polls we were going to take a risk because it was right to do so, and demonstrate through taking it that we knew our lead was conditional. Yes, the people were saying, we like the look of this guy and where he wants to take the Labour Party, but now prove it. Any sense of either complacency or caution and I knew the lead would melt under the hot sun of scrutiny.

When eventually party conference came round in October 1994, the public mood was still strong, but I was sure there lurked major doubts underneath. When a party has defined itself in a particular way which is not to the public's liking, the definition has an uncomfortable habit of sticking around, like the smell of decay in an old house. You can use some air freshener, you can throw open a few windows and you can jolly people up a little with some positive description of how it's going to be better; but the only thing that works, in the end, is to say: this place stinks, we're going to make it over, i.e. keep the structure, revolutionise the rest.

I assessed that there were three types of Labour: old-fashioned Labour, which could never win; modernised Labour, which could win and keep winning, which was my ambition from the outset; and plain Labour, which could win once, but essentially as a reaction to an unpopular Conservative government. The last couldn't win on its own terms with sufficient clarity, breadth and depth of support to be capable of sustaining victory through the inevitable troubled times of government. My favourite parable of the Gospel, the parable of the sower, always served as an example: the difference between plain Labour and modernised Labour was the difference between the seed that sprouted but never took real root, and the seed that yielded thirty, sixty, a hundredfold.

In order to keep winning, we needed to create a core of ideas, attitudes and policy that was solid, sustainable, strong; a sea wall that when the waves beat upon it was impregnable, that gathered friends to it and repelled foes. I knew that to do this meant confronting the old attitudes of the party not from time to time but every day, at every moment, on each occasion when they tried to reassert themselves. Conceding to them would matter not only in itself, but far more as a sign that the old house remained essentially untransformed.

I tried to see Labour as an ordinary, non-political member of the public saw us. I had many friends outside politics who thought the Tories were tired and should be put out. And what did they think of us? They thought we were for the poor; the downtrodden; for the union men; for the accused and the dispossessed. They thought we were liberals on law and order and peaceniks on defence. Herein lay the problem: all of these sentiments, in their place, are good and worthy—they are why I'm Labour—but only *in their place*. As dominant, complete definitions of where Labour stood and who it represented, there was no earthly way they formed a broad enough, deep enough or popular enough coalition. Defined in this way, we were a party of protest, not of government.

Moreover, these were the kindest ways of describing these attitudes. In fact, not in their place, such sentiments could be counterproductive for the country: union interests before public interest; a refusal to accept change where it was necessary; weakness on law and order and defence; attitudes that might be principled but could also be naive.

Under Neil Kinnock and John Smith we had of course broadened, deepened and become more popular, but it felt to me—and more importantly to the public—like a negotiation between us and our past. We were talking in an upbeat way, but there was a tinge of reluctance about it, a reverence for the old days that smacked of denial about how bad it had been. There was a care in speaking about the way things were that indicated an uncertainty, a lack of thorough conviction about the way things would be in the future.

I wanted us to be emphatic, to be in the political centre from belief, with passion, and with the total clarity that left our past behind, not in the sense that we didn't keep the structure of our traditional beliefs, including their central foundation—the commitment to social justice— but rather that new ways of developing such foundations were needed in the modern world. From the very beginning, I was determined to be the architect of something revolutionary, transformative and undeniable. I had kept the plan on Clause IV very tight. On the opening weekend of party conference, just before it began, I started the consultations with other key people.

Jack Straw, who had written a pamphlet on the subject, was delighted. So was Neil Kinnock. Robin Cook thought it was crazy because it would split the party, and warned it might be the end of me. Margaret Beckett raised an eyebrow. Donald Dewar said, "This should be interesting" in that funny Donaldish way. George Robertson, always sound, a former Defence Secretary and general secretary of NATO, was supportive. On the whole, opinion was mixed and apprehensive. I spoke to Gordon several times but was careful not to disclose how it was to be announced. I'm afraid distrust was already present, like a shadow between us.

I had wanted to do it right at the end of my conference speech, and so inflammatory was it certain to be that we decided not to say it in the bald terms: "Clause IV is going to be abandoned." This was not because we didn't dare to say it outside of the hall, but to say it in the hall itself could provoke a really adverse reaction which might mar the whole event. I was going to say we needed to decide what our aims and values really were for the modern world, and a debate would start soon (this took on John Prescott's point about the necessity of a proper discussion). Then we would wait for the purport to sink in. It was a device, but my consultations had shown we needed one.

Late on the Saturday we had a final vigorous debate about the slogan for it, and the use of the phrase "New Labour." Alastair invented the phrase "New Labour, New Britain." He said we should put it up in the hall as the main theme for the conference. Looking back now, it seems obvious that we should have done, but at the time there was a furious dispute, I can tell you. At one point there was even talk of a compromise, "new Labour," i.e. no capital "N." And it wasn't as trivial a point as you might think: New Labour with a capital "N" was indeed like renaming the party. Some of my inner circle warned there would be a dangerous reaction. Even Peter was worried. Finally, I thought, Let's go for it. There was indeed a reaction but it was containable, and the impact was massive, an emphatic signal that this was not going to be a minor refurbishment but a wholesale renovation.

When, at the conclusion of my speech, I spoke of the need to redraw the party's aims and values in its constitution (as George Robertson remarked, the hall was silent for a while, until the silence was broken by the sound of pennies dropping), and it was clear we were going to risk a vast internal party fight, the idea took hold that this leadership truly was different. This was red meat.

As if to underscore how difficult it was all going to be, the next day the party, at the insistence of the unions, passed a resolution reaffirming Clause IV. It was, ironically, helpful: it showed this was not a false wrestle put on for the cameras but a genuine fight, with real opponents and real pain. However, it also meant we had to win it or we were finished.

For me, I was absolutely clear: if the change was rejected, I was off. As we approached the twenty-first century, five years after the fall of the Berlin Wall and with even Communist China embracing the "socialist market" economy, if the British Labour Party was going to assert that it believed in state ownership of "the means of production, distribution and exchange," it meant we weren't serious. Such a position would confirm all the public's worst fears.

Of course opponents quickly shifted to asking: why have the internal row? This put opposition on a tactical, lower-ground basis. I retorted: there is a row only because you oppose the change. Either say you really do agree with the existing constitution, or accept the change.

The debate took six months. John Prescott finally came fully on board and that helped settle down the traditional wing of the party enormously. The bloc of Labourites who composed the Scottish Conference—who might have been tricky—passed a resolution in support of change, the first really big victory inside the party, setting the tone for the other swing voters to follow. If we could win in the heartland of the party, in Scotland where traditional thought was strong and where we might have anticipated resistance to such "middle-class" thinking, then we could win in most places, and even in the unions. The opponents tried to rally and rail, but they were hamstrung by the overwhelming support for change among the public, who didn't follow the detail but, as I anticipated, knew that it was really about whether the old Labour Party had changed or not.

The actual drafting was the product of an unusual collaboration between myself, Derry and Peter Hyman, with others providing commentary and suggestions. The initial draft was done sitting alone in Inverness in the family house of an old friend of mine, Mairi Stuart, just before the Scottish Conference. The final touches were put in place in our house in Islington, sitting in the bedroom with Peter Hyman, as downstairs our daughter Kathryn was having a birthday party. So I would go between games of pass-the-parcel and rewriting British social democracy.

The words mattered, to both party and public. For the party they had to convey genuine conviction. For the public, they couldn't be a fudge. They had to represent a clear move into the modern world.

So, we kept at the beginning the phrase "democratic socialism," but what came after was a plain statement of values which rejected any association of those values with the state as the principal economic actor:

> The Labour Party is a democratic socialist party. It believes that by the strength of our common endeavour, we achieve more than we achieve alone so as to create for each of us the means to realise our true potential and for all of us a community in which power, wealth and opportunity are in the hands of the many not the few, where the rights we enjoy reflect the duties we owe, and where we live together, freely, in a spirit of solidarity, tolerance and respect.

In the strange telepathic way they do things, the public had ranked in order of preference the outcome for my leadership: the best result was that I was in control of a party that agreed with me; the worst was that I was not in control of a party which disagreed with me; the acceptable outcome was that the party was prepared to go along with me. In the end we settled somewhere between the best and the acceptable. Although we were only a small group of co-conspirators, as time went on we drew significant numbers of people to us. A new generation of young supporters bought fully into the change. They were the true believers and are the only hope for the party's future today.

The battle over Clause IV more or less set the scene for the style and content of leadership in the years up to 1997. We hadn't anything like a fully formed corpus of policy. We were much less prepared for government than we should have been, given the eighteen years of Opposition, though actually it can be dangerous to formulate precise policy in Opposition that is uninformed by the experience and expertise that comes with government. How we would overcome the many obstacles, diversions, treacherous shoals and unknown terrain was not known. On the other hand, our compass was set in a firm direction, and the manner and attitude with which we would approach the challenges was clear. New Labour was not just a slogan. It was an attitude of mind. It would serve us well when we were tested in the next two years, allowing us to develop the harder-edged policy and make the tough decisions.

Sometimes the tests arose as the issues arose. In January 1995, we had to knock back any suggestion of taxing private schools. Indeed, schools were a constant object of controversy in those early days as I tried to wean the party off its old prejudices (though I think they may have called them beliefs). Ironically, in the light of her later defection from my supporters, it was over Harriet Harman, who had held various positions in the Labour government, including deputy leader, that the issue got hottest in January 1996.

When I had chosen to send my own children to the Oratory—a Catholic state school that had been funded by the government—it was a difficult enough moment. Alastair and I had a real set-to over it since he, and most especially his partner Fiona, who was a campaigner for comprehensive schools, really disapproved. (Comprehensive schools are state-funded and where children of all backgrounds and abilities are educated in a single school.) But I was determined that I couldn't let the kids down. Their education was important. They had enough to put up with as it was. To send them to a bad or average state school, when under the then rules governing admissions to Catholic schools we could have sent them to a good one, would be really quite wickedly irresponsible. As I said to Alastair: you and Fiona took hold of your children's secondary school, and changed it; I don't have that option. Also, there was always this somewhat absurd charge that we should have chosen Islington secondary schools for our children (they had been to primary school there) because that's where we lived. Without seeming complacent or taking things for granted, I couldn't point out the reality, which was that come the election we might well be living in Westminster. And, to be frank, with the state of Islington schools at that time, it is something that we would have tried to avoid anyway.

However, our situation paled into insignificance when Harriet, having sent one child also to the Oratory, decided to send the other to a grammar school, a state-run school that is allowed by law to select all its pupils on the sole grounds of high academic ability. This really was something. The whole of the Labour Party programme since the 1960s had been to abolish selection on the basis of academic ability alone and bring in comprehensive, non-selective schooling, which would serve students of all academic abilities. Grammar schools were by and large cordially detested by the party. Harriet's decision was therefore a real shocker.

Alastair wanted to send her a letter denouncing her decision. Bruce Grocott, my Parliamentary Private Secretary (PPS), who worked to keep me informed of all issues that affected me in Parliament, was appalled. Even my nearest and dearest in the office thought it pretty indefensible. Only Cherie came close to sticking up for her, since she always put the family first. As the news leaked, the party went into turmoil—after all, Harriet was a member of the Shadow Cabinet. Major slaughtered me on it at PMQs, finally having something he could really twist the knife on.

Alastair, as ever, held the line despite his own opinion, which was loudly communicated with much vigour. My view was absolutely crystal clear: it was her choice as a parent. On this, I was in a minority of one. The press smelt blood. It seems strange now but people really did tell me my leadership was on the line. No one could quite understand why I felt the need to defend her so vigorously.

To be honest, at first I wasn't sure why either, but as I licked my wounds over PMQs and reflected, I realised why the instinct was so strong: although Labour people would understand why Harriet might have to resign over this, no ordinary person would. Some woman politician decides to send her kid to a grammar school. She thinks it gives him the best chance of a good education. Her party forces her to resign. What do you think? You think that's a bit extreme; and not very nice; and a bit worrying; and is that what still makes me a bit anxious about those Labour people? Before we know where we are, we've really unsettled sensible middle-ground opinion.

I dug in. I went to the PLP the day after the Tuesday PMQs and defended her passionately. I also learned a great lesson: the row passed. Yes, it had been ugly for a while and as ever in the Westminster bubble everything seems so extraordinarily hyper, but in reality the world kept turning and the news moved on.

We were continuing to develop the orientation for policy across a range of issues. In May 1995, we had had the first of a series of discussions, internally in the office, about Bank of England independence to set interest rates. I was already firmly of the view we should do it. It was also part of the bigger analysis for business, unions, public service and welfare policy that I wanted to develop which would be plainly New Labour, and even if the most we could do was establish a direction, the direction should be clear.

In part this was about attitude; in part about policy; in part about reconstructing a different link between the party and the people. The attitude was clear: no compromise on the essentials, and making New Labour an indisputable fact of the political landscape; in policy, to figure out not the granular details but the guiding principles of policy positions; in the link between party and people, getting the former to behave like normal people and the latter to feel that, thus normalised, Labour people were their type of people.

All of this today sounds almost comically obvious, but not back then. We had become separated from "normal" people. For several decades, even before the eighteen years in the wilderness, Labour was more like a cult than a party. If you were to progress in it, you had to speak the language and press the right buttons. It went on so long it became natural to those in the party. Even I had to learn to do it—not that well, I may say—but without doing some of it, you got nowhere.

The SDP had been formed mainly for policy reasons, but they also masked a cultural disjunction between them and traditional Labour. I always remember in 1981 seeing on TV the Limehouse Declaration by the "Gang of Four"—Roy Jenkins, Shirley Williams, David Owen and Bill Rodgers—in which they spoke of their intention to leave the Labour Party. The actual declaration was important, of course, but what intrigued me was the photograph of the meeting. On the table was a bottle of wine. You may think this ridiculous, but I remember being shocked that they allowed themselves to be pictured with a bottle of claret. Then I became shocked at my shocked reaction. Didn't I have a bottle of wine on my table? Didn't many people? Yet I kid you not, at that time Labour members would have been aghast at such a picture. Beer, possibly; wine, no.

There was, in a sense, a cultural as well as a political divide between the party and the people. Normal young people went out on a Saturday night, had a few drinks and partied. Labour young people sat and talked seriously about the iniquities of the Tory government and the inevitable long-term decline of capitalism. I wanted us to reconnect completely at the cultural level. I wanted us to take the good bits of the Labour Party in the 1970s and 1980s—proper progressive attitudes such as equality for women, gays, blacks and Asians—and ally them to normality, bring them into the mainstream and out of the suffocating strictures of political correctness. So a woman should be able to be a woman and still be political. She didn't have to behave or seem like a man. That sense of ourselves as individuals has a very important political spirit attached to it.

The essential problem of Labour in the post-war period was that it had lost touch with its basic purpose. That purpose was always, at heart, about the individual. A more powerful state, unions, social action, collective bargaining—all of these were means to an end: to help the individual gain opportunity, to let him or her overcome limitations unfairly imposed by poverty, poor education, poor health, housing and welfare. It was all about opportunity not in general but in particular: for you, as an individual. That echoed and captured something deep within human nature: the desire to be free, to be the best you can be.

The problem for all progressive parties was that by the 1960s, the first generation of those helped in such a way had been liberated. Thus on the ladder of opportunity, they didn't want more state help; they wanted choice, freedom to earn more money and spend it. They fractured the homogeneous class base. They started to resent the freeloaders they paid for. Above all, they wanted a different relationship with the state: as partners or citizens, not as beneficiaries or clients. The private sector, driven by the market, shifted fast under such social pressures. The public sector got stuck. This is why by the end of the 1970s, Thatcher and Reagan were able to push forward major change.

For me, New Labour was all about understanding this social evolution. It wasn't at all about changing the basic values or purpose of progressive politics; on the contrary, it was about retrieving them from the deadweight of political and cultural dogma that didn't merely obscure those values and that purpose, but also defeated them.

What is more, it wasn't about "coming to terms" with such an evolution. It was about rejoicing in it, recognising that this was not an unfortunate reality that we had to learn to acknowledge in order to make progress; it *was* progress.

All of this may seem a long way back from Clause IV, policy changes and manifestos, but it was a critical part of orientation. I wanted Labour people to be ambitious and compassionate at the same time, and feel neither guilty about the first nor anxious about the second. We were normal human beings. We should be motivated and fascinated by the prospect of being agents of political change. We should be striving for happiness and fulfilment also in our chosen careers, in our personal life, in our enjoyment of art and culture.

Again I know it sounds a little bizarre, but back in the late 1980s there was a group of rock musicians called Red Wedge, fronted by people like Paul Weller and Billy Bragg, who came out and campaigned for us. It was great. But I remember saying after one of their gigs—and, by the way, Billy Bragg was someone I got to know later and really liked—"We need to reach the people listening to Duran Duran and Madonna" (a comment which went down like a cup of sick). I felt, in art and culture, we should represent all strands, avant-garde through to basic popular art that our voters might go to watch or listen to.

So, in a sense, for me, politics started with that very ground-level human reconnection of party and people. In late 1996, Alastair, who got all this completely, persuaded me to appear on the *Des O'Connor Show*. At that time, it was a very unusual thing for a politician to do. I was incredibly nervous. I had to prepare certain anecdotes, and get myself in a totally different frame of mind. It would be utterly unlike PMQs or a party conference speech. I didn't have to prove "fitness to govern" in terms of economic or social or foreign policy; I had to prove I was normal and could talk normally about the things people like to chat about. It was a risk, and I fear I made Alastair's life hell in the lead-up to it, but it worked. What astonished me, however, was that from then on, people sublimely uninterested in politics would feel I was accessible to them.

It meant we were back in touch, that this rather frightening cultural disjunction of the 1970s and '80s had been realigned. People were focused and prepared to listen. However—and this is also crucial—such a reconnection was only a beginning. Sometimes, political leaders make the mistake of thinking: That's enough, I've done it, they like me. That is gravely to underestimate people. That is actually just first base, no more than that.

Then they want answers. If you are in Opposition, people don't expect you to know it all. They're not asking for reams of detail, they just want to know where you stand—on spending and tax; on law and order; on defence; on Europe; on public services. Here two things are vital for an Opposition: keep it simple; and keep it coherent. By keeping it simple, I mean not surface only. I mean: clear.

For example, are you in favour of a tough approach on law and order or not? Do you support the war in Afghanistan fully or not? Are you for reform or status quo in public services? Do we need less, more or the same amount of public spending? Are you in favour of tax cuts, and if so, for whom? Big state, smaller state, different state?

Politicians, in one way rightly mistrusting the crudity of such simple positioning, don't like this, because once defined you are limited, and their instinct is to keep all options open. The holy grail is to have everyone onside; and I'm not saying I didn't pursue it fairly vigorously and, at points, more successfully than most.

However, you have to be able to answer those questions plainly and clearly. There can be qualifications and "get-outs," but the answers must remain comprehensible, because they define you. They add up to a political, not merely personal, character. This requires thought, detailed analysis and intellectual rigour. Politics is a far more intellectual business than is often realised. You may think: Well, if it's simplicity that's required, you don't need a whole lot of detail. Wrong. The simplicity is not born of superficial analysis. It is simple precisely because it is the product of being worked through.

It was here in the long period of Opposition, when every day, week and month had to be filled with something new or diverting, that the work I had done with Gordon and a range of other policy thinkers paid off. We had burrowed down; we had devilled; we had iterated and reiterated in order to get to grips with the governing principles in each area. So we needed more investment in public services. Fine. But how to pay for it? Growth? Tax rises? Are we against tax cuts or in favour of some? And how does that impact on spending? Is it investment first, then tax cuts? Or can you do both, maybe redistributing? If redistribution, of what sort? On the higher rate, or in other more covert ways?

I can't tell you how many times we went back and forth on these issues, so that by 1994, when we became more busy and the relationship more tense, we were already orientated. The pathfinder was already switched on: growth was key; investment not tax cuts; redistribute, but carefully and not touching income tax; keep the middle class onside, but where growth and some redistribution allowed, focus on the poorest; then, in time, you could balance tax cuts and spending.

Likewise on welfare. Throughout 1995 and 1996, we toyed with a jobs programme. In the end, we came up with the "New Deal" for the unemployed. The phrase was Gordon's, borrowed from Franklin D.

Roosevelt's economic programmes in the 1930s. He always liked that sort of thing. We chose a windfall tax on the privatised utilities as the means of paying for it (being often in a monopoly position, the utilities had ended up with bumper profits). Gordon pushed for the tax, but I was a little reluctant, fearful of alienating business opinion. In early January 1997, I had a set-to with him about it, mainly because his adviser Ed Balls had gone over the top in briefing it. In the end, we settled on a compromise which was less than he wanted, but still a hefty sum.

However, the real crunch came in the programme itself, where Gordon and I were on the same page precisely: along with the job opportunities for the unemployed, we insisted on a responsibility on the part of the unemployed person to take them—i.e. modern, not old-fashioned welfare. This was very controversial ground with a lot of the party. There was a huge outcry from union leaders and others (including Robin Cook) accusing us of introducing a type of workfare, though Robin's comments were in Shadow Cabinet and aimed at Gordon (with whom he had a long-standing feud that had begun deep in the history of 1970s Scottish politics). We stuck to our guns and saw the rebellion off.

But here's the point: each decision—to have a tax, to put it on the utilities, to use it for a new type of jobs programme—was born of a set of thoroughly worked-out positions on tax, on business, on welfare. Our thinking had been painstakingly orientated so that when we came to the policy, it was not only clear but also coherent. The position on welfare didn't contradict the business position. It could have done—we might have raised general corporation tax and funded a new type of jobs programme, but that would have been anti-business. We might have had a windfall tax on utilities and had an old-fashioned, traditional jobs programme, but that would have contradicted our message on welfare, namely that it was about a partnership between state and individual, not a handout. Instead, we chose carefully so that the policy was in balance and consistent with the overall New Labour position and message. In this way, it had broad appeal. Competitive business resented the utility windfall profits from privatisation, while people wanted action on unemployment but thought unemployed people also had a duty to help themselves.

I was obsessed by the thought that this Labour government had to be different; had to be able to govern for a lengthy term, as Tory governments seemed habitually capable of doing. In order to achieve this, there was no room for compromise on essentials. That is emphatically not to say we didn't compromise. We did. In 1995, I came out for a publicly owned railway system. I never had much faith in this particular privatisation of the Tories and felt it would lead to a hugely complex and possibly uncompetitive system; but on the other hand, I wasn't going to waste money renationalising it. On the NHS and schools we also compromised, sometimes more than I liked. However, when it came to those issues fundamental to New Labour—to its rationale, its heart, its political soul, if you will—there was no compromise at all. Often this was posed less in terms of what we would do than in what we wouldn't. But that was natural for Opposition; and in any event, it created the right political space for those things I was determined to move forward on, if and when prime minister.

So: no return to the old union laws; no renationalisation of the privatised utilities; no raising of the top rate of tax; no unilateralism; no abolition of grammar schools. And there were certain clear pointers to future policy: a tough line on antisocial behaviour; investment and reform in public services; pro-Europe and pro-U.S.; opportunity and responsibility together in welfare; encouragement for small- and medium-sized enterprises and even-handedness between business and labour (employees might have additional individual rights, but not collective ones).

At every stage of this (and the decisions came pretty fast and furious), I was reconciled to fighting, and to leaving if I lost. The party had to know I was not bluffing. If they didn't want New Labour, they could get someone else. The country had to know that if I was going to be their prime minister, I would be "of the party" but also removed from it.

At times—and this was a muted criticism from GB also—it seemed as if I was deliberately provoking the party. Genuinely I wasn't; but I was not going to defer. I was going to speak the same language to party and country. In so doing, I was going to encourage the sensible and modernising people in the party to step up and step out. Party leaders have a symbiotic impact on their activists. There is a subtle cloning process that goes on which, in turn, gives more strength to the leader.

Speeches I gave back then were different in content to the speeches in the early part of the twenty-first century, to be sure, but in tone they remained the same. Our understanding of what it meant to modernise changed with the experience of governing, but the will and determination to modernise never wavered. Of course, the other point to underline is that this will was born of belief. My settled conviction was that twentieth-century politics was coming to an end not only in time but also in substance. The old left/right distinctions remained, but needed amendment, confinement and definition.

So there it was: a basic belief—recovering Labour values from out-dated tradition and dogma and reconnecting the party to the modern world; a set of intellectual policy orientations coming from those values reapplied in the light of modernity; and finally a set of policy positions or decisions that reflected those earlier orientations and that basic belief. The commitment remained. The means of implementing it radically altered. The state and social action were a means of advancing the indi-vidual, not subsuming them. The objective was for the individual to ful-fil their potential and ambition; our role was as the enabler of this, not the controller of it, aiming not to limit that ambition or those goals but to open up their possibility to all. "For the many not the few," as the new Clause IV put it.

Every step, every declaration, every interview was dedicated to that coherent framework. The coherence itself is an essential component. Take the Tory Party of today. They wanted a modernising message. To an extent, they followed the New Labour handbook. They changed their position on gays, on investment in public services, on the impor-tance of society. They put away some of the old Thatcherite rhetoric, but the seed didn't take root. So when they thought it was in the bag, they relaxed. Suddenly the Eurosceptics were let out of the cage and indulged, and the Tories did less well in the 2010 election than expected. Now, of course, as a result of the coalition the Eurosceptics are conve-niently, for the Tory leadership, back behind bars. Why is Euroscepti-cism a mistake for a Tory Party trying to modernise? At first blush you may think: No, that's fine—after all, the polls show that's where the British people are. But it is a mistake because it immediately breaks the coherence of the modernising message. To a 25-to-45-year-old audi-ence, Europe is a fact. Live with it. (Whether you like it or not is another matter.) Let slightly wild-eyed anti-Europeans start talking about it with a passion that people instinctively distrust, and in a flash, the question mark over the party and its leader returns in bold print. Add into that any wavering on the economy, and the incoherence starts to worry the very voters you need to reassure. So, in a sense the final move towards modernisation was less a decision that could have ended with a conclusive election victory, and more the product of an election whose result was inconclusive. Having said that, they now have the chance to make it work, and to do in government what they did not do fully in Opposition.

Between 1995 and 1997, even after Clause IV, I was in a perpetual motion of reassurance. The more the poll lead went up, the more I did it. Members of the Shadow Cabinet would frequently say: Come on, enough, we are miles ahead. Each time they said it, I would get hyper-anxious, determined not for a single instant to stop the modernising drive. If I seemed obsessive, it was because I was. Reconnection was great and policy change was essential, but above all, people needed to know that when I was tested, I would stay true to that modernising appeal. Our opponents would say: it's all clever spin and PR. Day in and day out, with the party's reactionary elements as my foil, I would prove them wrong with a raft of modernising moves.

In June 1995 we had further outraged sensibilities by accepting an invitation, conveyed through the then editor of *The Times*, Peter Stothard, to address Rupert Murdoch's News Corporation conference on Hayman Island in Australia the next month. Again, now, it seems obvious: the country's most powerful newspaper proprietor, whose publications have hitherto been rancorous in their opposition to the Labour Party, invites us into the lion's den. You go, don't you?

We kept the invitation and my desire to go very quiet indeed. Poor Bruce Grocott was aghast. He was and is a wonderful guy—really sincere, decent and absolutely Labour to the innermost part of his being. In fact, the best of traditional Labour. He had been Mo Mowlam's inspired suggestion for my PPS. It was a great choice. (Bruce was succeeded by two equally great choices, David Hanson and Keith Hill. David was a great networker, respected even by those who disagreed passionately with me; and also a very tuned-in politician in his own right. Keith was a witty, lovable and really tough operator who hid his toughness beneath the wit; but the toughness was there when you needed it. Keith's great joke, which I found more amusing after I had left office, was to come and get me for PMQs at 11:57 precisely, throwing the door open and saying like a town crier: "Prime Minister, a grateful nation now awaits.") One enormous benefit was that I always knew what the party was thinking by reference to what Bruce thought. All the numerous volte-faces were pretty shocking to his system. He used to sit there as I explained my latest change to the party's theology and ritual, and his eyes would wander and he would shake his head or occasionally laugh and say: No, come on, this time you really are joking.

On this one, if I had told him I had a friend called Faust and he had cut this really great deal with some bloke called Satan, it couldn't have gone down worse. I also knew Neil Kinnock would hate it and feel, understandably, betrayed. The *Sun* had been vicious beyond vicious to him, and as a result really had achieved demon status for party activists. People would be horrified. On the other hand, as I said to Alastair, not to go was to say carry on and do your worst, and we knew their worst was very bad indeed. No, you sat down to sup; or not. So we did.

The long journey allowed me to craft the speech carefully. It had to be a speech that didn't pander. It had its pro-European part and commitments on poverty and the environment, but was also a clear articulation of New Labour from the point of principle not simply electability. Paul Keating, then Australian prime minister, went with us and as ever he was great company and a huge source of sensible advice delivered in the inimitable Keating manner. ("Don't ever put up income tax, mate," he used to say to me. "Take it off them anyhow you please, but do that and they'll rip your f★★★ing guts out.") He thought Rupert a bastard, but one you could deal with.

I thought Rupert an enigma, and the more I got to know him, the more I thought so. In the end—and I am aware of the shrieks of disbelief as I write this—I came to have a grudging respect and even liking for him. He was hard, no doubt. He was right wing. I did not share or like his attitudes on Europe, social policy or on issues such as gay rights, but there were two points of connection: he was an outsider, and he had balls. The "outsider" thing was crucial to understanding him. He remained both immensely powerful and, at certain quite elemental points, anti-Establishment. He would admire Mrs. Thatcher, but not necessarily the Tory Party with all its baggage, airs and graces. That gave me something to work with.

We had flown to Sydney after PMQs on the Thursday, and stayed overnight at Kirribilli House, the prime minister's place down by the harbour. We then flew up with Paul to Hayman Island on the Sunday, gave the speech the following day, and left an hour later to fly all the way back. We got to London in time to make a speech with Chris Smith, the Shadow Heritage Secretary, on the technology revolution on the Tuesday morning, and then did PMQs that afternoon.

The speech on Hayman Island went down well. I could see the executives were in awe (and a little fearful) of Rupert. Once he had introduced me in glowing terms (having given me credit, privately I think,
for having the brass nerve to come), they all rallied and I could feel we
were in with a chance of winning the *Sun*'s support.

The party were half appalled and half excited by the sheer vim of it
all. Indeed, back then we were moving at such a pace that they hardly
had the chance to recover from one shock to the system before another
came in its wake. It took their breath away, and though some of the criticism was strong, the mainstream of the party loved the fact we were
wrong-footing, disorientating and generally outfoxing the Tories. After
years of feeling like a whipped underdog, they rather liked the idea of a
bit of the swagger of a top dog.

At around that time in mid-1995, I set out a template for the Labour
Party approach to policy in a series of articles. Looking back, what
is interesting is that although the actual policies shifted significantly
with the experience of government, the basic philosophical positions
remained. In June, I wrote in an article in *The Times* that:

> The truth is that the electorate now sees Labour as the sensible main-
> stream party. We have changed. We admit the changes. But far from sim-
> ply ditching our past, we are proclaiming a positive message for the
> future. The new Clause IV is the most visible symbol of that change but
> it is not the only one. We have changed, too, the way we make policy.
> The education policy launched last week was not devised to please the
> National Union of Teachers. It was devised to meet the concerns of par-
> ents. The health policy we launched yesterday drew on the expertise of
> professional bodies and other experts in the NHS. But uppermost in our
> minds, all the time, was the patient.

We were constantly operating on two levels. One concerned the
campaigning genius of Alastair, Peter and the political team. They
were, of course, putting over the New Labour case, but they were also
whacking the Tories very hard, exploiting their divisions, underscoring
their weaknesses, using a devastating mixture of critique, ridicule and
bombast. It was fun, effective and professionally delivered. It carried us
through the by-elections which we were now regularly winning from
the Tories, even in the most unlikely places. As a machine, it was close
to unbeatable, like Manchester United at their best: exciting to watch,

unnerving for opponents and pretty much unstoppable. This was complemented by the rigorous attention to the need for policy positions that were centrist, credible and coherent, so that differences with the Tories didn't lead to vulnerability and so that the key message—Labour has genuinely changed, and not out of electoral calculation—would be reinforced.

Most of the articles about our position were written personally, crafted out of detailed policy discussion with David Miliband, Michael Barber, Jonathan and others. In what caused much jarring and tutting within the party, I even decided to own up to supporting changes Margaret Thatcher had made. I knew the credibility of the whole New Labour project rested on accepting that much of what she wanted to do in the 1980s was inevitable, a consequence not of ideology but of social and economic change. The way she did it was often very ideological, sometimes unnecessarily so, but that didn't alter the basic fact: Britain needed the industrial and economic reforms of the Thatcher period. Saying this immediately opened the ears of many who had supported the Tories in that period—not because they were instinctively or emotionally Conservative, but because Labour had seemed so old-fashioned and out of touch with individual aspiration. Our economic policy had appeared hopelessly collectivist; our social policy born of political correctness.

In another article for *The Times* in July 1995, I explained why Labour should be the party of social order and security at home, and internationalism and free trade abroad:

The only way to rebuild social order and stability is through strong values, socially shared, inculcated through individuals and families. This is not some lurch into authoritarianism or an attempt to impose a regressive personal morality. It is, in fact, about justice and fairness. The strong and powerful can protect themselves. Those who lose most through the absence of rules are the weak and the vulnerable. The first casualties of social breakdown are often the poor and disadvantaged. That is why the left should treat it seriously.

The left of centre should be the meritocrats of the twenty-first century. The Conservatives are in danger of becoming narrowly and insularly nationalistic. There is no future for that in a world of change. I am not saying it does not have popular appeal. It does. But it is not serious politics.

The Labour government I hope to lead will be outward-looking,

internationalist and committed to free and open trade, not an outdated
and misguided narrow nationalism.

It is a rejuvenated and revitalised left of centre that is placed to respond
to and shape this new world of change. If it can escape the constraints of
its past, learning from history not living in it, it is best equipped intellectually and philosophically for the new century. It is precisely to do this
that New Labour will continue to change.

My main worry was that the Tories would regain some political
sense, change leader and rejuvenate. It wasn't that John Major was bad.
However, he was plainly trying to keep together a party viscerally
divided over Europe, stretching the skin as tight as it would go to conceal the break, rather than conduct surgery and mend it. In a move
that could have worked, in 1995 he suddenly decided to hold a leadership election and force his opponents out in the open. It was a rather
brilliant tactic and had me worried. John Redwood stepped forward,
with the support of the Eurosceptic Tory press. "Redwood vs Dead-
wood," as the *Mail* put it.

But then, fortunately for me, Major made the same error as Labour
had in the 1980s: he appealed for unity rather than a mandate. So the
bold tactic was not accompanied by a bold strategy. Redwood was
defeated; but not for a cause. Michael Heseltine, who could have led the
Tories, remained marginalised.

It's a strange thing, the power of the appeal to loyalty in respect of a
leader. You have to be very wary of it. In particular, you have to define
what it is and what it isn't, or rather what it should be and what it
shouldn't. When prime minister, and in the darker days when I was
under fairly much routine attack by Gordon's people, my close supporters would sometimes complain that his supporters were disloyal. I would
always respond that they were perfectly entitled to challenge me, to put
forward an alternative, and to say I should go. What they shouldn't do is
undermine me. In other words—and obviously not trivially or serially—
if you come to the conclusion the leader is not up to it or is taking the
party fundamentally in the wrong direction, there is nothing disloyal in
being open and mounting a challenge. If the criticism is right, the challenge comes out of loyalty to the bigger cause: the party itself and its purpose. That is why I never had a problem with Gordon's people wanting
me out, provided it was for a purpose other than simply that of Gordon
doing the job rather than me. And for some of them, hostile to New

Labour, it was. What is always unacceptable is to chip away, to refuse the open challenge, to corrode. That is disloyal because it weakens the party; it doesn't change it or redirect it.

So I used to say: I don't mind the so-called disloyalty, I mind the fact that they want Labour to go back to election-losing ways. Major could have used the contest to assert leadership. Instead, the fight was messy and served to underline the fact that the Tories were unresolved in their essential direction.

In January 1996, we published the "Party into Power" document, a seemingly innocuous exercise in party management, but ultimately a very important change in the way the party developed policy. When I had read up on previous Labour governments, I had noticed that a destabilising factor was the relationship between party and government. When the party was called upon to exercise real power, there immediately came about a dangerous tension between activists and ministers in which the two always ended up divided from each other. The party wanted true "socialism" beloved of the activists; the government was focused on the people. They moved with remarkable speed into inhabiting separate political cultures. The result was an increasing disillusionment with the government from the party, which quickly communicated itself to the public.

The worst aspect was that this disillusionment then found easy expression in the party structures, notably the NEC and the party conference. The NEC became the equivalent of the government's moral inquisitor, trying to keep it to the straight and narrow; the party conference became the focal point for the dissension and a battleground for resolutions that usually asked the government to do something electorally suicidal. The "Party into Power" document effectively altered the rules so as to ensure that the routine resolutions didn't happen just by tabling a motion, but instead grew out of a managed process that required long debate and discussion in policy groups; and the NEC powers were sharply curtailed. We had to get the unions on board for the changes, and it was here that Tom Sawyer was invaluable, as a former trade unionist. With some reluctance and opposition, the party conceded the changes at the 1996 conference. They were vital when the going got rough in government.

None of this meant we were immune to the usual party backbiting and gossip. Several times in 1996, I was counselling the Shadow Cabinet to avoid damaging briefings and leaks and to stop fighting each other and fight the Tories. At the same time, I was trying to ward off attacks from the left that we had already diluted our principles in the quest for power. I decided, as I put it, to own up to the charges of betrayal and sell-out before we ever got there. I thought the bane of the left—the tendency to believe that the leadership is too right wing when usually the public worry is the opposite—was best brought out, acknowledged and confronted. In a message both to them and to the country, I said in effect: Don't be under any misconception; we are New Labour, we are going to govern as New Labour; it is not a gimmick; it is real; it is born of belief. I knew it wouldn't stop the charges of betrayal, but it would limit their salience and reach.

Roy Jenkins used to describe me as like someone carrying an immensely valuable vase across a wide room with a very slippery floor. Not for one moment could I let myself relax, my gaze be unfixed on the precious cargo, my mind diverted from the task in hand. Vast amounts of care and hard work went into the conferences. In 1994, I announced the change to Clause IV. In 1995, we announced a deal with British Telecommunications (BT) to promote skills, a connection with a major privatised utility sending the clear message that we would be good with business. In that speech, I also tried to reflect my wish for the country to modernise and to look outward and forward, and coined the phrase "Britain as a Young Country"—a phrase somewhat mocked, but illustrating my passion for Britain to capture some of the youthful optimism and energy of a country feeling confident of its future, not staring nostalgically into its past.

In 1996, I said our three priorities for government would be "education, education, education" (a line—the only one ever!—given to me by Jonathan). The purpose of focusing on education was for its own sake, obviously, but it also served to emphasise how we saw the role of the state: enabling the fulfilment of potential, not controlling lives or business. In the "New Labour, New Britain" guide we produced in 1996, we set out a clear compass in each area of policy. We had symbolic or token policies to illustrate direction, but carefully avoided over-promising or too much detail.

In this regard, Gordon was an indispensable ally. His natural caution made him disapprove of any hostages to fortune. He had seen the appeal of New Labour. He was determined to be seen as economically prudent, pro-business and, while he was always off to the left of me, it was all within bounds. He gave our position on the economy credibility, and that in turn enormously enhanced the credibility of the party's aspiration to power. In the 1995 Mais Lecture to the banking and finance community, I had set out our approach to the economy in close collaboration with him, emphasising our commitment to stability. In writing it, I got help from key City people who I knew would understand that the core purpose was to be the embodiment of sane, steady common sense. It worked, and reassured further.

Meanwhile, I was learning to cope with fame. Suddenly, I was one of the best-known faces in the land. There was huge interest also in New Labour from abroad. We were written about widely as the coming thing. We were the fashion.

However, at that point, there was still a link to reality in my daily life. I had no security, I drove the kids to school most mornings, I could go out to eat, see friends, be alone with the family. I was busy, to be sure, and the responsibility I was carrying was great, but it sat with relative ease on my shoulders. I looked incredibly young. People would stop me in the street and chat. Looking back, I see the days were blessed then. At the time, of course, it didn't seem like that.

Cherie and the children coped magnificently, but it is easy to forget how much their lives had changed. The children were, of a sudden, looked on differently by their classmates. Fortunately, because they carried on going to the same school, and as a family we went to the same church—St. Joan of Arc in Highbury, just up from the then Arsenal football ground—the faces were familiar, and though evidently we were regarded in a new light, the families we were close to remained close. They provided much normality. Our friends tended to be non-political and it made a comforting change from the pressure cooker.

Cherie decided to remake her image: get fit, look good, carry herself like the well-known figure she was becoming. In this, Carole Caplin was a great support, as she was to me when fitness became more of a preoccupation. She did a superb job for Cherie, made her look and feel good when Cherie was suddenly transported from one world (professional Bar) to another (tabloid press).

Carole was monstered by the media later when she had an affair with Peter Foster, a con man. Whole reams of newsprint were devoted to her, including stories that were completely made up and then became standard fare, like the fable about Cherie and Carole having showers together.

My close office were, it is fair to say, intrigued but generally dismayed by her. Alastair, in particular, couldn't understand it and strongly disapproved of it. He judged, in a sense rightly, that politics had no place for someone as exotic and apolitical as Carole. Personally, that's why I found her so refreshing.

Alastair was convinced she would sell her story. She never did. Whatever indignity was visited on her, she remained dignified. Contrary to the image assiduously and malignly created for her, she was kind, decent, hard-working and, above all, brilliant at what she did. The relationship with Foster was a big mistake, but it wasn't venal or badly motivated. It was rather the product of her almost obsessive refusal to compromise with people's opinions of other people. In this case, they were right and she was wrong, but that refusal to follow the crowd was what also made her innovative and creative in her work, a good friend and a reliable confidante for Cherie.

In retrospect, when the *Sun* broke the story of Carole's involvement with Cherie in 1994, it would have been better to have acknowledged her, been open and been supportive. Instead, entirely understandably given our nervousness about our position and how she was bound to provoke controversy, we hid her away in a safe house. But, of course, it only increased the fascination with her.

The problem, as I used to say to people who became close, is that knowing me is like catching a disease. My friends swiftly became targets. If a hostile part of the media couldn't get me, they tended to try to pick off people close to me. The truth is there is no one you cannot make out to be in some way odd, or a figure of ridicule, if you pry and probe into their life with sufficient ruthlessness.

But much of that came later. In those years before the election victory, we were working hard, but with the wind at our back.

Within the constraints and limitations of Opposition, we were as prepared as we could be. However, I have come to the firm conclusion that those constraints and limitations are a considerable disadvantage. You are woefully short on what is required to step into government and govern effectively, especially if you come into power after such a long period of Opposition. This is not about understanding the machinery of government; above all, it is about knowing the complexity of policy-making, financial management and prioritising. Knowing the committee structure and departmental highways and byways is no doubt important; but it is far more important to know how to focus on the essential details of preparation for implementing a policy which may seem easy enough stated in a manifesto, but when looked at in the hard light of day can be horrendously difficult to do. And parties tend to be really under-informed about the nature of how different commitments interact with public finances.

So, in policy direction we were pretty firm and clear. In the details, we were lacking. Nonetheless, as an election-fighting machine, we were exceptional. This we knew how to do.

When John Major called the election we were ready and waiting. We were ignorant of what lay ahead after we passed the winning post, but we had built up near-irreversible momentum towards it.

FOUR

HONEYMOON

The disadvantage of a new government is lack of experience in governing. It is also the advantage. Its very innocence, its immaturity, the absence of the cynicism that comes from perpetual immersion in government's plague-infested waters, gives it an extraordinary sense of possibility. From start to finish I never lost my optimism, self-belief or objective belief in what could be done, but you can never quite recapture that amazing release of energy and boundless "derring-do" that comes with the election of a fresh team—especially when it comes after eighteen years of one party's rule.

When I think of what we did in those first halcyon days, it was indeed quite remarkable. It wasn't born of arrogance; whatever people said, I never lost the impulse to guard against complacency, or the recognition that the ultimate boss was "the people." It came out of an unrestrained and genuine wish to drive the nation forward. We thought the unthinkable; did the undoable; the conventional became a constraint to be unshackled; what was traditional became old-fashioned.

One very early decision concerned me quite a bit, but I thought, To hell with it, I'm going to do it. At that time Prime Minister's Questions (PMQs) was scheduled twice a week, at 3:15 p.m. on Tuesdays and Thursdays for fifteen minutes. Even if another event was scheduled for earlier in the day, the morning would pass fitfully as my mind grappled with the manoeuvres, opportunities and bear traps of the forthcoming encounter. After it ended at 3:30 p.m. it reverberated in the mind: how it had gone, who had got the upper hand, what it had said about the mood of the backbenchers. My rational self told me it was all over and was usually forgotten within forty-eight hours; but there is no "rational" in the whole PMQs business. It is the emotional, intellectual and political repository of all that is irrational. Even as the Opposition leader—when I only had to ask the damned questions—it dominated my thoughts; I could only imagine what it would be like as prime minister.

One thing was obvious, though it may seem mundane: one of the keys to doing the job of a prime minister or president is to manage your time. Its importance is cardinal. Show me an ineffective leader and I will show you a badly managed schedule. This has nothing to do with the number of hours worked—I came across leaders who worked the most ridiculous hours, eighteen hours a day for frequent stretches of time—but whether time is used properly.

The schedule has to be based around the decisions that define the government, for which time must be made. In so far as it is possible to do so, the necessary formal routines have to be limited only to those that are vital. One of the first things Anji did for me on arriving in Number 10 was to uproot official dinners. I probably did no more than thirty, including the compulsory state banquets, during my whole time in Downing Street. Official dinners are almost always unnecessary. The host regards them as a chore, and here's the news: so do the guests. You eat late (the food is either rich or rubbish), and there is no greater political torture than the after-dinner speech. If it's business you're after, do it in a forty-five-minute meeting before dinner. Then you can go off with your family, and the guests can go off with their friends or close associates, let their hair down, and everyone is happy. Except protocol. And a happy protocol is almost invariably a sign of a badly run government.

Creating time for a leader is a near-sacred task. The person in charge of it is one of the most important in the team, and they have to be completely ruthless in saying no. The leader has always got to be the good guy. You bump into someone; they ask for a meeting; you agree, of course. What can you say? "You're too tedious, too unimportant and have nothing of any interest to say"? Of course not. You have to say yes. It's the job of the scheduler to say no. "But he agreed to see me." No. "But he said he wanted to see me." No. "But he said he had been meaning to call me himself to fix a meeting." No. "But . . ." No.

We used to have a phrase in the office called, in mock severity, "SO," which stood for "sackable offence." It applied to scheduling a meeting with people who were never to cross the threshold. It applied even if I had agreed to the meeting. It applied—I am a little ashamed to say—

even if I had expressed to the individual concerned my deep frustration with my own office for defying my wishes and not scheduling the meeting.

There was a particular old Labour grandee who used to be after me in order to give me "sound advice." He was a lovely man, but really. I naturally expressed my intense interest in seeing him. Kate, my PA, who was a hugely efficient naysayer, went AWOL for some reason or other. Someone else was temporarily manning the gate, and he got in to see me. After about thirty minutes of "sound advice," I was just about boss-eyed with boredom when the temporary gatekeeper put her head round the door and said, "Time's up."

"Oh, really," I said, "what a shame. I was really enjoying this."

"Well, in that case," she said, "I could leave you another half-hour because your diary has changed."

Prime Minister's Questions is of course of great gravity and import, but I could see from watching John Major that the physical and mental effort of each of the twice-weekly fifteen-minute slots absorbed the whole day: the morning and early afternoon were spent in preparation; meetings, if held at all, did not receive full concentration; the late afternoon and early evening were spent reflecting on what had happened. Two PMQs equalled two days. That's a lot of time.

I had hatched a plot before the election—somewhat disingenuously describing it in our party's manifesto as "making PMQs more efficient"—to change the two slots to a single one of thirty minutes. Not a big change, you may think; but I tell you, it was a revolution in saving time. Fortunately Paddy Ashdown, leader of the Liberal Democrat party, had indicated that he was in favour of reform, so I just took a deep breath and announced it, and it went through very quickly. If there had been any debate, it would most likely never have happened, but I was lucky we were a new government and the Tories were still reeling.

Later, when Robin Cook was Leader of the Commons, the half-hour slot moved to noon on Wednesday. Preparation would take place the night before and Wednesday morning would be clear, so while there was a period of complete absorption, it was limited in duration. By 12:30 p.m. the nightmare was over. Unless it had gone in a ghastly way, by mid-afternoon the mind had been released, and Thursday was free from its anxieties. It may have seemed a small reform, but for the personal well-being of the prime minister, it was vital.

It had its drawbacks: fifteen minutes may seem a very short time, but it's not when you're standing facing the howling mob gathered opposite the dispatch box—believe me, time passes very slowly indeed—so half an hour could be an ordeal, especially if the wicket was sticky and there was an "issue of the day" around which the questioning could coalesce.

PMQs was the most nerve-racking, discombobulating, nail-biting, bowel-moving, terror-inspiring, courage-draining experience in my prime ministerial life, without question. You know that scene in *Marathon Man* where the evil Nazi doctor played by Laurence Olivier drills through Dustin Hoffman's teeth? At around 11:45 on Wednesday mornings, I would have swapped thirty minutes of PMQs for thirty minutes of that.

Let us deal with some of the myths. When I describe the experience to Americans, who, along with the Japanese, seem to like watching it for some bizarre reason, they will sometimes say: "Oh, but you always seemed to enjoy it so much." If I did seem to be enjoying it, then it was a supreme instance of acting. I hated it. Others would say at the time: "You looked very relaxed at PMQs today." I never relaxed for a moment, and never had anything less than a full adrenalin surge.

I'm afraid it's also rather a myth that it's a great way of holding the prime minister to account. This thesis assumes that those asking the questions are interested to know the answers. In truth, the whole thing is a giant joust, a sort of modern, non-physical duel. The weapons are words, but my God they can hurt, and to devastating effect. For those thirty minutes, the prime minister is essentially on the "at risk" register. It is the unpredictability that is so frightening. Sure, your own back benches, if they are loyal, let you know the question, that is, let you know they are going to ask you an important question you very much want to answer, but to everyone else it's a blood sport and the prime minister is the quarry. If it goes well, you feel buoyed; if it goes badly, you feel not simply wretched but humiliated. There's no place like a full House of Commons for making someone seem a complete dolt.

And you can never tell. At times I would go in thinking: It's obvious what the subject of the day is, I have the answers at my fingertips, it should be a reasonable afternoon. Minutes later I would be tottering, having made some verbal faux pas or tactical blunder that had the place screaming in anger or, worse, derision. At moments like these, in a hole, there is an almost irresistible desire to keep digging. Your answers get longer and more convoluted; your tone becomes more shrill; your face gets redder as the paucity of your argument becomes plainer. You glance sideways, imploring your own benches to give some sign of support, and see the look of embarrassment on their faces. As you sit down, a few diehard loyalists give cheers which dissolve away in an apologetic murmur. Across the aisle, two sword-lengths away—from the days when Members carried swords—the gloating Opposition faces are contorted with glee and gratitude.

Over time I got better at it, and by the end was more often OK than rubbish, but the fear never abated for an instant. Even today, wherever I am in the world, I feel a cold chill at 11:57 a.m. on Wednesdays, a sort of prickle on the back of my neck, the thump of the heart. That was the moment I used to be taken from the prime minister's room in the House of Commons through to the Chamber itself. I used to call it the walk from the cell to the place of execution.

I would have got to the House of Commons around 11:30 a.m., having spent all morning in my office in Downing Street going through the papers, deciding tactics and strategy. In that last half-hour final decisions would be made, answers slipped through the door on questions I had asked, hurried last-minute consultations held about some unfolding event. The worst thing was stories breaking at 10 or even 11 a.m., usually around bad statistics of one sort or another, or something idiotic a member of the government had said. A line would have to be taken, facts would have to be given, though the full facts might not be known. A mistake by the prime minister in that bear pit is not a mistake: it is a deliberate deception, and all hell breaks loose around it.

By the end, I had much better karma in doing it. I got braver. I realised that in the end I had to confront the demons. It was no use praying more the night before, wearing the right shoes (I wore the same pair of Church's brogues every PMQs for ten years) or just hoping I would get by. I decided to analyse it, and try to work out how to do it to the best of my ability.

I remember as a schoolboy doing boxing, which was compulsory. I loathed it; I could never see the point of it nor understand its appeal. In the first fights, I was scared. I didn't want to hit my opponent. I didn't want him to hit me. I just wanted the thing over with. After a time, though, I chose to box properly, to stand my ground and fight. I did it with fear, but also with determination. Either do it properly or refuse to do it at all—that's also fine—but don't do it like a wuss. I didn't like boxing any better, but I respected myself more.

Gradually, I evolved a pattern of working for PMQs. It all started with a determination to be braver, to stand my ground and fight, consciously. Fear as a stimulus, in proper proportion, can keep you on your toes. Fear that tumbles into panic is all bad. In the early days, I wouldn't sleep well the night before or eat at all in the morning. The first thing I realised was the importance of being in the right physical as well as mental condition, so I changed my routine. I took a melatonin pill the night before so I got at least six hours' sleep. I made sure I had a proper breakfast, and just before the ordeal began, I would eat a banana to give myself energy. It seems daft, but I was finding that my energy levels, and thus my mental agility, were dropping after ten minutes. It really made a difference. At 12:28 I was still alive to the risks and up to repelling the assault.

Secondly, I faced up to what the fear was. The fear is being made to look a fool, or simply being outwitted. The way to prevent it was not so much mastering the facts, but mastering the strategy of debate. The right facts, properly researched, are utterly essential, of course. By the time I was in my stride I had a team of great talent, headed at first by the ultra-efficient Clare Sumner, then by Kate Gross, superb organiser and mistress of ceremonies. The key special adviser was Catherine Rimmer, brilliant head of research and with an extraordinary ability to master detail (also invaluable during the Hutton Inquiry). The team was topped off by Nicholas Howard, the wonderful master of the PMGs folder. Together, they gave me confidence that the factual basis of the answer was correct. However, the final component in winning was not the facts themselves but how they were deployed. The facts were the horse, the armour and the lance; the skill was in using them to best effect, which meant guessing the line of attack, working out how to parry and then laying out the counter-attack.

On a bad day with a no-win subject—and there were quite a few of those—the best that could be done was to fight it to a draw, but on a good or average day you had to go for a win. Winning gives your side confidence, it lifts them, it makes them think of the future as bright. Your own standing is enhanced. Losing is not only undignified, it hurts morale. A run of really bad PMQs can put the leader in jeopardy.

The night before I would go through the folder which held all the potential answers to all the potential questions, and the really complex factual areas were studied without the frantic pressure of Wednesday morning upon us. By 8 a.m. I would have whittled down the most likely areas of interrogation and then I would sit with a pad and work out the debating lines. Sometimes the best phrases came during PMQs, but this was rare in my experience. No one speaks quite so eloquently as they do when their eloquence has been honed, toned, constructed, deconstructed and reconstructed in the privacy of the antechamber.

By this method, I learned over time how to break out of defence and go on the offensive. It would also allow me to analyse the argument I was making with the facts—was it sustainable and persuasive, how would it play with their backbenchers as well as mine?

I discovered the force of humour, of light and shade. John Smith had been the first person I saw use humour to brilliant effect in the House, as in his demolition of John Major over the ERM debacle. Gordon, too, in his early days had been exceptional in using wit to demolish the Tory economic front bench when he had stood in for John in the late 1980s. Some of the lines he used against Nigel Lawson and the Tory Treasury team would have our side roaring their approval. We might be, usually were, weak on the argument; but it's amazing how much the weakness can be concealed by well-timed ridicule and well-judged wit. I tended to be more earnest, more like a lawyer with a case, but I have a sense of humour and I just needed the confidence to use it.

I learned how to disarm an opponent as well as blast them. They get angry; you get mild. They go over the top; you become a soothing voice of reason. They insult you; you look at them not with resentment, but pity. Under attack, you have to look directly at them, study their faces, your eyes fixed on theirs rather than rolling with anxiety.

Finally I realised that if you foul up, you move on. Easy to say; hard to do. When I had had a bad PMQs, the walk back to the room from the Chamber was almost as bad as the walk to it. We would always have a few minutes afterwards to deal with any consequential issues. For the poor old team, it was always tough when I messed up. The disappointment would be written large on their faces, even as they struggled to contain it. Jonathan Powell was usually the only one to voice the truth. "Thank God there's no more of that for a week," he'd say cheerfully as others would mutter about it being "a score draw, really," or some such bulls★★★.

Anyway, in those early days of May 1997, the twice-weekly PMQs was transformed into one. I never regretted that decision and subsequent prime ministers will thank me for it!

The next decision was of an altogether different and more fundamental nature. Some months before the election, Gordon and I formed the desire to give monetary policy—i.e. setting of interest rates—over to the

Bank of England. The so-called "independence" of the Bank had been a keen academic, economic and political debate going back decades.

I had no doubt it was right. I had been convinced long ago that for politicians to set interest rates was to confuse economics and politics, the long term with the short term, the expedient with the sensible. I had watched the game played out as governments carefully calibrated the interest rate movements with the electoral cycle. Everyone knew it was happening and why. The result was the country effectively paid a political premium on the interest rate. The contrast with the independent central banks of Europe, especially that of Germany, and with the U.S. Federal Reserve, was instructive and telling.

The issue, as I liked to say to doubting backbenchers and the serious experts who opposed the move, was not whether the Governor of the Bank was a more intelligent person than the Chancellor of the Exchequer. He might or might not be of superior intellect. But the decision-making process at the Bank was definitely of superior objectivity. I had talked about it often with Roy Jenkins, who had been Chancellor in the Labour government in the 1960s. Gavyn Davies—at that time with Goldman Sachs, and someone I often turned to for economic advice—had been immensely persuasive on the merits. I knew Nigel Lawson—a Chancellor I really admired—had wanted to do it. It was also the perfect riposte to those worried about the economic credentials of an incoming Labour government, so although the rationale was ultimately to put long-term economics above short-term politics, there were very good political reasons for doing so.

Gordon had come to the same conclusion, and so when I suggested it, he readily agreed. There was some debate about when it should be announced. I favoured doing it before the election to solidify our business credibility; he felt that it was sufficiently important to the way the markets would move that we should do it straight after the election, a proposition to which I eventually consented.

Gordon announced it on 6 May. It went well. Business and the markets liked it. The Tories opposed it but weren't really in the mood to create a major storm, and were unable to do so even if they had wanted to. For me, it was a very important moment. It defined not simply our approach to economic policy, but an approach to governing: it was not born from traditional left/right ideology; it drew people to the intelligent, radical centre ground; it spoke of our determination from the outset to protect and enhance our economic opportunity as a nation.

I allowed Gordon to make the statement and indeed gave him every paean of praise and status in becoming the major economic figure of the government. I did so firstly because I thought he deserved it, secondly because it was good for the whole thing not to look like a one-man show, and thirdly not doing so would have created considerable tension.

But it had an unfortunate and long-lasting consequence. I have many faults, but one virtue I have is that I don't mind big people around me. In my own office, I liked Alastair, Jonathan, Anji, Sally, Peter, David Miliband and others precisely because I knew they would tell me what they thought. That is not to say they were disrespectful (though the familiarity bred in Opposition wasn't always appropriate transferred into the more formal settings of government), but they spoke their mind. I welcomed it, and drew valuable advice and even confidence from it.

So when I consciously and deliberately allowed Gordon to be out there as a big beast, as the acknowledged second most powerful figure in the government, I did so without any fear of being eclipsed or outmanoeuvred. Indeed, the concept of manoeuvring seemed irrelevant. The office were less sanguine. Alastair in particular worried that a picture was being drawn that I was "the chairman" or "president," and Gordon was "the chief executive" or "prime minister," which, as he pointed out with vigour, easily translated into the person who simply does the glad-handing, and the hard-working serious guy who runs the country. So relaxed was I in my own sense of who I was and what I was doing that it didn't trouble me and I shrugged the warnings off.

In truth, too, as with the Bank of England independence, the broad framework on the economy, never mind anything else, was set by me. My notes to the office during those initial months were peppered with references to economic policy: getting the Comprehensive Spending Review aligned with the government's priorities, explaining what we wanted to do to create a more competitive economy, and jerking back hard on the rein if I thought there was a deviation from the essential pro-business, pro-aspiration line (stamping on the idea of taxing professionals more, or on taxing second homes, for example). Frequently, and at quite a micro level, a salvo would be fired off to keep the Treasury in check. Nevertheless, the perception—which later became damaging and undermining—was that I kept out of the economic policy space. The reality was that the train, the tracks and the destination were constructed in close interaction with Gordon, and on lines I shaped or was comfortable with. The driver was then given considerable freedom to manage the service. Not until very late on did I ever really yield control of economic policy.

We had had enough run-ins during the three years when I was leader for me to understand that there was a significant difference in our approaches. Only in the latter years did that difference start to become not just marked but fundamental. I was in no doubt that we came at politics from essentially divergent positions which of course converged, but did so as much for reasons of politics as for reasons of conviction. In the end, we were two very different people in terms of economic attitudes, with two very different backgrounds. Perhaps a better way of putting it is that we had different economic, financial and business instincts.

Basically, I understood aspiration. I like people who want to succeed, and admire people who do. When I was at the Bar—and the seven years I spent as a full-time barrister were immensely formative for me in many ways—I did a lot of commercial and industrial work and got on well with the risk-takers, those who didn't mope around, who had "get-up-and-go." I hate class; but I love aspiration. It's why I like America. I adore that notion of coming from nothing and making something of yourself.

This attitude had its downside. While the stories of my being dazzled by the wealthy are always ludicrously exaggerated (most of my close friends are not at all of that ilk), nonetheless I sometimes underestimated the ruthlessness and amorality that can go with moneymaking. Don't misunderstand me: many business people can be creative people for whom money is the consequence of their success, rather than the motivation. But others don't give a damn. And I tended on occasions not to comprehend fully the difference.

However, I didn't resent success, and on the whole that was a good thing for a progressive politician. I identified with it personally too. Did I want a nice home? Yes. Did I prefer a five-star hotel to a two-star? Yes. Did I appreciate that there was more to life than this? Yes. I never thought that enjoying life's good things led to indifference to the plight of those who couldn't. For me the opposite was true: what I wanted for myself, I also wanted for others. But I didn't feel it wrong to want it nonetheless.

When I was with a group of entrepreneurs, I felt at home. Gordon was completely different. He could analyse what a good business was and discuss the intricacies of this policy over that in order to promote it;

but he never *felt* it. I was a public-service guy who, if I had chosen a different path, would have liked running a business and making money. A bit of me thought: Wouldn't that be great? Now if I had really wanted that, I would have done it. I am, all said and done, a public service guy at heart. Gordon was a public service guy who, if he had chosen a different path, would have been a bigger public service guy. That's not to say he couldn't have made it in business—with his brain and determination he could have made it doing anything—but it would never have motivated him or possibly even interested him.

So, for me, top-rate tax was not about top-rate tax. Of course you can make a perfectly good case for wealthy people paying more, and around the edges—National Insurance and so on—I was content that they did, but I wanted to preserve, in terms of competitive tax rates, the essential Thatcher/Howe/Lawson legacy. I wanted wealthy people to feel at home and welcomed in the UK so that they could bring more business, create jobs and spread some of that wealth about. They weren't my priority; by which I mean that it wasn't a priority to run *after* them, and nor was it a priority to run *at* them. I was happy to leave well alone.

I knew if we put up the top rate of tax it would be seen as a signal, a declaration of instinct, an indicator whose impact would far outweigh its intrinsic weight. When Gordon suggested it prior to the election and I was given the usual opinion-poll guff showing 70 to 80 per cent in favour of it, I put in a complete *nolle prosequi*. For me, it was a total red line. After time, Gordon backed off.

To be fair, he took a more radical view on capital gains tax, which in turn helped the private equity industry enormously. He cut the rate down to as little as 15 per cent for those who held shares for a fixed minimum period, so those investing in companies, sorting them out and then selling them on, were paying far less than the income tax rate. Nevertheless, I felt it was done more as a political sign to those he thought were designating him anti-business, and a product of those who were advising him, rather than an act born of great conviction.

No matter; in that first statement on the Bank of England and his first Budget, he was pretty clearly New Labour. However, his seeming endorsement of the notion that I had vacated the economic sphere sowed seeds of distortion whose harvest was damaging. Of course, it is in the nature of politics that all the elements that ultimately bring about the downfall are there from the outset, albeit in mild form. Time merely enlarges and strengthens them. Even in those early days of power, indeed even from the moment of the phone call after John's death when I didn't immediately accede, there was a battle unresolved. Whether it was ever resolvable is another question.

Despite all this, the presence of such a big figure, the mere appearance on the landscape of someone who plainly was up to it as well as up for it, whose energy, intellect and political weight were undeniable, was a massive plus for the government. If there was a clash, it was at least a clash of the titans. If there were tensions, they could also have their creative side. In my Cavalier embrace of the middle class and his Roundhead identification with Labour tradition, there was surely a coalition of sorts that could be built and could function. So it seemed in those months following 1 May 1997, and so it was.

I have a somewhat weirdly optimistic view of the power of reason, of the ability to persuade if an argument is persuasive. It sometimes led me to believe that if a political goal is right, then it could therefore be attained. Evidently, politics does not work like that: there are goals that are absolutely desirable and entirely worthy, but utterly beyond reach.

My experience with the Liberal Democrats in those initial days of power was a case in point. From the off, I wanted to have them in the big tent. I regarded Roy Jenkins, who had left Labour in 1981 to join the Social Democratic Party (SDP), as a mentor. I grew to love him, actually, and thought him a decent, courageous and vastly rational and intelligent man. I also liked and respected Paddy Ashdown, and thought they had younger folk who were basically New Labour. I understood why the SDP was formed, why it failed, and why its failure was not one of ideas but of organisation and politics.

The Liberals were regarded as a motley crew of the vaguely serious, the not so serious and completely unserious. I had all the usual prejudices about blokes with beards in sandals and hideously coloured shirts whose greatest ambition was to be a really good campaigning local councillor, and women in baggy dresses who looked odd and talked about the importance of sex education.

After the amalgamation of the Liberal Party with the SDP, the new Liberal Democrats did rather resemble in their political contours the shape of two objects jammed together on the basis that they fitted when actually they didn't. They were a bit like the right and left wings of most parties, only more so, to paraphrase what Rick said of Louis in *Casablanca*.

It meant their activists tended to oddness. Now, I am an activist myself, and certainly in younger days a very active activist—so I should be careful here. But political activism always has that tinge of the odd-ball in it. I know that's a shocking admission of bigotry and preconception, but anyone who has ever swum in the waters of a political party and its membership knows what a peculiar habitat it is.

The Lib Dems could also be prone to gross opportunism. Now all politicians have to be opportunistic from time to time—seizing the opportunity is often what it's about—but in some of their local campaigns the Lib Dems had perfected this and taken it to the level of a science or art form. In particular, despite their official (and for the most part genuine) protestations of belief in racial and sexual equality, they were well up to fighting pretty dirty campaigns targeting the personal characteristics of their opponents.

Although they were a jumble, their leadership was sound, there were some outstanding people in their ranks and they were more or less aligned with New Labour politically. We had taken the Labour Party to the point which recognised that much of what the old SDP had been saying was correct; some of their prominent members had defected and joined or rejoined Labour; and truthfully, I was closer in political outlook to some of them than to parts of the old left of my own party. It made sense to try to draw them in. Could we go a step further and bring them into government? The traditional part of the Labour Party—and John Prescott especially—would go nuts at the thought; but this was a moment in time and it might never come again. I was certainly willing to give it a try. Paddy, his wife Jane, Cherie and I dined together regularly before the election. We liked each other and trusted each other. Paddy had real leadership quality and like me was unafraid of taking on his party.

In my party conference speech later that year, and greatly to Alastair's and Bruce's alarm, I specifically went out of my way to pay tribute in my own political heritage to Lloyd George, the British economists John Maynard Keynes and William Beveridge as well as Clement Attlee, Ernest Bevin and Keir Hardie. I had a belief—in part intuitive, in part reinforced by Roy Jenkins—that the twentieth century had been a Tory century precisely because good and talented people who should have been together were instead in separate parties fighting each other.

Reuniting these two wings of progressive social democracy appealed to my sense of history. It also derived from my general approach to politics. I had long before come to the conclusion that the party system, though necessary, was at one level irrational and counterproductive. It meant differences had to be either exaggerated or invented; it stopped sensible people cooperating to achieve sensible ends; complex problems that required thoughtful solutions were reduced to battles about slogans.

Hearing some of the Tory speakers during debates in the House of Commons in the 1980s, I concluded that were I an objective observer, what they were saying would have made a lot of sense. From a long time back, I would sit, converse and exchange views with Tories. None of this made me a Tory or diminished my commitment to my own political tribe, but it did illustrate the foolishness and even the futility of opposing for opposition's sake.

Above all, I realised that the battle for political supremacy between government and business, the state and the market, was essentially a twentieth-century hangover. A proper functioning state was obviously necessary to do what only government could do, as was a thriving and competitive private sector to generate the nation's wealth. Together, each in their proper sphere, they determined prosperity. I therefore concluded that while values and ends might differ and diverge—and in that lay real politics and ideology—the question of what means should be used to achieve those ends was plainly a practical one: what counts is what works. In terms of values and ends, it was hard, certainly so far as the Lib Dems were concerned at that time, to see where the great point of fundamental difference lay. Hence the decision to try to co-opt them.

In the frantic hours following the election, I spoke to Paddy. We agreed it would be premature to put them in the Cabinet (despite our cavalier attitude to our parties, we were both nervous about their respective reactions so soon after election), and unlike in 2010 I had won a huge majority. But we agreed we would begin a process of cooperation with an official committee that would try to draw up an agreed programme of constitutional reform.

Paddy was reluctant to do this, at least until after the constitutional committee had deliberated. I feared this would mean it wouldn't happen.

My fear, amply borne out by events when the Lib Dems ended up opposing our public service reforms on what were basically Old Labour grounds—however they tried to dress it up—was that while we could agree on the easy stuff—or, if not easy, the stuff that didn't touch voters' immediate lives—they would shy away from the painful but thoroughly necessary changes in schools, hospitals, pensions and welfare, which most directly touched voters' lives. In other words, for me the question was: is this cooperation for real? In the end, I'm afraid, it wasn't, not through a lack of good intentions or good faith on Paddy's part—he was totally straight about it throughout—but because of what I thought was their lack of the necessary fibre to govern. In the ultimate analysis, the Lib Dems seemed to be happier as the "honest" critics, prodding and probing and pushing, but unwilling to take on the mantle of responsibility for the hard choices and endure the rough passages. It will be fascinating to see whether the coalition conceived after the 2010 election holds. It may, since the Lib Dem desire for electoral reform is so intrinsic to them. But if that doesn't come about, I doubt the coalition will last long. However, I may be wrong . . .

Back in 1997, when a coalition would have been an entirely voluntary act between consenting parties, I thought that the opportunity for them to criticise, and thus take the easy way out, was just too tempting. The trouble is they get used to sitting on panels or TV shows and people nodding along with them because they are saying what people want to hear—which never really changes anything, I fear, and can lead them to opportunism that can be breathtaking.

I recall vividly when I was Shadow Home Secretary in 1993. Ken Clarke was Home Secretary. I like Ken, he's a proper stand-up politician. The Tories were foolish never to make him leader, though I was very grateful for that. He had proposed a set of wide-ranging reforms to the police. Some were smart (like changing pension requirements), others not so smart (as with their disciplinary code). Most were justifiable, but my God did the police hate them. The Police Federation—by far the most well-drilled union I ever came across—held a rally against the reforms at Wembley Arena, which was remarkable for two things. The first was the collective discipline of the coppers. The Fed's committee sat on the stage, with the audience in front of them. There must have been 10,000 police there, which was and is a really scary prospect. The massed ranks took their cue completely from the committee. When the committee applauded, so did the masses; when they sat on their hands, not a single person clapped. It was awesome.

The second remarkable thing was the performance of the Lib Dem speaker, Robert Maclennan, who was then their law and order spokesman. This story reveals the problem with them. Now the Lib

Dems' official position was as weak-kneed and liberal, with the smallest of "l"s, as you can imagine. They basically took civil liberties to the point where the worst punishment was a jolly good talking-to and the most important thing was to crack down hard on police brutality, all of which was a million miles from the heart and mind of your average British bobby.

I got up and spoke. Truth to tell I was a bit shamefaced, since I thought some of the reforms seemed entirely sensible, but I made a reasonable fist of sounding angry at the injustice of it all and was duly applauded.

Then it was Robert's turn. Now just a word about him. John Smith used to call his speeches in the Commons the work of a one-man crowd-dispersal unit. To describe Bob as a dull speaker was to fail completely to convey the full nature of the experience. If you had to follow him in the House as the next speaker and so had to listen to him, you could miss your opening just because he had reduced you to a catatonic state. By the way, he was also intelligent and decent and obviously so, and that didn't endear him much either.

So it was with the anticipation of considerable amusement that I saw Bob rise to address 10,000 coppers who I guessed would not appreciate being bored near to death by a Liberal. I can only describe his speech as one of the most electrifying I've ever heard. He knew what they wanted to hear. He had read their handouts describing the unparalleled iniquity of the proposed reforms. He gazed on their 10,000 expectant, upturned faces as he laid into the government not just with abandon, but with what appeared to be genuine, sustained and unstoppable outrage. By the time he had finished painting a picture of a country whose poor police were shackled and downtrodden while laughing criminals ransacked the nation, and all as part of a deliberate and heinous Home Office plot, the Fed committee, the 10,000 coppers, even the sound and lighting people were on their feet, stomping, roaring, baying for more from Bob the policeman's best friend.

However, it did all illustrate the problems with the Lib Dems. When it came right down to it, they were happier as critics than as actors. As time went on and I became more convinced we needed radical solutions to welfare and public services, not to say law and order issues, they gravitated naturally and contentedly towards an opposing position. The dream of getting them to reunite social democracy faded. Paddy was a leader really committed to the idea of uniting the progressive forces.

Charles Kennedy was a very decent guy, but not of the same commitment. Iraq was such a massive point of disagreement, and became such a huge recruiting and campaigning bonus to the Lib Dems, that after it our relations soured completely. It was a pity, but probably inevitable. To begin with, I thought that the sheer force of a reasonable position, reasonably argued, would win the day. Over time you learn that this is not so; change brings opposition, and opposition is much easier to advocate than change.

Another early reminder of this came with the changes to housing benefit we introduced in the summer of 1997, giving help to those with low income so they could pay the rent on their homes. They were entirely justified in order to stop abuse of the system, but suddenly and for the first time we knocked up against the need for a difficult decision as a government. The backbench revolt was immediate and large (with Lib Dems joining in). The size of the majority could take care of it, but there were ugly moments. When we then proposed further radical cuts to the welfare bill through reforming incapacity benefit, similar scenes were played out. We wanted to cut the welfare bill radically as the costs had risen sharply and now ran into billions. We were still handling the fallout from the recession of the early 1990s in terms of public finances. We had given a commitment—a very tough one, which Gordon stuck to, tenaciously and rightly—to keep to the previous government's spending totals for our first two years, but nonetheless wanted to get more money into health and education, and so were looking for every way we could to trim the welfare costs. In any event, it was clearly unhealthy for people to be subsidised on a life of benefit; and when they could work, then in their own interests, they should.

As with housing benefit, incapacity benefit had also become open to systematic abuse. In the 1980s, as long-term unemployment rose it suited the government quietly to allow large numbers of people, particularly in the old mining industries, to be transferred on to the incapacity register. They would thus count as sick, not unemployed, and the unemployment figures were reduced. All of us knew people in our constituencies who had spent years on benefit when their incapacity seemed, let us say, more than a trifle exaggerated.

The proposed changes had people chaining themselves to the railings of Downing Street in protest. They were usually chosen as protesters by virtue of being in wheelchairs, as if everyone on incapacity benefit was confined to a wheelchair, or all those in wheelchairs were unable to work—both of which positions I thought highly dubious. But that wasn't the point. Naturally, they elicited much sympathy.

Then at the end of July, as the summer recess approached, David Blunkett, a Labour politician who held several ministerial posts including Secretary of State for Education, announced the introduction of means-tested tuition fees, and so began the long and often slow march towards university reform. (These fees were to be paid according to the size of parental income, a loan to be repaid by the student once he or she started earning income.) Again cries of outrage and betrayal ensued.

It was all manageable, of course, but it was a portend.

We were a popular government, I still retained high approval ratings, but even back then, the signs were clear of storms and troubles to come.

I was learning, on the job, the trade of prime minister, the trade of decision-maker and responsibility-taker and, as I occasionally stepped back and surveyed it all, I could see where it was going. I could see the end even as I lived the beginning. I could see the rhythm of it all. The difference between beginning and end is not—major crises like wars excepted—simply in the nature of the events themselves. In other words, an event—let's say a scandal—can occur at the start, and because everyone is still in the throes of excitement at the new government it can be overcome reasonably easily. If it occurs later, it can be terminal. It depends less on the nature of the events than on their place in the cycle. The adversity, the intensity of the criticism, the fullness of the attack grow not in proportion to the decisions of leadership, but rather to the chipping away over time of its freshness, its appeal, its novelty and thus its persuasive power.

At first, in those early months and perhaps in much of that initial term of office, I had political capital that I tended to hoard. I was risking it but within strict limits and looking to recoup it as swiftly as possible. Over Kosovo, the first real life-and-death decision, I spent freely. But in domestic terms, I tried to reform with the grain of opinion, not against it.

If things went calm for a time, I wasn't in any great mood to disturb them. We were making changes. Devolution was one and that was historic. But much of the fruit was low-hanging. Some of it was even popular, like the minimum wage.

In public services, we had all the right language and all the right intentions, but the method tended to be one of driving change from the centre. The origins of later, far more radical change were discernible in those starting months, yet the policy prescriptions were too tame; the belief in the power of government itself to make the change on the ground was too trusting; and perhaps also we had an analysis that under-estimated the gravity of the problems and therefore the requirement for reform of a nature that was fundamental and structural.

The instincts were by and large spot on. The knowledge, the experi-ence, the in-depth understanding that grappling over time induces—these qualities were missing. There was a political confidence, even swagger about us; but it was born of our popularity with the country, not our fitness to change it as it needed.

That rhythm, too, was intruding and I was aware of it, for the first time. Of course I knew from the moment I became leader of the Labour Party that you never end as you begin. I understood completely that the business of politics was rough, the public could be fickle, the cracks and crevasses would appear soon enough, even in a carefully con-structed edifice of political advancement; and our edifice had been con-structed with immense care. But to contemplate it is one thing; to experience it is another. And feeling it first-hand both disconcerted me and sobered me.

No one ever believes a politician when he or she says this, but I was never desperate to be prime minister or to stay as prime minister. That's the honest truth. I don't mean I lacked ambition—I had plenty of that—but I did lack courage. I knew it would be brutal and ugly, and could end in tears.

In my moments of reflection on holiday in 1997, down in the south of France in the lovely old twelfth-century house we used to stay at in the Ariège—a beautiful and understated part of the country—I would think of the future. I would think of being released, of escaping with reputation and soul intact having served two terms, handing over to Gordon—let him have the damn thing—and being free again, free of all the anxiety, the responsibility, the living on a perpetual knife-edge where any slip could cut you to pieces. I thought of how good it would be to go, still young, just past fifty, still popular, still a friendly face in a friendly country. I would lead, of course, to the best of my ability. I wouldn't shirk the tough deci-sions. But I prayed they would not be those that could lose it all, could end in failure and humiliation. Get out before they stop listening, stop liking, and start loathing. That was my hope.

Yet I could sense the rhythm, feel its relentless and ever so slightly louder drumbeat, sense its effect on the country around me.

We were already starting to take the decisions that chip away at the stock of goodwill. It was amazing how even the most anodyne or seemingly consensual changes could result in a fierceness of response out of all proportion to the measure. Even David Blunkett's introduction of the literacy and numeracy tests—necessary to raise the low levels of eleven-year-old attainment from the roughly 50 per cent pass rate we inherited—caused shrieks of protest. I wasn't startled by it. But there was a slightly dangerous mood among the back benches that indicated they were profoundly unprepared for the travails of government. Having enjoyed the serenity of Opposition life, where everyone could imbibe some of the Lib Dem liqueur and just nod along, they were now having to grow accustomed to returning to their constituencies and getting an earful; not a really painful one, but nonetheless the change was a shock. At one of my regular PLP briefings, when the whole of the Parliamentary Labour Party would be invited to the Large Committee Room of the House of Commons to hear the leader's words of wisdom, I joked that when we were in Opposition, life was easy: MPs just went back home and blamed it all on the government; the trouble is, some of them still do. It's extraordinary how anyone who opposes the government is principled while anyone who is loyal is just a sycophant, when the support is usually far harder than the opposition, unless you are aiming for preferment.

I was learning that the very discipline I thought necessary in Opposition was every bit as critical, if not more so, in government; and that meant a constant interaction with the political troops. In turn, this was so much more difficult because suddenly the schedule was dominated by major meetings and functions.

Another lesson was therefore being learned. Foreign leaders had to be seen, those you needed or wanted to see and those you didn't. There was ceremony and protocol, much of which was unavoidable. There were summits, NATO, Europe, the G8. The summits were tiring and only occasionally productive. There was also the handing back of Hong Kong to China.

I travel fairly easily, but the Hong Kong trip, done in a day and a half, was exhausting. It was also my first real experience of China's leadership. It was an odd occasion. I was very attached to Hong Kong. I had visited reasonably often since my sister-in-law Katy was Hong Kong Chinese. She was very instructive on the subject of the return of the colony. Obviously she was Anglophile. Brought up a Catholic. Had lived a long time in the UK. But when I asked her if she felt sad at the return, she said immediately: No, I'm Chinese, it's natural to be part of China. Occasionally the British fail to see the fact that although we are often regarded in many parts of the world by the indigenous people as having been good colonialists, those people no longer want us as colonialists. In the end, however benign we were, they prefer to run themselves and make their own mistakes.

But at the handover ceremony I still felt a tug, not of regret but of nostalgia for the old British Empire. Later that night, I crossed the harbour to the Kowloon side in a tugboat, in the torrential rain to meet China's leaders. The lights fused at the landing place and the hotel quayside was lit by Chinese lanterns that swayed and jangled in the wind and the choppy water. I went upstairs feeling I must have looked about thirty (I aged quickly in the job as you can see), to greet Jiang Zemin and the assembled Chinese top brass. He completely threw me by talking with greater knowledge about Shakespeare than I could have possibly mustered and joking away as if it was the most natural thing in the world. He then explained to me that this was a new start in UK/China relations and from now on, the past could be put behind us. I had, at that time, only a fairly dim and sketchy understanding of what that past was. I thought it was all just politeness in any case. But actually, he meant it. They meant it. And relations with China did indeed make substantial progress from that day.

Equally, as part of the rhythm of government, came the inevitable personal scandals. I say inevitable, because there is no doubt that in any government, they will come. We made a very big mistake in allowing the impression to be gained that we were going to be better than the Tories; not just better at governing, but more moral, more upright. As a matter of record, I never said we were going to be purer than pure; I said we were going to be *expected* to be purer than pure, and I did so to stress the dangers. I came to regret the whole characterisation around the issue of so-called "sleaze." It was a media game, and in Opposition we played it. The goals were easy but the long-term consequences were disastrous. I was aware we were playing with Faust's companion, but with him onside, it was just too easy to score. And to be fair, I couldn't see us doing some of the things the Tories had done.

What I failed to realise is that we would also have our skeletons rattling around the cupboard, and while they might be different, they would be just as repulsive. Moreover, I did not at that time see the full implications of the massive increase in transparency we were planning as part of our reforms to "clean up politics." For the first time, details of donors and the amounts given to political parties were going to be published. I completely missed the fact that though in Opposition millionaire donors were to be welcomed as a sign of respectability, in government they would very quickly be seen as buying influence. The Freedom of Information Act was then being debated in Cabinet Committee. It represented a quite extraordinary offer by a government to open itself and Parliament to scrutiny. Its consequences would be revolutionary; the power it handed to the tender mercy of the media was gigantic. We did it with care, but without foresight. Politicians are people and scandals will happen. There never was going to be a happy ending to that story, and sure enough there wasn't. The irony was that far from improving our reputation, we sullied it. The latter months of 1997 saw two such "scandals," one personal, one financial.

On 1 August, just before I went on holiday, Alastair told me that the *News of the World* had a story about Robin Cook and Gaynor, his long-time assistant. In times gone by it was not exceptional for politicians to have mistresses, lovers and affairs, but because it was strictly against the mores of the times it was not considered proper to write about it. The irony is that while sex is written about more today, and people talk openly about sex and even have affairs openly, politicians are nonetheless expected to conform to traditional mores, but in a context where transgressions are far more likely to be publicly discussed. Leaders in the past—Kennedy, Lloyd George, and no doubt many others—led lives that would be completely unthinkable now, despite us living in more promiscuous times. While I tended to look upon such things with a fairly worldly eye (and assiduously avoided exploiting any Tory sex scandal before we came to office), I was nevertheless conscious of the fact that the rest of the world viewed it differently.

When the story about Robin broke, I was initially relatively insouciant about it, but Alastair thought it could be a real problem. We had to have a line; and that's where it got difficult. Robin was married to Margaret; he was having an affair with Gaynor. In the old days, this situation might have quietly carried on, but the question asked today is: who will he choose? Sitting in my little office on a Friday morning, on the day I was due to go on holiday, Alastair, Robin Butler and myself had to decide what to do.

Alastair phoned Robin Cook at the airport where he was about to go off with Margaret on holiday. An awkward conversation, as you can imagine. What to do? When I eventually talked to Robin I said: You will have to decide. If there is no decision, the danger is the thing runs away from us, creates a huge scandal and I don't in any event see how you can openly maintain both relationships.

Maybe I was wrong and maybe you think I was interfering unreasonably, but I couldn't see an answer to the basic problem: now we know about the affair, does it continue or does it stop?

And there's a Sunday deadline. And it's in the *News of the World*. All this is happening to some poor sod's private life and we have to sit there and try to give the best advice in the interests of not only Robin, but also the wider government. "Foreign Secretary leaves wife for another woman"; mildly interesting, but it soon passes. "Foreign Secretary in love fight—who will win?"; that could run for weeks.

Although it felt ugly, we had to be clear with Robin. You must speak to Margaret. You must choose. And I'm afraid you must do so before the Sunday-edition deadline of tomorrow lunchtime.

I know Margaret was very sore afterwards and felt Alastair and I pushed Robin to leave her, but it really wasn't so. The truth is he loved Gaynor and she was devoted to him. He made a choice. Next day he announced it. Because of the way Alastair handled it, it was treated reasonably sympathetically and the spotlight moved on with surprising speed.

As prime minister I was the recipient of numerous confidences and, via the whips, of numerous revelations. Here's the shocking or not so shocking thing: politicians really are like everyone else. Some are in marriages of love; some are in marriages of convenience; some are having affairs; some are straight; some are gay.

Up to a point, and a fairly distant point, the public tolerates sexual misdemeanour. The issue is not the fornication but the complication. The trouble usually arises when the media are able to discover, dredge or invent a "public interest" abuse in the course of the scandal: it was a security lapse; government information was compromised; he lied about it; he used government resources to pursue it. Then it can turn very awkward, but a plain and simple sex scandal—if there is such a thing— they will just about tolerate.

Financial scandal is different. Money is far more potent and dangerous than sex. Before the end of our first year we went through that as well, and in the course of it I learned a big lesson.

Before the election Bernie Ecclestone, the Formula One boss, had donated £1 million to the Labour Party. He had previously given money to the Tories, at which time the legislation requiring disclosure was not yet on the statute books. He came to see us on an industry matter relating to Formula One. Europe was looking to ban tobacco advertising in sport, and because Formula One was so heavily dependent on it, Bernie wanted time to have it phased in.

To be fair to him, he made no link whatsoever between the gift and the policy, and behaved entirely properly throughout. We already had the gift before the meeting, though there was, of course, always the possibility of further donations. I would have seen such a major figure anyway, given that the businesses associated with Formula One employ tens of thousands of people; and I would have taken the same policy decision to phase implementation of the ban over time.

However, it was a really stupid lapse of judgement on my part not to have immediately put a big Civil Service structure in place to ensure propriety was not only observed, but also seen to be observed. We didn't, and were duly, and in this instance fairly, whacked for it. (Though rather unfairly so was Bernie, since he had genuinely never made a linkage, not even implicitly.)

I was taught then and there that once in government, the rules on anything touching money were going to be applied very differently. Rightly so, you will say; but the essential problem—which grew over the years—was that parties need financing. There was a limit to how much could be raised from ordinary members, and high-value donors— as they were called—were absolutely crucial. Even in 1997, we were outspent by the Tories. In 1992, they had outspent us by a ratio of five to one, when 90 per cent of our money came from the unions who were, in my experience, the only funders who explicitly and insistently linked money to policy. I was determined to free us from that dependence; but once in government, no one believed a big donation could be made from the goodness of the heart.

Of course, in one sense the motives will always be varied or mixed. People give to charity for varied or mixed reasons, of which—don't get me wrong—desire to do good may be uppermost; but donating to political parties, at least in the UK, is not regarded as prima facie supporting politics, but as prima facie buying influence. So it all gets very sticky indeed. It was a sharp and telling portend of things to come.

It also taught me a lesson which, even after I learned it, I found difficult to apply. Part of the problem with scandal is that it steals up on you and takes you unawares. It then draws a vast media resource into spinning it out and developing it. Meanwhile, you are trying to find the facts, work out the line, think of what ground you can legitimately camp on. People's careers, their lives, depend on decisions taken in an instant, frequently imperfectly informed. When the storm is raging, your senses and decision-making capacity are upended, tossed about on the waves of some fresh "revelation," until you fear that you will never get to calmer waters and spot dry land.

Scandal is an absolute nightmare in politics. Take my word for it. The public may conclude that politicians today are lesser people than those of days of yore. That's cobblers. The difference is that the scrutiny is greater, and the transparency expected is of an utterly different nature; the hysteria with which the issue is publicly debated is many multiples of decibels louder; and the speed with which it moves is like the speed of a jet plane compared to the speed of a tractor. The people are the same; the context is a planet away from that of even twenty years ago.

And so the first months in government came to a close. Much to be proud of; huge changes set in train, not only in policy but in culture. We had embarked on an ambitious legislative programme with landmark changes to the constitution, the proposal for a minimum wage and Bank of England independence marking a major shift in the way the nation would be governed.

Though at this point as small as a child's hand, the clouds of the future were also gathering. We had lost our virginity on scandal. There were the first harbingers of future power struggles. But, all in all, it had been a good beginning. A new and untested government; yet we had not fallen flat on our faces. We had stood upright and were governing. We were satisfied. So was the country.

FIVE

PRINCESS DIANA

I returned from the summer holiday refreshed and alert. The first months since entering Number 10 had gone well. That was to be expected. The next would be tougher. That was also to be expected. There had been plenty of false starts, missed opportunities and imperfect decision-making, but the mood was so benign it seemed like a government blessed. Public moods are strange affairs. When they embrace you, the experience suggests they are deep, with firm roots. You wonder how they can change. Of course you know they do and will, but during them, if they are pronounced, they can float you along effortlessly or mercilessly push you back, as if the feeling, good or ill, will last forever.

The power of the media in shaping them is critical. When the mood is benign, it is truly benign: errors are charming eccentricities, gaffes are amusing, agonised processes of decision-making are simply a reflection of a profound sense of responsibility to get it right. When the mood is harsh, it is like running against a relentless headwind: each faux pas is magnified, previous transgressions are recalled and reiterated with renewed vigour, agonised decision-making is just incompetence. You are doing the same, and in the same way; but the manner in which it is assessed is completely different.

New Labour, New Britain did not seem like hubris. On the contrary, it chimed with something real in the mood of the country. Of course, in reality we were only scratching the surface on whole swathes of policy, on public services, welfare and pensions; but it didn't seem like that in those first few months.

The Conservative government had been controversial for all sorts of policy reasons, but that, in a sense, is normal politics. A new laissez-faire approach to industry, battles with the unions, foreign crises—each had taken its toll, though in many ways the agenda by which the Tories had governed was becoming reasonably common lore worldwide. However, they were also conservative with a small "c," and that was becoming outdated. They panned the Labour left in London for being pro–gay rights, for example. In the 1980s, it worked; in the late 1990s, it worked against them. Their stuffiness, their pomp, their worship of tradition, were of a metal stamped with the hallmark of a bygone age. John Major was in many ways different from all that and was quite capable of leading them out of it, but his problem was he was never really in charge.

The moment Labour started to throw off the chains of its past and behaved in a modern way in respect of the economy, and with common sense on issues like defence and crime, then the reasons to stick with the Tories fell away. The zeitgeist was free to turn less deferential, more liberal on social issues, less class-bound, more meritocratic. It didn't matter that I was the private-school boy and John Major the state pupil. I led a party in one mindset; he was shackled by a party in another.

This change of sentiment spread deep into the recesses of public life. Naturally that included the monarchy, which had its own personification of it: Princess Diana. She was an icon, possibly the most famous and most photographed person in the world. She captured the essence of an era and held it in the palm of her hand. She defined it.

This was gravely disconcerting for the monarchy as an institution, or a business, if you like. She so outshone the others in terms of charisma, ability to connect with the public, courage in embracing the new, that she was a rebuke rather than a support. That is not to say that she did not fully agree with the monarchy and all its hereditary tradition—she did—but her way of translating that into the modern idiom was so adventurous it throbbed with nonconformity; and thus danger. As she strode into hitherto forbidden places, vaulted carefully erected hurdles of propriety and demolished vast swathes of the norms of royal behaviour with an abandon that was total folly at one level and utter genius at another, the royal family watched with what I am sure was a mixture of helplessness and horror. Of course she was much too smart to give her support to any political party, but in temperament and time, in the mood she engendered and which we represented, there was a perfect fit. Whatever New Labour had in part, she had in whole.

I got to know her reasonably well before the 1997 election. A Labour peer, Lord Mishcon, had me round to dinner to meet her. My friend Maggie Rae knew those who knew her and had her to dinner as well. We kept in touch, and met from time to time.

She was extraordinarily captivating. The aura that already surrounded her was magnified by the radical combination of royalty and normality that she expressed. She was a royal who seemed at ease, human and, most of all, willing to engage with people on an equal basis. She wasn't condescending, she laughed normally, she conversed normally, she flirted normally. That was her great charm: put her with any group of people anywhere, and she could get on with them.

She had a strong emotional intelligence, certainly, but she was also very capable of analytical understanding. I had a conversation with her once about the utility and force of photographs and how they could be best used, which showed a mind that was not only intuitive but also had a really good process of reasoning. She had the thing totally worked out. Occasionally she would phone and say why such-and-such a picture was rubbish or what could be done better, and though not, as I say, at all party political, she had a complete sense of what we were trying to achieve and why. I always used to say to Alastair: if she was ever in politics, even Clinton would have to watch out.

She was also strong-willed, let us say, and was always going to go her own way. I had the feeling she could fall out with you as easily as fall in with you. She knew the full range of the power of her presence and knew its ability to enthral, and most often used it to do good; but there was also a wildness in her emotions that meant when anger or resentment were woven together with that power, it could spell danger. I really liked her and, of course, was as big a sucker for a beautiful princess as the next man; but I was wary too.

Anyway, for sure, just as we were changing the image of Britain, she was radicalising that of the monarchy; or perhaps, more accurately, her contrast with them illuminated how little they had changed. For someone as acutely perceptive and long-termist about the monarchy and its future as the Queen, it must have been deeply troubling. Above all, the Queen knew the importance of the monarchy standing for history, tradition and duty. She knew also that while there was a need for the monarchy to evolve with the people, and that its covenant with them, unwritten and unspoken, was based on a relationship that allowed for evolution, it should be steady, carefully calibrated and controlled. Suddenly, an unpredictable meteor had come into this predictable and highly regulated ecosystem, with equally uncertain consequences. She had good cause to be worried.

After the holiday and before my first visit to Balmoral for the prime minister's weekend with the royal family—a tradition stretching back to the time of Gladstone and Queen Victoria—I went to Sedgefield. It was great to go back as prime minister. I was proud of them, and they were proud of me. By and large that feeling persisted until the end. Despite the fact that ever since becoming Leader of the Opposition I had not been able to get back there with anything like the old regularity, they welcomed me each time I did. I would go to the local party's General Committee meeting and give my report, then spend an hour or two chatting, exchanging views, answering questions with people who had in many cases known me since 1983 and who had watched my rise; and in that room, I would be very frank. It was a privilege for me to be able to talk to people I genuinely trusted, under John Burton's watchful eye; and they felt it a privilege in return to have the access and feel part of history in the making.

I would visit the Dun Cow pub in Sedgefield Village or the working men's club. People were friendly but also respectful of the fact I was out for a pint or two and to relax. Politics was rarely discussed unless it was sat at a table over dinner with John and Lily Burton, Phil Wilson (later my successor as Sedgefield MP), Peter and Christine Brooks, really nice decent people, and Paul Trippett, a rough, tough but lovely and very smart man who was steward at the working men's club and became a close friend. We would chat, go through the constituency problems, and I would take their temperature on the big issues of the day. Collectively and individually, they had a great instinct for where the public was; and rarely, if ever, did they fail to help me feel my way. They also represented a very important strain of the British people. They might read the *Guardian* but weren't *of* the *Guardian*; they were not at all "London," and neither were they typical *Daily Mail* (a middle-class conservative tabloid). They were highly political, but knew lots of people outside politics.

They were yet another interesting example of how the old pigeon-holes into which people were put didn't fit any more. My politics represented that completely, but it was very hard to get the commentating classes to see it. Sedgefield was a "northern working-class" constituency, except that when you scratched even a little beneath the surface, the definitions didn't quite fit. Yes, of course you could go into any of the old mining villages—the Trimdons, Fishburn, Ferryhill, Chilton and so on—and find the stereotype if you looked for it, but increasingly it wasn't like that. The new estates were private estates of three- and four-bedroomed houses, and while the people who lived there couldn't be described as "middle class," neither were they "working class" in the sense of Andy Capp. They drank beer; they also drank wine. They went to the chippy; they also went to restaurants. They were taking one, two or even three holidays abroad a year, and not all of them in Spain.

This was a different Britain, and one in which I felt at home. There had been an article—usual *Daily Mail* stuff—about how I was a poseur and fraud because I said I liked fish and chips, but when in London living in Islington it was well known that I had eaten pasta (shock-horror). Plainly you couldn't conceivably like both since these were indications of distinct and incompatible cultures. The Britain of the late 1990s was of course actually one in which people ate a variety of foods, had a multiplicity of different cultural experiences and rather enjoyed it. This was as true "up North" as it was "down South." The world was opening up. My closest friends in Sedgefield symbolised that difference. There I was at ease and could be myself, and they were just them and that was fine by both of us.

Things had changed around our constituency house, as they had everywhere in our lives. There was a twenty-four-hour police guard, not as heavy as it became later, but always there. The roads had been changed to limit access, but it still felt like the one bit of our lives that remained constant. The surroundings were familiar and cosy.

My thoughts on the evening of 30 August 1997 were focused on the perpetual concern of getting an agenda together that made the changes match the rhetoric. I was worried that if people did not notice major change soon, cynicism would set in. I knew that we had the political initiative, and that the Tories were disconnected and ill-disciplined, but I also knew our media hold was fragile and based in many cases on convenience, not conviction, on both our parts. Once they decided they were going to go for us, if they couldn't get us on substance, they would try to get us on style, to make our strengths weaknesses and our very political success into a form of trickery. Also at some point, the right-wing media would understand we weren't actually a mild form of Thatcherism, and the left-wing media would realise New Labour was for real and not going to yield to the usual demands of the left.

Probably, too, I had been preoccupied getting the kids to bed—usually my job—settling them down (impossible with three aged thirteen, eleven and nine), fetching drinks, reading stories and hoping they would give us enough respite at least for a quiet meal together.

I went to sleep around 11:30. At about 2 a.m., something most peculiar happened. Cherie is difficult to wake once asleep, but I woke to find a policeman standing by the bed, which as you can imagine was quite a surprise. As I struggled into consciousness he told me that he had tried the bell but I hadn't heard it; that Princess Diana had been seriously injured in a car crash; and that I should immediately telephone Sir Michael Jay, the British ambassador in Paris.

I was fully awake now. Cherie had also woken up. I explained the situation to her, then rushed downstairs and Downing Street put Michael through. It was clear from the outset that Diana was highly unlikely to survive. Michael went over her injuries, informed me that her boyfriend Dodi Fayed and the driver had been killed outright, and the bodyguard was alive but unconscious.

I phoned Alastair. He had heard from media monitoring. (This was a system introduced by Alastair at Number 10 to ensure that all aspects of the media were summarised daily for my use and the staff's.) We were both profoundly shocked. I couldn't believe it. She was such a force in people's lives, so much part of our national life, so clearly, indubitably and unalterably alive herself, it was impossible to think of her dead.

At 4 a.m. I was phoned again, however, to be told that she was. Michael was full of praise for the way the French had handled it: the Interior Minister Jean-Pierre Chevènement, the Health Minister Bernard Kouchner, and President Chirac had been sensitive, cooperative and respectful. From that time onwards there was a constant round of calls and, through it all, we were trying to work out how it should be managed.

I know that sounds callous. I was genuinely in grief. I liked her and I felt desperately sorry for her two boys, but I also knew that this was going to be a major national, in fact global event like no other. How Britain emerged was important for the country internally and externally. I was the prime minister; I had to work out how it would work out. I had to articulate what would be a tidal wave of grief and loss, in a way that was dignified but also expressed the emotion and love—not too strong a word—people felt for her.

If the Queen had died, it would have been, in one sense, simple: there would be an expression of great respect and praise, but all of it, though deep, would have been nonetheless conventional. This was completely different. This was not a conventional person nor a conventional death; and there would not be a conventional reaction.

In addition to grief I felt something else, which stemmed from the last meeting I had with Diana. It had not been all that easy. She had wanted to come to Chequers and offered a date in June, which I accepted. Alastair—despite adoring her—and Number 10 felt that it was unseemly for me to see her before I had met Prince Charles, and it might be misinterpreted. Reluctantly I agreed, and we refixed for July. As astute as ever, she guessed the shifting of the date was deliberate and was cross about it.

She came for the day with Prince William. The weather was gorgeous and Chequers looked beautiful. The staff were thrilled she was coming, and she was gracious and friendly to all. We had been talking about what she could do for the country in a more formal way. It was self-evidently tricky to see what that might be, though she was enthusiastic to do something. She was undoubtedly an enormous asset and I also felt it was right that she be given the chance to shift the focus somewhere other than exclusively on her private life; but I also felt—and I don't know, maybe I would be less punctilious about it nowadays—that Dodi Fayed was a problem. This was not for the obvious reasons, which would have made some frown on him; his nationality, religion or background didn't matter a hoot to me. I had never met him, so at one level it was unfair to feel nervous about him, and for all I know he was a good son and a nice guy; so if you ask me, well, spit it out, what was wrong, I couldn't frankly say, but I felt uneasy and I knew some of her close friends—people who really loved her—felt the same way.

At that time, on a good day at Chequers, we would get the kids, the police, protection squad and the staff together and play football out on the back lawn where there had been a lovely grass tennis court in the 1930s. It was a fantastic pitch and we used to have great fun. Everyone except Diana and me went off to play, including William. Poor bloke, I think he wondered what on earth she had brought him for and he didn't much want to play football, but, like a good sport, he did.

Diana and I had a walk in the grounds. She reproached me gently but clearly for cancelling the June date. I wonder how I would deal with her today, but then I just broached the subject of her and Dodi straight out. She didn't like it and I could feel the wilful side of her bridling. How-

ever, she didn't refuse to talk about it, so we did, and also what she
might do. Although the conversation had been uncomfortable at points,
by the end it was warm and friendly. I tried my hardest to show that I
would be a true friend to her, and she should treat the frankness in that
spirit. I joined in the football game while she watched and laughed with
the staff, had her picture taken and did all the things she was brilliant at.
It was the last time I saw her.

As I contemplated her death and what I would say, I felt a sense of
obligation as well as sadness. I felt I owed it to her to try to capture
something of what she was. We were both in our ways manipulative
people, perceiving quickly the emotions of others and able instinctively
to play with them, but I knew that when she reached out to the disabled
or sick in a way no one else could have done and no one else in her
position ever had done, it was with sincerity. She knew its effect, of
course, but the effect could never have been as powerful as it was if the
feeling had not been genuine. I sat in my study in Trimdon as the dawn
light streamed through the windows, and thought about how *she* would
have liked me to talk about her.

Of course the numerous practicalities and logistics also needed to be
sorted out: calls to make and to take; how the body would come back;
the funeral; the business of government (would the Scottish referendum
campaign continue or not, for example)—everything from the significant to the utterly trivial required focus, since at these moments the
trivial can become significant suddenly and without warning.

However, all the time the main part of my mind was going over what
I would say. Robin Cook had just stepped off a plane in the Philippines
and had already said something, much to Alastair's irritation. I told him
not to worry; all that mattered was what I would say, and we agreed it
should be just before the church service in Trimdon Village at 10:30 a.m.

The Palace had, of course, put out a statement, but there was no
intention for the Queen to speak. Just before I left for church I had my
first telephone call with her, in which I expressed my condolences. She
was philosophical, anxious for the boys, but also professional and practical. She grasped the enormity of the event, but in her own way. She was
not going to be pushed around by it. She could be very queenly in that
sense.

By then I had worked out what I wanted to say. I scribbled it on the
back of an envelope, and discussed it with Alastair. I had talked to others of the close circle by now, but at this moment it was his advice and

input I needed. His judgement in these situations was clear, exemplary and forthright. The last thing you need at a time like that is a back-coverer, vacillator or sycophant.

The phrase "people's princess" now seems like something from another age. And corny. And over the top. And all the rest of it. But at the time it felt natural and I thought, particularly, that she would have approved. It was how she saw herself, and it was how she should be remembered. I also wanted to capture the way she touched people's lives, and to do so in a way that acknowledged her own life hadn't been smooth or easy. Failing to mention her problems somehow felt like being dishonest about her; and more than that, undermining what she meant to others. What they loved was precisely that she was a princess but still vulnerable, still buffeted by life's ups and downs, capable of healing their wounds because she herself knew what it was like to be wounded.

We drove the couple of miles to the green in the centre of Trimdon where the old church stands. It is a beautiful church with one of the few surviving Norman arches around its altar, a pretty garden and the graveyard that John Burton's wife, Lily, and her friends used to tend. Cherie and the children went on ahead inside. Alastair had arranged for a pooled press group to be present. I got out of the car and just walked up and spoke. It was odd, standing there in this little village in County Durham, on the grass in front of an ancient small church, speaking words that I knew would be carried around the country and the world. They would be a major part of how people thought of me. Even today people talk to me about it. You think of the great speeches, prepared over days and weeks, the momentous events that shape modern history and in which I played a part, the political battles, the crises, the times of elation, and despair; yet those few words scribbled on the back of an envelope probably had as much coverage as anything I ever did. The key thing is to put all of that out of your mind, don't think about how big it is, don't feed all the inner demons who suggest all the things that can go wrong. Just go out and do it.

Except in this case—and I know this sounds contrived—just before speaking I paused for a moment and thought of her, reminding myself that most of all I should speak for her. This is what I said:

I feel like everyone else in this country today—utterly devastated. Our thoughts and prayers are with Princess Diana's family—in particular her two sons, two boys—our hearts go out to them. We are today a nation in Britain in a state of shock, in mourning, in grief that is so deeply painful for us.

She was a wonderful and warm human being. Though her own life was often sadly touched by tragedy, she touched the lives of so many others in Britain—throughout the world—with joy and with comfort. How many times shall we remember her, in how many different ways, with the sick, the dying, with children, with the needy, when, with just a look or a gesture that spoke so much more than words, she would reveal to all of us the depth of her compassion and her humanity. How difficult things were for her from time to time, surely we can only guess at, but the people everywhere, not just here in Britain but everywhere, they kept faith with Princess Diana, they liked her, they loved her, they regarded her as one of the people. She was the people's princess and that's how she will stay, how she will remain in our hearts and in our memories forever.

I used the phrase "kept faith with Princess Diana" for a very particular reason. For some time before her death—and most of all recently, because of the relationship with Dodi—the jackals had been on the prowl. Parts of the media (the *Mail* especially) were gauging whether or not they could go for her. I knew they wanted to, and I had warned her of it when we met at Chequers, but they were nervous about it, unsure of the public reaction. So they contented themselves with laying down themes of criticism that could be developed, small barbs here and there, the occasional frontal attack, but nothing amounting to a campaign. The reason they held off was that her support was deep and quite visceral in its way, and people did keep faith with her. They were not going to let her be sacrificed. I knew that she would want those people to be recognised too. Would that support have continued in a future in which she remarried, grew older, became an even greater figure of controversy as well as renown? It is hard to say, but a decent part of it would surely have clung on. People knew her faults, and they didn't love her any the less for them.

The national mood was exactly what we thought: an outpouring of sadness. But already it was tinged with anger that she had been taken away. At first, the rage was turned on the paparazzi who had been following her. It is perhaps hard to convey what it is like to be a public figure and feel hounded. And for perfectly understandable reasons, many people don't feel sorry for the famous, most of whom have willingly taken that path. They often have a rich lifestyle. They take the upside, so the argument goes, and should jolly well put up with the downside. Anyway, small price to pay, isn't it?

Except in Diana's case it had gone way beyond a small price. She was literally hunted down. She was a very valuable commodity, a gold mine that was constantly plundered. The digging was deep and unusually desperate because the gains were so immense. Of course, media people say she was happy to pursue the media when it suited her, but this is a far less compelling argument than it seems. The truth is, in the full glare of media attention, you have no option but to engage with them, to try to mould their view of you, to try to prevent a different and often unflattering and unfair view from taking hold. In other words, sometimes this is a purely voluntary act, while at other times—as with Diana—there is no choice: either you attempt to feed the beast or the beast eats you. Now, at points she fed them more than was necessary, but that doesn't alter the basic fact: she was subject to a degree of persistent, intrusive and dehumanising harassment that on occasions was frightening, excessive and wrong.

That Sunday morning, the royal family attended a service in Crathie Church at Balmoral as usual. There was no reference to Diana. I knew the Queen would have felt that duty demanded that the normal routine was followed. There would have been no Alastairs in the entourage suggesting that possibly mentioning the tragedy might be sensible. The point is: the Queen is a genuine, not an artificial person, by which I mean there is no artifice in how she approaches things. While her absolute preoccupation was protecting the boys, it was to protect them first and foremost as princes. There would have been no question of them not going to church that day, hours after their mother had died. It was their duty as princes. Of course, to some of the public this looked incredibly, almost blatantly, insensitive.

I knew that swings in sentiment can come and go. I knew, too, that firmly set underneath there was a deep and abiding affection for the Queen. But this was a unique case. As the days passed, the crowds grew. Three books of condolence at St. James's Palace became four, became fifteen, became forty-three. The outpouring of grief was turning into a mass movement for change. It was a moment of supreme national articulation, and it was menacing for the royal family. I don't know what would have happened if they had just kept going as before. Possibly nothing, but in the eye of that storm, unpredictable and unnerving as it was, I couldn't be sure.

The refusal to lower the flags at Windsor Castle and the Tower of London was because Diana was technically no longer a member of the royal family, having been stripped of her HRH title. The flag at Buckingham Palace was not flying at all because, by tradition, only the Queen's personal standard is flown, and then only when she is in residence. She was staying at Balmoral because she didn't come to London in September. Again, by tradition. It was all very by the book, but it took no account of the fact that the people couldn't give a damn about "the book," actually disliked "the book," in fact, thought "the book" had in part produced the chain of events that led to Diana's death. In the strange symbiosis between ruler and ruled, the people were insisting that the Queen acknowledge that she ruled by their consent, and bend to their insistence.

Public anger was turning towards the royal family. At the same time, it hadn't abated towards the press who, sensing this, understood that they needed to direct it at the other target. And to be fair, they were releasing genuine public feeling and, like everyone else, struggling to read where it might all go.

There were also two camps inside Buckingham Palace. One was thoroughly traditional, and had not regarded Diana as an asset but as a danger. They felt that to give way to press and public pressure was to start down the slippery path to a populist-driven monarchy, which then led to the monarchy ceasing to be true to its station, and therefore losing its essential *raison d'être*. As admirably tough and principled as that approach was, it seemed hopelessly out of touch. While they may have understood the sadness of the people, they didn't understand the potential for rage.

The second camp in the Palace was to some degree represented by people such as Robert Fellowes, the Queen's private secretary and brother-in-law to Diana, who was a thoroughly sensible man. I don't know what he really thought of Diana—I think he saw both sides to her, loved the side he loved and shrugged at the other—but he was a professional and, as you sometimes find with well-bred upper-class types, a lot more shrewd and savvy than he let on. His deputy Robin Janvrin, who later succeeded him, was a Foreign Office official, also bright and completely au fait with where it was all heading.

At the suggestion of the Palace, I was to greet the body as it arrived from Paris. As I stood with sundry members of the Establishment out on the tarmac at RAF Northolt, I was acutely aware of the different camps. I had already decided in my own mind that this was a moment for the country to unite. There had to be love for Diana; respect for the Queen; a celebration of what a great country this is and how proud we were in having such a princess, and show ourselves able to put on something spectacular in her memory to the lasting admiration of the world. I therefore thought my job was to protect the monarchy, channel the anger before it became rage, and generally have the whole business emerge in a positive and unifying way, rather than be a source of tension, division and bitterness.

I also really felt for the Queen herself, who was in a hellishly difficult situation. On the one hand she had been worried about the impact of Diana on the monarchy as an institution, and on the other of course she grieved for the mother of the grandchildren she completely adored; but she didn't want to pretend to a view of Diana that was more conflicted than the public could accept, so her reluctance to step forward came about less through obedience to tradition and "the book"—though undoubtedly that was part of it—and more through a sincere desire to be true to what she really felt. My upfront and visible filling of the vacuum would have made her uncomfortable, and certainly some of those around her somewhat disdained it. It also emphasised their general unease with me and what I represented.

I am not a great one for the Establishment. It's probably at heart why I'm in the Labour Party and always will be. It's not that I mind them particularly, and, over the days that followed Diana's death, I did my level best to protect not just the Queen but also the court. I have to say, also, I found them polite, charming even, and never anything other than helpful people. So what I'm about to add may say more about me than them. I always felt that they preferred political leaders of two types: either those who were of them—or at least fully subscribed to their general outlook—or the "authentic" Labour people, the sort they used to read about, who spoke with an accent and who fitted their view of how such people should be. People like me were a bit nouveau riche, a bit arriviste, a bit confusing and therefore suspect. So I was also aware, during these days, that if it became too obvious I was trying to shape things, I could expect considerable blowback; and if I stumbled, I shouldn't expect help getting up.

It was strange standing there at Northolt watching the plane arrive, waiting for the coffin to be brought out, the press pack penned in their hundreds behind the fence, the awkward chit-chat with the others. You have to be so careful at such events. You stand around talking. The mood is sombre. Someone says hello; the natural inclination is to smile. Someone snaps the picture. Before you know it, you look as if you are behaving inappropriately, as if the only thing you did was grin. Diana was not wrong about photographs. When Cherie and I were getting out of the car for a memorial service or some other solemn occasion, I would always say, as much to myself as to Cherie, you can't afford to smile too broadly or laugh. Be on your guard.

For Prince Charles, it was really ghastly. He and Camilla were an obvious focus of intense interest and speculation. What could he do? Appear grief-stricken and he would be called a fraud. Appear calm and he would seem cold. It was an impossible situation, his every gesture interpreted or more likely misinterpreted, and people ready to pounce on any slip.

In this extraordinary, challenging time, his relationship with the boys rescued him. At that point I hadn't really seen them together, but as I saw more of them later, I realised that the relationship was close and deeply affectionate on both sides. Not surprisingly, since they were father and sons, you might say; but back then there were plenty of people who assumed that the strain between husband and wife had been transferred to father and sons. However, it wasn't so, and as the days wore on it became clearer, significantly easing the pressure on Prince Charles.

I had got to know him quite well before coming to office. He had made it his business to acquaint himself with leading members of what was likely to be the governing party. He was a curious mixture of the traditional and the radical (at one level he was quite New Labour; at another, definitely not), and of the princely and the insecure. He led a life in which naturally people deferred to him, and you wouldn't describe him as easy-going, certainly not in the way Diana was, but he was also sensitive to criticism and nervous about the public reaction to him.

I could never imagine him sitting in Maggie Rae's basement dining room in her terrace house in Hackney as Diana had, joshing with the other guests, everyone on first-name terms and beguiled into more or less complete informality. On the other hand, he had and has one very major and, to me, transcendent quality: he is enormously and sincerely committed. He does not sit on his backside biding his time until the moment of coronation comes. He genuinely cares about the causes he takes up, but more than that, he identifies them. He thinks about them deeply. And in his own funny way, when you get to know him better, he is less *de haut en bas* than many junior and transient heads of state. Probably he underestimates how much the public—now more than then—get him and are comfortable with him. They can smirk at the tree-hugging, talking-to-flowers business, and they can find it weird and unnatural when he refuses to play the game by their rules (as in that extraordinary moment when he and Diana had just become engaged and he was asked whether he loved her and said, "Yes, whatever 'love' means"), but they also know he does good work, believes in his duty to them and has commitment. That counts for a lot.

Towards the end of the second term, I was asked to advise on whether he and Camilla could or should get married. The scars of the Diana business were deep and lasting. It is fair to say that the Palace had become understandably neuralgic about anything that touched on it. I immediately said I thought it would be fine. They love each other; why not? Or are we really saying it's better they don't marry, as if marriage was somehow an insult? And by and large it was fine. There was, and from time to time still is, a media desire to go after and demonise Camilla, but the public have sussed her out too. They understand she is an uncomplicated, down-to-earth person who happens to love him. Is she Diana? No. Does she pretend to be? No. So let them get on with it. Now we are more sympathetic, more perceptive of the fact that the royals are both different and the same. In some ways, the furore around Diana's death was the point at which things turned. People not only felt the monarchy had taken a further and necessary step towards being more open to public opinion, but they also saw the human frailty and strength of its leading representatives and accepted both equally. The monarchy realised it could open up while remaining royal.

But during those days, it certainly felt touch-and-go. As the Queen stayed up in Balmoral and London became the capital of mourning for the world, the gulf between monarch and subjects became wider. Alastair and Anji had been inserted into the committee established by the Palace to handle the funeral and keep on top of the "situation" as it was unfolding. Both were evidently being of huge benefit to a machine not unnaturally struggling with the enormity of it all. Alastair was also guiding the press while alive to accusations of manipulating them, though frankly in crises like this, the difference between the two is hard to spot.

I wanted Anji in there because I knew that whereas Alastair would take a tabloid view of what needed to be done, she would speak for her very correct brand of Middle England. Between them, we had a chance to get the balance right. Some of the court were suspicious of such "interference," but most thought it practical and Robert Fellowes in particular insisted on it.

The funeral to be held the following Saturday was the main topic of debate. It had to be dignified; it had to be different; and it had to be Diana. There were endless discussions of the precise numbers of each category of people to be invited, the order of service and the role of Diana's family. Her brother Charles Spencer was a very strong and assertive character who felt extremely angry at the way she had been treated, certainly by the media and possibly by the royal family. Each decision was highly sensitive with multiple pros and cons, each had been worked and reworked. There was a big debate about whether the boys should walk behind the cortège with Prince Charles, and concern about the differing possible public reactions to him and to them.

Most of all, pressure was mounting on the Queen. I went out on the Wednesday and did a doorstep, supporting her strongly and asking for understanding that the priority was the children, as it should be. However, the fact that I was speaking only served to emphasise the fact that she wasn't. Indeed, if I hadn't spoken the previous Sunday and during the week that followed, literally no one in any position of authority would have been speaking. How bizarre would that have been, given this was the only news worldwide? Meanwhile, though Alastair and Anji were more or less working full-time on this, I was having to attend to government matters. We were cranking up the Northern Ireland business to get to a ceasefire by the IRA, and that was taking time; I had a major speech to the Trades Union Congress (TUC) the next week; there was a big education summit at Downing Street on the Thursday; and of course throughout I was taking calls from world leaders who rang to express their condolences.

On Wednesday afternoon, I decided to call Prince Charles. Part of my problem with the Queen was that there was no easy point of connection in age, or outlook, or acquaintance. I respected her and was a little in awe of her, but as a new prime minister I didn't know her, or how she would take the very direct advice that I now felt I had to give her. I totally understood how she looked at the whole thing and sympathised, but you didn't have to be a political genius to work out that this was a tide that had to be channelled. It couldn't be turned back, resisted or ignored. I didn't trust myself fully to go straight to her and be as blunt as I needed to be. So I went to Charles.

I called him from the den at Downing Street and realised straight away it had been the right thing to do. He was clearly of completely the same mind. The Queen had to speak; the royal family had to be visible. However tough it was for him personally, for all the obvious reasons, he and the boys couldn't hide away. They had to come to London to respond to the public outpouring. I was extraordinarily relieved. He agreed to take the message back. By the next day, Thursday, it was clear there would be a broadcast by the Queen herself. Alastair was able to steer the journalists gently on to that track, and almost immediately the tension started to dissipate and you could feel people moving back towards her.

At the Queen's request I called her on Thursday lunchtime, and we spoke about what would happen the next day and how it would be managed. She was now very focused and totally persuaded. It wasn't easy, but it was certain. The following day, the Queen, Charles and the boys visited the front of Buckingham Palace, which had turned into a shrine. There were some last-minute discussions about her precise words, but it was plain from the language and tone that once she had decided to move, she moved with considerable skill. The broadcast was near perfect. She managed to be a queen and a grandmother at one and the same time.

I had spoken to Prince Charles again and we had gone through the arrangements for the funeral one last time. The Palace had asked me to do a reading in church. It was a mark of how pivotal my role had been through the week, but I also know it would lead to a charge of "muscling in." Indeed, throughout, we were walking a tightrope, thinner and more frayed by the day, between organising everything to go well and "cashing in" or exploiting. And that was in those halcyon days; heaven knows what would have happened had Diana died some years later . . .

The funeral was all we could have hoped for. It was unusual—Elton John singing "Candle in the Wind," and doing it rather brilliantly—but it was also in keeping with Westminster Abbey. Charles Spencer made a strong attack on the press (I said to Alastair, mark my words, they will wait for the chance for revenge, and if it comes they will seize it savagely). There was also something of a rebuke to the royal family, but his speech was powerful and would reverberate.

I gave lunch to a huge assortment of kings, queens, heads of state and dignitaries. Hillary Clinton came, representing the U.S., and as ever it was good to see her. The scale of the whole affair was gigantic. On occasions like these, I tended to shut off from everything around and just concentrate on doing it. I was always glad when they were over.

The next day I did David Frost's television programme—which went fine—and then went to Balmoral for the traditional weekend, except that this time, of course, it was anything but the run-of-the-mill visit.

Balmoral Castle was built in the 1840s by Prince Albert for his wife and queen, situated between the villages of Ballater and Braemar. It is magnificent, the grounds simply stunning, and although the September weather is normally awful up there, it can be quite pleasant. On a sunny day, there is no more beautiful part of the world than that part of Scotland. The castle itself is very Victorian. There are no huge chambers or halls, the rooms are of moderate size, and some of the toilets are still the old water closets; not many are en suite, as they say.

I have to say I found the experience of visiting and spending the weekend a vivid combination of the intriguing, the surreal and the utterly freaky. The whole culture of it was totally alien of course, not that the royals weren't very welcoming. But I never did "country house" or "stately home" weekends and had a bit of a horror of the notion.

The walls are hung with the English painter Edwin Landseer's pictures of stags, scenes of hunting and of course Queen Victoria's servant Mr. Brown. There are footmen—in fact very nice guys, but still footmen. When I arrived for the first time on that Sunday, the valet—yes, you got your own valet—asked me if he could fold my clothes and generally iron the underpants and that type of thing, and so disconcerted me that when he then asked me if he could "draw the bath," I lost the thread completely and actually thought for a moment he wanted to sketch the damn thing. Using the bathroom on the other side of the corridor was a singular act of courage, sneaking open the bedroom door, glancing right and left and then making for it at speed.

There was a routine to everything. There was a proper afternoon tea, and the Queen would pour with, needless to say, a proper strainer, and a kettle was kept bubbling away so that the pot could be filled up. Breakfast was likewise straight out of Trollope, or, perhaps better, Walter Scott. Eggs, bacon, sausage, kidneys, tomatoes, kedgeree and kippers, all kept on a hotplate. Breakfast was huge. Lunch was huge. Dinner was huge. If you indulged thoroughly, you could have put on a stone in a weekend, but the royals never did. I always noticed that they ate very little.

The blessing was the stiff drink you could get before dinner. Had it been a dry event, had the Queen been a teetotaller or a temperance fanatic, I don't believe I could have got through the weekend. But this stuff—I was never quite sure what it was—was absolutely what was needed. It hit the spot. It was true rocket fuel. The burden and the head got lighter. The courage returned. The easy conversational intercourse with the royal family seemed entirely natural. The first two annual visits were, nevertheless, trying at all levels.

The second weekend, in 1998, was the anniversary of Diana's death and there was a service at Craithie where, on this occasion, the whole royal family was assembled, the only time in my experience it ever happened. Individually, it can be a little nerve-racking to be with them; en masse, all of them and just Cherie and me, well, you can imagine. Cherie had suggested we bring Euan, Nicky and Kathryn, at which I laughed hysterically and said on no account. Euan, for one, had a near-genius capacity for winding people up, as with his constant questions to Cherie about women's equality, a bait to which she always rose. The blood froze at the thought of what he would say to the Queen, let alone the Queen Mother who was also there.

Later, we went for the traditional barbecue that Prince Philip cooks, held in one of the estate cottages. This, too, is governed by convention and tradition. The royals cook, and serve the guests. They do the washing-up. You think I'm joking, but I'm not. They put the gloves on and stick the hands in the sink. You sit there having eaten, the Queen asks if you've finished, she stacks the plates up and goes off to the sink.

I had also spoken to William, who was not only still grieving but angry. He knew, rationally, why the week between Diana's death and the funeral had to be as it had been, but he felt acutely the conflict between public position and private emotion. He knew now, if he didn't before, what being a prince and a king meant. For all the sense of duty, the prison walls of hereditary tradition must have seemed too high a price to pay.

On the first visit in 1997, the day after Diana's funeral, I was shown up to see the Queen in the drawing room, which was exactly as Queen Victoria had left it. I was just about to sit down in a rather inviting-looking chair when a strangled cry from the footman and a set of queenly eyebrows raised in horror made me desist. It was explained that it had been Victoria's chair and that since her day no one had ever sat in it.

There were just the two of us, and after all that had happened, of course the papers were full of "Blair tells Queen" stories. No matter how sensible people are or how high their position—and the Queen was very sensible and her position very high—it wasn't going to be easy. Indeed, one of the perpetual embarrassments at Balmoral used to be the Sunday papers laid out on the drawing-room table as you had pre-lunch drinks. Inevitably there would be some screaming headline about me or her, sometimes both of us, which would lie there prominent yet unmentionable. Over time, as the media looked to cause trouble, and without having much scruple about how they did it, there would usually be some "story" timed for those very weekends about me insulting Her Majesty; or missing the Highland Games, the Saturday event to which the prime minister is invited (which I fear we did); or going to the Games, where one time the camera caught Cherie yawning . . .

To reiterate, I barely knew the Queen at this point. Had it all happened some years later, I would have been at ease and found it perfectly fine, to be frank. At this encounter, with the recent events still raw and the relationship in its infancy, I felt nervous. She did too. I talked, perhaps less sensitively than I should have, about the need to learn lessons. I worried afterwards she would think I was lecturing her or being presumptuous, and at points during the conversation she assumed a certain hauteur; but in the end she herself said lessons must be learned and I could see her own wisdom at work, reflecting, considering and adjusting.

It was a surreal end to a surreal week. Tragic, fascinating, unforgettable.

For myself, I had come through with general approbation. A poll showed the absurd rating of 93 per cent approval. I had, at least, the sense to know it was unreal; and also the realisation that earth-shattering though in one way the death of Princess Diana was, the tests of achievement for a prime minister and a government were rather different.

SIX

PEACE IN NORTHERN IRELAND

C hurchill was a leader who never saw a problem without enthusiastically, often adventurously, charging forward in search of the solution; but on Northern Ireland he was bleak. Writing in 1922, with an elegant simplicity that came to define the British political establishment's view of Ireland, he stated that "The whole map of Europe has changed . . . but as the deluge subsides and the waters fall short, we see the dreary steeples of Fermanagh and Tyrone emerging once again. The integrity of their quarrel is one of the few institutions that has been unaltered in the cataclysm which has swept the world."

There had been centuries of hatred in which religion and disputed territory were mixed in an evil chemistry, followed by a failed attempt at devolution in the nineteenth century, followed by the partition of North and South in the 1920s, followed by the civil rights uprising of the 1960s that sparked a bitter and brutal conflict lasting decades. Numerous attempts at peace were made with an inconsistent focus but a resolutely consistent outcome: repeated failure. In a sense Churchill can be forgiven his unusual and uncharacteristic defeatism.

When I told John Prescott prior to the 1997 election that I was determined to give peace a go in Northern Ireland, he snorted with derision. The attempt by John Major to put together a peace process had just collapsed in renewed terrorism, but Major had rightly divined that there was indeed a chance for peace. He had begun clandestine negotiations with the IRA and had started to put together some of the elements that could go to make up an agreement. He had brought in Senator George Mitchell from the USA, an immensely shrewd and capable wise oldish bird, to help bring people into early negotiations, and a ceasefire had been put together.

Though it had not held, it was clear something was stirring in the undergrowth of the Republican movement.

It was about time. One of the most extraordinary aspects of the entire tragedy was that anyone ever seriously thought there was going to be a winner: that the IRA believed that a nation as proud as Britain could be bombed out of Northern Ireland, where a majority regarded themselves as citizens of the United Kingdom; that the British government ever believed Irish nationalism was containable without paradigm change in the treatment of Irish Catholics; that the Unionists ever believed that on an island where a majority supported a united Ireland and were Catholic nationalists, they could ever refuse to share power with them.

What happened in those circumstances is in essence what happens in countless such disputes: the unreasonable drives out reason, by the use of unreason. The way this happens is very simple: those who do not hate, who want peace, who are prepared to countenance "forgive and forget" (or at least "forget") become slowly whittled down in number, seeming unrealistic, even unpatriotic to other members of their group. What starts as an unreasonable minority ends up consuming the reasonable in its snares and delusions.

Terrorism causes chaos and death, but also hatred of the perpetrators among the group targeted by them; human nature being what it is, the victim group regards the perpetrator group, not just the perpetrators, as responsible; the perpetrator group becomes the victim, and so the ghastly spiral continues. Then "the authorities" intervene, and such intervention is also bloody. Once the soldiers and the police feel the force of terrorism, they too become first victims, then perpetrators themselves. People often forget that British soldiers were originally dispatched to Northern Ireland in the 1960s not to take on the Nationalists, but to protect them.

The hatred had become entrenched and horribly vicious over the centuries. Old victories were celebrated with contemporary relevance, and the savagery of one side's actions in history was remembered as defining their present and future character. During one of the interminable sessions in Downing Street, I remember David Trimble, then leader of the Ulster Unionist Party (UUP), waiting in the Cabinet Room as I saw Gerry Adams of Sinn Fein in the den. When Gerry and I ended our meeting and came through to the Cabinet Room, David was leafing through a book from the shelves. It was a biography of Cromwell, which he took great delight in flourishing under Gerry's nose. To the Brits, Cromwell is an important historical figure; to the Irish he was a bigot and a butcher. I recall one meeting I had with Gerry and Martin McGuinness, a member of Sinn Fein and of the devolved Northern Ireland leadership, at Chequers. Cromwell's daughter had married the owner of Chequers, and the place is stuffed with Cromwell memorabilia. Showing Martin round, we came across Cromwell's death mask. "So you see," I said, "he really is dead."

"I wouldn't bet on it," he replied.

A culture had grown up around the dispute. The Unionists didn't simply have a political disagreement with the Nationalists, nor simply a religious difference; they had different music, a different way of speaking, a different attitude, a different nature. Naturally there was the Protestant/Catholic divide, and that too had cultural as well as religious connotations, but any theological dispute had long since been subsumed in the tribal one. Ulstermen (and it was all very male) were men of few words, literal, strongly spoken but polite, with a humour all their own and a tendency, not always unfounded, to distrust the world. The Irish were gregarious, flamboyant, of many colourful words, preferring to talk in generalities rather than particulars, with a keen sense not only of their status as victims but also of the wider world being more in tune with them than with their victimisers.

On one visit to Northern Ireland, I saw a remarkable demonstration of how the culture of opposition is enforced. Sinn Fein had invited the Palestinians to town. As I landed to stay overnight, I saw the Palestinian flag displayed along the Republican roads of Belfast, to welcome their guests. Next day I drove through the town to leave, and I saw arrayed along Unionist enclaves the white-and-blue flags of Israel. How they had got them, and how they had put them up overnight, I'll never know, but the moment those Palestinian flags went up, Unionist solidarity with Israel was total.

Ireland was also in my blood. My mother was from Donegal. Though living in the South, her family were Protestant farmers—fiercely Protestant. Her father had been a Grand Master of one of the Orange lodges, the largest Protestant organisation in Northern Ireland. An extraordinary example of the enduring nature of sectarianism was to be found in my maternal grandmother. She was a lovely woman, but was very much of her time and tribe, and in those days bigotry was unfortunately accepted as the norm. Later in life she had Alzheimer's, but one day as I visited her at her sickbed she had a startling moment of lucidity.

I had just begun to date Cherie. Obviously my grandmother had no knowledge of this, and indeed she did not really recognise me any more. As I patted her hand, she suddenly grabbed mine, opened her eyes wide and said: "Whatever else you do, son, never marry a Catholic." Everything else had disappeared from her mind, but left at the bottom was the residue of sectarian aversion.

We used to go to Ireland each year for our holidays to visit Mum's relatives. I loved those holidays. We would usually go to the Sandhouse Hotel at the resort of Rossnowlagh, near Ballyshannon. At that beach I learned to swim in the freezing Atlantic Ocean. I had my first go at chasing girls, aged about eleven. I was taught my first chords on the guitar. I drank my first Guinness.

The relatives were slightly strange, truth be told. There was Aunt Mabel, with one tooth. Then there was the even odder Great-Aunt Lizzie, who lived in a house at the top of the hill and was a miser. She wasn't just tight-fisted, she was an authentic miser who was apparently rich beyond the dreams of avarice but kept it all hoarded away. A large part of the extended family's time and energy was engaged in devising ways to part Great-Aunt Lizzie from her fabulous wealth. The chances of doing so while she was alive were plainly remote, but the family had high hopes of the will and testament. Great-Aunt Lizzie was regularly visited to be checked out for signs of imminent demise.

I remember Mum taking my brother and me to see her. She had expressed a desire to see "the boys," which Mum took as a good sign. I had never met her, but her fame was huge and I was overcome with excitement at meeting a real-life miser. Just as we went in the house, Mum said to us both: "Now look, Aunt Lizzie's house smells a bit." She paused. "Actually, a lot. YOU ARE NOT TO COMMENT ON IT. What's more," she went on, "Aunt Lizzie is giving us tea. If there are cakes, you eat them. YOU EAT THEM," she repeated.

"That's all right, Mum, I like cakes," I said.

She shot me a look. "Hmm," she said.

To this day, I mean honestly to this day, I can get neither the pong nor the cake out of my mind. The smell was a sickly, sweet, rancid odour that overwhelmed the senses, illuminating the true meaning of the word decay. The cake was obviously a relic of Great-Aunt Lizzie's last generous tea gathering, or possibly the one before. The combination of the smell and the cake made my stomach heave every so often as I sat there, until Great-Aunt Lizzie told my mother I was evidently not a well child. Even now as I write these words, I feel sick.

As we left the house—a little earlier than intended, since Mum began to worry that I really would throw up—I said to her: "But surely if she's a miser, she won't want to leave her money to anyone," an opinion that, as my mother remarked after Great-Aunt Lizzie died leaving us precisely nothing, was perceptive beyond my years.

Ireland was not just in my blood, but part of my experience growing up. We had friends there we saw every year. Then in 1969 we suddenly stopped going. It was not safe, Mum decided. The Troubles had begun.

I kept in correspondence with the friends, and their letters told me of how the bitterness was entering the stream of public sentiment. They were Protestant, of course. They described with increasing venom the gradual deterioration of their relations with, and then their view of, their Catholic neighbours, so I had some small but nevertheless direct understanding of the dispute.

Over the years, Britain would wake many mornings to the news of the latest terrorist attack or sectarian killing or a soldier's death or the further disintegration of community intercourse between Unionists and Nationalists. Ian Paisley—whom my grandmother revered—became a household name. As the 1970s rolled on into the 80s and 90s, the names of the failed peace attempts became imprinted on our consciousness. The reputations of the key players with whom I was to find peace were hammered out on the anvil of sectarian strife in this period: Gerry Adams and Martin McGuinness, John Hume, David Trimble, John Taylor, Peter Robinson and Paisley himself, naturally. They were part of it all, helped shape it all and created much of its history and its mythology.

Sometimes we forget the brutality of it: the torture; the maiming; the sheer, unadulterated vastness of the hatred. I thought of the hunger strikers often, particularly Bobby Sands, starving himself to death. I think of the pain, the unendurable horror, the blind courage required for such an act of self-destruction, realised not in a moment but over days and weeks of agony. People did things to each other and to themselves that now we can only look on with a sense of astonishment. For decades, such barbaric atavism defined Northern Ireland.

Why on earth did I think it could be settled? Jonathan Powell always used to put it down to what he referred to (I think jokingly) as my Messiah complex, i.e. I thought I could do what no one else could. In fact, it wasn't that. Or, at least, it may have been, but there was another reason too: I thought it was no longer in anyone's interest to tolerate conflict, not in Northern Ireland, but more important, not outside it. I thought the whole thing had become ridiculously old-fashioned and out of touch with the times in which the island of Ireland lived.

You might wonder what I mean by "no longer in anyone's interest to tolerate conflict." When was it ever? Of course, for the people inside Northern Ireland it never was, but it was fuelled by bigotry and by the pain of the Troubles, the period of political conflict in Northern Ireland. For the external world, the dispute in Northern Ireland was one in which too often people could express their emotional connection without ever having to live with the consequences, rather like the Palestinian cause. I don't mean by this that they actively sought to prolong the conflict, but they saw it pretty much from one side only. It was a rallying point. For communities with an Irish pedigree, it reminded them of their roots. They didn't really think it could be solved, so they never rallied to making peace.

Parts of the Irish-American community were a prime example. Thousands of miles from a lawlessness which they would never have tolerated for an instant, they would reflect on Irish history and folklore, the iniquities of the British, the cause of their kith and kin, and happily raise money used to kill innocent civilians and British soldiers.

The gallant attempts by Gladstone, Asquith and then Lloyd George to resolve the issue by devolution within the United Kingdom—which in the late nineteenth and early twentieth centuries undoubtedly could have worked (and nearly did)—were repeatedly broken on a wheel of sometimes opportunistic and always prejudiced rabble-rousing by Unionists and Tory MPs. Even great figures like F. E. Smith were prepared to use the dispute to cripple a United Kingdom government they did not like. For the politics of the Irish Republic, it was a useful unifying theme, giving point and purpose to the fledgling state as it gradually built itself. In the Second World War, Ireland was neutral, even mildly anti-British, though many brave and great Irishmen volunteered to fight the Nazis.

But times were changing as the modern world took form around us. Old attitudes clashed with new realities which had a youthful vigour. American statesmen like Teddy Kennedy began to dream of an Ireland at peace. Republican congressmen, who worshipped Margaret Thatcher and lauded her friendship with President Reagan, began to think it a trifle odd that they were supporting people who were actively trying to kill her. For British governments of whatever persuasion, the drain on resources and military manpower which Northern Ireland required made any prospect of peace extremely attractive.

But most of all, the Irish had changed, and with it attitudes to them. It is hard to understand now how the Irish were regarded by many British and Unionists. They were the butt of jokes, all revolving around stupidity. They were dismissively labelled "the bog Irish," to be employed as a builder's labourer but not in a bank. They were often regarded, I am ashamed to say, rather as some whites in South Africa regarded blacks in the era of apartheid: as inherently inferior. It seems incredible now, yet at one time it was true. And their politics were defined by the legacy of their relationship with Britain.

In the 1980s and later under Albert Reynolds with Bertie Ahern as a reforming finance minister, the Irish embarked on a remarkable process of self-transformation. They had joined the European Union and with the benefit of its generous programme of development, which they used with adroit intelligence, the country modernised. Dublin became a thriving go-ahead European city, and the economy boomed. U2 became one of the world's biggest bands, Bob Geldof was a hero, Roy Keane became the best football player of his time. Irish business, Irish art, Irish culture, in short Irish everything took off.

In the space of a few years it was no longer the backward old South that was looked down upon, but the North. The South was sprinting down the track towards the future, while the people of Northern Ireland were hanging around the starting blocks arguing about Protestants and Catholics in a way that obscured the race ahead in mists of irrelevance.

This was the factor that I thought gave us a chance of peace. For the Republic this was no longer a dispute to be clung to as a unifying symbol of Irish identity, but a painful and unwelcome reminder of Ireland's past. For decades, also, Unionists could point to Irish economic backwardness and their cultural and religious differences as making a fit between the two impossible. Now these elements were either fading or being reversed.

Even before taking office, I was working out a strategy. One of the first things I did on becoming Labour leader was to change our long-standing policy position on Northern Ireland. The Labour Party policy had for years been to try to negotiate a peace deal between Unionists and Nationalists on the grounds that we believed in a united Ireland and could be a persuader for it. It didn't take a political mastermind to realise that such a position wholly alienated Unionist opinion, and in doing so disabled any attempt to negotiate a deal based on that premise.

I knew I could never get a policy change through the party's usual policymaking machinery—certainly at that time—so I'm afraid I just popped up one morning on the *Today* programme not long after becoming leader and announced we would henceforth have a new policy: neutrality on the issue of a united Ireland or a United Kingdom. I also replaced Kevin McNamara, Shadow Secretary of State for Northern Ireland—a really lovely man but wedded to the old policy—with Mo Mowlam, who had held a junior Northern Ireland position under John Smith.

I then put us basically in a bipartisan position with John Major, fully supporting his foray into peacemaking. At the time, the bipartisan approach was very rare, partly because of the sharp moves to left and right of Labour and Tories, but also because it was thought to be bad politics. John Smith, however, had cannily backed Major in talking secretly with the IRA.

I decided to make it a full-blown demonstration not just of a change in Northern Ireland policy, but of a change in approach to being in Opposition. As I expected, people thought it mature politics; no one believed Northern Ireland should be a focus of partisan point-scoring. We held this approach up to and through the 1997 election. I cultivated ties with David Trimble and the Unionists. I sent messages showing interest in Sinn Fein. I met Bertie Ahern, also a Leader of the Opposition, and we got on immediately like the proverbial house on fire. The Taoiseach John Bruton, prime minister of the Republic of Ireland, was a great guy but was plainly going to lose.

Our victory of 1 May 1997 had released new energy everywhere. Challenges that mired a tired and psychologically demoralised government now inspired an energetic and confident team to have a go. I often reflect that such audacity could only be given wing in the first flush of enthusiasm that greets a profound moment of change.

The first few weeks taught me a lot about the nature and complexity of this challenge. While I was at my first European summit, news came through that the IRA had killed two off-duty police officers, shot in the head as they walked down the street. Two lives ended; two families in mourning. I was repelled. I had sent warning messages to the Sinn Fein leadership before the election. It didn't seem a wildly optimistic start.

I had also decided that my first major speech as prime minister would be on the subject of Northern Ireland and peace. I had been mulling over what to say for some time even before the election, and had talked about it with David Trimble. Once in Downing Street, the diplomat John Holmes, who had done sterling work under Major, joined us and became an integral part of the team. Jonathan Powell was the key operative in the government effort from the outset.

I was never entirely sure why or how Jonathan became so important on the issue, but he did. You can always exaggerate in such situations and say "Had it not been for so-and-so this would never have happened," but in this instance it is no less than the unvarnished truth. Without him, there would have been no peace. Every talent he had—and he has many—seemed to be displayed to best effect in pursuit of this peace agreement. He was diligent, quick-witted, insightful, persistent, inventive and above all trusted—in so far as anyone was—by both sides. He and Adams struck up a genuine friendship. The Unionists respected him and he got the best out of the Northern Ireland Office, the UK department that ran government business in Northern Ireland, which all parties affected to despise and which was the object of innumerable complaints, but which in fact did a superb job in well-nigh impossible circumstances. His invariable calmness was also a great foil for the mood swings which Northern Ireland produced in me.

I say invariable, but there was one meeting which I had on the Drumcree madness when he erupted in a way I had never seen before. The Drumcree people were the unreasonable of the unreasonable of the unreasonable. In the premier league of unreasonableness, they left every other faction, in every other dispute, gasping in their wake. There was one guy, Breandan MacCionnaith, who represented the residents of the Garvaghy Road . . . But first let me explain Drumcree in a nutshell.

The Unionist marches often went through Catholic and even Republican areas. Not unreasonably the Nationalists and Republicans didn't like it. Somewhat unreasonably they wanted them banned. Wholly unreasonably the marches would provoke violence. Of the several hypersensitive routes, Drumcree was the most sensitive. Part of the route of the annual march there went down over a hundred yards of Garvaghy Road, a highly Republican neighbourhood. There was a Parades Commission that had to decide whether to allow it or not, and then the police, poor things, had to keep order.

The whole thing was a nightmare. Banning it caused tens of thousands of Unionists to take to the streets. Allowing it caused riots in

Republican areas. Part of the peace process was trying to resolve it. The residents were led by this Breandan MacCionnaith. He was so unreasonable that in the end I became rather intrigued by him, much to Jonathan's disgust. He took unreasonableness to an art form. He conceded nothing, and I mean nothing. I'm not just talking about the substance of meetings, I mean where a meeting should be held. Who should be there. Who shouldn't be there. When it began. When it ended. What its purpose was. Who spoke first. Who spoke last. Who spoke in between first and last.

A great belief of mine is that when you are negotiating with someone, the first thing is to set the atmosphere at ease; signify a little glimmer of human feeling; exchange a few pleasantries; and above all start by saying something utterly uncontroversial with which disagreement is impossible. Get the other person's head nodding. It's that nod which establishes rapport, and which is an early, tiny sign that all is not lost. I might say: "I know you feel strongly about this." Well, of course they do; that's why there's a dispute; and there would be a nod.

Breandan MacCionnaith was completely and totally nodless. If I said to him, "I know you feel strongly about this," he would say, "I don't feel more strongly about this than anything else." So I'd say, "Yes of course, sorry, but obviously you do have strong feelings." "Who are you to tell me about my feelings?" he would reply. When I said that the purpose of the meeting with Orangemen (members of the Orange Order or lodge) and residents was that we could resolve the dispute satisfactorily for everyone so that peace broke out, he said, not a bit of it; the purpose was to dispatch the Orange Order and their oppressive provocation of ordinary decent residents on the Garvaghy Road to the dustbin of history, or some such. In the end I would say, "What about . . ." and then pause, just to hear him start to say "No" before I'd even explained the proposition. If I tell you Breandan MacCionnaith didn't stand out dramatically for his unreasonableness (though he did ultimately clinch gold medal), you might understand how unreasonable all parties were.

Strangely it was with the Orange Order that Jonathan lost his cool. We were having one of those interminable, circular and unproductive meetings around whether, where, how the march might be done, and the Orange Order (in the main fairly polite) were making their points. One of them made a childish remark about my involvement. Suddenly I became aware of a rumbling to my right followed by Jonathan leaping to his feet, virtually throwing himself across the table, face red with anger, shouting: "How dare you talk to the British prime minister like that? How dare you?"

We were all speechless with amazement. Except Jonathan, who was full of speech, somewhat repetitive but making his point with great clarity. The Orange Order chap was quite shaken. So was I. As I say, I'd never seen him like that before. We had some words afterwards along the lines of "You should have taken your tablets this morning," and I've never seen him like that since. No one ever quite behaved normally around the issue of Northern Ireland. The incident also raised an interesting reflection on the nature of the PM's job: you have to absorb a large amount of abuse. Not crude shouting down or protests, but your motives constantly questioned or traduced, your words misunderstood or misrepresented, your attempts to do good seen as attempts either to further your own interests or even to do bad.

I had a constant problem of trust, mostly with Unionists but often with the other side too. It derived partly from the necessarily tricky path that had to be woven through the hazardous thickets of Northern Irish politics, and deals of every description—side, secret and surface—abounded; but it was more to do with the general point that people find it hard to accept political leaders might genuinely be trying to help. So, in respect of Northern Ireland, you might think the involvement relatively selfless: the conflict was *the* issue in Northern Ireland (no Labour voters there) but not really an issue in United Kingdom politics (indeed, the more you solve it the less salient it becomes); fantastically difficult; inordinately time-consuming. In terms of pure political self-interest, stakes high if you failed, low if you succeeded.

Yet all the way through the process, the good faith of the government, never mind its good government, was in question. In the end I decided people operate at two levels in relation to political leadership. At one level, they vest all their hopes, expectations and, most of all, once in government, their frustrations on the leader. You are the focal point, and therefore the focal point for criticism. At this level you aren't measured against a reasonable yardstick but against perfection. Unsurprisingly, you fall short.

However, at another level, less visible but real, people indeed take a more mature view and if you are really trying, you get credit for it. Nevertheless, as I say, a great capacity for absorbing abuse was a necessary part of the job.

There was another trait that served me well in Northern Ireland. I don't really get on my high horse. I am not big on the "dignity of office" stuff. I rested my authority on motivating and persuading people, not frightening them. It's possible I took this too far, at times, and it may also be true that on occasions a bit of hauteur and bossing, even bullying, would have served me better, but there it is: it's my nature. In Northern Ireland, it worked. People could be really very insulting without much provocation, yet if you fell out with them over it, the consequences could be unpredictable. So by and large I didn't.

In those first months after taking office, I was trying to give shape to our strategy. I made the speech at the Royal Ulster Agricultural Show on 16 May and deliberately set out to woo and bring onside Unionist opinion. The setting itself was indicative—right in the heart of the Unionist community. Acting on David Trimble's advice, I made it clear I valued the Union and then, in a passage that caused a lot of sucking through teeth, said that I doubted we would see a united Ireland in the lifetime of anyone present. Since some of those present were in their twenties, it was quite a bold pro-Union statement. It was the weirdest place to give a major speech, in a tent where outside prize bulls jostled with ruddy-faced farmers while the potential future of the land was being made.

Despite the murders of the two police officers (and the IRA sent messages essentially saying it had been unauthorised), we gave the IRA five weeks to renew the ceasefire, which in the past eighteen months had lapsed. This they did on 19 July 1997.

Weeks later the British and Irish governments agreed to establish an Independent International Commission on Decommissioning (IICD). The issue of decommissioning was one very unfortunate legacy from the previous administration which was to become a big ball and chain round our legs in the years to come. Under Unionist pressure, John Major had agreed that a vital precondition of peace and power-sharing was for the IRA not merely to embrace peace but to decommission their weapons. Of course, at one level this is entirely reasonable: if you are for peace, you don't need weapons; but on another level, it carried an implication for the IRA of surrender, of not merely embracing peace but of apologising for ever having been to war, and it complicated their internal management horribly. Gerry Adams and Martin McGuinness were trying to bring their movement with them. Like all such situations, there was a spectrum of Republican opinion. There were real hardliners. They would stay hardliners. The important thing was not to let them have traction on the middle ground. The prospect of the IRA being forced to destroy their weapons gave them such traction, but there it was; to renege on John Major's commitment was impossible, so it just had to be managed. The IICD bought us some time and space.

George Mitchell had been doing great work drawing up principles of non-violence and common positions—a commitment to exclusively peaceful means for all parties in government, for example, things that were broad but set a framework for the much bigger negotiation to come—and had been chairing talks before we came to office. Sinn Fein immediately said they would abide by the Mitchell principles, but the IRA refused to give the same commitment. That didn't exactly reassure Unionists, but we persevered and identified three strands to the negotiation which had begun when John Major was prime minister: how Northern Ireland would be governed under a devolved system of power-sharing; relations between the United Kingdom and Northern Ireland (East–West); and relations between the Irish Republic and Northern Ireland (North–South).

The talks began in September without David Trimble. Republican dissidents set off a bomb on the second day. On the third day, the Unionist parties other than the Democratic Unionist Party (DUP), Paisley's party, entered the talks.

There were further talks the next month and then I went over on 13 October to have my first meeting with Gerry Adams and Martin McGuinness. Up to then, no British prime minister had met either of them. It was a big moment. A crucial question was whether or not I shook hands with them (no Unionist leader did until 2007). I decided just to do the thing naturally. So they walked in, we shook hands.

When asked about it afterwards, I said I treated them like any other human being, but later the same day I got a taste of Unionist sentiment. I was invited by Peter Robinson, the DUP deputy leader, to visit a shopping centre in his constituency. I was never sure whether he set me up or not. I'll assume not.

The place was full of the most respectable elderly grannies doing the shopping. Like something out of a bad dream, however, they suddenly morphed into very angry protesting grannies, shouting, swearing, calling me a traitor and waving rubber gloves in my face. I was perfectly happy to listen to them, but the Royal Ulster Constabulary (RUC)—with what I thought was a trifle too much eagerness—turned it into a major security incident and physically carried me into a room for my own safety.

Amusingly, I didn't get what the rubber gloves were about at all. I thought they had just finished doing the washing-up or something. When I told Jonathan, he roared with laughter and said, "No, it's because you should have worn rubber gloves when shaking hands with Gerry Adams."

The next few months were a complicated trek through a very dense and dangerous jungle, as we tried to get to the uplands where we could see our way to a negotiated deal. Our path was constantly, though fortunately temporarily, barred by unhelpful events. One Loyalist group reinstated their ceasefire. Good. Then another Loyalist group broke theirs and had to be excluded from the talks. Bad. In February 1998 there was a real crisis when the IRA killed two people in Derry. Sinn Fein were excluded for seventeen days. Then the dissident Republican group the Irish National Liberation Army killed Billy Wright, the Loyalist Volunteer Force leader, inside the Maze prison. More upheaval.

Throughout I was never off the phone to David Trimble and Unionist leaders, desperately holding them in while, not entirely unreasonably, they regarded the continual outbreaks of sporadic violence as somewhat inconsistent with the Mitchell principles.

To assuage Nationalist opinion and under pressure from the Irish, I also ordered an inquiry into the Bloody Sunday shootings in 1972, when British troops had opened fire on protestors in Belfast, killing a number of people. Nationalists claimed they were peaceful protestors. An inquiry at the time by Lord Widgery, the then Lord Chief Justice, was widely condemned as a whitewash and we agreed to meet the twenty-five-year demand to have another inquiry. It certainly assuaged opinion at the time. It also turned out to be a long-running saga, however, lasting twelve years at a cost of nearly £200 million. Until it reported in 2010, I considered it a classic example of why you should never conduct inquiries into anything unless utterly impossible to resist, or in the most truly exceptional circumstances. They rarely achieve their aim. However, the report when published proved me wrong. It had been worth it, an exhaustive and fair account of what happened.

Somehow or other we staggered into early April when we had decided to try to broker agreement around the three strands that had been the basis of the talks under John Major. We fixed a date for the meeting. The fascinating thing about the Good Friday Agreement is that the way it came about was far more by accident than design. I was due to stay a day to give an agreed deal my endorsement, the detailed work having been done by officials. I ended up staying for four days and nights and engaging intimately in the detail of one of the most extraordinary peace negotiations ever undertaken. At critical points throughout those days the deal was lost; but in the end, and by the squeakiest of squeaks, we got it through. I can truthfully say I have never been involved in anything quite like it. And it did make history.

Talking of "history," there was a hilarious moment when I first arrived. I had heard from David Trimble on the phone the night before that although an immense amount of detailed work by officials had indeed been done, not only was none of it actually agreed, it also looked as if it was very unlikely to be agreed. I decided to be in practical, workmanlike, non-rhetorical mode when I addressed the press outside Hillsborough, the stately home that is the perquisite of the British Secretary of State for Northern Ireland. "Today is not a day for sound bites," I began eagerly, oozing impatience to get down to work and irritation with anything flowery or contrived. Then—and heaven only knows where it came from, it just popped into my head—I said, "But I feel the hand of history upon our shoulder," which of course was about as large a bite of sound as you could contemplate. In the corner of my eye I could see Jonathan and Alastair cracking up. I decided to say no more and quickly went back into the building before being taken to the negotiations, held at Castle Buildings at Stormont.

Stormont, the seat of the Northern Ireland government in the years following partition until the whole system collapsed, is typical of the extraordinary buildings with which Britain told the rest of the world of its own importance. Built in the early twentieth century, it is an imposing edifice with grounds to match and a grandeur that is impressive, stately and strong. Some lunatic, however, had decided that Castle Buildings—the modest annexe—should be where we met. There should be a warrant out for the person who designed it. There were next to no facilities, it was ugly, cramped and, worst of all, had no soul. I am rather sensitive to my surroundings. I love good design, find energy in beauty, particularly of architecture, and I like to work in an environment that pleases the eye and refreshes the soul. Castle Buildings was the antithesis.

However, never mind the damn building, it was clear that we had badly misjudged Unionist readiness to deal. Of course David Trimble was under perpetual pressure from Ian Paisley, who turned up outside Castle Buildings to condemn the whole thing as a monstrous sell-out.

I had also taken the precaution of talking the evening before to John Alderdice, the leader of the cross-community Alliance Party. John was the thoroughly reasonable leader of a thoroughly reasonable party, which meant they stood no chance of winning. Nonetheless, they exercised some swing influence in the centre and John, especially, was a quality politician who knew the Unionist community well. He told me bluntly the thing was a non-starter for David Trimble.

I went up to the room on the fifth floor that was to become my living quarters, my cell, for the next few days. I beetled along the corridor to see George Mitchell, who was in jovial mood but somewhat unnerved me by telling me jauntily that he thought the deal was undoable.

I took the decision then and there to take complete charge of the negotiation. I spoke again to David Trimble, who was in favour of leaving things until after Easter. I started going through the detail of what he needed. The previous night I had familiarised myself with the complexities of the different strands of negotiation. It was like being back at the Bar reading up the next day's brief. I am lucky in being able to digest a large amount of information quickly, an invaluable training which the law really provides.

One myth about me is that I prefer the broad brush to the detail. In truth, it's impossible as prime minister to be across the detail of everything, and in addition, too much detail creates an immediate wood/trees problem. But sometimes—at moments of crisis or negotiations like this, or some of those back-breaking European treaties or Budget agreements—the detail is absolutely of first importance. At such times, I would immerse myself in detail.

I did so now, and just as well. David had pages of amendments, and, naturally, one side's improvement to the text would be the other side's loss. With not much genuine basis for so doing, I promised David I would deliver what he needed.

I next got hold of Bertie, who had just arrived. Bertie is one of my favourite political leaders. Over time he became a true friend. He was heroic throughout the whole process, smart, cunning in the best sense, strong and, above all, free of the shackles of history. That is not to say he had no sense of history; on the contrary, his family had fought the British, had been part of the Easter Uprising, were Republicans through and through; but he had that elemental quality that defines great politicians: he was a student of history, not its prisoner.

His mother—to whom he was close—had just died, and the previous night he had watched over her body. It was good of him to come at all. Now he had to contend with me telling him that the North–South part—i.e. the all-Ireland part, so dear to his constituents—would have to be rewritten. It was not the news he wanted, but here's where Bertie showed his mettle and his character.

On 7 April 1998—and many times later in the years to come—he could have put the traditional past perspective of his country before a living, evolving vision of its future. Instead, he chose repeatedly to put the future first. His support and his ingenuity were recurring mainstays of the progress in the search for peace. His officials were really capable, and they took their cue from him. His presence and mine, his personality and mine, in a way symbolised the new, modern realities which were extinguishing old attitudes. In a sense we personified the opportunity to escape our history, British and Irish, and move on. Nonetheless, he left me in no doubt that rewriting the North–South pact would be a blow to the Nationalist side.

The next thing was to see David Trimble with his full team. Here was a strange phenomenon about the difference between the two sides. When you saw the Republicans, you saw unity in motion. They had a line; they took it; they held it. If it appeared to modify in the course of a meeting, it was an illusion—the modification had been pre-built into the line, and the line was sustained. Gerry Adams was the leader. You would no more have had one of the delegation raising eyebrows during his remarks, let alone uttering words of dissent, than you would have had Ian Paisley leading a rousing chorus of "Danny Boy." Per contra, the UUP had the most alarming way of conducting meetings. You would think you had them all jolly and sorted and then one of them, usually not the leader, would make a depressing or downbeat comment and helter-skelter they would all follow in leaping off the cliff. Even more alarmingly, it could happen on the most apparently minor issue. As for supporting their leader, they didn't regard that as their job. At all. Not merely eyebrows, whole hairlines would be raised in mock bemusement as their leader spoke, generally insinuating that whatever he might be saying, don't let that kid you for a moment they were going down that path.

They also had an innate and powerful tendency to think they were being had. It wasn't always without justification, but that wasn't the point. That's just how they were. David Trimble would go back and explain what he thought was a reasonable outcome, only to be clattered around the head with innumerable objections, qualifications, additional points, amendments, requests for clarification and so forth.

Whenever I used to think leading the Labour Party was hard, I would think of David and feel grateful.

Having conceded a lot to David, I thought we might get a smooth enough ride with him and his colleagues in delegation. I was quickly disabused of such a fond notion. Ken McGuinness, a big, hale, hearty and actually rather decent man, who was in charge of security for them, had a whole new raft of changes. Disconcerted, I tried to accommodate them. Then Reg Empey, David's deputy, began the helter-skelter by saying: Why not take the whole thing off the table and start all over again? The room swayed. I sent Jonathan off to talk to Ken about security, and pretended Reg hadn't said what he said (which was hard since he kept repeating it). I was throwing concessions around like confetti, since I knew the danger was they would just march out. Putting off until tomorrow what you didn't want to do today had served Unionists well for decades, if not centuries. I knew delay was fatal.

I had a now-or-never sense. Truth be told, at that point I would have bet the house on "never." Jonathan, though, was insanely upbeat and said it could be done. Bertie had had to return home for his mother's funeral. When he got back, he just took the decision that he would agree to the North–South amendments. It was a big step. He simply took it. Progress!

We then got the Irish and UUP in the one room—my office—to talk it through. Bertie's decision gave the Unionists heart. We decided overnight that they should come up with an agreed text.

Jonathan and I got a couple of hours' sleep after meeting other parties (all of them had to be seen regardless of whether or not they could add anything, because otherwise backs were put up and feet might walk). When we returned, to our consternation the Irish and UUP had only talked around the issue and had not agreed anything. Frantic work ensued. I decided to let the UUP draft a text and the Irish amend it. By midday we had what I thought was an agreed text, and on the trickiest of issues.

Foolish thought. I said that the Republicans showed military discipline in presenting their case and supporting their leader. That is true, but they weren't the only party on the Irish side. There was the Irish government and the Social Democratic and Labour Party (SDLP), the moderate Nationalist party, and they would be locked in the same frenetic dance with each other as were the Unionists. The SDLP thought that they often got ignored because we were too busy dealing with Sinn Fein. "If we had weapons you'd treat us more seriously" was their continual refrain. There was some truth in it. The big prize was plainly an end to violence, and they weren't the authors of the violence. Their real problem was that strategically they decided they would never go into government with the Unionists unless Sinn Feinn were at the table too. This was understandable, because in the past Sinn Fein had collapsed the show by claiming the SDLP were selling out. They therefore had somewhat of the same problem the UUP had with the DUP.

Nonetheless, it meant that they gave up their trump card. They used to attack me for "handing Sinn Fein the veto," but actually *they* had, since without Sinn Fein there could be no government with the SDLP. But the point was this: they were always looking to stymie Sinn Fein if they could. When Bertie had told the Irish side—for these purposes the whole spectrum of Irish opinion—the concessions he'd made, they revolted.

The result was, in the afternoon, the thing fell apart. Again Bertie came to the rescue. I explained we could not now go back to the UUP with the old text. They would walk. Reluctantly he agreed they would negotiate on the basis of the UUP draft, and faced everyone else down.

Once that happened, on Strand One (the governing of Northern Ireland) the Unionists conceded to work off the SDLP proposals. Crucially—and this was David Trimble's huge contribution—they agreed that there would be a system guaranteeing genuine power-sharing across Assembly voting and in the Executive. (The Northern Ireland Assembly has full authority to make laws and take decisions on the functioning of the Northern Ireland government departments. It also elects members of the Executive, which has the responsibility for administration.) Up to then, Unionism had always said it should be a majority vote, ignoring that, practically speaking, this could mean supremacy of the majority, i.e. them, in Northern Ireland. Instead, now there would need to be cross-community support for things to happen and the government seats on the Executive would have to be shared out fairly.

The thing started to come together again. We breathed a sigh of relief. Again too soon. Sinn Fein had resented the way the SDLP got agreement with the UUP. They felt cut out, and issued a press release that there would be no agreement.

At this point, I should say something about the world beyond the negotiating madhouse which we were inhabiting. We were in a cocoon. We might as well have been in outer space. As the hours then the days passed, I had little sense of the fact that outside Castle Buildings had gathered an army, a convocation, a full-blown live happening of the world's media. It was the start of 24-hour-a-day news, and they came in their droves, with a lot to say and nothing to say, if you get my meaning.

I didn't really imbibe the full purport of this until after the event, which is just as well, since had I thought about it, I would have quailed at the political risk we were taking. As time went on, the stakes became ever higher as it was clear I was putting my whole prime ministerial authority on the line for a deal. Failure was going to be not just bad, but potentially dangerous, with both streets—Unionist and Nationalist— inflamed, possibly literally.

Alastair and John Holmes, the other part of the team, were perform- ing to the highest standard. Alastair was rather brilliantly trying to feed the media beast without a lot of meat in the sandwich, conscious that one word out of place could provoke some party or other to feel slighted. John was the perfect foil for Jonathan and me, working up the detail, providing ideas, being brilliantly creative and letting us take care of the politics. Mo Mowlam was glad-handing and looking after people, but a little removed from the negotiations.

The moment Sinn Fein told the waiting hordes of media there would be no agreement, collective hysteria broke out. The result, as no doubt Gerry and Martin intended, was that we had to scuttle off to them and try to bring them back. They were negative. Martin bluntly said he couldn't recommend it. I suggested that they went away and came back with their amendments. I knew the Unionists would go nuts if they thought we were asking Sinn Fein for ideas on their docu- ment, but I couldn't think of another option. Everyone had to be kept in play. The see-saw was in a state of constant imbalance, as first this side and then that felt cheated, or taken advantage of, or let down.

Here I discovered another piece of bizarre psychology about the whole thing: it was a zero-sum game to all of them, and not only in terms of negotiating detail—"You suggest this. We oppose. You like this. We don't," etc. Walking around the building they would spot the other's expression. If one looked happy, the other looked for a reason to be sad. If one was down, the other immediately went up. It was unbe- lievable. At crucial moments, when we had just scrabbled one party back on board, I would be terrified in case they went out of the room look- ing satisfied in front of those waiting to come in for the next meeting.

We had one bonus, however: there were a huge number of different elements in the deal. At one level this complicated things, but at another it gave us lots of dimensions to play with. Unionists might feel unhappy with conceding on the way the Executive worked, but they could be brought round by a good deal on North–South bodies. There was always another card in the hand.

Sinn Fein came back with forty pages of detailed changes. I was aghast when I received the document. I used to be a lawyer; forty pages of amendments means a lot of negotiating. I assumed all were to be taken seriously, and needless to say, they would have made Unionist hair curl and would have unified their delegation. It was here that Mo played an important part in the negotiation. Mo's idea of negotiating with Sinn Fein was rather smart. She heard them out, took receipt of the document, as it were, then ignored the overwhelming majority of the points, focusing on the one or two things that might matter. The rest sort of fell by the wayside. It seemed very odd to me, but it worked.

The point which she correctly identified did matter was the IRA men behind bars for various terrorist acts and killings. She took an extraordinarily forward position on this. Basically, she thought the issue not of enormous consequence to Unionism; after all, prisoners had been released before in the 1970s, and people more or less expected something similar. She offered Sinn Fein the release of them all within a year; they came back on board.

Then I started to reconsider. It seemed to me inherently implausible that Unionist opinion wouldn't object to "IRA killers" being out on the street. I asked Alastair, who thought the notion abhorrent to the British public, never mind Unionist Northern Ireland. I asked John Steele, a senior and very sensible Northern Ireland Office (NIO) official, who gave his view in civil servant language—which I was beginning to be able to translate—and told me the whole business was barking. (I think he said it wouldn't be "frightfully helpful.")

But I was stuck. I had agreed with Gerry that they would be released. I went back to him to renegotiate—never a good tactic. In the end, I did something very "Tonyish" and he did something very "Gerryish": I privately assured him we would do it in one year if the conditions allowed, but publicly and officially, it would be two. He agreed, and what's more, never called in the promise or used it publicly to embarrass me.

So: Irish government OK. UUP OK. SDLP satisfied. Sinn Fein back on board. We had an agreement. I called President Clinton and asked him to phone Gerry Adams to bind them in, which he did. He was a total brick throughout, tracking the negotiation, staying up all night, calling anyone he needed to call, saying anything he needed to say and much more besides, and being supremely on the ball, and typically, with that instant knack of his, getting right to the political nub.

The hours passed as we went back over the detail yet again, filling in the gaps, sorting out the administrative glitches, working at what we would say and with whom.

It was of course ludicrously optimistic to think we had an agreement. Even though we had carried on through the night, now having been almost forty-eight hours without sleep, the wretched see-saw slipped again in the early hours of Good Friday morning, 10 April 1998. The Irish—still fretting a little over how the North–South part would be received—added a section to that strand, creating two new North–South bodies (thus indicating Ireland would act on a unified basis) in the areas of trade protection and the Irish language.

Now you might think cooperation on these two issues would be relatively uncontentious. In fact the Unionists screeched to a halt. It turned out there was some obscure language called Ullans, a Scottish dialect spoken in some parts of Ulster which was the Unionists' equivalent of the Irish language. By this time, nothing surprised me. They could have suggested siting the Assembly on Mars and I would have started to draft options.

Everyone was now tired and fractious. I had an awful meeting with Bertie and David Trimble, in which Bertie did not take quite the same relaxed view of the importance of Ullans as I did, suggesting that maybe David would like to speak some of the "fecking thing" to hear what it sounded like; and David taking umbrage at the idea that the dialect was a Unionist invention, explaining solemnly and at length the Scottish roots of Ullans with all the sensitivity of a landowner talking to the village idiot.

The episode sent David Trimble's delegation down the helter-skelter, and fresh amendments started flying out. Alastair, meanwhile, had hinted to the media, who were now pretty fractious themselves, that we had an agreement, which in all good faith he thought we had. When I told him of the impasse, he expressed himself in terms of which only Alastair was capable, to the effect that if I thought he was now going to tell the world's media that contrary to what he had told them earlier, we had failed to secure an agreement after all because of a Scottish Ulster dialect called Ullans, and so the war in Northern Ireland would go on, such an announcement, on his part, was more than a tad unlikely. I was at my wits' end. Even calls from Bill Clinton yielded nothing. Here again, Jonathan was superb. He dealt with the Unionist concerns one by one, calmed their delegation, tried to put it back into balance.

We whittled it down to two issues—one real, the other surreal—but by now the border between the two was becoming harder to discern. The surreal issue was the Unionist desire to close down somewhere called Maryfield. At first there was confusion, since we thought that the Unionists were saying "Murrayfield" had to close, and even I winced at the prospect of demolishing the Edinburgh home of Scottish rugby that I had visited often as a teenager. But it was a measure of our now complete isolation in the negotiating cell that I neither asked why Unionism might want to erase a rugby pitch, nor was unprepared to do it.

After a few minutes, we elicited to my relief that Maryfield was in fact the name of the secretariat established under Mrs. Thatcher's hated Anglo-Irish Agreement in the 1980s. The secretariat basically did nothing, and in any event would be superseded by our agreement. Maryfield was just an office, so the whole business was entirely symbolic. Then it transpired they didn't simply want the secretariat shut—that would happen anyway—they wanted the physical building closed. "Fine, we'll use it for something else," I said.

"No," they said, "we want Maryfield shut. Closed. No longer in use. For anything."

It was as if the building had become a political manifestation of the dispute, which I suppose in a sense it had. By now, I didn't care. I would have taken a crane and concrete block round and demolished it myself if it meant they signed up.

The Northern Ireland Office cavilled. "Why do they need it closed? Can't we use it for filing?"

"Guys," I said, "please don't ask why. From now on Maryfield is a thing of the past. It's over. Part of history. Raze it to the ground." I never did find out what happened to it. Probably everyone forgot about it.

The serious issue was one in which I had a lot of sympathy for David. He and Unionism as a whole were worried that if the Republican movement reneged, if they failed to decommission, how would they be excluded from government? Of course, the Unionists could walk out; but, reasonably enough, they felt it shouldn't be them that would have to bring the thing down.

For Sinn Fein, any talk of exclusion was anathema. They had point-blank refused such a suggestion earlier. Reopen it now and we would lose the whole show. I explained to David. He went away crestfallen and his delegation walked into a closed session.

I sat and reflected with Jonathan. We were within inches, but I could tell it was not going to work. David couldn't swing it. Heaven knows what would be going on in that delegation room, but if it were positive, my Great-Aunt Lizzie was a philanthropist. "We've got to do something," I said. I was pacing the room. I had a thought. "Let's write him a letter, a side letter." The letter guaranteed that if within the first six months of the Assembly, Sinn Fein didn't deliver on decommissioning, we would support changing the provisions within the agreement to allow exclusion. It was very typical of the intricate nuance of the negotiation: we didn't say we *would* exclude, we said we would support changing the agreement so as to exclude.

We drafted at speed, Jonathan at his laptop, me dictating, and both Jonathan and John Steele offering comments. I signed it, and sent Jonathan racing down to the delegation room. At first he couldn't get in. Eventually, like the message from the governor halting the execution just before they turn the switch on, he brought it into the packed session. John Taylor, David Trimble's other deputy who by turns could be incredibly helpful or incredibly unhelpful, read it, looked up and said, "That's fine by me."

I sat in trepidation and anxiety for a further hour (not least because I'm afraid I had told none of the other parties about the side letter) while each member of the delegation gave their views. David called up to my room. "We're going to run with this."

We had a deal.

The next hours passed in a blur. We were beyond exhaustion, light-headed almost. George Mitchell announced the agreement. Bertie and I gave statements. There was general euphoria. At long last I was released from the hellhole Castle Buildings had become.

I had lost all sense of time. As I got into the car to drive away and the close protection team said we would be at the airport in twenty minutes, I realised with a start that I was off to Spain. Like all of us, I had thought this would be a quick negotiation and had booked a visit to Spain, taking up the invitation of the Spanish prime minister José María Aznar, whom I only knew slightly at that time, for me and my family to come and spend some days with him. I knew he was a tough negotiator and a strong, successful party leader, but little else. We were from different political families, he being leader of the Partido Popular, the Spanish Conservative Party, and I thought it worthwhile to get to know him. I knew about his toughness because we had been together at the Amsterdam Treaty negotiation at the end of May 1997, just weeks after I had come to power and a year into his first term.

In Amsterdam I had had all sorts of complicating demands, some correct, some hangovers from the previous government, and I was negotiating hard. It was my first international deal and I didn't want to mess up. José María had one major sticking point: he needed the treaty to reflect Spain's special position as the recipient of European support and as a "big" country along with other "bigs," not a "small." This was a real problem for the other "bigs," notably the Germans led by Helmut Kohl.

The Dutch tried the old tactic, with German encouragement, of leaving the Spanish demands till last. The idea was that you settled everyone else and then put the thumbscrews on the remaining recalcitrant, who got bullied or shamed into submission. "Europe needs you. How can you disturb Europe's stability at a moment like this? Have you no sense of history? Do you want to be responsible for a European failure?" etc. A load of old nonsense, but effective in a large number of cases.

But not with Aznar. They waited until everyone had settled into their roles at the negotiations, including me, and then offered him a compromise, not a bad one but not a good one. He said, no, I told you my terms. Ah, yes, but we need to know your bottom line, they said. That is my bottom line, he replied. He then said: I'm going into the next room to smoke a cigar. Which he promptly did.

They tried everything. Wim Kok, former prime minister of the Netherlands, went in and made his disapproval clear in a mildly Dutch Protestant way. Jacques Chirac tried to lord it over him in a very French way. Helmut Kohl finally rose to his feet and carried his considerable weight into the next room, looking like a juggernaut in search of a hedgehog. He came back mystified. The hedgehog had inexplicably refused to be squashed. Kohl turned to me. "You're new like him," he barked. "You go and try."

I went into where José María was sitting, just him, his interpreter and his cigar, on which he was puffing away as if he hadn't a care in the world. We dispensed with the interpreter and spoke French. I gave him a spiel about how important it was, how this negotiation hung in the balance, how only he could save the day, and ended by saying how truly disappointed everyone would be, especially Helmut, if he didn't compromise. "I know. I am so sad," he said with an enormous grin. "Can you give them a message from me? Tell them I said on what terms this treaty was acceptable to Spain and I said it at the beginning. And until now, they never asked me again. But if they had, I would have told them those were the terms acceptable to Spain. And look," he said, pulling something out of his pocket, "I have so many more cigars to smoke." He got his terms.

The family and I had been due to pass a few days before Easter with him. Such was my confidence on the Ireland negotiations—crazy, I know—that I decided to send Cherie, the kids and my mother-in-law on ahead, telling them I would join them shortly.

Now this was a real mark of Aznar. They arrived on the Wednesday, forty-eight hours before me, during which time he hosted them all with enormous kindness and effusive goodwill. I think I and most leaders would have been a tiny bit disconcerted having to entertain the family of another leader, and moreover a family they'd never met, with young kids to boot; but he took it all with perfect equanimity and it formed the basis of a lasting personal friendship that had important consequences at a later date.

At Belfast's RAF Aldergrove I somehow got onto the plane, and took a call from the Queen to congratulate me. I think until then I really hadn't understood the enormity of the achievement. I thought I bet she doesn't do this often, and indeed she doesn't. I then fell asleep for the whole journey.

It was the early hours of the morning when I finally crept into bed beside Cherie, who woke and also congratulated me. I slept again until mid-morning. When I got up I went in search of my host, only to find him somewhat alarmingly closeted with my mother-in-law. "Oh, you needn't have bothered turning up," she said, "we've sorted everything."

"Sorted what?" I said.

"Gibraltar of course," she said.

Well, she would have done as good a job as anyone.

After a couple of days with the Aznars we went to spend some time with Derry's friends Karin and Paco Peña—the flamenco guitarist—in Córdoba. I completely fell in love with Córdoba, a beautiful place. The Mezquita was the highlight, but the whole city was enchanting. Paco had a delightful old home in the centre of town with a traditional courtyard and, perhaps less traditionally, a barrel of sherry at the top of the stairs to the balcony, to slake the thirst of any passing guest. It was a week of wonderful relaxation. Paco taught me some classical guitar, we visited tapas bars and sherry vaults and generally passed an agreeable time.

The impact of the Good Friday Agreement, as it was already being called (except by Unionists who insisted in calling it the Belfast Agreement), reverberated around the world. I was constantly stopped and congratulated, and it was one of the few times in the job I can honestly say I felt content, fulfilled and proud. There weren't many more!

Back home, reality swiftly took hold. The thing is, the Good Friday Agreement was a supreme achievement—without it, nothing else could have been done—but it wasn't the end, it was the beginning. It was a predictor of the course that the peace process should take if all went well. The implementation then had to begin; and whereas the agreement could be described as art—at least in concept—the implementation was more akin to heavy manufacturing.

The first challenge was to have a referendum in the North and South endorsing the agreement and then an election in the Assembly so as to begin the procedure for getting a working Executive. The Northern Irish were, to be fair, hugely supportive of the agreement—at least as an idea. However, they didn't know the detail, and in the euphoria of the moment certainly hadn't contemplated the true ramifications. Very soon, they started to.

In a typical twist, the agreement was formally agreed to by the UUP, but never by Sinn Fein. The UUP might therefore have been expected to be the more upbeat, but no: as soon as the agreement was signed (fortunately David Trimble quickly got his party executive to endorse it), Unionist tremors, never far below the surface, broke out. Such doubts were magnified by the political equivalent of the Hubble telescope by what happened next.

The deal on prisoners included the power in the United Kingdom government to transfer IRA prisoners to the South. Rather unwisely, Mo decided to transfer from England to Ireland the "Balcombe Street Four," members of the notorious gang which had carried out assassinations and terror attacks for the IRA in the 1970s. Then the Irish government, having taken receipt of the prisoners, released them on parole to attend Sinn Fein's Dublin Conference without telling us. The prisoners received a ten-minute ovation on prime-time telly while Unionists looked on in utter horror.

It is true to say that that decision very nearly wrecked the train as it was leaving the station. It certainly put it on one rail for the duration of the referendum campaign and subsequent election to the Assembly, all of which had to happen within roughly ten weeks of the Good Friday Agreement being signed.

John Major and I visited to calm things. Then I went with William Hague, former leader of the Conservative Party. I wrote out pledges in my own hand, promising no seat in government for those of violence and other such things. Bill Clinton issued a statement of support from the G8 in Birmingham, which I was also chairing.

It was an anxious time. We got a majority of Unionists to back the agreement in the referendum (55 per cent to 45 per cent). David's party won the Assembly election over the DUP, and the SDLP were the second biggest party. But we had learned a lesson: there was still a long way to go. Although we had the map, we were miles from journey's end.

It took us another nine years to put it all together in a final working solution. Each of those years was fraught, and many times we were close to admitting failure. Deadlines were missed and negotiations over minutiae took months, but we kept going.

There was never again a negotiation as comprehensive as at Castle Buildings, but there was a constant stream of meetings over one, two or three days, which we usually tried to hold in a nice place. Looking back, it reads like a roll call of stately homes: Hillsborough, Weston Park, Leeds Castle, St. Andrews. The parties always feigned reluctance to be taken out of their natural habitat in order to have the discussions to move the process forward, but I had a hunch they were probably like me: if you were going to have a hellish time arguing back and forth, you might as well do it in a pretty environment. It also served to free people up, in some strange way—if we had had the meetings in the middle of Belfast or in Downing Street, people would cling to cherished positions, but somehow a new setting produced a new attitude. Or at least sometimes it did. Anyway, that was my justification for the partnership between the Northern Ireland peace process and something from the pages of *Country Life*.

I could go through, by chronology, all the tortured and tortuous steps between June 1998 and May 2007, but you can be grateful that I won't. Essentially it took another fifteen months or so, even after the June 1998 Assembly election, to get the Executive up and running. The Executive was chosen according to an erudite voting formula named after the Belgian mathematician d'Hondt (whose name can be added to the proud list of famous Belgians). Let me not attempt the impossible by explaining it to you. Suffice to say, it meant Martin McGuinness and another Sinn Fein member, Bairbre de Brún, became ministers, in charge of education and health respectively; itself a historic moment.

The reason for the delay in setting up the Executive was the endless wrangle over decommissioning. There was also a long-running dispute over policing, because in the new Northern Ireland the RUC had to be changed into something all parts of the province could accept. The process was suspended in February 2000, reinstated in May 2000 and lasted until October 2002 when, again over the IRA disarming and various other things, it was suspended. It stayed that way up to May 2007. In the meantime, Ian Paisley's DUP overtook David Trimble's party as the largest Unionist party, and Sinn Fein overtook the SDLP. It took approximately three and a half years of negotiation before the historic day dawned when Ian Paisley and Martin McGuinness sat down in government together and we could say the peace process, though not ended, had fructified.

But throughout the setbacks, the steps forward that were immediately displaced by steps back, the declarations succeeded by new declarations succeeded by clarifying declarations, the accusations against us were legion (usually all sides could agree at least on the perfidy of the British government). We experienced, as a modus vivendi, the roller coaster of emotions in which hope and despair coexisted on an almost daily basis.

The Good Friday Agreement came to be a vastly different exercise in negotiation, and the document vastly more compendious, than originally thought. If I hadn't been a (relatively) new prime minister, if I hadn't ended up, by a mixture of happenstance and good fortune (though it seemed at the beginning ill fortune), taking charge of the negotiation and then passing the point of no return in the search for a solution almost without knowing it, we would probably never have reached agreement.

Every conflict is, of course, different—each has its own genesis, its opposing traditions, its shared history, its variegated array of dimensions to resolve—so lessons in resolution are difficult to draw, but I came to the conclusion by the end that there were indeed core principles that have a general application. Rather than describe each and every event of the nine years of implementation, let me describe what I think are the central principles of resolution and weave some of the key events of the years into the exegesis.

1. At the heart of any conflict resolution must be a framework based on agreed principles. One of the things I always try to do in politics is to go

back to first principles: what is it really about? What are we trying to achieve? What is at the heart of the matter?

In Northern Ireland we had a basic disagreement which made the conflict very hard to resolve: one side wanted a united Ireland, the other wanted to remain in the United Kingdom. Sometimes people say to me: Northern Ireland can't be as hard as the Middle East, surely. In fact, in this respect it is even harder. In the Middle East peace process, there is an agreement as to the eventual outcome: a two-state solution. In Northern Ireland, there is a profound and actually irreconcilable argument whether Northern Ireland should remain in the United Kingdom or unite with the South and become part of the Irish state. Because we couldn't resolve this issue, we had to search for principles that would allow peace while leaving that issue open for the future.

It seemed to me that the first principle was really what was called the principle of consent. If a majority of people in Northern Ireland wanted to unite with the South, then there would be unity, but until then, Northern Ireland would be part of the United Kingdom. It was this principle that Republicans could not accept historically, arguing that the partition of Ireland was constitutionally invalid and that the island as a whole should be treated as the voting constituency. Obviously this meant peace was impossible. So they had to be brought to accept the principle of consent, explicitly or implicitly.

The question then was: on what basis and on what principles would Republicans accept it? The answer, which then underpinned the formation of the Good Friday Agreement, was peace in return for power-sharing and equality, i.e. the IRA war would end if there was a government in Northern Ireland which was truly representative of all parts of the community and there was genuine equality of treatment for Protestants and Catholics alike. Hence the need for reform of the police and the courts, and hence the acknowledgement of the Irish language. Those wanting a united Ireland would have to accept partition, at least until they were in the majority; but in return, within a divided Ireland, they would receive fair and equal treatment and recognition of the aspiration to a united Ireland. Hence also the North–South bodies.

Once those core principles were agreed, everything else then became a matter of intensely complicated, hard-fought, often malfunctioning engineering, but based on a valid design concept accepted by all parties.

Without such a framework of principle, progress in conflict resolution is difficult, if not impossible. It is an enduring reference point. It constitutes guidance. It also traps the parties within it. Once they accept the framework they can't argue things inconsistent with it; or if they do, the inconsistency tells against them. So, if there is an agreed programme for policing, based on the principle of equal treatment, how can there be a paramilitary army operating alongside it? Actually, once the principle of peace for power-sharing is agreed, the rationale for the IRA—founded to create a united Ireland without the consent of the Unionist majority—disintegrates. Likewise, once equality of treatment is accepted as the basis of governing, how could Unionism continue its opposition to Sinn Fein members in the government, provided of course they were committed to peace?

In this way, establishing the core principles shapes the process and makes the reconciliation possible.

2. Then to proceed to resolution, the thing needs to be gripped and focused on. Continually. Inexhaustibly. Relentlessly. Day by day by day by day. The biggest problem with the Middle East peace process is that no one has ever gripped it long enough or firmly enough. The gripping is intermittent, and intermittent won't do. It doesn't work. If it was gripped, it would be solved.

In the case of Northern Ireland, we had a very detailed agreement across a range of issues. There were new bodies set up, new strains of working to be executed, a panoply of interlocking arrangements to be carried forward. Each of these then had to be negotiated further in the precise detail, and all of it required a perpetual grip.

On policing, for example, we had a vast number of unresolved questions. We asked Chris Patten, a former Tory Northern Ireland minister and former chairman of the Tory Party, to head up an inquiry into how it could be done. He did a brilliant job, and his report was the cornerstone for policing reform; but believe me, each bit of it was refined and refined again—sometimes to his understandable annoyance—as we tried to keep the see-saw in balance.

Decommissioning was the real bugbear. For the reasons given, this was extraordinarily sensitive for the IRA. And at one level Unionists understood it was more symbolic than real. In truth, if the IRA destroyed their weapons, they could always buy new ones. In other words, peace didn't ultimately depend on destroying weapons but on destroying a mindset.

We had a *Roget's Thesaurus* debate about this. In the end, the IRA agreed to "put the weapons beyond use" rather than destroy them—but how to tell if this had been done? We devised a means whereby two international statesmen—Martti Ahtisaari, former president of Finland, and Cyril Ramaphosa, a leading light of the ANC—took on the task of certifying the weapons were "beyond use." Those poor guys were ferried around the Irish countryside examining weapons dumps, which they did with incredible good grace. Cyril was a smart, stand-up guy who I always thought should have been a contender for leadership of the ANC. Martti was that rarity in politics, and in life: a person as modest as he was capable (and he was a very modest man).

But then how did we know that these weapons were *all* the weapons? A Canadian general, John de Chastelain, who by coincidence had been to the same school as me in Edinburgh, headed up the IICD. At this time the Executive was suspended. David Trimble was trying to put it back together but needed real action on decommissioning. The IRA were still deeply reluctant. They kept doing only 90 per cent of what was needed, and in this context that might as well have been zero per cent.

We went to Hillsborough after much negotiation, while John was taken to witness an IRA "act of decommissioning." We were to await the news that the act had taken place—a bit like in the old days when crowds gathered to hear the news that the king's marriage had been consummated. John then disappeared off our radar—literally. The IRA held him incommunicado, and while they let him witness the act, they wouldn't let him describe it at all, in any way—a bit like the herald being unable to say with whom the king had been abed, or when exactly it had happened, or what room they were in, or something about the nightdress, or how joyful they were; in other words, anything to give the thing some damn credibility. In this case, the crowd waiting for the news was awash with scepticism bordering on downright distrust.

Finally poor John turned up to do his heralding. It immediately became clear that he, as a man of integrity and honour, felt bound by the IRA stricture on total confidentiality. We decided nonetheless to field him to a press conference, whose only lasting historic significance is that it should be compulsory viewing for all students of press conferences.

John gave them the bald statement that in effect it had happened, but he resolutely refused to say more. In answer to the question "What was decommissioned?," he replied: "Well, it wasn't a tank"—a bit like the herald, when asked with whom the king had consummated his marriage, saying, "Well, it wasn't a donkey."

This did then for David Trimble, I'm afraid, and I blame myself for it. Even Sylvia Hermon, one of his MPs, who was the most decent, sensible and clear-sighted of the lot and just a thoroughly lovely woman, said she couldn't support reinstating the Executive on this basis.

It was as well that John was a patient man; he required patience in saintly quantities. He was put upon, mucked about, abused, disabused, and took it all in the interests of peace. To his enormous credit, he stuck with it and his reputation as a straight guy was an invaluable part of the whole process. The point is that in each phase of this wrangle—and there were many—the thing had to be gripped throughout.

3. In conflict resolution, small things can be big things. This is not just about gripping, it is also about putting aside your view of what is important in favour of theirs. And not being prissy about finding such things below your pay grade. Your pay grade covers anything important to the parties you are serving; as defined by them.

Occasionally in my new role in the Middle East, people say to me: Don't you find it demeaning to be arguing about where some obscure roadblock should be positioned or whether permission can be given to rebuild two hundred yards of road in some remote part of Palestine? I say: No—if it matters to them, it matters to me.

I used to know the precise whereabouts and could describe the structure of each and every one of the watchtowers the British Army used in South Armagh. For the IRA this border country was their country, where many of their key activists lived. The watchtowers were a constant source of friction, symbolising that the British Army was still after them. Our military, of course, regarded the towers as a vital point of surveillance, especially on dissident Republicans coming up from the South to commit acts of terror. They could point to attempts foiled and lives saved. So it was delicate and the removal of the towers had to happen bit by bit, and each step had to be focused on.

For both sides in a dispute, symbols are crucial. They need to be handled with care. In Northern Ireland, each aspect of the new policing regime, from the cap badge, which is worn on a policeman's helmet to signify which regional police force he is a part of, through to the precise method of recruiting, had to be painstakingly circumnavigated.

Very often, such small things can be traded. With each part of the Northern Ireland negotiation, someone was always having to compromise, someone was always upset. In such a dispute, both sides are in a state of more or less permanent complaint, about each other or about the mediator. Both sides think only they are making concessions, only they truly want peace, only they are acting in genuine good faith. I would regularly have identical conversations in consecutive meetings with the two sides, each convinced it had made all the movement and the other had made none.

I remember once talking to a group of Unionists some time after the Good Friday Agreement. One of them said to me—and not aggressively, but quite sincerely—"Tell me what we have really got out of this agreement." I said: "The Union. That's pretty big, don't you think?" In other words, the basis of the deal meant that the principle of consent was avowed; and so as long as a majority desired it, the Union would remain. That, after all, was the *raison d'être* of Unionism. But he didn't really see it like that. He just saw a string of concessions to bring "the men of violence" to stop what they should never have been doing anyway.

So the small things matter because in the minds of the key parties, they often loom large with a perspective we can't always grasp.

4. Be creative. Use the big or small things, singly or in combination, and if necessary invent a few more, to unblock progress. Here is where Jonathan particularly was brilliantly inventive. At times the impasse seemed insurmountable. Right at the end we had set a deadline for reconstituting the Executive on 26 March 2007. So many deadlines had come and gone that they were a devalued currency. They were better than no currency, however, and although they were always rejected by the parties, to my mind they always served some sort of purpose; but this time the Irish side put their foot down in unison. No budging from this deadline. We had been three years or more trying to get Ian Paisley into a deal and it was now or never, do or die, etc. So 26 March had to be it. At the last minute, as I suspected might happen, Ian Paisley told me he couldn't carry his party for March. It had to be May. The Irish were sceptical. Sinn Fein were furious. Everything teetered on the brink.

I thought it crazy to bring the whole thing down for the sake of two months. Jonathan came up with the idea of giving the DUP their two months, but asking them in return to agree to a face-to-face meeting between Ian Paisley and Gerry Adams, who had never met before. We made the offer. The DUP accepted and then Gerry Adams went along with it.

Then—and yes, it really does come to this—we had to negotiate not just the choreography of the actual meeting but its furniture. It came down to the shape of the table. The DUP wanted the sides to sit opposite each other to show they were still adversaries. Sinn Fein wanted everyone to sit next to each other to show they were partners and therefore now equals. Robert Hannigan, a great young official who had taken over as the main Number 10 person, then supplied the final piece of creativity: he suggested a diamond-shaped table so they could sit both opposite and with each other. The deal was done.

In the creativity, you cannot always think of everything, but you should be wary of doing anything that forfeits trust.

By the way, trust, as a political concept, is multilayered. At one level no one trusts politicians, and politicians are obliged from time to time to conceal the full truth, to bend it and even distort it, where the interests of the bigger strategic goal demand it be done. Of course, where the line is drawn is crucial, and is not in any way an exact science. (And don't get too affronted by it; we all make these decisions every day in our business and personal lives.) Without operating with some subtlety at this level, the job would be well-nigh impossible.

But the public are quite discerning, and discriminate between politicians they don't trust at a superficial level, i.e. pretty much all of them, and those they don't trust at a more profound level. This level of trust is about whether the public believe that the political leader is trying to do his or her best for them, with whatever mistakes or compromises, Machiavellian or otherwise, are made. This is the level of trust that really matters.

I heard an interesting example of this once from, of all people, Nelson Mandela. Mandela—or Madiba as he is also called (his clan name)—is a fascinating study, not because he's a saint but because he isn't. Or rather he is, but not in the sense that he can't be as fly as hell when the occasion demands. I bet Gandhi was the same.

I always got on well with Madiba, partly I think because I treated him as a political leader and not a saint. He knew exactly how he was used by people—including me—to boost their credibility at certain points, and provided he liked you, he was totally prepared to do it. The most fascinating thing about him was his shrewdness. He was wily, clever as in the French word *habile*, smart and completely capable of manipulating a situation when it suited his higher purpose.

We were discussing how he changed and reformed the ANC from a revolutionary movement to a governing party—no easy task. They used, of course, to commit specific acts of violence, called terrorism by the apartheid regime but regarded by the ANC as a legitimate means of achieving freedom. Madiba decided they had to drop the campaign of violence, and also knew that if he approached it from the point of view of principle, he would be bitterly opposed and would divide the movement, perhaps split it. So he contrived a tactical reason for suspending it. He told the ANC cadres that he was as committed as them, but that tactically they should suspend violence for a period, so that later all options would be open to them and more achievable. Of course once it was suspended, it remained suspended in perpetuity.

Such tactical manoeuvres were the warp and woof of the Northern Ireland peace process. Again at the last minute, after the negotiation over the St. Andrews declaration of October 2006, up popped the issue of what oath would be sworn by those taking office in the reconstructed Assembly and Executive. All manner of permutations were gone through to find a mutually acceptable formula. Naturally the DUP wanted a very clear commitment to the police in the oath itself, to ensure security and stability. Sinn Fein didn't like the wording and wouldn't commit until it was clear the Executive was in being, so there was a synchronising issue as well as a language problem.

In the end they agreed a timing and, roughly, a wording, but over the following weeks it started to fall apart. Gerry Adams had agreed to call an Ard Fheis (a council meeting of Sinn Fein) to endorse it, but only if Ian Paisley had clearly stated in advance that such an endorsement would allow the Executive and Assembly to be revived. For once, roles were reversed, with Gerry Adams demanding clarity and Ian Paisley producing waffle. I then had the idea that I would reinterpret the waffle and so deliver Gerry his reassurance.

I had a Christmas holiday in Miami. The sun shone, but that was about it as far as holidaying went. Because of the time difference I had to start my calls at 5 a.m. Frequently the Paisleys would be out visiting friends so calls were missed. I took horrendous chances in what I was telling each the other had agreed to—stretching the truth, I fear, on occasions past breaking point—but I could see the whole thing collapsing because of the wording of an oath of office. Somehow, with creativity pouring out of every orifice, we got through it.

The point is you need to be nimble, flexible and innovative. I often reflect on issues like settlements, Jerusalem or refugees in the Middle East peace process; in each case, ingenuity will find a way through, but ingenuity—in abundant supply—there will have to be.

5. The conflict won't be resolved by the parties if left to themselves. If it were possible for them to resolve it on their own, they would have done so. Ergo, they need outside help.

This third-party assistance is vital in many different ways. Obviously it can produce much of the ingenuity necessary as stated above. It can also help reassure the parties of each other's good faith. In the Middle East, talk to any Israelis and they will say, with utter sincerity, Of course I want peace.

I remember saying to the head of Israel's military intelligence—a man with a tough assignment—that he had to understand Palestinians didn't believe Israel was serious about creating a Palestinian state. "They think you want just to swallow them up," I said.

"That's not true," he replied. "I'll tell you a story. A guy who owns a Rottweiler goes into a bar and says, 'Who owns the chihuahua dog outside?' 'I do,' says someone. 'Then help me,' the man says, 'because your chihuahua's killing my Rottweiler.' 'That's ridiculous,' says the chihuahua's owner, 'how can a chihuahua kill a Rottweiler?' The man replies: 'He's stuck in his throat.'"

But ask an Israeli whether the Palestinians want peace and they'll say, "No. Don't talk to us about settlements and occupation. We got out of Gaza, we took our settlers with us, and we got Hamas and rockets." You can play the same type of conversation back, with a Palestinian about the Israelis.

The point is the outside party does not just help negotiate and mediate: they act as a buffer, a messenger and, crucially, as a persuader of good faith in a climate usually dominated by distrust. They also help define issues and indeed turning points. Northern Ireland provided a graphic example of this. In reality, there were two distinct phases to the peace process: the first was from the Good Friday Agreement up to the suspension of the Assembly and the Executive in October 2002 over the IRA failure to decommission; the second was from the fall of David Trimble in 2003 through to May 2007. The intervening period of around a year was like an intermission, though much happened.

The first phase was the period of what we might call creative ambiguity, during which people moved slowly, warily (and occasionally not at all) from very entrenched positions. No one seriously thought that the day after the Good Friday Agreement the IRA were going to disband; they were going to wait to see if the Unionists delivered their side of the bargain, and until then the IRA would hold the use of force in reserve.

On the other hand, we had to pretend this was an orderly and structured transition. So there were fudges, things said and done that had little intellectual or political consistency except that of seeing us through each set of obstacles.

This was particularly true of relations with the Republicans. They had their history, even quasi-theology, to uphold as a revolutionary movement. They had to honour their dead and imprisoned. But they had also to conform to the language of a peace agreement they couldn't be sure would be implemented. As with the decommissioning saga, there were a series of half-steps, all clothed in fairly obscure Republican-speak, with which they were trying to convince Unionists, without destabilising their own internal politics.

Additionally, as well as being a paramilitary force fighting the British, they were also a para-police force in Republican areas. I remember telling one of my constituents in Sedgefield about how the IRA would knee-cap drug dealers and beat up rapists, and I could tell that for the first time he might warm to the Republicans. Of course, none of this was going to stop overnight; yet none of it could possibly be reconciled with the rule of law as set out by the Good Friday Agreement.

For a time, the creative ambiguity around all this served us well. The terrorism stopped. The bombs stopped. No British soldiers died. No police officers were assassinated. But none of this was the same as saying the normal processes of law and order now ruled Northern Ireland. This was demonstrated by the murder of Robert McCartney in January 2005. He was defending a friend who was being beaten up in a bar by IRA men, who then dragged McCartney outside and stabbed him to death.

The killing was in many ways the final turning point. His family, all Republicans, refused to be silenced, and his sisters, fiancée and friends campaigned for his murderers to be brought to justice. The IRA didn't quite get the point and issued a statement asking, in effect, if shooting the culprits would help, but it brought to the forefront the essential decision that the IRA had had to make since the suspension of the Assembly and Executive in October 2002.

And here's where the third party can also help. After the suspension in 2002, I went to Belfast to make the most important speech I had made on Northern Ireland since May 1997. This speech came to be known as the "acts of completion" speech. Essentially I said: Creative ambiguity was our friend in the initial phase; it allowed us to get the caravan moving; it helped us round the myriad impasses in the first stages. But now it is no longer our friend; it is what is holding us back, because until it is absolutely clear that violence in whatever form will be given up for good—and if it is, power will be shared—then we can't make further progress. In place of "creative ambiguity" there now had to be "acts of completion" to demonstrate beyond doubt that the past is behind us.

It was a carefully worded speech, and it was also powerful because it was plain and unadorned. From then on, my constant refrain to Gerry Adams and Martin McGuinness was that the IRA no longer served any purpose but that of sustaining rejectionist Unionism—they were now stymieing the very thing they said they wanted, namely power-sharing.

The same, of course, is true of the militant wing of Hamas today. They are the best friends of the "one-state" Israelis. Their adherence to violence provides not the justification for negotiation, but the excuse for exclusion.

However, spotting this, defining it in a persuasive way and using that definition to move the process on is something that often comes easier from a third party than from either of the main players.

6. Realise that for both sides resolving the conflict is a journey, a process, not an event. Each side takes time to leave the past behind. A conflict is not simply a disagreement characterised by violence. It has a history and it creates a culture, with traditions, ritual and doctrine. It has a mind and soul as well as a body. It is enduring, and it is deep.

Changing all of that is an undertaking of immense ambition and intense introspection. People can change, but people are also very set in their ways. The "ways" have to be "unset" so that the change can progress. The first time I met Gerry Adams and Martin McGuinness, they were not just hesitant or distrustful, they were sitting down with the enemy. For countless meetings at first, Martin would not simply want to negotiate, most of all he would want to explain his side's purpose, its pain, its anger and its expectations. It took time before he came to regard me as a partner and even a friend. So if it was like that for him, imagine what it was like for an ordinary IRA volunteer, perhaps one personally abused by a soldier or RUC officer, or whose family had suffered and had been born and bred to believe it was an injustice deliberately perpetrated by evil-minded people.

The two sides rarely see each other's pain. Even the most progressive

Israelis I know can seldom understand the humiliation of a middle-aged Palestinian man being searched by a young Israeli soldier at a checkpoint in front of his family (and let us assume not always with exemplary politeness). Palestinians will justly mourn the latest innocent Palestinian victims of an Israeli raid, but find it really hard to sympathise with the parent of an Israeli child blown up in a suicide attack.

Then there are attitudes which, to us, seem absurd, comic even, but to them are defining. I remember before the 1997 election a leading Orangeman describing me as unfit to be prime minister because my wife was a painted jezebel who claimed her allegiance to Rome. When I first heard it, I puzzled over it, misunderstanding Rome as the seat of the Italian government rather than the Vatican and wondering what on earth Cherie had been saying to Romano Prodi, the Italian prime minister.

The notion that there is ever going to be one moment in time when peace occurs is an error. The peace has to mature, put down its own roots to displace the roots of conflict, and allow over time a different set of attitudes to take shape and make their impact.

Sometimes I used to try to describe it by this analogy: it was like a car driving away from a crash. The sight of the wreckage does not disappear straight away. It grows more faint over time. There is a constant look in the rear-view mirror even while the eyes strain to see the road in front. The passengers are shaken up, and the memory of what has happened competes for space in their minds with the hope that better times are ahead. There is no immediate release from the pain; it continues far and deep and only gradually diminishes before eventually disappearing.

What this implies for the process is that you have to work at persuading each side that the other's faltering steps as they travel the journey are not born of a lack of good faith or a change of mind about peace, but are a natural consequence of the experience they have been through. It is an unavoidable feature of resolving the conflict.

7. The path to peace will be deliberately disrupted by those who believe the conflict must continue. Be prepared for such disruption. Do not be deflated by it. People often forget that the worst terrorist attack in the history of the Troubles came *after* the Good Friday Agreement, not before it. Thankfully it was also the last.

On Saturday 15 August 1998 at 3:10 p.m. a massive bomb went off in the market town of Omagh and twenty-nine people died. Many others were badly injured. Still more will bear the mental scars for life. Among the dead was a woman pregnant with twins, whose mother and daughter also died, and four youngsters from Spain and their escort who were on an exchange visit. The bomb was the work of the dissident group the Real IRA, formed in protest at Sinn Fein's embrace of the peace process. In the event the Catholics killed outnumbered the Protestants. The terrorists had given a warning, but for the wrong place, and the police had unwittingly moved the crowd right into the path of the bomb.

I was on holiday in the south-west of France at the time, in a little village called Miradoux. We were staying with our friends Maggie and Alan, he having been secretary to the PLP and she an old friend who gave Cherie and me a billet in her house in Stoke Newington when we searched for our first home as a newly married couple.

I was informed around 3:30 p.m. By 5 p.m. the savagery of the attack was clear. I gave a short press statement on the steps of the village church in a suit borrowed from one of my security people, my emotions a mixture of shock and anxiety as to the consequences for the process.

The next morning I went to Northern Ireland and visited the injured. Even now I cannot think of it without tears. I met a girl who lost her sight but was determined to make the best of her life, as she later proved, and I met the father of the pregnant woman. If the families had been angry or taken it out on me—"If you hadn't started this, they would still be alive," a sentiment voiced by some—I could have kept my composure; what completely broke me down was their quiet dignity, their limitless sadness for the loved ones they would never see or hold or speak to again.

Even at that point of supreme human tragedy brought about by evil beyond understanding, I had to think politically. We were faced with a choice: either to throw our hands up in horror and say, "These people will never make peace," or to use the horror as the reason to go on, to say, "These people want this process to stop, and our response is to drive it faster and further."

In the event, and to the great credit of all (helped by another presidential visit by Bill Clinton), the key participants in the process chose the latter course. What could have been a turning back, was a turning point. The Real IRA never recovered. Gerry Adams and Martin McGuinness condemned the attacks unequivocally. David Trimble rose to the occasion. And most of all, so did the people. One of the bereaved said to me, even as he mourned the loss of his wife: "Don't be put off, carry on, and make my wife's memorial a lasting peace in Northern Ireland so that no one ever again feels as I do this day."

This attitude is in contrast to the Middle East where, unfortunately, the opposite usually happens when a terrorist attack occurs. The response there is often to clamp down in a way that alienates the peacemakers as well as the terrorists, and to see violence by a faction as showing the futility of trying to make peace with those not part of the faction. The problem is the moment such a course is taken, the keys to the process are put in the hands of the terrorists. Their purpose is to lock up the process. That's the sick rationale behind the terror. Once you concede that terror does indeed lead to possession of the keys, they're in charge. Keep the keys firmly in the hands of the peacemakers.

Terror is the starkest example of the extremes trying to block progress, but pressure to lock up the process also comes from perfectly respectable and democratic elements on both sides who accuse their own party of selling out. David Trimble was subject to an unrelenting barrage from those in the DUP and elsewhere who saw each concession as a betrayal, and the process as a whole as a sell-out of their community. To the outsider, this seems unreasonable and unpersuasive; not so to the insider. David, I think, took the view that I did too little to assist him; I took the view he never quite stood up for the positive, tending rather to share and sympathise with the Unionist propensity to see plots and conspiracies against them. But he had an extraordinarily difficult hand to play, and if he didn't always play it as I would have done, he played it with a courage that rightly won him the Nobel Peace Prize.

8. Leaders matter. Any peace process calls for political risks, even a sense of political adventure and certainly political courage, sometimes even personal courage. The quality of leadership matters; it is a *sine qua non*.

The point is: the easiest thing for the parties in any conflict to do is hold firm to established positions. An ideology, even a sort of theology, will have grown up around the conflict, reflecting the partisan nature of it. Everything is seen through the prism constructed by such partisan ideology. To hold to it is to tread a familiar path, which may lead nowhere, but whose surface is well worn, whose landmarks produce instant recognition, and where the leaders' followers feel most comfortable.

By contrast, like Moses with the Israelites, striking out in a new direction whose destination is uncertain, whose obstacles are formidable and unfamiliar and when at least some of the followers will accuse the leader of betrayal, is tough; and it requires the quality that motivates the best political leadership: a desire to do good.

We were very lucky in the quality of leadership we had. David Trimble was instrumental. He began it when it seemed impossible, kept at it when it was most difficult, and paid the ultimate political price (though I have no doubt that his reputation in history is fully secure).

Then in the most unlikely of roles, Ian Paisley—for years the wrecker, the spoiler, the scourge of all in Unionism who sought accommodation—took over and completed the process.

Ian Paisley was definitely a strange political figure, a product of the unique concatenation of political circumstances in Northern Ireland. He is a genuine and committed Christian, a true God-fearing man; he is a passionate Unionist; he is clever, shrewd, occasionally even sly. He had a great grasp of strategy and tactics and could spot the difference between the two.

The unanswered question is: did he change or did the situation change? He would say the latter, and that he was always prepared to make peace if the IRA forswore violence. But I think two things also happened to change him. First, after a long and debilitating illness which, as he used to remark, he knew he would survive (though many hoped his wish was misplaced), he had a sense of impending mortality, political and personal, and wanted to leave behind something more profound and enduring than "no surrender." There was a really rather moving moment during the course of the talks at St. Andrews in October 2006, when it was discovered that he and his wife Eileen were celebrating their fiftieth wedding anniversary. At the end of the meeting, there was a little ceremony at which each party congratulated him, including Gerry Adams, and Bertie then presented him with a piece of wood from a tree at the site of the Battle of the Boyne. He made a gracious and benign reply (and Ian was perfectly capable, even when being congratulated, of being neither of these things) and I felt this was a man looking into his own soul and feeling differently. He hadn't exactly matured; but he had in some indefinable sense broadened.

The other change was that Ian was nothing if not a politician with his ear firmly tuned into the people. In the course of late 2006 and early 2007, he heard the people telling him it was time for peace, and even, in particular, time for him to make the peace. During those meetings, time and again it was Ian who wanted to push forward, Ian who was prepared to seek creative solutions, Ian who took care always to leave the door open. He and I would often meet alone in the Downing Street den. Jonathan used to be highly amused when I described the meetings, which almost always dealt with the issue at a spiritual rather than temporal level. It's true: we were both fascinated by religious faith as well as being people of faith. He gave me a little prayer book for Leo.

Once, near the end, he asked me whether I thought God wanted him to make the deal that would seal the peace process. I wanted to say yes, but I hesitated; though I was sure God would want peace, God is not a negotiator. I felt it would be wrong, manipulative, to say yes, and so I said I couldn't answer that question, that only he could and I hoped he would let God guide him.

People could never understand it when I used to say how much I liked him. But I did. I think my granny's reverence for him made me have a soft spot.

On the nationalist side, too, there were leaders of real calibre. John Hume was, is, a great political figure and genuine titan. He had vision and imagination and foresight when others were resolutely still in blinkers. Seamus Mallon and Mark Durkan, the leaders of the SDLP, were moderate and reasonable, and felt both qualities counted against them. They were always in a difficult position. The trouble was Sinn Fein had to be brought in from the cold, and so inevitably more time, energy and focus were given to them. This caused deep resentment; but it was an unfortunate and inevitable consequence of making peace. Nevertheless both Seamus and Mark were significant figures in their own right. Both, incidentally—and I don't know if the SDLP have a special training school for this—were masters of the sound bite, really first-class speakers, who outside of Northern Ireland's politics would have been major players in any political party.

Of Bertie and his contribution, I have spoken. Then there are Gerry and Martin. They were an extraordinary couple. Over time I came to like both greatly, probably more than I should have, if truth be told. Again, either would have been a big political leader in anyone's politics. They did not merely understand, they were supreme masters of the distinction between tactics and strategy. They knew the destination and they were determined to bring their followers with them, or at least the vast bulk of them.

A lot was written about the Provisional Army Council and their membership of it and thus their relationship with the IRA. Many people, including a large part of British intelligence, thought Sinn Fein and the IRA were indistinguishable. When Gerry and Martin would say they would have to talk to the IRA about something, the joke was always they could look in the mirror and ask.

I always thought the relationship was more complex than that. The idea that they could just instruct the IRA never felt right to me. I don't doubt that on many occasions the difference between Sinn Fein and the IRA was an artifice, a divide used for tactical reasons. I know that both could be clever and manipulative; but so can I. And my sense was that, in certain situations, they were persuading and negotiating with others, not giving orders. I came to the view that the SF/IRA relationship was a bit like that of the Labour leadership and the Labour Party National Executive Committee (NEC), the governing body of the party: yes the leadership is powerful, yes it usually gets its way, but not always and rarely without a lot of persuasion and negotiation.

Throughout, the fear of Gerry and Martin was a split, as had happened before to Republicanism, with disastrous consequences. This meant taking their people step by step, leading them, cajoling them and not always being totally upfront as to what the destination really meant. It was a tough task and they performed it with immense skill.

Ultimately, they understood that the IRA's existence had become not the way to a just settlement, but the barrier to it. It took real political courage to implement that insight, and whether you like them or not, and no matter how strongly you disapprove of their past actions, they had courage in abundance.

Then there were the leaders of the minor parties, often the odd ones out in the conflict but whose leadership, when there was nothing in it for them, was rather inspiring. People like David Ervine of the Progressive Unionist Party, the Alliance leaders, and the marvellous women's coalition whom I used to see just to remind myself there were normal people in Northern Ireland.

There were Ronnie Flanagan and Hugh Orde, the two chief constables I dealt with, whose very special position as head of the Northern Ireland police meant they had a role to play which was of the essence. They played that role not in an overtly political way, but with political sense.

I also like to think that, in this instance, at least, I chose well in the people I appointed. Secretaries of State and ministers performed really well. They were very different, mind you: Mo Mowlam, Peter Mandelson, John Reid, Paul Murphy, Peter Hain, were all unusual people in their own right, but really talented, and each made a significant, even crucial, contribution.

Whether they were already in place or were appointed later, leaders mattered. Every step required decision-making that was complicated and a political sense that was acute. But it is not just the leadership internal to the key parties that matter: external circumstances must also be propitious.

9. The external circumstances must militate in favour of, not against, peace. I have described how the changes in the south of Ireland helped create the context for progress. Such a change is almost invariably crucial in a conflict. These conflicts rarely invoke strong feelings only in the immediate zone of dispute. Kashmir, Sri Lanka, Kosovo: in any of these cases, external players also have a role to play, for good or ill.

The classic example is the Israel–Palestine dispute. The ramifications are region-wide, even global. The external players, especially in the Arab world, are vital. Actually, there's a potential change in their attitude to peace: for years the Palestinian cause was used and often abused, but now they, like Israel, fear Iran and its influence in the region.

Starting with the Crown Prince Abdullah Peace Initiative in 2002, the Arab nations no longer want to exploit the dispute, but to settle it. It offers an enormous opportunity to Israel. Likewise, a world troubled and threatened by a global terrorism based on a perversion of Islam needs the dispute resolved. The objective conditions are today benign. That is why grasping the possibility and pushing on to peace is so self-evidently right. But it will take perseverance. Which brings me to:

10. Never give up. Simple but essential; never stop working on it and never give up on it. This is not just about gripping the conflict; it is about refusing to accept defeat. As we used to say in Northern Ireland: if you can't solve it, manage it until you can solve it; but don't walk away and leave it untended. A peace process never stands still—it goes forward or back. You have to believe a solution is possible even when others don't, even when conventional wisdom is against you, even when those most intimately concerned—the parties themselves—have given up hope. And remember: it is better to try and fail than not to try at all.

★ ★ ★

These are my ten principles. More or less, we applied them to Northern Ireland. There were many times it did indeed seem hopeless, but fortunately something or someone kept hope alive.

The historic day came about on 8 May 2007, just over nine years after the Good Friday Agreement, when I went to Stormont to witness the reinstatement of the new Executive government of Northern Ireland. Ian Paisley was the first minister, his deputy was Martin McGuinness.

That day I saw things that had you predicted them ten years before, people would have laughed, ruefully maybe, but still laughed. The meeting with me, Bertie, Peter Hain, Ian Paisley and Martin McGuinness, the latter two of them sharing jokes, the three others of us sitting there a trifle dumbfounded, wondering if we were in a dream; the ceremony itself, where up in the balcony previously sworn enemies were sitting together exchanging pleasantries as if the previous decades had never happened. People who had wanted to kill each other were now wanting to work together. Remarkable, moving and satisfying.

At the gates of Stormont there was another protest. Every time we set foot in Northern Ireland there were protests—large, small, peaceful, violent, some Unionist, some Republican—always showing how divided the politics of Northern Ireland was from that anywhere else. That day for the first time there was a protest not about Northern Ireland, but about Iraq. When I saw it, I felt that Northern Ireland had just rejoined the rest of the world.

SEVEN

"WE GOVERN IN PROSE"

Y ou campaign in poetry, you govern in prose," the former governor of New York Mario Cuomo once said. In the summer of
1998, after just over a year in office, an uneasy feeling gripped me.
I had come to power believing the Labour Party was its own worst
enemy. I looked back on a century of existence and saw a party that was
essentially Her Majesty's Loyal Opposition. The periods of government
were intermittent, and the psychology was not that of the decision-
maker but the protester.

However, we had come on an incredible journey of change. The
party had accepted things that would have been unimaginable even a
decade before. I had always thought if you led from the front, bold and
striking out in a perpetual advance, they would stick with the leadership; and so they did. It wasn't merely the product of eighteen years of
Opposition; there was a cadre of people who believed in New Labour
and understood it, instinctively and emotionally as well as intellectually,
but they were small in number, uncertain in influence and still feeling
their way, as in a sense I was.

The body of the Labour Party, and particularly the older generation—
not all, but most—were for a Labour Party modernised from the ways
of the 1940s, but they stopped around the 1960s. Roy Hattersley was
typical of this group: absolutely solid against Militant, in favour of a private sector alongside the public sector, and knowing Labour had to be
sensible on defence. In other words, for him and many others, the
Labour Party had to stop being extreme and go back to its proper set of
positions. This was a mindset away from the destructive nonsense of the
Labour turmoil of the 1980s, yet there was still a long way to go in terms

of the way the world had changed. To cease being extreme was necessary, but it was also insufficient.

For most of this older generation—old right, as well as old left—it was enough that New Labour had taken us out of the darkness of Opposition, but they didn't believe in it. Actually they thought New Labour had no beliefs, and bought the then conventional Tory press opinion that it was in essence a marketing construct, a PR creation; head without heart. They were convinced a winning formula had been discovered, which was clever, but not sincere.

In order to circumvent the party, what I had done was construct an alliance between myself and the public. Throughout 1994–7 and certainly in this early period of government, the alliance was firm and unshakeable. The party had little option but to accept it. Any sign of indiscipline invoked the memory of all those years of Opposition. Now we were on the up; why on earth go back? It was a simple, crude, electorally perfect argument to keep the party in line, and it meant I could go out on the end of a branch, knowing that the strong and steadfast trunk of public opinion was supporting me.

But it was high-risk. I knew also that as time passed, the branch would get longer and thinner and the trunk ever more likely to be shaken and its strength tested.

One of the roots of my unease was that, in Opposition, the public will support a leader taking brave decisions because they are taken in respect of the leader's party, and the public are to some extent spectators; in government, however, decisions are taken in respect of the people. They are participants. Their lives are in play.

I had studied our party history closely, and concluded that to win, the party had to move beyond itself, and the leader had to be more than a party leader; but I also derived an appreciation of the danger which all progressive parties face, when instead of the alliance being one between leader and people, it becomes one between party and people against the leader.

You might ask why that is a danger; surely the party simply ditches its leader, finds a new one more in tune with what the public want, and marches on to electoral success. The danger is that while the party and the public may be in common opposition to the leader, they can be opposed for very different reasons. With progressive parties, the public can become disillusioned for all sorts of reasons—in our case it was to do with insufficiently rapid progress on public services, the cost of fuel, taxes, crime and immigration, often centre-right concerns; but the progressive party is itself more likely to be disillusioned because it thinks the leadership is insufficiently radical in a traditional leftist sense—spending and taxing too little, sacrificing cherished positions and doctrines, doing too much for the middle class and not enough for the poor. Nonetheless, the party convinces itself that the public dissatisfaction vindicates its own dissatisfaction. The result is not electoral success but disaster.

I remember back in the early 1980s, in the course of one of my many failed attempts at becoming a parliamentary candidate, being harangued by a questioner as to why Labour had lost in 1979. His basic pitch was that we had trimmed to the right, betrayed our class, forgotten our left roots, etc. I was trying desperately to keep hold of myself, knowing it was crazy in party terms to dispute this thesis, while also knowing that the thesis was crazy in public terms. I mumbled something vaguely conciliatory and cowardly. Another person started up; then another; and I couldn't help myself. I erupted: "If the public thought Labour wasn't left wing enough, why on earth would they vote Tory?" I said, "Are they stupid? Did they think the Tories under Margaret Thatcher were going to be more left wing than Labour under Jim Callaghan? Are you really saying they are that dumb?" And of course they *were* saying that.

As we completed the first Comprehensive Spending Review in mid-1998—which would put an end to the tough self-imposed public spending constraint which applied for the first three years after 1997—I was also uneasy because something wasn't right with the way we were governing. The rhetoric and intellectual analysis were fine—investment plus reform; hand up not handout on welfare; rewarding the good, getting rid of the bad in teaching; cutting waiting lists in the NHS—but there was a gap between the quality of the rhetoric and the quality of the reforms themselves.

We still had 1.3 million people on waiting lists to become inpatients, most waiting over six months. However, the waiting didn't start with becoming an inpatient, it started with trying to get a doctor's appointment. At the time there were no minimum standards in terms of getting to see a doctor. After the doctor, the waiting began to get on the consultant's outpatient list. That could take months. Only after waiting on the outpatient list could you get on the list to become an inpatient. The six months waiting often wasn't six months at all; it could be twelve or eighteen or even more.

The NHS was great, heroic even, in terms of dealing with emergencies and the chronically ill, but as a service, it was uneven, good when good, truly appalling when bad. It was certainly underfunded, but money was not the only problem; and more money was therefore not the complete solution.

Across the piece it was the same. We were starting to cut class sizes for infants. It was what we had promised. It was what we were delivering. Some extra money was flowing into school buildings. But the truth was that we still had 40 per cent of eleven-year-olds leaving primary school without being able to read or write properly. David Blunkett's literacy and numeracy strategy was starting to take hold and, again, making a difference. But we both knew the real challenge lay in secondary schools. There were only thirty London secondary schools that got over 70 per cent of their pupils to five good GCSEs (General Certificates of Secondary Education, exams taken by 14-to-16-year-olds; grades A to C are considered "good"). In my heart of hearts I knew I wouldn't send my own children to most inner-city secondary schools. Discipline was variable, sometimes awful. Teachers were often, unsurprisingly, demoralised. There was often no organised school sport in the inner city, and sometimes little out of it.

In welfare, we were getting people off the dole. With the economy in reasonable shape and after Bank of England independence, there was a sense of macro-stability for the long term. So naturally, unemployment was falling. We took this as a sign that our tougher welfare policies were working. But, again, I felt the rhetoric was considerably ahead of the actual measures.

There was another question that dogged my thoughts in those days— still relatively halcyon—in the summer of 1998, one to which I returned over time with increasing anxiety and impatience. It was about the quality of our social analysis. I could see that society was fracturing into elements that defied traditional centre-left theory. There was a middle class, to be sure. It was growing. It encompassed the solicitors and the bank managers and middle executives. It also drew in the higher-end skilled workers, the technicians, the new computer analysts, the creative industry middle-rankers.

But to talk of a "working class" just seemed odd, correct but some-how uncomprehending. The term encompassed those on the minimum wage, the casual or temporary workers, the lower-paid nurse even, the shop floor. But it was also used to describe those at the bottom of the heap, the "non-working class" if you like—in a phrase we coined for government, the "socially excluded."

In time I began to realise you couldn't and shouldn't lump these two categories together. The right-wing phrase "the underclass" was ugly, but it was accurate. These people at the bottom didn't have dysfunctional working lives. They had dysfunctional lives, full stop. Their children were disruptive at school, if they attended at all. Their parents were often separated or abusive or just plain inadequate.

The consequence of this was felt also in crime and antisocial behaviour. As I said earlier, I had come to prominence around the time of the James Bulger murder in 1993, when I drew the easy but ultimately flawed conclusion that our society had broken down; but of course it hadn't as a whole, only in part. I was to come to the right conclusion only at the very end of my premiership: instead of focusing general social policy on this class of people, they need specific, targeted action. In the summer of 1998 I could see the symptoms of such breakdown very clearly: in the schools, on the streets, in the statistics for law and order.

That wasn't all. We had come to power with a fairly traditional but complacent view of immigration and asylum. Jack Straw, the Home Secretary, was greatly influenced by his own heavily Muslim constituency of Blackburn, where these issues were live and real. On the other hand, Jack was sensible and no softie on lawbreakers. We were unprepared for the explosion in asylum claims through 1998 and 1999. Within our first three years, the number of claims trebled, quadrupled even. I'd thought we had a pretty tight framework, but we sent a few placatory signals and this, together with a growing economy creating jobs and that we were an English-speaking country, set off an influx of claimants. Added to that, worldwide immigration flows were increasing. We weren't the only ones with a problem, but we were virtually the only ones with a set of statistics that were even roughly accurate and so were quickly dubbed the asylum capital of Europe. Suddenly from a manageable 30,000 claims per year for asylum, we were looking at 100,000. Moreover, the backlog of claims was scary and getting scarier. The system was utterly incapable of processing the claims.

Essentially, Britain, like all European countries, had inherited the post-war, post-Holocaust system and sentiment on asylum. The painful stories of refugees fleeing from Hitler and the Nazis and being turned away produced a right and proper revulsion. The presumption was that someone who claimed asylum was persecuted and should be taken in, not cast out. It was an entirely understandable emotion in the aftermath of such horror.

Unfortunately it was completely unrealistic in the late twentieth century. The presumption was plainly false; most asylum claims were not genuine. Disproving them, however, was almost impossible. The combination of the courts, with their liberal instinct; the European Convention on Human Rights, with its absolutist attitude to the prospect of returning someone to an unsafe community; and the UN Convention of Refugees, with its context firmly that of 1930s Germany, meant that, in practice, once someone got into Britain and claimed asylum, it was the Devil's own job to return them.

And, of course, many thought it was indeed the work of the Devil to try. The first attempt at tightening the law in 1998 produced a hysterical reaction and compromises had to be found to steer it through.

But the reality was that the system for asylum was broken, incapable, adrift in a sea of storms, and required far tougher action. The Civil Service machine charged with putting it right wasn't greatly inclined to the radical action the system needed.

Here, too, there was a gap, which was between what we thought the Civil Service problem would be, and what it turned out to be. In Labour mythology, the Civil Service is made up of closet Tories, snakes in the governing grass, lying in wait for the naive Labour minister whose radical policy is strangled before it can perform. In this fantasy—and it is fantasy—they are the Establishment's ideologues and the Establishment is the Tory Party, the true party of government, the fuddy-duddy repository of the old Britain of colonies, aristos and fox hunters. In this scenario, the senior mandarins are forever poised to strike down the progressive action a Labour government wants to take and propel forward the heinous plots of the right wing.

God, if only. The reality was not they were poised to strike, sabotage or act. The problem with them, as I indicated at the beginning, was inertia. They tended to surrender, whether to vested interests, to the status quo or to the safest way to manage things—which all meant: to do nothing.

Wholly contrary to the myth, they were not the least in thrall to the right-wing Establishment. They were every bit as much in thrall to the left-wing Establishment. Or, more accurately, to a time and a way and an order that had passed, a product of the last hundred years of history.

The Sir Humphrey character in the TV series *Yes, Prime Minister* was a parody and a fiction, but he was the closest parody could get to fact. Sir Humphrey wasn't left or right; he just believed in managing, in keeping things upright, in the status quo, not so much because of the status but more because of the quo; a quo he knew and could understand and one that to move from was a risk. And risk must at all costs be avoided.

This Civil Service had and has great strengths. It was and is impartial. It is, properly directed, a formidable machine. At times of crisis, superb. Its people are intelligent, hard-working and dedicated to public service. It was simply, like so much else, out of date. Faced with big challenges, it thought small thoughts. It reckoned in increments when the systems required leaps and bounds.

They didn't think New Labour too left wing—on the contrary, they thought us sometimes too right wing—but crucially they thought we were iconoclastic and recklessly so, when they were the keepers of the high places, the temples of inherited wisdom.

They also, along with the judiciary, bought the idea that New Labour's and my preoccupation with antisocial behaviour, family breakdown, asylum, etc., was a preoccupation born of our driving desire for the right levels of populism to get and retain power. They didn't see it as born of a genuine wish to improve lives in a world in which the old ways of doing so wouldn't work.

So in 1998, I began with Sir Richard Wilson, the new Cabinet Secretary (head of the Civil Service), the first stages of Civil Service reform. And to be fair, he got behind them thoroughly. But—and this is a criticism of me, not him or the Civil Service—they were like many of the other reforms: talking the right language but shying away from the really radical measures.

And this was what was making me uneasy. I started to worry that confronting the party with the need to change was the easy part; confronting these non-political interests and public opinion was the hard part—but also the necessary one.

I was learning rapidly, and what I learned was fascinating but also daunting. The problems were deep, and systemic. During the winter break in 1998, in between dealing with various crises, I got out the 1997 manifesto and reread its promises on public services and crime. I laughed at their modesty. The challenge wasn't meeting them. The challenge was: so what? An increase in the numbers treated, though the waiting lists of 100,000 had not been reduced. Infant class sizes to be under thirty—not in all class sizes, just five-, six- and seven-year-olds. Halving the time it took juvenile offenders to come to court—not all offenders, just youngsters, and that reduction from historic highs. New Labour, New Britain? It was ridiculous.

But to go deeper, to start changing systems was a whole different order of political as well as practical task. Adjust a system and people hardly notice. Change it and out of every channel come the interests the system maintains.

As I write now, looking back, I sense in my speeches and meetings an anxiety that something was missing, some dimension barely glimpsed, let alone understood, but important, crucial even. Now, of course, I know what was wrong. But then I was seeing as through a cloud.

This was reflected in my Labour Party conference speech for 1998. A couple of weeks before, we had had a Cabinet away day at Chequers. We had the usual presentation from Philip Gould about polling and the Tory Party's complete incapacity. Worries on delivery were coming through. I remember telling them about a person who wrote to me back in May 1998 beginning the letter of complaint: "Now you've been in power for some years . . ." The impatience was starting. The point was I shared it.

As Philip intoned about the Tories, I looked around the room. We were in the Great Parlour upstairs, a kind of huge drawing room with seventeenth-century Dutch wood panelling and a fine large mahogany dining table, though the room was never used for dining. Above the main chair where the prime minister sat was the same picture of Walpole that hangs in the same spot in the Cabinet Room in Downing Street. Walpole was the first and longest serving prime minister (just under twenty-one years); he held office at the whim of the Crown, was often detested, but also very effective. The hint of a smile in his portrait always reminded me a little of John Smith. Benevolent, except when crossed; in which case, dangerous.

I thought of the history of the room. I thought of Chamberlain, who loved to tend the Chequers rose garden personally and whose private diaries are still on the shelves. Chamberlain: denounced by history. A comparison to Chamberlain is one of the worst British political insults. Yet what did he do? In a world still suffering from the trauma of the Great War, a war in which millions died including many of his close family and friends, he had grieved; and in his grief pledged to prevent another such war. Not a bad ambition; in fact, a noble one.

One day, meandering through the bookcases, I had picked up his diaries and begun to read the account of his famous meeting with Hitler prior to Munich, at the house in Berchtesgaden high up in the Bavarian mountains. Chamberlain described how, after greeting him, Hitler took him up to the top of the chalet. There was a room, bare except for three plain wooden chairs, one for each of them and the interpreter. He recounts how Hitler alternated between reason—complaining of the Versailles Treaty and its injustice—and angry ranting, almost screaming about the Czechs, the Poles, the Jews, the enemies of Germany. Chamberlain came away convinced that he had met a madman, someone who had real capacity to do evil. This is what intrigued me. We are taught that Chamberlain was a dupe; a fool, taken in by Hitler's charm. He wasn't. He was entirely alive to his badness.

I tried to imagine being him, thinking like him. He knows this man is wicked; but he cannot know how far it might extend. Provoked, think of the damage he will do. So, instead of provoking him, contain him. Germany will come to its senses, time will move on and, with luck, so will Herr Hitler.

Seen in this way, Munich was not the product of a leader gulled, but of a leader looking for a tactic to postpone, to push back in time, in hope of circumstances changing. Above all, it was the product of a leader with a paramount and overwhelming desire to avoid the blood, mourning and misery of war.

Probably after Munich, the relief was too great, and hubristically, he allowed it to be a moment that seemed strategic not tactical. But easy to do. As Chamberlain wound his way back from the airport after signing the Munich Agreement—the fateful paper brandished and (little did he realise) his place in history with it—crowds lined the street to welcome him as a hero. That night in Downing Street, in the era long before the security gates arrived and people could still go up and down as they pleased, the crowds thronged outside the window of Number 10, shouting his name, cheering him, until he was forced in the early hours of the morning to go out and speak to them in order that they disperse.

Chamberlain was a good man, driven by good motives. So what was the error? The mistake was in not recognising the fundamental question. And here is the difficulty of leadership: first you have to be able to identify that fundamental question. That sounds daft—surely it is obvious; but analyse the situation for a moment and it isn't.

You might think the question was: can Hitler be contained? That's what Chamberlain thought. And, on balance, he thought he could. And rationally, Chamberlain should have been right. Hitler had annexed Austria and Czechoslovakia. He was supreme in Germany. Why not be satisfied? How crazy to step over the line and make war inevitable.

But that wasn't the fundamental question. The fundamental question was: does fascism represent a force that is so strong and rooted that it has to be uprooted and destroyed? Put like that, the confrontation was indeed inevitable. The only consequential question was when and how.

In other words, Chamberlain took a narrow and segmented view—Hitler was a leader, Germany a country, 1938 a moment in time: could he be contained?

Actually, Hitler was the product as well as the author of an ideology that gripped several countries, of which Germany was one. By 1938, fascism was culminating in a force that was not going to act according to Chamberlain's canons of reason, but according to the emotions of the ideology. He misunderstood the question and so answered wrongly.

But, my God, how easy to do. By contrast, Churchill spotted the right question and answered it correctly. Churchill: loathed in many quarters, distrusted so much that the King didn't want him in Baldwin's government; accused of errors in the Dardanelles in the First World War and in the gold standard policy of the 1920s; very nearly not appointed prime minister in 1940 and only becoming so when Halifax refused.

There he had sat at the same table in Chequers, occasionally delivering his broadcasts. He loved Chequers. He sacked the cook for not making the soup properly; turned the Long Gallery into a cinema; often stayed in bed until midday as he barked instructions to his secretaries; began dinner around 10 p.m., all washed down with vast amounts of champagne and brandy, and finished work at 2 a.m. Loved his holidays!

So there I was at the away day, gazing at my colleagues round this famous memory-soaked table, a repository of so many words and meetings, and thinking not of war—not then—but of how the unease I felt was related to wondering if I was asking the right fundamental question. I knew the party had to continue to be led strongly and planted firmly in the centre. When I spoke, I focused not on polling or the Tories but almost entirely on the overriding need to modernise, and in particular how we couldn't just be advocating more money in public services.

The unease was this: maybe the real problem wasn't the party's failure to embrace modernisation; or, at least, not only that. Maybe it was that the country didn't really buy it. What if instead of taking on the party, I had to take on the public, my allies, the strong trunk holding up my branch? It was not a thought designed for repose.

We were riding high, the country, though impatient, was still essentially supportive; the Tories were nowhere, we were politically supreme.

Why risk that? So, yes, we should drive through reform, but not to a depth or at a pace that overwhelmed people, that disorientated or destabilised them. Truth be told, we were also still learning. In March 1998, we had published a Welfare Reform Green Paper, offering greater support for those who need help in society and to provide a better system to ensure those who want to work can do so; had started tax credits; begun the Sure Start programme for children, creating centres to deliver a good start in life for every child, including education, child care, health and family support; introduced a minimum wage; the literacy and numeracy strategy, a national curriculum for primary school children aged five to eleven; and the education action zones for the inner city, where local businesses and schools come together to raise school standards in specific areas. There was NHS Direct coming in (phone and Internet access for the general public where they can call or log on to diagnose health-related problems before speaking directly to a doctor) and the first antisocial behaviour legislation, practical help to tackle aggressive, intimidating or destructive behaviour that damages or destroys another person's quality of life. There was activity and there was impact.

But in each case, again I felt it was unsatisfactory. We now had some decent policy reform nuggets going beyond the very limited commitments we had made in the 1997 manifesto, but that is what they were— nuggets, no more. Literacy and numeracy hours set aside for teaching were a step forward for primary schools, but what about failing comprehensive schools, particularly in the cities, which were the real Achilles heel of the state school system? And failing local education authorities with bad management and bad results? And the teaching profession? Tax credits, and the various measures in the Welfare Reform Green Paper—including new "stakeholder" pensions above the existing state pension that would be offered at a low cost to employees by their employers, and new welfare-to-work incentives, new "employment zones" to target extra help to the unemployed and a unified Employment Service and Benefits Agency—these were all very well; but what about the 1.7 million and rising on incapacity benefit (a weekly payment for people who become unable to work due to illness or disability), signed off work for life with precious little incentive even to start looking for employment? We talked of the dramatic reduction in the numbers unemployed, but this masked the huge rise in numbers on incapacity benefit that had taken place under the Tories and was continuing under us, and the Green Paper proposed only tinkering changes in this crucial area.

Similarly, NHS Direct was a concept for the future, and specific strategies for tackling cancer and other chronic conditions, alongside extra doctors and nurses, were making a difference in the health service, but they were partial responses to the chronic endemic problems of rising waiting lists, long waiting times, outdated working practices and without proper choice for the patient within the NHS. So serious was the NHS situation that the annual nightmare of "winter pressures," when there are more illnesses, had us holding our breath and hoping that the NHS would not collapse entirely in the first winters after 1997. And the criminal justice system seemed impervious to any reform beyond the further entrenching of rights for offenders and ever more bureaucratic processes encumbering the police and the courts.

To bridge the gap between reform and aspiration, we set alongside these piecemeal reforms a swathe of performance targets to eliminate the longest hospital waiting times, raise school literacy and numeracy and GCSE scores. There were also new national agencies and structures to drive improvement, such as the National Commissioning Frameworks, which sets out the system for planning and funding the education and training for young people up to the age of twenty-five and for young offenders in custody; the National Institute for Clinical Excellence in the NHS; the National Literacy and Numeracy Strategies, and a new National College for School Leadership with mandatory leadership qualifications for new head teachers, to raise standards in education. These were sensible steps to improve accountability for extra funding and spur departments and their agencies to greater efforts. We were to go further and—as I describe later—publish a full "NHS Plan" in July 2000 which highlighted greater staff flexibility, greater decentralisation and the reduction of waiting times as key priorities. These were to be achieved alongside the step change in NHS spending and the transformation of the NHS estate starting to take place thanks to the recent Comprehensive Spending Review.

But as we flogged the horse harder for only partial improvements, it became clearer to me that only so much could be done by driving improvement from the centre through targets and piecemeal top-down reform, even with the significant extra funding coming through. I increasingly came to see the centralised systems themselves, and the disempowerment of front-line managers and the denial of user choice

which they entailed, as a fundamental part of the problem. I wondered—as did some of the newer and more radical faces in my Policy
Unit, although this was still heresy in the party, not least among most of
my ministers—whether we had been right to dismantle wholesale GP
commissioning in the NHS and grant-maintained schools in education,
instead of adapting these concepts of local self-governance to spread
decentralised management across the state health and education systems,
but without the inequity inherent in the underfunded Tory reforms we
inherited.

From talks with capable voluntary and private sector providers only
too willing to engage in public service delivery but prevented from
doing so, I also chafed increasingly at the restrictions placed in the way
of good independent providers establishing themselves within health,
education and the other public services. This seemed to me a classic case
of the confusion between means and ends which had dogged the left for
a generation—and which it was New Labour's mission to overcome.
For public services to be equitable, and free at the point of use, they did
not all need to be provided on a monopoly basis within the public sector, controlled in a rigid way by national and local bureaucracies often
deeply resistant to innovation and genuine local autonomy.

In short, our mantra was "investment and reform together"—
emphasising rhetorically the big difference in the public services
between New Labour and Old Labour (investment without reform)
and New Labour and the Thatcherite Tories (reform without investment). But where was the scale of reform to match the scale of the
investment coming on stream?

In welfare and law and order, I similarly worried that we had a good
mantra—"rights and responsibilities together"—but no comprehensive
policy thrust to underpin it. It wasn't just the benefits system. Another
acute concern of mine was antisocial behaviour. What were we actually
changing on the council estates (built for those less well-off in society)
to eradicate the constant barrage of low-level crime which made a misery of so many lives, and to break the grip of worklessness passing from
generation to generation? More police officers, and police modernisation—which we took forward with, for example, the introduction of
auxiliary community support officers able to do much of the community policing job in a more focused way—were only partial responses;
the police also needed better, more immediate tools for the job in terms
of sanctions, which meant a shake-up of the criminal justice system. We

had to move from concept to policy, and were doing so only fitfully and painfully.

I was starting to think more systematically about New Labour and its relationship with the welfare state we had inherited and pledged to preserve and improve. The welfare state and public services, as we recognise them, were created after the tumultuous events of the Second World War, but their origins lay in the early budgets of Lloyd George, in the groundbreaking economics of Keynes, in the combination of vision and mastery of detail that was Beveridge. The state would provide.

Capitalism had driven the Industrial Revolution. Unregulated, unrestrained, untamed, its giant wheels rolled over the great mass of the people, squeezing work and profit out of them. But it was also bringing them together, letting them see how they toiled and sweated not as individuals but as a collective machine, and not for their own benefit but for the benefit of the owners of capital.

Out of such common struggle came the trade unions, the cooperative societies, the great engines of collective spirit and will to confront the grinding wheels of capital. For some, such confrontation was for the purpose of eliminating capitalism; for others, to make it fairer.

Out of this struggle came the idea that to change society, there had to be political organisation and there had to be democracy. The mass was the majority. They should take command of the laws of the land. Those who had too much should yield to those who had too little. The ones who took the profit by their capital should yield to those who made it by their labour.

Out of this idea came the notion of the state, not in the sense of the ultimate authority, but in the sense of the political and social expression of this collective will; the state not as in the phrase "the grand affairs of state," but as in the state as benefactor, as provider for those who couldn't provide for themselves.

So the state grew, first in the field of pensions and National Insurance, then in education, then finally after the war in the National Health Service. The state also regulated: health and safety laws; mining; the Protection of Children; redundancy and unfair dismissal legislation in the 1960s and 1970s. The state would protect. Its power would regulate, restrain and tame the power of capital.

But, in time, two things happened with profound political consequences for progressive politics, not just in the UK but everywhere where the same process of change had occurred. First, as the state ame-

liorated the conditions of the people, so the divide became more apparent between those who wanted to humanise capitalism and those
who wanted to eliminate it. For fifty years or more, this put the Labour
Party on the rack, meaning that its divisions were not just about means
but about ends, giving it a fatal incohesion right in its guts. Second—
and for the purposes of reform, of more consequence—the state grew,
and as it grew, its very success became its problem. Suddenly, alongside
the vested interests of capital could be seen very clearly the vested interests of the state. Bureaucracies are run by people. People have interests.
And whereas the market compels change, there is no similar compul-
sion in the public sector. Left to its own devices it grows. Governments
can change it, but governments use the public sector, depend on it and
are part of it.

Moreover, and partly as a result of what the state has achieved, as
prosperity spreads, the beneficiaries of the state find they are also its funders through their taxes.

In the 1930s, before the state's full power had been developed and
when the mass of the people were still "the mass of the people," the
middle way in politics could be easily defined. It was a public sector,
owning assets and regulating in the interests of fairness, alongside a private sector suitably constrained. Harold Macmillan's book *The Middle
Way*, written in 1936, was extraordinary for its time. It accurately
reflected where social democratic politics should have been. But such
politics only got there in the 1960s.

And that was the point. By the 1960s we had caught up with the
1930s. Anthony Crosland's book *The Future of Socialism* was a magnificent essay in bringing Labour to the reality of life in the 1950s, but we
only really imbibed it and digested it by the late 1980s.

Whatever the enormous impact of the Thatcher reforms had been on
the private sector of the 1980s, we had inherited a public sector largely
unreformed; and we weren't instinctively inclined to reform it. The state
was still as it had been since 1945. In fact, had Clement Attlee come
back to earth in 1998 and examined modern Britain, much would have
astounded him. But the welfare state, rather like Whitehall, he would
instantly have greeted as an old friend.

There was a further political complexity of which I was all too
acutely aware, and which bore directly on the issue of reform and the
unease I felt. As I say above, the people today are largely beneficiaries
and funders of the welfare state and public services. Unfortunately, what

this means is that simultaneously they want more of them and to pay less for them. And, again unfortunately, they are perfectly within their rights to hold these apparently contradictory sentiments.

It also makes them sorely prey to those within the service who tell them change will harm them. It always makes me hoot when the polls are trotted out showing how respected and trusted are doctors' opinions on the NHS, and how despised the opinions of politicians (and in 1998 the British Medical Association attacked us for the first time), when it is so obvious that those who are running a service have a self-interest as well as a public interest to serve, and when for most of the politicians, there is no reason other than public interest for taking them on.

So all this I knew. And if I am honest, I hesitated to probe fully my own doubts about the true radicalisation of what we were attempting. What we were doing up to then was working well politically, and well enough on the ground.

In the NHS, we were beginning to reorganise the system itself. Power to commission was being devolved to primary care trusts, local organizations working with local authorities, themselves run by GPs. Increasingly, they would hold the budgets and negotiate with the hospital trusts. But the reality was that a large part of the commission was already accounted for, in ensuring emergency admissions, operations, consulting appointments and so on. And there was no alternative provider to which they could turn. Likewise, GPs had a complete monopoly. Competition, even in the event of a hopeless service, was literally banned. So the different bits could negotiate with each other, but if they were unhappy, there was not a lot they could do.

We had, of course, increased the investment and there were extra staff being recruited and so on, but not enough to notice in what was a massive organisation, the biggest single employer in Europe.

It had been our pledge to remove the so-called divisive internal market of GP fundholders and ordinary GPs. This was a limited market experiment. Some GPs loved it. Others hated it. It did indeed make for a two-tier system. As grammar schools had. The trouble with this criticism was that an unreformed system also had its tiers. The middle class will always find a way to make the system work, or at least answer to them in some form or other. So good schools, comprehensive or not, would be in good neighbourhoods.

Throughout that period, then, roughly March 1998 to December 1999, we went through enormous policy introspection as the Green and

White Papers flowed, the policy wheels turned and the Civil Service toiled. I debated with policy experts, think tanks and the Number 10 unit headed by David Miliband, but had, as I have said, a growing hunch that our approach was not right. Not that it was wrong or having no effect—it was—but that it was incomplete at best, short of a dimension that was not peripheral but core.

The extraordinary thing was that there was no outside body, or institute or centre of learning that provided the dimension, with the possible exception of the work Richard Layard did for us at the London School of Economics on the New Deal. I used to pore over the latest offerings from various highly reputable academic or scholarly quarters, and find nothing of any real practical help. The trouble was that they essentially wanted to discuss the ideology behind the issues of reform. In a bizarre way, they focused on the politics—but that was not what I needed help with. I needed to know the practical answer. To me, to charge for the NHS or not is a political or ideological question, but the fastest way to cut waiting lists is not.

While we were trying to come up with solutions—"what counts is what works"—the sobering truth was that the system of welfare and public services was vastly complex, and "what does work?" was the question I kept referring to, without a great amount of external intellectual sustenance being provided. So we continued with the approach we had taken—driving from the centre—but we shied away from deep systemic reform. As a result, we could not produce change that was self-generated or self-sustaining, but change only generated and only sustained from the centre.

Nevertheless, at the party conference in 1998 the speech flowed. It set out the third way—not old left nor Thatcherite right; we had enough momentum to show things were changing; and to be fair the basic message was one of constant challenge, at least to the party. It was strong on devolution within the nation and partnership outside of it with Europe and America. It had all the right themes, pressed all the right buttons and, on the whole, generated the right responses.

As I sat afterwards with the close political family—Jonathan, Peter, Alastair, Anji, Sally, Peter Hyman—I knew we were still at the start of the journey, knew we still had a mountain to learn about as well as to climb, and my feelings were mixed, impatience and frustration knocking shoulders with the pride in achievements and political success; and of course there was also this glimmering of an appreciation that the rhetoric and the reality were out of alignment.

Another part of the problem was that there was increasingly no real interest in a policy debate. The Tories were in many ways *hors de combat*, still licking their wounds and, aside from Europe, not much bothered in opposing a government that, by governing from the centre, was making it pretty hard for them to get orientated.

Moreover, the media had settled into a mode, developing over time, whereby without a major controversy or visual focal point, there was no real interest in describing policy. For instance, they had been more engrossed in the Harriet Harman and Frank Field *pas de deux* than in the intricacies of the pension debate, Harriet being the Secretary of State for Social Security and Frank being the Minister for Welfare Reform. Admittedly, this saga was fairly engrossing. Harriet was not really a policy wonk and this portfolio required a lot of wonkery. Frank was not really politically astute and it required a lot of political astuteness.

The result was a severe mismatch, like a kind of "dating agency from hell" mistake. Frank was hugely persuasive on the big picture, but I couldn't seem to get him to focus on the practical policy. Harriet was desperate to be supportive of the policy, without quite understanding that it was her job to devise the damn policy.

Frank used to lock himself away in his office to "think the unthinkable," but the problem was not so much that his thoughts were unthinkable as unfathomable. Harriet fussed and fretted. They would sit in the Cabinet Committee disagreeing with each other, which was more than mildly disconcerting. The upshot was that we tried to steer policy out of Number 10, but it was hard. And, of course, the policy area itself was incredibly hard. The results were less than satisfactory.

I removed Harriet in the July reshuffle, which she took well, to her credit. When I refused to make Frank Secretary of State, he resigned. It was embarrassing, and though I both really liked and respected Frank—a genuine free independent spirit—I was also relieved. Some are made for office, some aren't. He wasn't. Simple as that.

After party conference we began preparing in earnest for the Queen's Speech. Although for the reasons given I was not wholly satisfied with the welfare reform package, it was to be the centrepiece of the speech. The weeks prior to it—and it was rather late that year, on 24 November, delayed by the leftovers from the previous packed parliamentary session—were a direct lesson in how the agenda can be hijacked by events from the grave to the trivial, or at least the sensational.

On the morning of 27 October, Jonathan Powell and Alastair Campbell suddenly interrupted the usual slew of meetings to pull me into the Downing Street dining room. The two of them together always meant trouble. What they told me made my eyes get wider and wider until I was like someone with goitre. It was one of those laugh, frown, gasp, sad routines.

Ron Davies, the Secretary of State for Wales, had been robbed by a black male prostitute on Clapham Common. My mind was fairly boggling, and we asked Ron to come into Number 10.

"It's all very easy to explain," he began. "I had been in Wales for the weekend, I drove up to London, and to stretch my legs I decided around midnight to go for a walk on Clapham Common." Puzzled looks from listeners. "I bumped into this Rasta bloke and we got talking, you know, as you do." Eyebrows raised further. "He said: Why not go for a curry? I said: Fair enough, and got in his car." Mouths start to fall open. "Then we met up with a few of his mates and suddenly I was set upon and robbed. Could have happened to anyone."

Stunned silence, then almost in unison, "Er, not really, Ron."

I know it's all absurd and, set out like that, comic; but it was also someone's career and life just about to disappear down the drain. That is what is so unbelievably cruel about political life. Of course it was the dumbest thing. In Ron's statement, which I helped to draft, I described it as "a moment of madness," but I knew his career couldn't be salvaged. The problem was not anything to do with sex or not, it was the misjudgement. I felt desperately sorry for him. I had known him since we came into Parliament together in 1983. He was a talented operator, though most people felt he was too talented an operator for comfort. But no one really deserves what he got.

And, naturally, it followed the same course as virtually every resignation I ever dealt with. At first they understand and comply. Then, as the enormity sinks in, they rebel and finally they become resentful. Ron followed that pattern precisely. And, of course, the hounding they get is a horrendous pressure on them and their family. Ron's was a resignation that was inevitable.

Over time, however, I became increasingly resentful of how resignations were forced. And so much depended on the circumstances of the revelation.

Unbelievably, a few days after Ron went, the *News of the World* trapped Nick Brown, whom we had moved from chief whip to be the Agriculture Minister in the July reshuffle, with someone who they said was a rent boy. When Alastair told me—and rather innocently I had never been sure Nick was gay—the room did sway a bit. Two gay scandals in one week. And there I am, completely committed to equality between gay and straight. Chris Smith had just bravely come out as the first openly gay Cabinet Minister. People knew Peter Mandelson was gay. I was a little alarmed at the public becoming a trifle wide-eyed themselves at everything.

To be fair to the *News of the World*, they came to us with the story on the Thursday before the Sunday publication, and Alastair heroically persuaded them to run it with Nick coming out as a gay man. The result was the story turned from a sordid scandal into an honest confession and Nick was saved.

He had been very angry at being moved from chief whip, and I knew he was more or less continually working for Gordon and against me, and had actually probably been doing so all along. But when the revelation came, he was saved, not least because he wasn't chief whip, though mostly because we went out of our way to save him. And here's where you just can't get all aggrieved as leader. You would think he would be grateful. Not a bit of it. He carried on believing he had been hard done by and that I was out to get him, when, of course, I could have got him there and then and finished him off. But we didn't because we were not like that. It was always odd to be described as having this incredibly ruthless machine, when actually we had plenty of ruth; indeed, on occasions far too much of it.

Just before Christmas 1998 there was a huge resignation, one that in time I came bitterly to regret and in respect of which I still reproach myself, though when I reread Alastair's diary on it and its accurate account of what the media furore was like, it is hard to see how it could have been toughed out.

Essentially, Peter Mandelson had been given a loan by Geoffrey Robinson, the Paymaster General, to buy a house. The sum was large, certainly in those days: £373,000. Peter was Secretary of State for Industry, and the department was inquiring into Geoffrey's business dealings, an inquiry established in response to a Tory complaint, and set up well after the loan was made. Peter hadn't disclosed the loan to his permanent secretary. He should have. That he didn't do so was, I had no doubt, nothing to do with being dishonest. In fact, Peter had had nothing whatever to do with the inquiry into Geoffrey, and neither would he have. If he had disclosed it, the affair would possibly have been manageable, though in the event the media just went for the whole thing rather than that one aspect.

As was my wont with "scandals" at that time, I pulled in the Lord

Chancellor Derry Irvine and Charlie Falconer, who had until recently been Solicitor General, as two good forensic minds. Both thought it very difficult.

I pushed the issue away for two days, and in any event was intensely preoccupied with the proposed U.S. military action in Iraq at that time. The *Guardian* had broken the story, and the rest piled in. It was wall-to-wall mayhem. Several members of the Cabinet called to say it was hopeless. Good old Jack Cunningham, whom we had moved from Agriculture to be Minister for the Cabinet Office, went out to defend the position, but even he found it hard. At least Parliament wasn't sitting, thank God.

By 23 December, I felt I couldn't sustain it. I steeled myself and told Peter, who accepted my decision with extraordinary grace. I also sacked Geoffrey. And I told Gordon that Charlie Whelan, his spokesperson, had to go as well.

My feelings were beyond rage; more real sadness and a sense of doom. The truth is I don't know that Gordon's people leaked it—you never do know—but only two people were party to the agreement for the loan, and I was sure as hell Peter hadn't told anyone, since he hadn't even told me. And it was the *Guardian*, not the *Mail* or the *News of the World*, to whom the story had been given; it was therefore more likely to be a party source such as Charlie Whelan, since the *Guardian* was more or less the party in-house paper at the time.

One thing was for sure: whoever it was had done it with complete malice aforethought. This was not a story, it was a political assassination, done to destroy Peter; but it was done also to damage me and damage me badly, without any regard to the impact on the government.

I sat in Chequers that Christmas Day and contemplated. Peter was a brilliant Secretary of State, had real verve and imagination, and was loved by his department (and believe me this is pretty rare). He was an important part of the government, and a crucial part of New Labour. This would end his career. Knowing all that, someone gives the story to the *Guardian*. What is the mentality of such a person? Determined, vengeful, verging on wicked. It frightened me because of what it might mean. People always think politicians behave to each other like something out of a Jeffrey Archer or Michael Dobbs airport novel, but in my experience, they don't. There is rivalry, backbiting, undermining, but little that you could describe as really dark. But this was.

I knew, in one sense, sacking Charlie Whelan was unjust because, as I say, I really didn't know that he was responsible; and to be fair, he denies it. I also knew, however, that if I didn't sack him, then a terrible lesson, with possible momentous consequences, might be learned for the longer term. So, after a bit of toing and froing, he went.

At the time I was certain Peter had to resign. Now I am not so sure. The trouble is, it's impossible to appreciate fully what it is like to be at the centre of a media frenzy, unless you have gone through it.

When they have decided to go for someone, they start with the story. That story may be true, but it is then embellished. If resistance is met, they just up the pressure until the frenzy is the journalists' equivalent of the screaming abdabs. If resistance continues, they basically say: right, we will continue running this story until the person resigns. The problem then becomes not the story but the total submersion of the government agenda. Nothing but nothing gets through.

Being prepared to wait that out is really hard, believe me. Towards the end of my premiership, when caution had finally been abandoned to the winds, I did tough it out (when there were calls for Tessa Jowell and John Prescott to resign), but it is a ghastly power struggle, and you worry as prime minister and leader of the party at the collateral damage and feel a responsibility to avoid it.

However, I still wish I had sat it out. It was an early trial of strength with the media and I backed down. To be fair, I also felt Peter had been stupid and wrong in not telling his permanent secretary; as happened with his later resignation in 2001, he didn't always help in the handling. But you know something? In the end that's beside the point. The point is not actually one about friendship or loyalty. It's about the country. There's a limited pool of talent in politics. A special talent—and he was and is very special—should have been saved in order to serve. When Gordon was prime minister and Peter asked my advice as to whether he should go back into government, I answered affirmatively without hesitation. His absence from my government was a huge loss; his presence in any government is a huge asset. Simple as that. So it's not just on policy that you learn in government.

On Boxing Day, I went off to the Seychelles. Poor old Alastair. He would call me up saying the press were terrible, I was being panned, and I was sitting in the sun or on a boat fishing or just generally relaxing, playing football with the protection team and the locals. It would drive him crazy. He felt he was bearing the brunt when I was "swanning off," but he never understood me and my holidays. The truth is I had had a bellyful, and needed some sun and an environment as far removed from Westminster, Whitehall, Downing Street and Fleet Street as could be imagined. Alastair tried calling a few times to sort out the details of the Whelan business, but eventually gave up in frustration. I had said Whelan had to go, and the details didn't trouble me. He was going.

The reason I had had a bellyful, however, was not only the rash of resignations. November and December 1998 had also been dominated by Iraq. On 11 November, I had met with George Robertson, the Defence Secretary, Robin Cook and the Chief of the Defence Staff, General Sir Charles Guthrie. Saddam had thrown out the weapons inspectors, who had written a damning report on the outstanding issues relating to weapons of mass destruction and Saddam's continuing ambitions to develop a programme for them. President Clinton was contemplating a military strike. Charles took me calmly through the options and the likely casualties were we to participate. As ever, he was straightforward, clear and strong. The next day I took the Cabinet through it, with George warning that this was the most serious development in respect of Saddam since the Gulf War.

On Saturday 14 November, we met in Downing Street again in the morning. We were set for air strikes to begin at 4 p.m. Suddenly the news came that Clinton had decided to pause, since Saddam had sent a new letter saying he would readmit inspectors. Then we got the letter. It was full of holes, typical Saddam rubbish. Over the next eighteen hours, finishing at 4:30 a.m. on Sunday, I was in constant contact with Bill. The action was suspended, much to the relief of Robin, who had been troubled by it. I was determined to keep the U.S. alliance intact and functioning at what was a crucial moment.

The inspectors went back in, but it was clear Saddam was just messing about. Finally, when their report came in mid-December, it was damning again. This time Bill decided we had to act, and we did so with four days of aerial strikes in Operation Desert Fox. It was a nerve-racking time, and the operation was a limited success. The general feeling was that Saddam had got away with it again.

EIGHT

KOSOVO

The awakening from Opposition to government lies in the tough nature of decision-making. In Opposition you can, if skilful enough, mask contradictions, conceal choices, blur distinctions, cast a cloak of ambiguous consensus over discordant, spiky and unpalatable decisions. So it looks smooth. In government, it is all jagged edges. The moment you choose and start acting on the choice, the edge starts to cut.

My awakening on domestic policy took place over time. Probably I only fully found my voice on domestic reform in the last term. The awakening on foreign policy was, by contrast, abrupt. It happened over Kosovo.

The categorisation of policy into foreign and domestic has always been somewhat false. Plainly a foreign crisis can have severe domestic implications, and this has always been so. Two things make the distinction even more misleading today: first, the world is far more integrated, so home and abroad tend to come together; second, as a global media develops, foreign crises are often played out in real time and graphically on our TV screens. They swiftly become domestic challenges. This can be because they impact on domestic life—as with the world economy or immigration—but also because people's sympathies and emotions are involved. When Israel attacks Gaza, for instance, the vivid nature of war and its attendant suffering is displayed immediately in our homes in the remotest parts of Britain. We are engaged in a way that, decades ago, would have required a kind of Midlothian campaign to get people aroused.

Yet even this description almost trivialises what is happening. It is not simply that people get affected by what they see; it is that they care about other people. Their feelings are genuine. They see starving children in Africa and are moved to act. They witness injustice and expect their government to help correct it. While they may care most about what happens within their borders, they are not indifferent to misery beyond them.

The culmination of all these things, more forcefully today than ever before, is to make the world interconnected not just economically or in self-interest but emotionally, the heart as well as the head. When we talk of an interdependent world, we mean that we are linked, that challenges and solutions tend to be in common, that problems in one part of the world can easily trigger reactions in another; but also that we feel at a human level more connected across national boundaries than ever before. The space we live in feels more shared, more held in common. Travel, mass media, the Internet and modern communication all pull us in one direction: together. Personally, I like this. I am comfortable—no, more than that, excited—by a world that is opening up, allowing us to experience and learn more about each other. However, even if I resented it, I would have to accept it as a fact, possibly *the* fact, of modern politics.

In the course of this, foreign policy and domestic policy interact and overlap; yet we still devote much to pretending they don't. Having read widely, I knew a lot about history before becoming prime minister; but about contemporary foreign affairs, I knew little. The 1997 campaign was fought almost exclusively on a domestic policy basis. If you had told me on that bright May morning as I first went blinking into Downing Street that during my time in office I would commit Britain to fight four wars, I would have been bewildered and horrified.

That's the way it is. I can't remember an incoming American president who fought a foreign policy campaign to reach the White House; or who didn't, in the course of his administration, end up being preoccupied with it. The conventional wisdom among all political strategists is that to base a campaign on, or become immersed in, foreign policy is a disaster, the beginning of the end. (As I found out, to a great extent that is true.) The reason is that the public think it's both important and at the same time very distant from their daily preoccupations.

So, at one level, the public understand the need for the big international picture. At another, to them it is round after round of summits, banquets and political chummery. It seems so remote—"What's it got to do with us?" is the cry. What you come to realise as a leader is that although this feeling may be understandable, it is also wrong. The very nature of the interdependence makes it so. Globalisation pushes people together. The challenges are faced together, and the solutions—in part, at any rate—have to be found together. Therefore, it is unlikely that a challenge in continent A, if it is truly serious, will not lead to a challenge in continent B. The phrase "global community" is a cliché, but it's also true. It's the way we live now.

There is another consequence of the interaction between foreign and domestic policy: the foreign policy itself has to be conducted in a different way. Global challenges require global solutions. Global solutions require global alliances. Global alliances can't be constructed on the basis of narrow national self-interest. They have to be based on shared global values.

Take climate change, which is *the* global challenge. The solution is a global agreement. The agreement requires developing and developed nations—China and India, America and Europe—to agree. Their national interest lies in a collective bargain. That bargain won't work unless it is fair to countries at different stages of development. By this process of reasoning, the national interest relies on a multinational accord that is based on a shared perception of fairness.

The effect of all this is that a traditional foreign policy view, based on a narrow analysis of national interest and an indifference unless that interest is directly engaged, is flawed and out of date. I happen to think as Gladstone did that it is also immoral; but even if I didn't, I am sure that in the early twenty-first century, it doesn't work.

This of course became the dominant debate over foreign policy during my time as prime minister. By the end, I am afraid, I was in a small minority when this thinking resulted in military action, but it was more widely accepted, at least in theory, when it came to the economy, the environment and other issues. It also utterly confused left and right until we ended up in the bizarre position where being in favour of the enforcement of liberal democracy was a "neoconservative" view, and non-interference in another nation's affairs was "progressive." But more of that later.

When Kosovo emerged as an issue at the end of 1998 and erupted in the first months of 1999, the jagged edge of foreign policy and decision-making was immediate and painful in effect.

Essentially, the problems caused in the wake of the break-up of Yugoslavia, following the collapse of the Berlin Wall, were still reverberating. The wounds of the Bosnia conflict were not fully healed. In particular, Serbia remained under the dictatorship of Slobodan Milosevic. Religious, ethnic and nationalist tensions abounded. Kosovo—a small territory about the size of Yorkshire or Connecticut, with roughly a million inhabitants of whom a majority were Muslim Kosovan Albanians—remained part of Serbia, which was a Christian Orthodox nation. Relations between the Serb rulers and their Kosovan subjects were dire.

The outcome of the Bosnian conflict divided the former Yugoslavia into a number of countries according to the Dayton Agreement of late 1995, achieved by the energy and ingenuity of the American diplomat Richard Holbrooke. Though it had taken two years for the West finally to intervene—in which time more than 200,000 people died—when it did so, the partition allowed some sort of peace.

In December 1998, Paddy Ashdown had sent me a note after his visit to the region. He reported that generally things were improving; but in respect of Kosovo, things were deteriorating. The KLA—the Kosovan paramilitary "liberation" army—was rearming in the face of Serbian military preparations for what looked like an invasion. Paddy's anxieties were reinforced by our intelligence people at the end of 1998, who reported strong evidence that Milosevic was about to authorise a major Serb assault. Already in the past months, hundreds of thousands of civilians had been displaced, and around 2,000 had died.

In October 1998, a temporary agreement was made, and some civilians returned under the assurance of the international community that it was safe to do so. But since then, displacements and killings had continued.

This was ethnic cleansing. What's more, it was happening right on Europe's border. In the first two months of 1999, the international community started to crank itself up to act. There was a conference at Rambouillet in France that tried to broker an agreement. Resolutions were passed, statements were issued and daily declarations were made about the unacceptable nature of what Milosevic was doing, but the killing and cleansing carried on. On 15 January at Račak, a small village in Kosovo, forty-five civilians were executed. Further condemnations were sent forth. The cleansing only intensified. Thousands were now dying.

Finally, in March, military action was taken, in the form of NATO strikes against Milosevic's forces. This continued up until June 1999 when, faced with the prospect of ground troops—at least from the U.S. and the UK—Milosevic retreated in disarray, a defeat that led to the erosion of his authority and, in time, his removal from power. Some 750,000 refugees returned.

The Kosovo conflict taught me many things, about government, about leadership, about myself. When I reread the material now and contemplate the situation as it evolved, I marvel at it. It also completely changed my own attitude to foreign policy.

So many things stand out. The first is that without doubt the primary instinct of the international community was to act, but within very tight limits, and if at all possible to put together a deal, virtually any deal, that removed the issue from the headlines. There was a desire to pacify, but not to resolve.

Second, from the outset I was extraordinarily forward in advocating a military solution. I look back and can see that throughout, to the irritation of many of our allies and the consternation of a large part of our system, I was totally and unyieldingly for resolution, not pacification.

Third, the strengths and weaknesses of Europe in this type of situation were laid painfully bare: brilliant at ringing statements of intent, which then evaporated into thin air when the consequences of seeing them through became apparent. This whole episode convinced me of the need for strong European leadership and for a proper European defence strategy.

In addition, I put the most colossal strain on my personal relationship with Bill Clinton. It says a huge amount about him and is to his unalloyed credit that he allowed the pressure to be put on him in the way that I did so. It also says a great deal about America and its preparedness, in the ultimate moment, to recognise the necessity of the moment and act.

Kosovo was a very tough issue for U.S. opinion. Unlike later conflicts in Afghanistan and Iraq, it was quite hard to describe the direct American interest. There was no real appetite in the public or among the politicians for any action, let alone major military action involving ground forces. The U.S. view was more or less that it was Europe's problem on Europe's frontier, thousands of miles from America, and the Europeans should summon the will to deal with it.

In discussions with officials and our military, I realised very fast that there was no way this was going to be resolved by diplomacy alone, and that military force would be necessary. Following our failure to intervene in Bosnia and the disaster of Sarajevo, Milosevic did not feel— unsurprisingly—that there was the will in the West for strong action, believing instead that he could do more or less as he wished. As a result, the advice I was getting was that without at least the threat of military action—and one that was credible—there was little prospect of stopping what were appalling scenes of brutality and oppression. Even then, the advice was that he was going to test our resolve and see whether we would put our forces where our mouths were.

From early January, I set about trying to build a consensus for action. My strategy was basically to engineer a set of strong declarations and keep diplomatic negotiations going, but make it plain that in the event of those failing, we were bound to act.

Why was I so keen to act? I saw it essentially as a moral issue. And that, in a sense, came to define my view on foreign and military intervention. I also saw it as an act of enlightened national self-interest, for I believed that if we left the issue to fester or allowed ethnic cleansing to occur unchecked, it would eventually spill over into other parts of Europe.

However, my primary motivation was outrage at what was happening. Here were ordinary civilians being driven from their homes and turned into refugees, killed, raped, beaten up with savagery and often sadism, whole families humiliated or eliminated. God, had we learned nothing from Europe's history? It was shocking. And in one way, even more outrageous was the sense in some quarters that, yes, well, it was shocking but did we really want to be involved?

Later, when I visited refugee camps in Macedonia and heard the stories of heartbreak and misery, I felt proud of what we had done, since these refugees would return home, but very uncomfortable at how close we had come to abandoning them.

Now we look back and most people would say: well, of course we couldn't have abandoned them; although we very nearly did—not because the political leaders who hesitated were bad people or poor leaders, or because they didn't feel as much as I did about the suffering and cruelty, but as we figured out what could be done in early 1999, it wasn't simple. Kosovo was part of Serbia. Serbia had an army that was powerful by reputation. Beginning wars is relatively easy; it's ending them that's hard. Innocent people die; unintended consequences develop; bad situations can be made worse. It is the uncertainty, the absence of clarity until hindsight delivers it—too late—that makes leadership difficult.

Through Kosovo I came to the view—rightly or, some may think in the light of Iraq, wrongly—that in such an uncertain landscape, the only way of finding direction was first to ask some moral questions: should this be allowed to happen or not? Should this regime remain in power? Should these people continue to suffer injustice?

If the answers were no, then that didn't mean you reach for the military solution. You need to try all other alternatives. You need to ask if such action is feasible and practical. People often used to say to me: If you got rid of the gangsters in Sierra Leone, Milosevic, the Taliban and Saddam, why can't you get rid of Mugabe? The answer is: I would have loved to; but it wasn't practical (since in his case, and for reasons I never quite understood, the surrounding African nations maintained a lingering support for him and would have opposed any action strenuously).

Posing and answering a moral question doesn't inexorably lead to a military solution, but it establishes a framework that can do so. And it is a structure with a plainly different starting point from that of traditional foreign policy, which is: is this in our country's interests?

Of course, my broader argument, based on the theory of global interdependence, is that this moral question is part of the national interest; but historically, such a broad view was distrusted. With some justification, it was thought of as leading to zealotry, to subjective and not objective criteria of judgement, to the heart leading the head rather than being in alignment with it. I have some sympathy with this view. The opposite view to mine is not the product of a moral disability; it is born from a perfectly natural reservation about the unforeseeable ramifications of morally motivated intervention. My point is not to denigrate or deplore the moral limitations of such a view, but rather to say that non-intervention also has unforeseeable ramifications. Non-intervention in Bosnia in the early 1990s might have seemed sensible at the time, but not in retrospect. And, of course, it led directly to Milosevic believing that he could get away with the operation in Kosovo.

During 1991 and 1992, ethnic cleansing had been pursued as a policy, organised by Milosevic and carried out with extreme brutality by the

Yugoslav National Army. Out of a population of just over 4 million, 200,000 Bosnians were killed, and a similar number were injured. Rape and pillage took place on a scale unbelievable in a relatively developed country in the late twentieth century. The UN was helpless. As the fighting started, its force in Sarajevo pulled out and left the civilians of that city to their fate, where 12,000 died. Thousands also died in Croatia and many hundreds of thousands were displaced across the region. Even after peace came, it left Milosevic intact, i.e. the peace pacified, but it did not resolve. As I sat in early 1999 trying to work out a way through, I was conscious that the same reluctance which had characterised our attitude in the early 1990s remained.

I worked on two groups: the Americans and the Europeans. For the latter—meaning essentially Jacques Chirac and Gerhard Schroeder, with the Italian prime minister Massimo D'Alema also intimately involved, given the proximity of the fighting to Italy—I tried to stoke up concern and also push the line that not resolving this was only going to lead to further trouble. Very early on, they were prepared to commit to the necessary expressions of disgust at what was happening and demand that it stop, but were insistent that any military threat should explicitly rule out the use of ground forces.

This, naturally, was an utterly hopeless negotiating tactic with Milosevic. It signalled from the outset that there was a limit to our seriousness of intent, and that provided he could withstand an air campaign, he could survive. It is amazing that people constantly miss the importance of the fact that any threat made in international affairs must be credible. The absence of credibility actually increases the likelihood of confrontation. The recipient of the threat doesn't believe it, so he carries on; then the very choice you are trying to avoid—go to war or not—is the one you are forced to make. I saw this time after time after time. We are about to witness the same wretched business over Iran. Back up a demand with a credible threat, and the demand has a good prospect of being satisfied. If you seem unsure about how far you will go to enforce a demand, a confrontation becomes almost inevitable.

So, from the off, I was somewhat isolated on the European side. To be fair, Gerhard had real internal and specifically German worries about participation in military action—for obvious reasons. Germany had become constrained by its constitution and its politics in signing up to any use of German forces. But, as time went on, he became more and more emphatic that ground troops should not in any circumstances be used, not only German forces but any country's. It was the first real rift in my relationship with him. I understood his problem, but he was a smart guy and he could surely see our problem: if it became clear that only ground forces could do the job, then either we committed them or we didn't do the job. Hundreds of thousands of refugees had then gone back to Kosovo in the summer and autumn of 1998 on our assurance that we would not permit a renewal of ethnic cleansing.

As we began the preparatory discussions for a NATO offensive, one other thing became crystal clear: even if we took action only by air, 85 per cent of the assets used would be American. In truth, without the U.S., forget it; nothing would happen. That was the full extent of Europe's impotence.

I began to engage with Bill Clinton over the possibility of military action, not just by air, but if necessary through the use of ground forces. By this time, my relationship with him had become close. We were political soulmates. We shared pretty much the same analysis of the weakness of progressive politics. We were both quintessential modernisers. We were both informal in style and young in outlook for our age. And both of us were at one level easy-going; but when you reached right down, there was a lot of granite providing the foundation.

He was the most formidable politician I had ever encountered. And yet his very expertise and extraordinary capacity at the business of politics obscured the fact that he was also a brilliant thinker, with a clear and thought-through political philosophy and programme. The myth he suffered from was the myth of his electability. In this respect, again, there were similarities with the predicament of New Labour.

The third-way philosophy that we both espoused was not a clever splitting of difference between right and left. Neither was it lowest-common-denominator populism. It was a genuine, coherent and actually successful attempt to redefine progressive politics: to liberate it from outdated ideology; to apply its values anew in a new world; to reform the role of government and the state; and to create a modern relationship between the responsibilities of the citizen and those of society—a hand up not a handout on welfare, opportunity and responsibility as the basis of a strong society. It was a way of moving beyond the small-state, "no role for society" ideology of the Republicans; and the big-state, anti-enterprise ideology of much of the traditional Democratic base. It was we who should be the good economic managers; the people who understood crime; the ones that got aspiration and empathised with it.

He completely recoiled from the rainbow coalition politics so favoured by parts of the left at the time. His famous speech against the black activists who preached hostility to whites, in which he told them bluntly he wouldn't countenance it, transformed in a moment the image of the Democrats as people in hock to minority radicalism.

Over time, the right wing brilliantly created the legend that people voted for him because he was just a really clever political operator; and of course a large part of the left joined in with the same chorus. In fact, people voted for him because they were smart. They didn't buy a slick politician; they bought a sensible, modern, worked-out programme, based on a philosophy that seemed far more relevant to the late twentieth century than what they had been offered so far.

Even as personalities, we were less dissimilar than people often thought, but as a political class act I deferred to the master. He had it all. His superb intellect was often hidden by his manner, but he had incredible analytical ability, was genuinely interested in policy debate—possibly, occasionally, too much so—and constantly on the lookout for new ideas.

He was quick-witted. He would have shone at PMQs. When I visited him in the Oval Office in 1996, just before my election campaign and his re-election, we sat there, me feeling very awed, hoping as you do that the meeting isn't too short ("Blair snubbed"), praying it overruns ("Blair welcomed"), but in either event begging to avoid disaster. Neil Kinnock, who as Labour leader visited Washington during Ronald Reagan's time, was done enormous damage both by the content of the meeting (Reagan bluntly said Labour's unilateral nuclear disarmament policy was crazy) and by the fact that Reagan mistook Denis Healey, travelling with Neil as the Shadow Foreign Secretary, for the British ambassador. For me, it was both a thrill to be there and a relief when it ended. But Bill couldn't have been kinder or more welcoming—and it did overrun.

If the president isn't going to do a full press conference—and it would be inappropriate to do that with an Opposition leader—he often does an impromptu few words in the Oval Office, as the press file through to take pictures. As we sat there and the cameras rolled, someone (Peter Riddell of *The Times*, I think) asked Clinton if he thought he was sitting with the next British prime minister. Tricky. Saying "Not a question for me" looks a bit cold; saying "Yes" would be diplomatically unthinkable. Quick as a flash, Bill says: "Well, I just hope he's sitting with the next president of the United States."

He also had inimitable resilience. When you reflect on what Bill went through during the impeachment saga, you have to sit down. It's too much. How could he, how did he, survive it? But he did, and left office with an approval rating over 60 per cent.

He did it first and foremost by refusing to let it dominate his view of his presidency, even if it did indeed dominate the media's. This is where the resilience was so fundamental to his success and survival. He used to tell me that every day he got up, determined to carry on governing. They would be talking about Monica Lewinsky; he would be launching a health-care plan. They would be dilating on the impossibility of him still being there; he would still be there, putting forward a new welfare programme. Whatever they did to him, he would carry on doing what he could for the people. He just got up and got on with it.

The second reason is that, as I suggested earlier, the public have always taken a more measured and human view of the sex lives of politicians than the media hysteria surrounding them would indicate. They understand; they empathise, and, to some extent, they indulge. It's not that they approve, but their disapproval is tempered. Their disappointment is qualified in its intensity by their knowledge that they too fall from grace, they too err and they too need forgiveness. While some take the view that their political leaders should be above reproach in this regard, others think that there are more important measures by which to judge them, such as: are they doing a good job for the nation?

So even Bill's "not telling the truth" they understood as him not wanting to embarrass his family. And then of course his persecutors overplayed their hand, and by the end were as much in the dock as he was. I was also convinced that his behaviour arose in part from his inordinate interest in and curiosity about people. In respect of men, it was expressed in friendship; in respect of women, there was potentially a sexual element. And in that, I doubt he is much different from most of the male population.

He was preternaturally cool under fire. By sheer happenstance, I was with him when major parts of the saga broke. The first time, in February 1998, the main revelation from Monica Lewinsky appeared, and I was in the White House. We had to do a press conference. As we stood in the ballroom, waiting behind the curtain to go through, we chatted away. I was more than a little nervous. I didn't for an instant think of doing anything other than being completely supportive. He was a great guy, a good president, and above all he was a friend. I am very, even excessively, loyal to friends.

It was one of those surreal moments in politics. At the press conferences there is a stated topic—actually, believe it or not, in this case it was
Saddam and the WMD. He was obstructing the inspectors yet again and
the international community was gearing up. We thought a military
strike a real possibility. Here was an issue of pressing life-and-death
importance. But then there is the issue the media wanted to get their
teeth into: Monica. So it was obvious which one would provide more
interest.

Just before we walked out to the stage, Rahm Emanuel, at that time
one of Bill's senior advisers, said to us, "Don't f*** it up." We didn't.
Bill was dignified. I was supportive. Given the circumstances, all in all it
was a triumph.

Later, on the day of another event—a third-way progressive politics
conference, where Bill and I were due to speak along with the president of
Bulgaria (a lovely guy called Petar Stoyanov) and Romano Prodi
(bizarre line-up)—a fresh revelation broke, namely the tapes of the Starr
interview. It was wall-to-wall. The pressure was mounting on Bill and
the attacks were absolutely vicious. His opponents could smell blood
and they were going for it.

As it turned out, the tapes were less sensational than at first had been
hoped or feared, but the day was more surreal than the last occasion. As
I entered the build-up to do the seminar, Bill and Hillary took me to a
small office where we talked. It was there that I witnessed the
indomitable Hillary determination, nerve and strength. If ever I wondered how important a part of Bill's rise she had been, I knew it from
then on. She was angry and hurt in equal amounts and large amounts—
that was clear—but no way was she going to allow it to destroy what
she, as well as he, had built. And if anyone had the right to be angry
with him, she had, nobody else.

People often asked me about their relationship. There was a common
assumption among many people, including other leaders, that theirs was
a marriage not of convenience exactly, but political partnership; that this
kept them together, despite it all. I used to say: you know what I think
it's all about? I think they love each other. That's the real revelation. Yes
it's a political partnership, yes it is buttressed by mutual ambition, but
when all is said and done, the ambition is the awning under which true
love shelters, not love which gives shelter to the ambition.

I didn't quite know what to say as the three of us sat there together.
Hillary just explained calmly and forcefully: this wasn't going to drive

him out. He would stay, fight and win. We talked for a time about it all, then we went to do the seminar and of course Bill was articulate, interesting, relaxed. I sat there at points open-mouthed in admiration of the chutzpah.

Later that day he and I went to do a meeting with students at Montgomery Blair High School outside Washington. We were supposed to deliver a speech on education policy. When we arrived there were thousands of students in the gymnasium. It was like a rally; they were shouting, stomping their feet, singing. We threw away the scripts and worked the crowd like two old music-hall queens. He got a fantastic reception and it lifted him.

By that time—September 1998—Kosovo was already making its presence felt. When we got to early 1999 and I had worked out what we needed to succeed, I realised it all depended on my relationship with him. If he could be persuaded, we had a chance. If not, the Europeans on their own would never act. We would repeat the mistake of Bosnia, not learn from it.

In January and February, Bill and I spoke regularly. The diplomatic offensive was still going on, but so was the Milosevic offensive against the Kosovan Muslims. The descriptions coming out of atrocities—Račak was the most reported, but was not exceptional—were pitiful. This was horrible: a civilian population slowly being ground into the dirt and for no other reason than being a different religion. The leader of the Kosovans, Ibrahim Rugova, came to see me. He was a thin, unwell man who had had throat cancer. He begged for help. "They are killing us," he said. He gave me a present, a small piece of purple-and-white Kosovo crystal. "I have little to give," he explained. I used to keep it on my desk in the den in Downing Street.

Bill and I agreed to take military action through NATO in a series of air strikes. At the beginning, and despite my intense misgivings, it was stated unequivocally that there would be no ground troops. Without that statement, there would have been no air action, so I thought it worth agreeing to. We could work out how to unravel it later.

Preparations were made. Suddenly in late March, the eviction, cleansing and killing of Muslim Kosovans quickened. Milosevic was mounting the campaign that had always been presaged. Now we had to act. The air strikes began, in which UK planes took part. I made a statement in the House, and we had broad cross-party support. Paddy, though he had announced in January that he was standing down from the Lib Dem leadership, was still leader at this point, and was strongly supportive. He also sent me a note warning that ground forces would be necessary.

My first full-scale military campaign got under way. Basically, Kosovo demonstrates the fundamental, unavoidable and irredeemable limitations of a pure air campaign against a determined opponent who cares little about losing life. It followed what is now a familiar path for such campaigns. Air strikes do real damage and are visually forceful; they weaken an enemy's infrastructure and demoralise the military and certainly the civilian population; they can deter, inhibit and constrain—what they can't do is dislodge a really dogged occupation of land by an enemy willing to sustain losses and wait it out.

At the beginning, the targets are plentiful. With modern technology and weaponry, these are swiftly taken out. The question then arises: now what? The targets get more interspersed with civilian areas. "Collateral damage"—a ghastly phrase that I tried to ban—grows, and the wrong targets get hit. (In this case, not just civilian, but in a terrible accident, the Chinese Embassy in Belgrade.) The enemy is being damaged, but not being beaten. Frustration grows, as does a sense of unfairness, at least in Western nations, at a purely air campaign. "Planes versus soldiers" is not thought quite fair. All of it increases the pressure on the political leaders. If you are not careful, the aggressor starts to assume the mantle of victim.

Worse, in this case, after a few days it became clear that NATO itself had certain severe limitations in running such a campaign. We had a hopelessly, almost laughably, complicated committee procedure for clearing targets, which frequently delayed decisions. Wes Clark, the Supreme Allied Commander Europe in charge of NATO military operations, was a good guy, fired up, committed, but in no way did he have the necessary media and communications infrastructure which a campaign like this, dominating the world news, required. Javier Solana, NATO Secretary General, was also first class, but caught between the differing views (not to say egos) of his political bosses.

To cap it all, there were now hundreds of thousands of refugees streaming across the border, swamping the surrounding nations, especially Macedonia. After two weeks, I thought enough was enough. The thing couldn't go on like this. It was going to be a disaster.

I then took a clear decision. I had only been in power eighteen months, but already I was contemplating that I might have to leave. I spoke to Alastair and Jonathan and then called the close team together. I said: I am willing to lose the job on this, but we are going to go for broke. We are going to take even more of a fronting-up, out-there, leadership position and stake it all on winning. The response so far to what was a monstrous and unpardonable outrage had been pathetic. We were going to try to grip it and I would use all my chips with President Clinton to get a commitment to ground troops on the agenda.

The team were fabulous at moments like that. Some of them thought it more than a little strange that a government committed to changing Britain's public services and cutting unemployment should put its life on the line for a military adventure in the Balkans, but they all jumped to it to make it happen.

First, I contacted NATO and spoke to Wes and Javier. To my surprise, rather than resenting help, they welcomed it with open arms. We went to NATO. I took Alastair with me, not for my press but for theirs. I recall seeing Wes in his office. Suddenly his mobile went. It was a journalist asking about the campaign. He spoke to him briefly and returned to our conversation. "How often does that happen?" I asked. "Oh, all the time," he replied. He was doing the military side brilliantly, but was immensely frustrated at the lack of political cohesion and commitment. He warned me, rather nicely and in a kindly way I thought, that I shouldn't think all leaders felt like I did. Alastair stayed on to work his magic and organise a proper comms infrastructure. Wes told him that he should watch my back. This was good of Wes but I knew already I was way out on a limb.

I then spoke to the generals, in particular the decent German in charge of the air campaign. The generals, including our own very capable Rupert Smith, were unanimous: you can't win this by an air campaign alone.

Paddy went out to the Balkans again, and returned convinced we were not winning. After thirty days, he said, we have yet to stop Milosevic taking any action he wants to take against the Kosovans. The number of refugees was growing; the targets were shrinking. The Macedonian prime minister sent me a message through Paddy: "My people are frightened because they think NATO has a plan and they are not being told about it. I am even more frightened because I know NATO hasn't got a plan."

I spoke once more to President Clinton and then followed up with a personal note. I put forward plans for better coordination, changes in targeting procedure, changes in the media operation.

A week later I sent another note. In the meantime, I had visited one of the refugee camps myself. However specious such visits are, it allowed me to speak with greater authority. In this second note, I went over our call of the night before, during which I had again raised the issue of ground forces. Unsurprisingly, Bill had recounted all the objections, even of planning such a thing, since the fact of the planning would inevitably leak out. In the note, I pressed the need for the logistics to begin now, because unless that happened, we might be too late to do anything before the winter came, given that a ground campaign could take months to implement.

I then really went over the score. I saw our military. The Chief of Defence Staff, Charles Guthrie, was someone I really liked, respected and relied on, as I say. He was of the same view as me, but I said if we needed a ground offensive, we should be prepared to offer 50,000 UK troops, with the U.S. supplying 100,000–150,000. I knew that very few, if any, other European nations were likely to join in and we would be relying on the Americans. Not unreasonably they would say: Well, if you're so keen, what are you prepared to commit? Even Charles's eyebrows were raised. It was an outsized gamble. And also Gordon, again not unreasonably, was starting to question the cost.

The air strikes continued, but as each day passed, the absurdity of ruling out ground forces became ever more apparent. Of course, the figures for the number of troops staggered everyone. But here's what is interesting about leadership. These are the decisions that define. They separate out. They are the distinguishing features of high command.

It goes like this. You have a strategic objective. Let us say you have embarked on achieving it. You come to an obstacle. The cost of removing it seems vast. Everyone not sitting in the leader's chair can have a discussion about it. The cost is very high, says one; the objective is very important, says another; the pros and cons are mighty, says a third. The leader has to decide whether the objective is worth the cost. What's more, he or she must do so unsure of what the exact cost might be, or the exact price of failing to meet the objective. Both of these have to be judged and measured according to an inexact science. Those not in the seat can point to the cost or the price, but they don't have to say which prevails. Their responsibility may be acute, but it isn't ultimate. That responsibility sits with the leader.

In this context, by the way, indecision is also decision. Inaction is also action. Omission and commission both have consequences.

So, yes, a ground war in the Balkans. Are you crazy? But if the alternative is a victory for Milosevic, what price peace in the wider region then? What price NATO credibility? What price deterrence to dictators?

So however high the cost, my decision was that the price of allowing Milosevic to triumph was so high that it couldn't be countenanced. Therefore, if the only way of avoiding the price was a ground campaign, we had to do it.

It was, nonetheless, let us say, a minority view . . .

As late April dragged into May, my anxiety redoubled. NATO had the situation more under control though I was still uncertain of how the situation would go forward and resolve itself. We at least had a serious case to deploy and were deploying it. But the fact remained: Milosevic was still there and there was no sign he was prepared to withdraw. The diplomatic track continued, but it was unclear that it was leading anywhere acceptable, certainly anywhere acceptable to me. By then I had come to believe that nothing except his unequivocal defeat would do.

But the enthusiasm of our European allies for a ground offensive had not burgeoned; on the contrary, the opposition to it was as firm as ever. On 18–19 May, I wrote two notes, one to President Clinton, the other to key fellow European leaders.

In the note to Bill, I agreed again that we needed to prepare for a ground offensive. I advocated a force of around 150,000 with half coming from Europe, and half of that from the UK. It was a pretty bold suggestion since I had no clear reason to believe Europe would contribute any troops other than UK ones, but I bet that if the U.S. committed, the Europeans would feel shamed into support, especially if the Brits were putting in by far the biggest number.

I also tried to amend the proposal being put forward by Massimo D'Alema for a forty-eight-hour pause in the bombing, the purpose of which was to see if Milosevic would strike a deal. I was really worried that if we just accepted this proposal *simpliciter*, it would give Milosevic exactly what he wanted. So I suggested that along with the pause, there should be a UN Security Council Resolution (there were signs Russia might support one if there was a pause) giving Milosevic an ultimatum: take it or leave it; and if he refused, reconvening immediately with the prospect of a ground operation.

The tone of the note to Bill was apologetic for continuing to press on ground forces, but unyielding on the necessity of confronting the issue. Milosevic was still absorbing the punishment, but the targeting was now

harder and harder. A civilian convoy had been hit, causing more criticism of our campaign. I could see where this was heading, and a messy
compromise was an acute possibility which I wanted to avoid at all
costs.

For the Europeans, I made the point starkly: is the bottom line
"NATO must not lose," or is the bottom line "NATO must not use
ground troops"? If it is the former, how can we rule out ground troops
when the military advice is unanimous that we cannot guarantee victory by the air campaign alone?

I buttressed both notes with telephone calls. The one with Bill
began very stickily indeed. A series of press reports had suggested the
U.S. were being pressured by me to commit and I was having to stiffen
him. He pointed the finger at my press operation (of course everyone
believed Alastair single-handedly shaped the news everywhere). He
was genuinely steamed up. I denied it vigorously (and truthfully). It
turned ugly for a bit until, having got it out of his system, the conversation turned back to the issue and for the first time I could feel he was
manoeuvring his side into supporting a ground operation. It was a
big step forward. I also realised how difficult it was for him. Virtually no
one was urging that course on him and he knew full well the Republicans were lining up to cane him either way: weak, or foolhardy.

It was as well our relationship was strong enough to overcome what I
call the "winding-up syndrome" of political courts and courtiers. It was
a phenomenon I came across so frequently, and it used to do so much
utterly pointless damage.

By and large politicians are an odd mix of rhino hide and super-soft
tissue. They need the hide just to get through the day, since slings and
arrows are more or less constant. At another level, their natural insecurity often makes them acutely sensible of how they are seen, whether
they are duly respected by their peers, who is out to get them and who
supports them. It is unbelievably easy to forget this. Things can be written and said about another leader without you even being aware of
them, but they are attributed to you, and in the blink of an eye a relationship has soured. I always say in politics that other than when you
really need to, you should avoid making enemies deliberately, because
you make so many entirely accidentally.

In this process, the "winding-up syndrome" plays a big part. Leaders
have teams around them. The members of the teams owe their positions
to the leader. For the most part they are loyal, sometimes fiercely so. They

are always on the lookout for a slight, and scour the press. More sinisterly, they also know their leader's inner fears and insecurities, and become adept at manipulating them.

I had a great team and was really lucky that Anji and Jonathan, especially, were very ready not to suspect or see a conspiracy behind every criticism or move made. But I lost count of the times I had to say: You don't know who put that story there; I don't know; what's more we will never know, so let's stop bothering about it. I therefore got the "winding-up" a lot less than most, but I saw it go on perpetually around other leaders and indeed other Cabinet members. The worst time was in and around any Cabinet reshuffle when the speculation would be rampant, and if anyone's name appeared in the papers, it was naturally assumed to be put there by the "Downing Street machine."

The most bizarre example of this was in 2004 over the then Secretary of State for Work and Pensions, Andrew Smith. Andrew was a capable minister, nice guy, never going to be Chancellor but hard-working and effective. The press started to say I was ready to sack him. It may well be that the GB people had put the thought in the press mind or his (see— that's me being a victim of the syndrome, because actually I really don't know).

Anyway, he was convinced he was for the chop. He came to see me and said he was going to resign before he was pushed. The reshuffle was due in the next days, and I had the outline of it. I was not going to sack him—in fact, I had never thought of it, and told him so—but so wound up was he that he obviously didn't believe it and said, no, he really preferred to go rather than suffer the indignity of being sacked. So he went.

You have to be fantastically careful of being wound up by people who love the chatter and the intrigue and the "behind the arras" stuff, or even by very well-intentioned close staff who genuinely believe you are being badly done by. Paranoia is the worst condition for a political leader to suffer from.

However many voices were whispering in Bill's ear that the famed Blair machine was trying to upend him and grandstand. Fortunately he didn't let it bother him for long. And on the decision that mattered, he was moving in the right direction and with considerable courage.

Over the next two weeks, it became apparent that the American resolve to see this through had hardened. Clinton was arriving at the decision to prepare and if necessary implement the ground-force option—at least in his own mind, but it is remarkable how quickly such things are communicated almost by osmosis through the system. Press reports to that effect started to circulate.

On 27 May, we spoke again and I followed it up with another personal note. He was not fully convinced, but we were on a trajectory. I also pointed out that a victory against Milosevic could be the signal to offer a whole new future to the Balkan countries, within Europe.

Interestingly, on 1 June, David Miliband sent me a note from Florida, where he had been at the same time as the president; David minuted that he thought Clinton's mind was made up and now the issue was only how he could persuade the American people.

As our resolve grew, so Milosevic's started to collapse. We were nearing the end. As European leaders met on 3 June, the UN negotiators led by President Martti Ahtisaari of Finland went to Belgrade. Milosevic was prepared to capitulate. Over the coming days, there were some ups and downs but essentially it was over. On 10 June, the agreement for the complete and unconditional withdrawal of Serbian forces from Kosovo was concluded.

There was an extraordinary epilogue, which arose in this way: the idea was for the Serbian forces to withdraw, and then NATO would go into Priština airport. On Friday 11 June, we awoke to news that there was a delay, and suddenly we were told Russian forces intended to occupy the airport. Throughout, of course, the Russians had been strongly opposed to the military action, which was one reason why we couldn't get a UN Security Council resolution. They were obviously very closely connected to the Serbs. If they then took over the main airport, it would turn everything into a fiasco.

Russian planes demanded airspace to fly through Hungary to get to the airport. Russian tanks were on their way from Bosnia. At this point Wes Clark decided we had to take the Russians on. He wanted to order General Mike Jackson, the British on-the-ground NATO commander, to fight for control of the airport if necessary. Wes was Mike's commanding officer for these purposes. It was, therefore, very tricky. Did we really want British forces fighting Russians? I didn't think so.

Wes was absolutely right to be mad at the Russians. It was a total breach of the understandings that had been made. It was inflammatory and it threatened the peace.

I came out of a meeting to take the increasingly frantic calls ricocheting around the system. Charles Guthrie thought we should be extremely cautious. Contrary to all propriety in chains of command, I called Mike

Jackson myself. Fortunately he was a very sound and solid citizen, brave though not daft; but also in a difficult position: Wes was his commander-in-chief. Mike explained an order was an order. What should he do? The U.S. forces hadn't arrived. Only the Brits were on the spot. To fight, or not to fight? Mike clearly thought fighting the Russians was completely crackers. I told him to play along, ignore the order and stay cool. He sounded relieved.

Finally, after a couple of days of farcical toing and froing, the Russians said it had all been a mistake and the matter was settled. I often wondered what would have happened if I had told Mike to obey the order to fight. Doesn't bear thinking of, really.

The Russians were very weird to deal with at this time. Yeltsin was a man of considerable courage and had done a great thing for his country in defying the coup against the democratic forces after the Gorbachev changes in Russia. But by the time I knew him, he had become, let us say, a bit unpredictable. I recall meeting him at an international summit shortly after the Kosovo conflict. We had exchanged some pretty harsh words about it, but it was all over now, so he came across the room to greet me with one of his famous hugs. I was happy to be embraced, as it signalled that the feud was a thing of the past and now we could all get on. The hug began. The first ten seconds were, I thought, wonderfully friendly. The next ten began to get a little uncomfortable. The following ten started respiratory problems. I finally got released after about a minute and staggered off in search of a stiff drink. I think he made his point.

I got to know Vladimir Putin far better than I ever knew Boris Yeltsin. It was a relationship that began really well, and though over time it cooled—as a result of Iraq, but more perhaps as a result of the worsening Russia–U.S. relationship—I never forgot the initial warmth, and never gave up trying to understand what made him as he was and is.

One thing I did get completely: when Russia was the Soviet Union, although it had the wrong system of government and economy, it was nevertheless a power; it was treated with respect, even feared. It counted. I understood how glasnost, perestroika and the fall of the Berlin Wall may have liberated Russia from Communism, but it also made it seem to lose its position in the world. Yeltsin, for all his strengths, was not someone capable of regaining that position. Putin was; he is quintessentially a nationalist.

I also had a serendipitous connection with him. Our friends the

Strozzis, whose villa in Tuscany we used to visit, were Russian on Irina's side. They are a remarkable family. He is a professor whose ancestor has been associated with Machiavelli, and she is a strong-minded and delightful person. Together they have produced two extraordinarily talented daughters who both speak five languages. Irina's family had fled during the Revolution and settled in France, where she and her brother Vladimir were brought up, but they continued to be engaged with Russia. A good friend of Vladimir's was the then mayor of St. Petersburg, Anatoly Sobchak, who was also the patron of Putin. I met Sobchak at the Strozzi villa in 1996, and once more before his premature death in February 2000 (supposedly from natural causes).

This gave me a point of connection with Putin, who had been Yeltsin's prime minister before running for president himself. As prime minister, Putin had prosecuted the war in Chechnya with vigour and, some said, brutality. Though I understood the criticism, I was sympathetic to the fact that this was also a vicious secessionist movement with Islamic extremism at its core, so I understood the Russian perspective as well.

I met him just before he took over as president in 2000, when others at that time, including Jacques Chirac, gave him something of a cold shoulder. Of course, in time that all changed and their relationship became very close as mine waned. Back then, Putin wanted Russia to orient towards Europe, and our first meeting was in St. Petersburg, the most European of all Russian cities. He admired America and wanted a strong relationship with it. He wanted to pursue democratic and economic reform in Russia. We were the same age and, it seemed, shared the same outlook.

We met at the Mariinsky Theatre to see an opera conducted by Valery Gergiev. Putin had chosen the opera carefully: *War and Peace* by Prokofiev, written as a morale booster for Russian nationalism and caricaturing Napoleon as Hitler. It was an extraordinary occasion and all of Russian top society was there. One thing happened which I often recalled to myself in future years. Vladimir and I walked through the beautiful corridors of the magnificent nineteenth-century building. In a similar situation in the UK, I would have been greeting people, shaking hands, engaging and being engaged; with Vladimir I noticed people fell back as he approached, not in fear or anything; but a little in awe and with reverence. It was a tsar-like moment and I thought: Hmm, their politics really isn't like ours at all.

Vladimir later came to believe that the Americans did not give him his due place. Worse, he saw them as circling Russia with Western-supporting "democracies" who were going to be hostile to Russian interests.

In vain, I tried to get him to see that actually we supported those countries in their wish for democracy, not because we saw them as a strategic bulwark, enfeebling or encircling Russia, but because we genuinely believed that if they wanted to have the same freedom as us, we should allow and encourage it. I even proposed (and got accepted at NATO) a new arrangement for cooperation with Russia, which gave them a far greater involvement in NATO decision-making.

But in time, my efforts failed. Iraq; National Missile Defence which, in a sense understandably, they saw as aimed at them; the weakness, as they saw it, of the American efforts to construct a proper partnership; and most of all, the Western belief that under Putin's leadership Russia began to exhibit undemocratic and tsarist/KGB tendencies—all of this conspired to put him in a position where he believed it was better for Russia to be "independent" (i.e. difficult) and to pursue a foreign policy of a very nationalist kind.

However, I never lost that initial feeling for him or the thought that had circumstances transpired or conspired differently, the relationship could have prospered. And that's how politics is.

Another reason for the difficulty in my relationship with Vladimir was that I think he found my approach to foreign policy intervention at best odd and at worst dangerous. To him, major powers should work out their interests in a fairly traditional, hard-headed way and implement them. Talking of moral causes was a serious mistake. It destabilised when stability was key. It started a row about rights and wrongs, which just got in the way of necessary power-brokering.

I'm afraid, however, Kosovo had not diminished my appetite for such intervention where I thought it essential to resolve a problem that needed resolution, and where a strong moral case could be made.

In Sierra Leone in early 2000, a further challenge presented itself. It is one of the least discussed episodes of my ten years as prime minister, but it's one of the things of which I am most proud. However, the important thing is the lesson it can and should teach us.

The tale of Sierra Leone—and I hope its future chapters are brighter—is a metaphor for what happened to Africa. Fourah Bay College in Freetown has a link with Durham University, where my father taught. It used to be one of the top universities in Africa and as good as many European ones. In the 1960s, Dad would go out to teach in Freetown. At that time, Sierra Leone was a country freed from colonial rule, with a strong governing infrastructure and a GDP per head around that of Portugal.

Between then and the late 1990s, the country went on a downward spiral that was as tragic as it was entirely avoidable. By the time we came to power, the democratically elected government looked as if it would be toppled by a collection of gangsters, madmen and sadists known as the Revolutionary United Front (RUF), and the country's abundant natural resources—particularly its diamonds—were being systematically plundered. The people were caught in the middle.

When the government tried to insist that the future should be decided by an election, its supporters were subject to a campaign of medieval brutality. When I visited after calm was restored, I drove through village after village. Every third or fourth person would have a part of their right arm missing. The RUF's response to the demand for a vote had been to cut off the voting hand of the people—literally.

Preceding our intervention was the usual round of negotiations, agreements, declarations and general attempts to find common ground between factions who had none. For two years, the diplomatic saga dragged on. A UN force was sent, but, as ever, was mightily constrained, both politically and logistically.

Britain, the former colonial power, had an especial interest. We contributed some observers and military advisers to the force, but it was plain the situation was going nowhere but downhill. Ceasefires came and went. In May 2000, it suddenly turned really ugly as the RUF renounced the latest ceasefire and went on the rampage.

President Ahmad Tejan Kabbah, who was a kindly and decent man, had just come to see me to beg for help. When the RUF finally threatened to take over the whole country, there was a simple decision: did we leave it to the UN force, who had already shown that they couldn't really contain the RUF, or did we decide to act ourselves?

As usual, Charles Guthrie was clear and unambiguous. He said: We have out there a force of a thousand or more men. We can send more. We can send a battleship. If you want us to sort out the RUF, let's do it. The instructions were given.

The British had been defending the airport at Lungi. Their mission was expanded, and over a number of weeks they did indeed sort out the RUF. Their action gave the UN a chance to bolster its force. The RUF leader Foday Sankoh was arrested, and during the following months there was a build-up of the international presence, a collapse of the rebels and then over time a programme of comprehensive disarmament, with the former RUF soldiers being gradually absorbed back into Sierra Leone society. The country's democracy was saved.

After that experience, I became ever more convinced that there had to be a proper, well-equipped standing force for Africa, preferably African in nature, with a mandate to intervene and be deployed in situations such as Sierra Leone. The problem in much of Africa is conflict. You can ship in enormous amounts of aid, but unless you deal with the root causes—fights over resources and territory, weak or corrupt governance—the aid is only ever going to be a sticking plaster and, as such, subject to being ripped off and the wounds reopened at any time. I advocated such a force, and with Kofi Annan pushing hard, the UN eventually agreed it. It's still in the making today, though the capability has grown. Without addressing these gaping inadequacies in practical politics, all that development aid will salve our conscience but not the countries most in need of salvation.

During the Kosovo conflict, I had the opportunity to address the Economic Club of Chicago. In that speech on 24 April 1999, I set out what I called a "Doctrine of the International Community," a rather grand title for what was really a very simple notion: intervention to bring down a despotic dictatorial regime could be justified on grounds of the nature of that regime, not merely its immediate threat to our interests. It was an explicit rejection of the narrow view of national interest and set a policy of intervention in the context of the impact of globalisation.

It was such a break with the past that I was careful to hedge the doctrine with limitations, in case it was thought madly quixotic. Even so, it drew predictable criticism for making foreign policy a moral cause. Interestingly, in the light of later military campaigns, many on the Republican right took issue with it, seeing it as contaminating a proper and prudent regard for the only thing that matters: the American national interest. But, of course, my point was that this interest had to be more broadly defined in the new era.

I set out five major considerations when considering intervention.

First, are we sure of our case? War is an imperfect instrument for righting humanitarian distress; but armed force is sometimes the only means of

dealing with dictators. Second, have we exhausted all diplomatic
options? We should always give peace every chance, as we have in the
case of Kosovo. Third, on the basis of a practical assessment of the situation, are there military operations we can sensibly and prudently undertake? Fourth, are we prepared for the long term? In the past we talked
too much of exit strategies. But having made a commitment we cannot
simply walk away once the fight is over; better to stay with moderate
numbers of troops than return for repeat performances with large numbers. And finally, do we have national interests involved?

In retrospect, applying those tests to Iraq shows what a finely balanced
case it was, and why I never thought those who disagreed were stupid or
weak-minded.

But the doctrine itself comes down not only to a debate about foreign policy, but also to a judgement, and a judgement rather familiar
across the board in politics: how best to bring about change, assuming
change is necessary or strongly desirable. Change can happen by evolution, and it can happen by revolution. This is true of the way a
country proceeds towards freedom. Russia in 1917 is a case in point. It
could have changed through Kerensky and in a step-by-step social
democratic advance, but it happened in fact by Bolshevik revolution.
It is true also of more mundane areas of politics: public services or the
economy can be changed by gradual reform, or they can be changed
sharply, as with the Thatcher revolution in industry in the 1980s.

But here is the point: if a system is malfunctioning, it does need to
change, whether that change be gradual or abrupt.

In some cases of regimes that are oppressive and dictatorial, there is
nonetheless a process of evolution that is discernible in the right direction. The reforms may be slow, but there is a direction and it is benign;
or at least, it is not threatening.

In other cases, the regime's very nature lies in its oppression. It has
chosen to be what it is. It will not change, not by evolution, not by the
exercise of its own will—because that will is directed towards oppression—and for a long time, at least, it will not change by the will of the
people who, because they are oppressed, lack the means to overthrow
the regime. Its malign nature will deepen.

Even with regimes like this, the answer cannot be always to intervene.
They may pose no outside or external threat; or it may be easily contained
diplomatically. It may—as with Mugabe—be simply politically impractical
to intervene.

But where there is such a threat and intervention is practical, then a judgement has to be made. If change will not come by evolution, should it be done by revolution? Should those who have the military power to intervene contemplate doing so?

The dangers are evident. As I said earlier, such an attitude can lead to rash adventures and to consequences worse than those of the oppression. That's the case some would make on Iraq, to which we shall come later. But non-intervention also has its consequences, as again I said earlier. In each military campaign I engaged in, there was a history of non-intervention before the intervention. Milosevic had removed autonomy from Kosovo in 1989, and the tension and suffering had built for almost a decade. Bosnia was the epitome of the non-interventionist philosophy; and of its consequences. In Sierra Leone, through all sorts of cobbled-together compromises, non-intervention or mild intervention had held sway for several years. In other words, evolution had failed. The only thing that was going to work was solving the problem, not pacifying it. And of course in a different part of Africa, in the small state of Rwanda, the non-interventionists succeeded in holding back those who took the genocide as a call to arms.

No one can say the problems of the Balkans are now solved. Sierra Leone remains poor, as does too much of Africa. But the Balkans, which for a century or more was a byword for instability, today has at least the prospect of a better future. Croatia has opened accession nego-tiations with the EU, and Slovenia is a full member. Sierra Leone is a democracy. Its government has changed without bloodshed. Next door, Liberia is on the same agonising, difficult journey into the future, and its former leader who supported the RUF is awaiting trial.

When revolution comes through intervention, and when that inter-vention is based on a desire to bring freedom and democracy, the strug-gle will still be arduous; the setbacks will be legion; those who exclaim that it would all have been better if left well alone will have their day, and regularly; but I doubt history will make the same judgement. Even if brought about by the pain of war, at least the grip of oppression is broken after such a revolution. A proper evolution, however fraught, can begin.

This is a fascinating debate. At the special meeting of the five perma-nent members of the UN Security Council in New York in September 2000, it led to the adoption of the Brahimi Report, which laid out the plan to create a standing UN force for peacekeeping in Africa, a direct effect of the success of the Sierra Leone intervention. It also led to the

UN adopting in 2005 the principle of the "Responsibility to Protect," the idea that states have a duty to safeguard their citizens from mass atrocities, and that the international community has a duty to intervene if a state fails in this responsibility.

But however much it fascinated me (and some others), it didn't cut much ice with the British public.

Throughout 1999 and particularly around Kosovo, we were aware the government was losing support. Its focus—my focus—seemed to be on a faraway place; and there was plenty to do at home, not least in health, education and crime. And, indeed, we were trying to do it; but not unnaturally, the headlines were full of tanks, bombs and airplanes.

It was not all bad. We won the first Scottish Parliament elections, the first time in the twentieth century that the government polled ahead in the local elections for city and town councils. Not that I should call them "local"—the entire thing was itself a revolution of sorts.

Attempts to devolve power to Scotland, Ireland and Wales had been made ever since the United Kingdom was formed, and time after time they failed. It was the same commitment to devolution, very roughly, that had engulfed and nearly destroyed the Liberal Party of the late nineteenth century, and in the 1970s it was on devolution (among other things) that the last Labour government had come unstuck, when the so-called West Lothian Question had dominated debate and defeated the devolution legislation.

The West Lothian Question was named after the Labour MP Tam Dalyell's constituency, since he was the person raising it. The question itself was very simple: if by devolution you reserve certain issues such as health or education to a Scottish Parliament so that English MPs no longer have a say in them, how can it be right or logical that Scottish MPs can still vote on issues of English health or education? It was a perfectly sensible question, and an interesting example of a problem in politics to which there is no logical answer.

However, my answer to it was that, though not logical, a devolution arrangement was not as unfair as it seemed. The truth is English MPs dominate the Westminster Parliament, which passes the Budget and makes the laws. In deciding the Budget allocation to the Scots, for example, English MPs could always outvote them. And, of course, constitutionally, in theory whatever powers Westminster bestowed, it could usurp. So though the West Lothian Question was valid, the arrangement that gave rise to it was, in the context of balance and weight between England and Scotland within the Union, justified (or at least justifiable). Anyway, insofar as there was an answer, that was it!

I was never a passionate devolutionist. It is a dangerous game to play. You can never be sure where nationalist sentiment ends and separatist sentiment begins. I supported the UK, distrusted nationalism as a concept, and looked at the history books and worried whether we could get it through. However, though not passionate about it, I thought it inevitable. Just as the nation state was having to combine with others in pushing power upwards in multinational organisations to meet global challenges, so there would be inexorable pressure to devolve power downwards to where people felt greater connection.

We didn't want Scotland to feel the choice was status quo or separation. And it was a central part of our programme for Scotland. The Scots were notoriously prickly about the whole business.

I always thought it extraordinary: I was born in Scotland, my parents were raised there, we had lived there, I had been to school there, yet somehow—and this is the problem with nationalist sentiment unleashed—they (notice the "they") contrived to make me feel alien.

Language had to be used carefully. They were incredibly sensitive to the fear that the Scottish Parliament would turn out to be a local council (which it never was). The Scottish media were a PhD dissertation about chippiness all unto themselves. They could spot a slight that to the naked eye was invisible (because it was non-existent). Once I gave an interview on why the Parliament should have tax-raising powers, in which I said: "If even a parish council can, why shouldn't the Scottish Parliament?"—which led to the headline "BLAIR COMPARES PARLIAMENT TO PARISH COUNCIL," which even by their standards was quite some misinterpretation. Funnily enough, I quite liked them. They were hard to deal with, but it was sort of fun at the same time.

The best example of their chronic obsession with an English plot (or domination by "London," as it became) was over the 1997 manifesto proposal to have a referendum on whether there should be a Scottish Parliament. As the legislation to devolve trundled through Westminster, I knew the only way we could avoid the trap that previous governments had fallen into was to negate the possibility of the legislation being sabotaged by the House of Lords. Their Lordships weren't in a great mood with us either, since they too were being subject to reform in the shape of the removal of the hereditary peers. At that time, the Lords was essentially controlled by small "c" and large "C" Conservatives who by and large didn't like devolution since it represented constitutional change. I knew they would seize any opportunity to derail the measure unless it could be made somehow constitutionally or politically improper for them to do so. And of course the West Lothian Question gave them, as it had in the 1960s and 70s, legitimate grounds on which to camp.

While Leader of the Opposition, and despite heavy misgivings from George Robertson, then Shadow Secretary of State for Scotland, I devised the gambit of offering a referendum not after the legislation, but before it, so that people could take a decision on the principle first. The strategy was clear: to devolve after a hundred years of waiting. The tactic was obvious: get the people to say yes, then the Lords could not say no.

It produced the most contorted cries of outrage from assorted nationalists and hacks, convinced it was designed to scupper the whole thing. It was even called undemocratic. I had the most contrary conversations and interviews where I would be asked: Isn't having a referendum vote just a way of denying Scotland its due and proper Parliament? I would say: Er, but the Scots are the ones voting. Ah, they would say, but suppose they vote no? Well, I would say, in that case I assume they don't want one. And so on. Amazing.

In the event they voted yes; the House of Lords could only cavil at the periphery of the legislation, not attack its core; and devolution came about. I think it was the right thing to do. I hope it was.

In early December 1999, the Tory MP Shaun Woodward came to see me. He had been the star of the 1992 Tory campaign. He was clever, articulate, plainly someone who had joined the Tories because Labour were so crazy in the 1980s, was economically and socially liberal, abhorred the Tory prejudices around gay rights particularly, was also out of sorts with them over Europe—in fact over their whole attitude to the modern world—and wanted to defect.

He approached Cherie first, and then he and I talked. I thought he was genuine. Naturally it would be a great coup, but I also thought he would make a great addition to our team. Getting him a seat would be tough (though in the end we did). Defecting can be an act of opportunism. It can also be an act of courage. In his case, I thought it was courage. Alastair handled it brilliantly, as ever, and it was announced just before Christmas.

It solidified our grip on the centre ground, and expressed, in a way speeches couldn't, the open-door policy we had towards people who thought the country had to move on from Thatcherism but not go back to Old Labour. These were the people who were successful, or wanted to be, who were in favour of a competitive market economy and who were socially liberal and compassionate. It was a strain of thought that had little purchase on the media mind, which thought in very traditional left/right terms, but it had its constituency in the country.

However, I was well aware that while such people applauded the vision, the words and the direction, they would need to know the path was being followed with the necessary vitesse, and that the destination could be reached. For that ever to happen, we were going to have to be a lot more radical in our approach. We were successful politically, incredibly so; but politics is for a purpose, and the frustration both within me and around me was beginning to mount.

NINE

FORCES OF CONSERVATISM

T he "forces of conservatism" speech at the party conference in September 1999 had marked a sharpening of the analysis and a hardening of the soul. Pushing to get out of me was the desire to be a leader who led and challenged all the way. To the outside world, not much had changed. Inside, I knew I was changing.

As we began to try to drive change in the public services, in welfare, in law and order, it became obvious that there were major small "c" conservative interests within the services that were hostile to change, essentially vast vested interests that were pretty unscrupulous about defending themselves on the spurious grounds of defending the public interest.

I began to reflect on change and progress, and how it occurred. I saw a pattern in which conventional thinking had a grip which, when loosened, unleashed a fairly serious backlash; and how then once change occurs and takes root, it in turn becomes the conventional wisdom. I applied it not just to reform but to progress in human rights, in women's rights, in defeating racism and apartheid, to left as well as right. It was a good argument and a radical one, but it had a slight Year Zero feel to it, as though I was saying that there was nothing of merit prior to New Labour. So while the argument was right, the tone was a fraction misjudged—and in politics, fractions multiply fast.

Of all the things that were completely obvious about the difference between Opposition and government, one thing came on us to my great and entirely unjustified surprise: the gap between the commitment and the execution. We would take a decision, announce it; feel that soon the consequences would be manifest, even if it took time for their fullest impact to be felt.

The two years of spending controls inherited from the Tories had ended. In the Budget of 1999 we had started to relax things. In the public borrowing requirement of November 1999 we had announced a major investment in public services, but it was like turning on a tap and seeing only a trickle come out. We had proclaimed 1999 as the "year of delivery"—a phrase that somewhat came back to haunt us. Truthfully there had been progress, but it was very incremental, not only because the money had not really started to flow, but also because as the "forces of conservatism" speech had indicated, there was a structural problem that money alone couldn't solve. Across the piece—in schools, universities, the NHS, law and order and criminal justice—we were still only tinkering, not transforming. The speech was actually self-critical as well as system-critical. As 1999 wore on and the year 2000 turned, I began to look at how we propelled the whole question of reform further and faster.

First, however, we had the occasion of the millennium itself. I will remember the entry into the twenty-first century chiefly for two things: the Dome and the millennium bug. One should never have been, and was; the other should have been, and wasn't.

When I think back on the time, effort and panic preparations for the "Y2K," or whatever it was called in the jargon, I can't think of more time wasted to less effect. The only comfort was that the whole world was convinced about it. Basically, if you recall, computers were not supposed to be able to handle the numerical transfer to the year 2000. People cursed the hubris that had led mankind to think a computer would be an infallible object of progress. Predictions were made of catastrophe, crisis meetings were held, and around the planet we braced ourselves for the calamity that never came. Margaret Beckett, who had held various positions in the Labour government, including Foreign Secretary, and I would have meetings about it, at the end of which we would both agree we hadn't the foggiest idea what the experts were talking about. David Miliband tried to explain it once, and I honestly didn't have a clue what he was talking about and didn't ask him to explain it again.

David had never quite recovered from a meeting I had had as Leader of the Opposition with Bill Gates, then in his heyday as the computer maestro transforming our times. David was smart and modern on technology. I was non compos mentis on the subject, being a genuine technophobe. He tried to tutor me before the meeting, alarmed that I would behave in a way inconsistent with the New Labour "we are at the cutting edge of the technological revolution" mantra.

I didn't disappoint his expectations. I got all my terminology muddled up and, to the horror of David and the young "beautiful people" in the office, asked Bill how his mainframe was or something like that, a question that produced consternation mixed with giggling from the staff and a curious gulping sound from Bill. I had heard the term "mainframe" somewhere or other and thought I would astonish my audience by showing off my knowledge. I merely astonished them.

Anyway, the Y2K crisis came and went with no one in the end really noticing. The only good thing was that I had never agreed to spend much money on it. That's the funny thing about decisions as prime minister: some are about doing things, but equally important are those about *not* doing things. They all come thick and fast, and sometimes you don't recognise them as decisions. They tend to be the things you say "no" to.

Unfortunately, one thing we had said "yes" to was continuing with the Dome. I think as bad decisions go, it wasn't a frightful one. Part of the problem—and I really don't mean this as an excuse—is that we inherited the decision, and by the time we took office around £100 million had been committed, so cancellation costs would have been significant.

Actually, the original idea wasn't bad either. Michael Heseltine, a former deputy prime minister in the Conservative government, had had it, and like a lot of his ideas it was big and bold and brassy. The concept was similar to that of the Crystal Palace Exhibition of Prince Albert, and the London Exhibition—which John Prescott remembered—of the Coronation year. We would put on a great British exhibition and situate it on the reclaimed swampland around the Greenwich gasworks. The trouble was that it was never wholly clear what would go in the exhibition, and the futuristic theme we wanted was fine at the broad-brush level, but elusive in the detail. So it sort of fell between multiple stools: future, technology, play, science, entertainment. It was a kind of jack of all trades and master of none.

That said, it wasn't dreadful. It just wasn't brilliant. The Dome team—headed by Jenni Page—worked like crazy and the whole thing was, in a sense, a miracle, given the scale of ambition. Six million people came to it, and many of them enjoyed it. We all became increasingly defensive about it, until we got to the stage—me, Peter Mandelson and

Charlie Falconer especially—where if it had consisted of a man slapping everyone around the face with a wet fish, we would have stoutly held it to be a work of genius.

The simple points were that in this day and age, it wasn't really a suitable project for government, and it never quite struck a note sufficiently attuned to the millennium. If we hadn't inherited it, we would probably never have embarked on it. As David Yelland, the then editor of the *Sun* told us, a brilliant new hospital would have been a better government priority.

To be fair, Gordon was always against it, but I thought the pain of cancelling too great, and in any event, considered it worth a go. At the Cabinet which gave the green light, opinion was pretty evenly divided. John Prescott swung the day. I had had to leave early. He came into the chair and in a swashbuckling JP sort of way, rammed it through, mostly because he knew I wanted it and a little because he thought the idea had flair. Which it did. It just lacked sense.

The Dome itself was superb, designed by Richard Rogers, and of course we look at it now as a city landmark, instantly recognisable and giving the whole of south-east London a lift. In addition, of course, we reclaimed the land, built thousands of homes, a health centre and a school. It is also now the best entertainment venue for rock and pop in the country, possibly in Europe.

While it was in retrospect a mistake, the hysterical trashing of the whole project was never justifiable. However, it was explicable. The night of 31 December 1999 I shall never forget. I have always been awful about "great" days and anniversaries—I shouldn't be like this but I am. I never "got" birthdays except for the giving and receiving of presents. Christmas Day was and is always a wonderful family time, but somehow I'm always relieved when it's over.

I was on duty and working the night of 31 December, and yes, OK, a millennium is a big deal, but—as I feel most New Year's Eves—I could quite happily have gone to bed early, had a good night's rest, and woken up the next day refreshed and able to contemplate at leisure the fact that another year had gone.

Anyway, you get the point: it's not really my thing. So I looked forward to the evening of the turn of a new millennium with all the fervour of a visit to the dentist. Actually, I would have preferred a visit to the dentist. As it turned out, it would have been less painful, quieter and certainly less stressful.

First off, I had to go and start the Millennium Wheel, with an attendant spiralling fireworks display. We left Downing Street on foot, with me feeling an inchoate and gathering sense of dread. At times like these, Cherie would be heroic and perfect as a foil: she was—or at least put on a great act of being—thrilled by the whole prospect.

As we moved among the crowds in Whitehall and made our way to the Embankment, people were incredibly friendly and celebratory and my mood temporarily lightened. Somehow we got to the point near Hungerford Bridge where Bob Ayling, the chief executive of British Airways, was waiting for me to start it all off. Bob had taken over running the millennium celebrations and had done a great job under hellish pressure.

"What happens when I start it off, Bob?" I said above the din.

"Well," he said, "not much since it's not actually quite ready." He was unflappable. I liked that. Because I was definitely flapping. Bob turned his attention to the fireworks. "What'll happen is that when you press the button, they'll go off right down the Thames."

Right, I thought. I got to the little podium; there were cheering crowds; I think I made a little speech—emphasis on the "little"—of a generally inane nature; and then pressed the button.

A few desultory fireworks sprang to life, but by a cruel stroke which afflicted all our millennium celebrations, they failed to go off in quite the spectacular fashion envisaged. Indeed, as fireworks go, I had attended somewhat livelier events at Highbury Fields in Islington on Guy Fawkes Night.

And, of course, the Millennium Wheel was not yet working. "I don't think that really matters for tonight," Bob said cheerfully.

"It does if it's called the Millennium Wheel," I said sourly, the dread returning.

But there was no time to sulk. We had the Dome Party with the Queen to look forward to.

We were due to get there on the new Jubilee Line extension. The Tube was itself part of the development for the celebrations, and new stations were being opened. Again, a great idea; again, as the new year approached, it was a source of continual fretting. We had contractors' disputes, union disputes and political disputes. The problem was that everyone knew they had us over a barrel—the deadline couldn't exactly be moved, and without the extension, we couldn't get people down to the Dome. We had left it tight. I had promised all manner of torture to my staff and ministers responsible. And I didn't like the "Fingers crossed,

Prime Minister" gallows humour emanating from the London Underground management. It was a massive undertaking to get it finished, and John Prescott performed minor miracles bludgeoning people.

But millennium night was the first time it would be running. The initial nerve-racking moment came when we got to the train: would it work? Would the doors open? Would it just grind to a halt?

Anyway: it did work. It let us in and let us out, and so we got into the Dome, which was thronging; except that it wasn't quite. There didn't appear to be hordes of people. A lot, yes. Packed to the rafters, ready to party, no. "Where is everyone?" I asked our guide from the Dome.

"I think the connecting train from Stratford station has broken down. The station is effectively shut."

The room swayed. "What?" The Stratford station, vital to transport people to the Dome, had some wretched electrical fault and was malfunctioning. I thought of the public waiting there, the panic rising. "I've got to see Charlie," I said.

When Peter Mandelson had resigned, Charlie Falconer had taken over as the minister responsible. Charlie took more abuse over the Dome than it is possible now to imagine. He was wondrous throughout. Every time I saw him after yet another mauling—complete with barbs about his weight, looks, character and manner of speaking—I would say to him, "How are you, Charlie?" and really mean it. He would always reply that he was loving the job and was so grateful to me for the chance of doing it, all without any apparent hint of irony. I found it awesome. His performance over the Dome was an amazing feat of self-immolation.

I found him upstairs at the VIP reception. "Charlie," I said, "what the hell's going on at Stratford?" He explained the breakdown. "Oh Jesus, Charlie, how many people are waiting there?"

"A few thousand, I'm afraid. Sorry."

I looked at him melancholically. "What on earth will we say when the media find out?"

"Um, I'm afraid they will have found out already since the editors are all there waiting."

I fear I did grab him by the lapels at this point. And I adore Charlie.

"What? What? What the hell are the media doing there? You didn't, no, please, please, dear God, please tell me you didn't have the media coming here by Tube from Stratford, just like ordinary members of the public."

"Well, we thought it would be more democratic that way."

"Democratic? What fool thought that? They're the media, for Christ's sake. They write about the people. They don't want to be treated like them."

"Well, what did you want us to do," Charlie said, feeling he should be fighting his corner a little, "get them all a stretch limo?"

"Yes, Charlie," I thundered, "with the boy or girl of their choice and as much champagne as they can drink; or at least have got them riding in the Tube with us."

I am ashamed to say I then shouted and bawled at him for a bit longer, while the more sensible of our party tried to find out what to do. Eventually we heard they were on their way, though possibly not in time for midnight. "Please don't tell me it doesn't matter if they're not here for midnight, Charlie, or I will club you to death on the spot," I recall saying. In the end some got there, some didn't; and anyway, the media coverage was more or less set in stone from that moment.

Meanwhile, a fresh knot of anxiety had gripped me. We had persuaded the Queen and Prince Philip to come down to the Dome to join in the fun. I don't know precisely what Prince Philip thought of it all, but I shouldn't imagine it's printable. I suspect Her Majesty would have used different language but with the same sentiment. However, we all had to go through it with a cheery face and she put on her best. We sat down together. We looked at the programme.

There was an acrobatic show prior to midnight. Now this was spectacular. They were way up in the Dome performing extraordinary feats, flying through the air. They were dressed in a riot of colour and really did look and act most impressively.

Then an appalling thought struck me, and chilled me to the innards. They were doing their wild thing right above where the Queen was sitting. "Well, that is remarkable," Prince Philip said, brightening a trifle. "You know they're doing that without safety harnesses?" I swear I knew what was going to happen. I felt like someone in one of those sixth-sense movies who can see the future: from sixty feet up, one of the performers was going to fall in the middle of a somersault, hurtle down and flatten the Queen. I could see it all. "QUEEN KILLED BY TRAPEZE ARTIST AT DOME." "BRITAIN'S MILLENNIUM CELEBRATIONS MARRED." "BLAIR ADMITS NOT ALL HAS GONE TO PLAN." Britain's millennium would indeed be famous; I would go down in history forever.

I kid you not, I joke about it now but at 11:30 p.m. on New Year's

Eve 1999, I was absolutely convinced. I have never been more relieved than when it all stopped.

Then came the ghastly singing of "Auld Lang Syne." Another decision; to link arms with the Queen or not. We looked at each other. I realised helplessly that to do it was ridiculous, but not to do it was stand-offish. I made my choice, stretching out my arms. She kept her options open, holding out one arm. But what the hell, she was alive, and that was the main thing.

The rest of the evening passed in a blur. We finally got home around 2 a.m. "I thought the evening was rather fun," Cherie said as we clambered into bed.

"Darling," I replied, "there is only one thing I am going to thank God for tonight, and that is they only come round every thousand years."

The next morning I was back to the reality of the day job. We were now two and a half years into office. For the way governments work, it is a blink of an eye. For the way the public think, it is an eternity. The "forces of conservatism" speech was the product, in a sense, of my frustration at being unable to align the two time zones. Some of the criticism from commentators and the public was undoubtedly unfair, but some—indeed the core of it, namely that change was too slow and insufficiently radical—I believed myself. Hence the speech.

I was learning how complex the institutions of public service were, how multiple their pressures, how vast their demands and how great the expectations were of what could be done and in what period of time. The millennium may have been an exceptional moment in the calendar, but the 1999/2000 NHS "winter crisis" came with the monotonous predictability of death and taxes. And two and a half years in, people expected better.

It is hard now to look back and realise just how inevitable such crises appeared. This time it was a flu bug. It produced the sad cases of individual misfortune. It centred around a lady called Mavis Skeet, who was not given proper treatment and died. Her family naturally were outraged. The intensive care units of the hospitals were finding it hard to cope. There were stories of people being turned away; people treated on trolleys; people waiting hours in Accident and Emergency rooms.

Quite apart from routine cases and the flu epidemic, there were patients waiting so long for operations for heart disease that they would die while waiting. I received a letter from a woman whose husband, I think, had been a *Northern Echo* photographer and whom I had worked with, who had died in such circumstances. I felt it horribly, felt the responsibility and felt, perhaps worst of all, the gnawing doubt as to whether it was just time we needed or something more profound in terms of the way the service was run. If it was the latter, we weren't scaled up to do it. And to be very frank, I wasn't entirely sure what the answer was. That's what I mean by learning.

I had an increasing worry on health and education, which was that while the Tory reforms may have been badly implemented and badly explained, their essential direction was one that was in fact nothing to do with being "Tory," but to do with the modern world. These reforms were all about trying to introduce systems where the money spent was linked to performance and where the service user was in the driving seat. They were often divisive and even misguided in policy detail, but the overall approach was born of the same social and economic trends that had given rise to support for privatisation and tax cuts.

I could see a trend that was about breaking down centralised and monolithic structures, about focusing on the developing tastes of consumers, about ending old demarcations in professions; and this trend seemed to me to be related to how people behaved, not how government behaved. The precise shift in the way the private sector was organised and managed seemed, and not unnaturally, to have its echo in the challenges facing the public sector.

In crime and in welfare policy, I figured the Tories had not really thought it through and had only really begun to think radically at the end of their time. But in the NHS and schools it was different—there were elements of the changes they had made that we needed to examine and learn from, not dismiss.

The trouble was, at the time there was not a great appetite in the Labour Party for such thinking. Indeed, it was heretical. In particular, at the helm of the NHS, I had put Frank Dobson. This, in itself, indicated how little I understood when first in office. The truth is Frank was genuinely and, to be fair, avowedly Old Labour. He was one of the many who considered New Labour a clever wheeze to win. He didn't understand it much, and to the extent that he did, he disagreed with it.

The hierarchy in the department and in the NHS, though truly dedicated and fine public servants, believed sincerely that there was an incompatibility between private sector concepts like choice, and the basic equity of the NHS as an institution. It was the age-old problem of the policy becoming the principle, so the policy of the NHS for 1948—perfectly appropriate for its time—became the hallowed principle for all time.

So I was turning all this over in my mind during 1999 and beginning a conversation with my nearest and dearest political associates. But I had two problems: the first was Frank Dobson, the second was money. I knew that the underinvestment in the NHS was clear and the Tories had not understood it, or maybe hadn't wanted to. When we compared our spending with any similar country, the disparity was plain. Money was not sufficient. But it was necessary.

The winter crisis was the immediate manifestation of the problem. But that was all it was. The true problem lay deep within the service: the funding and how it was run.

I had had a series of seminars with health professionals that the excellent Robert Hill (my adviser on health and author of NHS Direct) had put together for me. It was fascinating. From within the NHS, there were people who fully endorsed the NHS principles of equity, but were chafing at the bit about how the service was managed; how outdated its practices were; how there was an incompetence in some of its systems that led to consequences that were truly inequitable.

I had also had a conversation or several with Gordon about NHS funding; but as I anticipated, he was fairly adamant against doing anything big on it. Incidentally, I make no criticism of that. It was his job as Chancellor to run a tight ship in respect of the finances and repel boarders, as it were.

So I had to get the money, in order to get the reform; and in order to get the reform, I had to get a top team who believed in it.

I did the first in a somewhat unconventional way. I was due to do my annual new year *Frost* programme interview.

David Frost was still far and away the best interviewer around on TV, far better than those who sneered at him for not being sneering enough. He wasn't rude or hectoring, but had an extraordinary talent for beguiling the interviewee, leading them on, charming them into indiscretion, tripping them, almost conversationally, into the headlines. I lost count of the number of times Alastair would say to me, "What the hell did you say that for?" after a Frost encounter. I would say, "What?" and he would explain and I would go: "Oh."

Also, David had the revolutionary notion in his head that the audi-

ence wanted to hear what the person answering the questions had to
say, rather than the person asking them. By this device, he got people to
say much more than they intended and on a much broader range of top-
ics. You would always end up with four or five news stories out of the
interview. And of course by being insistent but not aggressive, he made
it far harder, psychologically, for the interviewee not to answer directly.

Anyway, in this instance there was no need to worry about what I
might say inadvertently. I had decided to say it advertently. I decided to
commit us to raising NHS spending to roughly the EU average. Naturally, there were a plethora of methods for calculating what that was.
There were armies of statisticians and accountants who worked it out
and came to different conclusions from each other, but the basic point
was fairly clear and the signal such a commitment sent would have its
own determinative impact.

On Saturday, Robert Hill and I worked through the possible permutations. I talked again to Gordon, who became more adamant. But I was
convinced, as a matter of profound political strategy, that this decision
had to be taken and now.

I also knew by then that we had a chance of getting the reform. In
late 1999, Alan Milburn had replaced Frank in the department. Alan
had been Minister of State and really shone there and was fully simpatico with the direction of change. Frank had resigned in order to concentrate on the mayoral contest for London.

I admit, at this point, that I had not discouraged Frank from resigning,
partly because I thought it would free up the Department of Health. It
did, however, leave us with a big problem for the mayoral race. The truth
is that Frank had about as much chance of beating Ken Livingstone in a
contest to be London mayor as Steptoe and Son's horse had of winning
the Grand National. At a later point of this saga, when in the course of
the election I was trying to lift my team's spirits, I said gamely that I
thought Frank would just win it. To which Anji said: "If you think Frank
Dobson can beat Ken Livingstone in London, I'm calling a doctor."

So there was a big mess looming in London; but by the time I did
Frost, I knew what I wanted and I had who I wanted at the helm.

I did the interview and, to David's pleasure, I didn't need my confession to be extricated, but averred it fully, openly and right speedily, as it
were. It was one of the few examples I can remember of going on a programme with a story in mind and emerging from it with the same story
on record.

There were a few days of tin-helmet time with Gordon, but he could see the inevitability of it and anyhow the politics made it impossible to oppose. It was a straightforward pre-emption. But it was a pre-emption that was both necessary and justifiable. It then allowed me to get on with the other part of the plan: to work with Alan on a serious proposal of reform.

We talked about it and agreed that we would work over the coming months to produce a proper, fully-fledged plan of transformation for the NHS. After some toing and froing we agreed it should be a ten-year plan. The aim should be to change fundamentally the way the NHS was run: to break up the monolith; to introduce a new relationship with the private sector; to import concepts of choice and competition; and to renegotiate the basic contracts of the professionals from nurses to doctors to managers.

The most important element was that it implied a resolution of what had been revolving in my mind for some time. We had come to power in 1997 saying it was "standards not structures" that mattered. We said this in respect of education, but it applied equally to health and other parts of the system of public services.

In other words, we were saying: forget about complex, institutional structural reforms; what counts is what works, and by that we meant outputs. This was fine as a piece of rhetoric; and positively beneficial as a piece of politics. Unfortunately, as I began to realise when experience started to shape our thinking, it was bunkum as a piece of policy. The whole point is that structures beget standards. How a service is configured affects outcomes.

That is, unless you believe that centrally managed change works best. This is where the change in thinking had deep political as well as service implications. Part of the whole thought process that had gone into creating New Labour was to redefine the nature of the state.

Except on law and order, I am by instinct a liberal. That is one reason why I used to go out of my way to praise Lloyd George, Keynes and Beveridge; and why I always had respect as well as affection for the mind of Roy Jenkins.

In a world in which the individual sought far greater control and power over their own lives, it seemed inconceivable to me that any modern idea of the state could be other than as an enabler, a source of empowerment, rather than paternalistic, handing out, controlling in the interests of the citizens who were supposedly incapable of taking their own decisions. That intuition, that gut feeling then obviously had to be translated into the praxis of state institutions. Really it was as simple as that; a symmetry between the policy and the philosophy.

From early 2000 onwards, with the funding issue resolved, at least in general terms, Alan and I and a close team of advisers started to work out what would become the ten-year NHS Plan.

Meanwhile, we were working in other policy areas to similar purport. Andrew Adonis had taken over as my education adviser. I can't remember exactly how he came to us. He had been an academic at Oxford and member of the Social Democratic Party. He had been committed to writing a biography of Roy Jenkins (which the pressure of work prevented him from completing) and had been a journalist for the *Financial Times* and the *Observer*. His arrival was fortuitous and gloriously productive. He was totally decent, had a first-class intellect, and was not afraid to think without ideological constraint. He completely "got" New Labour.

Of course, there was resentment of him because of the SDP past. By the way, it was similar with Derek Scott, who advised me on pensions and macroeconomic policy. Derek was really tough-minded and acerbic, and added a new dimension to the team. He had, however, the diplomatic skills of Dirty Harry. Meetings with the Treasury would turn into war zones and he could go off faster than the average firecracker. But, funnily enough, I liked having him around.

Andrew, by contrast, was such a thoroughly nice guy that even diehard SDP-haters found it difficult to dislike him. Not that a few of them didn't try really hard, mind you.

David Blunkett, like me, was undergoing the same reconsideration around standards and structures, and of course Andrew greatly urged in this direction. David had pulled around him a strong team as well, with people like Michael Barber and the permanent secretary of the department Michael Bichard, who was one of the best. So we also began rethinking our way through school and university reform, with the same principles as in health.

Criminal justice was altogether a different bag of nails. There the problem was and is profound. Over time, it led me to a complete reappraisal of the nature, purpose, structure, culture, mores, practice, ethos—you name it—of the whole system. It was and is essentially dysfunctional. But more of that another time.

Suffice to say, as one of my longer year 2000 notes put it, we needed to become more searching, more radical, more groundbreaking in our approach to the whole post-war settlement around public services and the welfare state, right across the board.

Throughout the first half of the year, we beavered away, especially on the NHS. In March, I made a statement to the House on NHS modernisation, which paved the way for the later July plan.

At the same time, the mayoral race trundled on with entirely predictable outcomes. There were two stages: first, the race for the Labour nomination; second, the race for the office itself.

As to the first, we put our all into securing Frank the nomination. We had a formidable machine in those days and it did its job formidably. The feeling about Ken among the top brass was unbelievably strong. And, of course, stupid. I don't exempt myself. I didn't feel visceral about it, as John and Gordon did. I rather admired Ken's style, his quirkiness, which made him stand out as different, and his ability to communicate. I also exaggerated the dangers of his policy positions, not wilfully, but just out of force of habit when describing an opponent's politics. It shouldn't be like that; there is always a risk in politics that when you disagree with someone, you magnify the disagreement. Two shades of grey become black and white. A mistaken policy becomes a disastrous one.

Ken as a Labour candidate was going to be a problem for a very simple reason: he disagreed totally with the public/private partnership John Prescott and Gordon had designed for the Tube. Since London transport in many ways defined the job, it was going to be difficult to have a Labour candidate dedicated to stopping the Labour transport policy.

I supported the policy, but felt strangely less sure about its modernising nature. I also thought Bob Kiley, who Ken wanted to bring in to run the Tube after a successful spell as chief of transport in New York, had something to commend him.

But John had the contempt of Northern Labour for London Labour, and didn't trust Ken or some arriviste New Yorker. And Gordon just detested him. Also Neil Kinnock expressed himself very strongly as only Neil could. And in any event, I had, as I say, not discouraged Frank from resigning to stand, so Ken was therefore obviously not the leadership candidate.

In time, I learned to let go and realised the stupidity, indeed the futility, of imposing the leadership line in situations where the whole point was to devolve power. It was, in fact, a hangover from the days of Labour Party indiscipline. There was such a fear of departing from the line that a sense of perspective easily got lost. So, in the end, I decided that, all in all, an independent Ken victory may be the least worst option, given Frank as mayor was undoable.

But we still had the party election to go through. Frank won, but due to union votes. Not a great New Labour outcome. I saw Ken at Chequers just before the result and asked for a pledge of loyalty if Frank won. He gave it, but without enthusiasm, and I was not really surprised when after the result he announced he would stand as an independent. I didn't really blame him. Interestingly, some of the London Party people who were supportive of me, but a little leftish, told me they were going to vote for Ken come what may; and that I had just been daft in opposing him, because, as they said, if Ken doesn't stand, don't think Frank will be mayor. He won't. They were probably right.

At the last moment, just before the primary got under way within the Labour Party, I made a last-ditch attempt to switch horses.

There had been some whispers that Mo Mowlam might consider entering the list. Now this was a wholly different order of proposition. Mo would give Ken a real run for his money. I asked her if she was serious. She said she was. I latched on to the idea. I invited Frank and his wife Janet round to Downing Street and had a drink with them in the flat. Alastair was there, and Cherie popped in. I explained I thought it would be difficult for Frank to win and explored whether he might contemplate standing down. The answer was firm; he wouldn't. I can't say I was surprised, and he probably, and with some justification, felt let down by me even broaching the subject.

In the end, Mo was not really prepared to press it either. My relationship with her also was not quite what it had been.

One of the problems in politics is that when you are leader—and it is, I guess, the same in any organisation—you have to take personnel decisions that can be highly fraught. There are only a certain number of top jobs and there are many more applicants or supplicants than appointees.

Reshuffles are hard enough. Sacking people is always a ghastly business, but so is failure to promote in accordance with the person's estimation of themselves. There is often a yawning gap between their judgement about their capacity and yours.

Mo had been fabulous in Northern Ireland—just what the situation needed—but when I came in late 1999 to consider a change there (as usual it was unhelpfully discussed in the press, and as usual even more unhelpfully ascribed as part of a Downing Street operation, which was completely untrue—I would never have done that to Mo), I had a one-to-one discussion with her out on the terrace of Number 10.

She was not averse to moving, though she was annoyed at the stuff in the media, which was understandable. But she then startled me by saying (and she was nothing if not blunt): I am the most popular person in the government; Robin Cook is unpopular and tarnished; you should make me Foreign Secretary. It was a bid I was completely unprepared for, and I'm afraid I showed immediately that I thought it was unthinkable.

And there is the problem. The moment the chasm opens up between their revealed sense of their capability and your revealed sense of their capability, the relationship never recovers.

Mo had been an early supporter of mine. She had real political sense. She was immense fun to be around. She handled her illness with beautiful dignity. She *was* the most popular member of the government.

Her unique brand of what I can only call "Mo-ness" was a healthy culture shock in Northern Ireland. I shall never forget the moment in the peace negotiations when in front of some fairly orthodox Irishmen, she came into my room, took off her wig, slapped it on the table, put her feet on the desk, belched loudly and opined, "Well, this isn't a barrel of laughs, is it?" and proceeded to tell them how many other things she would prefer to be doing right then, starting with vigorous sexual intercourse. In a matter of seconds she altered all hitherto fixed canons of behaviour recognisable in previous British Secretaries of State. But I quailed to think of what this attitude would do when thrust upon the slender sensibilities of foreign ministers and tricky international summitry. I wasn't sure the Foreign Office—the grand building imbued with the spirit of Palmerston and Grey and Halifax and even Peter Carrington—was quite ready for "Mo-ness." So it wasn't to be.

Incidentally, it is an amazing thing about the Foreign Secretary job—everyone wants it. It is not simply that the Foreign Secretary is one of the "great offices of state," but also because you basically spend your time with people who are polite to you, on the global issues of the day, and travel the world generally dispensing goodwill and opinions to those who seem relatively keen to receive them. Not for you the hairy-handed sons of toil badgering you over fuel prices, or complaining about the government's clearly ill-motivated refusal to spend money on this service or that, or the minutiae of road schemes. You are too lofty to be troubled by such ephemera. Your stage is the world; your discourse is of strategic interests too rarefied and majestic for ordinary souls; your attitudes can be balanced and measured in a way wholly inconsistent with the rough and tumble of the domestic scene. Even in the House of Commons—the nearest you ever come to the brute side of life—you can still talk of things and places and pronounce names that have the average Member of Parliament nodding along in gratified incomprehension.

So people want it. One of the reasons why I had such huge regard for Jack Cunningham, a great example of a serious grown-up in the Labour politics of the 1980s and 90s, was that he had been John Smith's choice as Shadow Foreign Secretary. I moved him to make way for Robin Cook, who was not Jack's favourite person. He took the decision—if he resented it he never showed it—and got on with things. Such people are rare.

All this, however, is to digress. The mayoral election was doomed to be messy; and so it proved. Ken duly stood as an independent, trounced Frank and became mayor. I was careful, though, not to go over the top in attacking Ken during the campaign and kept lines of communication open. After the race, we settled down to a proper relationship with remarkable ease, something he deserved real credit for.

Throughout these months, despite the politics of London, fresh tremors in Northern Ireland, the hijacking of a plane at Stansted by (ironically in the light of future events) Afghans escaping the Taliban, May Day riots by anarchists who defaced the Cenotaph and all the normal flotsam and jetsam, I was still burrowing into the geothermals of public service reform.

The intricacy of the issues involved was really hard to unravel and reconstruct. At this stage, I was still feeling my way, holding endless meetings with advisers, experts and those within the services. I was trying to get a sense of how change might be fashioned, formulated and most important put in place on the ground, in real situations with real people.

I found it all intensely frustrating. At points, I wanted to give up everything else and just spend days on the front line, learning what it was like to manage a service, what its real pressures were, what could be done within the conventional parameters and how the parameters might be changed.

Also here I bumped up against the single most difficult thing about making change in any organisation. It's what I call "taking away the givens." By this I mean as follows. Usually, you operate in any organisa-

Right: me and Mum, with Dad holding my older brother Bill in the mid-1950s

Below: my dad on his way to work. Fostered by a rigger in the Govan shipyards, he went on to become an academic, a barrister and a Conservative

Left: always happy in the sun. We lived in Australia till I was five

Left: at my school, Fettes, in spring 1971 with friends Amanda Mackenzie Stuart and Chris Catto

Above and right: in 1972, I left the north and came to London for a year. Alan Collenette and I promoted rock bands

Above: Cherie and me on our wedding day, at the Chapel of St. John's College, Oxford, 29 March 1980

Above: the Labour Party candidate in the Beaconsfield by-election, May 1982

Left: Cherie's father first secured me an invitation to visit Westminster. On the terrace of the Houses of Parliament with Cherie, 1984

Left: Michael Foot, leader of the Labour Party, came to support my campaign in Beaconsfield

Above: the people of Trimdon, where we had our constituency home, supported me loyally during my twenty-five years as the Member for Sedgefield. I won the constituency in June 1983

Below: with Shadow Cabinet colleagues, a few months before the crushing general election defeat of 1992. From left, Gordon Brown, John Smith, Neil Kinnock, Margaret Beckett and me

Above: one of many happy moments with Cherie, Euan, Nicky and baby Kathryn at our house in Islington, 1988

Above: relaxing with friends Marc Palley and Peter Thomson, whom I met at Oxford. Peter was probably the most influential person in my life

Left: Derry Irvine, my pupil master in chambers, taught me a great deal in the early years. I was later to appoint him Lord Chancellor

Above: my relationship with my oldest political friend, Geoff Gallop, has been sustained from student days

Right: the saddest of days. With Gordon at John Smith's funeral in Edinburgh, 20 May 1994

Left: we announced that Gordon was not going to stand as Labour leader on 1 June 1994

Above: alongside John Prescott and Margaret Beckett, the other two candidates for the Labour leadership, June 1994

Right: that summer we made a holiday detour to recruit Alastair Campbell. From left, Neil Kinnock, me, Alastair and Glenys Kinnock with Kathryn, and Alastair's children, Calum and Grace, August 1994

Right: drafting the new wording of Clause IV in March 1995 with John, now deputy Labour leader

Above: John Prescott, Gordon Brown and I launch the Labour Party manifesto alongside a Shadow Cabinet team that included Jack Straw, far left, and Robin Cook, second row, third right. London, 3 April 1997

Above: reviewing the election coverage with the team, including Alastair Campbell and David Miliband, on the last Sunday before polling day, 27 April 1997

Above right: watching the election night results with John Burton, my constituency agent, Trimdon Labour Club, Sedgefield, 1 May 1997

Right: going to vote at Sedgefield, 1 May 1997. Hordes of photographers were in tow

Right: expectant family and friends at the Sedgefield count. Kathryn holds my dad's hand; Cherie's mum is in the front row, far right, and her dad second row, third right. 1 May 1997

Below: Neil Kinnock, John Prescott and Peter Mandelson among colleagues and supporters as the celebrations begin, Royal Festival Hall

Above: as dawn broke on 2 May 1997, I made my victory speech on the South Bank. I could see the cheering crowds massed all along the Embankment

Right: the new prime minister, celebrating with Cherie, 2 May 1997. This was not just a win, it was a landslide

Inset, above: the moment our lives changed. Kathryn waves from the window of our old home as Cherie and I head to the Palace

Above: walking along Downing Street for the first time, I felt the emotion run like a charge through the crowd

Below: after an hour's sleep, Cherie and I arrived at Buckingham Palace on the morning of 2 May 1997. Supporters lined the streets

Right: as prime minister, on the steps of No 10. We were the youngest family to have lived there since the 1850s

Above: down to business with, right to left, Gordon Brown, Charlie Whelan, Peter Mandelson and Alastair Campbell, Downing Street, 10 July 1997

Clockwise from above right: some of the inner team. Peter Mandelson could tell you what people would be thinking tomorrow; Anji Hunter, possessed of a naturally intuitive political instinct; Jonathan Powell, a key operative in government; Sally Morgan, superbly attuned to the party; Philip Gould, chief pollster, and central to our strategy

Above: in the sunshine of the Downing Street garden, at the end of May 1997 with Bill Clinton.

Above left: with Bill and Hillary Clinton and Cherie at Tower Bridge the same day

Left: the Clintons meet the family at Downing Street

Below left, and below: as fellow third-way progressives, Bill and I had a natural bond

Above right: on the international stage at the G7 summit in Denver, Colorado, with Bill Clinton and Helmut Kohl, centre

Right: Prince Charles and I flank Chris Patten, the last governor of Hong Kong, at the handover ceremony to China, 1 July 1997

Right: among leaders at the NATO summit, July 1997. Helmut Kohl makes a point to me as, left to right, Jacques Chirac, Jean Chrétien, Jean-Claude Juncker, Walter Neuer and Romano Prodi look on

Top left: Princess Diana chatting to Kathryn
during a visit to Chequers, 6 July 1997

Top right: it fell to me to address the nation about
Diana's death, outside Trimdon Church, 31 August 1997

Right: face to face with Prince Charles on the
airstrip of RAF Northolt in north-west London,
as Diana's body arrived back from France

Above: Prince Charles, Prince Harry, Earl Spencer,
Prince William and Prince Philip follow Diana's
coffin, borne by soldiers of the 1st Battalion,
the Welsh Guards, 6 September 1997

Above: Prime Minister's Questions was the most nerve-racking, terror-inspiring and courage-draining experience of my prime ministerial life. Facing the Tory front bench led by John Major during the devolution debate, 6 June 1997

Right: Jack Straw looks on from our side during a debate in 1998

Below: the four other Tory leaders I faced were, from left, William Hague, Iain Duncan Smith, Michael Howard and David Cameron

Above left: at Stormont in Northern Ireland, after days of negotiation, I announced the Good Friday Agreement on 10 April 1998. Mo Mowlam and Paul Murphy look on. Other key figures in the talks included, *clockwise from top right*, Ian Paisley; Seamus Mallon and John Hume; Martin McGuinness and Gerry Adams; Jonathan Powell; and Bertie Ahern

Left: pushing for a yes vote in the peace agreement referendum, with David Trimble and John Hume, County Antrim, 21 May 1998

Right: three months later, bombers struck in Omagh, killing twenty-nine and injuring many more. Bill Clinton was quick to visit the scene at this terrible time, 3 September 1998

Above and right: with Nelson Mandela at the European Council meeting in Cardiff, June 1998

Right: with Cherie, meeting a family of Kosovan refugees, Macedonia, 3 May 1999

Below: talking to the press after visiting the border between Yugoslavia and Macedonia, 3 May 1999

Above: with General Sir Charles Guthrie, left, and General Mike Jackson, right, at the British army HQ near Skopje in Macedonia on the same visit

Above left: Millennium night celebrations on the Embankment in London—the fireworks did not go quite to plan. 1 January 2000
Above right: singing "Auld Lang Syne" with the Queen and Prince Philip at the Dome, 1 January 2000

tion within boundaries of thought and of practice. These become "givens." So in the NHS, it is a given that the surgeon performs operations, and the GP is a general practitioner who doesn't touch the surgeon's knife. The nurse doesn't (or didn't then) hand out complicated prescriptions. The more hospital beds, the better the service. In the private sector you pay; in the public sector you don't.

Or in a school, you have a standard national curriculum. Or in the Civil Service, you have a set career path. Or in the courts, there is a trial process that is hallowed.

Challenging these "givens" within which the system operates can be hard. They are always there for a reason and, historically at least, often a good reason. Changing them can be even harder. A whole web of custom, practice and interest has been created around them; yet for the organisation to make progress, they must be changed.

So we began a reconsideration of the basic principles on which these services were run, trying to measure them not against the "givens" but against the contemporary reality, the potential and possibility opened up by change, the parameters we would want if we were relieved of all political constraint and just exercised freethinking.

I used to call the experts in and say if you had a completely free hand and you could do what you want, how you want: what would you do? The picture I started to build up conformed to my own instinct, but it was clear the services would require radical change.

Thus the ten-year NHS Plan. I didn't think I would last ten years and neither did Alan, but we were conscious of the need to set a framework to construct a platform that would place the NHS on a different trajectory. The pace might be quicker or slower, but the direction would be irreversible, at least if we were allowed the chance to show what reform could do.

But we had to proceed with the utmost care. There was party opposition—John Prescott was often hostile; the Treasury sceptical though at that point merely mildly obstructive; the unions wary and (rightly) suspicious; and the professions within the services basically dominated by the traditionalists.

There was another challenge. People could accept there were areas of clear and obvious failure in the public services. It wasn't, to be fair, hard to persuade people we needed to change the way we dealt with the NHS winter pressures. It wasn't hard to persuade people to do something with failing schools, by which I mean schools that were to all intents and purposes basket cases—10 per cent, 15 per cent, 20 per cent of pupils getting five good GCSEs—but that was nowhere near the ambition I wanted.

I take an essentially middle-class view of public services, and you can't understand anything I tried to do to reform them without understanding that. I sent my own children to state schools; they were good state schools—but I wanted them to be even better. And they were, at least then, reasonably rare. It wasn't simply the schools getting 10 per cent, 15 per cent or 20 per cent of their kids to the right level that concerned me, but the schools getting only 50 or 60 per cent.

It wasn't reducing waiting times for inpatients from eighteen months to six months that was the final goal; I thought six months totally unacceptable. I knew I wouldn't stand for my own loved ones waiting that long. Why should anyone else? And why should it be an impossible dream to alter the system so that the best happened?

So we had a much greater ambition for change. The trouble was for many people, including, ironically, the public we were wanting to serve, a coasting or average service seemed fair enough.

In any event, though there were people prepared to settle for less than they deserved, there was a large swathe of New Labour support that voted for us precisely because they shared that middle-class mentality. By the way, none of that means "working-class" people want less; but the very fact that I feel that the phrase now goes in inverted commas shows something (and not just about me!). The aspirant working class aspire to be middle class.

It all comes back to the same thing. Most people are ambitious for themselves and their family and don't feel guilty about it. Neither should they. It's just they should not begrudge such ambition or achievement for others and should feel a sense of obligation to help bring it about for those less fortunate or successful.

The problem, however, was that though much of the party could accept radical reform in the event of chronic failure, most would not accept that radicalism in the case of passive mediocrity. So we had a battle to change structure, to alter the "givens"; we also had a battle to change attitudes, to promote excellence not at the expense of equity but as a legitimate goal in its own right.

Probably, too, we were still in the process of education through empirical experiment. The NHS Plan, as it was written, still bore marks of political and intellectual immaturity. But it was a radical departure from where we had been.

Before that, I had a law and order agenda to address. We had begun the first antisocial behaviour legislation a couple of years before. Increasingly, for me, this fitted within a whole agenda around the antiquated and failing criminal justice system. The objective was to start treating criminal justice like a public service. I know that sounds odd, but here was the issue: because it concerns profound and rightly revered questions of human liberty, the focus in the criminal justice system was and still is on the interplay between prosecution and defence. In the adversarial inquisition that follows, the system is governed by the priority of doing justice to the process of finding someone guilty or innocent.

Of course, that is and always should be central, but in focusing so rigidly on this aspect, in the real world, whole legitimate areas of public and individual concern become marginal. How the system functions as a service is one. The witnesses, the victims, everyone basically other than the court itself, have to fit around the interplay between prosecution and defence. Cases are cancelled. Defendants don't turn up. Warrants don't get executed. The police don't have time to deal with minor offences. Behind each one of these things is a person, a victim who goes unnoticed—until they turn up in court, that is, when often they go through a traumatic and prolonged process that adds insult to their already grievous injury.

And all this takes place against a background where crime is so much more prevalent than in the mid-twentieth century. People can go over the reasons for this endlessly, but it amounts to this: the system doesn't fit the reality of modern living. It's a horse in the age of the motor car. It's a wonderful thing but it doesn't take you far enough, fast enough.

I was preoccupied with antisocial behaviour, and was personally completely intolerant of it. I remember when our home was in Stavordale Road, near the Arsenal Tube station in Islington, and I had to go out to dinner. I walked down to the station. As I passed the end of our street, a bloke was urinating against a wall. I stopped. "What are you looking at?" he said. I said, "You, you shouldn't be doing it." He took out a large knife from his coat. I walked on.

I hated it. I hated the fact that he did it. I hated even more the fact that I didn't stop him. I hated the choice I was made to make: stop him and risk ending your life because someone urinated in the street—hardly the stuff of martyrdom—or walk on.

Day in, day out, across our cities, towns, suburbs, villages and hamlets, such vignettes are played out. It's the same in most European cities and in the U.S. it can be worse. Absolutely rightly, people resent it powerfully. It offends their most cherished sensibilities. Out and about around the country, that was what people talked about; and I listened with a genuine desire to act.

I felt we had gone really badly wrong as a society and had to correct it. I didn't feel it as some fragment of nostalgia; I felt it was a classic challenge of the modern world and our system had to be modernised to meet it. I wrote several personal, private notes about reform in the criminal justice system. Jack Straw got it. I'm afraid Derry didn't. He half pretended he did to humour me, but he took the *de haut en bas* view that it was all populist gimmickry, as did most lawyers, judges and assorted bigwigs.

We had an additional problem, too, arising out of the fact of being a Labour government. The *Mail* had turned pretty poisonous. Worst of all, for those people like its editor Paul Dacre who are essentially tribal Tories, the gravitational pull of opposition meant that even if they agreed with what was being said, they disagreed with it because of who was saying it.

A whole section of the right went into a completely nonsensical civil liberties mode, at the same time as complaining of how we had to be tougher on crime. I don't mean the whole civil liberties critique was nonsense—I didn't concur with it, but I respected it—I mean right-wing law and order types who suddenly discovered that preserving the liberty of suspects was what they had really been about all along.

It was the beginning of the unholy coalition that after Iraq proved such a force, a sort of *Daily Mail/Guardian* alliance, whose only real point of unity was dislike of me, but who found in the reforms plenty to dislike if they were minded to; and they were. So, over time, the coalition of support New Labour had built, got weakened by a coalition of opposition that on the one side was born of conviction and on the other of expedience. But its existence meant getting heard was a challenge.

As I set about making my case for reform of criminal justice, I did so with what can only be described as mixed success.

First, I decided to make the philosophical case about the nature of our society, how it had changed, how we could retrieve the sense of values lost if we were prepared to think afresh. Unfortunately, I decided to visit this sociological essay upon the good matrons of the Women's Institute Triennial Gathering at Wembley.

Quite what I was thinking of when I embarked on such a rash and ill-starred venture, I don't know. I can only think the birth of Leo might have had something to do with it.

One reason why I had been a tad distracted at the time of the "forces of conservatism" speech, and didn't calibrate and recalibrate it in my normal fashion, was because Cherie had just shocked me profoundly by telling me she was pregnant.

The announcement some weeks later had been greeted with the usual run of a) astonishment—"You mean the prime minister has sex? And with his wife?"; b) cynicism—"Alastair Campbell commanded it as part of a diversionary tactic"; and from our children, c) mild disgust.

The birth itself was bizarre. There I was in a corridor with my detectives, listening and waiting as Cherie did a bit of preliminary shrieking and groaning, then going in and staying with her as he was born. The midwives were wonderful—just really sensible, down-to-earth, no-nonsense people. Cherie was unbelievable. There are times with that woman when I am in awe. She kept working until the last minute. Gave birth on time and to order. Got out that night. And she was forty-five. It was pretty impressive.

It was a kind of global event. The next day I wandered out of Downing Street to say a few words as a proud dad, etc. I made the mistake of holding a mug of tea which had a picture of the other three kids on it, which was considered very cheesy, and I suppose it was. But for once I really did feel proud.

I then went back in for the official photo of Leo, having decided we would ask one photographer to do it and sell the pictures, giving the proceeds to charity. We asked Paul McCartney's daughter, Mary, to do it. She was great, and the photos were superb. This was a minor miracle since the other kids—teenagers by then—behaved sensationally badly throughout the shoot and I could tell Mary thought they should have been given Anti-Social Behaviour Orders.

I then had to do the proper modern dad thing and take paternity leave. It was bliss. Not because I adored looking after Leo (I'm afraid looking after babies at the eating, sleeping and other thing stage has never been my idea of fun, though I always did it). But I had two weeks to relax, miss PMQs and think about my speech to the Women's Institute, whom I had been told were a generally delightful and well-disposed group of people and before whom I had decided to drop my pearls of wisdom.

So on the morning of 7 June, just before PMQs (what was I thinking of?), I beetled along to Wembley. I remember reading the speech through in a little anteroom and having a vague premonition that maybe it might have been a little more appropriate as a lecture to a bunch of professors. Afterwards, and though I say it myself, the thing that was most annoying was it was actually a good speech—thoughtful, well argued, and even if neither of those things, worthy of comment or critique.

I set out my reason why the absence of good manners among so many people was not a trivial thing but something that masked a decline in proper conduct that then expressed itself in far more serious ways. I talked about parents who sided with their children rather than the teacher who disciplined them; about how the essential courtesies are so often disregarded, and the culture to which this gives rise. I explained how we had to try to reverse this, not by pretending the clock could be switched back, but by recognising the world had changed and required a different system for enforcing good conduct in the absence of the pressure of tradition and family.

I thought the Women's Institute might see the sense of all that, and strangely, had there been fewer of them and had they been prepared to listen, they probably would have.

Instead, as I proceeded on to the platform and looked out at 10,000 of them and started my speech, I had an uncomfortable feeling. I am acutely audience-sensitive—you have got to be in my profession—and somehow I knew this wasn't quite ringing the bell.

About ten minutes in, when I was starting to plough on and getting more and more uneasy, a whole lot of shouting and slow handclapping suddenly started up. The audience were revolting. To be frank, there's not a lot you can do in a situation like that. You more or less freeze.

I looked across at the Women's Institute leadership on the platform. They were not encouraging. Eventually they intervened in a slightly "We're sorry you're having to listen to this but can you please—and sorry to be a nuisance about this—let him drone on a little longer" sort of a way.

That quietened the masses somewhat, but only after a bit of grumbling and barking, and it was fairly clear I was on sufferance that might at any moment be revoked. The fact that the platform was showing the sort of leadership of your average French Revolutionary Committee in the presence of Madame Defarge didn't help. I resolved to cut my losses, make some trivial extempore remarks and get the hell out of there. Which I duly did. To be fair, the leadership recovered a little to thank me for my presence and generally did a bit of pro forma buttering up. I smiled wanly and appeared to take it all in good humour, despite my largely unkind thoughts towards them all.

As I got into the back of the car to take me to Parliament and PMQs (and what a mirthless laugh the prospect of facing William Hague after that experience gave rise to), I shook my head. "What a disaster," I said to Anji.

The great thing about Anji was her indestructible and occasionally incredible optimism. She perked up when others perked down. She saw the silver lining long before the cloud. She was a positive life force, bashing down whole fields of negativity, basking the environs around her with beams of light, joy and hope amid the darkness.

She did not fail on this occasion. "Apart from the interruption I thought it went rather well," she said.

"Keep it plausible, darling," I replied.

Later that evening, over a drink, after a day of bulletins of humiliation and exuberant delight among my foes, and under Cherie's influence, I got the giggles about the whole thing. After all, as she said, it had been a speech about the decline of good manners.

The second happening around the decision to make the case for reform of criminal justice didn't fare much better, though its consequences were more far-reaching and ultimately satisfactory.

As part of the discussions with senior police officials about crime and disorder, I had been debating with them how to short-cut the normal and lengthy processes for establishing guilt in respect of more minor criminal offences.

Here was the problem. When I sat down with police who worked the beat, as I did fairly regularly, one thing recurred time and again. I used to ask: When someone is found drunk and disorderly, say, or creates a disturbance or assaults another but the assault is not severe enough to result in any very serious sentence, what do you do? And more often than not, the reply came back: Nothing. It's not worth it.

"Let me tell you what happens in the real world," I remember one policeman in Kent telling me, and he recounted how, for even a minor charge, there were reams of paperwork, a barrage of hearings and meetings and consultations with prosecutors and witnesses and how, most galling of all, the offenders who were habitual and knew the system, knew that it could be gamed. So they acted more or less with impunity.

That, along with other similar conversations, convinced me that, whatever the theory, obliging a full court process for minor offences meant in practice they didn't get prosecuted. I had become a complete adherent of the zero-tolerance analysis—if you let people get away with the small offences, the big ones follow. You create a culture of "anything goes," of disrespect; of tolerating the intolerable. And though all these offences could be called minor, the adjective was relative. I never even tussled with the bloke urinating in my street, but I never forgot the incident.

So if the reality, whatever the textbook says, is that the minor offences go unpunished, the whole system is in disrepute. It was an argument I was to have many times over the years. I didn't win it, certainly not in the way the argument was won about choice in health, or academies in schooling (state-funded schools open to all students established and managed by sponsors from a wide range of back-grounds), or tuition fees for universities. But sometime or other, a government will have to relearn the lesson. Banging on about law and order while accepting the "givens" of the existing legal system gets you nowhere.

After some debate, we alighted on the idea of giving the police the power to administer on-the-spot fines, "fixed penalty notices" as they came to be known. We had a fierce battle over it in the relevant Cabinet Committee. Even the Home Office wanted to scale back. The police were up for it and I was convinced it would give them an additional instrument of law enforcement. Today, hundreds of thousands of them are given and they are accepted as part of the system, though in my view they could still be used more broadly, and the amount of the fine should be increased radically. But they are there, to be built on.

I decided to announce this at a venue even more weird and inappropriate for the subject matter than the WI.

My Oxford friend Pete Thomson had always sung the praises, rightly, of the inestimable Hans Küng, a Catholic priest turned professor at the University of Tübingen in Germany. Hans was a distinguished scholar and author who had fallen out with the Vatican over his views on papal infallibility, and was considered a radical. He had also written books such as *On Being a Christian* which were great works, reaching out to non-Catholics. He was years ahead of his time in the interfaith field, too. I fell out with him over Iraq, as I did with many people, but he was always courteous and generous.

At Pete's prompting, Hans invited me to give a lecture at Tübingen.

It is a beautiful ancient city, one of the few that escaped Allied bombardment. John Burton had once played there with his folk group. There is no plaque, though I should imagine there were a few records broken in the local taverns.

The speech was again about the nature of a changing society and its rules and order. For the purposes of domestic consumption back home, we had a passage in the speech about louts and on-the-spot fines. If we hadn't, as Alastair rightly pointed out, we were going to Europe for "nul points" with the British electorate.

Rather foolishly, I let him write the passage about the fines. It was a great piece of Alastair tabloidery. Except that, as can happen with this genre, it went too far, suggesting we would march the offender up to the nearest cashpoint and solemnly watch as they were forced to take out their money and pay the fine—i.e. a real on-the-spot, on-the-spot fine. Literal, but not practical.

"You watch how this goes on the news," he said confidently as we settled into the seats of the RAF plane flying us back. "It'll go big." And in that prediction, limited as it was, he was undoubtedly right.

Unfortunately, it was a classic example of a big argument being obscured by a small error. On-the-spot fines indeed came in, but they were more or less missed in the embarrassment of our not being able to defend them by reference to "cashpoint justice."

It didn't much matter in the end. The seeds of a far bigger development—a new framework of antisocial behaviour legislation—were sown.

The public presentation of the reform I wanted was not going well. The philosophical dimension had been felled by the WI; the policy dimension was stuck in the medieval vaults of Tübingen. Now it was the turn of the personal dimension.

It is always unconscionably dangerous for a prime minister to have teenage children. It is the proverbial accident waiting to happen. I have been blessed by having the most fantastic, generally understanding and only quietly rebellious children. When I remember what I was like at their age, I shiver to think of myself as a teenager transplanted to Downing Street.

I recall, back in the mists of time, my dad greeting me off the train at Durham railway station as I came home after my first year at Oxford. My unwashed hair was roughly the length of Rapunzel's and I had no shoes and no shirt. My jeans were torn—in the days before this became fashionable. Worst of all, I was wearing a long sleeveless coat I had made out of curtains my mum had thrown out. All my dad's friends were at the station, and their kids looked paragons of respectability beside me.

Dad saw the old curtains and visibly winced. They did kind of stand out. I took pity on him.

"Dad," I said, "there is good news. I don't do drugs."

He looked me in the eye and said: "Son, the bad news is if you're looking like this and you're not doing drugs, we've got a real problem."

As children go, my kids are great. But that's the point—children do go.

Euan was sixteen and had just sat his GCSEs. To be frank, and if he doesn't mind me saying so, they weren't a huge cause for celebration, but he and his friend James, a lovely guy who became a Labour candidate in the 2010 election, decided to go out and celebrate nevertheless.

Around 11:30 on the night of 6 July, I was proceeding in an upwardly direction to my bed, when I thought I would look in on the said Euan, who I assumed must have been back in his room by then. The assumption was false. There was no Euan. Not in his room, not in the flat.

Cherie was away with her mum and Leo, taking a short break in Portugal.

Where the hell was Euan? I only knew he had been out with James. I phoned James's mum, and got James's number. I phoned him. He was not making a massive amount of sense, but the gist was he had last seen Euan wandering off in the general direction of Leicester Square.

I panicked. This is where being prime minister poses a few unusual challenges. I wanted to go and look for him. You do. You want to rush out and get busy. But I could hardly saunter up to Leicester Square and do a walkabout at midnight. I spoke to the policeman by the door at Downing Street, explained what had happened and threw myself on his mercy. Like a complete trooper, he announced he would go and search for Euan.

The next couple of hours were desperate. In my worry, I temporarily forgot the fact I had a huge programme on the next day. I was due to be down in Brighton, first to visit the Black Churches of Britain Conference, and then to do a special edition of *Question Time*, featuring just me, and centring on—yes, you guessed it—law and order and antisocial behaviour.

The wonderful Downing Street copper somehow tracked him down, and at around 1:30 a.m. he turned up with a very sorry-assed-looking Euan, plainly still the worse for wear, having been arrested near Leicester Square Tube station for underage drinking and being drunk in a pub-lic place. The circumstances and timing were not, shall we say, absolutely desirable.

I got no sleep that night. Around 2:30 a.m. Euan insisted on coming into my bed. Alternately, he would go into a mournful tirade of apology and then throw up. I loved him and felt sorry for him, but had a police cell been available I would have been all for moving him there.

Somehow, eventually, it was morning. The news had come out at roughly the time when Euan was being ushered back in the door of Downing Street. Police stations serve many admirable and necessary purposes, but they aren't places to keep secrets. Alastair, who I had to speak to about press handling, thought the whole thing hilariously funny, going into what he thought was a very amusing riff about how *Question Time* would be, linking it without any sense of self-awareness to the debacle of cashpoint fines. I'm afraid I was completely beyond it all. I can make do with only a little sleep, but not no sleep. By some means—I suppose it must have been the train—I got down to Brighton and, clutching a prepared speech, went to where the Black Churches were having their conference.

I didn't quite know what to expect. I didn't know much about them then, though I came to know much more later in my time. In particular, I hadn't realised how similar they were to American Black Churches—lively, inspirational, participational, all-singing and all-dancing.

When I walked in, there was a great roar of welcome. Of course, they all knew about Euan. It was big news. And it was meat and drink, if you'll pardon the expression, to them. There was the prime minister's son, falling from grace, yielding to the devil alcohol, straying from the righteous path; and here was the prime minister coming among them. Well, you can imagine.

It was like a revivalist convention. People were blessing and praying and calling out the Lord's name. The main man, a total inspiration and lovely human being, got them all to hold hands and pray for me, for my family, for Euan. I did, at one moment, want to point out that, OK, he was drunk and shouldn't have been, but all this seemed a little exces-sive—it's not as if he was a proper criminal or anything.

But I didn't and it wouldn't have mattered a jot if I had. To them, the boy was lost and now was found, and that was all that mattered.

It certainly did revive me. I threw away my speech, got thoroughly into the spirit of it all and have to admit gave them as good as I was getting, cavorting shamelessly around the stage like some TV evangelist, doing a bit of whooping and hollering myself and having a ball.

By the time I got to the *Question Time* studio, I was fighting drunk on the Lord's spirit. When the first questioner asked me a nasty question about whether my son's antics didn't make a mockery of my claim to be concerned about law and order or some such, I practically bopped him—verbally at any rate—and continued in that vein. "What did they slip into your tea at that religious thing?" Alastair asked afterwards. "We should send you down there every week. On second thoughts, maybe not," he added.

We stopped off at a pub on the way back, much to the amusement of the locals. They were all thoroughly supportive of Euan and I heard in turn each customer's tale of a similarly misspent youth. At moments like that, the British are very decent folk.

Once those various alarums and excursions were out of the way, Alan and I settled back down to the detail of the NHS Plan. We were having scores of meetings on it, several a week—examining, re-examining, re-re-examining over and again.

I realised that to sell it to a doubting and nervous party we would have to sweeten the pill of reform at points. Progressive parties can take their medicine and, once taken, feel and act better—but a spoonful of sugar helps it all go down. We had a number of positive factors to play with: the extra money; the extra staff: more NHS work to be secured from consultants in their starting years; more help for cancer and cardiac patients; an end to most mixed-sex wards; an increase in some types of hospital bed.

In return, we were opening up all the contracts of the professionals for renegotiation; breaching new ground with the private sector; changing the way the service worked to make it far more user-friendly; and, in essence, prefiguring an NHS that started to import twenty-first-century business concepts into the heart of the service.

Rereading it now, I can see all its limitations. Today it would be considered less than bold. And there were errors in implementation, to be sure. We paid more for the consultants' and GPs' contracts than strictly necessary (this later became a strong bone of contention with the Treasury), but in the long run, I considered it worth it. We set in place tracks of reform that in time would carry the system to transformational change. So: GP contracts were generous, but when we put the new contract into legislation, we inserted the right to open up local GP monopolies to competition. Nurses were given far more power; old demarcations between junior and senior doctors were collapsed.

The door was edged open for the private sector. The concept which, in time, was to result in foundation hospitals was introduced. (These were created by the Labour government to devolve decision-making from central government. The NHS Services in the foundation hospitals can be directed more to the needs of the local community.) And the whole terminology—booked appointments, minimum guarantees of service, freedoms to innovate—spoke of a coming culture of change, oriented to treating the NHS like a business with customers, as well as a service with patients.

For me, the process was itself extraordinarily revealing and educative. I started to find my proper points of reference when thinking of reform; began to articulate the concepts more clearly; assumed a more substantial confidence in the direction of change. I stopped thinking of it as a gamble with questionable empirical evidence, and started realising it was a clear mission whose challenge lay not in whether it was right, but in how it was carried through.

I date from that time, too, my clear break with the thinking that had dominated even New Labour policy up to then: that the public and private sectors operated in different spheres according to different principles. New Labour had indeed weaned the party off its hostility to the private sector, but now we moved on from the 1990s version of New Labour to something more consistent with a twenty-first-century mindset.

The truth was that the whole distinction between public and private sector was bogus at all points other than one: a service you paid for; and one you got free. That point is obviously central—it defines public service. But it doesn't define how it is run, managed and operated. In other words, that point is critical, but at all other points, the same rules apply for public and private sector alike, and those points matter enormously.

For a public service, even one like the NHS, in the negotiation of contracts for buildings, IT equipment, technology, it is like a business. When it cuts costs, as it should if it can, it is like a business. When it employs or fires people, it is like a business. When it seeks to innovate, it is like a business.

So I began to look for ways, all ways, of getting business ideas into public service practice. Just as the private sector had moved from mass production and standard items to just-in-time, customised products, so should public services. Just as people could shift custom if one company's service was better than others, so should customers of public services be able to do so. Just as private sector service was driven by risk-taking and innovation, so we should be freeing up the front line of public services to do the same.

I also came to have a sense, at times too obvious, of impatience with the view that all such talk was a betrayal of public service ethos. It seemed to me perfectly clear that if the status quo resulted in a poor service, then that was the true betrayal of that ethos; and so, if the poor service arose from the wrong structure, the structure had to change. In any event, I could see that so much of the language of defending "our public services" was just obscurantist propaganda designed to dress up a vested interest in the garb of the public interest.

We took care in how we presented the plan, which was scheduled for launch at the end of July, just before the recess. I always liked to announce a few big things before the long summer recess.

It can be up to three months. Robin Cook—in his reforming zeal when Leader of the House of Commons—tried to shorten it, a proposal in which the media delighted and at which MPs groaned. Personally, I loved the long summer break. It gave everyone space to contemplate, holiday, work it all out and get in shape for the party conference season. Life is so frenetic when Parliament is sitting. And, of course, the media environment in which ministers work is so incredibly altered, with tons more media obligations. The pace of modern politics is breakneck, so a long recess really helps.

But the MPs need to be sent off for summer with a clear strategy. Hence, the end of July was always a busy time, as busy as I could make it.

Before we got to the NHS Plan we had a stack of other things to do. We presented our Annual Report as a government to Parliament. This was one of our wackier innovations. The idea was entirely sensible: go through what the government had said it would do, and what it had done during the year. A sort of State of the Union address.

I finally binned it after the 2000 Report which I presented in mid-July to Parliament. It was a bit rushed. We ticked off the items we had achieved. Except some we ticked, we hadn't done. There was a memorable so-called achievement we listed and ticked off, which was the building of a new sports stadium in Sheffield. The only problem was it didn't exist. William Hague gave me a real old drubbing. Peter Brooke, a wonderful old Tory grandee, got up and asked what was the purpose of the photograph on page so-and-so, which turned out to be a picture of a packet of contraceptive pills. Tricky one to answer, that. Anyway, some ideas work, some don't. This didn't.

I decided that by bending over and inviting people to come and kick the government's backside we weren't advancing the cause of human progress much, and certainly not the cause of Her Majesty's Government. So although binning the idea generated a certain amount of additional embarrassment, I was more than happy to suffer it to save a perpetual hiding being handed out each year.

On 27 July 2000, I presented the NHS Plan. It went well. There was enough to satisfy the backbenchers that it was a Labour document. And we had put down the markers for New Labour.

Around the same time, Andrew and I first formulated the academy idea for schools. It was still in its early stages, but the idea had germinated. It was based, in part, on the old Tory policy of independent technical colleges, but they had only created ten of them and then sort of shelved the policy. However, it aligned neatly with our thinking elsewhere: to give schools independence, to set them free from the local authority system of hands-on control; and to let them innovate, including in how they employed staff.

The public service and welfare reform agenda for the second term was gradually becoming defined. As we departed for the recess, I was in a reasonably jolly mood. I was no longer feeling my way, but finding it.

However, one cloud was gathering, and starting to spread with a rather deep shade of darkness. Gordon was managing the economy with all his power and skill, and that was no small thing—it gave the whole government ballast and weight—but there was a worrying pattern emerging that was more than conventional Treasury caution. It was clear that the direction of reform was not shared; not agreed; and not much liked. I noticed that the term "marketisation" of public services started to be used in discussions between us, especially when his adviser Ed Balls was involved, and the term was not meant as a compliment.

The cloud did not obscure the sun or sky at that point, but it made me uneasy. I wanted a radical manifesto, and so did he—but did the term "radical" mean the same thing to each of us? And how would he feel about the second term and the succession? An election was less than a year away if we were to go four years, the right time for a government which believes it can win again.

But, as I set off down to Tuscany and then to the Ariège in France, I felt we were in good shape to win a second term and win it well. Little Leo was proving a complete, unalloyed blessing: gorgeous, happy, a joy to others and to himself. It was weird having a small baby again; and weirder still in Downing Street. But right from the off, he was carried from room to room, from the switchboard to the foreign policy unit, a pocket-size piece of benign innocence existing in the maelstrom of the world-weary activities of government.

In the beautiful and venerable garden of the Strozzis' trattoria in Tuscany, I wondered what the intervening months would hold in store. My conjecture ranged widely. But not for one moment did it stray into the realms of floods, fuel protests and foot-and-mouth disease. Just as well, really.

TEN

MANAGING CRISES

I left for holiday at the end of July with the focus on public service reform. I came back at the end of August and found naturally that the focus had shifted to the thought that an election could be anticipated in May 2001; this was the run-up. The moment you begin a pre-election period, everything starts to be shaped around the election. The focus alters. The mind starts to think politically; the perpetual analysis and reanalysis about public sector reform gets displaced by polls, focus groups, anecdotal evidence of public opinion; the party people, exiled for years in the Siberia of party drudgery far from the centre of government, suddenly re-emerge in the halls of the Kremlin with renewed self-importance; and the wheels of the election machine start to turn.

For most of the party, the upcoming campaign would be centred on one simple ambition: to be the first ever Labour government to win two successive terms in office. For me, it was going to be about winning a mandate for more fundamental change. For me, the arguments about direction were long settled. The first term had proved we could govern. The second term had to be about what we were governing for: getting beyond the old established British ways, based in my eyes on a vision of the country no longer possible or desirable, and making us fit for the future. My boundless, at times rather manic lust for modernisation could occasionally be misdirected, but I was sure the basic thrust was correct: we needed to modernise the whole idea of the 1945 welfare state and public services, out-of-date systems of law and order and immigration, and our view of our role in the world. We had to use the twenty-first century as an occasion to renew ourselves as a nation. Thatcher had done the right thing in liberating enterprise and industry, but in becoming so obsessed with Euroscepticism, I felt she had still indulged the country in a view of itself that was simply no longer compatible with where we needed to be now, in this the year of the millennium.

I hadn't by any means worked out all the right policy answers, but I had worked out the crucial failing of the first term: the mistaken view that raising standards and performance could be separated from structural reform. This was true virtually across the board; and especially so in the public services. Above all, we had to divest power away from the dominant interest groups, unions and associations, and put it into the hands of people, the consumer, the parent, the patient, the user.

So I came back after a long and good holiday rested, but also fidgety and anxious. I had to frame the political argument right to win. I had to frame our manifesto right to give ourselves a proper mandate for proper change. We had hoarded our political capital in the first term. We had to keep it high to win again and win big. But I knew the moment was fast coming when I would have to spend it. And by now, if I had ever been in any doubt at the beginning, I knew that this would mean a second term that was an awful lot tougher, more challenging and less popular than the first.

As if to bring this home to me, from the moment I was back until nine months later when we won the election, I was embroiled in the most bizarre mixture of divine and man-made crises.

Within hours of my return, I was posed one of those extraordinarily sensitive and difficult decisions that can occur at any time and frequently come in batches. The British troops in Sierra Leone had been brilliant, and were successfully reasserting the control of the democratic government, but sadly a group of soldiers from the Royal Irish Regiment caught up in the fighting had been kidnapped by the RUF. We received intelligence as to where they were. Charles Guthrie asked to see me urgently in my den in Downing Street. He told me that they could mount an SAS (Special Air Services) rescue operation, employing the elite of our armed forces.

As ever with Charles, he had the courage to recommend a course of action rather than simply leave the decision to me, but he warned me that casualties were likely. The RUF are crazy and well-armed people, he explained, and there is a risk both to the hostages and to the rescue force. The alternative was to continue trying to negotiate and hope somehow we could prise them out through that route. We could probably buy them out, but we both quickly agreed that would be a disastrous signal which would only provoke a rash of copycat kidnappings.

We sat there for a few moments staring at each other. It would have been nice to have called for more work to be done; to have probed for greater detail; to have asked for the plans and the drawings and goodness knows what else they would have been doing at SAS HQ in Hereford. But I knew that while it could all be seen, and seen again, the decision would remain the same.

"Are you guys up for it?" I asked somewhat redundantly.

He snorted. "The guys are always up for it, as you know."

"OK, let's do it."

We got all the hostages back, but we lost an SAS soldier. Charles called me up in the flat and told me himself. I wandered around the flat for a while, imagining who he was, what he looked like, how he had felt going into the operation, the nerves, the adrenalin, the realisation that death might be moments away, and I reflected on a life lost, a family in mourning. We could still be negotiating and he could still be alive.

"I'm really sorry, Charles," I had started to say, "the trouble is if we hadn't acted—"

"You don't need to say that," Charles broke in. "For what it's worth, I have no doubt it was the right decision. It is very sad that we lost a man. But they are professionals. They know the risks. They do it because they want to do it and because they believe in it. There will be a lot of grief back in Hereford but also a lot of pride."

With an election in the offing, it had been decided that I should do a regional tour in order to "reconnect with the people." There is always something a trifle dubious about the "connecting with the people" business. In modern politics, you have to pretend to be living the life the ordinary person leads, when, of course, you can't and don't do the shopping in the supermarket, fill up the car, go down to the pub for a few beers, the quiz night and a bit of banter. But everyone nowadays has to go through the elaborate pretence that the prime minister could and should do all that, otherwise he or she is "out of touch," the worst criticism that can ever be made.

I can't tell you how many cafes, fish and chip shops and shopping malls I would go into, have money thrust into my hand (yes, the prime minister must have real cash jingling in his pocket) and buy something, all in the interests of showing I was a "regular bloke." One of the main reasons it's total rubbish is that prior to going in, the place is staked out by armed detectives, the shopkeeper is quizzed for security and politics, there are around twenty cameramen and film crews, a few random protesters, passing eccentrics, ordinary but bewildered members of the public and occasionally a police helicopter whirring overhead. Which all amounts to something a trifle different from how your regular bloke usually buys his coffee or CDs. But it all had to be gone through, and the office—Alastair particularly—would get very snooty and irritated if I tried to complain that it was all daft.

The classic was me and Gordon buying ice creams on a trip to a park and playground in the 2005 election. The conversation with Kate Garvey went something like this: "Go and buy ice cream from that van there, one for you, one for Gordon, to show togetherness and being normal."

"No," I said, "it's absurd. I don't like Mr. Whippy ice cream, except with a chocolate bar stuck in it; and does Gordon look like your average ice cream buyer? Come on, it's ridiculous, we're two guys in suits, one is the prime minister, the other is the Chancellor of the Exchequer. What's normal about it?"

"Just do it," she said menacingly, "and don't get a bar; it'll make you look greedy." (Advice I ignored.)

Such visits usually would provide a proper quotient of amusement. As I wandered round the park that day, I met a working-class mum, grandmother and baby in a pram. "You're better looking than on TV," the older woman remarked, sizing me up like a piece of meat.

"You can come again," I said jauntily.

"I just 'ave," she said, a story Kate regaled to an embarrassed Gordon.

Before the rounds of interviews anywhere near election time, I would have to go through a list of the price of everyday things like a pint of milk, a pound of butter, a shoulder of lamb. Bread used to produce lengthy debate about which type of loaf, white or brown, nothing too wholemeal, nothing too unhealthy, all of it done in the belief that if I knew such a fact, it would mean I might be going down to the shop near Downing Street (not that there was one) and collecting the groceries, which of course I wasn't. But people have great faith in the power of such trips to "connect" with the public, and who's to say they're wrong.

However, though I went along with it all, I always used to question the premise. The public aren't stupid; they know the prime minister doesn't really tootle off to the supermarket like they do. They don't want to know that he actually does live like one of them, but they want to know that he could; and more important, they want to know that he feels like them, that they could get on.

This is nothing to do with upbringing or class or background. You can be an Old Etonian and get along with people; you can be from Trimdon Colliery and be hopeless with them. It's about temperament, character and attitude. It's also about being authentic. To be sure, if you aren't naturally a bloke people would like to have a beer with and you're running for office, it is a problem. It may be irrational, but it's true. I always used to say to people about George Bush: don't underestimate his appeal as a normal guy. You might not agree with him, but if you're a voter, you would never think you would be uncomfortable or feel inadequate if you met him socially; you would think he would be nice and easy with you. And you'd be right.

You can just about get over a lack of such normality provided you don't pretend to be other than you are. Some politicians, and I'm one of them, enjoy chatting about things and meeting people. I am infinitely curious about them. (Clinton's great political strength was an endless capacity to be fascinated even by the most unfascinating people because he was always willing to learn from them.) But other politicians aren't. If you aren't, don't obsess about it. Serious-minded, severe even, can still win, provided it's authentic.

Though I always complained about doing these regional tours because of the questionable PR premise, and the time away from Number 10 and from pushing forward on policy, and despite the unreality and occasional surreality of it all, I would always learn something from being out and about, in particular from talking to front-line staff or businesses. They were useful not so much as a barometer of opinion, but as a means of finding out whether what I was being told in Downing Street bore any resemblance to the facts on the ground. Very often it didn't.

At the beginning of September, just before we left to do this tour in the North, there were reports of fuel protests in France. The price of oil had been steadily rising to over $30 a barrel, the highest for more than ten years. Prices at the fuel pump began to rise sharply.

Fuel duty had been a bone of contention for years. In order to sort out the public finances, the previous government had established a "fuel duty escalator," which meant that the duty would rise by a certain percentage above inflation. It was also given an environmental justification—the first green tax—but no one took that reasoning very seriously. It helped bring the borrowing requirement back under control, and while the price of crude oil remained low, the rise in duty could be effectively masked by the low price of the raw product. So it suited government fine. Of course, when the oil price began to spiral upwards and carried the price of petrol at the pump with it, it was a different matter.

The French tend to protest at anything and don't need much excuse to get out on the street, but in Britain it was not traditionally the done thing. Suddenly the anger at the rising price of petrol concentrated attention on the fact that UK fuel duty was the highest in Europe. On 8 September, the fuel protests from France, which we had been watching with a rather uninterested complacency, spread to the UK.

The fuel protesters were a motley bunch. There were farmers, long-distance lorry drivers, the self-employed and the anti-government. They were not from the usual protesting stock with which the left is familiar; these were what your Marxist would call the petty bourgeoisie, not that there was anything petty or petit about them. They had a genuine grievance. But they were strongly anti-Labour, I suspect.

They were also smart enough to target the Achilles heel of the fuel industry, and thus the economy, and thus the government. Oil comes into the country and is refined at vast refining plants, of which there are not many, before being transported by lorry to petrol stations. Without the refining plants, no blood flows to the arteries. Petrol stations don't have a lot of capacity, so they fill up every forty-eight hours or so. Day in, day out, this system gets the fuel out to the forecourt and hence to the customer, be they a farmer, a business or a member of the public.

The trouble is at the time when I had to know this, I didn't. And neither, it seems, did anyone else in a position of authority, so when we heard of some protests at two refineries—Buncefield and Stanlow—the enormity didn't sink in.

We went on our tour, the normal round of schools and hospitals and "connections with ordinary people." We stopped for lunch at a small country hotel just outside Hull, where we were due to talk at a party event and then go for a dinner to celebrate John Prescott's thirty years as a Hull MP. We ate a leisurely meal, as we had a bit of time to kill. There was a travelling media pack and I passed some time with them discussing the upcoming presidential election in the U.S. I recall having an intriguing discussion about terrorism and its potential to grow into a world-wide threat.

The fuel protesters were using the good old trade union picket tactic which Mrs. Thatcher had outlawed, and stopped the lorries leaving the refineries. Anji Hunter told me the protests were spreading. Shell, who had reported that some of the protests were violent, wanted police escorts for their drivers. I was beginning to get the first real stirrings of unease—about forty-eight hours too late.

By the time we got to Hull, the thing had turned really ugly and protesters were ringing the Hull City Hall. Like a storm breaking out of nowhere, the media and the protesters suddenly came together in a great clap of thunder. You might think that employing Arthur Scargill-like tactics of picketing and intimidation in order to bring the nation to a halt would have called the media forth into a barrage of condemnation. Had it been Scargill, president of the National Union of Mineworkers in the 1980s during the miners' strikes, probably it would have, but since this was about the price of petrol—something dear to their readers' hearts—and the protests were aimed at a Labour government, the opposite happened and the protesters quickly became street heroes, fighting for the rights of ordinary people against an insensitive administration.

One of the hardest things at a time like this is to carry on and do all the things in the schedule, when you are desperate to stop it all, go into a quiet corner and think. Sitting in an anteroom to the main chamber in the magnificent Hull City Hall, I was really agitated. I knew I had messed up big time. My antennae should have been twitching. I should have realised that for your ordinary motorist, the rising cost of filling the car was a big, not an insignificant one (after all, the children's nanny, Jackie, had been complaining about it for weeks). I should have understood the total vulnerability of the system to the protest; and the attraction of the protest to the media. Sitting there with a twenty-point lead in the polls, I had just opened up a massive breach in our defences.

The Chinese restaurant where the dinner for John Prescott was to be held was already thronging with protesters. The police advised me to call it off. I accepted gratefully. I had to think.

We got out of a side door of the City Hall, and after being pursued down the street by a mob, we got into the hotel. I was trying to get some sense of the seriousness of it all from Number 10. Alastair was in full crisis mode, but the rest of the machine seemed curiously paralysed, reacting to the scene as it was unfolding with a mixture of endless process and hand-wringing that was not pretty to behold.

You always have to know when to delegate and when to take the thing very purposefully and very clearly into your own two hands. Leadership without delegation is usually a mess—nothing gets done as people fret about whether they are doing what the leader wants them to do, and the leader has too many things on the go to concentrate long enough to give adequate instruction. But when it is crisis time, forget delegation. That's the moment you're there for: grip it, shape it, decide it and solve it.

After a restless night—I wished I had gone back to London the previous evening—we got to the station very early. As I stepped onto the train, much to the surprise of the travelling public, a lady said to me: "Don't give in to them, they're Tories, you know. You stand up to them." That was one view, certainly. There would definitely be others.

On the train I formed a strategy. We had to defeat the protest and reopen the refineries, that was for sure; but we also had to make sure the Pre-Budget Report addressed the fuel question, i.e. stand up for proper government, but don't be daft and refuse to listen. Unreasonable people sometimes make reasonable demands.

First things first. The crisis was now fully blown. The media were revelling in it. Panic buying of fuel was the order of the day, and the images of queues of cars, petrol forecourts crowded or closed, and general chaos were irresistible, and the media weren't in a mood to resist them. They were lashing the chariots of fury on, the protesters were cheered and the government got lambasted for "doing nothing" to solve the crisis which the media were actively encouraging.

I was really angry about it. I felt that a Tory government would not be treated like this. But, having vented a bit to Jonathan, Anji and Alastair, I realised that anger—or even worse, self-pity—was just pathetic. We were where we were; we just had to get out of it.

I called in the ministers. Jack Straw was, as ever, practical and focused. Gordon said it was important that this was not seen as a tax issue (we had a slightly unreal exchange over the next days as he kept telling me it can't be seen as a tax issue and I kept telling him that unfortunately it was seen as a tax issue and nothing was going to change that). Stephen Byers, the Trade and Industry Secretary, was calm.

But no one seemed to have much of an answer. Fuel supplies had literally stopped, and the country was at a standstill. I called in the oil companies and the police. The military were already being activated, but all they had were a few very old tankers, nothing like what was necessary. Hopeless!

At times like those, you know what the phrase "the buck stops here" means. The oil guys were very polite, but they sort of didn't regard it as their problem. The police seemed to have been getting mixed signals. One officer said they were doing their best to try to make sure the protests were peaceful and that there was proper dialogue with the protesters. As I looked at him, I realised what the problem was: they were all very reasonable people, and they wanted to be very reasonable.

Oh Lord, I thought. I could feel my heart starting to bounce, the anger in my gorge, my jaw tightening. I was about to blow my top when I decided to use icy calm instead. More prime ministerial.

I looked at the police officer. "Tell me what you are going to do to stop the protests."

"Stop the protests?" he said, his eyes narrowing slightly. "You mean you want us to prevent them taking place?"

"Yes," I said, very calm. "And I want you the oil companies to instruct your drivers to cross the picket lines, and if they don't, for reasons anything other than fear of violence to their person, I want you to sack them. And I would like the army to come in and if necessary drive your tankers, and if they meet with any violence from protesters, I want you the police to deal with them very firmly, and if not, to let the army take care of them. They're very good at it."

The police officers brightened. They understood. No more nice cuddly neighbourhood policing, but go after them hard. The army, as ever, couldn't wait to get started. The oil guys looked a little nonplussed, but I threw in some vague remarks on public anxiety about their excessive profits from the rising oil price and they at least understood they had to become active, rather than reactive.

I summed up a list of action points, arranged for a Cabinet Office Briefing Room (COBR) crisis-response meeting for me to chair the next day, and ended the meeting satisfied we were at least gripping it and beginning the process of turning things around.

I then went off for a press conference. The only thing to do at a time like this is to show you are on top of it and give a general appearance of being in charge, whatever the panic underneath. I did well, though foolishly said that within twenty-four hours we would have the situation "on the way back to normal." I choose words carefully—it's part of my very useful training as a lawyer—but these words were foolish because subtlety doesn't often translate into clear communication. It was taken as saying that within twenty-four hours everything would be back to normal. Impossible, of course. But apart from that, it was OK and served its purpose.

The next thing was to take away some of the moral high ground from the protesters. Alan Milburn said we should focus on the impact on the NHS, and Alastair agreed. They were running short of supplies. The fuel protesters—and this was how ludicrous the whole thing became— were allowing tankers through for "emergencies" based on their assessment of "emergency." Depending on the negotiation between them and a hospital, fuel would be allowed through or not. It was intolerable, but gave us a chance to exploit their weakness; in the end, who were they to decide life or death?

So we sent nurses out to the picket lines to argue with the protesters. Alan gave a very strong statement echoing my position and we could feel support for them beginning to ebb. It was the first successful PR blow. It also shows the invaluable assistance good teamwork in politics can give. It's not usually thought of as a team game, but it is, especially in a crisis. Everyone around me put their hands to the pump, as it were. Instead of fretting—or worse, sitting around moaning—people like Alan actually tried to think of ways of solving it.

The Tories also messed up. I write about William Hague elsewhere, but I doubt if the Hague of today would have made the mistake of the Hague then. He more or less backed the protest; not quite, but more or less. Opportunity always knocks for an Opposition leader, but sometimes it's best not to answer and leave it knocking. The public start with one mood, and when the mood changes, if you're not careful and you have tried to exploit it, you're high and dry.

The public were angry at the price of petrol; and in large numbers they backed the protesters' case. But the country grinding to a halt is not a great idea, and the public know it. The consequences come home of what is really, as they know in their heart of hearts, grossly irresponsible action. After about four days of standstill, the sentiment that "enough is enough" started to percolate through the national consciousness. Slowly but surely we got back to normal.

I have had many harsh things to say about the unions over the years, but I have to say on this crisis they reacted magnificently. They were fulsome in condemning the protesters, making the valid point that unions doing the same were regarded as acting like wildcat strikers. For the first time in memory, I was praising John Edmonds of the GMB (Britain's General Union) and Bill Morris of the TGWU (Transport and General Workers' Union), and was actually really grateful to the Trade Union Congress.

I asked Jim Callaghan to come out and support us, and he gave a statement to the *Today* programme backing the government and me personally (though he declined an interview for them on the basis that he would be asked about the comparisons with the stoppages of the 1970s). The Confederation of British Industry, our top business lobbying organisation, finally woke up and weighed in on the side of sense.

From 13 to 16 September, the situation continued to be bad, but was improving daily. We set up a committee with the oil companies to lay plans for averting such a protest in future. By 17 September, more than 60 per cent of petrol stations were open again. Panic buying had stopped.

It was over; but the damage to the government had been considerable. You really have to hand it to the media—once the thing collapsed, we were roundly taken to task for not acting soon enough and not doing more to prevent the protests spreading. It was extraordinary, comic even. Without a blush they were castigating us for not stamping on a fire they were actively helping light under us. I think, after that, I realised two things. The first was that there is no point getting steamed up about them; they are what they are, and to get angry is just to waste energy (this is a very good precept, but as time showed, rather hard to adhere to). The second thing was that life will always be different for a Labour leader compared to a Tory leader. Provided you know that, it's OK; but it is different, and you have to know it.

The fallout from the fuel protests meant we went into party conference at the end of September in slightly chastened mood. A poll showed us eight points behind the Tories.

Polls are an absolute nightmare. All leaders will tell you they don't pay attention to them, but all leaders do. The problem is they can be an instant snapshot of public opinion (i.e. real, but superficial and therefore potentially transient) or they can indicate a trend (i.e. potentially of lasting significance). You never know which it is.

But they matter because quite apart from anything else, your supporters and the media dwell on them. They help create a mood, which itself often then reinforces the polling. You watch any U.S. election and it's amazing the degree to which the polls create the weather. In part the media, and indeed all of us to a degree, distrust our own instinct—we may think "X," but then a poll shows "Y," so we think, Well, maybe "Y" is right after all.

The result of this can be not merely confusing; it can reduce the disposition to argue a case. One of the weaknesses of polls, as I learned, is that they don't measure the degree to which people are open to persuasion. So the snapshot may well say "Y," but actually the public could be brought to think "X."

Over time, I became less concerned with the polling (which may have coincided with the fact it became less amicable!), but I would still always cast a nervous eye at it. Then there was Philip Gould and his focus groups. Philip was a fantastic support, at times as crucial as a morale enthuser as a political strategist, but I used to laugh at how extraordinary the confluence was between his own thoughts and what the groups seemed to say. Also, so much depended on the individual people. Though pollsters always swore blind these groups were selected on a very "scientific" basis, the truth about any group of people chosen like this is that they are utterly in thrall to their own mood on the day, any recent experience, what they think they should think, and above all to the voice in the group which speaks most definitively and so influences the dynamics that will occur within any collection of strangers sitting in a room together for the first time. I always wanted to attend one secretly and then at the end jump out and confront them with all the vicious calumnies they had just been uttering against me!

But so frenzied is the political desire to sniff the prevailing winds accurately that huge emphasis and sanctity is placed upon polls. You begin to realise how the ancient temple priests must have felt in pagan days, trying to read the entrails. I bet they were much like Philip and one of his groups, and the conclusion they arrived at was not greatly different from where they thought things were moving anyway. So they, and polls, should be treated with the utmost caution. But they never are.

In this instance, the eight-point Tory lead did seem genuinely transient, but it was an indication we had taken a hit. I decided we had to answer what I thought was a basic underlying problem. People thought we were an all-powerful government, the Tories were rubbish and there was no real Opposition. Now, of course, to us sitting there dealing with the daily grind, it wasn't like that at all—we felt under unbelievable pressure all the time—but the public, egged on by the media, could see signs of hubris and arrogance. That was part of the reason why they took the side of the protesters so readily: they didn't really want us to lose the fight, but a bit of a kicking might serve us right.

We had also just had an unfortunate run-in with Britain's pensioners. One of the greatest myths of human existence is that as people get older, they get more benign, more long-suffering, more relaxed and more phlegmatic in how the world treats them. Not in my experience.

Your average Rottweiler on speed can be a lot more amiable than a pensioner wronged, or, to put it more accurately, believing they are wronged. Around this time, I remember distinctly visiting a housing development to open a new nursery, going down the path shaking hands with a few well-wishers. Out of the corner of my eye, I caught sight of an old-age pensioner, a woman no less, with a placard that read: "Blair, you are a c★★★." I couldn't believe it. I was really shocked. She looked like your typical sweet granny. I almost stopped to remonstrate, but then wisely thought better of it.

My mother-in-law—by the way, a wonderful mother to Cherie and an inestimable support to the family—used to keep me informed of the views of pensioners, and as lobbyists go she was up there with the best of them. I used to reflect on how much money was spent on expensive Westminster lobby firms all paying a fortune to get the ear of some junior minister, and here right at the centre of Downing Street was one woman giving a rolling masterclass in the art of targeted persuasion. However, it was a mono-theme: the government's scandalous treatment of pensioners.

What was fascinating, and more than a little unnerving, was that there seemed to be little or no correlation between the largesse bestowed on them and the volume of complaint. When, some years into government, we were hurling the money at them, somehow or other there would be one age group or tier of pensioner that we would miss, and then the rest would take great pride in their solidarity with those who had been so callously forgotten.

I exaggerate to make a point. There were those who were genuinely grateful for the measures we introduced, which did amount to the biggest ever boost to the earnings of the oldest, least well-off and most vulnerable pensioners. Those measures on their own were always a riposte to the absurd notion in parts of the left that we had betrayed our "traditional" vote. We did things no Tory government would have contemplated, never mind done. And we did it for good motives, though as I say the gratitude was not always commensurate with the generosity.

But in the summer of 1999 we had messed up. We had applied the usual rules for uprating the basic state pension in line with inflation, which was low. The result? A 75p rise per week. We were still in our two-year period of keeping to tight spending limits. Those were the rules. We applied them.

The pensioners, unsurprisingly, were not impressed. Though my mother-in-law put the case a little too graphically, it was clear we had a serious problem. We rectified it in the Budget by increasing the amount, but, again, damage was done.

I decided at the 2000 party conference to apologise and eat a portion of humble pie. We had some blowback from Gordon and Alistair Darling who felt it dangerous to admit we were wrong; but I felt it was worth it. Anyway, we were wrong!

The rest of the speech was concerned with uplifting the party by installing some pride in what we had done; energising them by laying out what we had still to do; and giving them some battle lines on how much we could lose under the Tories.

The speech went well. I learned one other lesson in the course of it. I really work out during a big speech. It's a physical not just a mental or rhetorical act. And I sweat. Before the speech we were in the hotel suite trying to work out what to wear. I had chosen a very good shirt/tie combination. Unfortunately the shirt was blue, and by the end of my speech it was very visibly wet through. Naturally, the headlines were about "BLAIR SWEATING UNDER PRESSURE" etc. From then on, I always wore a white shirt for a big speech!

After the conference season, well into the autumn, the atmosphere continued to be difficult. There was nothing particularly wrong; but nothing particularly right either. The media environment was tricky. Alastair was talking about moving on, as was Anji. This was deeply unsettling.

Part of the problem with New Labour was that, in the beginning, it had been the creation of a very tightly knit group. It was only really towards the end that a new generation of talented young people came on board properly who were able to take positions of leadership and broaden our base. The senior politicians around me were good and strong players; but JP was obviously not inclined to New Labour; with Gordon it was difficult to sell. At one level, he was; but the tensions in the desire to push ahead more radically with reform were starting to surface; and in any event his preoccupation was the succession and he always worried that anything difficult would undermine the inheritance. David Blunkett, of course, was fully behind the push, but others like John Reid and Charles Clarke were still on the way up. Robin Cook went along with it—partly because of the appalling relations between him and Gordon at that time—but you wouldn't rely on him if it turned sour. Jack Straw was supportive but not a force pushing at the frontier.

So I was acutely conscious that it rested on my shoulders, that I had to drive and keep driving; and I hadn't yet properly matured or hardened. That may seem an odd thing to say, but I felt that I had a lot to learn and a lot of inner strength still to develop. I didn't feel courageous much of the time. I knew if push came to shove I would be, but there was much more nervous anxiety lingering near the surface of my psyche than showed—maybe that's always true of people in this position—and at one level I felt needy.

Cherie was a great support, of course, but she wasn't there during the working day, so naturally the people I worked with really mattered. They were an outstandingly talented team, and I felt a bit like a football manager might when he realises he has a dream team that is perfectly balanced, with elements of genius and masses of commitment. Needless to say, he doesn't want to lose any stars.

In time I learned to escape this bind—and it is a bind; there are other great players out there. Change is refreshing, it challenges old ways; but I was still developing and I thought I couldn't manage without the old team.

Only later did I realise the strain Alastair was under; and only later did I, in a sense, move to a place that required different skills to the many that he has. At that stage, communication was still paramount. Of course communication is always important, but in those early days it was at the crux. Later, I put policy there, and then communication assumed a lesser, though still critical role.

Alastair was getting exhausted and ratty, and he was getting set upon by the media, whom he was coming to loathe and was therefore not handling quite right. Both he and Anji were also people to whom I selfishly and needily transferred much of the pain and the strain. They lightened the load, but in doing so, they burdened themselves. And it was a heavy burden to bear.

In those late months of 2000, I was trying to persuade both to stay, trying more than I should have and more than was wise. But there it is: you live and learn.

We were still pressing away on getting the policy fundamentals in place for the reform agenda. I was working flat out devising the direction of structural reform for schools, the NHS, criminal justice, welfare and the Civil Service. I was intensely frustrated by my lack of detailed knowledge in each discipline and was constantly trying to expand it. Of course, it is impossible for any prime minister to be at the centre of all disciplines or to be the complete master of any, except in bursts of activity usually associated with a crisis, but nonetheless I was meeting groups of front-line professionals who understood the case for change and wanted to lead it. They improved my understanding as I got to grips with the tangle of complexities that lie in the navigation of any process of change. I was sure now that we could set sail, confident of a really radical second term. In every area I had a fairly firm compass. I was growing in confidence about the arguments, increasingly sure that we were heading in the right direction. The only problem was, I wasn't clear about how much support I had getting there.

Meanwhile, events were colliding with my programme, pulling it this way and that. We had severe flooding in many parts of the country, a natural disaster but one which necessitated vast amounts of time and focus. I went on several visits to lift spirits and make sure that everything that should be done was being done. The damage floods can do is extraordinary, unbelievable, billions of pounds' worth with remarkable speed and ease. When I visited the flooding in York everyone was very stoic, but it was obvious it would be months before things returned to normal. With the risk of flooding increasing due to climate change, insurers, government and businesses—and entire towns and villages—were having to rethink policy. In the end, we committed to a billion-pound investment in flood defences.

Then came the Hatfield rail crash on 17 October, when an Intercity express train derailed on the line from London to the North-East, which was one I travelled on regularly. Four people died, and it was a big shock, especially coming just over a year after the Ladbroke Grove crash, in which thirty-one people had been killed.

It led to a major examination of the state of the railways, the arguments about privatisation were reopened, and there was much agonising about what to do. The cause had been an unnoticed crack in one of the gauges, which was serious since it meant other such cracks might exist. We met the rail chiefs at Number 10 and JP, who was in charge of transport, was very heavy on them. He was probably right to be so, but I was immediately concerned about an entirely different problem.

The railway companies, encouraged of course by the Department for Transport, went on a very risk-averse course of action, which basically put all the trains on a go-slow. I knew that the moment the immediate shock of the accident evaporated, human nature being what it is, the public would go back to normal and what they would want would be the damn trains running on time, and there was no hope of that.

For about the next year, there was a pantomime played out between me and the department. I was desperate to get them to return to normal schedules, believing they were being too cautious. They were resistant, thinking I was taking risks. The number of meetings I had; bangings on the table, exasperation; exchanges of varying degrees of politeness with JP.

The later months of 2000 continued to be dominated by events piling in thick and fast. In October, Milosevic fell—a great moment, the streets of Belgrade alive with emotion and hope—and Donald Dewar, the First Minister of Scotland, died. He had been an excellent colleague, and though we were never close friends, I felt a strong tie to him. I trusted him. He had genuine integrity. Because of Derry and his wife Alison (to whom Donald had previously been married), I knew his children well. I had visited him a few weeks before his death, when he was recovering from an earlier illness which presaged a brain haemorrhage, in his flat in New Town in Edinburgh. Though I had known him for years, I had never visited his home and was rather astounded to see his very valuable collection of Scottish Impressionists and prints. "I never knew about this," I said.

"I never told you," he replied, very Donaldish.

Politically, I always felt that, underneath it all, Donald was rather New Labour. He had a good mind and also a good spirit about him, an impatience with ideology and a hearty common sense about human nature. His loss in Scotland was irreparable. He was a father figure; a creator of Scottish devolution; and clearly a man of stature. His funeral was a very sad affair. I felt strangely like an outsider. It was very Scottish and very GB-dominated—he gave a brilliant oration, Gordon at his best.

I was also spending a lot of time on European business. The forthcoming Nice summit in early December was looming large, where we were going to decide the new voting rules for the EU, a mind-blowingly complex interaction of individual and national interests struggling to serve the collective European interest. I had Jacques Chirac to dinner at a pub in my constituency to discuss it all, where he managed to say that the food was superb, but with a little too much smirking from his entourage for my liking. Outside the pub, fox hunters were protesting.

Fox hunting; now there's a tale. One of the strangest parts of politics is how you get into situations of unbelievable controversy without ever meaning to or wanting to. The fox-hunting subject resulted in one of the domestic legislative measures I most regret, along with the Freedom of Information Act. Both were great progressive causes (at least to some); both were the cause of inordinate political convulsion, and for what purpose, God only knows.

But fox hunting brought the most grief. The issue itself crossed boundaries of opinion in a remarkable way, zigzagging through swathes of Middle England, working-class heartlands and old-fashioned aristo-crats. The thing was you could never tell people's reactions to it. You had dyed-in-the-wool Tories for whom a ban was their ultimate politi-cal fantasy; and you had solid Labour blokes, whose right arm would have withered away rather than put a cross in the Tory box, who wanted to kill me because of the proposal to ban it.

People used to say it's a class thing—and for some it was. For others, it was an animal thing. I remember a secretary from the Downing Street administrative support group coming to see me at Chequers while I was working in the study, and telling me with tears in her eyes that at long last justice for the poor little fox was to be secured. I used to have meet-ings with my advisers or the whips and just sit there and say: but people cannot feel that strongly about it; it's impossible. Well, they do, they would tell me. And they were right. Gerald Kaufman—sensible, sane, loyal Gerald, who had served in the Shadow Cabinet—said to me: if you don't do this, I could never support the government again. He didn't really mean it, of course; but he wished he did. The passions aroused by the issue were primeval. If I'd proposed solving the pension problem by compulsory euthanasia for every fifth pensioner I'd have got less trouble for it.

And here is a real political lesson. You have to "feel it" to succeed in politics. That's where instinct comes from, the emotional intelligence. By and large I do feel it, and so, on most issues, I get it. On this one, I had a complete lapse. I didn't "feel it" either way. I didn't feel how, for fox hunters, this was part of their way of life. I didn't feel how, for those wanting a ban, this was fundamentally about cruelty. Result? Disaster.

I was ignorant about the sport. I thought it a bit weird that people wanted to gallivant around hunting a fox, but having read my Trollope I understood it is a part of our history. What I didn't understand—but boy, I understood it later—was that it is a rather large part of our rural present.

I made a fatal mistake by not shutting the issue down at the outset. Instead, I let it get running out of the blocks. Expectations were raised. On a TV programme I stupidly gave the impression it would indeed be banned. Of course I had voting form, having voted to ban it or said I wanted to or signed some petition or something. Anyway, I repeated my "position" rather than reconsidering it. The moment I did so, I was defined. And so trapped. By the end of it, I felt like the damn fox.

The trouble was, as I say, I just couldn't get it, but Philip Gould, doing his polling, began telling me it was now an issue of trust. Sally Morgan, Hilary, Ann Taylor—influential senior Labour figures, the "if necessary we'll take the world on and screw them all" brigade—were telling me: fail to do this and you have a leadership problem. "I can't believe it," I kept saying rather pathetically. "Start believing it," they would reply.

If I told you the contortions and permutations I went through to avoid this wretched business, you wouldn't credit it. We had regional referenda, partial bans, civil penalties, criminal penalties—you name it, we considered it.

The protesters were predominantly Tory, of course, and at long last they had something to protest about. And protest they did, following me round blowing trumpets, clanging cymbals, shouting, singing, howling, chanting. It was quintessentially British. I remember George Bush was here for a visit when they were out all over the place, and he asked what it was about. I explained. "Whatever did you do that for, man?" said George, as ever getting right to the point.

Unfortunately, "Whatever did I do that for?" was the question I began to ask myself after I started to educate myself about fox hunting—i.e. did what I should have done before I embarked on this rash undertaking. The more I learned, the more uneasy I became. I started to realise this wasn't a small clique of weirdo inbreds delighting in cruelty, but a tradition, embedded by history and profound community and social liens, that was integral to a way of life. It was more broadly based and less elitist than I thought, and had all sorts of offshoots among groups of people who were a long way from being dukes and duchesses.

None of this means I wanted to take it up myself, or even that I especially liked it—"Vote Labour or the fox gets it" was quite a popular slogan in several elections—but banning it like this was not me. Not me at all. Fox hunting mattered profoundly to a group of people, who were a minority but had a right, at least, to defend their way of life.

During the course of our summer stay with the Strozzis, we visited the beautiful island of Elba. We went to lunch with some of their friends and there happened to be a woman who was mistress of a hunt near Oxford, I think. Instead of berating me, she took me calmly and persuasively through what they did, the jobs that were dependent on it, the social contribution of keeping the hunt and the social consequence of banning it, and did it with an effect that completely convinced me.

From that moment on, I became determined to slip out of this. But how? We were obliged to allow Parliament a debate and the result was never in doubt: there would be a ban. In the end, there was a masterly British compromise—it was banned in such a way that, provided certain steps are taken to avoid cruelty when the fox is killed, it isn't banned. So it's banned and not quite banned at the same time. Hmm. Anyway, it was the best I could do, but not an episode of policymaking I look back on with pride. And I should think not, I hear you say.

When the law later came into force in 2004, Hazel Blears was in the Home Office. She phoned me up and said, "The police are asking: do you want this policed vigorously so we can get some prosecutions under our belt?" After I replied, she said, "I thought you might say that."

It reminds me that I won a bet with Prince Charles about this. Of course, he thought the ban was absurd, and raised the issue with me in a slightly pained way. I would explain the political difficulties. I'm not sure he ever quite grasped it—not surprisingly, since as I have confessed, I didn't either, until too late. The wager was that after I left office, people would still be hunting. "But how, if you're going to ban it?" he asked.

"I don't know, but I will find a way," I replied.

Prince Charles truly knew the farming community and felt we didn't understand it, in which there was an element of truth. Our farmers had a specific and uniquely British set of challenges: they had been through the devastation of Bovine Spongiform Encephalopathy (BSE), a cattle disease, and at that time still couldn't really export beef except in very limited circumstances; farm prices had fallen; fuel costs had risen; floods had hit them hard. But the worst was about to come.

During the last months of 2000, we were holding regular meetings to prepare for the summer 2001 election. In November, we had an away day at Chequers and I very firmly said the danger was complacency; we had a real fight on our hands and we had to up our game. We were back in front in the polls but I deliberately told Philip to downplay that and focus on the difficulties. We had an almost 20 per cent deficit on right/wrong direction, and though the Tories didn't seem to be breaking through, I set out what I thought they could do if they galvanised a patriotic, anti-Europe, anti-immigrant vote and combined that with a sense of cynicism and apathy about us.

I said we had to get to the big choices about the future. I emphasised the need for reform as well as investment, and put at the heart of our appeal an offer of increased personal prosperity, through both a strong economy and improved public services.

Peter and Gordon had been rowing about the euro, with Peter ill-advisedly talking to the media about our position on the single currency. As usual, Gordon overreacted, but I was getting worried about the number of colleagues who had it in for Peter and the sheer venom of the GB lot towards him. As my close ally, Peter was at that time, of course, a target for Gordon's supporters.

Then in early 2001, Peter was forced to resign for the second time. It was typical of the way so-called scandals erupt, hot mud is poured over all concerned and the victims are eliminated before anyone quite has the chance or the nerve to wait until the mud is seen to stick or not. Even more than on the first occasion, I deeply regretted it afterwards.

The *Observer* ran a medium-size story about Peter having raised money for the Dome from the Hinduja brothers, Indian businessmen and philanthropists, then securing a passport for one of them. As ever, the way the story was handled turned into the issue, not the allegation itself. It is a real lesson in such things.

There would have been no problem if Peter had merely passed on the passport request or even asked that it be expedited, provided he had also sought to ensure that the proper procedures had been followed. As it happened there was absolutely no reason why S. P. Hinduja should not have been given a passport—he qualified, and as a wealthy and successful businessman, there was no issue about whether he could support himself.

But here's what happens in such situations: I'm busy, Alastair's busy,

Peter's busy (there had been another, far bigger story in the *Sunday Times* about Peter and Gordon which had preoccupied him). The story is medium-level. If you are not careful—and we weren't—you get the facts just a fraction off, and then you are in the proverbial hurricane.

Peter said—and Alastair repeated to the media—that Peter's private secretary, not Peter himself, had passed on the request. In fact, it transpired that Peter had mentioned it to Mike O'Brien, a Home Office minister.

It seems almost pathetic now when you look back on it. Because a wrong statement had been made to the media, they were able to turn it into a full-blown scandal. Peter, with the GB people strongly against him, was pretty much alone and without support except from me. It seems utterly bizarre, given what Peter subsequently became to the Labour Party during Gordon's premiership, but back then he was as isolated as you can be in politics.

Wednesday came. PMQs day. Nightmare. Alastair's and Derry's view was that it was irretrievable. Jack Straw felt the same and was worried because there was a note of the Peter call, and it was therefore bound to come out. I called Peter in before PMQs and told him he had to go. He felt Alastair was pushing me. He wasn't; it was my decision. I agreed to an inquiry into the affair, headed by the former Treasury solicitor, Sir Anthony Hammond, whose report five weeks later cleared Peter of any wrongdoing. It was a miserable though redeeming finale to a sorry episode.

Peter fought his seat bravely at the election and won it, and then clawed his way back with his usual genius, but I missed him desperately in Cabinet between 2001 and 2005. He would have been such a strength.

Back then, however, election fever started to incubate in the Westminster hothouse. I set out in a note the campaign structure, the key dividing lines, the future vision of the nuts and bolts of how we would fight the campaign. It wasn't going to be easy, managing conflicting egos and personalities, letting everyone think they were directing it while making sure I was.

We aimed for a May 2001 election, but an event took place that meant a complete upheaval of all previously laid plans. I was in Canada to address the Parliament and meet my friend Jean Chrétien, the Canadian prime minister. He was a very wise, wily and experienced old bird, great at international meetings, where he could be counted on to talk sense, and, as Canadians often are, firm and dependable without being pushy. All in all, a good guy and a very tough political operator not to be underestimated.

While we were there, we were told that the Ministry of Agriculture had been informed of a case of foot-and-mouth disease at an abattoir in Essex. You're given a piece of information like that and your first reaction is: is that a big deal? The answer was yes. A very big deal. Two days after the disease had been found, the European Commission imposed a complete ban on all British meat, milk and livestock exports. Was that not an overreaction? I asked. No. OK, so this is really serious. Jean Chrétien immediately identified it as a crisis. "Watch that, young Tony, watch it very carefully. That's trouble." We put movement restrictions on all livestock. I asked anxiously from Canada whether we could be sure of lifting the ban within a week. If only I had known.

For the next few days, I remained abroad but was also living on UK time, trying to get some order into the response. Nick Brown, the Minister of Agriculture, appeared to be doing well, and for once the ministry was fully apprised of the gravity of the situation.

Four days after the first case, another outbreak was confirmed, this time at the other end of the country in Tyne and Wear. There then followed near enough three months of almost constant focus on what was the worst ever outbreak of foot-and-mouth disease in Europe, and one of the worst in world history.

Foot-and-mouth affects all hooved animals, but doesn't necessarily kill them, and nor does it make their meat unfit to eat. Some countries—Argentina, for example—have areas where the disease has existed for decades. But of course it isn't great for the export market, and the average consumer isn't exactly going to be rushing out to buy infected meat. It has never migrated to humans, although the fear is there that it could. It's a disease that is at one level not serious in terms of life and death, even of the animal, but its practical consequences on the livestock industry are devastating; if it is not eradicated, then, to all intents and purposes, the effect is terminal.

What had happened was that infected meat had somehow got into the country, possibly illegally, and had contaminated a farm. Animals are transported around the whole country, and as the incubation period can be up to ten days, the disease was only discovered—and livestock movements halted—several days after it began to spread. The result, as we quickly appreciated, is that we didn't have the foggiest notion how many animals were affected, or where they were.

What's more, the disease is airborne and can be carried on the soles of shoes. Footpaths, walking trails and other elements of rural tourism were all potential sources of it spreading. Within days, we were having to shut down the British countryside. The only way to deal with it is to slaughter the infected herd. There is a huge debate about whether to vaccinate against foot-and-mouth disease, a debate that ricocheted around the public discussion during the course of the crisis. The blunt truth was that EU requirements based on scientific study meant that even vaccinated animals had to be slaughtered eventually, and in any event vaccination couldn't be guaranteed effective in sheep; and sheep could spread the disease to cattle.

Animals were having to be taken away to slaughter but not, of course, in the abattoir, so burning funeral pyres started to spring up. One was situated near the Heathrow flight path, to delight the passengers hoping to spend a few days in rural idyllic Britain. The pictures of the pyres went round the world. Rumours abounded; so-called human cases were detected (it didn't matter they were all later found to be false). When we shut down the tourist sites, it was assumed it was because of the risk to people. The Americans are great tourists, but they are hopeless when it comes to these types of things. The American tourist influx virtually ceased, on the basis that if they came to Britain they would all go back with two heads.

By the time I had got back home from my transatlantic trip, there was a palpable sense of crisis. I had thought the ministry and Nick were pretty much on top of it. They were somewhat jealously guarding their patch on it and were happy to consult, but I sensed that Nick was feeling pressurised by me and didn't want to yield up control. Jonathan alarmed me by describing how the Number 10 switchboard had accidentally put him in on a call between Gordon and Nick, with Gordon telling Nick not to give in to my "presidential style"—interference which was not greatly helpful.

As the cases grew, and the bitter facts of the shutdown started to affect jobs, livelihoods, export orders, businesses, tourist attractions, hotels, B & Bs—i.e. the whole infrastructure of rural Britain—I was feeling distinctly queasy and, yes, frightened by it. I let it go for a few more days of the ordinary meetings, queries, debates and instructions and then I thought, No, this isn't going to work.

The National Farmers' Union leader was Ben Gill. Both he and his deputy, Richard Macdonald, seemed to me eminently sensible and sane citizens. They were representing a community that was literally seeing their entire past, present and future go up in smoke. There was pain, panic and real grief out there. Ben and Richard were forthright: the only answer was slaughter and the only way to do it was fast.

The challenge was how to do it. We could throw resources at it, but throw them where? At the weekend, I got down to Chequers early. It always helped me clear my head. I read all the papers, spoke to a few people. The chief vet Jim Scudamore was a good bloke, but he was overwhelmed. We all were. I got as detailed a briefing as I could. Then I just sat and thought.

Sometimes in a crisis, you have to demonstrate activity to keep spirits up, but the actual machinery is working away effectively. Sometimes the machinery itself is non-existent or inadequate and then you have to think first. Otherwise the activity is useless or, even worse, counter-productive.

The basic challenge was one of logistics. You had to have enough vets to inspect the herds where cases were suspected. You then had to be able to do the slaughter. You then had to have the capacity to dispose of the carcasses. You then had to have a system of compensation that was ratio-nal and quick, and a system of welfare for the burgeoning cases of hard-ship. You then had to have a plan for reopening the countryside and a strategy to entice the tourists out of their funk. And you had to do it all while tracking the disease to make sure you weren't opening too early or proclaiming victory too soon. On the other hand, restoring confidence to the battered and bruised rural community could not come a moment too soon.

When I got back to Downing Street on Sunday I decided to grip the whole thing, and got my close advisers together. By some master-stroke—not mine, I hasten to add, but Richard Wilson's, the Cabinet Secretary—our chief scientific adviser, Sir David King, was invited to join the inner circle. If anyone tells you that scientists are impractical boffins, refer them to David. What he told me sounded a trifle wacky, but over the weeks to come it was to be of priceless value in defeating the disease. Essentially, by means of graphs and charts he set out how the disease would spread, how we could contain it if we took the right culling measures, and how over time we would eradicate it.

The officials were extremely sceptical. So was I. How could he predict it like that, with so many unknowns? But, almost *faute de mieux*, I followed his advice—and blow me, with uncanny, almost unnatural accuracy, the disease peaked, declined and went, almost to the week he had predicted. Remarkable, though it was not without my undergoing a deep immersion in every detail. By the time it was under control in the summer, I knew everything there was to know about it: how it started; how it was spread; the methods of containment; the pros and cons of slaughter and vaccination; the different reactions of sheep and cattle; the impact on humans; the workings of farms and abattoirs; the numbers of animals normally slaughtered in a week and the number we eat in a year (a lot, by the way).

But I also learned more about crisis management and the utter incapacity of the normal system to deal with abnormal challenges than I had ever needed to learn before. Though the public naturally thought we mishandled it and no one gave us any thanks for any of it, actually when I look back and reread the papers, reminding myself of the sheer horror, depth and scale of the crisis, it is a total miracle we came through it.

ELEVEN

A MANDATE FOR NEW LABOUR

The 2001 election was an odd, disjointed affair. The outcome was never in doubt. It resulted in another landslide majority. Our well-constructed and well-oiled political machine whirred effortlessly—or so it appeared—over the complicated and bizarre contraption that was the Tory Party. And perhaps for those very reasons, it was odd and disjointed.

I learned two things from the campaign. The first was that, increasingly, there was simply no media interest in policy at all, unless it was accompanied by visible, high-impact controversy. The second was that the TB/GB story was unlikely to have a happy ending, at least so far as my time as prime minister was concerned.

The foot-and-mouth crisis was in its last stages. The disease wasn't beaten completely or culled out, but it was waning. We were on top of it, and it was not going to dominate the election. The decision to postpone the election for a month had been right. However, there was now a will, among the electorate as well as politicians, for the mandate of the government to be retested.

I had shaped the 2001 manifesto very carefully and deliberately. I had decided that we had been, understandably, erring on the side of caution; and now was the time to strike out boldly. I had learned much about government and, above all, I had learned that unless driven, the risk was not some hidden agenda that the system harboured secretly, the risk was inertia. We had seen enough, done enough, experienced enough, to know how to do the whole thing better and more radically.

I was now clear that public service reform needed major structural change, including a much closer relationship with the private sector. I had become convinced that the law and order agenda was the prisoner of a system of criminal law and criminal justice that simply didn't measure up to the nature of twenty-first-century society and the types of crime and types of criminal. I wanted a new emphasis on science, technology and small businesses to form part of a modern enterprise and industry policy. I had come to the conclusion that on welfare, we had to focus far more particularly on social exclusion and the danger of families becoming isolated outside society's mainstream. In respect of the euro, I was still wedded to the economic test of convergence, but I wanted to make the political case far more clearly; and if the economics could align, I was prepared to risk all in a referendum on joining the single currency.

So the manifesto was one I was more or less very happy with. The one exception was over university reform and tuition fees, where I backed away from a clear commitment since there were remaining major policy differences in the party and of course with the Treasury. However, all in all, it set out a plain, unadulterated New Labour position.

The campaign got off to a bizarre start and didn't much depart from the bizarre until it ended. We decided to launch the campaign not in the old, boring, "men in suits sitting on a platform in a conference centre" mode, but at a school, to emphasise the importance of education to the second term. I went to St. Saviour's and St. Olave's Church of England Secondary Girls' School in Southwark in south London, met some of the students, visited a classroom or two and then we had assembly. Being a church school, some hymns were sung and then I got up to speak. It was one of those moments. I was in front of a stained-glass window, we were praying and singing. Then I was addressing the serried ranks of teenage girls, all of whom were of course under voting age, about how we couldn't return to the boom and bust era of the Tory years. As I began, I felt an almost irresistible desire to giggle at the utter absurdity of it, but I soldiered on, to their bemusement and my embarrassment, and then got out as quick as I could.

It was, of course, inappropriate, and there were shrieks of self-righteous anger. Anji and Kate Garvey were brilliant at organising such things and indeed were brilliant generally; but apparently our extraordinary machine had, for once, sprung a gasket or whatever gaskets do. The school took it well, especially as the head teacher got roasted for allowing it.

In part, we were victims of our own mythology. Everyone assumed it was a masterstroke. Well, it must be, mustn't it? After all, we were the sultans of spin, blah blah blah.

The interesting question, however, is why we thought it necessary to have a "new style" launch at all. People assume that politicians are constantly looking for better ways to present because they condone the triumph of presentation over substance. Actually, the politicians are reacting to the situation, not creating it.

Your average politico is at their happiest talking policy, believe me. They love it. I do too. I could talk for hours about the ins and outs of education or health reform. I was genuinely intrigued by analysis of the criminal justice system and the debate and balance between civil liberties and effective law and order. It is one of the supreme myths about politicians that they are talk-show hosts who have to learn about policy; more often they are policy wonks who have to learn to be talk-show hosts.

As the media have become more geared to sensation, scandal and impact, so the politicians have had to look for more devices and strategies to generate interest. I came to the sad conclusion through the 2001 campaign that the best I could hope for was that underneath some whizz-bang piece of marketing creativity or twist to a story, we might squeeze some policy. But there was never any chance of having the policy out there centre stage.

When a government is in its first months and it is a novelty, and some of the policies mark a sharp break with the philosophy of the previous government, then policy can be out in front, able to speak and be heard. But as time goes on and the agenda becomes familiar—even if the actual policies are new—interest fades and very quickly a sense of "we've heard it all before" takes over.

To be fair to the media, it was hard in circumstances where the Tories didn't really engage, except on Europe. But even so, it was dispiriting and it meant that when we tried, as with the launch at the school and cocked up, it only allowed them to confirm for the public that we were indeed only interested in "spin." But we knew for sure that if we did a conventional general election launch, it would go nowhere.

Throughout the campaign, with the polls showing us anywhere between ten and twenty points ahead and varying only slightly, we attempted to fire the whole thing up only to find that the squib exhibited perpetual signs of dampness. After a rally at Croydon, sitting in my hotel room, I took a call from Bill Clinton. It was eerie how he could read my mood from several thousand miles away.

"Just phoned to see how you're doing," he said.

"Great," I replied.

"No, I know what you're feeling," he said. He then explained to me how in the 1996 campaign against Bob Dole, he had been a certain winner from the outset. All this did, he said, was make the media mad and the public think it was a shoo-in. He knew that at this moment I would be fretting and fearing that the public would react against it.

"OK, you're right," I said. "So what's the answer?"

The answer, he went on, was to fight the campaign as if it were neck and neck, to show the people how much you want it, how much you are prepared to fight for it, and how grateful you are for every last vote you are going to get. "Show them you are desperate for their mandate, and the more you're up in the polls, the more desperate you should become."

It was good advice. I took it. From then on, I didn't care how bad the Tories were, I just scrapped and fought and clawed my way through as if my life depended on every vote. It didn't change the media mood, and heaven knows if it changed the outcome, but it gave me a sense of energy and the party a sense of urgency.

The Tory campaign was indeed abject. I had puzzled over William Hague. He was a truly outstanding debater, he had a good mind and a high-grade intellect. There was lots of real quality in him and about him. I thought he had definite leadership character. In different circumstances and at a different time, he could have been—and very possibly may still be—a great leader and even prime minister.

As I listened to him, however, I wondered if it is possible to love words too much. Such was his ability and use of words and humour, his capacity to weave clever conceits and amusing demonstrations of wit, that he expended too much of his mind on that and too little on the purpose for which the conceits and wit were devised. The result was that although he often humiliated an opponent, he less often beat them in argument.

While he was formidable and I could not underestimate him, he and the Tory high command inexplicably based their campaign on Europe. There were perfectly sound opinion poll and media reasons for such a strategy: polls showed Tory policy hugely preferred to ours; the Murdoch press, the *Mail* and the *Telegraph* were all very Eurosceptic and therefore strongly supportive of the Tory position. The problem was that very senior Tories like Ken Clarke were against such a strategy and the issue had the capacity to divide the party badly. What's more, while Euroscepticism was just about tolerable, there were—as there always are with such issues—those who wanted to take a position that was already at the outer edge of respectability and push well beyond it. The leadership stance gave them permission to go even further and there's where the public's position on Europe couldn't be entirely guessed by reference to the polls. True, if asked, they supported the Tories on it, but it was never going to determine the election. It wasn't their priority, so the Tory focus on it gave the Tories a curious, lopsided look that swiftly turned into the thought among the public that, well, maybe they just weren't ready to govern. Once such a thought takes hold, the election's over.

Obviously, the single most important thing was for us to avoid a serious mistake. Of course, the media knew that too and tried to work out how to force us to make one. We had crafted our essential practical message: a lot done; a lot to do; a lot to lose. It was simple. No one could deny the economy was strong and the money was now beginning to flow into schools and hospitals (though the commitment to keep spending tight for the first two years had hampered things—the decision was right but it had constrained us). And it was a first term; surely we should be given the chance to complete what we had started. The memory of the Tories was still fresh enough for the "a lot to lose" line to resonate.

Naturally, I wanted a more elevated campaign which moved the country beyond the choices of the past, beyond Thatcherism in a sense. In my weekly personal notes to the inner team at Downing Street just as the election got under way, I spelt out what was wrong with Thatcherism, having spent much of the previous time reassuring people about what had to be kept.

Where Mrs. Thatcher was absolutely on the side of history was in recognising that as people became more prosperous, they wanted the freedom to spend their money as they chose; and they didn't want a big state getting in the way of that liberation by suffocating people in uniformity, in the drabness and dullness of the state monopoly. It was plain that competition drove up standards, and that high taxes were a disincentive. Anything else ignored human nature.

Where she was wrong and running against a tide of history, however, was in her attitude to Europe and her refusal to countenance the fact that the majority of people were always going to have to rely on public services and the power of government to get the opportunities they needed. The government should change; the public services should be reformed; but she just went too far in thinking everything could be reduced to individual choice. She was in that sense a very traditional Tory, but with the added impatience, like my dad, with anyone who hadn't succeeded—she had, so why hadn't they? In that way, though she "got" one side of human nature, she appeared to ignore another.

The result was she had a view of Britain that was at one level correct and necessary—regaining our spirit of enterprise and ambition—but at another, completely failed to take account of the changing position of Britain in the world, however enterprising we were, by dint of population, size and geography; and allowed a desire for people to stand on their two feet to cross into a profound lack of compassion for those who were left behind. She was essentially uninterested in social capital.

I saw our role as taking Britain on a further stage of modernisation, creating public services and a welfare state that combined investment with reform to make them personal, responsive, entrepreneurial and, so far as the welfare side was concerned, based on responsibilities as well as rights and entitlements that were earned. There was no doubt in my mind that this was where the majority of the public stood, where the sensible, serious centre ground could congregate and where we could define an agenda that was essential third-way material: personal ambition combined with social compassion.

As for Britain's place in the world, it seemed to me self-evident that we had to exercise power through alliances. We had the two best— Europe and America—so why not keep them strong and use them? This argument was less easy to make popular; but its strength was clear, and although its supporters might be fewer in number, they were high in quality. Business, in particular, understood the point thoroughly.

The trouble was, from the off, it proved wholly impossible to get coverage for any of this elevated stuff. I decided to use a series of speeches on Britain's future as the washing line on which to hang the various parts of the agenda and so try to stimulate a vigorous policy debate. The speeches were thorough and, though I say it myself, well argued. I wrote most of them personally, along with help from chief strategy adviser Matthew Taylor, Andrew Adonis and David Miliband. But within days of the campaign starting, it was plain that whatever else it was going to be, an intimate account of the nation's future policy choices it was not!

The day we launched the manifesto, 16 May 2001, was an almost comic illustration of the point. If elections were to be judged on the success of the election-day launch, the landslide would have been the other way. I doubt it is possible to have more mishaps, missteps and mis-adventures in a single day's campaigning.

We chose to do a big serious manifesto press conference, with ministers wheeled out to describe the next Parliament's programme. I decided to give the whole thing real edge by setting out clearly our design to bring the private sector into the running of public services. There was still an overwhelming tendency among senior politicians and advisers to see this as part of a plan—to their mind, unnecessary—to veer rightwards to appease the right-wing media. I kept trying to explain that I actually believed it—which I think may have made it worse. When you considered public service systems in other countries, it seemed to me axiomatic that certain core lessons stood out. Health care systems in which there was a mixed public/private provision, or which at least demanded some individual commitment and gave some individual choice, did best. Monolithic systems either were in the process of being changed or were failing. It was true that the failing of the U.S. system was the numbers of poor people left out, but—and this was an uncomfortable truth too many ignored—for those who were covered, the standard of care and its responsiveness (together with the second-order things like food, the environment, the ability to switch appointments and so on) were often much higher than a purely state-run service. Surely it must be possible to combine equity and efficiency.

Also in the U.S., charter schools were just starting, and the results of the Swedish education reforms were starting to come through, so there was a wealth of empirical evidence from around the world as to what changes were being proposed, by whom, for what purpose and with what success.

All of this was anathema to the various interest groups that were determined to keep the status quo but just spend more money; yet I knew that any sensible, objective observer would want to know that we were open to new ideas, whatever the party traditions seemed to dictate.

So the 16 May launch was a much bigger moment than it appeared. There were all sorts of scratchy behind-the-scenes issues around who spoke when and on what, with people slightly resenting my insistence on dominating it, but I just wanted to be sure that the desire to secure a radical second-term mandate was plain and unvarnished. Some of the ministers, like David Blunkett and Patricia Hewitt, entered fully into the spirit, sensing, as I did, that a second term was pointless unless it broke new ground, and that this meant taking more profound risks.

But, as ever, in our wish to make it all properly organised and run smoothly, we were a bit of a parody of ourselves, with ministers given their two minutes—otherwise the whole thing would be too long—and then retreating into the shadows. Nonetheless, it passed relatively without incident; which is more than can be said for the rest of the day.

I was due to visit Queen Elizabeth Hospital in Birmingham, where we were to open the new cardiac centre that was going to become (and indeed today is) one of the foremost and advanced in Europe. I met Gisela Stuart, the excellent local MP, at the entrance. Gisela was unusual in that she is German, speaks with a slight but noticeable German accent, and had won a seat in the Midlands—which only shows that people are not as prejudiced as you think. She was smart and very New Labour. As we entered the hospital a woman called Sharron Storer, who became rather famous as a result of the encounter, approached me and started to harangue me about the treatment her partner, a cancer patient, was receiving at the hospital. Of course, there turned out to be a multitude of disputes as to whether he had been badly treated or not, with the hospital staff protesting loudly, but their protests were drowned out by the fact of the prime minister getting an ear-bashing from someone "telling the truth" about the NHS and how dire it was.

Naturally for the media, already bored to death with a campaign whose outcome seemed not to be in doubt, it was manna from heaven. She became an overnight star. There was a great rejoicing that at last Labour's slick machine had run into a "real" person. There was a running theme—pushed hard by the *Mail*—that we were not meeting "real" people, but that everything was stage-managed. In fact, I've never come across a campaign in an election that wasn't stage-managed (though whether well or badly is another matter). And of course we were meeting lots of people.

Here's the thing: a person is not a "real" person unless they are bawling out a politician; unless there's a scene; unless there's anger, and preferably rudeness. Only a scene gives the news its impact. The truth is that most "real" people—I mean real "real" people—don't behave in that way at all. Most Britons are polite. They listen. They may disagree, but they do so reasonably. You meet plenty of them, but they aren't "real" because they are not combustible.

A curious but highly significant phenomenon was developing: the celebration of the protest. Let's say a politician attends a meeting at which there are a thousand people present, and one of them shouts something. The other 999 people can be supportive, or at least reasonable in their opposition, but the lone disruptive voice is presented as representative when the chances are it isn't. Most people don't make a scene, so by definition the sole protester is atypical, not typical.

I recall a visit to Hebron in Palestine after I left office, when I went to the Ibrahimi Mosque where the New York Jewish settler Baruch Goldstein had murdered Muslim worshippers in 1994. There was a single voice of protest who shouted at me, who turned out to be a member of Hizb ut-Tahrir, an Islamist group banned in certain countries and totally unrepresentative of most Palestinian opinion. The next day it was literally the only news out of the visit. The protester was interviewed, and his opinion debated and analysed. All other voices were delegitimised. No one else got a look-in.

It's a key development in the reporting of modern politics, and the more people realise it, the more they attempt to disrupt. It has now become absolutely the paradigm within which the news is created. Throw something, heckle, confront, storm the stage and you lead the news, with your views thereby legitimised. The politician looks astounded or affronted, cannot retaliate (with an exception I am about to relate) and thus there's only one winner. That is why more and more people do it. Not for an instant does it advance debate or necessarily represent opinion. Any argument conducted in heat is a clash of views, not an exchange of views. No matter; it's news!

Anyway, this, rather than the manifesto, was obviously going to dominate. I sort of staggered off round the cardiac centre, realising that the big launch day was written off.

But things were only just warming up. After a quick lunch, I heard the news that Jack Straw had got slow-hand-clapped at the Police Federation Conference. He told me afterwards—and Jack, to be fair, was very grown-up about such things—that what was amusing was that the audience reaction appeared completely divorced from the content of his speech. Not being daft, Jack had decided in the middle of an election campaign to give a pretty routine and fairly hard-line law and order speech; but they were having none of it. He could have doubled their pay and they were going to boo him. (Well, that might have stopped them.)

So by late afternoon, you would have thought the nation was in revolt at this government they were about to re-elect with another land-slide. Part of the problem when the Opposition is useless is that the public feel strangely disenfranchised. This was how many Labour people felt during the Thatcher years. It's why after 1992 Labour started to consider electoral reform. We had lost four elections in a row. The system must be faulty, mustn't it? Whereas, of course, we were at fault. So this sense of alienation is not, in fact, reasonable. Actually, it's worse than that; it is profoundly undemocratic. It's the losing side feeling it shouldn't have lost and trying to manufacture a rerun, or a change of the rules.

Here is where a progressive government is often treated differently from a Conservative one: the Tory side thinks it really should be in power, and if it isn't, someone isn't playing fair. When Labour was out of power for eighteen years, the attempts by some groups (like parts of organised Labour in the miners' strike) to upend the democratic result was widely and rightly seen as wrong, whatever sympathy people felt for individual miners. But when, as in our time, the boot was on the other foot, such opposition was regularly portrayed as an entirely justifiable protest by people inexplicably denied their legitimate voice.

There was thus a weird disconnection between public opinion as expressed in the polls (and indeed in the result), and the public opinion apparently struggling under the oppression of a government, against whom severe action had to be taken because there was no alternative, since the democratic system was for some reason or other not working as it should. Towards the end of my time in office, this meant that those who leaked government papers, for example, were treated as people's heroes rather than condemned for a breach of confidence.

On that day, the interaction between government and governed was given a monumental, vivid and impactful expression beyond the media's wildest dreams. John Prescott was doing a campaign meeting in Rhyl, North Wales. There was the normal motley crew of protesters outside to jeer him on the way in. As he walked down the gauntlet, a big bloke, with an amazing mullet hairstyle from the 1970s, slapped an egg on him; John turned round and give him a sharp left hook, which sent him sprawling. After that, well, you can imagine. Even if instead of our manifesto launch of profound and detailed policy nuggets we had got up and danced the can-can, it wouldn't have mattered.

I had been doing a TV programme with voters, compered by Jonathan Dimbleby. Alastair had kept the incident with John from me before the programme, which was recorded just after it took place and before it could be assimilated into the questioning. As I got into the car afterwards, glad to have got out of the studio more or less intact, Alastair said cheerfully: "Um, there's some more news. John Prescott just thumped a voter."

I misheard him. "Someone's hit John?" I said. "That's awful!"

"No," he said, "John did the hitting. He just belted someone."

You know when they say in books "His jaw dropped"? Well, it happens. My jaw dropped.

There began a period of intense reflection, analysis, introspection, retrospection and general panic about what to do. We knew we had twelve hours before the press conference the next morning, and we had to have a line by then. The deputy prime minister assaulting a member of the public, even one who slapped an egg on him, was at one level mind-boggling and grave. At another, it was mind-boggling and comic.

Looking back, I know now the comic wins out, but I can assure you it wasn't clear-cut at the time. How the comic won out provides an interesting insight into how instinct in politics is so important; and also a sense of proportion, even when all around you proportion is being chucked overboard.

I personally felt the thing was extraordinarily funny. The egg was funny. The mullet was funny. The left hook was funny. The expressions on both their faces were funny. But there was no getting away from another point of view, and some of the women in the operation were voicing it loudly: you can't have the deputy prime minister doing that. It was undignified. It was macho. People would be repelled, appalled, ashamed, etc.

The Southern women took this view strongly. Anji, surprisingly, was of the same mind, but I wondered later whether that wasn't because Adam Boulton from Sky News (whom she subsequently married), with whom she may well have discussed it, had taken a position of such disgust about it and was very up on his high horse. Anji's instincts were normally superb. Even the usually certain Sally was uncertain. So was Alastair, though that may have been Fiona's influence. But most of the blokes and the Labour Party staff, men and women, were riotously with John.

I decided an apology at least might be in order, to take the sting out of it, genuflect a little in the direction of the soft Southerners. So I phoned John. I began at my most mellifluous. Sorry about what happened. Dreadful of him to do that. Must have been a shock. Really, in the heat of the moment, not surprising. After about five minutes of this guff, John interrupted me. "I know you," he said, "I know what you're up to. You want me to apologise."

"Well—" I started to say.

"Aye, well, I'm bloody well not. So you can forget it."

I got a little more steely and became insistent; and as ever with John, when he knew I was really serious, he was prepared to accommodate. So we agreed some form of words and the call ended.

I got home and felt uncomfortable. The news was of course near hysterical, the Tories jumping all over it and the Liberals being very "Liberal-ish," i.e. wet. But I still couldn't quite bring myself to feel I should condemn it.

I went up to the flat where Cherie was waiting. "What a day!" I said. "My God, what was John thinking of? People say it's terrible," I said, testing her out. She's a QC, liberal, lives in London.

"Oh, don't be ridiculous," she said with a snort. "Why shouldn't he hit him? The other man hit him first." You see, she is also a Liverpool girl. "Well, what would you have done?" she said. "Put on one of your smiles and ask him not to do it again? He got what he deserved. John's just a man."

I phoned John Burton. He and all the boys were exactly of that view. "I think it's great," said John. I rate John's judgement very, very highly. I know world leaders with less good judgement than John. What's more, he told me the women were of the same view up North. When the news had come on in the Trimdon Labour Club, everyone had cheered as JP hit the guy.

That settled it. However, there remained the question of how to deal with it at the press conference, when the media would undoubtedly be tut-tutting about it. I decided on the essential line: no more apology, no resigning, no nothing. Some of the team still voiced concern, but by then I had my bearings. How to express the line was a little trickier. The trouble is, you can't actually defend the deputy prime minister hitting a voter. On the other hand, we had now decided not to condemn it.

We puzzled over it, sitting in the room preparing for the press conference. David Blunkett was there and he too was strongly of the John Burton school of thought. As the minutes ticked by—and this was world news, incidentally—we fumbled over various formulae.

"The thing is," I said eventually, with about a minute to go, "John is John, really. Nothing more you can say." It was like the former soccer star Eric Cantona's approach: you say something so enigmatic that people just move on in a somewhat confused way. So that's what I said.

"What do you mean 'John is John'?" they said.

I shrugged my shoulders expressively. "I mean John is John."

And so the great scandal subsided. The Cherie/John Burton view also started clearly to predominate. People—or at least a lot of people—loved it. A politician turns human—wow! After forty-eight hours, back in my own patch in Sedgefield I was regularly accosted by voters, including older women, who echoed Cherie's remark. "Well, what would you have done?" they said. "You wouldn't have hit him, would you, laddie?"—and they didn't mean it as a compliment.

And so the election launch that began with a manifesto replete with serious policy prescription for the nation's future, ended in a mullet, an egg and a punch that sank the serious policy to the bottom of the political sea.

John Prescott always brought something unique to the Labour Party, and to the government. He could be maddening; he could be dangerous; he could be absurd; he could be magnificent. But dull, placid, uneventful and forgettable were words that would never be associated with him.

Neil Kinnock once described him as someone with a chip on both shoulders, which was true, though I always thought they somewhat balanced each other out; whereas Neil's single chip could be more troublesome.

What did John bring to the party? A lot, actually. When John Smith died and the issue arose as to who should be deputy—it being reasonably clear I was going to win the leadership—the safe bet was certainly Margaret Beckett. She had been part of the pre-1992 economic team; she was capable and was undoubtedly a safe pair of hands. John could not be described as that; but he brought an authenticity, an appeal to the party's traditional wing, especially within the union movement, and he had something else that I valued greatly: in a tight spot, I thought you could count on him. You couldn't necessarily count on him in terms of individual policy items, or more generally in terms of New Labour, but, on the basis of the tiger-shooting analogy (would you venture into the jungle with this person?), he passed muster. I wasn't so sure of Margaret. I liked and respected her, but if things got really ugly, I wasn't sure she would step up and throw a protective cordon round me; whereas John, I thought, would do so. I never took a position in the election of a deputy. Some of my closest people voted for Margaret, but the very fact I didn't go all out for her sent a signal that I could live with John. In any event he was the party's preferred choice. They wanted a bit of yin and yang, and if I was very yin, he was certainly thoroughly yang.

The contrast between the two of us couldn't have been greater. I was the private-school, Oxford-educated barrister. He had been a ship's steward, doyen of the union movement, and was proud of his working-class roots. He is one of the most fascinating characters ever to hold really high office. Nowadays, of course, John would not be John. In that, he is very similar to the Labour politician Dennis Skinner. Dennis is a really brilliant guy—first-rate mind, great wit, huge insight into people—but was brought up in the days when exceptionally clever people were regularly failed by the education system, or just fell between the cracks of poor schooling, and the narrow-minded views of parents and communities. But they are, thankfully in one sense, a dying breed. John had failed his eleven-plus—the exams that decided whether he went to a grammar school or a comprehensive school—which must have made a terrible impact on him and been responsible for at least one of the chips on his shoulders. Yet he was naturally very clever and incredibly hard-working. Which is why, in the end, it's not sensible to base your school system on such a test at age eleven.

However, all those days have passed and now John would most likely have taken a job in industry or the public sector as a manager and probably never have gone near a trade union. Instead, he was a major link with a part of Labour's roots that might be withering, but still had reach and depth in critical parts of the political forest.

Despite failing his eleven-plus he had been to Ruskin College in Oxford (as had Dennis Skinner) and was a lot more intellectually interested and capable than he let on. This latter part of him I also liked. He would start from a position of natural hostility to any New Labour policy, but if the matter were argued properly, he was prepared to listen; and eventually, if he saw merit in the proposal, he was prepared to be persuaded. That doesn't mean to say that he always went along—frequently he didn't, and it's fair to say that some of those around me came to see him as a liability because he was a rallying point for opposition in the drive for reform.

Later, he came to have a relationship with Gordon that was unfortunate. Gordon had backed Margaret strongly and put his machine to work for her, so the initial relationship between him and John was not good, but over time I urged Gordon to make peace with John. "Don't underestimate him," I used to say, "and if you want to be leader, don't have him as an enemy. He couldn't necessarily make someone leader; but he could stop it happening."

Gordon took the advice and, from my point of view, a good deal too much. It's not that John was ever personally disloyal—he wasn't—but Gordon pitched his own position on reform in such a way that it was obviously more simpatico with John's; so it changed the constellation of forces around me.

John also came to the view that Gordon and I were interchangeable as leaders, with Gordon's position a little left of my own, but no less attractive for that (possibly more so). He therefore bought the idea that the handover was only fair and right, since Gordon was after all simply a slightly different version of New Labour. In particular, he backed the view that on public services and welfare we had gone far enough in the "market" reforms, reforming the system in relation to the economic situation of the day, whereas I was strongly of the view we hadn't gone far enough.

Two consequences flowed from this. The first was that on city academies, the introduction of new health service providers and on greater conditionality in welfare, I could frequently count on the support of neither the deputy prime minister nor the Chancellor. Although in the end John was just about persuaded—he waxed eloquent on the failures of the traditional state comprehensive school system in Hull, his constituency—it was a struggle, and it took many painful hours of meeting, discussion and debate.

The second was that by the end, in 2006–7, John agitated strongly for me to go, partly because of his own problems with the media turning savage on him, and partly because he really didn't think it mattered electorally if I was swapped for Gordon. By then, I had decided I would have to go anyway; but, unsure of whether I was sincere and also partaking of the general assumption that no one would ever voluntarily give up Number 10, he told me in the spring of 2007 that he would resign as deputy prime minister if I didn't go. He didn't mean it in a disloyal way, and funnily enough, I didn't take it that way; he just genuinely believed that it was in the interests of the party that Gordon became leader.

That said, there were countless times over the years where I needed his support and where he gave it with great courage. He knew he was there, to an extent, as the brake on New Labour. He knew therefore that his own credibility rested on his ability to wring changes out of me. He knew that every time he went with me, he sacrificed some of that credibility. But he did so.

Over Clause IV, the aims and values of the Labour Party constitution, he moved from a position of doubt to a position of positive advocacy, because in the end he was convinced it was right. Once convinced, he became the staunchest proponent of change. After 11 September—indeed at any moment of crisis on foreign policy—he stuck by me one hundred per cent, giving crucial support at moments when any hint of a split between us would have been deeply corrosive.

So all in all, and given the gigantic stresses and strains imposed on any relationship at the top of the political tree, I have to say I was lucky to have had him as deputy.

As a minister, he could be at points too enthusiastic about the power of government, intervene too readily, mix too much bureaucracy into the policy pie; but he could also be innovative and imaginative. He brought the shipping industry back into the UK by getting the Treasury to change the rules on flags of convenience (a flag flying on a ship that does not signify the ship's true point of origin). He led the negotiations at Kyoto and helped the UK to become the only country in the world to meet its Kyoto target on reducing greenhouse gas emissions. He played a vital role in housing, chairing the housing policy committee to drive forward the White Paper proposals to improve the planning system of towns, cities, housing and businesses in the UK. In his ten years, the government secured decent homes for two million more people. He also represented the UK internationally and headed the China Task Force, leading on cross-departmental accords on trade and investment and other areas. His civil servants, once they got used to his moods and saw beneath the rough exterior, liked him and respected him.

His foibles were usually on the endearing end of the spectrum—though some women I know strongly disagree with that assessment. He was definitely old-fashioned, not great at working with a certain type of middle-class woman, and though sound on the policy on gay rights was led more by his head than his heart, if you know what I mean. He was also completely paranoid about smart, young, well-spoken intellectual types. With these, he was like a pig with a truffle. He could smell out condescension, a slight, an air of superiority or a snub at a thousand paces; and once smelt, he would charge after it with quite shocking abandon. Whole swathes of younger advisers, used to the subterranean soil of collegiate debate and temperate exchange of views, would be pursued with manic fervour until forced from their hiding place and sliced into tiny bits. It was made all the more alarming for them by the fact that they would usually be entirely oblivious as to how they had caused such offence.

I confess I was highly amused by this, even though I shouldn't have been really. Back in the late 1980s when I first came to prominence and got elevated to the Shadow Cabinet, John was just like that with me. Peter and I were part of what he called the "beautiful people set," and that was as big an insult as he was capable of bestowing.

I suppose what made it all bearable, even acceptable, for me at least, was that it was all so transparent. Though John could be extremely cunning, to say he wore his heart on his sleeve would be a severe understatement. He put the whole body map there. At Cabinet, he would occasionally sit like a grumbling volcano ready to erupt at any moment. The proximate cause of the eruption would more often than not be one of the women intervening. Patricia Hewitt was certain to get him moving. She was, in fact, a really good minister and was excellent at the Department of Health, taking truly difficult decisions with immense determination, but at Cabinet, she would usually raise the women's angle. John would make some slightly off-colour remark if he was in a sour mood. I would then bring her in again, just for the sheer entertainment of watching him finally explode. She would patronise him in the most wonderfully insensitive fashion: "Now, John, that's a very, very good point you've just made, and it's always so worth listening to you."

He genuinely made me laugh. It was a bit like "How do you solve a problem like Maria?" in *The Sound of Music*, though the similarity between John Prescott and Julie Andrews pretty much stops there. Laughing at him or with him was equally good. I always used to tell him that his confrontations with the English language were part of his appeal, but he worried about them, was embarrassed by them, and when it came to things like standing in for PMQs, he was put in genuine dread. Threatening to have a meeting abroad on a Wednesday was the only way I knew of terrorising him; he would palpitate with the horror of the approaching encounter, but he got up and he did it, with a kind of swaggering blunderbuss approach that the House quite liked. The only time it could be a real problem was when he was meeting foreigners and required interpretation, where his manner of speaking defied the talents of most interpreters, who generally needed extensive therapy and counselling after one of these sessions.

He also knew me very well, and knew especially when I was trying to hoodwink him into something or circumvent him or when I was retreating only with a plan to advance again. He was ultra-sensitive to his position not being taken seriously enough. A meeting would be convened and he would come in steaming and puffing to complain vigorously. I developed a specialism in how to handle such situations: the thing was to let him speak and not interrupt or hit back; but rather to absorb and let the anger naturally subside.

Perhaps his most alarming trait was his habit of starting a conversation in the middle—no beginning, no context, no explanation of what the problem was. I remember a time when it looked as if I was going to bring the Lib Dems into the Cabinet—the papers were full of it—and JP was horrified. Some days had passed since the issue was live, so it was not in my mind. But it was in his.

I was working at the Cabinet table, my head full of some policy conundrum or other. In storms John. "Where's fookin' Menzies?" he begins. It wasn't a promising start. He then began searching under the Cabinet table. "Come on, where is he?" I had literally no idea what he was talking about. He raged about the room. I finally cottoned on: Menzies is of course the proper name of the senior Lib Dem person we all knew as Ming Campbell. John had been ruminating on the press reports of Lib Dems coming into the Cabinet, and by some process had decided it was Ming—and had for some reason not known he was called Ming, or maybe thought "Ming" was some private-school nickname and was therefore suspect—and was going to put a stop to it.

I protested in vain that Ming was not joining the Cabinet, and neither was he lurking underneath the Cabinet table. After a few minutes of expletives, John went to leave. As he got to the door, he turned round and said: "So do I have your word he's not coming in the Cabinet?"

"Yes," I said.

"Well, just to let you know," he replied, "I'm not fookin' havin' it."

He was deeply suspicious of the aristocracy of course, and therefore the royals, but he treated them with respect and decorum nonetheless. For their part, they were half nervous, half intrigued by him. He and Prince Charles corresponded regularly on issues, and as John had responsibility for some rural affairs, it was a relationship that was always a little tricky. John was a vigorous opponent of hunting and there was no persuading him out of that, period.

Shortly after their first meeting, I bumped into Prince Charles. "I had a meeting with Mr. Prescott recently," he said.

"Ah," I said, "how did it go?"

"Fine, fine," Prince Charles replied with a somewhat distracted air, "except . . ."

"Yes?" I said encouragingly, knowing some Johnism was about to emerge.

"Well," he said, looking round to see we were undisturbed, "does he ever do that thing with you?"

"What thing?" I said.

"Er, well, when he's sitting opposite you, he slides down the seat with his legs apart, his crotch pointing a little menacingly, and balances his teacup and saucer on his tummy. It's very odd. I've never seen someone do that before. What do you think it means?"

"I don't think it means anything really," I said.

"Hmm. You don't think it's a sort of gesture or sign of hostility or class enmity or something?"

"No," I said, "he does that with me often."

"Yes," he replied, clearly unconvinced, "but—"

"You mean," I interjected, "he's making a working-class point against you, upper class, and me, middle class?"

"Well, it could be," he said.

"No, I think he just likes drinking his tea that way."

"Yes, you're probably right," he said, plainly puzzled and unpersuaded, "it's just I've never seen it done before."

So there you have him. A one-off. Occasionally my bane. More often my support. But genuine, unvarnished and, in the ultimate analysis, true. And in my profession, you can't say better than that.

The day after John and his punch, we just had to get on with it. I went up to Manchester. There was the usual round of visits to provide background pictures: not too few, so as to provide variety; not too many, so as not to provoke additional unnecessary risk.

After the events of the manifesto launch, it was not surprising that we wanted to keep a grip. But it was frustrating. The trouble was we were in a rhythm. The media wanted a story and the only story was a stumble. We wanted to focus on record and policy, where we thought we were strong and the Tories weak. The result was that the two campaigns never really met; they ran on parallel lines.

From time to time I would call Peter Mandelson and keep him informed of the campaign and get his advice. He was fighting up in Hartlepool, showing his steel and his fortitude in doing so. I thought it might be best for him to stand down, but he was determined not to and he was right. If they were going to pull him down, he wasn't going without a fight. Later, I wondered about the difference between us. Of course, fighting to stay as prime minister and fighting to stay as an MP are a world apart from each other.

At that point in June 2001, I was fairly clear about myself: I was ready to go before the third election. I was less clear about my motives. I liked to think it was because I could walk away; I was not obsessed with being prime minister; I had a hinterland and another mission in my interest in religion. But I had a nagging doubt that part of it was just cowardice; part of it was wanting to be free of the burden, of the pain it brings, of the sometimes near-intolerable weight of responsibility. Did I want to go for unselfish reasons, or for reasons that were in fact utterly selfish? Was I kidding myself about my desire to keep power? Was I kidding myself about the desire to lay it down? Was I fearful of outstaying my usefulness or, in reality, fearful of the bitterness and rancour of the fight to stay?

Peter Mandelson could have taken the easy way out after his second resignation. He would have gone straight into the Lords and would still have been EU commissioner. But he chose to stand his ground, to make the point that he had nothing to be ashamed of and that his detractors, who liked to say how hated he was, would be proved wrong in his own patch.

The election was difficult for him. I told him to stay out of the national limelight and to focus on the local, make it a fight about Hartlepool's right to choose their MP, not have the decision taken for them by a media out to get him. He did so with aplomb, and with down-to-earth political skill. Of course the London media travelled up, baiting him, being unremittingly negative, cynical and unpleasant about him, and naturally poking fun at the whole idea of Peter being capable of getting on with "the Northern working-class folk of Hartlepool."

Of course, as ever, such stereotypes were ridiculously simplistic; and, being sensible, the people of Hartlepool decided that Peter had done a lot to put the place on the map and had defended and supported it, despite not being from there himself. In the end, his majority decreased only slightly. But in one sense the problem that Peter had was reflected in the wider problem of the campaign.

We managed to reassert our grip. Events came and went. We had celebrities out in abundance. That again added some spice. The regulars like Alex Ferguson, some of the cast of *Coronation Street*, the actors Richard Wilson and Michael Cashman turned out of course, and other *EastEnders* stars like Michelle Collins. In a rather wonderful turn, Sir John Mills came out for us and introduced me at rallies. Well into his nineties, he remained fit and sharp and very clear. He wasn't natural Labour; but he was supportive of me. Charlotte Church sang for us at one rally, as did Lesley Garrett. Mick Hucknall, lead singer of the UK band Simply Red, was staunch in his support.

To this day, I'm never sure of the effect the celebrity thing has. I don't dismiss it, as some do. When you are trying to capture the mood—and this is more often so for a progressive party—celebs can reinforce, even boost the message. They add some glamour and excitement to what can often be a dreary business. What they can't do, of course, is substitute for the politics. In fact, if they try to, they become immediately counterproductive. If they begin lecturing the people as to why or how they should vote, it's nearly always a disaster. The public feel they are overstepping the mark and put them and their political fellow travellers in their place. They clearly don't determine the outcome, but properly used, they help. And frankly, given the difficulty in rousing the damn thing, we needed the help.

I went through a carefully calibrated analysis of the marginal seats—Dartford, Gravesend, Basildon, Loughborough, Weymouth, Forest of Dean, a roll call of the seats Labour thought for decades we could never win and now were looking to keep—and the solid Labour parts of the inner cities, northern shires and old industrial communities, in order to deal with the argument that, as we gained new voters, we would somehow lose interest in our traditional heartlands. As press conference gave way to meeting, which gave way to event and then rally, and interview piled upon interview, the frustration began to tell on me. And also the worry.

At one level, the campaign was going brilliantly. We were well ahead in the polls. *Pace* the Prescott punch (and possibly even because of it) we were making the running. Whatever the paddling underneath, and as ever, some of it was frantic, not much was disturbing what looked like a comfortable and serene ride to victory. As it became clearer that the Tories had no magic potion and could not achieve breakthrough, they started to fall apart at the seams. Their right wing started to say silly things, as when the then Shadow Health Secretary Liam Fox—actually clever—let his guard down and remarked: "All we hear from Labour is poverty, poverty, poverty, la, la, la. It's just boring for Conservative members." A partially true statement, but unwise. Then Oliver Letwin—the Shadow Treasury Secretary, and also clever—let the cat out of the bag about how the Tories wanted spending cuts of around £20 billion.

Here's where modern politics becomes ridiculous. Past a certain figure, amounts of money are, for a large part of the public, completely without meaning in terms of scale. "We will spend £500,000 on new school toilets" sounds, at one level, quite a lot. £1 billion sounds just enormous, while £20 billion is beyond wildest dreams or nightmares, and all sense of relativity is lost. Most Treasury forecasts of GDP or revenue can be out by that amount and not much account taken of it, but put it in a headline and it seems revolutionary. It was a total mystery to me why the Tories ever thought it was sensible to quantify what they were planning to do, since it was as plain as a pikestaff (and by the way always is, which is why it's daft as an Opposition to get into this game) that any such figures would be subject to reassessment were a new government to be elected.

However, such pronouncements indicate instinct, direction of travel, an underlying intent. For a Tory Party put out of power because it underinvested in public services, it was about as dumb a move as only the very clever can organise. Labour pounced. The hapless Mr. Letwin spent the next days in hiding. The Tories weren't sure whether to endorse, explain or expunge, and so did all three simultaneously. It gave me something to run on, preoccupied the media at least for a few days and thus gave us respite; and it provoked other criticisms from within the Tory Party to surface. The anti-Europeans went anti. The pro-Europeans went pro. The public went: they're not ready yet, are they?

But even as I revelled in the chance to put the Tories down again, and keep them down, I sensed my own political mortality. Yes, the campaign was succeeding. Yes, the media were in one sense with us, *The*

Times supporting us for the first time; yet peering beneath that, and looking at what really lay there, I felt a deep sense of isolation. The papers on the left, like the *Guardian*, were of course urging our re-election, but on the basis of fear of the Tories, and expressly warning the government and me that any reform of public services would be fiercely resisted. Likewise the *Mirror*. On the right, the *Sun* and the *News of the World* were advocating that we be given the benefit of the doubt, but were vigorous against Europe and thought we hadn't gone far enough on reform.

The point is: no one bought the package. Except the people, of course. Many of them did. They were the New Labour believers. There were more of them than was thought. They were the people who in 2005 made certain we would not lose. They "got" the balance, the newness of the political approach: personal tax rates held steady (or reduced) but investment increased; pro-business but pro-fairness at work (not pro-union); reform along with the spending on public services; a tough approach to responsibility in law and order and welfare; a strong supporter of the U.S. and a player in Europe. They knew Mrs. Thatcher had been right to make Britain competitive, but they also wanted a compassionate society. They were liberal about private lives; hard line on crime. They had no difficulty with a modern Britain. They wanted it, and disliked and distrusted Little England attitudes.

There was a constituency for New Labour all right, but it was not reflected in the media and it was still in its adolescence in the Labour Party. Around me, at the top, were people who for one reason or another were lukewarm. Those who supported it—like John Reid, David Blunkett, Tessa Jowell, Charles Clarke, Alan Milburn, Hilary Armstrong and John Hutton—were on their way up, with still some distance to go; or, like Peter, were under a lot of attack. Go back to May 2001 and none of the major posts—deputy prime minister, Chancellor, Foreign Secretary, Home Secretary—was held by an out-and-out moderniser.

Yet I had now become militant for radical change. I was absolutely clear that in each of these areas, we had an argument that was strong, right and could win the country. Here was the rub: I couldn't get the argument heard. I don't mean I didn't make it—I did, loud and clear—but it was not really listened to. It found insufficient echo among other Labour speakers and very little within the media. The result was a campaign and mandate that meant different things to different people. I was completely certain: the manifesto and the mandate was one for New Labour, but the absence of serious policy discussion meant there was no sense of that being so. If you had asked ordinary people, they would have said: You've done OK, the other lot aren't ready, carry on. It was an election fought in prose, when I was trying to make poetry out of it.

At the time, at one level, what did it matter? We won, and handsomely. But it gave rise to a dangerous confusion among the party, part of which believed that what had won the election was not really New Labour but a benign economy, some extra cash and the parlous state of the Tories. I was absolutely sure the only route to victory was New Labour; even without a focus on policy, that essential radical centre-ground position had somehow still been established and come through. But it was not clear to the party or to the media.

The turnout was low, and the myth was born that the true victor was indifference. We were assailed by cynical over- and undertones. Of course, turnout is often a function of how close people think the result may be. The 1992 turnout was higher than 1997; 2005 higher than 2001. It is actually a very unreliable guide to the feelings about the government.

But, hard as I tried, it meant that as the campaign came to a close, though we were out-of-sight winners, there was a tinge to the victory that discomfited me, and made me realise that reform in term two was going to be a rocky road indeed.

Nonetheless, election night was the opposite of 1997, when everyone except me had been euphoric. This time I was fairly euphoric, while everyone else felt a little flat. After all, it was the second biggest win in the history of British politics—two landslides in a row was impressive. (George Bush phoned me after the election to say, "Man, how did you do that?") As the results rolled in and it was plain it was going to be overwhelming, this time I did permit myself a drink and some celebration. But I also had decisions to make.

One was internal to the office. Anji was keen to go. John Browne, the boss of BP, had offered her a job. I, of course, thought her mad to give up being at the heart of Number 10, even for the sake of working for a company the size of BP and a person of John's reputation and talent. Frankly I couldn't believe it, and I spent significant time before and during the election trying to get her to reconsider.

Eventually, she relented and agreed to stay, but for her it was a mistake. She repented of relenting, and finally left at the end of the year, though not before seeing me through the challenge of 11 September.

It was a terrible wrench. She was one of my oldest friends. I trusted her totally. The prime minister's job is a lonely position, and given that my political isolation was acute for the reasons stated, someone like that, in whom you can have complete confidence, is a godsend. She had developed into an outstanding operative—charming, vivacious, spreading lots of happiness and contentment, while retaining a formidable ruthlessness and capacity to scheme. She was a solid voice for Middle England, had no ideological baggage and was calmness personified in a crisis.

I learned a lesson: never try to keep someone who's moved on in their mind or who wants to go.

On the morning of 8 June, I put Anji in a new position with added power. I hastily moved Sally to the House of Lords (the Queen can formally appoint a Lord on the recommendation of the PM or of the House of Lords Appointments Commission) and made her a minister, which she took with remarkably good grace and from which experience she profited enormously, so that when she took charge of government affairs and political liaison some months later, she had turned into a quite exceptional political manager and was invaluable in the travails of the second term. I had soon realised I missed her badly; and that her skills, more attuned to the party than Anji's, were equally required.

Partly because much of the reform had to be driven from and through Number 10, I knew that we had to strengthen the centre of government considerably, and I made major changes. It is a feature of modern politics that nothing gets done if not driven from the top. Once the framework is set, the departments know their direction and they know what they should do, but leaving it up to them to do it is highly risky, unless the individual ministers fully buy into the vision; and even then, they need to have the power of the centre of the party behind them.

My impatience with the scale and ambition of our reform was now carved in granite. I was going to do it, come hell or high water. I needed to be able to solve the tricky questions of policy detail that added up to the general shape of the change; and I needed to track whether and how the change was being introduced. I had also become aware that the length and breadth of foreign policy issues were creating a requirement for a wholly different order of service. Summits were proliferating, and the scope of foreign policy decisions and their consequences meant leaders, and not foreign ministers, inevitably took on bigger roles.

This was never popular with the traditionalists. There was a lot of talk of centralising government; wanting to be a president; overweening (even manic) desire to have absolute power. It was complete tosh, of course. The fact was you couldn't get the job done unless there were clear procedures and mechanisms in place to implement the programme. There was so much to do in foreign policy terms, where an interdependent world was exponentially increasing the impact of multilateral and foreign policy decisions. And, in domestic policy, changing public service systems inevitably meant getting into the details of delivery and performance management in a radically more granular way. Increasingly, prime ministers are like CEOs or chairmen of major companies. They have to set a policy direction; they have to see it is followed; they have to get data on whether it is; they have to measure outcomes.

There was, again, a lot of exaggerated nonsense about targets and so on in the public sector. Some criticism was valid. Targets can be too numerous. Sometimes different targets conflict, which is a recipe for incompetence. Sometimes they are too prescriptive. All of that was valid.

However, as I used to say to ministers and civil servants, if that is true, cut them down to the essentials, unwind any conflicts, grant a sensible discretion on how they should be met—but don't think for an instant that in any other walk of life you would spend these sums of money without demanding a measurable output. Inputs we had aplenty, but I knew, as the money spent increased, it would be on the outputs that the focus would come; and rightly so.

To ensure the delivery of my top public services priorities we established a Delivery Unit, headed by Michael Barber, who had been David Blunkett's adviser in the Department of Education. The concept of the Delivery Unit was Michael's idea. It was an innovation that was much resisted, but utterly invaluable and proved its worth time and time again. It was a relatively small organisation, staffed by civil servants but also outsiders from McKinsey, Bain and other private sector companies, whose job was to track the delivery of key government priorities. It would focus like a laser on an issue, draw up a plan to resolve it working with the department concerned, and then performance-manage it to solution. It would get first-class data which it would use for stocktakes that I took personally with the minister, his key staff and mine, every month or so. The unit would present a progress report and any necessary action would be authorised.

We reduced radically the number of unfounded asylum cases that way; drove up literacy and numeracy in schools; applied it to NHS waiting lists, street crime and a host of other things. It was like an independent private or social enterprise at the heart of government. In the process, whole new areas needing reform would be illuminated, since often it became clear that the challenge was systemic, requiring wholesale change to the way a public service worked, rather than a centrally or bureaucratically driven edict.

We also created a Strategy Unit, to look ahead at the way policy would develop, the fresh challenges and new ideas to meet them. That also was highly successful. It allowed us to take a medium- and even long-term view of certain issues that were looming but not imminent. Whereas the Policy Unit handled the day-to-day and focused on managing the departments to produce the policies and their implementation that derived from the manifesto or the departmental plans, the Strategy Unit was trying to construct the next policy platform. Of course the two overlapped, but in areas like pensions, welfare to work, public health and further education, the Strategy Unit was constantly putting issues on the agenda that, even if not urgent today, would become tomorrow's crises unless prepared for.

In addition, I strengthened the foreign policy team. Instead of one poor soul covering all foreign policy for the prime minister, which usually meant they worked fourteen-hour days and were never able to interact with other parts of our system or those of other countries in the way they needed to, we formed a unit of four or five, with one senior person on Europe and another on the rest of foreign policy, and some other officials to help. This hugely helped Downing Street to cope with the mounting burden of foreign policy challenges.

I wanted to go further in the machinery of government. I was really passionate about antisocial behaviour and petty crime and the misery it caused people. I also believed we needed a completely new approach to organised crime. This area was to prove incredibly frustrating. I had a plan to reorganise the whole way the criminal justice system worked: to reduce crime, the fear of crime and their social and economic costs, to speed up the process of cases through the system, to dispense justice fairly and efficiently, to promote confidence in the rule of law and to promote confidence in the system.

The decision I didn't take was to move Gordon. When people look back, they always think that was the crucial moment when moving him could have been achieved politically; and that therefore this was an opportunity missed. On balance, I still disagree. He was recognised as an outstanding Chancellor. He was a big figure, a towering figure in many respects. He had a solid media and party following. Moving him would have seemed, and been written up as, a piece of petty spite on my part, as a jealousy move, a self-interested one rather than a disinterested one. And who would I have put in his place? At that point only Robin Cook or Jack Straw could have filled the position. In truth, neither would have been as good—more amenable, maybe, but not as formidable. The Gordon problem—the combination of the brilliant and the impossible—remained.

I think he believed I would move him, so when I tried to say to him the second term must be different from the first and you must cooperate, he immediately said he knew I wanted to get rid of him. What was an attempt to have a frank way of putting the thing on an even keel only further destabilised the vessel.

I did move Robin from Foreign Secretary and put in Jack Straw. Robin had done well, but four years was considered a long time doing that job. It wasn't necessarily wise politically, however. From then on, he was a potential danger. Indeed, I had the same problem with Jack in 2005. The trouble is no one ever wants to stop being Foreign Secretary. As I have said, of all the jobs, that's the one they get to thinking is theirs and should jolly well continue being theirs until the end of time, or at least the end of the government, and even then some harbour the thought that they had done it so well, shouldn't it be elevated above the squalor of party politics?

At the first PLP meeting after election, the PLP were in truculent mood. Unbelievable—second landslide in a row, what's there to complain about? The tension I had felt during the campaign was coming to the surface: the PLP felt they had won on one basis; I felt I had won on another.

However, before either of us had much time to moan about the other, within less than nine weeks of our victory the world would change, and the fate of my political leadership—along with many other things of far greater importance—would change with it.

TWELVE

9/11: "SHOULDER TO SHOULDER"

I t is amazing how quickly shock is absorbed and the natural rhythm of the human spirit reasserts itself. A cataclysm occurs. The senses reel. In that moment of supreme definition, we can capture in our imagination an event's full significance. Over time, it is not that the memory of it fades, exactly; but its illuminating light dims, loses its force, and our attention moves on. We remember, but not as we felt at that moment. The emotional impact is replaced by a sentiment which, because it is more calm, seems more rational. But paradoxically it can be less rational, because the calm is not the product of a changed analysis, but of the effluxion of time.

So it was with 11 September 2001. On that day, in the course of less than two hours, almost 3,000 people were killed in the worst terrorist attack the world has ever known. Most died in the attack on the Twin Towers of the World Trade Center that dominated the skyline of New York. It was a workplace for as diverse a workforce as any in the world, from all nations, races and faiths, and was not only a symbol of American power but also the edifice that most eloquently represented the modern phenomenon of globalisation.

The explosion as the planes hit killed hundreds outright, but most died in the inferno that followed, and the carnage of the collapse of the buildings. As the flames and smoke engulfed them, many jumped in terror and panic, or just because they preferred that death to being on fire. Many who died were rescue workers whose heroism that day has rightly remained as an enduring testament to selfless sacrifice.

The Twin Towers were not the only target. American Airlines Flight

77, carrying sixty-four people from Washington to Los Angeles, was flown into the Pentagon. A total of 189 people died. United Airlines Flight 93, bound from Newark to San Francisco with forty-four on board, was hijacked, its target probably the White House. It came down in Somerset County, Pennsylvania. Its passengers, realising the goal of the hijack, stormed the cabin. In perishing, they saved the lives of many others.

It was an event like no other. It was regarded as such. The British newspapers the next day were typical of those around the globe: "AT WAR," they proclaimed. The most common analogy was Pearl Harbor. The notion of a world, not just America, confronted by a deadly evil that had indeed declared war on us all was not then dismissed as the language of the periphery of public sentiment. It was *the* sentiment. Thousands killed by terror—what else should we call it?

Opinions were forthright and clear, and competed with each other in resolution, not only in the West but everywhere. In the Arab world, condemnation was nearly universal, only Saddam ensuring that Iraqi state television played a partisan song, "Down with America," calling the attacks "the fruits of American crimes against humanity." Yasser Arafat condemned the acts on behalf of the Palestinians, though unfortunately, most especially for the Palestinian cause, the TV showed pictures of some jubilant Palestinians celebrating.

The most common words that day were "war," "evil," "sympathy," "solidarity," "determination" and, of course, "change." Above all, it was accepted that the world had changed. How could it be otherwise?

The reason for such a description was also not hard to divine. The first attempt to attack the World Trade Center, in 1993, had been foiled, but the planning this time had obviously been meticulous. The enemy had been prepared to wait until it had accumulated the necessary means and opportunity.

However, more than that, a terror attack of this scale was not calculated to do limited damage. It was designed for maximum casualty. It was delivered by a suicide mission. It therefore had an intent, a purpose and a scope beyond anything we had encountered before. This was terror without limit; without mercy; without regard to human life, because it was motivated by a cause higher than any human cause. It was inspired by a belief in God; a perverted belief, a delusional and demonic belief, to be sure, but nonetheless so inspired.

It was, in a very real sense, a declaration of war. It was calculated to draw us into conflict. Up to then, the activities of this type of extremism had been growing. It was increasingly associated with disputes that seemed unconnected, though gradually the connection was being made. Kashmir, Chechnya, Algeria, Yemen, Palestine, Lebanon; in each area, different causes were at play, with different origins, but the attacks, carried out as acts of terror, were growing, and the ideological link with an extreme element that professed belief in Islam was ever more frequently expressed. Until 11 September, the splashes of colour on different parts of the canvas did not appear to the eye as a single picture. After it, the clarity was plain, vivid and defining.

We look back now, almost a decade later when we are still at war, still struggling and managing the ghastly consequences which war imposes, and we can scarcely recall how we ever came to be in this position. But on that bright New York morning, not a cloud disturbing the bluest of blue skies, we knew exactly what was happening and why.

We knew that so far as we were concerned we had not provoked such an outrage. There had been acts of terror committed against us: Lockerbie, the USS *Cole*, the U.S. embassy in Tanzania. We had tried to retaliate, but at a relatively low level. They were individual tragedies, but they did not amount to a war. They were the price America paid for being America. The other conflicts we reckoned were none of our business; or at least they were the business of our diplomatic corps, but not of our people.

So those carrying out such acts were wicked; but they weren't changing our world view. George Bush had won the presidency after the controversies of the most contested ballot in U.S. history, but the battle between him and Al Gore had focused mainly on domestic policy. At my first meeting with him—Camp David in February of the same year—his priorities were about education, welfare and cutting down on big government as he saw it.

So there was no build-up to 11 September, no escalation, no attempts to defuse that failed, no expectation or inevitability. There was just an attack—planned obviously during the previous presidency—of unbelievable ferocity and effect. No warning, no demands, no negotiation. Nothing except mass slaughter of the innocent.

We were at war. We could not ignore it. But how should we deal with it? And who was this enemy? A person? A group? A movement? A state?

I was in Brighton that day, to give the biennial address to the Trades Union Congress. Frankly, it was always a pretty ghastly affair for both of us. As I explain elsewhere, I was frustrated they wouldn't modernise; they were frustrated with my telling them how to do their business. Not that they were ever slow in telling me how to do mine, mind you. And sure-fire election-losing advice it was too. They ignored my counsel; and I ignored theirs. For all that, we sort of rubbed along after a fashion, and in a manner of speaking, and up to a point.

The great thing about Brighton is that it is warm, closer than Blackpool to London, and retains the enormous charm of yesteryear. Blackpool can be a great town and has a unique quality, but it needs work done on it. Brighton was where Neil Kinnock, posing for photos on the pebble beach on the day he became Labour leader in 1983, lost his footing and fell in the sea. You can imagine the pleasure of the assembled press. It must have been replayed a thousand times and became a slightly defining misstep; unfairly so, of course; but such things are never fair. In public, you are always on show, so always be under control. The trick, actually, is to appear to be natural, while gripping your nature in a vice of care and caution. Don't let the mask slip; don't think this is the moment to begin a new adventure in communication; don't betray excesses of emotion of any kind; do it all with the ease and character of someone talking to old friends while knowing they are, in fact, new acquaintances.

Over time, I began to think there was never a moment when I could be completely candid and exposed. You worried that even sitting in your living room or in the bath, someone would come to photograph, question and call upon you to justify yourself. I became unhealthily focused on how others saw me, until, again over time, I refocused on how I saw myself. I realised I was considered public property, but the ownership was mine. I learned not to let the opinion of others, even a prevailing one, define my view of myself and what I should or should not do.

The TUC took place in early to mid-September, and the party conference a couple of weeks later. Both always made September a little nerve-tingling. From the TUC you could get a sense of where the party were liable to be in terms of contentment and/or otherwise. Trouble at the first usually presaged trouble at the second. The 2001 TUC was no exception. Having just won our first ever consecutive full term, in a second landslide victory, you would have thought it an occasion for general rejoicing. "I think mostly they'll want to congratulate you on the victory," Alastair said to me, po-faced, as we boarded the train.

"Do you think so?" I said, perking up.

"Don't be ridiculous," he replied.

Sure enough, the mood as I arrived at lunchtime was the usual mixture of sweet and sour, but with the sweet a decided minority. I went straight to the Grand Hotel. We had an hour and a half before I had to go to the new Conference Centre a hundred yards or so along the beachfront. I worked in the bedroom as the team gathered in the living room of the suite. Just after a quarter to two, around 8:45 Eastern Standard Time, Alastair was called out of the room by Godric Smith, his very capable deputy. Alastair came back in, turned on the television and said, "You'd better see this." He knew I hated being interrupted just before a speech, so I realised I'd better look. The TV was showing pictures of the Trade Center like someone had punched a huge hole in it, fire and smoke belching forth. Just over fifteen minutes later, a second plane hit, this time graphically captured live on-screen. This was not an accident. It was an attack.

At that moment, I felt eerily calm despite being naturally horrified at the devastation, and aware this was not an ordinary event but a world-changing one. At one level it was a shock, a seemingly senseless act of evil. At another level, it made sense of developments I had seen growing in the world these past years—isolated acts of terrorism, disputes marked by the same elements of extremism, and a growing strain of religious ideology that was always threatening to erupt, and now had.

Within a very short space of time, it was clear the casualties would be measured in thousands. I ordered my thoughts. It was the worst terrorist attack in human history. It was not America alone who was the target, but all of us who shared the same values. We had to stand together. We had to understand the scale of the challenge and rise to meet it. We could not give up until it was done. Unchecked and unchallenged, this could threaten our way of life to its fundamentals. There was no other course; no other option; no alternative path. It was war. It had to be fought and won. But it was a war unlike any other. This was not a battle for territory, not a battle between states; it was a battle for and about the ideas and values that would shape the twenty-first century.

All this came to me in those forty minutes between the first attack and my standing up in front of the audience to tell them that I would not deliver my speech but instead return immediately to London. And it came with total clarity. Essentially, it stayed with that clarity and stays still, in the same way, as clear now as it was then.

Immediately I saw that, though it was a war, because of its nature it would have to be described and fought differently. It was, in a profound sense, a battle that was ideological, the mores and modus vivendi of religious fanaticism versus those of an enlightened, secular system of government that in the West, at least, incorporated belief in liberty, equality and democracy. It was also a battle about modernisation, a clash not so much between civilisations, but rather one about the force and consequence of globalisation.

All around the globe, the new technology—the Internet, computers, mobile phones, mass travel and communication—was opening the world up, casting people together, mixing cultures, races, faiths in a vast melting pot of human interaction. With this, came the reaction. In the West, it often took the form of virulent nationalism, waves of anti-immigrant feeling as people saw their traditional identity being weakened and their control over the world around them being surrendered, economically and culturally.

Within Islam, other, deeper forces were at work. Many distrusted globalisation, worried about the way it changed society, worried about ceding authority to it. Many disliked Western culture, its brash insistence on liberal attitudes, its sexual freedom, its individualism that could and sometimes did lapse into hedonism. All of this would have produced its own reaction. But what deepened it and turned it into a powerful radicalising potency was peculiar to Islam. For centuries, Islam had not only been a dominant religious movement in the Middle East and beyond, but had also achieved political dominance and led the world in science, art and culture.

For hundreds of years after the death of Christ, as Christianity was spread first by those scorned and persecuted by the Roman Empire and then as the official religion of the Empire, it became the accepted or enforced religion of countries that today we know as Muslim: Egypt, Palestine, Lebanon, Syria, Iraq. There are still pockets of Christians in each today, though less than there were; and they descend from Christian communities that pre-date Islam.

By the seventh century, Christianity was riven by division, schisms and battles over what was heresy and what wasn't. Once martyred and persecuted, the Christians then hounded not only those who weren't Christian, but also those Christians who disagreed with the orthodoxy. For a religion based on compassion and love, it was a dismal picture.

When Islam began, and within the space of twenty or so years was established by the Prophet Muhammad into the government of what we now know as Saudi Arabia and beyond, it was in part an attempt to take the Abrahamic faiths back to their roots and develop them into a principled, rational and moral way forward for the world. The message of the Prophet was given to him by the angel Gabriel from God—the Koran therefore being the direct recital of the word of God.

At least to begin with, Islam was a welcome contrast with the state of Christianity. Where Christian armies would routinely butcher their foes, Islam showed mercy. Where other religions were forcibly suppressed, Islam showed tolerance. Where priests and prelates often lived lives of debauchery and vice, the followers of Islam seemed genuine disciples of devotion and discipline to God.

As Islam expanded far beyond Mecca and Medina, it was often looked upon as a liberator, even by some of the Christian communities such as the Nestorians in Iraq. In time, of course, as it became more powerful it also became more dictatorial. Non-believers were offered a choice—conversion or taxation—and the price of the latter became uncomfortably high. Nonetheless, there is a fair case for saying that up to and through the Crusades, and until around the European Renaissance, Islam was the greater repository of civilised thought.

The history of Islam—its origins, its rise, its present predicament—is essential to understanding the significance of the events of 11 September. It is precisely here that I made a mistake: I misunderstood the depth of the challenge. I was ignorant of the pervasive nature of the phenomenon. As at 11 September 2001, I accepted what most accepted: this act was perpetrated by a small group of fanatics wholly unrepresentative of Islam who could and should be crushed.

If I had known then that a decade later we would still be fighting in Afghanistan, I would have been profoundly perturbed and alarmed.

I hope I would have still taken the same decision, both there and in respect of Iraq. To have tried to escape the confrontation would have been a terrible error, an act of political cowardice. What I know now does not make me any less committed to the fight we began on the day of the event itself. On the contrary, it is even more clear to me that the battle has to be fought with every means at our disposal, and fought until it is won.

What is clear now is the scale of the challenge, which in two senses is different to what we originally contemplated. The first is that in the mindset that is modern Islam, there is one spectrum, not several. At the furthest end of the spectrum are the extremists who advocate terrorism to further their goal of an Islamic state, a rebirth of the caliphate that came into being in the years following the death of the Prophet. It is true they are few in number, but their sympathisers reach far further along the spectrum than we think. While many do not agree with the terrorism, they "understand" why it is happening.

Still further along the spectrum are those who condemn the terrorists, but in a curious and dangerous way buy into bits of their world view. They agree with the extremists that the U.S. is anti-Islam; they see the invasion of Afghanistan or Iraq as invasions of Muslim nations because they were Muslim nations. They see Israel as the symbol of Western anti-Islamic prejudice. This group stretches uncomfortably far into the middle of the spectrum.

Then you have, of course, a large number, probably the majority, who condemn the terrorists and their world view.

But—and here is the second point—even this group have not yet confidently found their way to articulating a thoroughly reformed and modernising view of Islam. In other words, it is true they find the terrorism repugnant and they wish to be in alliance with the Western nations against it, but this does not yet translate into an alternative narrative for Islam that makes sense of its history and provides a coherent vision for its future. What this means is that very often countries in the Arab and Muslim world will offer their people a disconcerting and ultimately self-defeating choice between a ruling elite with the right idea, but which they are reluctant or fearful to advertise, and a popular movement with the wrong one, which they are all too keen to proclaim.

The combination of all of this means that this battle is not, I'm afraid, one between a small, unrepresentative group of extremists and the rest of us. Or at least, it is not only that. It is also a fundamental struggle for the mind, heart and soul of Islam.

In that struggle we are necessary participants, both because we came under attack and also because those who must lead Islam to change need our support. In the final analysis, of course, it is a struggle that must be won from within. Such struggles don't last an electoral cycle; they last a generation.

Back in the instant following the cataclysmic act of terrorism that stunned, shocked and appalled the world, the issue was clear: the madmen had declared war. They would be rooted out and eliminated. No one doubted it. No one—or very few—disputed it, or the action that followed.

Be under no illusion whatever—and the period since then is littered with illusions—there were only two ways of dealing with this phenomenon. One was to manage it; to have left the Taliban in power but ringed them with sanctions and alliances; to have adopted a purely soft-power approach to the challenge. Some indeed advocated this strategy (though not many did so on 12 September), and I do not dismiss it. It is the true alternative to what we actually did. The idea would have been to have worked for gradual reform and the appearance of a new Islam over time. So we would have been provoked to war; and resisted the provocation.

The other way, the way we chose, was to confront it militarily. I still believe that was the right choice, but the costs, implications and consequences were far greater than any of us, and certainly me, could have grasped on that day.

To win in this way would not and does not require simply a military strategy to defeat an enemy that is fighting us. It requires a whole new geopolitical framework. It requires nation-building. It requires a myriad of interventions deep into the affairs of other nations. It requires above all a willingness to see the battle as existential and to see it through, to take the time, to spend the treasure, to shed the blood, believing that not to do so is only to postpone the day of reckoning, when the expenditure of time, treasure and blood will be so much greater. Who knows which is right? No one. We will only know later. Just as our knowledge was limited on 11 September 2001, so our knowledge remains limited now. In such circumstances, in such conditions of understanding, the only course is to follow instinct and belief. There is nothing more to do. That is what I did in those days following the tragedy.

All these years on and still fighting, people look at the situation and ask: What went wrong? This ignores the possibility that it is not so much a case of "what went wrong," as that the nature of the struggle means that it will turn and twist and evolve over a long time. We thought back then that the equation was relatively simple: knock out the Taliban, give Afghanistan a UN-supervised election, provide billions for development, and surely the outcome is progress. And, of course, without an enemy using terror to disrupt and destabilise, without the tribal and warlord factions of a failed state, if the people had been allowed to do what they wanted, they would indeed have decided for progress. In fact, in so far as they could, they did, and at every election came out and showed what they wanted and what they didn't. But even with our support, even with the activity of our forces and the aid we give, the people's will for order has not yet been able to overcome the countervailing will for chaos.

However, the conclusion from this is not that we give up; still less that if we had never bothered, we or the people would be better off. The conclusion is that the war is brutal and long. And that is exactly what makes it all the more important to win.

The paradigm through which we see all this today is that we cannot see the end in sight and meanwhile we are losing brave and committed soldiers in a fight whose outcome is uncertain. But in any serious war, such an issue is at some point reached and the question then is whether to retreat or to press forward. The soldiers are not being killed because the cause is any less just and not necessarily because it is being badly prosecuted; they are being lost because the enemy is fighting us; because for them, too, the stakes are high and because they can see the possibility, if they last out, that we will lose heart or cobble together some ignominious deal in which we will trade the essential principles we are fighting for, in return for calm. Then they will re-emerge stronger, and their ideology with them.

So it is important to recall why the war in Afghanistan happened. It did so because on that fateful day, terrorists harboured by the Taliban and trained in Afghanistan showed that they would kill innocent people on a hitherto unknown scale, to drive us out of alliance with those in Islam who want peaceful coexistence and force us to leave that world to the ideology of religious extremism, to government by fanatic or dictator. We did not seek them out. They sought us. Had it not been 11 September, it would have been another occasion.

In the immediate aftermath, too, we were unsure of where the next strike might come. For some time afterward, we had an emergency procedure in place if a plane was over London or any major city and had lost contact with air traffic control. Basically there was a series of escalations of alarm up to the point where I could be asked to authorise bringing the plane down. Fighters were on standby ready to go up in the air and shoot it out of the sky if so ordered. It only happened once. I recall it, as you can imagine, vividly. I was at Chequers at the weekend and was called urgently to the phone. A passenger plane had been out of contact for some time, and was heading over London. I had the senior

RAF commander authorised to get my decision. The fighter jet was airborne. For several anxious minutes we talked, trying desperately to get an instinct as to whether this was threat or mishap. The deadline came. I decided we should hold back. Moments later the plane regained contact. It had been a technical error. I needed to sit down and thank God after that one!

As I left the stage of the TUC—ironically given a better reception than any I ever enjoyed—I was already putting in train the emergency meetings that would take the proximate decisions for Britain's security. I also fixed calls with the key world leaders, including of course President Bush. I took calls from the main ministers and the Cabinet Secretary on the train back to London.

It was a strange journey as we sat in the carriage riding through the peaceful and beautiful Sussex countryside, such a contrast to the fevered concentration of the conversations about a world whose security had just been turned upside down. At that point, though, as I have said, I was relatively calm, clear in my own mind about what had to be done.

Back in Downing Street and during the first of several emergency sessions with ministers and officials, we ran through the measures we had to take. Flights over London were suspended, the police and security services were put on red alert. The intelligence people were dispatched to ferret out any possible plots here. Every part of Whitehall was buzzing and alive with activity. At such moments the machine is at its best, covering all bases, setting an agenda for the decision-making, joining up the disparate parts in some sort of semi-automatic cohesion. It was impressive. I was glad of the steady hand of Richard Wilson and his senior Civil Service colleagues.

I spoke in turn to Putin, Schroeder, Chirac and Berlusconi, and the next day to President Bush. The collective sense of solidarity was absolute. Everyone was fully behind the U.S. It is hard now to realise just how fearful people were at that time. For all we knew, there were other attacks about to happen. At any moment, we expected to hear of some fresh atrocity.

I saw my role as that of galvanising the maximum level of support. I knew that when the immediate impact of the event diminished, there was always a danger of backsliding; and I also knew the key thing was to assemble as broad a coalition of support for action as possible. On the night of 11 September, I set out our position as a country in a broadcast from Downing Street:

This mass terrorism is the new evil in our world. The people who perpetrate it have no regard whatever for the sanctity or value of human life,
and we the democracies of the world must come together to defeat it and
eradicate it. This is not a battle between the United States of America
and terrorism, but between the free and democratic world and terrorism.
We, therefore, here in Britain stand shoulder to shoulder with our
American friends in this hour of tragedy, and we, like them, will not rest
until this evil is driven from our world.

"Shoulder to shoulder" came to be something of a defining phrase. I
chose the words carefully. I was aware this was a big commitment that
would come to be measured not in words but in actions; and I knew the
road on which we were going to travel "shoulder to shoulder" was
going to be rocky. How rocky, as I say, I did not know, but I think and
hope that had I known, my words would have been the same.

I took this view for reasons both of principle and of national interest
(and, incidentally, have never believed the two are mutually exclusive).
As a matter of principle, I was sure that we should see the atrocity as an
attack not on the U.S. per se, but because the U.S. was the leader of the
free world, it was therefore an attack on us too. It was also in our
national interest to defeat this menace and if we wanted to play a major
part in shaping the conduct of any war, we had to be there at the outset
with a clear and unequivocal demonstration of support. I believed in the
alliance with America, I thought its maintenance and enhancement a
core objective of British policy, and I knew that alliances are only truly
fashioned at times of challenge, not in times of comfort.

Over the next days, I rallied support. I hosted Silvio Berlusconi who, as
ever, was straightforward in his commitment to the U.S. I visited France
and Germany and they too were on board, though I noticed with a little
anxiety that Jacques Chirac particularly was urging caution in respect of
any response. Parliament was recalled and I made a statement. Opinion was
universally—among Opposition leaders at least—supportive.

On 20 September, I travelled to the U.S. By then, my position as the
world leader strongly articulating the need for comprehensive and
strategic action was pretty well established. My concern throughout was
to make sure America felt embraced and supported, felt a real arm of
solidarity stretched out towards them. The fear, but above all the sense
of anger and outrage, would be enormous. How it was channelled
would be a product not just of how America's leaders spoke to their

own people, but of how the outside world expressed its sympathy and also its readiness to share responsibility.

Of course, the other crucial point was that many Britons had lost their lives. I met families of those who had died. Such encounters are always the hardest thing you do. You have to retain the dignity of office but you genuinely feel the grief, and can often not help expressing it in tears. One woman I met was pregnant. Her husband had flown over for a meeting in the World Trade Center. He and his child would never see one another. Other parents mourned the loss of their only son, whom they plainly idolised. I was shocked by the hideous random nature of terrorism. Dead just because you happened to be there. No other reason. No other explanation. Just the merest happenstance.

Having landed in New York, we went to St. Thomas Church on Fifth Avenue. The mayor Rudy Giuliani was there. I liked him instantly. He was under immense pressure but he seemed to be not only coping, but stepping forward and giving a strong sense of leadership. I had a message from the Queen that was to be read out, and then gave a short reading myself. The Queen's message was strong and clear. The words I quoted were from Thornton Wilder's novel *The Bridge of San Luis Rey* about five people who die when a bridge collapses over a gorge:

> But soon we die, and all memory of those five will have left Earth, and we ourselves shall be loved for a while and forgotten. But the love will have been enough. All those impulses of love return to the love that made them. Even memory is not necessary for love. There is a land of the living and a land of the dead and the bridge is love, the only survival, the only meaning.

As we stepped outside the church, a battery of cameras and journalists assailed us and I spoke some words which I had thought about on the ride from the airport:

> I can only imagine what it must have been like for the people of New York for the past nine days. My father's generation went through the Blitz. They know what it is like to suffer this deep tragedy and attack. There was one country and one people which stood by us at that time. That country was America and those people were the American people. As you stood by us in those days, we stand side by side with you now. Your loss is our loss. Your struggle is our struggle.

I felt Rudy next to me relax and take comfort as I spoke. I could see on the faces of people we walked past an intense, earnest desire to know if they had friends at this moment of trial; if America was alone or with others; if the world meant the words spoken and would follow through with deeds. I wanted to assure them that this was so, that at least Britain would not be wanting, that what we said we meant, that we would be at the front and not the back.

We finally got to Washington, an hour late for the meeting with President Bush, who was to address both Houses of Congress that night. As I drove up to the back entrance of the White House, the one I used on so many occasions, where the immaculately dressed marines stood to attention either side of the door, I wondered how I would find George. We had spoken on the phone a few times. We had already started to exchange ideas. After the initial shock, he had handled himself exceptionally well, and plainly had the American people right behind him.

I went into the Oval Office. He was there putting the finishing touches to the speech. It had been agreed I would sit in the gallery to hear it, side by side with George's wife Laura. He was unbelievably, almost preternaturally calm. We even had dinner together. I reflected that faced with a similar speech, I would have been closeted away, drafting and redrafting. I would have been dismayed at having to entertain someone. I offered to slip away but emphatically he said no, stay, let's talk, and we did until it was time for him to go over. I suddenly realised two things about him (and at that time I did not know him nearly as well as I came to): the first was that he sincerely welcomed the friendship I and Britain had showed. He didn't just appreciate it; he found it a source of strength. Second, he was not panicking or fretting or even plain worrying. He was at peace with himself. He had his mission as president. He hadn't asked for it. He hadn't expected it. He hadn't found it. It had found him. But he was clear. The world had changed, and as president of the world's most powerful country, he was tasked with making sense of that change and dealing with it.

As we got into the lift, he as ever exchanging a bit of banter with the lovely George Hannie, the maître d' of the White House flat, I asked him if he was nervous. "No, not really," he replied. "I have a speech here and the message is clear." I marvelled at it, looked carefully at him; but yes, he did indeed appear completely at ease.

It was the first time I had seen a speech to Congress. (In 2003 I would deliver one myself.) It was an extraordinary affair, something that only the U.S. could do with that elan and confidence. As the president spoke, you could feel the representatives come together around love of the nation, the pride, patriotism and self-belief exuding from every pore of that wonderful arena of mahogany, brass and stone, rich in history, certain of the future. George singled me out in the gallery alongside Laura and I duly took a bow, somewhat self-consciously.

As I looked down on the assembled ranks, so forthright, so determined, so sure, I reflected on what lay ahead. I assumed we could dislodge the Taliban. I had already worked out that it should be done by a tactical manoeuvre of offering them a choice: yield up bin Laden and the terrorists, or be removed from power. And then what? I knew little about Afghanistan, but I did know it was a country that over the centuries had been invaded, occupied and plundered yet always seemed eventually to swallow and spit out the invaders.

Some months before, sitting in the Long Gallery in Chequers surrounded by the portraits of the previous tenants and Cromwell memorabilia, including his swords at the Battle of Naseby, I had stumbled upon a three-volume set of diaries. They were by Field Marshal Roberts, an officer and then head of the British Army in the mid- to late-nineteenth century, including the time of the Indian Mutiny. They were fascinating reading, and gave a brilliant first-hand account of what it was like to be a young officer, recounting the events of the mutiny, how it spread and how it was put down, conveying a vivid sense of that part of the British Empire. They described battles in Hyderabad and Peshawar and then in the Hindu Kush, in Kandahar, Helmand and Lashkar Gah, names all too familiar today.

They also showed the remarkable spirit of the British soldier. As the mutiny took hold—and it all arose out of the false rumour that native Muslim soldiers in the British Army had had their rifles greased with pork—the British troops were pushed back and towns were overrun. The native soldiers, well trained and well equipped by the very people they now set out to kill, fought fiercely. For a time, things hung in the balance. Nawabs, the princes of India, calculated which way it would go, some joining the mutiny, others giving provender to the rulers.

Roberts gave one incredible account of how, as they prepared to storm a redoubt of the mutiny, there was a fierce argument among the soldiers, as to who should have the honour of going first into the breach that the artillery would make in the city wall. To go first was certain death. But the competition to do it was, for all that, intense. Eventually, to their great delight, the argument was won by Scots High-landers. Duly they went in first; duly they died. But how the pride of their regiment swelled at the endeavour.

In these diaries, Afghanistan was regarded differently from today: more bleak, more savage, more ungovernable. As the Russians discovered a hundred years later, the country had its own way.

So I had committed us; but I did so knowing that war is unpredictable, and in Afghanistan especially so. Partly as a result of this, I thought it essential that the battle we were about to embark upon was not simply a war to punish. It had to liberate. Yes, the cause was the attack on the Twin Towers, but once the engagement began, it couldn't just be a retaliation, a reprisal, a redress of a wrong done to us. It had to be of bigger reach, intent and purport. Precisely because this struggle was connected with an ideology that was not confined to Afghanistan—indeed had been imported into Afghanistan—the ambition had to be greater. All this would add to the weight of it and the responsibility to see it through.

Overnight on 20 September we flew into Brussels for an emergency European Council the next day. I had deliberately decided to go to the U.S. before the Council met, so that when I arrived I could speak directly of what I had seen and experienced in New York and Washington. Europe had stayed very strongly behind the U.S., but now when we came to the point of action, you could never be sure. In the event the Council went well, and came out with a satisfactory statement unifying people in condemnation and recognising the need for action. The memory of the events was still uppermost in the minds of politicians and public alike; the news was more or less given over to it and would remain so for several weeks as more details emerged, the human stories of tragedy, sacrifice, suffering and heroism became clear, and the implications were analysed and sunk in.

Those implications were vast. If the terrorists could have killed more, they would have. If instead of 3,000 it had been 30,000, they would have rejoiced. For world leaders wondering and worrying where the next hostility would come from, the contemplation not only of what had happened but what might happen was continuous, urgent and nerve-racking.

In those initial days, even before the war began, and long before Iraq was on the agenda, certain thoughts crystallised and became decisions. One I have described: that this could not be a battle fought on the ideological low ground; it had to be fought on the high ground—our values versus theirs. The goal was not simply to remove the Taliban but to replace them with democracy, to rebuild the country. This was not just a matter of idealism, it was also about understanding why Afghanistan had become a failed state, why it had become a breeding ground for terror, why it had descended into this horrible, cruel mix of anarchy and despotism. Like it or not, from then on, we were in the business of nation-building.

Second, the prospect of any such group, or a state which sympathised with them or shared a similar outlook, obtaining nuclear, chemical or biological weapons—the so-called WMD trinity—was unthinkable. If they got hold of them, there could be little doubt on the evidence of 11 September that they would use them. Indeed, in the days following the attack, anthrax was sent to top Congress, White House and other officials, and the news was full of alarm at the possibility of some form of chemical attack. It was obvious to me that our attitude towards the trade, transfer and development of such weapons had to be of a wholly different kind. A new signal had to be sent out, a new urgency established in order to make it clear that such a possibility constituted a direct threat to our society.

This was immediately plain, not least out in the Middle East. The issue of Saddam and his ten-year obstruction of weapons inspection was not upfront, but from then on, it was there in the background. There was no decision at that point as to how to deal with him; nevertheless, that he had to be confronted, brought into line or removed, was on any deeper analysis, fairly obvious.

Third, how could such an attack have been planned, developed, supervised and executed without a hint of anyone knowing? If such a plot could be hatched in the USA, where else could similar plots be taking place? From this point on, it seemed to me that the balance in civil liberties between protecting the rights of the suspect and protecting the rights of the citizen had changed. Of course care had to be exercised, and as a lawyer I was only too well aware of the risks of jeopardising our way of life in the name of safeguarding it; but once 11 September had demonstrated this terrorism's capacity and intent, governments round the world—especially those closely allied to the U.S.—saw the need to take new measures of security and perhaps a new approach to it.

All of these decisions—taken certainly with contemporaneous support and understanding—were to have far-reaching consequences for the future of both the country and the government. We felt we had been attacked. But more than that: we felt we had been warned.

As I got back to Chequers late on Friday 21 September, I was tired yet also galvanised. If I could have seen into the future, I would also have been deeply disturbed.

The next weeks were spent in a frantic but essentially well-organised process to put together the military operation to remove the Taliban, and the reconstruction plan for Afghanistan.

Despite the pressure, George was determined not to rush—"I don't want a $10 million missile hitting a $10 tent just for effect," he remarked memorably. He agreed to an ultimatum to the Taliban, so that people could see we had offered a way out if they chose to take it. But it was clear they wouldn't take it.

I was writing regular notes to him, raising issues, prompting his system and mine: humanitarian aid; political alliances, including in particular how we co-opted the Northern Alliance (the anti-Taliban coalition) without giving the leadership of the country over to them; economic development; reconciliation in the aftermath of a hopefully successful military operation. Above all, I was globetrotting—to the Middle East, Pakistan, Russia—trying to ensure that we kept the support we had. I wrote a personal, private note to my own staff and senior officials, setting out how we needed to get all parts of the system, ours and the Americans', better coordinated.

The UN under Kofi Annan's guidance was being helpful and from the outset I was determined that they should help take the strain of the politics. Fortunately, in Lakhdar Brahimi they had a sensible interlocutor with the Afghans, one who was experienced and savvy.

The meetings abroad went well too. I visited President Putin. At this point, we remained strong allies. He and I sat in a small anteroom in the Kremlin. I always thought how difficult it was to position Moscow culturally. St. Petersburg was clearly European, but Moscow was to itself, unplaceable in a broader context, even unfathomable, but impressive in a somewhat intimidating way.

Putin was anxious to help. Through Chechnya he knew the influence of this extremism. He saw a common link between all these different arenas of struggle. Back then, also, he saw the possibility of Russian renaissance and a resurgence of Russian power as compatible with, or even furthered by, being allied to the U.S. It was one of my regrets that we never got together a proper strategy for allowing him to fulfil that ambition with the UK, as opposed to what eventually happened, which was an attempt to fulfil it in contradistinction to us. Maybe that was always a fond hope. He and George got on well personally, but Vladimir thought the Americans treated him and Russia with insufficient respect or consequence, and as time wore on he decided to pitch Russia to the international community as the country willing to stand up to America. In Iraq, he found an issue upon which such a role could be played, and he played it with his customary vigour. The UK should have made greater efforts; in particular, the Americans tended to underestimate him, and that was never a good idea.

Nonetheless, in late 2001, we sat and conspired on what we could do to ensure that the former Soviet satellite countries ringing Afghanistan would be supportive or compliant in respect of any action to come. At one moment, he even suggested we fly together that night to Tajikistan to lobby its president personally, a notion I adored, but which my travelling staff quailed at.

President Musharraf of Pakistan was in a difficult position: his government had worked with the Taliban government; the borders between Afghanistan and Pakistan were porous; the tribal and political links were strong, yet he was an ally of ourselves and the U.S., of course.

On 5 October, we flew in on an RAF plane equipped with special anti-missile devices. I had thought it somewhat of an overreaction, until the moment we began our descent into the airfield. The plane circled sharply, spiralling down in a careful manoeuvre, and as we landed and the rubber squeaked on the tarmac, the crew burst into applause. They were plainly relieved. As we drove in from the airport to Islamabad, I saw roads and streets shut down, but lined nonetheless with large crowds standing up on the embankments, the men in white robes, the women usually veiled, staring, with neither enmity nor friendship obvious.

I was ushered into Musharraf's study in the Presidential Palace. All through the meeting a bodyguard hovered near the door, coming in and standing over us each time the servants brought in tea or refreshments. Musharraf himself was clear in his condemnation of the Taliban and in his offer of help and support. He knew the attack had changed everything. He told me something I reflected upon a good deal in later years: in the 1970s General Zia had made the fatal error of linking Pakistani nationalism to devout Islam, in the course of which he had adopted the manner of a religious as well as a political and military leader, proudly showing the mark on his forehead from being pressed to the ground in prayer. The connection between the two, Musharraf explained, had furthered radicalism in the country, heightened the issue of Kashmir and made reconciliation with India harder.

"Surely," I said, "economic development is the key challenge for Pakistan."

"Of course," he said, "but the reality is today Pakistani politics is about nuclear weapons and Kashmir."

"What can we do to help?" I asked, expecting an answer to do with aid or India.

"Do Palestine," he immediately shot back. "That would help."

I came away pleased with his support, but uneasy at how clearly he felt the ultimate success of the mission was in the balance.

On all these visits I had the full inner team with me. I also had the enormous benefit of Sir David Manning, who had become my chief foreign affairs adviser and who had been in the U.S. at the time of the 11 September attacks. I had by this time already strengthened the core team of Downing Street and I now had the redoubtable Stephen Wall as the European adviser. They were both examples of the best types of mandarin. David was cool, calm, very good under pressure, and creative too, always ready with a strategy to resolve an impasse. Over these months, he was a titan in the team, truly invaluable. Stephen was very professional and proficient, of course; but underneath you could tell he was a riot of strong emotions, opinions and insights which he longed to have you seize upon and implement. Some you could, some you couldn't. But grey, he wasn't; and I liked that.

Meanwhile, on 7 October the military campaign started. It was largely a bombing campaign, with limited boots on the ground. The Northern Alliance were also advancing. We had identified four core objectives: deny al-Qaeda its Afghan base; deny them an alternative base outside Afghanistan; attack them internationally; support other states in their efforts against them.

From the first attacks in October 2001, the UK was involved alongside coalition forces led by the U.S. under Operation Enduring Freedom (OEF). Royal Navy submarines fired Tomahawk missiles against the Taliban and al-Qaeda networks, and RAF aircraft provided reconnaissance and air-to-air refuelling capabilities in support of U.S. strike aircraft. The U.S. flew missions from Diego Garcia, part of the British Indian Ocean Territory, under permission from the UK government.

UK troops were first deployed in November 2001, when Royal

Marines from 40 Commando helped to secure the airfield at Bagram. A 1,700-strong battle group based around 45 Commando was subsequently deployed as Task Force JACANA. Their role was to deny and destroy terrorist infrastructure and interdict the movement of al-Qaeda in eastern Afghanistan. In several major operations, Task Force JACANA destroyed a number of bunkers and caves, and it also provided humanitarian assistance in areas previously dominated by the Taliban and al-Qaeda. It withdrew in July 2002.

The International Security Assistance Force (ISAF), which aimed to assist the Afghan Transitional Authority in creating and maintaining a safe and secure environment in Kabul and its surrounding area, was created in December 2001 in negotiations led by the British, authorised by United Nations Security Council Resolution (UNSCR) 1386 and successive resolutions (the latest of which is UNSCR 1776 of 2007). Major General John McColl led the first ISAF mission with contributions from sixteen nations. As well as providing the headquarters and much of the supporting forces for the ISAF, the UK contributed the brigade headquarters and an infantry battalion. Our contribution initially peaked at 2,100 troops, later decreasing to around 300 personnel after the transfer of ISAF leadership to Turkey in the summer of 2002.

The Taliban had collapsed by the end of 2001, remnants melting back into the Pushtun populace in southern Afghanistan and the Pakistani tribal areas. It was important to ensure that Afghanistan did not return to ungoverned space within which terrorist training and preparation could flourish. International forces therefore remained to provide security and stability, to combat residual Taliban and al-Qaeda elements, and to support the development of Afghan security forces.

At that time, the coalition was still intact, the weight of opinion with us, the objectives clear. In view of what happened subsequently, it is worth stating what the goal was. The analysis we had was that Afghanistan had been a failed state; the Taliban had taken over; and as a consequence extremism under their protection was allowed to grow. An additional destabilising factor was the drugs trade. Afghanistan had become the source of 90 per cent of the heroin that found its way onto the streets of Europe.

Now, years later, people say: But the mission isn't clear, or it's confused. It isn't, and it wasn't. To us then, and I believe this to be true now, there is no neat distinction between a campaign to exorcise al-Qaeda, or to prevent Taliban re-emergence, or to build democracy, or to ensure there is a proper, not a narco, economy. There is no "or" about it. Allow the Taliban to re-emerge, fail to build governance, and you will have the same failed state with the same consequences. The problem is not that we have tried to do too much; it is that to do it requires a complete and sustained engagement, backed by the resources and the will over a very long period.

Up to and through 2004, while the huge scale of the challenge was clear, things nevertheless seemed slowly to be working. I will come later to the decisions of 2006, by which time it was clear that progress had stalled, but from 22 December 2001 when the interim government was installed, through to the 2004 presidential elections when turnout was 70 per cent and large numbers of women voted, through even to the provincial elections in autumn of 2005, Afghanistan seemed to be basically on the path to being a better state, despite the constant diversions, excursions and setbacks aplenty.

By the way, I am emphatically not saying we did everything well or could not have done many things better. So it is with any such situation. But above all, I certainly misjudged the depth of the failure of the Afghanistan state; and the ability of the Taliban to immerse themselves into the local communities, particularly in the south, and to call upon reinforcements from across the border in the mountainous highlands that seemed a law unto themselves. Thus immersed, they were able by a continuation of intimidation, organisation and sheer malevolence to reassert control of parts of the territory, or at least to disrupt the work we were doing.

Also, their fanaticism meant that the end justified the means. They would kill, terrorise and torture without compunction or conscience. Villagers, uncertain of which masters they were going to have to deal with, hovered between support for the allies and obedience to their local religious extremists. Meanwhile, the central government in Kabul, led by Hamid Karzai, struggled to have their writ run.

What happened was that even as 2001 wore on, even as the news eventually moved on—at first reluctantly, but then gladly—what had been a supreme international effort started to resemble more and more an effort by the U.S. and its closest allies. We didn't get another 11 September. The stories of chemical attacks gradually slipped away. The world consciousness of a menace needing to be confronted slowly melted, losing its shape and its prominence, as life got back to and seemed normal. Hesitantly at first, but then picking up confidence, several strands of opinion emerged that were to have a deeply corrosive effect on the will to keep going.

The first of these was that over time, and as the pictures of allied bombing missions made their impact, the strength of Muslim support for the campaign started to waver. The mindset that our enemies sought desperately to impose—namely that this was a war against a Muslim nation—gained traction. Much more fundamentally, from the outset this was seen as an essentially Western affair. There were Turkish forces involved and later others, but for Arab and Muslim opinion, the offensive was conducted for America, not against terrorism. Those elements deep within Islam that saw it as a victim reasserted themselves, questioning our motives, seizing on any language of an unfortunate nature. Both George and Silvio had used the word "crusade." It was completely obvious that they were using it in a generic sense, as one would refer to a crusade against drugs or crime, a term commonly used in our politics; but it was twisted to suggest they used it in reference to the Crusades of old. Many of the Arab and Muslim governments did not see—perhaps unsurprisingly—the cause of democracy as one to which they should rally.

The moral force with which the action had been launched began to dissipate in Western circles as well. For a few years after Afghanistan retreated from the top of the bulletins, this dissipation seemed to make little practical difference, but it meant that time and time again when we needed top-quality focus, it wasn't there, except from the U.S. and UK; and it was clear we could not do it all on our own. The Europeans were with us, but within limits set by their own public opinion, which was prepared to support the mission in general terms but was deeply reluctant to commit forces and to suffer casualties.

Without doubt things could have been done better and differently; but the principal reason for progress stalling was that our enemy began to sense the boundaries of our endurance and the strength or otherwise of our stomach for the long fight. In both Iraq and Afghanistan they started to understand that we were unprepared for a fight that might mean we take substantial losses; that if they showed they were prepared to carry on, day in, day out, in territory they knew well, and with a people who had seen so much brutality and oppression over the decades, then they could win, not by superior force or greater resources or a broader appeal, but by dint of perseverance.

In my darker moments, I would consider the parable in which Jesus asks: "Which of you, intending to build a tower, sitteth not down first, and counteth the cost, whether he have sufficient to finish it?" We had counted on a long steady march; we had of course counted on immeasurable difficulties along the way. But we had not counted on the deep grip this extremism could exercise on the imagination, will and way of life of its adherents.

The fact was that even many who were not extremists nevertheless shared the sense that they were justified in fighting us; that this was a battle between the West and the people of Afghanistan. Such an argument was patently false, since the people of Afghanistan had shown in an election what they desired. I tried to counter it by constructing a broad strategy based on values that required soft as well as hard power.

In my conference speech of 2001, I set out what I thought could and should be a new order of things. I drew a historical parallel with the defeat of revolutionary Communism. Military strength played its part, of course—if the Soviet Union had not understood that its might would be confronted with our might, it could have triumphed despite what was right—but ultimately it was defeated by the strength of an idea: human freedom. In time, people saw Soviet Communist regimes for what they were: dictatorships. Communist economies in practice were disasters. Communist societies deprived their people of all that motivates and enriches the human spirit. Along the way our mistakes were manifold, but our insistence on waging a battle was right.

As the twenty-first century opened, those battles for political ideological supremacy had fallen away. Even in China—socialism with Chinese characteristics—the system had become a balance between market and state. Other than in North Korea, the collapse of the Berlin Wall had indeed ushered in a new era.

Now we were confronted with a new battle—one about culture and religion more than politics per se, yet the route to victory was, in my judgement, the same: stand up militarily, but realise that the way to defeat a bad idea is with a better one. I thought we had to provide a comprehensive strategy for changing the world and in doing so exhibit the values that, at our best, we believe in and act upon.

Western nations have many faults, but as I always used to say, there's a simple test of a country: are people trying to get into it or get out of it? On the whole, immigration not emigration was our problem. In the final analysis the people were the boss, not the politicians. We also stood for justice; so I set out how, as part of this broader fight, we had to show our determination on Middle East peace, our concern for Africa—"a scar on the conscience of the world"—and our commitment to the environment. We had to demonstrate, in sum, that what we wanted for ourselves, we wanted for all.

The premise of my speech was the world's defining characteristic of interdependence.

Round the world, 11 September is bringing governments and people to reflect, consider and change. And in this process, amidst all the talk of war and action, there is another dimension appearing. There is a coming together. The power of community is asserting itself. We are realising how fragile are our frontiers in the face of the world's new challenges.

Today conflicts rarely stay within national boundaries. Today a tremor in one financial market is repeated in the markets of the world. Today confidence is global; either its presence or its absence. Today the threat is chaos; because for people with work to do, family life to balance, mortgages to pay, careers to further, pensions to provide, the yearning is for order and stability and if it doesn't exist elsewhere, it is unlikely to exist here. I have long believed this interdependence defines the new world we live in.

I set out the need for concerted action across the range of international issues and described the challenges of globalisation. I then said:

The issue is not how to stop globalisation. The issue is how we use the power of community to combine it with justice. If globalisation works only for the benefit of the few, then it will fail and will deserve to fail. But if we follow the principles that have served us so well at home—that power, wealth and opportunity must be in the hands of the many, not the few—if we make that our guiding light for the global economy, then it will be a force for good and an international movement that we should take pride in leading. Because the alternative to globalisation is isolation.

Confronted by this reality, round the world, nations are instinctively drawing together. In Quebec, all the countries of North and South America are deciding to make one huge free trade area, rivalling Europe. In Asia, ASEAN. In Europe, the most integrated grouping of all, we are now fifteen nations, with another twelve countries negotiating to join, and more beyond that. A new relationship between Russia and Europe is beginning.

And will not India and China, each with three times as many citizens as the whole of the EU put together, once their economies have developed sufficiently as they will do, not reconfigure entirely the geopolitics of the world and in our lifetime?

When we act to bring to account those who committed the atrocity of 11 September, we do so not out of bloodlust. We do so because it is just. We do not act against Islam. The true followers of Islam are our brothers and sisters in this struggle. Bin Laden is no more obedient to the proper teaching of the Koran than those crusaders of the twelfth century, who pillaged and murdered, represented the teaching of the Gospel.

It is time the West confronted its ignorance of Islam. Jews, Muslims and Christians are all children of Abraham. This is the moment to bring the faiths closer together in understanding of our common values and heritage, a source of unity and strength.

I also gave a strong defence of America, not just as a nation but as a concept:

America has its faults as a society, as we have ours. But I think of the Union of America born out of the defeat of slavery. I think of its constitution, with its inalienable rights granted to every citizen still a model for the world. I think of a black man, born in poverty, who became chief of their Armed Forces and is now Secretary of State Colin Powell, and I wonder frankly whether such a thing could have happened here. I think of the Statue of Liberty and how many refugees, migrants and the impoverished passed its light and felt that if not for them, for their children, a new world could indeed be theirs. I think of a country where people who do well don't have questions asked about their accent, their class, their beginnings, but have admiration for what they have done and the success they've achieved. I think of those New Yorkers I met, still in shock, but resolute; the firefighters and police, mourning their comrades but still heads held high.

I think of all this and I reflect: yes, America has its faults, but it is a free country, a democracy, it is our ally and some of the reaction to 11 September betrays a hatred of America that shames those that feel it.

So I believe this is a fight for freedom. And I want to make it a fight for justice too. Justice not only to punish the guilty, but justice to bring those same values of democracy and freedom to people round the world.

And I mean: freedom, not only in the narrow sense of personal liberty, but in the broader sense of each individual having the economic and social freedom to develop their potential to the full. That is what community means, founded on the equal worth of all. The starving, the wretched, the dispossessed, the ignorant, those living in want and squalor from the deserts of Northern Africa to the slums of Gaza, to the mountain ranges of Afghanistan: they too are our cause.

This is a moment to seize. The kaleidoscope has been shaken. The pieces are in flux. Soon they will settle again. Before they do, let us reorder this world around us.

Today, humankind has the science and technology to destroy itself or to provide prosperity to all. Yet science can't make that choice for us. Only the moral power of a world acting as a community can. "By the strength of our common endeavour we achieve more together than we can alone" [a quotation from the new Clause IV].

For those people who lost their lives on 11 September and those who mourn them, now is the time for the strength to build that community. Let that be their memorial.

As with all visionary speeches, it attracted both plaudits and sneers. I had written it myself, virtually straight out. There was none of the usual agonising. The redrafts were minimal. I sat in Chequers in the study overlooking the Rose Garden, as the first autumn colours began to appear, and wrote. I remember picking up from the desk a silver-and-gold inkstand that had been a present to Chamberlain in 1937, with a Latin inscription that translates as "To stand on the ancient ways, to see which is the right and the good way, and in that to walk." I felt we were on the eve of a mighty decision about the world's future. I wrote easily because I wrote what I thought.

Looking back, it was extraordinarily idealistic; but it was also a strategy. And it rested on one very important but highly contestable decision.

In the Chicago speech of April 1999 I had already set out a doctrine that put intervention—if necessary, military intervention—at the heart of creating a more just international community of nations. I had enlarged the concept of national interest, arguing that in an interdependent world, our national interest was engaged whenever injustice or danger existed. So I came to this new challenge with what was already a highly developed instinct for the bold approach and for being prepared to intervene rather than let be.

In essence, there are two views of how foreign policy should be conducted. They are often presented as a choice between idealism and realism, but that is unfair to both schools of thought. The idealist believes that a foreign policy driven by principle is the only one that works, because it is the only one that changes and persuades. The realist believes that by realpolitik we save lives and money and conflict, and that is surely worth achieving. They are simply two different analyses of what is effective.

Because it was such a shocking and terrible act, 11 September threw the world's pieces into the air. It was accepted totally as altering our view of the world fundamentally. At that moment, people were completely prepared to intervene radically so that the pieces settled in good order and harmony.

But as time passed, people wondered whether maybe its consequences hadn't been exaggerated; perhaps it really was just a one-off, in which case, the argument developed, should we just try to manage this situation, maybe evolve it over time, but above all tranquillise it? As the mission became more painful and the will of the enemy to keep on fighting grew clearer, such an argument became increasingly attractive. Maybe this extremism could be cauterised. Maybe with a big push on Israel and Palestine, for example, we would evolve out of it. Maybe if we sought a lesser ambition and merely managed world affairs, recognising that different cultures have different ways, we could all get along better. So, they argued, it's not really a "War on Terror"—how unhelpful such intemperate language sounds. This isn't really to do with Islam or indeed religion. The disputes that seemed to be connected are possibly not connected, but local. To bring democracy to these nations is to try to enforce Western ideas on non-Western peoples. It's a form of cultural colonialism born of ignorance. So the argument went.

To which the response of people like myself was that we had been given a warning and we should heed it. You can't categorise al-Qaeda as a simple offshoot of some weird fanatical ideology. In later time, as I studied the issue closer still, I saw the significance of the Iranian Revolution. While it was true that in 2001 Iran was hostile to the Taliban and Saddam, and therefore to al-Qaeda, the hostility was centred on the Shia/Sunni divide, not on the methods or world view of either. The battle was about who would lead a reactionary movement within Islam, not who could construct a progressive movement.

I looked at the storming of Mecca in late 1979 by Sunni extremists, anxious in case the Shia Muslims were stealing a march. It had been put down with total firmness, and the House of Saud had also learned its strength. From then on, there was an increasing disposition to allow religious forces to fashion Saudi society.

I also believed that the answer to one threat was not to conjure up another. I examined how in Afghanistan we had supported what became the Taliban in order to stop the Russians, precisely in the name of managing the situation; how we had armed Saddam to be a brake on Iran; and how in each case the consequence of such "realism" had been simply to create a new, and potentially worse, source of instability.

Above all, though, I conceived of 11 September as making all previous analyses redundant, or at least duty-bound for re-examination. We could no longer presume that countries in which this virus persisted were none of our business. In the choice between a policy of management and a policy of revolution, I had become a revolutionary. No more did I think this situation could be managed safely. It had to be set on a path of fundamental change.

In January 2002, with the memory still present of a happy few days in the sun with the family and baby Leo in Sharm el-Sheikh in Egypt, I visited Bagram airport in Afghanistan. I stepped off the C130 transporter to see that a red carpet had been rolled out. We were warned not to step off it since large parts of the airfield were still mined.

As I came down the steps to be greeted by Karzai, I looked at the assembled guard of honour. They had been hastily put together, their uniforms begged, borrowed or stolen from what appeared to be the armies of the world. The men were thin; the place was a mass of burnt buildings and craters.

As Karzai and I walked down the line inspecting the guard, photographers and cameramen were ahead of us trying to take pictures, clashing with the Afghanistan security detail, who would throw them off the carpet, which they then bounced back onto, like something out of a comedy sketch, the two of us having to react normally with cameras trained on us, as this St. Vitus's Dance was performed in front of us.

"I want you to meet my Cabinet," Hamid said. We walked to a bombed-out building by the edge of the strip, went inside and sat on makeshift benches and plastic garden chairs. One man, introduced to me, I think, as the arts and culture minister, sat quite motionless. He had lost one eye, and the good eye stared at me, not leaving my face for an instant. It never blinked.

They spoke of their hopes and fears. Hamid knew exactly what to say and how to say it. His perfect English, his perfect poise and assurance, lifted my spirits. I came away inspired by their heroic expressions of determination, but daunted by what a few small glimpses of the country's condition had told me.

This would take time. But how long, and how hard it would be, I did not know.

THIRTEEN

IRAQ: COUNTDOWN TO WAR

A s I thought on how to answer the question put to me at the end of my evidence to the Chilcot Inquiry into the Iraq War in January 2010, I felt sick, a mixture of anger and anguish. "Do you have any regrets?" This wasn't a question being asked or answered in the quiet reflections of the soul; not something that could be weighed, considered and explained with profundity and penetrating clarity or even an easy honesty.

It was a headline question. It had to have a headline answer. Answer "yes" and I knew the outcome: "BLAIR APOLOGISES FOR WAR," "AT LAST HE SAYS SORRY." Choose a variant. The impact would be the same. Those who had opposed the war would rejoice; those who had supported it would be dismayed, imagining their support and in some cases their sacrifice had been in vain. Answer "no" and you seem like some callous brute, indifferent to the suffering or perhaps worse, stubbornly resistant, not because of strength but because you know nothing else to do.

So I said I took responsibility, accepting the decision had been mine and avoiding the headline that would have betrayed. However, it was an answer that was incomplete.

The anger was at being put in a position in an inquiry that was supposed to be about lessons learned, but had inevitably turned into a trial of judgement, and even good faith; and in front of some of the families of the fallen, to whom I wanted to reach out, but knew if I did so, the embrace would be immediately misused and misconstrued. But the anger was selfish, trivial—comparatively at any rate—and transient.

The anguish remains. The principal part of that is not selfish. Some of it is, to be sure. Do they really suppose I don't care, don't feel, don't regret with every fibre of my being the loss of those who died? And not just British soldiers but those of other nations, most of all of course the Americans, but also the Japanese and Dutch and Danes and Estonians and Spanish and Italians and all the others of our coalition. And the Iraqis themselves, and not just those who were the casualties of our forces in war, but those who died at the hands of others, whose deaths we failed to prevent. The diplomats, like the wonderful Sergio Vieira de Mello, who gave their lives in a cause they never advocated. The random casualties of the vagaries of war, like Ken Bigley, and the private security guards taken hostage with Peter Moore.

To be indifferent to that would be inhuman, emotionally warped. But it is not that accusation that causes the anguish.

The anguish arises from a sense of sadness that goes beyond conventional description or the stab of compassion you feel on hearing tragic news. Tears, though there have been many, do not encompass it. I feel desperately sorry for them, sorry for the lives cut short, sorry for the families whose bereavement is made worse by the controversy over why their loved ones died, sorry for the utterly unfair selection that the loss should be theirs. Why did it have to be their child, their husband, their family, at that time, in that place, on that journey or mission or appointment?

The reason fate could make that choice derived from my decision. But then there were the myriad chance factors that conspired to bring about the circumstance of each life lost.

The anguish arises from an urgency to act, to commit, not to feel, but to do.

I am now beyond the mere expression of compassion. I feel words of condolence and sympathy to be entirely inadequate. They have died and I, the decision-maker in the circumstances that led to their deaths, still live.

I used the word "responsibility," incomplete though it is, with deliberation.

I can't regret the decision to go to war for the reason I will give. I can say that never did I guess the nightmare that unfolded, and that too is part of the responsibility. But the notion of "responsibility" indicates not a burden discharged but a burden that continues. Regret can seem bound to the past. Responsibility has its present and future tense.

Even out of office, playing now a wholly different role, I am still engaged in the same struggle that gave rise to the events I shall describe. When I say I think about Iraq and Afghanistan and their consequences and their victims every day of my life, it is true; but more than that, I use that reflection to recommit to a sense of purpose in the bigger affair, a business as yet unfinished. I cannot, by any expression of regret, bring to life those who died; but I can dedicate a large part of the life left to me to that wider struggle, to try to charge it with meaning, purpose and resolution, and keep my responsibility intact and functioning, in however small or large a way. I can't say sorry in words; I can only hope to redeem something from the tragedy of death, in the actions of a life, my life, that continues still.

One other thing before I start: many who read this will have disagreed with the decision, maybe strongly; maybe you just can't bring yourself even to debate it now. I am sorry about that too. But for the moment let each of us go back to the beginning and I will try to explain what was going on in my mind.

The trouble with debating Iraq is that, by and large, people have stopped listening to each other. There are probably more "uncommitteds" among the public than generally thought. In my experience, "the people"—as opposed to the players, the commentators, the hangers-on, the aficionados in the narrowly obsessive beltway of politics—have an innate appreciation of the complexity of decision-making. They come to a view instinctively. They are prepared to shift it from time to time. They understand leadership is a hard business. And they have a different process of reasoning from politicians, at once both startlingly superficial and at points more profound. Nowadays they won't think of Iraq much. But if they did, they would remain reasonably open to persuasion.

Not so those who feel strongly and have taken a keen interest. Their minds are made up, and the conventional wisdom—certainly among progressives—has hardened pretty much to granite; and is negative: it was a mistake. It is also, of all the decisions I took, the one that even closest friends disagreed with; indeed, not so much simply disagreed with, but found hard to comprehend. My oldest political friend Geoff Gallop used to say not that he took a different view from me, but: "Just can't understand why you did that, Tony." Many supporters will acknowledge I did it for the correct motives, but still regard it as "the stain" on an otherwise impressive record. And of course those who aren't supporters regard it as final proof of villainy.

I understand entirely why people take this view. The stated purpose of the conflict was to enforce UN resolutions on Saddam's WMD, and we found no WMD after taking control of the country. We thought there was an active WMD programme and there wasn't. The aftermath, following Saddam's removal in May 2003, was bloody, destructive and chaotic. If we had found actual WMD, the view would be different; and if we had ended the conflict in May 2003 and the aftermath had been like Kosovo, the debate would be rather distant and academic. But the former seemed to disintegrate the *casus belli*; and the latter has served to keep the fact and consequence of it constantly in our thoughts.

So that is one reason, and a perfectly comprehensible one, for the conventional wisdom; but there is another reason. Politics today works by reference to paradigms of opinion that are formed, harden fast and then become virtually unchallengeable. People have a short time to reflect and consider; issues are weighed quickly, little care is put into what goes on the scales and so judgements are made with a speed and severity that a more deliberative process would eschew. Once such judgements are made, stories are written that tend to reinforce the judgement. Stories to the contrary are ignored, until eventually to challenge the judgement is deemed almost delusional. Balance is an alien concept in today's world. It wants opinions that are certain and are made fast.

For these purposes, therefore, my task is a modest one: not to persuade the reader of the rightness of the cause, but merely to persuade that such a cause can be made out. It is to open the mind. I have often reflected as to whether I was wrong. I ask you to reflect as to whether I may have been right.

The intelligence on Saddam and WMD turned out to be incorrect. It is said—even I have said—that how this came to be so remains a mystery. Why should Saddam keep the inspectors out for so long when he had nothing to hide? Even when he let them in, why did he obstruct them? Why bring war upon his country to protect a myth? Was it really, to paraphrase the former UN weapons inspector Charles Duelfer, as paradoxical as this: that he thought the U.S. and its allies were bluffing when we threatened force and actually we were sincere; and we thought he genuinely had WMD when actually he was bluffing?

When I went back over all the facts again for the purposes of the Chilcot Inquiry, I reread in full the final Iraq Survey Group Report from 2004, and had greater time to reflect on its purport. Compiled by the U.S./UK team headed by Dr. David Kay and then Charles Duelfer to determine the truth about Saddam and WMD, the report was published in two stages. The first, while David Kay was heading the group, concluded in 2003 that Saddam had no active WMD programme. That took the news headlines, and unsurprisingly led to the view that therefore the intelligence was just plain false, that Saddam had evidently been in compliance with the UN resolutions and that the war was unjustified. The caveats entered by Dr. Kay were largely overlooked, including his assertion that Saddam was possibly a greater threat than we had known, a remark seen at the time as inexplicable, given the primary finding.

The second report, from Charles Duelfer, was not published until September 2004. It received far less attention, yet this was the complete analysis. Under the pressure of the challenges of the time in Iraq, I didn't digest it in full. Furthermore, it was only some years later that Charles Duelfer published his book describing in detail the compilation of the report. For the purposes of the Chilcot Inquiry, I studied both. What had been inexplicable was there explained.

The ISG team under Duelfer had managed to conduct interviews with the key personnel from the regime, the top associates of Saddam. In an extraordinary process lasting some months, an FBI agent, George Piro, also secured interviews with Saddam himself. The team uncovered tapes of meetings that Saddam had had with senior staff at which the WMD programme was discussed. The real story emerged. And it's worth reading.

Essentially, after sanctions were imposed, Saddam's regime became severely constrained. The constraint became even tougher when revelations from Saddam's son-in-law about his continuing interest in development of WMD were broadcast to the world in 1996. (He was later lured back to Iraq and killed.)

Saddam made a tactical decision. From the mid-1990s onwards, Saddam's policy became to remove sanctions at all costs. The active WMD programme was shut down. The material that had not been destroyed by the inspectors in 1991 was disposed of. He knew he could no longer risk producing WMD and trying to conceal them.

However, he retained completely his belief in the strategic importance of WMD to his regime and its survival. He believed that the use of chemical weapons had been vital in repelling the Iranian soldiers who, filled with religious zeal, had thrown themselves in waves against Iraqi forces in the Iran–Iraq War. Only their use had, he thought, compensated for the superior number of Iran's forces. The gassing of the Kurds had delivered not just a military but a psychological blow to their hopes of challenging Saddam, so these weapons had played a pivotal role in suppressing internal dissent. Saddam knew that Iran was acquiring nuclear weapons capability, and believed Israel had that capability already. For him, the acquisition of such nuclear capability would serve his basic purpose: to be the dominant force in the Arab world.

He therefore did indeed conceal or remove any evidence of an active programme for nuclear, chemical or biological weapons. However, what the ISG discovered was that this was merely a tactical decision to put such a programme into abeyance, not a strategic decision to abandon it.

The ISG concluded:

> Saddam wanted to recreate Iraq's WMD capacity—which was essentially destroyed in 1991—after sanctions were removed and Iraq's economy stabilised, but probably with a different mix of capabilities to that which previously existed. Saddam aspired to develop a nuclear capability—in an incremental fashion, irrespective of international pressure and the resulting economic risks—but he intended to focus on ballistic missile and tactical chemical warfare (CW) capabilities.

This conclusion on nuclear weapons was actually endorsed by the Butler Report of July 2004, though that was written prior to the full ISG Report of September 2004. The Butler Report concluded:

> As a result of our Review, and taking into account the evidence which has been found by the ISG and debriefing of Iraqi personnel, we have reached the conclusion that prior to the war the Iraqi regime had the strategic intention of resuming the pursuit of prohibited weapons programmes, including if possible its nuclear weapons programme, when United Nations inspection regimes were relaxed and sanctions were eroded or lifted.

In pursuit of this strategic ambition, Saddam kept together the scientists and technicians necessary to reconstitute such a programme; he imported dual-use goods in breach of the sanctions, and maintained laboratories undisclosed to the UN that could quickly be reactivated for

WMD purposes. These activities were financed by illegal manipulation of the oil-for-food programme in which some oil revenues were allowed in order to buy food and medicine.

According to the senior officials the ISG interviewed, the Iraqi Intelligence Services (IIS) maintained throughout 1991 to 2003 a set of undeclared covert laboratories to research and test various chemicals and poisons. They went on to say:

> ISG has no evidence that IIS Directorate of Criminology (M16) scientists were producing CW or BW agents in these laboratories. However, sources indicate that M16 was planning to produce several CW agents including sulfur mustard, nitrogen mustard, and Sarin.
>
> The existence, function, and purpose of the laboratories were never declared to the UN.
>
> The IIS program included the use of human subjects for testing purposes.

All of this emerges in the interviews conducted by the ISG that were, of course, the sticking point in the Hans Blix inspections between November 2002 and March 2003 (his difficulty in getting access to inspect). They are not evidence that supports the intelligence of an active WMD programme on which we relied. So the true facts are different from those we thought to be true as at March 2003. But the true facts do provide the clearest possible basis to assess that he was indeed a threat and, in particular, that the charge that he was in breach of the UN resolutions was fully correct.

The danger, had we backed off in 2003, is very clear; the UN inspectors led by Blix were never going to get those interviews; they may well have concluded (wrongly) that Saddam had given up his WMD ambitions; sanctions would have been dropped; and it would have been impossibly hard to reapply pressure to a regime that would have been "cleared." Saddam would then have had the intent; the know-how; and, with a rising oil price, enormous purchasing power.

Now, you can dispute many parts of this thesis. Maybe he would have decided he didn't need WMD after all; had he tried to develop them, maybe the international community would have acted; in any event, it could all have taken time. But if you read the ISG Report, the picture that emerges is of a regime whose only constraint was one externally imposed. The nature of it was utterly dark. For example, a small point: the descriptions of the experimentation they conducted on humans for research into biological poisons—admittedly for assassination purposes, not WMD—are indicative.

My point here is not to persuade that we were right to remove him, but only to make those who adhere to the conventional wisdom at least pause and reflect. I don't claim that the thesis is an indisputable one, that had we failed to act in 2003 Saddam would have re-emerged stronger, a competitor to Iran both in respect of WMD and in support of terrorism in the region—the opposite case can be made—but it is surely at least as probable as the alternative thesis, namely that he would have sunk into comfortable, unmenacing obscurity and old age; and his sons, groomed to succeed him, would have reformed.

The same is also true for the moral case against what we did, which, in essence, comes down to the chaos and death that followed Saddam's removal. There is no moral judgement that can or should be based on mathematics: here's the number Saddam killed; here's the number that died after his fall. Such a calculation is necessarily invidious. However, since so much is said about the numbers of Iraqis who died after March 2003, it is at least worth conducting the debate on the best evidence available, not the worst.

To the question "Is Iraq better now than in Saddam's time?," there is really only one sensible answer: of course. The best estimate of those who died under Saddam is as follows:

- Iran–Iraq War, 1980–8: 600,000 to 1.1 million total fatalities from both countries (Anthony Cordesman, *The Lessons of Modern War*, Vol. II, p. 3)
- Anfal Campaign against Kurds, 1988: up to 100,000 Kurdish fatalities; many more injuries and displaced persons (Human Rights Watch, "Genocide in Iraq," 2003)
- 1991 Invasion of Kuwait/Gulf War: 75,000 fatalities (Milton Leitenberg, "Deaths in Wars and Conflicts in the 20th Century" Cornell University, Peace Studies Program)
- 1991 campaigns/reprisals against Shia: 50,000 fatalities (Leitenberg)
- Other political killings over the years: 100,000 or more (Human Rights Watch, "Justice Needed for Iraqi Government Crimes," December 2002)

But this only tells a part of the story. As Saddam came to power in 1979, Iraq was richer than either Portugal or Malaysia. By 2003, 60 per cent of the population was dependent on food aid. Millions were mal-nourished, and millions were in exile. One statistic above all tells us what Saddam's Iraq was like. According to the UN, by 2002 the number of deaths of children under the age of five was 130 per 1,000, a figure worse than that for the Congo. By 2007, as a result of the coalition and then the Iraqi government introducing proper immunisation and nutrition programmes, this figure had fallen to just over 40 per 1,000. The difference equates roughly to 50,000 to 60,000 children's lives saved each and every year.

Before anyone says "Ah, but it was sanctions," it should be remembered that Saddam was free to buy as much food and medicine as he wanted. He chose not to do so, in order falsely to claim it was the West causing the deaths of Iraqi children. In the Kurdish area, despite Saddam and despite sanctions covering them too, the death rate for children was half that of central and southern Iraq.

One third of all Iraqi children in the centre and south of Iraq suffered from chronic malnutrition by 2003. The deaths from diarrhoea and acute respiratory infections were easily preventable. Even in the midst of the war that followed, between 2005 and 2007 malnutrition for the population was reduced to under a quarter of what it was in the era of Saddam.

These were the deaths we never saw; the carnage we never witnessed; the grief that never appeared on our television screens. But they were every bit as real as the tragic loss of life after Saddam was removed.

What was that loss of life? Here, again, "facts" were seized on and rapidly became unassailable. Frequently it will be said that 500,000 or 600,000 died between 2003 and 2009. Once claimed, it just passes into the cuttings and is then repeated.

The origins of this figure lie in the report of the leading medical journal *Lancet* published in October 2004 which purported to be a scientific analysis of deaths in Iraq. The figure they gave—600,000—led the news and became dominant, repeated as fact. Later the methodology on which this report was based was extremely challenged; its figures charged with being inaccurate and misleading; and the assessment made comprehensively questioned by other publications. This got practically zero publicity.

The International Red Cross, who did a detailed examination of all the evidence, concluded that the Iraq Body Count, plus the wealth of data from the Iraq Living Conditions Survey and Family Health Survey, is the most accurate estimate. The Brookings Institution, which compiled its own findings, came to a similar view as the Iraq Body Count (a group which, by the way, was against the war). The figures both came out with are between just over 100,000 and 112,000.

That is 112,000 too many, but a far cry from half a million. However, the additional point is their finding that the majority—almost 70,000—were killed not by coalition forces but in the sectarian killings of 2005–7 that were the work of al-Qaeda and Iran-backed militia.

Again, this is stated not to prove that removing Saddam was therefore better for Iraq than keeping him, but just to put in the balance what Iraq was really like under Saddam, and what it was really like when he went. What it is really like today we will come to.

So this is not just a case of "if we knew then what we know now." On the basis of what we *do* know now, I still believe that leaving Saddam in power was a bigger risk to our security than removing him, and that terrible though the aftermath was, the reality of Saddam and his sons in charge of Iraq would at least arguably be much worse. None of this in any way dismisses the force of the criticism that we failed to foresee the nature of what would follow once Saddam was gone. The planning for the aftermath is a point of fierce debate and I shall come to it. The truth is we did not anticipate the role of al-Qaeda or Iran. Whether we should have is another matter; and if we had anticipated, what we would have done about it is another matter again.

It is for these reasons that I am unable to satisfy the desire even of some of my supporters, who would like me to say: it was a mistake but one made in good faith. Friends opposed to the war think I'm being obstinate; others, less friendly, think I'm delusional. To both I may say: Keep an open mind.

Whereas I must accept the reality of what happened in removing him, those who take a different view must accept there would have been a reality if he and his sons were still in charge of Iraq. Look at the twenty-five-year history of his reign and tell me the next five, ten, fifteen or twenty years would have been better.

However, I am leaping ahead. Let us go back to the time of 2001–3 and begin at the beginning. There are two ways of describing what happened: one by reference to the psychology of the decision-making; the other by reference to the chronology of events. I will begin with the nature of the decision.

First, perhaps by way of a preliminary, we should dismiss the conspiracy theory part of the story. There was no big "lie" about WMD. You can examine the intelligence I had received on various government websites. The Joint Intelligence Committee (JIC) reports were spread over many years, and all assumed an active chemical and biological programme. There were those in the international intelligence community who disputed the extent of the programme, but no one seriously disputed that it existed. UN Resolution 1441 of November 2002, unanimously passed, said as much.

The reason for this was very simple. In 1981, Israel had bombed the nuclear weapons research facility at Tuwaitha near Baghdad, on good evidence that this was part of an active and accelerating programme to acquire nuclear weapons capability. The chemical and biological programme continued. In 1988, as part of the Arabisation policy, to clear Kurds out of the country just north of Baghdad, there were several chemical weapons attacks on Kurdish villages in which 100,000 or more people were killed, including one on Halabja in which several thousand were eliminated in one day.

In March 1990, the *Observer* newspaper journalist Farzad Bazoft was hanged, supposedly for spying on military installations. As part of the ceasefire after the Gulf War following Iraq's invasion of Kuwait, weapons inspectors were put into Iraq in order to locate and destroy their chemical and biological munitions. Concern was less, it has to be said, about their use on the Iraqi population, but more about their potential use in Scud missiles, which had been fired on Israel during the course of the conflict, and the potential, therefore, for their use in wider regional battles.

The weapons inspectors listed the material they found, but also the material they didn't. In a report in January 1999, subsequently much quoted, they said they listed the large amounts of WMD material unaccounted for.

From the outset there had been obstruction. By March 2003, when conflict began, there were no fewer than seventeen separate UN resolutions on the Iraqi refusal to cooperate with the inspectors. In 1998, the inspection team had left in protest. As I said earlier, in December 1998 President Clinton and myself authorised an air attack on Baghdad with the aim of degrading their facilities. It made the point, but no one was sure how effective it had been. The assumption, pretty much universal, was that the programme continued.

I write this not as the justification for the 2003 conflict, but to recall a sense, now stored deep at the back of the memory bank, of what Iraq under Saddam was really like. His government was, internally, a source of appalling brutality and oppression; and externally, a cause of instability and conflict. Some flavour of this can be found in reports from 1999.

The situation of human rights in Iraq is worsening and the repression of civil and political rights continues unabated. The prevailing regime of systematic human rights violations is contrary to Iraq's many international obligations and . . . remains a threat to peace and security in the region. (Interim Report by Max der Stoel, UN Special Rapporteur on Iraq 1991–9, to the 54th Session of the UN General Assembly [UNGA], 14 October 1999)

Gross human rights violations are taking place systematically in Iraq . . . while the Iraqi government has used every opportunity to publicise the suffering of the population under the sanctions regime . . . it has exercised a complete news blackout on the atrocities that its security forces have been committing. (Amnesty International Report, 24 November 1999)

The point is that while none of this without more justifies war, it does underline the absurdity of the notion that Bush effectively stuck a pin in the atlas and decided, inexplicably, to go to Iraq. It is true that what happened in the first Gulf War, when the decision was taken not to go on to Baghdad after having expelled Iraq from Kuwait, influenced U.S. thinking. It did so for a perfectly valid reason: following the March 1991 ceasefire, Saddam engaged in a further bloody suppression of his population in which thousands more died and in which his grip on the country tightened.

Through the oil-for-food programme, the international community had tried to alleviate the suffering of the people. Such a programme was necessary because of the sanctions that remained in place, precisely because of WMD and other concerns over Saddam. But it never really worked; the money was constantly filched by Saddam, his sons and his associates. The result, as I have said, was that the food and medicines often failed to get through.

The issue of oil raises another allegation: that it was all about oil. Although fatuous as an explanation, it gained enormous currency and still has its adherents today. In truth, if oil had been our concern, we could have cut a deal with Saddam in a heartbeat. He would have readily given more in return for the lifting of sanctions and the threat of inspections. After the 2003 conflict, and as part of the UN resolution, we established a UN-administered framework for ensuring that money from oil production went to the Iraqis, and today, for the first time in decades, that money is being used to rebuild Iraqi infrastructure, schools and hospitals; and is one reason why GDP per head in Iraq in 2010 is three times that of Iraq in 2003.

At this point it is perhaps worth dealing with the very serious charge that sanctions were containing Saddam and would have continued to do so, thus eliminating the threat he posed. So, the argument goes, war was unnecessary.

The fact is that by 2001, the existing sanctions framework was disintegrating. It was because of this that discussion began in the UNSC, in mid-2001, for a replacement sanctions policy. Saddam had successfully conned people into believing sanctions were responsible for the appalling plight of his people. Sanctions were being breached. He was taking billions illicitly out of the oil revenues.

The discussion focused on so-called "smart sanctions," which were to be more targeted. The argument that those "smart sanctions" would have constrained Saddam simply doesn't stand up to detailed scrutiny. The "smart sanctions," as originally conceived, depended crucially on the surrounding countries to Iraq changing policy and preventing leakage of illegal goods and services, which was a major factor undermining the original framework. To this end, the initial draft of the new "smart sanctions" policy contained strong prohibitions on such trade and other key restrictions on Saddam.

I doubt the sanctions would have been effective, even with these in place. But without them, there was no chance. As the discussion proceeded, several countries objected to the tougher provisions and they were dropped. In particular, the strong prohibitions on surrounding nations were taken out. As Kenneth Pollack wrote in his book on the subject, *The Threatening Storm: The Case for Invading Iraq*, this left the policy neutered. He said there were seven preconditions for sanctions to work, and concluded that none of them would have happened.

No, right or wrong, we did it for the reasons given, and for the thinking that lay behind those reasons. So: what were they?

But for 11 September, Iraq would not have happened. People sometimes take that as meaning I'm saying Iraq posed the same threat as Afghanistan, i.e. there was a link to al-Qaeda. I'm not. It is correct that some in the U.S. system thought there was such a link. It is also correct that there was strong intelligence that al-Qaeda were allowed into Iraq by Saddam in mid-2002 (with severe consequences later) and that he was certainly prepared to support terrorism, as he did in paying money to families of Palestinian suicide bombers. But the assessment of the threat was not based on Saddam's active sponsorship of terrorism or terrorist groups.

(There is an interesting sidebar to this. It later emerged that al-Zarqawi, the deputy to bin Laden, had come to Iraq in May 2002, had had meetings with senior Iraqis and established a presence there in October 2002. This intelligence has not been withdrawn, by the way. Probably we should have paid more attention to its significance, but we were so keen *not* to make a false claim about al-Qaeda and Saddam that we somewhat understated it, at least on the British side.)

The link with 11 September arose in this way. As I wrote earlier, the real shock of that attack in which 3,000 people died—the worst single terrorist attack in the history of the world—was that it indicated a mind-set on al-Qaeda's part of unlimited destruction, i.e. if it could have been 30,000 or 300,000, the better from their perspective. This was not a targeted terror attack to achieve a definable and realisable political objective; it was a declaration of all-out war in pursuit of a religiously motivated objective. It was therefore of a different order from anything the world had faced before.

At the same time, the issue of WMD had grown. Again, now that history has been rewritten so as to impose the worst possible construct on the action taken, it seems almost as if the whole issue of WMD was a convenient invention to justify a decision already taken. In fact, the issue of proliferation—and not just of nuclear but also of chemical and biological weapons—was a source of growing anxiety even before 11 September. The various conventions and treaties in force were conspicuously lacking in enforceability. The activities of A. Q. Khan, the Pakistani scientist who brought Pakistan to nuclear status, were the subject of a vast amount of behind-the-scenes discussion, debate and concern in the intelligence community. His expertise was alleged to be for sale. We were pretty sure that some countries like Libya had active chemical or biological or nuclear programmes.

After 11 September, the thinking was this: if these terrorist groups could acquire WMD capability, would they use it? On the evidence of 11 September, yes. So how do we shut the trade down? How do we send a sufficiently clear and vivid signal to nations that are developing, or might develop, such capability to desist? How do we make it indisputable that continued defiance of the will of the international community will no longer be tolerated?

In this regard, there grew up a distinction that was neither helpful nor sensible. Often, and most of all in respect of Iraq, people would say: is it regime change you are after, or WMD? The true answer is that though in one sense these are separate questions, in another, of course, the two are connected. If, for example, Iran was a well-governed, democratic nation at ease with the world and was trying to acquire nuclear weapons capability, our attitude would be very different. We would still have concerns and would still oppose it, but the context of risk and threat would be dramatically altered. And the point is if they were democratic, they probably wouldn't be seeking such capability. In other words, the appreciation of the danger is in part governed by the assessment of the regime. In a very profound sense it was in the nature of the Saddam regime that the ambitions for WMD were to be found, and the risks to be judged.

An example of this muddled thinking is to be found in the constant assertion that whereas the U.S. had a policy of regime change, the UK had a policy to do with WMD. Therefore, it is said, we were on different sides of the argument and eventually the UK was pulled onto the U.S. ground.

It is instructive to read the Iraq Liberation Act of 1998 passed by President Clinton. It was then that U.S. policy became regime change, but it did so—as the Act makes clear—because of the WMD issue and Saddam's breach of UN resolutions. It wasn't to do with the moral case against Saddam; it was precisely to do with the WMD threat, and arose out of his defiance of the will of the international community.

Therefore, as the impact of 11 September reverberated around the world, and I as a leader contemplated the future potential for risk, the possibility of terrorists acquiring WMD was at the forefront of my mind.

It was true that, in certain respects, you could say that groups like al-Qaeda and regimes like that of Saddam's were on opposite sides. Al-Qaeda was aiming at governments, and often those in the Arab world. Governments—and especially dictatorships—inherently dislike and distrust those who operate outside their influence. Fanaticism disturbs those who rule through order imposed with an iron fist. All of this was true, and remains true.

But I thought I could see something deeper, that at a certain level down beneath the surface there was an alliance taking shape between rogue states and terrorist groups. There was a common enemy: the West and its allies in the Arab and Muslim world. They shared a fear of Western culture, attitudes and thought. Rightly, as the adoption of such thought was a material threat to them. There was a reason why Saddam of all the Arab leaders was so vociferous in opposition to the Saudi peace initiative, launched with much courage by the then Crown Prince Abdullah in 2002. Peace between Israel and Palestine was a threat to all those of an extremist hue, as it is today. It would mean coexistence. To groups like al-Qaeda, this was anathema. To regimes like Saddam's, it was a threat. A calm region, on a path to change, would not be an easy region for the likes of him or his sons.

This sharing of a common enemy was buttressed by a common set of attitudes: indifference to human life; the justification of mass killing to achieve ends abhorrent to most people; and a willingness to involve religion and the history of Islam in pursuit of such ends.

Would someone like Saddam want al-Qaeda to be powerful inside Iraq? Absolutely not. Would he be prepared to use them outside Iraq? Very possibly. Was there a real risk of proliferation, not only from Iraq but elsewhere, leeching into terrorist groups which would not be averse to using WMD? I certainly thought so.

Actually, I still think so. How many times did I hear, in respect of the Iranian government, people tell me that they, as Shia, would never forge an alliance with Sunni groups in the Middle East? But where they conceive it serves a tactical purpose, they do—because they share with those groups an interest in instability and a passionate aversion to "Western" values, which they rightly see as a long-term threat to their grip on power.

I also felt that the Middle East should be viewed as a region whose problems were ultimately interlinked and whose basic challenge was very simple: it was urgently in need of modernisation. It was an alarming melange of toxic ingredients: a wrong-headed view of the future; a narrative about Islam that was at best inadequate and at worst dangerous; and governed by regimes that could be allies of the West but be otherwise under immense internal strain. The leaders were often well intentioned, but presiding over systems that were inherently and deeply unsustainable. So the leaders would be open to the West, but their societies would not be. The discourse between leaders in that world and in ours could agree on the need to root out extremism, but the discourse on their streets would frequently represent that extremism.

This was exemplified by the attitude to Israel. At leadership level, though highly critical, and sometimes with good cause, of Israeli governments, the leaders basically wanted peace. What had been used as a rallying cry was now an irritant, and moreover a source of internal disaffection. Whereas at one time they wanted to use the issue, now they just wanted it solved, out of the way, off the agenda. And though back then Iran was perceived as less of a threat (a point they would make against the Iraq War, of which more later), there was even at that time a growing anxiety about Iranian influence and intention. They might dislike Israel, but they never feared it. Iran was a different order of worry altogether.

But, as even a cursory reading of local Arab press would indicate, at street level and among the educated commentariat, Israel was hated. It became a means of siphoning off the demand for change inside, by focusing political energy and commitment to an external cause, an injustice not just to Palestinians but to Muslims everywhere, a vital and persistent proof that the West was inimical to Islamic interests and to Islam itself.

As I have argued before, the most combustible combination politics knows is a people faced with a choice between an undemocratic government with the right idea, and a popular movement with the wrong one. That choice was there in abundance in the region and beyond. In the case of Saddam, this was almost inverted, which meant that his influence within the region was both poisonous and regressive to those who, like many of the Gulf states, wanted desperately to take their people on a journey to the future.

I looked at the region and felt the chances of a steady evolution were not good, and undoubtedly worse if Saddam remained in power. I never quite understood what the term "neocon" really meant. To my bemusement, people would say: It means the imposition of democracy and freedom, which I thought odd as a characterisation of "conservative." But what it actually was, on analysis, was a view that evolution was impossible, that the region needed a fundamental reordering.

George Bush's State of the Union address in January 2002 was famous for its "axis of evil" remark, linking Iran, Iraq, Syria and North Korea. It indicated that America was set on changing the world, not just leading it; and, as Afghanistan had shown, if necessary by force.

From my perspective, there were two drawbacks with the way the thesis was expressed by its supporters. The first was that (and this is less a criticism of George, who was always wary of the term) by wrapping it in partisan language—"neocon"—it caused obvious problems for those from the progressive wing of politics, like me. Second, as I said in my September 2001 conference speech (and like a broken record thereafter), I believed that resolution of the Palestinian issue was of essential

strategic importance to resolving this wider struggle. It hadn't caused
the extremism, but resolving it would enormously transform the battle
lines in defeating it.

However, leaving those problems aside, I had reached the same conclusion from a progressive standpoint as George had from a conservative
one. The region needed a fundamental change. And this change was to
be of a different character. In the 1980s we had armed Saddam as we had
the mujahideen in Afghanistan, so as to thwart Iran in the one case and
the Soviet Union in the other. It was a tactical move but a strategic mistake. This time, we would bring democracy and freedom. We would
hand power to the people. We would help them build a better future.
We would bring not a different set of masters, but the chance to be the
masters, as our people are of us.

And hadn't we shown that such idealism was indeed achievable? In
Afghanistan they were preparing for their first election, and the Taliban
at that time were seemingly banished. In my first term, we had toppled
Milosevic and changed the face of the Balkans. In Sierra Leone, we had
saved and then secured democracy after the ravages of the diamond
wars. We had the military might of America, not to say that of Britain
and others. There was no way Saddam could resist: he would lose, or he
would go voluntarily, in the knowledge that the alternative was invol-
untary removal.

So if there was a message to be sent about defiance of the international community, it should be sent to Iraq. If there was a regime
whose detestable nature and penchant for conflict was clear, it was Saddam's. If there was a people in need of liberation, it was surely the Iraqi
people.

It didn't turn out like that. Precisely because the roots of this wider
struggle were deep, precisely because it was a visceral life-or-death battle between modernisers and reactionaries, precisely because what
was—and is—at stake was no less than the whole future of Islam—the
nature of its faith, its narrative about itself, and its sense of its place in
the twenty-first century—precisely because of all this, there was no way
the forces opposed to modernisation, and therefore to us, were going to
relinquish their territory easily. They were going to fight as if their survival depended on it, because it did and it does. Let the values of
democracy put down their own roots; let Western-funded development
help the people prosper; get people right in the heart of the Arab world
to see the benefits of a modern approach to work, leisure and life, and

the narrative about the West as enemies, as infidels, would collapse and be seen as the self-serving nonsense that it is.

And they were going to fight using the one weapon almost impossible for any government, even one in a strong tradition of government, to handle: terrorism. The truth is that the insurgency among Sunni groups, albeit with some high-visibility terror attacks thrown in, was disruptive but manageable. What precipitated the deluge and very nearly broke the country apart were the al-Qaeda-led attacks of indiscriminate terror in markets, shopping malls and even mosques, killing large numbers of ordinary civilians and spreading fear and panic; complete with highly discriminate attacks focused specifically on Shia places of worship and holy sites and on the Shia population itself that were designed to fan— and did fan—the flames of sectarianism.

On its own, even that could have been defeated. But what lent it devastating force was that terror in combination with the steady build-up of Iranian influence among extremist Shia groups, and then finally with al-Qaeda, whose use of terror and then improvised explosive devices (IEDs) against UK, U.S. and other forces, led to the draining of support for the whole venture. We may have begun fighting Saddam; we ended fighting the same forces of reaction we are fighting everywhere in the region, beyond it and even on our own streets.

In other words, left to itself, the country could have just about managed. What made the task all the harder, occasionally verging on the impossible, were the activities of the outside influences, hell-bent on chaos and destruction. Both al-Qaeda and Iran knew what was at stake in Iraq. Neither was going to let the nation stabilise without a fight, and as our will weakened, theirs grew. It was then only through Prime Minister Nouri Maliki showing (frankly unanticipated) leadership qualities—and the Bush decision to surge—that the balance of will to win was shifted back towards the forces of democracy and modernisation.

It had been hard, harder than anyone foresaw. The problem, however, with the line that the aftermath "proves" that the removal of Saddam was wrong is that it involves an acceptance of something that, on reflection, we should find unacceptable. We remove Saddam. The people are given the chance of a UN-sponsored democratic process and a large sum of cash to rebuild their country. They want to take it and show that desire in an election. However, the removal of Saddam provides the opportunity for terrorist and anti-democratic forces to disrupt the country. This causes a bloody war. Therefore, the argument goes, leave Saddam in place. Thus the Iraqis, a bit like the Afghans, are presented with a choice: the brutal dictator they have, or being overrun by terrorists who will impose their own dictatorship. So they can have a secular tyranny or a religious one.

As one Iraqi put it to me on my visit to Baghdad shortly before leaving office: "So you're saying [meaning the Western critics]: We can have Saddam or rule by terrorist; but we can't have what you have? Surely we had to defeat Saddam; now we must defeat terror. But there must be a better choice for our future."

The trouble is that the enemy we are fighting in Iraq and Afghanistan have discovered one very important facet of the modern Western psyche: we want our battles short and successful. If they turn out to be bloody, protracted and uncertain, our will weakens. In particular, the loss of our soldiers demoralises and depresses us. Instead of provoking feelings of anger, determination or even revenge, it arouses a sense of the pain not being worth it, of a battle that is too much, too heavy, too laden with grief. And of course in the media age of today, it is played out in real time, in real life—and in real life, war has never, not from first to last, been anything other than horrible. Ironically, the last to lose heart are the warriors themselves, the soldiers who joined the army as volunteers and who want an army prepared to fight. But the public tires long before, emotionally exhausted and psychologically unnerved. The result in Iraq was that as time wore on, there was a fatal sagging of the will that was really only restored by the surge and the Iraqis' determination to avoid the abyss.

The fact is, in Iraq, there were two conflicts: a relatively short one to remove Saddam, and a prolonged one to rid the aftermath of the destabilising plague of terror. It was in that second conflict that horrendous numbers of casualties were suffered, both of innocent Muslim Iraqi civilians and of U.S., UK and other Allied soldiers. But to have conceded to such often externally inspired and guided terror would have been a disastrous setback for the wider struggle.

So the argument raged fiercely back then and rages fiercely today. History, as ever, will be the final judge. At this point, I don't seek agreement. I seek merely an understanding that the arguments for and against were and remain more balanced than conventional wisdom suggests.

This was not Suez, where in 1956 Britain and France, against America's wishes, sought to topple Nasser and failed. It was not Vietnam, which was a battle fought against a genuine insurgency (though one clearly not universally supported in the country) and where the insurgents won.

Forgotten in all the inevitable controversy over Iraq was the impact on other regimes at the time of the action. In early 2003, Libya began its negotiations to come clean on its nuclear and chemical programmes and eventually yielded them up and destroyed them. In October 2003, Iran, at first shocked by the U.S. action, came back to the negotiating table on its nuclear programme for the first time since August 2002. North Korea came back to the six-party talks demanded by President Bush. The activities of A. Q. Khan were the subject of radical action by the Pakistan government and finally shut down. Proliferators and purveyors of WMD material hastily drew in their horns. The adverse consequences of really hard-line American attitudes are well known, but there were also important and benign consequences. People reckoned Bush was tough enough to do anything, and they took notice. As I knew from private conversations with leaders in the Arab world, their reaction at the time, whatever the public stance, was one of silent approbation for an America that appeared to brook no nonsense from anyone. As the conflict continued and the mood of their street turned, so that approbation changed; but they never wanted a weak U.S. president. They knew their own neighbourhood. And a little bit of fear about what America might do was no bad thing.

The chronology of events leading up to March 2003 was marked by the steady build-up to conflict. The U.S. mindset after 11 September had altered radically and fundamentally. The extremism within Islam, based on a perversion of its truth, had declared war on the U.S. Even more so than those like me on the outside, those inside the American administration were clear: we had to take a wholly new look at the world. States that harboured terrorists or succoured them were potential enemies, as were states engaged in WMD. The possibility of the two coming together—terrorists and so-called "rogue" states developing nuclear, chemical or biological weapons—was too great a risk to contemplate. In a little-noticed move at the 2002 G8, the key nations agreed billions of dollars to protect or eliminate sites of former Soviet states with WMD. Each nation agreed to undertake and did undertake comprehensive anti-terror legislation, tightened money-laundering rules that might be connected with trade in terror or WMD, and bore down on any radical groups fomenting extremism.

At the first meeting with George in February 2001 at Camp David, Iraq was raised in the context of the new sanctions resolution that I described earlier, but there was no great sense of urgency. George was set on building a strong right-wing power base in the U.S., capable of sustaining him through two terms, and was focused especially on education and tax reform. We got on well, but fairly gingerly. Actually, Cherie probably hit it off better with Laura Bush than I did with George at first. I liked Laura immediately—modest, unassuming, but with obvious true strength just beneath the surface. It can't have been easy moving into such a powerful family, and Barbara must have made a formidable mother-in-law (though far more lovable than her public image sometimes suggested). Laura had that inner, quiet belief in herself that gave her a thick carapace of toughness for the ordeals that lay ahead.

George had a great sense of humour, was self-effacing and self-deprecatory in an attractive way, but the fact remained he was conservative and I was progressive. There weren't many social issues we seemed to agree on; and on climate change, we were poles apart, as it were.

It was not my first time at Camp David—I had been there with Bill. But that made it odd too. Last time, Bill and I had been sitting out in the sunshine in February 1998 debating how the centre left could get itself out of its perennial inadequacy of short bursts of power in an otherwise steady line of conservative government. It was exactly the kind of stimulating, intellectual, conceptual conversation that Bill loved, and as ever I would learn constantly, adding my own analysis and always surprised and encouraged by how our thinking converged.

This was not George at all. By the way, this was not because he wasn't smart; he was very smart. One of the most ludicrous caricatures of George is that he was a dumb idiot who stumbled into the presidency. No one stumbles into that job, and the history of American presidential campaigns is littered with the political corpses of those who were supposed to be brilliant but who nonetheless failed because brilliance is not enough. No one who isn't clever could survive that ordeal of the nine-month election duel, which itself usually follows a couple of years of hard graft. It's the same with UK politics, for a different reason: PMQs. An idiot couldn't survive one

session. To survive and hold your head up over a period of time—
let's say a year of being Opposition leader—you have to be clever,
significantly past a basic intellectual threshold, otherwise you will be
eaten alive.

But to succeed in U.S. politics, or that of the UK, you have to
be more than clever. You have to be able to connect and you have to be
able to articulate that connection in plain language. The plainness
of the language then leads people to look past the brainpower
involved. Reagan was clever. Thatcher was clever. And sometimes
the very plainness touches something else: a simplicity that is the
product of a decisive nature. Now that simplicity can be impulsive;
or it can ignore the complexity of the issue; and it can, of course,
sometimes lead to the wrong decision. But it isn't born of dumb-
ness. And you can produce a clarity of decision and action that, in
situations calling for such clarity, is both powerful and beneficial.
There are leaders who agonise too much; who are forever weighing
up; whose consideration of the options becomes an end in itself
and a substitute for clarity of decision. Of course it's good to think
before you act, but the thinking has to be of finite duration and
the action must follow. This is true in and of itself, but it is also
true because when leading a country, or indeed any organisation,
failure to act is an action with consequence. Inaction is a decision
to maintain the status quo. Maintenance of the status quo has its
own result, and usually its own dynamic. So removing Saddam had
enormous consequence. Failure to remove him would not have
been free of consequence. We can debate the nature of such consequence and how profound it would have been, but unquestionably,
there would have been one.

George had immense simplicity in how he saw the world. Right or
wrong, it led to decisive leadership. Now you may disagree strongly
with the decisions, but the opposite also has its problems.

As we sat outside the main building at Camp David, on the balcony
in the February sun, and chatted on a "get to know you" basis, it was
obvious he was a world away from Bill Clinton. But he was also tough
and clear and knew exactly what he wanted.

The visit to Camp David had been a welcome break in my preparations for the 2001 election, which was shortly to be postponed by foot-
and-mouth disease. I had come through a difficult patch following the
fuel-duty protests, I was at least ten points ahead in the polls and feeling
confident. I could tell he was dealing with me in expectation he would

still be dealing with me a year later. So we both wanted to get on with each other.

Camp David is set high up in the woods around Catoctin Mountain Park in over 140 acres. It is a collection of log cabins, very much American-style but well done. The main building houses the president's eating place, a cinema (where, believe it or not, we watched *Meet the Parents*), and various study and entertainment rooms. It is fully equipped. It has its ranch feel to it, but it can very fast transform itself into a theatre of action.

I liked it. There were plenty of grounds to walk around, paths that weaved in and out of the trees. The media were carefully kept outside and allowed in only for press conferences. There was a gym and a chapel, and the food was good. It was a great place to relax and to scheme, and is only a short helicopter ride from the White House lawn, so its attractions are manifest.

In the months that followed that visit—whose chief news value was my choice of casual clothes, as usual not quite right, and an odd comment by George about us using the same brand of toothpaste—I probably thought more about Iraq than he did.

Since the bombing raid on Baghdad in December 1998, there had been on/off military and diplomatic activity aimed at Saddam, though not with much success. Following my re-election in June 2001, there was a protracted discussion between the U.S., UK, French, Germans and Russians about the new sanctions regime to get Saddam to allow UN inspectors back into Iraq. There was an ongoing concern about Russian commercial interests. When Vladimir and I discussed sanctions at the July 2001 Genoa G8 summit, he joked he was all in favour of them, provided we compensated him for the $8 billion that Iraq owed Russia.

The U.S. had plans for a repeat exercise of 1998 if Saddam refused to comply, but essentially the whole context was one of steady but not urgent diplomatic pressure, with myself as perhaps the staunchest advocate of strong action, though even I was not thinking in terms of Saddam's forcible removal.

In July 2001, I even wrote to President Khatami of Iran thanking him for his support for our draft resolution on Iraq. For some time I had been told that Khatami offered a realistic chance of remaking our relationship with Iran and bringing it back into the fold. I was sceptical but willing to try.

In August 2001, U.S. and UK military commanders patrolling the no-fly zones in southern Iraq informed us that the threat to coalition aircraft had increased substantially, and at the very end of August, U.S. F-16 planes were in action over Basra. But none of it made many news headlines.

With the attack on New York and Washington on 11 September 2001, all of this changed. As I explained before, suddenly the whole nature of the security threat altered: from one that was low-level, to one that was of supreme significance; from one that could be dealt with in time, to one that was urgent, immediate, pressing and dominant.

At a stroke, the American attitude shifted. Saddam had been an unwelcome reminder of battles past, a foe that we had beaten but left in place, to the disgruntlement of many. But he had not been perceived of as a threat. Now it was not so much that the direct threat increased, but he became bound up in the U.S. belief that so shocking had been the attack, so serious had been its implications, that the world had to be remade. Countries whose governments were once disliked but tolerated became, overnight, potential enemies, to be confronted, made to change attitude, or made to change government.

Above all, there was a sense of an emergency. In this time, the failure to act was indeed an action with its own consequence and that consequence might be profoundly adverse. At that moment, the fear of history's judgement was not the fear that came with action, but with inaction. How to change the world was a tough challenge to answer; not to answer it, to be paralysed in indecision, was deemed the greater risk, by a large margin.

The immediate question was how to deal with bin Laden, al-Qaeda and the Taliban, but it was obvious that the U.S. was limbering up on the wider issues to do with WMD. In November 2001, President Bush issued a stark general warning to those governments developing WMD; and to Iraq in particular, to let inspectors back in. A cross-party group of senators reminded George in a strongly worded letter in early December 2001, calling for the removal of Saddam, that U.S. policy was regime change.

In January 2002, under pressure, Saddam began the process of reopening negotiations with the UN over weapons inspectors. But his compliance with UN resolutions had been minimal, as the following table compiled for the PLP for discussion at a Cabinet meeting in July 2002 shows.

Table of requirements that Iraq has to meet under various UN Security Council resolutions, and the regime's record of compliance.

Requirement	Is Iraq complying?
UNSCR 661—6 August 1990 Iraq must comply with SCR 660 (leave Kuwait)	37-nation coalition expelled Iraq
Trade embargo on Iraq, except fuel and medicine	No
UNSCR 686—2 March 1991 Iraq must return all stolen Kuwaiti property	No
UNSCR 969—3 April 1991 Iraq must respect the border with Kuwait agreed in 1963	Yes
Iraq must accept destruction, removal or rendering harmless of its WMD	No
Iraq must declare the elements of WMD programmes	No
Iraq must cooperate with UNMOVIC and IAEA inspections	No
Iraq must accept all responsibility for direct damage due to its invasion of Kuwait	No
Iraq must cooperate in accounting for missing Kuwaitis and others missing since the Iraq invasion of Kuwait	No
Iraq must not commit or support international terrorism	No
UNSCR 688—5 April 1991 Iraq must end repression of its civilian population	No
Iraq must allow access to international humanitarian organisations	No
Iraq must cooperate with UN Secretary General on needs of Iraqi civilians	Yes

UNSCR 707—15 August 1991	
Iraq must complete full, final and complete disclosure of its WMD programme	No
Iraq must give UNMOVIC and IAEA unconditional and unrestricted access	No
Iraq must cease any concealment or movement of its WMD	No
Iraq must fully respond to questions or quests from IAEA/UNMOVIC	No
Iraq must allow UNMOVIC/IAEA flights without interference	No
Iraq must halve all nuclear activities other than legitimate use of its isotopes	No
Iraq must provide IAEA/UNMOVIC with any necessary logistical support	No
UNSCR 715—11 October 1991	
Iraq must cooperate with UNMOVIC/IAEA monitoring	No
Iraq must enact penal laws to secure enforcement against WMD in Iraq	No
UNSCR 949—15 October 1994	
Iraq must not use force to threaten its neighbours or UN operations	No
Iraq must not enhance its military capability in southern Iraq	No
UNSCR 1051—27 March 1996	
Iraq must report to IAEA/UNMOVIC shipment of dual-use WMD items	No
UNSCR 1284—17 December 1999	
Iraq must cooperate with UNMOVIC	No
Iraq must cooperate with Tripartite Commission	No
Iraq must cooperate with oil-for-food programme	No

Of course, as ever, as the conspiracy theories abound in this area, it is assumed that the U.S. took a decision to remove Saddam by military force in late 2001, and from then on, war was inevitable. It wasn't. And it's just not how politics works. Or human beings. And in the end human beings take political decisions.

What had happened, as I say, was that the U.S. attitude to risk had been turned upside down. Iraq was now definitely on the agenda. There was a predisposition to believe that Saddam was incorrigible. There was the certainty that he had an ongoing WMD programme. There was a belief that the world would be better off with him out of power. All that is for sure. It was still a long way off a decision. Instead of the tortuous and transparently insincere process he engaged in, had Saddam done what Gaddafi had the sense to do in Libya, the issue may have been resolved. If he had thrown his doors open, condemned instead of supported the attack of 11 September, made it clear that he understood the rules of the game had fundamentally altered, then he would have found an open mind on the other side of his open door. But then probably he wouldn't have been Saddam.

The point is: the decision to confront Saddam flowed in the U.S. mind from 11 September; but the confrontation could in theory have remained and been successful as a diplomatic exercise.

I know because I was talking to George throughout. He may have thought action at some point was necessary, and towards the end of 2002 it all became a lot clearer to him. But in those early and middle months of 2002, it wasn't like that. And, as I will recount, even late in 2002 and early 2003, we could still have avoided a conflict. Of course, now people point to the fact there was military planning as showing that the diplomacy was all a show. Such planning was inevitable and right, not because war was inevitable but because it was an option and that option had to be planned for.

The first time we got to grips with it properly was on my visit to Crawford, George's ranch in Texas, in April 2002. It is pretty much in the middle of nowhere, 1,600 acres with a house and guest house and various outbuildings. As usual, I turned up mob-handed, with Grandma and Leo in tow. It was all very odd. Cherie used to like the family to travel with me, but frankly when I was working, I preferred to be on my own and undistracted, able to concentrate entirely on the matter in hand, not having to worry about Leo feeling bored, Grandma complaining or making sure everyone got on together! So I was never at my best on these mixed business/social occasions, alternately irritable and intense.

However, George and Laura made us incredibly welcome, far beyond normal host duty. The weather, unbelievably and to my chagrin, was quite cold. I had assumed Texas was pretty much sunshine all year round (wrong, I know) and had been looking forward to it after the British winter. It was also rare for me to give up a weekend at home. I tried to keep those free of official functions unless absolutely necessary. However, this was an exception and I figured that the best way to get inside George's mind on this was to do it out of Washington or even Camp David.

From my standpoint, by this time I had resolved in my own mind that removing Saddam would do the world, and most particularly the Iraqi people, a service. Though I knew regime change could not be our policy, I viewed a change with enthusiasm, not dismay. In my Chicago speech of 1999, I had enunciated the new doctrine of a "responsibility to protect," i.e. that a government could not be free grossly to oppress and brutalise its citizens. I had put it into effect in Kosovo and Sierra Leone.

That said, because of the difficulties such an act required, because war should be the last not the first resort, I had come to a firm conclusion that we could only do it on the basis of non-compliance with UN resolutions. Tyrant though he was, Saddam could not be removed on that basis alone.

In later times another myth came to light, based on observations by the then UK ambassador to the U.S., Sir Christopher Meyer. He alleged that while at Crawford, I had pledged "in blood" that I would support America, had signed up for regime change and then articulated it in a speech in Texas the day after.

Actually, he was never present at the Bush meeting; wasn't even in the same building; I made no such commitment—in fact I emphasised the UN route; and my speech in Texas was entirely consistent with my other public pronouncements.

But there it is—the myth, once it has been born, becomes the reality.

However, I was clear about two things. The first was that Saddam had to be made to conform to the UN resolutions, that the years of obstruction and non-cooperation had to end. The second was that Britain had to remain, as a country, "shoulder to shoulder" with America. This is not as crude or unthinking a policy as it sounds. It didn't mean we sacrificed our interest to theirs; or subcontracted out our foreign policy. It meant that the alliance between our two nations was a vital strategic interest and, as far as I was concerned, a vital strategic asset for Britain.

It implied we saw attacks on the U.S. as attacks on us, which I did. It argued for an attitude that did see us genuinely as at war, together, with a common interest in a successful outcome. I believed then, as I do now, that the U.S. could not afford to lose this battle, that our job as an ally who faced a common threat should be with them in their hour of need. I know all this can be made to sound corny or even, as some would have it, self-deceiving in terms of our effect on U.S. decision-making. I was well aware that ultimately the U.S. would take its own decisions in its own interests. But I was also aware that in the new world taking shape around us, Britain and Europe were going to face a much more uncertain future without America. As the defeat of Communism showed—and let's be clear, without America, it would not have been defeated—our alliance with the U.S. mattered. My experience in needing Bill Clinton to act on Kosovo, which he did and which arguably saved the Balkans, had shown that we had recent and not merely historical reasons for knowing our need of America. So when they had need of us, were we really going to refuse; or, even worse, hope they succeeded but could do it without us? I reflected and felt the weight of an alliance and its history, not oppressively but insistently, a call to duty, a call to act, a call to be at their side, not distant from it, when they felt imperilled.

At the press conference in the Crawford school library, with the flags of the U.S. and UK behind us, we delivered a strong message. It was basically: change the regime attitude on WMD inspections, or face the prospect of changing regime.

Behind closed doors, however, our talk was more nuanced. We shared the analysis about the nature of the Saddam government, its risk to security and also the wider problem of the region. My concern then and subsequently was to locate the question of Saddam in the broader context of the Middle East as a region in transition. Even then, though less clearly than today, I saw the disparate issues as essentially part of the same picture. Therefore I made a major part of my pitch to George the issue of the Israel–Palestine peace process. To me this was the indispensable soft-power component to give equilibrium to the hard power that was necessary if Saddam were to be removed.

That process was in a mess. Following the intifada of 2000, there had followed a terrible passage of events with Palestinians engaged in terrorist attacks and severe Israeli retaliation resulting in a vastly increased weight of occupation. The process so near to breakthrough (or so it seemed) at the tail end of the Clinton administration was now in total disrepair. Patching it up and putting it back on track was, for me, utterly crucial to creating the conditions in which the tougher, harder measures could be taken without a revolt on the Arab streets and upset across the Muslim world. Already, just six months after the atrocity of 11 September, the appetite for action was waning and enthusiasm for any sort of military confrontation minimal, to say the least.

Days before leaving for Crawford, I had had a meeting at Chequers with senior army officers. The meeting was not specifically in preparation for Crawford, but to kick around the basic questions about what military action might entail. There had been discussion about whether our aim was focused on WMD or regime change. I had emphasised that the two were linked, and also that it was hard at this point to say that the nature of the WMD threat specific to Iraq had changed demonstrably in the last few years. It was the assessment of risk that had.

The new Chief of Defence Staff, Sir Mike Boyce, a submariner and former navy chief, and Sir Anthony Pigott, a general who had studied the military options, gave a presentation. They warned it could be a bloody fight and take a long time to remove Saddam. The U.S. were engaged in preliminary planning, but it was hard to read where they were going with it. We needed to get alongside that planning and be part of it. Of course, as ever, this presented a dilemma: if you wanted to be part of the planning, you had to be, at least in principle, open to being part of the action. Early on, because I could see that this might have to end with Saddam's forcible removal, I resolved to be part of the planning. From around April, we were then fairly closely involved even in the early stages of U.S. thinking.

None of this meant that war was certain. It wasn't and indeed a constant part of the interaction between George and myself through those months, probably up to around November, was acute anxiety that since we were planning for the possible, that meant, in the media mind, it was inevitable. We had the basic concepts ironed out: Saddam had to comply with UN resolutions and let the inspectors back in; he couldn't, on this occasion, be allowed to mess about—his compliance had to be total; and if he refused, we were going to be in a position where we were capable of removing him. So the diplomacy and the planning proceeded along separate but plainly at certain points connected tracks.

It made domestic politics, however, highly uncomfortable. Naturally people were reading the reports, assuming everything was decided and taking positions accordingly. If we said war was not agreed, they asked if we were planning; if we accepted we were doing some form of planning, that meant war was indeed therefore agreed. The notion of a contingency was too subtle. And, to be fair, many of the noises emanating from parts of the U.S. system did suggest that there was only one direction in which policy should go.

We flew back from Crawford with some really tough thinking to do. I made a statement on the Middle East peace process, following George's commitment to me to re-engage with it. We had the Budget to get settled, on which I was having meetings with Gordon, on the whole reasonably satisfactorily. We had finally agreed a policy on the rise in National Insurance tax, the amount paid by employees to build up an entitlement to certain social security benefits including the state pension, to pay for the NHS.

Around this time, also, and for the first time since we had been in government, relations with the press finally really soured. The frustration of the right wing at the state of the Tory Party was boiling over into ever more personal and vitriolic assaults on me, any passing minister who looked vulnerable and on those who worked closely with me.

We had the extraordinary saga of the Queen Mother's funeral. The Queen Mum had died at the ripe old age of 101. The nation was generally sad at her passing. She had been such a familiar and solid British figure over the decades, much loved and remembered for her stoicism and grit during the war, when she insisted on staying in London through the Blitz.

The arrangements for a big state event such as this are always complicated. She was going to lie in state in Westminster Hall for a week, before the actual funeral service. From my office, Clare Sumner, a civil servant and a lovely, capable and very straight young woman, got in touch with Black Rod, a retired general, about the protocol. For some reason unbeknown to me, there had been an issue over what I did or where I stood or some such (I can't even recall the detail it was so trivial), which had been resolved without any problem, so Clare thought, and she agreed to do exactly as Black Rod wanted. I never even knew of the issue until afterwards.

The *Telegraph*, *Spectator* and the *Mail on Sunday* then ran stories about how I and Alastair (who had known absolutely nothing of it either) had interfered with the Queen Mother's funeral, caused consternation and distress, how disrespectful to muscle in, etc. All complete rubbish. For once, and stupidly, I took it seriously and we decided to go to the Press

Complaints Commission. It was the last time I made that mistake. To be fair, the person who was the full-time executive was perfectly sensible, but of course the PCC panel was made up of the editors. Then we were told that the source was very close to Black Rod. So the PCC felt they couldn't adjudicate. But it left a bitter taste.

Then Steve Byers, who had been a good minister, decided to resign. He had endured weeks of constant battering, being called a liar and a cheat and a villain and the rest, over his refusal to sack his press aide Jo Moore (who had sent an email on 11 September saying it was a good time to "bury" bad news), and various issues to do with the railways. There was absolutely no justification for his resignation but I could tell he had had enough. You have to be superhuman or maybe subhuman to endure it all, with your family reading it and your friends pitying and your enemies crowing, and I could tell he was just shot through. The reshuffle gave me a chance to bring in David Miliband as a minister, barely a year after his election as an MP.

We had a Cabinet meeting in June at which John Prescott launched a scathing attack on Peter Mandelson and others who, he said, were upsetting the balance between New Labour and Old. I hit back pretty hard and said it was a difficult time but that's what government's like and we couldn't, as I think I said at the time, "wet our knickers" every time we hit a rough period.

Anyway, you get the picture: the usual mix of the historic, the transient and the trivial. And throughout, now an insistent and pervasive backdrop, Iraq and what we were going to do about it.

Iraq will be looked back on for many reasons, but one interesting study is around the fact that it was the first war fought on the ground in the new era of transparency and twenty-four-hour media. Literally every day, stories would appear moving the debate this way and that and in line with developing patterns of reporting, always hardening speculation into fact. At times we would not be sure whether we were driving the agenda or being driven by it. On holiday in France in August 2002, I took a call from George, who was equally frustrated by the fact that everyone assumed we had made up our mind and that the march to war was inexorable.

However, in one sense it was not surprising that they felt this way. At a meeting just before the holiday towards the end of July, Mike Boyce made it pretty clear that he thought the U.S. had decided on it, bar a real change of heart by Saddam. Geoff Hoon, then Defence Secretary, described the options—basically for a generated start, i.e. slow build-up;

or a running start, i.e. fast-moving; and also as to where the troops would move in, at that time the preference being for them to come in from the north. So it's impossible not to read the accounts of the meetings during that time without an assumption of a decision already taken.

But here is the difference between everyone else and the final decision-taker. Everyone else can debate and assume; only one person decides. I knew at that moment that George had not decided. He had, as I say, concluded a conceptual framework in which the pivotal concept was that Saddam had to come fully into compliance and disarm, but he had taken no final position on the way to make him.

In late July, I sent George another personal, private note setting out the case for going the UN route; and stressing again the Middle East peace process. David Manning, foreign policy adviser at Number 10, went to Washington, talked it through with Condoleezza Rice, the U.S. National Security Advisor, and then direct with the president. I followed up with another call.

The debate around the UN within the administration was pretty fierce. We agreed to meet after the summer break.

I reflected with the closest team on the different strands of the challenge. If it came to war, how did we do it with least bloodshed? That was the military question. On the basis that we did it, how did we maximise the coalition? That was the UN question. And how did we do it without provoking uproar across the Middle East? That was the Arab question.

When I returned from holiday I did a press conference in Sedgefield. It was strange how I always relaxed there, even in the most unrelaxing moments. I also had my lines clear. I was going to be very tough: we had to deal with Saddam; it was right to do it; we had to send an unvarnished and plain message on WMD to the world.

One other rather fateful decision was taken at that time. Reasonably enough, people wanted to see the evidence on Saddam and WMD. This evidence was contained in intelligence. It was not practice, for obvious reasons, to disclose intelligence. We decided we had to do it. Many times afterwards, I regretted this decision. The "dossier," as it was called, later became the subject of the most vicious recrimination and condemnation. In reality, it was done because we could see no way of refusing it, given the clamour for it. The very unprecedented nature of it was, however, part of the problem. Both opponents and supporters of action against Saddam were urging us to share with the public the intelligence we had.

Two things should be said in retrospect about the dossier. First, contrary to *ex post facto* wisdom, it was considered at the time—September 2002—dull, and not containing anything new. The infamous forty-five-minutes claim—a quote from the 22 September government dossier which said that Iraq could deploy WMDs within forty-five minutes—was taken up by some of the media on the day but not referred to afterwards, and was not even mentioned by me at any time in the future, including in the crucial parliamentary debate on 18 March 2003, which authorised military action. Of the 40,000 written parliamentary questions between September 2002 and the end of May 2003 when the BBC made their broadcast about it, only two asked about the forty-five-minutes issue. Of the 5,000 oral questions, none ever mentioned it. It was not discussed by anyone in the entire debate of 18 March 2003. So the idea we went to war because of this claim is truly fanciful.

Second, it would have been far better to have just published the Joint Intelligence Committee (JIC) reports, i.e. the intelligence reports based on the raw material. We debated this, but understandably the intelligence services felt this was a breach of tradition too far. But had we done so, much grief—as well as many completely unfounded allegations about lying, making up the intelligence, etc.—would have been avoided. Or maybe not . . .

In the light of all the different allegations about the dossier, it is just worth nailing down a few of the myths. The dossier itself was the work of the JIC. They zealously and rightly protected its authorship. What it said, as the four concluded inquiries have now found, was an accurate summary of the material. Neither myself nor Alastair wrote any of it. I wrote the foreword only.

It is said, rightly, that the March 2002 JIC report on Iraq warned that the intelligence on Iraq was "sporadic" and "patchy." What is then omitted is what it went on to say, which was: "But it is clear that Iraq continues to pursue a policy of acquiring WMD and their delivery means." By September 2002, of course, further intelligence had been received. The final report reflected this and was firmer. But then the evidence was greater. Shortly before the dossier, fresh intelligence was received about a mobile production facility that had just been created. This led to the description of Saddam's programme as "growing."

It may be worth dealing with a further issue at this point. There was evidence given to the Chilcot Inquiry that shortly before the outbreak of war, intelligence was received that Saddam might not be able to assemble WMD quickly. This was reported in the media coverage of the inquiry as meaning that, in effect, I was being warned that the threat was less than supposed. Actually, the intelligence was that Saddam had taken measures to conceal his programme, including dismantling and storing certain equipment. The overall impact of the intelligence was not that he had given up on his programme but that he was hiding it from the inspectors. I was specifically told this intelligence confirmed his WMD programme. So, far from being a warning to desist, it confirmed the need to persist.

Anyway, no doubt after a fifth inquiry there will still be calls for more. The truth is we believed, without any doubt at all, that Saddam had an active WMD programme. Given his history, we did so for pretty good reasons. There was no intent to deceive. Indeed, such an intention would have been in any event absurd, since once Saddam was out, the truth would be out also. The ISG Report, as I indicated earlier, explains both why we were in error and also what remained accurate.

On 7 September, prior to the publication of the dossier, we had gone back to Camp David. At this meeting we had one objective: to get George to go down the UN route, i.e. to agree that before any action we would pass a UN resolution and give Saddam a final chance.

This was not an easy sell. The U.S. context, politically, was completely opposite to ours; and the UN did not play well there. The meeting was a little tense, though by then George and I had a really good personal chemistry. In the end, one to one, I got his acceptance, not as a favour but because I think ultimately he bought the idea that this was going to be a whole lot easier if we had a coalition behind us. I said that I really feared the consequences of U.S. unilateral action; or U.S./UK joint action. I had written him a note prior to the meeting setting out my concerns and saying the very unpredictability of the outcome meant that a coalition was wise. We had to try for peace, even if eventually we did go to war. This was not Kosovo or even Afghanistan. It was going to be far tougher.

It's true to say, however, that at that point the downside risk of military action revolved around how easy or hard it would be to remove Saddam, and any humanitarian fallout. There was, of course, also the Sunni/Shia issue, but never at that stage—or indeed until after Saddam's removal—was the true threat perceived: outside interference by al-Qaeda and by Iran. The view of our military and intelligence was that though Saddam did sponsor terrorist groups, there was only hazy evidence of any al-Qaeda link; and after the Iraq–Iran War, with its one million casualties, it was assumed that Iran would be relatively compliant. The issue of the Sunni minority suddenly turned from rulers to ruled was extensively canvassed. But the main question was about Saddam's capability of withstanding a military campaign and about the degree of support he might have. This is highly relevant to debates about the planning for the aftermath.

Once George declared he was in favour of going the UN route, the visit relaxed. Dick Cheney had been there for part of the time, and made it clear he was not for going down the UN route. He was unremittingly hard line.

Dick is the object of so much conspiracy theory that it's virtually impossible to have a rational discussion about him. To those on the left, he is, of course, an uncomplicated figure of loathing. Even for the middle ground, they tend to reach for the garlic and crucifixes. You have to go pretty far right to find Dick's natural constituency.

My take on him was different from that of most people. I thought he had one central insight which was at least worth taking seriously. He believed, in essence, that the U.S. was genuinely at war; that the war was one with terrorists and rogue states that supported them; that it stemmed from a guiding ideology that was a direct threat to America; and that therefore the only way of defeating it was head-on, with maximum American strength, with the object of destroying the ideology and allowing democracy to flourish in its stead. He would have worked through the whole lot, Iraq, Syria, Iran, dealing with all their surrogates in the course of it—Hezbollah, Hamas, etc. In other words, he thought the world had to be made anew, and that after 11 September, it had to be done by force and with urgency. So he was for hard, hard power. No ifs, no buts, no maybes. We're coming after you, so change or be changed.

Of course, this attitude terrified and repelled people. But, as will be obvious from what I have written, I did not think it was as fantastical as conventional wisdom opined. It is one struggle. Our enemy has an ideology. It does threaten us. The ultimate answer is in the spread of democracy and freedom. It is even possible to conceive of this, in different language, as being a progressive position, certainly where removing someone like Saddam was concerned.

My problem with the way he put it and wanted to do it was that the manner of doing it was incomplete. Precisely because the war was based loosely around an ideology, the fight had to be waged and won at the level of ideas and in a way that would appeal not to us, but to those who had fallen or might fall prey to that ideology. In other words, it couldn't be a hard-power strategy alone. It had to encompass more than military might. It had to engage the people out in the Middle East, in the Muslim world, and had to build alliances within that world. This wasn't some namby-pamby peacenikery; it was a critical part of winning. That was why, for example, progress to a Palestinian state was of such huge importance. It wasn't a sideshow; it was central to the main stage on which the struggle was being played out.

Therefore, also, when it came to human rights and prisoner issues, we had to be showing by our actions the strength of our alternative ideas and, however constraining it might be, the truth was that in the reality of modern communications, in an age of information that was transforming the arena of public debate, this was not a weak-minded concession, it was an absolute imperative.

So there was much to be said for his insight, but the methods and messaging assumed the world of the 1980s, not the early twenty-first century.

By the end of September, we had a clear commitment for a fresh UN resolution. This also greatly helped with the concerns of our Attorney General, Peter Goldsmith, about the legality of action without one.

My speech at party conference that year came together with surprising ease. Though I dealt with Iraq and foreign policy, I reserved most of it for a huge push on reform. We were now well into our health, education and crime plans and I felt, at long last, both more confident about the case for them and more comfortable with the ministers fronting them.

A staunch friend as always, Bill Clinton turned up to the conference to spread a bit of stardust and remind them I was progressive and knew well at least one American other than George. He even went out to a Blackpool McDonald's for a burger and fries, much to the amusement, astonishment and bemusement of the sprinkling of late-night diners. He had an endless ability for rapport with ordinary people, liked it, got something from it, felt reinvigorated from it. I could do it but was always a little shamefaced, never sure whether I was intruding or foisting myself on strangers. He would just love it, "shooting the breeze," as if having a McDonald's in Blackpool was what he did every Tuesday night as a matter of course. Kevin Spacey was there too, a really fun guy, who turned up with Bill for Northern night (attended by Northern MPs and Northern Labour Party advocates) and did a brilliant impersonation of him. Also performing was Paul Rodgers, the lead singer of

Free and Bad Company, and so a set of completely bizarre pictures of all of us were taken, with the party activists in awe at the spectacle.

I always reckoned that even the ones who didn't like me (quite a few) or didn't agree with me (a large proportion) still admired the fact I counted, was a big player, was a world and not just a national leader. It's not a reason for doing anything, by the way, but the British, whatever they say, prefer their prime ministers to stand tall internationally. Most foreign leaders wouldn't have turned a head if they wandered down Guildford High Street. The U.S. president, yes. Others, not really, maybe Sarkozy in later times, but probably not Chirac even at the time. However, Brits would want to know that in a French city people would recognise me. Our leaders should stand out, and if not cut a dash, at least make an impact. The problem is as time has gone on and the world has changed, and Britain's relative size and weight have shifted, it becomes harder to do. Not less desirable; just harder.

Again I stress: it's not the reason for acting in Afghanistan and Iraq or anything else, but our alliance with the U.S. gave Britain a huge position. Those who thought our closeness to America was a problem in the rest of the world could not have been further from the mark. On the contrary, it gave us immediate purchase. There was no greater nonsense than that our alliance with the U.S. lost us standing in the world. The opposite is the case. This was true even in the Middle East. It was true in spades in China and India. I remember once debating the pure politics of Iraq with Robin Cook. He said to me: It will be a disaster electorally; remember Wilson and Vietnam—he didn't side with the U.S. I know, I replied, and just remind me of the result of the 1970 election again? I'm not, by the way, commenting on the decision; only the pure politics of it.

In October 2002, we had evidence of the continuing terrorist threat when a nightclub in Bali was bombed, leaving just over two hundred dead, including many tourists, mainly Australian. It was an ugly jolt to any complacency. It was followed by the Moscow theatre hostage attack in which over a hundred died. A little later in February 2003 we had our own scare when we were told of a potential attack on Heathrow. We had the usual emergency meeting. The options included shutting the airport, but I feared that the consequence would be devastating for British industry and the airlines. Instead, I decided to put up a big presence around the airport as a deterrent, including armoured vehicles and heavily armed patrols. It worked, but the press accused us of inventing the whole thing as a pretext for stepping up the "war on terror."

The UN resolution was duly debated and passed in November 2002, and shortly after, the weapons inspectors, led by Hans Blix, were allowed back into Iraq. Hans was a curious fellow. He was smart and capable, and I liked him, but his problem was that he felt the weight of the politics of the inspection. This was quite natural, but in truth he just needed to do his job. If Saddam was in compliance, fine. If not, fine. That was his judgement. But it was ours as to the consequences. Instead, he first said Saddam wasn't complying; but then, as he could see the result of such non-compliance, shifted more to the position that Saddam might comply. And it wasn't clear whether the facts had changed or his appreciation of the political implications. He kept saying, "I have to decide for war or peace," and I kept saying, "You don't. Just tell us your honest assessment." However, to be fair, he was in a pretty impossible position and, as I shall relate, was actually very helpful in a last-ditch attempt to resolve the issue peacefully.

By this time in late 2002, our military were well alongside the U.S. The options were still being canvassed. There were essentially three "packages" for our potential involvement. One was purely logistics support. The second was air and sea, with special forces. The third was for full-on "boots on the ground," i.e. the participation of UK ground forces inside Iraq. Mike Boyce, who had grown in stature and confidence as time went on, was clear that the optimum from the British perspective was package three. He said he would have a real problem with the army if they were not fully involved, and such involvement alone gave us far greater influence in shaping U.S. thinking. This was also my own instinct.

The new year turned and with it a sense we were in the final phase. The inspectors were in. The first Blix Report in mid-January was clear: Saddam was not complying. A further report would come in a month. The UN resolution passed in November had been silent on the need for a further resolution prior to any military action. There were legal debates as to whether it was necessary, and Peter Goldsmith was again anxious about it. The Russians had become negative, and it was perfectly possible a second resolution would be vetoed.

I was still thinking it might be possible to get a second resolution—George was adamant he didn't need one. Jack Straw and others warned me that, without one, I might be unable to survive the expected House of Commons vote.

I was about as isolated as it is possible to be in politics. On the one hand, the U.S. were chafing at the bit and essentially I agreed with their basic thrust: Saddam was a threat, he would never cooperate fully with the international community, and the world, not to say Iraq, would be better off with him out of power. My instinct was with them. Our alliance was with them. I had made a commitment after 11 September to be "shoulder to shoulder." I was determined to fulfil it.

On the other hand, my isolation within Cabinet, let alone the PLP and large parts of media and public opinion, was colossal. And worrying, not because I might go down—in a sense, so what?—but because so much was at stake. War and peace. The struggle against terrorism. The future of our treasured alliance. The reputation of the country and its armed forces. Above all, people's lives. Either way, people's lives, since "peace" would not be peace for those in Iraq under the boot of Saddam.

As I pondered in December 2002 and took a short winter break in January 2003, I tried to work out what was the right thing to do. I was past expediency, past political calculation, past personal introspection. I knew this could be the end politically. I just wanted to know: what is the right thing?

I could see by now, and following the first Blix Report, that barring something unanticipated, the likelihood was war. We could opt out, of that I was sure. Package one was designed with that in mind. George had regularly given me the chance to take it and stay out of the conflict, coming in only for the aftermath. We had many allies by then. Thirteen out of twenty-five EU countries were onside. The coalition would eventually number over thirty different nations. But many were taking the route of avoiding the initial fighting.

I remember that Christmas at Chequers. As ever, there was the massive tree in the Great Hall, the decorations, the festivity done with a ritual and solemnity that time had long made hallowed. My family came, as did Cherie's. The house was busy, bustling and brimful of Christmas spirit. Leaving everyone to take pre-Christmas drinks, I went up to the Long Gallery, my place of quiet reflection, with its ancient books, some dating from the time of Caxton. I sat and thought. What did I truly believe? That Saddam was about to attack Britain or the U.S.? No. That he was a bigger WMD threat than Iran or North Korea or Libya? Not really, though he was the only leader to have used the term. That left alone now, with these inspections ending the same way as the last, he would threaten the stability of the region? Very possibly. That he would leech WMD material or provide help to terrorists? Yes, I could see him doing that. Was it better for his people to be rid of him? For sure. Could it be done without a long and bloody war? You can never be sure of that. Did I want more time? Yes, but to allow me to probe every other way of doing it, rather than because I believed the nature of his regime would ever change. Would a new Iraq help build a new Middle East? I thought that possible.

Did I think that if we drew back now, we would have to deal with him later? That I thought was clear: yes, there was no way this man, with his past, was going to be anything other than a source of instability. At some point, especially if strengthened now, he would be back to his old tricks.

So, in or out? In, I concluded. And if in, better in fully and not partly. I still thought it possible to avoid war. I still thought it possible that other alternatives, diplomatic or through a coup of some sort (there was much private Arab talk of such a thing), could be available to avert conflict. I was determined, at the least, to try to persuade the Americans to get more time. But I had said I would be with them, and if conflict could not be avoided, I would be in with the whole and not half a heart.

If you had told me then that we would not find WMD after we toppled Saddam, and that following his removal there would be six years of conflict as we grappled with the terrorism so cruelly inflicted upon the Iraqi people, would my decision have been different? I ask that question every day. So much bloodshed. So many lives so brutally affected or destroyed. Yes, a new Iraq is now emerging and at last there are signs of hope. But at what cost?

And then I think of leaving him there in power. I remember the stories some of the Iraqis have told me since of what life was really like under Saddam. The killings, the torture, most of all the fear. "You trusted no one except the closest family," I remember one man saying. "No one." In the worst days of 2006 when Basra seemed overrun with militia, I recall asking someone from there if it would not be better if it had never happened. "Are you serious?" he said. "It will take time. Iraq was a broken country. For some, now it's worse. It's true. But no, you have no idea what it was like. And at least our future is in our hands."

But back then, I could not foresee the future; I could only try to navigate my way through the present. In February 2003, a million people marched in London against the war. There had never been a larger demonstration, reminding me of my isolation and the responsibility of the decision I was about to take.

FOURTEEN

RESOLUTION

The weeks in the build-up to military action on 19 March were probably the most difficult in all the ten years of being prime minister. The inspectors were back in Iraq and producing reports, but they were inconclusive. The Blix Report of 27 January 2003 was the first formal report of the inspectors. In his oral briefing of the United Nations Security Council on 9 January, he had said that many outstanding issues were unresolved by the Iraqi declaration in December 2002; and that the information sought by the inspectors had not been forthcoming.

In the 27 January submission, the inspectors made it clear that, in terms of process at least, Iraq had somewhat opened up, but the November 2002 UN resolution had called for cooperation by Saddam to be "immediate, unconditional and active." The submission is important since it provides essential context to understanding the decisions being taken by me and others. Blix said as follows:

> Resolution 687 (1991), like the subsequent resolutions I shall refer to, required cooperation by Iraq but such was often withheld or given grudgingly. Unlike South Africa, which decided on its own to eliminate its nuclear weapons and welcomed inspection as a means of creating confidence in its disarmament, Iraq appears not to have come to a genuine acceptance—not even today—of the disarmament which was demanded of it and which it needs to carry out to win the confidence of the world and to live in peace.

He then went on to describe, in detail, what his current understanding was of the various programmes. This is worth reading since it gives an insight into the difficulty of trying to deal with a regime like that of Saddam.

Chemical weapons

The nerve agent VX is one of the most toxic ever developed.

Iraq has declared that it only produced VX on a pilot scale, just a few tonnes and that the quality was poor and the product unstable. Consequently, it was said that the agent was never weaponised. Iraq said that the small quantity of agent remaining after the Gulf War was unilaterally destroyed in the summer of 1991.

UNMOVIC, however, has information that conflicts with this account. There are indications that Iraq had worked on the problem of purity and stabilisation and that more had been achieved than has been declared. Indeed, even one of the documents provided by Iraq indicates that the purity of the agent, at least in laboratory production, was higher than declared.

There are also indications that the agent was weaponised. In addition, there are questions to be answered concerning the fate of the VX precursor chemicals, which Iraq states were lost during bombing in the Gulf War or were unilaterally destroyed by Iraq.

I would now like to turn to the so-called "Air Force document" that I have discussed with the Council before. This document was originally found by an UNSCOM inspector in a safe in Iraqi Air Force headquarters in 1998 and taken from her by Iraqi minders. It gives an account of the expenditure of bombs, including chemical bombs, by Iraq in the Iraq–Iran War. I am encouraged by the fact that Iraq has now provided this document to UNMOVIC.

The document indicates that 13,000 chemical bombs were dropped by the Iraqi Air Force between 1983 and 1988, while Iraq has declared that 19,500 bombs were consumed during this period. Thus, there is a discrepancy of 6,500 bombs. The amount of chemical agent in these bombs would be in the order of about 1,000 tonnes. In the absence of evidence to the contrary, we must assume that these quantities are now unaccounted for.

The discovery of a number of 122 mm chemical rocket warheads in a bunker at a storage depot 170 km south-west of Baghdad was much publicised. This was a relatively new bunker and therefore the rockets must have been moved there in the past few years, at a time when Iraq should not have had such munitions.

The investigation of these rockets is still proceeding. Iraq states that they were overlooked from 1991 from a batch of some 2,000 that were stored there during the Gulf War. This could be the case. They could also be the tip of a submerged iceberg. The discovery of a few rockets does not resolve but rather points to the issue of several thousands of chemical rockets that are unaccounted for.

The finding of the rockets shows that Iraq needs to make more effort to ensure that its declaration is currently accurate. During my recent discussions in Baghdad, Iraq declared that it would make new efforts in this regard and had set up a committee of investigation. Since then it has reported that it has found a further four chemical rockets at a storage depot in Al Taji.

I might further mention that inspectors have found at another site a laboratory quantity of thiodiglycol, a mustard gas precursor.

Biological weapons

I have mentioned the issue of anthrax to the Council on previous occasions and I come back to it as it is an important one.

Iraq has declared that it produced about 8,500 litres of this biological warfare agent, which it states it unilaterally destroyed in the summer of 1991. Iraq has provided little evidence for this production and no convincing evidence for its destruction.

There are strong indications that Iraq produced more anthrax than it declared, and that at least some of this was retained after the declared destruction date. It might still exist. Either it should be found and be destroyed under UNMOVIC supervision or else convincing evidence should be produced to show that it was, indeed, destroyed in 1991.

As I reported to the Council on 19 December last year, Iraq did not declare a significant quantity, some 650 kg, of bacterial growth media, which was acknowledged as imported in Iraq's submission to the Amorim panel in February 1999. As part of its 7 December 2002 declaration, Iraq resubmitted the Amorim panel document, but the table showing this particular import of media was not included. The absence of this table would appear to be deliberate as the pages of the resubmitted document were renumbered.

In the letter of 24 January to the president of the Council, Iraq's Foreign Minister stated that "all imported quantities of growth media were declared." This is not evidence. I note that the quantity of media involved would suffice to produce, for example, about 5,000 litres of concentrated anthrax.

Missiles

I turn now to the missile sector. There remain significant questions as to whether Iraq retained SCUD-type missiles after the Gulf War. Iraq declared the consumption of a number of SCUD missiles as targets in the development of an anti-ballistic missile defence system during the 1980s. Yet no technical information has been produced about that programme or data on the consumption of the missiles.

There has been a range of developments in the missile field during the past four years presented by Iraq as non-proscribed activities. We are trying to gather a clear understanding of them through inspections and on-site discussions.

Two projects in particular stand out. They are the development of a liquid-fuelled missile named the Al Samoud 2, and a solid propellant missile, called the Al Fatah. Both missiles have been tested to a range in excess of the permitted range of 150 km, with the Al Samoud 2 being tested to a maximum of 183 km and the Al Fatah to 161 km. Some of both types of missiles have already been provided to the Iraqi armed forces even though it is stated that they are still undergoing development.

The Al Samoud's diameter was increased from an earlier version to the present 760 mm. This modification was made despite a 1994 letter from the executive chairman of UNSCOM directing Iraq to limit its missile diameters to less than 600 mm. Furthermore, a November 1997 letter from the executive chairman of UNSCOM to Iraq prohibited the use of engines from certain surface-to-air missiles for the use in ballistic missiles.

During my recent meeting in Baghdad, we were briefed on these two programmes. We were told that the final range for both systems would be less than the permitted maximum range of 150 km.

These missiles might well represent prima facie cases of proscribed systems. The test ranges in excess of 150 km are significant, but some further technical considerations need to be made, before we reach a conclusion on this issue. In the meantime, we have asked Iraq to cease flight tests of both missiles.

In addition, Iraq has refurbished its missile production infrastructure. In particular, Iraq reconstituted a number of casting chambers, which had previously been destroyed under UNSCOM supervision. They had been used in the production of solid-fuel missiles. Whatever missile system these chambers are intended for, they could produce motors for missiles capable of ranges significantly greater than 150 km.

Also associated with these missiles and related developments is the import, which has been taking place during the last few years, of a number of items despite the sanctions, including as late as December 2002. Foremost amongst these is the import of 380 rocket engines which may be used for the Al Samoud 2.

Iraq also declared the recent import of chemicals used in propellants, test instrumentation and guidance and control systems. These items may well be for proscribed purposes. That is yet to be determined. What is clear is that they were illegally brought into Iraq, that is, Iraq or some company in Iraq circumvented the restrictions imposed by various resolutions.

The recent inspection find in the private home of a scientist of a box of some 3,000 pages of documents, much of it relating to the laser enrichment of uranium, support a concern that has long existed that documents might be distributed to the homes of private individuals. This interpretation is refuted by the Iraqi side, which claims that research staff sometimes may bring home papers from their workplaces. On our side, we cannot help but think that the case might not be isolated and that such placement of documents is deliberate to make discovery difficult and to seek to shield documents by placing them in private homes.

Any further sign of the concealment of documents would be serious. The Iraqi side committed itself at our recent talks to encourage persons to accept access also to private sites. There can be no sanctuaries for proscribed items, activities or documents. A denial of prompt access to any site would be a very serious matter.

Find persons to give credible information: a list of personnel

When Iraq claims that tangible evidence in the form of documents is not available, it ought at least to find individuals, engineers, scientists and managers to testify about their experience. Large weapons programmes are moved and managed by people. Interviews with individuals who may have worked in programmes in the past may fill blank spots in our knowledge and understanding. It could also be useful to learn that they are now employed in peaceful sectors. These were the reasons why UNMOVIC asked for a list of such persons, in accordance with Resolution 1441.

Some 400 names for all biological and chemical weapons programmes as well as their missile programmes were provided by the Iraqi side. This can be compared to over 3,500 names of people associated with those past weapons programmes that UNSCOM either interviewed in the 1990s or knew from documents and other sources. At my recent meeting in Baghdad, the Iraqi side committed itself to supplementing the list and some eighty additional names have been provided.

<u>Allow information through credible interviews</u>
In the past, much valuable information came from interviews. There were also cases in which the interviewee was clearly intimidated by the presence of and interruption by Iraqi officials. This was the background of Resolution 1441's provision for a right for UNMOVIC and the IAEA to hold private interviews "in the mode or location" of our choice, in Baghdad or even abroad.

To date, eleven individuals were asked for interviews in Baghdad by us. The replies have invariably been that the individual will only speak at Iraq's monitoring directorate or, at any rate, in the presence of an Iraqi official. This could be due to a wish on the part of the invited to have evidence that they have not said anything that the authorities did not wish them to say. At our recent talks in Baghdad, the Iraqi side committed itself to encourage persons to accept interviews "in private," that is to say alone with us. Despite this, the pattern has not changed. However, we hope that with further encouragement from the authorities, knowledgeable individuals will accept private interviews, in Baghdad or abroad.

I am sorry to quote at such length, but it is critical to understand the context in which WMD were being debated in the run-up to the outbreak of conflict. We the key allies had no doubt that Saddam had an active WMD programme. We had worked really hard to get Resolution 1441 through. There could be no doubt that the only reason for the inspectors being allowed back into Iraq was a threat of military action. The build-up of American forces was likewise the only conceivable reason for what cooperation there was. But that cooperation fell short of what Resolution 1441 demanded. And the history of dealing with Saddam did not exactly lead to belief in his fidelity to the UN.

By this time, UK troops were also being prepared for the possibility of war. Several statements were made to Parliament in January along these lines. I still pinned some considerable hope on getting a diplomatic breakthrough. For me too, the prospect of a second UN resolution was central. We had left unresolved the issue of whether a breach of Resolution 1441 was in and of itself a justification for action. There was a legal dispute about it; but it was swiftly apparent that the law and the politics were inextricably intertwined. If people disagreed with war, they tended to think a second UN resolution specifically and expressly authorising military action was legally necessary; if they agreed with removing Saddam, they didn't. And whether there was such a resolution depended on President Chirac and President Putin agreeing, or at least not vetoing, the new resolution.

At this point, it is perhaps sensible to deal with the issue of the advice of the Attorney General, Peter Goldsmith. Again this has been extensively, indeed exhaustively, canvassed before the Chilcot Inquiry, but again it has become the object of ingrained myth designed to show that the war was plainly illegal, that Peter really thought so and that he was pressured into changing his mind, not for good legal cause but for base political reasons.

It is therefore worth just restating some of the legal ideas and concepts behind the judgement that Peter eventually came to. The previous UN resolution in the early 1990s specifically authorised the use of force to make Saddam comply with the UN inspection regime. In particular, Resolution 678 stated that it:

> authorised Member States to use all necessary means to uphold and implement its Resolution 660 (1990) of 2 August 1990 and all relevant resolutions subsequent to Resolution 660 (1990) and to restore international peace and security in the area.

So the UNSCOM inspections mechanism was established at that time to disarm Saddam, backed by the explicit authorisation of force if he failed to do so. This resolution was still extant. Therefore there was an argument right from the outset that the authority to use force remained in being.

Its revival was the basis for the 1993 and 1998 military action against Saddam, when at that time he was in breach of the UN resolution and effectively threw inspectors out of Iraq. By 2002, Resolution 678 was still in place. But it was felt—and set out in a note to me in March 2002— that because of the passage of time, we should have a fresh UN resolution specifying that Saddam was in breach of the UN resolutions in order for 678 to be the basis of further action. Hence we went down the UN route—i.e. a first UN resolution was a legal necessity.

Resolution 1441 in November 2002 was the fresh UN resolution. It specified Saddam was in breach; it gave him "a final opportunity" to comply; it called for him to give "immediate, unconditional, and unrestricted access" to the inspectors and, unusually, it said that failure to do so would in itself be a "further material breach."

Now it is true that it didn't explicitly state that military action was to follow. But it expressly reaffirmed Resolution 678, and a French/Russian attempt to insert language to the effect that any military action required yet another resolution was rejected. It did call, though, for an assessment to be made by the Council in the event of breach.

So of course a case could be made that a further resolution expressly authorising force was necessary. But it was equally valid to argue that it wasn't; 1441 was clear; and that if there was not in fact full compliance, Saddam was in material breach, 678 still applied and action was lawful.

Again, my purpose here is not to say it was beyond argument; simply to assert, rather, that there was at least as much, if not more, on the side of legality as not.

The truth is that the international community jointly agreed 1441 and then got buyer's remorse once it became clear Saddam was still not really playing ball. As I say, had Saddam taken Gaddafi's decision and really changed, 1441 would have meant no military action. This was accepted by George on several occasions. But Saddam didn't; yet the consequence of that failure was not accepted in the spirit, at any rate, of 1441.

There was, naturally, a spirited debate inside the legal fraternity of the Foreign Office and the Attorney General's department. At first, though Peter thought 1441 shifted the argument considerably, he was still of the view that, to be sure, we should have yet another resolution. It was all about what the UNSC had in mind when passing 1441.

Eventually, when he spoke to Sir Jeremy Greenstock, who had been the ambassador at the UN negotiating 1441, he moved closer; and then after a debate with the U.S. lawyers he was finally persuaded. What persuaded him was the account of the negotiation, and in particular the fact that France and Russia had failed in their attempt to link any military action to a new resolution.

So, of course, there were pros and cons on the legal case but in the end Peter came down in favour of military action being legal, provided it was clear that Saddam was still not giving full compliance. And Blix, for all his ambiguity, was clear on that point even up to the outbreak of hostilities.

However, politically, as well as to put the issue beyond any legal claim to the contrary, a second resolution was certainly desirable. Above all, it would reunite the international community.

Unfortunately, during the course of February, despite my best endeavours—and my God I tried—the division in the international community grew larger, not smaller. Europe was now split down the middle. As I say, thirteen out of the twenty-five members were in favour. The ten new accession countries came out strongly for the U.S. position—and were roundly abused by Jacques Chirac for it! But the "old versus new" Europe paradigm was misleading—Spain and Italy both supported action. Allies of the U.S. outside Europe, such as Japan and South Korea, also rallied. So did many of the applicant countries for NATO. Australia gave unflinching and determined support under John Howard.

But public opinion in many traditionally supportive countries, like Turkey, was strongly anti. Canada decided they couldn't support without a new UN resolution, as did Mexico.

Basically, there were nations for whom the American alliance was a fundamental part of their foreign policy. They tended to back the U.S. Then there were those for whom the alliance was important, but not fundamental. They backed off. As happens in these situations, the dynamic of disagreement then started to fashion new alliances, with France, Germany and Russia, in particular, moving to create an alternative pole of power and influence.

I thought this was highly damaging; but I also understood it was inevitable. They felt as strongly as I did; and they weren't prepared to indulge the U.S., as they saw it. They thought conflict would harm relations between the West and Islam, and of course the more they said this, the more they rather played into that analysis and strengthened it.

For me, the choice still remained the same. I agreed with the basic U.S. analysis of Saddam as a threat; I thought he was a monster; and to break the U.S. partnership in such circumstances, when America's key allies were all rallying round, would in my view then (and now) have done major long-term damage to that relationship.

I had one last throw of the dice, however. The problem which sensible opinion had with it all was the feeling that it was a rush to war. Now, the U.S. position was that this was all very well, but they had close on 250,000 troops down in the region and they couldn't simply wait until a diplomatic dance, which they had fair evidence for thinking would be interminable, was played out. Their position was: Resolution 1441 was a final chance; he didn't take it; if we give him time, we just allow him to mess us around as he has before; he won't reform; we're kidding ourselves if we think he will; so let's go and get the job done.

The inspectors' reports were at best inconclusive; but they certainly weren't evidence of "immediate, unconditional and active compliance." The U.S. was champing at the bit. President Bush was actually losing support by waiting. The international community was split. UK public opinion was split. The party was split. I was between numerous rocks and innumerable hard places.

The strain on everyone around me was almost unbearable. At home in Downing Street, I was a bit like a zombie; eating meals distractedly; not hearing questions the kids asked; trying to keep family life normal but with all of them acutely aware it was all very abnormal, not least because of how I was behaving. I forced myself on occasions to relax and stop working, but the issue was like an incessant throbbing ache that wouldn't go away, wouldn't let you forget it for an instant, and didn't stop reminding you of the necessity of dealing with it.

Gradually I did deal with it. I sat and reasoned it all through. I knew in the final analysis I would be with the U.S., because in my view it was right, morally and strategically. But we should still make a last-ditch attempt for a peaceful solution. I decided to do two things. First, to make the moral case for removing Saddam in response to the protesters' moral case against war. Second, to try one more time to reunite the international community behind a clear basis for action in the event of continuing breach.

On the day of the massive demonstration in London—15 February— I was due to make a speech to the Scottish Labour Party Spring Conference in Glasgow. I didn't sleep well, going over the arguments in my head, but I was determined to make the point that whatever their feelings about the ghastly reality of conflict, people should not be able to hide from the ghastly reality of Saddam continuing in power. In my hotel in Edinburgh (where we were staying for security reasons) I sat and worked from the early hours.

The Caledonian is a wonderful old hotel situated at the end of

Princes Street. From the suite I could see Arthur's Seat rising up behind Edinburgh Castle, that magnificent fourteenth-century edifice within whose battlements the Tattoo takes place each summer, where the pipes and drums are the musical backdrop to a display of ancient Scottish military might. I used to go as a teenager while still at Fettes, even though it was during the school holidays. Somehow, looking out of the hotel window at the rock and the castle and all the familiar sights of Edinburgh, my mind settled as it needed to in order that I write this speech.

The conference centre in Glasgow was ringed with security. The protesters were out in force. My speech was heard respectfully by the party members. Actually, people were interested in the argument. When I came to the core of the speech, I described the case in these terms:

> The moral case against war has a moral answer: it is the moral case for removing Saddam. It is not the reason we act. That must be according to the United Nations mandate on weapons of mass destruction. But it is the reason, frankly, why if we do have to act, we should do so with a clear conscience.
>
> Yes, there are consequences of war. If we remove Saddam by force, people will die and some will be innocent. And we must live with the consequences of our actions, even the unintended ones. But there are also consequences of "stop the war."
>
> If I took that advice and did not insist on disarmament, yes there would be no war—but there would still be Saddam. Many of the people marching will say they hate Saddam, but the consequences of taking their advice is that he stays in charge of Iraq, ruling the Iraqi people. A country that in 1978, the year before he seized power, was richer than Malaysia or Portugal. A country where, today, 130 out of every 1,000 Iraqi children die before the age of five—70 per cent of these deaths are from diarrhoea and respiratory infections that are easily preventable. Where almost a third of children born in the centre and south of Iraq have chronic malnutrition. Where 60 per cent of the people depend on food aid. Where half the population of rural areas have no safe water.
>
> Where every year and now, as we speak, tens of thousands of political prisoners languish in appalling conditions in Saddam's jails and are routinely executed. Where in the past fifteen years over 150,000 Shia Muslims in southern Iraq and Muslim Kurds in northern Iraq have been

butchered; with up to four million Iraqis in exile round the world, including 350,000 now in Britain.

This isn't a regime with weapons of mass destruction that is otherwise benign. This is a regime that contravenes every single principle or value anyone of our politics believes in. There will be no march for the victims of Saddam, no protests about the thousands of children who die needlessly every year under his rule, no righteous anger over the torture chambers which if he is left in power will be left in being.

The succeeding days were a whirl of diplomatic activity, speeches, press conferences and phone calls. I was now running on pure adrenalin, utterly focused, clear in my own mind and watching as other leaders came to their final decisions. Some broke in favour of the U.S.; some against; some broke for cover. It was an agonising time for practically everyone. The stakes were high, as high as anyone could remember. George was clear: bar something extraordinary and unforeseen, America was going to remove Saddam. The whole might of the U.S. armed forces was mustered around Iraq.

The irony, as I pointed out to George, was that as American intentions became more plain, so of course the attitude of Saddam shifted to more cooperation. This was reflected in the Blix Report of 14 February. Just as that of January had pointed to a breach of Resolution 1441, so the report of February pointed towards greater compliance. But it pays to reread the report now. It was clear that compliance was stepped up significantly as the prospect of military action became more real, but it was also clear that the problem was unlikely to be resolved unless those running Iraq had a genuine and not transitory change of heart. The report described the finding of imported material for longer-range missiles in breach of UN resolutions; the difficulties of tracking down the anthrax and VX nerve agent, without greater Iraqi cooperation; and it concluded: "If Iraq had provided the necessary cooperation in 1991, the phase of disarmament—under Resolution 687 (1991)—could have been short and a decade of sanctions could have been avoided. Today, three months after the adoption of Resolution 1441 (2002), the period of disarmament through inspection could still be short, if 'immediate, active and unconditional cooperation' with UNMOVIC and the IAEA were to be forthcoming." They were hopeful that Iraq could be disarmed; but the report still concluded compliance had yet to conform to the requirement of the UN resolution of three months before.

Even in his report to the UN on 7 March, here is what Hans Blix said about Iraq's cooperation. Having stated that it was increasing, which, as he put it in somewhat of an understatement, "may well be due to outside pressure," he then addressed the matter of interviews and documents:

> It is obvious that, while the numerous initiatives, which are now taken by the Iraqi side with a view to resolving some long-standing open disarmament issues, can be seen as "active," or even "proactive," these initiatives 3–4 months into the new resolution cannot be said to constitute "immediate" cooperation.

Most of all, on the crucial matter of interviews, Blix was never going to get cooperation. That only came after March 2003 with the ISG. So though both we and Blix wanted more time, it is highly doubtful that it would have yielded anything other than the (wrong) conclusion that because Saddam had no active WMD programme, therefore he was not a threat.

This issue of interviews was absolutely of the essence. In the end it was how the ISG got to the truth of the whole business. The reality was that he was never going to allow his top people to spill the beans. In December 2002, after Blix and UNMOVIC entered Iraq, we had intelligence (and this remains valid) of Saddam calling his key people working on weapons together and telling them anyone who cooperated with interviews outside of Iraq would be treated as an enemy agent. Later, in 2004, the ISG uncovered evidence of a meeting of over four hundred scientists chaired by Taha Ramadan, the vice president of Iraq, just before the inspectors returned, in which he warned them of dire consequences if the inspectors found anything that interfered with the lifting of sanctions. Of course the obligation under 1441 was just the opposite: to disclose anything relevant to the inspections. The ISG also found that once inspections resumed, foreign experts were hidden from the inspectors.

So in hindsight, my effort was probably futile in any event, although at the time I thought interviews might indeed yield something.

But as one ambiguous report succeeded another, opinion polarised further.

Public opinion in most of Europe was pretty fiercely against. In Spain, José María Aznar told me that there was only 4 per cent approval for military action. I told him that was roughly the number you would get in a poll of people who believed Elvis was still alive. But he was a tough guy and was going to stay firm with America. He believed, like me, that the prospect of a link between WMD proliferation and terrorist groups was too real to be countenanced; and now was the moment to take a stand with the one regime, Saddam's, that had used WMD.

But he also, like me, thought it critical, if at all possible, to get a fresh UN resolution authorising action. Jack Straw, Hilary Coffman, Sally Morgan, all those closest to me were advising that without a UN resolution specifically agreeing military action, the politics was going to be difficult and possibly terminal. I asked Alastair what he thought my chances were of having to resign. "Around twenty per cent," he said. "More like thirty per cent," I replied, "and rising."

Cabinet meetings were regular and on the whole supportive. Robin was clearly manoeuvring for the exit, but doing it, to be fair, with transparency and no ill intent (at that time) towards me personally.

Clare was being her usual self. One of the most bizarre things said about the build-up to war is that it was a kind of one-man mission, discussed with a few special advisers on the famous sofa in the den, with the Cabinet excluded. Actually, it was *the* topic at virtually every Cabinet meeting for nigh on six months, with not just me but Jack and Geoff Hoon briefing extensively, and everyone not just having the right to have their say, but saying it.

It was also the only military action expressly agreed in advance by the House of Commons. The Opposition leaders were briefed throughout and the intelligence and military chiefs made available to them.

Both Opposition leaders behaved honourably and decently. Charles Kennedy was going to be anti-war, that was clear, but he conducted himself in a sensible and friendly fashion and I think understood that I was also in a difficult position.

Iain Duncan Smith had long been an advocate of taking on Saddam. His view was that Saddam was a threat, he would never change and he had to be confronted. He had written a very powerful pamphlet on the issue in early 2002. Like the Thatcherite ex-ministers and followers, he was Eurosceptic but passionately in favour of the American alliance. He gave solid backing and I was really grateful for it. What's more, unlike many of his colleagues, he wasn't a fair-weather friend, but remained of the same view even when the going got tough.

It was reasonably clear fairly early on that I would need Tory votes to be sure of winning in the House of Commons, and we were already committed to a vote before the action. So I knew I would win the vote itself. But—and it was a big "but"—the Tories were, perfectly justifiably, making it clear that if there was a "no-confidence" motion following the vote on the conflict, then they would side with the rebels. In that case, I would be out. Therefore I had to win well, and in a way that deterred any on my own side taking their opposition as far as agreeing they would vote against the government on a "no-confidence" motion.

On Wednesday 5 March, as France, Germany and Russia issued a joint statement separating themselves from the U.S., Jack came over after PMQs. He was genuinely alarmed and worried about the political fallout. "If you go next Wednesday with Bush and without a second resolution, the only regime change that will be happening is in this room." He said it as a friend and colleague; and he meant it.

I discovered that Andrew Turnbull, who had succeeded Richard Wilson as Cabinet Secretary in September 2002, was quietly looking into the Labour Party rules and what they meant for government in the event of my falling. It would have had to be led by John Prescott and there were a series of bureaucratic consequences that Andrew was trying to work through. He wasn't, by the way, doing it sneakily; he was quite within his rights to investigate all possibilities, and this was certainly one. But when I heard, I laughed a little uneasily and I thought: These really could be the last days in office.

I was going flat out to see if there was any juice left in the diplomatic tank. On 7 March, things got more complex still when Putin made it clear he would veto any second resolution. I knew I had about ten days in which to try to buy some time for the inspectors. I still thought it possible—though the odds were lengthening—that we could get a Saddam capitulation; or, another idea floating around, that we could agree a special blue beret (i.e. UN-backed) inspections force that would effectively take over the disarmament process. Meanwhile, I had come up with my own idea, on which I had been working with Hans Blix and some of the non-aligned countries on the UNSC.

There are five permanent members of the UNSC. Then there are another ten non-permanent members who rotate between the nations. These are drawn mainly from South American or African or Asian nations. Each of the permanent members has a veto. The non-permanent members don't.

My idea was really born out of the essential ambiguity in the UN inspectors' reports that Hans Blix presented. As will be seen, the reports were, as the Americans rightly said, evidence that the November 2002 UN resolution was being breached. Therefore, they said, as a matter of policy and also as a matter of law, military action was justified.

However, it will also have been seen that you could say politically: OK, there has not been full compliance, but there has been some. And it was obvious that the areas of non-compliance could be identified, in particular the failure to allow interviews outside of Iraq, the non-production of relevant documents, the refusal to provide evidence of destruction of the illicit materials, and so on. I conceived of the following idea: that we draw up a document with the UN inspectors, identifying the clusters of unresolved issues; that we spell out, on the back of it, the demands to which Saddam must yield forthwith; and that we give a limited time—seven days—for beginning total compliance, otherwise military action would follow. Blix thought Saddam could do it. I undertook to persuade the U.S. It would be a very hard sell.

Again, interviews were my main point of focus. In this regard, I ended up having a rather troubling series of conversations with Hans Blix. I said to him that we had to take the key people out of Iraq. That was the only way they were going even remotely to dare being honest. He was reluctant. They could be killed, he said, or their families tortured. He didn't feel he could take that responsibility. I was a little exasperated. If they're going to kill them, I used to say, what does that say about Saddam and compliance with 1441? Anyway, in the end he relented.

Those around me had come to the following view: if we put a resolution with such a timeline to the UNSC and it got vetoed, we could live with it, provided we got majority UNSC support. This was now a political not a legal issue.

For the week between 7 and 14 March I had a crazy schedule of calls. Since many of those to whom I was talking were on Eastern Standard Time, I would often be calling into the early hours of the morning. It was indeed a hard sell to George. His system was completely against it. His military were, not unreasonably, fearing that delay gave the enemy time—and time could mean a tougher struggle and more lives lost. This was also troubling my military. We had all sorts of contingency plans in place for what Saddam might do. He might set the oilfields on fire, release chemical or, worse, biological material, or attack Israel. His past record gave us no confidence in his trustworthiness or his humanity.

There was both UK and U.S. intelligence warning previously of this risk.

Nonetheless, I felt it worth a try. Ricardo Lagos, the president of Chile, was an ally, a really smart, sensible man, a progressive politician but with the courage to do tough things. Both he and President Fox of Mexico were in acutely uncomfortable positions: big allies of the U.S., but with their public opinion overwhelmingly against war.

I set out my case for delay in a note to George. We then had a call. It was tricky but I laid it on the line and reluctantly he agreed. We got the document prepared with the Blix people. It had five crucial tests in it. It would, especially on the interviews, have flushed out the regime thoroughly on what they were hiding and on whether they had any good faith.

Chile and Mexico were prepared to go along, but only up to a point. Ricardo made it clear that if there was heavy opposition from France, it would be tough for them to participate in what would then be a token vote, incapable of being passed because of a veto—and what's more a veto not by Russia, but by France.

Unfortunately, the French position had, if anything, got harder, not softer. They were starting to say they would not support military action in any circumstances, irrespective of what the inspectors found. They were clearly enjoying a new and very strong trilateral relationship between themselves, Germany and Russia. It was effectively becoming an alternative pole of power, standing up to and taking on the U.S., and was bringing them some benefits in terms of Muslim and Arab sentiment.

I decided we should table the five tests anyway. We did so in the early hours of Thursday 13 March. They were immediately rejected by France. Jacques Chirac gave a very strong statement saying he would not support military action whatever the circumstances. Dominique de Villepin, at that time Foreign Minister and someone I actually liked but who just disagreed with me on this, also then rejected the tests per se. This was before the Iraqis even responded. Ricardo then explained that, in this case, he couldn't really participate in an obviously futile charade at the UNSC. The UN route was blocked.

Meanwhile, we had resolved our own legal issues.

On 7 March, Peter Goldsmith had submitted his final opinion. As I said earlier he had been over to Washington and had had detailed discussions with the administration lawyers. He set out the arguments for and against and on balance came out in favour. Later, much was made of the "pressure" on Peter to do so. The truth is he was, and is, someone of genuine integrity. He really wanted to be sure. It was difficult. The world is full of lawyers, and on this, every lawyer was having his or her shout. He felt the responsibility keenly, as he should have. There was clearly a case against in law; but there was also a case for. He debated, discussed, reflected and decided. His opinion was balanced. The argument was balanced. He did his job.

He was also one of the few lawyers who, in charge of an administrative function, had real executive capability. The changes Peter made to the role of Director of Public Prosecutions, to the Crown Prosecution Service and to criminal justice made a huge difference to the quality of the system. He put up with my frequently expressed impatience (and not always expressed politely) with the courts over their immigration, terrorism and asylum rulings. He was a stickler for proper process. But within those bounds, he was a radical, with the ability to translate the radicalism into real change.

George and I were due to meet in the Azores on 16 March, partly to bind in Spain and Portugal who were both supportive and both of whose prime ministers were under enormous heat from hostile parliamentary and public opinion. It was clear now that action was inevitable, barring Saddam's voluntary departure. George had agreed to give him an ultimatum to quit. There was no expectation he would, however. Alastair, Jonathan Powell and David Manning were working hard with the Bush team, Condoleezza Rice in particular, to draw up the right statement with the right phrasing.

The mood in the UK continued to be highly volatile. On 11 March, Donald Rumsfeld inadvertently put the cat among the pigeons by suggesting at a press conference that owing to Britain's internal politics, it may be that we shouldn't be part of the initial military action. Some thought he was trying to put the wind up us. It was clear to me that it was just a cock-up. He was actually trying to be helpful. It didn't help, however, and by then the military were absolutely determined, rightly, that they would be part of the action from the outset, and took amiss any sense that we might be in the second rank.

Robin Cook came and said now that it was clear that a second resolution was impossible, he would resign, and perfectly amicably we set about drawing up resignation statements. I understood the importance of the second resolution in terms of political survival and so forth. I confess I always thought it a bit odd in terms of the moral acceptability of the course of action or not. It bestowed more legitimacy, it was true, but whether we got a second resolution or not basically depended on the politics in France and Russia and their calculation of where their political interests lay. We had acted without UN authority in Kosovo. It would have been highly doubtful if we could ever have got UNSC agreement for either Bosnia or Rwanda. I never even thought about it for Sierra Leone. Yet it would be hard to argue that, morally, in each of those situations, we should not have intervened. What's more, if the going got tough, as we have found in Afghanistan, the mere fact of UN authority does not necessarily bind people in.

However, had we got it, of course the politics, at least for a time, would have been far easier. But we didn't and so the choice was clear, as it was for many nations' leaders at that moment: in or out? We could count on roughly thirty to be in the military coalition, but it was plain the U.S. and UK would bear the brunt.

On the morning of 16 March, Jonathan, Alastair, David, myself and other officials got up early and flew to the Azores. It was a slightly surreal event. On the face of it we were still pushing for a political solution. There were some last-minute hopes of an Arab initiative to get Saddam out; or of a Saddam capitulation. George was content to adopt the line that we were going to hold out every last hope for peace. We sat and talked for a while in the strange little waiting room outside the main room where the meeting had taken place. It was at the Lajes airbase and the facilities were basic, as most military airbases are, the rooms functional, the decor pretty plain save for some *azulejos* (Portuguese tiles) on the walls. It was a beautiful island—that much we could see from the flight in—but we saw little of it.

We rehearsed again the main arguments. He was completely calm. He thought we had to send out a message of total clarity to the world: have anything to do with WMD and we were going to come after you. More even than me, he was focused on the possibility of terrorist groups getting hold of WMD material. "I am just not going to be the president on whose watch it happens," he said. "I love my country and these people threaten it by their hatred for us."

It's easy to mock the simplicity of the George Bush view of the world. Some of it does indeed appear Manichaean. On the other hand, the simplicity was born out of a very direct analysis which it was hard to dispute. For all its faults and the limitations natural in any entity containing humanity, America is a great and free country. There's lots of things about the U.S. which I find incompatible with the way we Europeans think about things: guns and capital punishment and the prison system and some of what seems indifference to inner-city poverty, for example. But plenty of Americans also disagree with those things.

None of that should diminish its strength, its appeal or its essential goodness as a nation. I know that "goodness as a nation" sounds odd, but they and we have systems of government and basic rights and freedoms that are "good." Now some nations can't achieve those freedoms yet, but are on their way and will get there. I believe China is such a nation. It has unique problems. It has the world's largest population and more than fifty different ethnic varieties within it. It will take time to develop politically. We should be sensitive to the stresses and strains of that development.

But you look at other nations and you see no sign of benign evolution. You see, instead, power corruptly wielded, a nation held back, people oppressed and a future denied. There is no house on the hill which makes the present struggle worthwhile; just a horizon full of deeper despair as far as the eye can see.

For those people in that bleak wilderness, America does stand out; it does shine; it may not be a house in their land they can aspire to, but it is a house they can see in the distance, and in seeing, know that how they do live is not how they must live.

So when I look back and I reread all the documents and the memories flood back to me of all those agonised and agonising meetings, calls and deliberations, I know that there was never any way Britain was not going to be with the U.S. at that moment, once we went down the UN route and Saddam was in breach. Of course, such a statement is always subject to *in extremis* correction. A crazy act of aggression? No, we would not have supported that. But given the history you couldn't call Saddam a crazy target.

Personally, I have little doubt that at some point we would have to have dealt with him. But throughout I comforted myself, as I put it in the Glasgow speech, that if we were wrong, we would have removed a tyrant; and as a matter of general principle, I was in favour of doing that.

Nonetheless, I was also aware that the very split in international opinion meant that we were absolutely at the mercy of events, and in wars events are usually of the unforeseen and unpleasant kind. So as we left the Azores, I knew the die was cast. I was aware of my isolation, my precarious grip on power, and—stomach-churning thought—my total dependence on things going right, not wrong. What's more, this was the first time I would be committing ground troops to an action to topple a regime where we would be the junior partner, where we would not be in charge of all the arrangements. It is true that in Afghanistan British troops were engaged on the ground, but the initial action was an air campaign. This time we would be fighting Saddam's forces, who had been through two wars themselves, and would be fighting to protect their privileged place in the Iraqi hierarchy.

Above all, as I stared out of the window of the BA plane chartered for the day trip and looked at the coastline of the Azores fading into the distance, I knew lives would end or be altered as a result of this decision. I was calm too, but calm because now my fate was sealed along with the fate of countless others. I was doing what I thought was right. But by God, I wished I wasn't doing it.

We returned. We held an emergency Cabinet on the Monday. Robin had resigned and so didn't attend. I took everyone through the arguments again. I had finally got George to commit to the Road Map, which was of enormous importance to the Middle East peace process. Essentially it provided the framework, as it still does today, for the steps towards peace. It had been resisted by the Israelis (ironically in view of their later strong advocacy of it), and the U.S. system was at best lukewarm, but it was holy writ for the Palestinians, the Arab world and the EU. After much wrangling and debate, we got the U.S. signed up to it and we even got a specific commitment to it in the U.S. ultimatum to Saddam.

Apart from Clare Short, the Cabinet were supportive. All my most loyal people weighed in. As ever on these occasions, John Prescott was a rock. Derry Irvine came in with a very helpful intervention saying that if France had not threatened to veto any resolution authorising action, we could probably have got a second resolution and the problem was that we tried so hard to get a second resolution that people assumed, wrongly, we needed one legally.

Then came 18 March and the debate in the House of Commons. The Bush ultimatum, with our changes all incorporated, was balanced, not bellicose, and strongly supportive of the Iraqi people. And, critically for me, it played up the Middle East peace process. I had worked on my speech—the most important speech I had ever made—late into that night and Tuesday morning. At times like this, I just put my head down to write.

The argument came easily. I went through the history of the perpetual flouting of international law and UN resolutions, the ejection of the inspectors, the military action in 1998. I explained why we couldn't allow this to go on; how after 11 September we had to send out the clearest possible signal that the security paradigm had changed and so should our toleration of rogue regimes that used or developed WMD.

In one passage, which I regretted and almost took out, I made reference to the 1930s and to the almost universal refusal, for a long time, of people to believe Hitler was a threat. I was careful not to conflate Saddam and Hitler and specifically disowned many of the glib comparisons between 2003 and 1933. But I did mention how joyful people had been at Munich when they thought action had been averted.

Now I would put it differently. Actually there *is* a parallel, but it is less about the lead-up to action and more about the general ideology of this extremism based on a perversion of Islam and our attitude to it, and our attitude to the rising threat of fascism. In both cases, there is enormous reluctance to believe we are necessarily in a war. In both cases, our longing for peace blinds us to our enemies' determination to have their way. In both cases, we excuse behaviour on the part of people and states that in other circumstances we would abhor. In both cases, it seems all a bit remote from us and therefore we ask: Why do we need to intervene?

I summarised the basic case in this way:

> Let me tell the House what I know. I know that there are some countries, or groups within countries, that are proliferating and trading in weapons of mass destruction—especially nuclear weapons technology. I know that there are companies, individuals and some former scientists on nuclear weapons programmes who are selling their equipment or expertise. I know that there are several countries—mostly dictatorships with highly repressive regimes—that are desperately trying to acquire chemical weapons, biological weapons or, in particular, nuclear weapons capability. Some of those countries are now a short time away from having a serviceable nuclear weapon. This activity is not diminishing. It is increasing.
>
> We all know that there are terrorist groups now operating in most major countries. Just in the past two years, around twenty different

nations have suffered serious terrorist outrages. Thousands of people—
quite apart from 11 September—have died in them. The purpose of that
terrorism is not just in the violent act; it is in producing terror. It sets out
to inflame, to divide, and to produce consequences of a calamitous
nature. Round the world, it now poisons the chances of political
progress—in the Middle East, in Kashmir, in Chechnya and in Africa.
The removal of the Taliban—yes—dealt it a blow. But it has not gone
away.

Those two threats have, of course, different motives and different origins, but they share one basic common view: they detest the freedom,
democracy and tolerance that are the hallmarks of our way of life. At the
moment, I accept fully that the association between the two is loose—
but it is hardening. The possibility of the two coming together—of terrorist groups in possession of weapons of mass destruction or even of a
so-called dirty radiological bomb—is now, in my judgement, a real and
present danger to Britain and its national security.

Let me explain the dangers. Three kilograms of VX from a rocket
launcher would contaminate 0.25 sq km of a city. Millions of lethal doses
are contained in one litre of anthrax, and 10,000 litres are unaccounted
for. What happened on 11 September has changed the psychology of
America—that is clear—but it should have changed the psychology of the
world.

Of course, Iraq is not the only part of this threat. I have never said that
it was. But it is the test of whether we treat the threat seriously. Faced
with it, the world should unite. The UN should be the focus both of
diplomacy and of action. That is what 1441 said. That was the deal. And
I simply say to the House that to break it now, and to will the ends but
not the means, would do more damage in the long term to the UN than
any other single course that we could pursue. To fall back into the lassi-
tude of the past twelve years; to talk, to discuss, to debate but never to act;
to declare our will but not to enforce it; and to continue with strong language but with weak intentions—that is the worst course imaginable. If
we pursue that course, when the threat returns, from Iraq or elsewhere,
who will then believe us? What price our credibility with the next
tyrant?

I also dealt with the divisions in the international community and
in particular with how I wish Europe had negotiated with the U.S. In
retrospect, I fear this only heightened the fact of my isolation, but it

is interesting to speculate whether with different leadership, a different outcome along the lines I describe could have been achieved.

What we have witnessed is indeed the consequence of Europe and the United States dividing from each other. Not all of Europe—Spain, Italy, Holland, Denmark and Portugal have strongly supported us—and not a majority of Europe if we include, as we should, Europe's new members who will accede next year, all ten of whom have been in strong support of the position of this government. But the paralysis of the UN has been born out of the division that there is.

I want to deal with that in this way. At the heart of that division is the concept of a world in which there are rival poles of power, with the U.S. and its allies in one corner and France, Germany, Russia and their allies in the other. I do not believe that all those nations intend such an outcome, but that is what now faces us. I believe such a vision to be misguided and profoundly dangerous for our world. I know why it arises. There is resentment of U.S. predominance. There is fear of U.S. unilateralism. People ask, "Do the U.S. listen to us and our preoccupations?" And there is perhaps a lack of full understanding of U.S. preoccupations after 11 September. I know all this. But the way to deal with it is not rivalry, but partnership. Partners are not servants, but neither are they rivals. What Europe should have said last September to the United States is this: with one voice it should have said, "We understand your strategic anxiety over terrorism and weapons of mass destruction and we will help you meet it. We will mean what we say in any UN resolution we pass and will back it with action if Saddam fails to disarm voluntarily. However, in return"—Europe should have said—"we ask two things of you: that the U.S. should indeed choose the UN path and you should recognise the fundamental overriding importance of restarting the Middle East peace process, which we will hold you to."

Finally I dealt with the issue of regime change.

I have never put the justification for action as regime change. We have to act within the terms set out in Resolution 1441—that is our legal base. But it is the reason why I say frankly that if we do act, we should do so with a clear conscience and a strong heart. I accept fully that those who are opposed to this course of action share my detestation of Saddam. Who could not?

The brutality of the repression—the death and torture camps, the barbaric prisons for political opponents, the routine beatings for anyone or their families suspected of disloyalty—is well documented. Just last week, someone slandering Saddam was tied to a lamp post in a street in Baghdad, their tongue was cut out, and they were mutilated and left to bleed to death as a warning to others. I recall a few weeks ago talking to an Iraqi exile and saying to her that I understood how grim it must be under the lash of Saddam. "But you don't," she replied. "You cannot. You do not know what it is like to live in perpetual fear." And she is right. We take our freedom for granted. But imagine what it must be like not to be able to speak or discuss or debate or even question the society you live in. To see friends and family taken away and never daring to complain. To suffer the humility of failing courage in face of pitiless terror. That is how the Iraqi people live. Leave Saddam in place, and the blunt truth is that that is how they will continue to be forced to live.

So the moral case for action—never absent from my psyche—provided the final part of my speech and its peroration, echoing perhaps subconsciously the Chicago speech of 1999.

We won the vote handsomely in the end, by 412 to 149. My team—both civil servants and special advisers—had been utterly magnificent, giving me the most powerful, sustained and sustaining support.

I went back to Downing Street. Everyone assumed the U.S. would begin its bombing campaign the next day. In fact, the action started with British forces, including special forces securing the oilfields to prevent an ecological disaster.

We were at war. How long, bloody and difficult was soon to become apparent.

FIFTEEN

IRAQ: THE AFTERMATH

The problem with a military campaign to which a large part of opinion—public and most important media—is opposed is that this part continues to have a point to prove. Unless they can be somehow co-opted at least to a neutral position, then they approach the conflict with a strong desire, conscious and subconscious, to see it fail. I don't say that in the sense that they wish for disasters to befall coalition troops or the local people; but they are unreconciled. They feel forcefully that the campaign is wrong. They want to say: we told you so. However much they try to resist it—and in the case of Iraq, some didn't try hard—they see each setback as a rebuke for those who advocated the action. This had crucial consequences for the later phases of Iraq.

Right from the outset, I was keen to put the operation back under a UN badge as swiftly as possible, and to reunify the fractured transatlantic alliance. If the going got tough, we would need that alliance.

That the planning for the aftermath was inadequate is well documented. The lessons, set out in the compendious U.S. Inspector General's Report in 2009 and in the Rand Report of the same year, have been pored over, examined and, to a great extent, learned.

The military campaign of conquest was a brilliant success. The civilian campaign of reconstruction wasn't. But disentangling what was avoidable error, what were the unpredicted and unpredictable challenges and what effect each had, is difficult even now. The U.S. has admitted that its plans for reconstruction were poor. We in the British sector could have done better; but frankly for the area for which we were responsible, the plans were adequate and in any event were quickly ramped up and any inadequacy addressed.

The problem is that even if there had been the most intensive and fully adequate planning for the aftermath, all that would have meant was greater concentration of effort on things that ultimately weren't the cause of the bloodshed.

The pre-war preparations threw up three principal areas of concern. First and foremost we feared a humanitarian disaster, as a country dependent on food coupons lost the tightly controlled system of government distribution. This occupied most of our thinking and was the subject of numerous interactions inside government and between the U.S. and its main allies.

When people say that there were warnings that the planning for the aftermath was not up to the mark, that is absolutely true. What is forgotten, however, is that those warnings were about eventualities that fortunately didn't materialise. Somehow, despite the inadequacy, there was no humanitarian disaster. The food was distributed. The system worked.

The second principal concern was over the possible use by Saddam of chemical or biological weapons. We spent much time and money trying to protect people against such a possibility. In the event, for obvious reasons, that never happened.

Finally, we were concerned that Saddam would set fire to the oilfields and spark a major ecological disaster. This was prevented by timely and targeted intervention early in the campaign by British troops.

Had we not done so—and we discovered the oilfields were indeed mined and ready to be fired—the effect would have been to pollute the entire area of the south of Iraq, its marshes, its biology and wildlife and the surrounding sea. Saddam had driven the Marsh Arabs—over 100,000 of them—from the marshlands that they had helped preserve, and so already there were signs that the marshes were deteriorating. But an oil slick would have been horrific in its consequences.

However, of course, what troubled us most was the military campaign itself. Above all, in terms of our armed forces, we worried whether the Saddam army whose Republican Guard, in particular, had had the run of the country, with highly privileged positions of power, would fight to the last. The casualties in such a scenario would be large.

So the operation began. In a statement to the House of Commons on 24 March, following the European Council of 21–22 March, I set out our aims and initial action undertaken.

We are now just four days into this conflict. It is worth restating our central objectives. They are to remove Saddam Hussein from power, and to ensure that Iraq is disarmed of all chemical, biological and nuclear weapons programmes, but in achieving these objectives we have also embraced other considerations. We want to carry out this campaign in a way that minimises the suffering of ordinary Iraqi people, brutalised by Saddam; to safeguard the wealth of the country for the future prosperity of the people; and to make this a war not of conquest, but of liberation. For this reason, we did not, as some expected, mount a heavy bombing campaign first, followed by a land campaign. Instead, land forces were immediately in action, securing oil installations and gaining strategic assets and retaining them, not destroying them. The air campaign has been precisely targeted. Of course, there will have been civilian casualties, but we have done all that we humanly can to keep them to a minimum. Water and electricity supplies are being spared. The targets are the infrastructure, command and control of Saddam's regime, not of the civilian population. We are making massive efforts to clear lines of supply for humanitarian aid, although the presence of mines is hindering us.

By contrast, the nature of Saddam's regime is all too plainly expressed in its actions. The oil wealth was mined, and deep-mined at that. Had we not struck quickly, Iraq's future wealth would even now be burning away. Prisoners are being paraded in defiance of all international conventions. Those who dare speak criticism of the regime are being executed.

Now let me give the House some detail, if I may, of the military campaign. In the south, our aim was to secure the key oil installations on the Al Faw peninsula; to take the port of Umm Qasr, the only Iraqi port to the outside world; and to render Basra, the second largest city in Iraq, ineffective as a basis for military operations by Saddam against coalition troops. In the west, in the desert, our aim is to prevent Saddam from using it as a base for hostile external aggression. In the north, our objective is to protect people in the Kurdish autonomous zone, to secure the northern oilfields, and to ensure that the north cannot provide a base for Saddam's resistance. Then, of course, the vital goal is to reach Baghdad as swiftly as possible, thus bringing the end of the regime closer.

I hope that the House will understand that there is a limit to how much I can say about the detail of our operations, especially those involving special forces, but with that caveat, at present British and U.S. troops have taken the Al Faw peninsula; that is now secure. The southern oil installations are under coalition control. The port of Umm Qasr, despite continuing pockets of resistance, is under allied control, but the waterway essential for humanitarian aid may be blocked by mines and will take some days to sweep. Basra is surrounded and cannot be used as an Iraqi base, but in Basra there are pockets of Saddam's most fiercely loyal security services, who are holding out. They are contained but still able to inflict casualties on our troops, so we are proceeding with caution. Basra international airport has been made secure. The western desert is largely secure. In the north, there have been air attacks on regime targets in Mosul, Kirkuk and Tikrit. We have been in constant contact with the Turkish government and the Kurdish authorities to urge calm.

Meanwhile, coalition forces led by the American 5th Corps are on the way to Baghdad. As we speak, they are about sixty miles south of Baghdad, near Karbala. A little way from there they will encounter the Medina division of the Republican Guard, which is defending the route to Baghdad. That will plainly be a crucial moment. Coalition forces are also advancing on al-Kut, in the east of Iraq. The two main bridges over the Euphrates south of Baghdad have been taken intact. That is of critical significance.

The air campaign has attacked Iraqi military installations, the centres of Saddam's regime and command and control centres. More than 5,000 sorties have taken place, thousands of Iraqi soldiers have surrendered and still more have simply left the field, their units disintegrating. But there are those, closest to Saddam, who are resisting and will resist strongly. They are the elite who are hated by the local population and have little to lose. There are bound, therefore, to be difficult days ahead, but the strategy and its timing are proceeding according to plan.

The European Council began with tragedy. I got in to Brussels late on Thursday night. We were staying overnight on 20 March in the UK Representative's home, a lovely old house on a nineteenth-century Brussels terrace. There are very beautiful parts of Brussels (unfortunately not including any of the EU buildings) and this was one of them. It is that very particular mid-century architecture, large rooms with very high ceilings and those plain, long, thin double doors.

I was woken early on Friday morning to hear that eight British marines and four U.S. soldiers had been killed in a helicopter collision in Kuwait. It was an ominous sign. Up to then, in the combined operations in Kosovo, Sierra Leone and Afghanistan, we had lost only a handful. The horrible feeling that this was going to be very, very tough returned to me. As ever, I imagined the families, the knock on the door, the grieving widow, the fatherless children, the sheer tragedy of it all.

Both Jacques Chirac and Gerhard Schroeder came over to me at the beginning of the Council and gave their condolences in a sincere and touching manner. I was very grateful for it. It also allowed us to discuss how we might now reunite the international community.

My aim was to persuade the U.S. that as soon as the fighting stopped, the whole political process should be put under the UN. They could then supervise the elections. They would have the formal power of decision-making, even if obviously the de facto power rested with the U.S. We could then say: OK, we all disagreed over removing Saddam. But now he's gone, let us agree we all have an interest in a stable, friendly and well-governed Iraq.

In this regard, the Council went better than expected. It agreed on the need for oil revenues to be held in trust by the UN and for the Iraqi people. It agreed that the UN should have a strong post-conflict mandate, and that the new provisional government should, for the first time in decades, be generally representative of all sections of Iraqi opinion. Since the 1960s, the Shia (60 per cent of the population) and the Kurds (20 per cent) had been effectively excluded from power. Now was the chance for them to participate in the running of their country.

The U.S. was harder to persuade. Colin Powell was very much in favour, pretty much for the same reasons as me. Dick Cheney, Donald Rumsfeld and much of the administration thought the UN bureaucracy would just snarl things up. The task, as ever, was to persuade George. We were due to meet on 27 March. I wrote him a detailed note explaining why the UN had to be involved. I stressed once again the seminal importance of the Middle East peace process. When we met at Camp David, we went through the note pretty much line by line. Once he had studied the note carefully it was clear that he would end up coming down on the UN side. That was good, but the fact that it was a struggle indicated the nature of the problem.

The Americans' belief was that the UN got in the way. My belief was that you had to construct a coalition to win and the UN was the easiest conduit to such a coalition. This isn't simply a matter of waging a war that is a guerrilla campaign rather than a conventional war. There have been guerrilla wars fought before. It is that, with modern technology and modern news and communication, the reality of war is played out in real time in people's living rooms across the world. It is a spectacle.

What the spectators see—and, above all, the lens through which they see it—is a vital component of winning or losing. Of course, public opinion has always played its part in warfare. But now, there are embedded media with the front-line troops. Everyone gives a running commentary. The collective news footage is not just vastly greater; it is of a quite different nature from what has gone before. I sometimes wonder whether some of the wars of old, including the Second World War, could have been fought in the way they were if the media of today had been there with the technology they now have. Think of Dresden or Hiroshima.

The point is that the visual impact of real war completely eclipses analysis, context or explanation. It becomes its own story because the images are so shocking. In those circumstances, it is of the essence that the narrative about why we are doing it, the purpose, the objectives, the moral as well as geopolitical rationale, is clear and sufficiently agreed and accepted so that it can overwhelm the visual force of the images of war.

This is so for virtually any modern military engagement. It is abundantly so for any engagement that will take time. That is why building a coalition to topple Saddam mattered; it is why, above all, reuniting the international community post-Saddam was going to be vital. If the post-Saddam Iraq could be made a task for all of us, then, yes, it is true there would be irritating amounts of UN bureaucracy, but there would be the immense bonus of international buy-in. Or, at the least, a greater prospect of it.

It was a hard sell with George and even harder with Dick. But in the end we got agreement "in principle" that the UN should come in.

I tried to mend fences by going from Camp David straight to New York to see Kofi Annan. I had and have a great respect and liking for Kofi. His position throughout Iraq was quite impossible. He did his level best to steer a sensible course. He was, personally, I am sure, opposed to the action, but he saw entirely the sense of the UN coming back into it and was grateful I had made the effort to see and consult him.

In the light of what came to be a familiar criticism of UN exclusion, and because it provided Clare Short with the ostensible reason for her resignation a few weeks later, it is worth pointing out that from the outset Kofi made it clear he did not seek the "lead" role for the UN. He wanted the UN to be at the centre of things but thought (rightly) there was no way the UN could take the lead until the country stabilised. What he wanted—a "central" or "vital" role, as it came to be called—was what he got.

In the days and weeks that followed, there was a continual round of meetings, updates, conference calls and the steady progress of the forces on the ground.

I used to meet the core group—the Chief of Defence Staff, the heads of intelligence, Jack Straw and Geoff Hoon—early in the morning; and then have the War Cabinet at nine. The War Cabinet meetings were marked by Clare's continued agonising over whether she should stay in the government or resign; and usually very detailed debates about individual items. I tried to keep it focused but it was difficult, frankly. However, it kept everyone united. There is a charge—bolstered by some of the Civil Service grandees (though not others)—that there were mistakes in Iraq because not enough was discussed in the bigger Cabinet. It really is nonsense. I wasn't there during the Second World War or the Falklands, but if Winston Churchill or Margaret Thatcher used to do everything through formal Cabinet meetings, I would eat my proverbial hat. It's like any other walk of life. You can't take decisions by vast committees of people. You can debate, discuss and absorb views that way, but you can't run a war, organisation or company that way. It just doesn't work; at least, not in my experience. But then again, that might be my fault . . .

The American and British forces performed brilliantly. Indeed, from 19 March to the effective end of Saddam's government was less than two months. In fact, on 14 April in a statement to the House of Commons, I said that though the conflict was not over, in essence the regime had already collapsed. It had been an extraordinarily well-executed and brisk military campaign. I outlined what had been achieved so far:

> The south of Iraq is now largely under British control. The west is secure, and in the major town of Al Qaim fighting is diminishing. In the north, Kurdish forces have retired from Kirkuk and Mosul, leaving U.S. forces in control. U.S. forces are in and around Tikrit. They are meeting some resistance. But in essence, all over Iraq, Saddam's forces have collapsed. Much of the remaining fighting, particularly in Baghdad, is being carried out by foreign irregular forces. In Baghdad itself, the Americans are in control of most of the city but not yet all of it.

> As is obvious, the problem now is the disorder following the regime's collapse. Some disorder, frankly, is inevitable. It will happen in any situation where a brutal police state that for thirty years has terrorised a population is suddenly destroyed. Some looting, too, is directed at specific

regime targets, including hospitals that were dedicated for the use of the regime. But it is a serious situation and we need to work urgently to bring it under control.

Basra shows that initial problems can be overcome. I am particularly proud of the role that British forces, ably led by Major General Robin Brims, have played in Basra.

Iraqi technicians and managers are now making themselves known to British forces. Together we are restoring many key services. Most public health clinics are operational. UK forces have supplied oxygen to Al Basra general hospital and are providing other medical support where they can. About two hundred policemen have reported for work. Joint patrols started on 13 April. In surrounding towns, looting has either ceased or is declining, local patrols are being re-established and cooperation with city councils is going well.

The casualties on the British side for such a military operation were mercifully slight—fewer than thirty deaths, each one a personal tragedy, but an extraordinary low count on such a major undertaking.

As the army moved through the south, taking out Iraqi resistance, mopping up any renegade elements, they were, through the excellence of the engineering unit, also repairing bridges, electricity, water and power infrastructure. Detailed plans were developed for rehabilitation and repair work. Though it is true that Clare's attitude did hamper the civilian efforts, the army commitment more than made up for it, and in any event, frankly, any failings of Clare could have been easily remedied, had the security situation remained benign.

The U.S. effort, through the Office of Reconstruction and Humanitarian Assistance (ORHA), was a mess. On the other hand, the truth is that until American forces got into Baghdad and obtained a real sense of what the real-life situation was, there was a limit to what could be done. I will come to how that effort progressed. But right at the outset, let's be very clear: it would be so easy to say that the reason for the subsequent difficulty lay in planning failures, in terms of the civilian capacity to rebuild Iraq. It isn't true. The plain fact is that with the money and effort committed, any defects would have been overcome, had the problem been administrative or bureaucratic. What went wrong was on the security side. Some of the civilian decisions may not have helped and I will come to those also. But the notion that they were the root of the problem is just false, a delusion I'm afraid, and one that matters, because in future conflicts we have to be aware of the limitations of this approach. Reconstruction is essential. It can't happen in a violent environment. I saw that in Iraq and Afghanistan. I've also seen it since in Gaza and the West Bank.

The only issue is whether with better preparation, the security situation itself would have been better. If that preparation had yielded in and around Baghdad different or more troops, it is possible it would have. Down south, where the British were and where soon enough we were joined by 20,000 troops from other nations, it is less clear. For much of 2003 the south was relatively calm.

But I doubt any change would have prevented the al-Qaeda and Iran factors emerging; and it was those that from 2005 to 2007 almost tipped the country into the abyss.

In those initial weeks, all seemed according to plan. The regime had no support among the people at large. Many towns declared themselves open to coalition forces. Pockets of fighting continued but, without a local base of support, they were quickly eliminated and the south—Shia and heavily anti-Saddam—was swiftly subdued. Indeed, by 12 April, local police patrols resumed in Basra.

Baath Party officials were being captured or were surrendering to U.S. forces. When the notorious Abu Ghraib prison complex was taken—notorious then and to become even more notorious later—it was found empty. Saddam had released all the prisoners, at least the criminal elements. It should have warned us—along with the intelligence that Saddam had allowed al-Qaeda to establish a base inside Iraq in early 2003—that his tactics were not to fight our superior force but to let the country be overrun and then attempt to plunge it into chaos. But at this point, the reception accorded to the forces, if not that of garlands of flowers, was certainly more that of a liberating force than an occupying one. Towards the end of April, a million Shia pilgrims attended the main Shia festival in Karbala, something Saddam had forbidden to them.

On 27–28 April, things were sufficiently quiet even in Baghdad for General Garner, head of ORHA, to be able to host a political and reconstruction meeting with over two hundred Iraqi delegates and representatives of the coalition force nations. At the end of June, the first new Basra political council was established.

Before then, I had myself visited Basra on 29 May. The British troops had been brilliant. I saw the forces at the Presidential Palace and then at the port of Umm Qasr. The port was being de-mined and they were preparing to reopen it. The potential of it was enormous, all of it lost during the Saddam years. But it could have been—and in the heyday of ancient Iraq it was—one of the great ports in the world. When, just before leaving office in 2007, I made a speech in the Emirates and said that Basra in time could become like Dubai or Abu Dhabi, I was much mocked. But the truth is it could, and today is expected to double its capacity in the next three years, having already increased it dramatically since the days of Saddam.

I visited a school newly refurbished by the British troops. Basra was quiet and relatively peaceful. Up in Baghdad, the statue of Saddam was wrenched from its pedestal and broken into pieces to cheers. It was a great moment. Stupidly I gave an interview to the *Sun* and allowed myself to be drawn into a vainglorious remark about how I had almost lost my job over the war. (Rather less important than the soldiers losing or risking their lives, you might think.) But all in all, at that point the campaign had been hard and bloody but successful and short. By the end of May, roughly five hundred coalition troops had been lost, over four hundred of those American, and according to the Iraq Body Count around 8,000 Iraqis had died, obviously significant numbers of them combatants.

The humanitarian disaster had not happened. The oilfields had been protected. The resistance of Saddam elements had crumbled. The warnings of doom had been wrong.

We thought we were at the end of the main military campaign. Actually, we were at the beginning of what then became a quite different phase of operations; but this one hard, bloody, protracted, and at times during those years, the result was most definitely in doubt; even today it is fragile.

In this phase, the absence of international unity in the original decision, and the vested interests of many to prove that it was a mistake, counted heavily against us. I got a taste of this during a visit to Russia at the end of April. Vladimir Putin launched into a vitriolic attack at the press conference, really using the British as surrogates for the U.S., and then afterwards at dinner we had a tense, and at times heated, discussion. He was convinced the U.S. was set on a unilateralist course, not for a good practical purpose but as a matter of principle. Time and again, he would say, "Suppose we act against Georgia, which is a base for terrorism against Russia—what would you say if we took Georgia out? Yet the Americans think they can do whatever they like to whomever they like." Chechnya was another example, though as I pointed out I had actually supported suppression of terrorism there.

I realised then how deep was his feeling that Russia had just been ignored by the U.S. and his determination that they should see it eventually as a mistake. The difficulty was that I half agreed with him about the unilateralism. There was an arrogance to it that was not so much wrong as counterproductive to our cause. But it didn't mean that the action per se shouldn't have been taken or that the analogies he was drawing were accurate. The truth is that the India–Pakistan dispute over Kashmir did erupt into sporadic violence and there was terrorism coming out of Pakistan. But, though elements of state organisations might be involved, that was a long way from saying the Pakistan government was a terrorist government, or Pakistan was a rogue state. China's issue with Taiwan was of internal Chinese unity. It was not really an external threat to anyone. Chechnya did indeed exhibit some of the same characteristics, but frankly if the U.S. or Britain had gone into Iraq as hard as Russia had in Chechnya, there would have been bedlam.

I respected Vladimir for being as direct as he was. Though we disagreed, we kept lines open. But the chance to forge a really strong U.S./Russian partnership had been lost. If I were the U.S. I wouldn't allow the same thing to happen with China. Bind them in and treat them as an equal, not in form alone but in substance.

There was also another more pressing and more embarrassing issue for the coalition. We were actively searching for the WMD. We were sure we would find them. This was the moment I was waiting for. It would draw a line under one major issue.

As our troops went further into Iraq, so we would get daily reports. Sometimes we would try to inspect plants or sites and get thwarted. Other times we would think we had made a find and be disappointed. As the weeks wore on, I became more and more agitated. By the time of my visit to Basra at the end of May, Donald Rumsfeld had somewhat unhelpfully suggested that we may never find WMD, a prediction that turned out to be true but needed to be handled with some care. It was, after all, the *casus belli*.

When in Basra, I met Jerry Bremer, who had just taken over the running of ORHA, soon to be the Coalition Provisional Authority (CPA). I told him that he should not hesitate in asking for anything he needed from us, and advised him to use the same tactic with his own administration. "Don't hold back," I said. "If you need it, demand it. I will back you up and I'm sure your president will too." Unsurprisingly, he seemed a trifle overwhelmed, but very capable and committed.

Following that conversation, however, I redoubled our efforts on helping, not just in respect of our field of operations down in Basra, but in what we could do to support the U.S. in the rest of the country. It was set to be my principal preoccupation over the coming months.

The visit was a real wake-up call. Though I could see that much was being done, I could also see we were in danger of having won the war, then losing the peace. The expectations of the people were enormous. The complexities of tribal and religious life manifest. This was a huge challenge and there was no cause whatever for complacency.

On my return I called the key ministers together and gave a series of instructions to get our help to the U.S. on a better footing. We had thought they would handle the centre of the country and we the south. I realised after that visit that unless they succeeded, we would fail. I had sent John Sawers, my former key foreign policy adviser, to Baghdad. He came to the same conclusion: the American operation needed a drastic boost. I also sent a strong note to George and we then spoke by phone.

Fortunately, on 22 May, the UN had passed unanimously UN Resolution 1483 which gave the UN a key role in all aspects of Iraq's development. It put us back on a multilateral path. I argued strongly for the appointment of a really top UN operative to go into Baghdad. After some deliberation, Kofi agreed. At my urging he chose Sergio Vieira de Mello, the High Commissioner for Human Rights, and a man with a first-rate record and experience.

However, my attention soon got diverted elsewhere. On 29 May, the BBC's *Today* programme contained as its top story revelations from its defence correspondent Andrew Gilligan. In it, he focused on the forty-five-minute claim in the September 2002 dossier. As I've said, this claim was in the dossier, it was highlighted by some papers the next day in a form we should, in retrospect, have corrected. But it then disappeared off the radar.

The claim turned out to be wrong. Also, unknown to me, or to the Secretary of State, or indeed to the Joint Intelligence Committee (JIC), there had been internal Ministry of Defence debate about it. One of those taking part in the debate, though not directly responsible for the dossier, was a Dr. David Kelly, a Ministry of Defence intelligence expert of about twenty years' experience.

The BBC broadcast did not claim, simply, that the intelligence was wrong on the forty-five minutes. What Gilligan said was:

What we've been told by one of the senior officials in charge of drawing up that dossier was that actually the government probably knew that that forty-five-minute figure was wrong even before it decided to put it in . . . Downing Street, our source says, a week before publication ordered it to be sexed up to be made more exciting and ordered more facts to be discovered.

There could hardly have been a more inflammatory or severe charge. Mistaken intelligence is one thing. Intelligence known to be mistaken but nonetheless still published as accurate is a wholly different matter. That is not a mistake but misconduct. What's more, directly attributed to Number 10.

In view of five separate inquiries into this and the vast quantities of ink, time and energy expended on it, it would be tedious to go back over every fact, every argument, sub-argument and all the very painful personal grief that it caused. Dr. Kelly, a decent and honourable man, took his own life. The two top people at the BBC, Greg Dyke and Gavyn Davies, resigned. Alastair and numerous officials went through several months of absolute hell over an allegation that was untrue. Probably my own integrity never recovered from it. Quite a consequence, really. As a result of it, something else happened: the division over the war became not a disagreement but a rather vicious dispute about the honesty of those involved. A difficult situation became and remains an ugly one.

Of course, as I have said, the blunt and inescapable truth is that though Saddam definitely had WMD, since he used them, we never found them. The intelligence turned out to be wrong. But here is where the relationship between politics and the modern media plays such a crucial role.

The intelligence was wrong. We admitted it. We apologised for it. We explained it, even. But it was never enough, in today's media, for there to have been a mistake. The mistake is serious; but it is an error. Humans make errors. And, given Saddam's history, it was an understandable error. But it leads to a headline that doesn't satisfy today's craving for scandal. A mistake doesn't hit the register high enough. So the search goes on for a lie, a deception, an act not of error but of malfeasance. And the problem is, if one can't be found, one is contrived or even invented.

I'm not saying we handled the allegation well. But it was a global fire-cracker that set blazing a whole series of conspiracy theories that in turn, at the very moment when we needed to unify people, divided them in the sharpest way possible. Before it, we were in error; after, we were "liars."

The basic facts are, actually, straightforward. As each inquiry in turn found—and on the evidence there was no other finding possible—each of the points in the original broadcast was wrong. The forty-five-minute claim was not put in the dossier by anyone in Downing Street or anyone in government, but by the JIC. We didn't "probably know it was wrong" and neither did anyone else. We never ordered the dossier to be "sexed up." Dr. Kelly was not one of the officials involved in drawing it up.

Worse, Gilligan then went on in an article in the *Mail on Sunday* to allege that Alastair was the author of the whole claim, i.e. invented it, a charge that brought Alastair into the forefront of all the anti-war protest and was just an unbelievable thing to write, unless you were really sure it was true; which, of course, manifestly it wasn't, and by then both ourselves and the JIC had denied it.

It was never clear if Dr. Kelly, who though he admitted talking to Gilligan denied making the allegation, really did brief him in terms that justify the story.

But what followed set the pattern for the interaction between ourselves and the media in the years that followed. Relations between myself and the BBC never really recovered; and parts of the media were pretty off-limits after it.

The problem was that the BBC hierarchy couldn't see that it wasn't an allegation we could let pass. Look, if political leaders had to chase up every false or distorted story about their motives, they would be full-time press fact checkers. But this was qualitatively different. People were giving their lives in Iraq. They could forgive an error. They couldn't forgive a deception. Besides anything else, it meant I had deliberately misled the House of Commons. That in itself, if true, would mean resignation and disgrace.

From the outset, I tried to get Greg and Gavyn to see it. Here's where my friendship with both was a hindrance not a help. The *Mail* had been running a campaign attacking them as stooges. They wanted to prove their independence. Greg had also been personally anti-war and couldn't really see that as Director General of the BBC he had to remain neutral.

All I needed was for them to accept that the story was untrue. They could attack the government all they liked, but the allegation of impropriety should be withdrawn. They wouldn't. Gavyn kept saying it wasn't the function of the BBC governors to investigate the truth of the allegation—a bizarre position since that was precisely what they should have done. Greg—who could be very obstinate—tried to maintain that the broadcast was accurate because the forty-five-minute claim was wrong, which, as I constantly said, was not the point.

Anyway, I could bore you to tears with my side of the issue and no doubt they could with theirs. What happened subsequently was more serious and tragic.

The Gilligan allegation led to a rash of others. The Foreign Affairs Committee decided it should investigate, and we were slap bang into what turned into a six-month battle of immensely time-consuming, wearing, dispiriting and draining efforts to clear our collective name.

It became apparent in early July who the source was for the Gilligan story. Dr. Kelly offered himself up. He admitted that he had also talked to Susan Watts at *Newsnight*, but her reports had been a lot milder and less inflammatory, though even those had the quite wrong allegation that there had been a dispute over the forty-five-minute claim between the intelligence services and Downing Street, which was not the case. There had never been a discussion of it, since we never knew of it until the JIC put it in the dossier.

I will never know precisely what made Dr. Kelly take his own life. Who can ever know the reason behind these things? It was so sad, unnecessary and terrible. He had given such good and loyal service over so many years. Probably, unused to the intensity of the pressure which the Gilligan broadcast generated, he felt hemmed in and possibly vulnerable to internal discipline if his role emerged. I don't know and shouldn't really speculate. I met his family later at Chequers, at my request, and very dignified and sensible people they were. The awful irony was that for all the controversy caused, Dr. Kelly himself had long been an advocate of getting rid of Saddam.

How Dr. Kelly's name came out was the subject of a significant part of the Hutton Inquiry. That too was the subject of brutal media allegations, particularly against Alastair. It was suggested that he had leaked the name in breach of instructions from the Ministry of Defence. He hadn't. It was simply that once we knew it was Dr. Kelly, and since the Foreign Affairs

Committee was engaged in investigating the forty-five-minute claim and broadcast, we would have been at risk of a charge of concealment from them had we known the source of the leak and refused to say. In fact, the whole thing was handled by Dr. Kelly's line management, the permanent secretary at the Ministry of Defence, Sir Kevin Tebbit, and by Sir David Omand, the Security and Intelligence Coordinator in the Cabinet Office, at my insistence. His name was released on 10 July, and unsurprisingly the Foreign Affairs Committee immediately said they would interview him.

On 15 July he was interviewed. He denied he could have been the source of the Gilligan story since he disputed it. In particular, he said he had never thought or said that Alastair was responsible for inserting stuff into the dossier. The Intelligence and Security Committee (ISC) was also conducting its own inquiry. He had to give evidence to them as well; and in the course of it said he thought the dossier was "a fair reflection of the intelligence that was available and presented in a very sober and factual way."

I had a rough PMQs on the back of it all on 16 July. The BBC were refusing to say whether Dr. Kelly was their source. The Foreign Affairs Committee had decided that he wasn't and reprimanded the government. I was outraged by the BBC position. It was all very well for them to hold to the traditional journalistic practice of not revealing their source, but this was patently an exceptional case. Here someone was being described as the source. They could confirm or deny his involvement. They didn't need to name who it was, if it wasn't Dr. Kelly. Just say that there was someone else. But, of course, they didn't dare, since if they admitted it was only Dr. Kelly and since he had denied saying what they alleged, they would have had to have withdrawn the story as originally broadcast. This, they were damned they were going to do.

That evening I flew to the U.S. The next day I was due to address both Houses of Congress. It was a big moment. I wrote the speech on the way over and the next morning. It was one of the most important and, in my judgement, best speeches I made.

This is a battle that can't be fought or won only by armies. We are so much more powerful in all conventional ways than the terrorists, yet even in all our might, we are taught humility. In the end, it is not our power alone that will defeat this evil. Our ultimate weapon is not our guns, but our beliefs.

There is a myth that though we love freedom, others don't; that our attachment to freedom is a product of our culture; that freedom, democracy, human rights, the rule of law are American values, or Western values; that Afghan women were content under the lash of the Taliban; that Saddam was somehow beloved by his people; that Milosevic was Serbia's saviour.

Members of Congress, ours are not Western values, they are the universal values of the human spirit. And anywhere, any time ordinary people are given the chance to choose, the choice is the same: freedom, not tyranny; democracy, not dictatorship; the rule of law, not the rule of the secret police.

The spread of freedom is the best security for the free. It is our last line of defence and our first line of attack. And just as the terrorist seeks to divide humanity in hate, so we have to unify it around an idea. And that idea is liberty. We must find the strength to fight for this idea and the compassion to make it universal. Abraham Lincoln said, "Those who deny freedom to others deserve it not for themselves." And it is this sense of justice that makes moral the love of liberty.

In some cases where our security is under direct threat, we will have recourse to arms. In others, it will be by force of reason. But in all cases, to the same end: that the liberty we seek is not for some but for all, for that is the only true path to victory in this struggle.

And this is not a war of civilisations, because each civilisation has a unique capacity to enrich the stock of human heritage. We are fighting for the inalienable right of humankind—black or white, Christian or not, left, right or a million different—to be free, free to raise a family in love and hope, free to earn a living and be rewarded by your efforts, free not to bend your knee to any man in fear, free to be you so long as being you does not impair the freedom of others. That's what we're fighting for. And it's a battle worth fighting.

And I know it's hard on America, and in some small corner of this vast country, out in Nevada or Idaho or these places I've never been to, but always wanted to go, I know out there there's a guy getting on with his life, perfectly happily, minding his own business, saying to you, the political leaders of this country, "Why me? And why us? And why America?"

And the only answer is, "Because destiny put you in this place in history, in this moment in time, and the task is yours to do."

And our job, my nation that watched you grow, that you fought alongside and now fights alongside you, that takes enormous pride in our alliance and great affection in our common bond, our job is to be there with you. You are not going to be alone. We will be with you in this fight for liberty. And if our spirit is right and our courage firm, the world will be with us.

The reception was ecstatic. They got up and applauded throughout, a total of thirty-five times. But then they have always been generous to their speakers.

In later times, congressmen and senators have frequently mentioned it to me. The thing is: it did have an argument to it, and though the Republicans loved the tough security stuff, the Democrats could agree on the broader agenda in the speech involving climate change, Middle East peace, Africa and social justice. The problem was that this, in a way, describes my political weakness. The right agreed partly; the left, partly. But very few in whole!

After the speech Cherie and I went back for dinner with George and Laura, who were, as ever, gracious and welcoming. I think he was genuinely impressed with the speech and it was a relaxed and generally happy evening. At that point, we had won. Saddam had gone. From George's perspective, the regime had been changed and with relative ease. From mine, the UN was now back in the mix and there was a prospect of the international community coming together again. It was the last easy evening contemplating Iraq.

We left reasonably early. Alastair had gone back to the UK. I was due to fly to Japan and South Korea for a long-promised visit. Cherie and I drove to the Andrews Air Force Base outside Washington. It would be a long flight. We changed into BA sleeper suits and went to sleep. In the middle of the night, Sir David Manning woke me. "Very bad news," he said.

David was calm, matter-of-fact, and a brilliant adviser, someone of deep integrity, great loyalty and not insignificant courage. He had been a massive support throughout the whole Iraq business. He was due to leave soon and go to Washington as ambassador. "David Kelly has been found dead," he said, "suspected suicide." It was a truly ghastly moment.

Of course, in a rational world, it would be a personal tragedy. It would be explained by the pressure on him. It would be treated as an isolated event. I knew there was not the slightest chance of that happening in our media climate. It would be treated as a Watergate-style killing. It would provoke every manner of conspiracy theory. It would give permission for any and every fabrication of context, background and narrative. The media would declare it was a scandal. They were absolutely capable of ensuring there was one.

I often go over the decision to hold the inquiry into Dr. Kelly's death, taken in those early hours, exhausted, on the flight across the Pacific, by means of the unsecured plane phone. I spoke to Charlie Falconer, who had succeeded Derry as Lord Chancellor. He agreed to find a judge. It had to be someone utterly impeccable, impartial, someone whom no one could allege was New Labour or even knew us. If necessary, we would do it in public, though I had no idea just how much there would be and how long it would take. Eventually, Charlie came back with the suggestion of Lord Hutton, the former Northern Ireland judge, a law lord who had helped carry out the judicial work of the House of Lords, someone who definitely fitted the description. He was indeed, by all accounts, of unimpeachable integrity. We appointed him then and there.

Maybe I should just have slogged it out. Maybe I should have just refused to be overwhelmed by the ferocity of the onslaught. But, though, naturally, I was wanting to clear my name, that wasn't the main motivation. From the outset, deprived of a real policy attack on New Labour, this alternative attack of being a government of "spin," of "deceit," of me as a "liar," had taken root. It was part of what modern politics was becoming: personal attack, not political debate. In normal circumstances, in debates over the run-of-the-mill type of political issue, such brutal exchanges didn't go far. It was in the 2001 election that the Tories had first called me "Bliar."

However, this was about a decision to go to war. In this instance, could we really just tough it out? Weren't we obliged to have it investigated? Maybe. Maybe not. But at that time, I felt: enough is enough. Let it all be brought out in the open. Let us be utterly transparent. Let the truth be told. Then surely, with an objective judgement by a professional judge, people will accept the ruling. Surely. Surely? On balance, I still think it was worth it. Maybe, in time, it will be seen for what it is; but back then, after six diverting months, it was hard to see the positives.

I won't go through each and every point of the evidence. Read the report, I recommend. It was unprecedented for the prime minister and all senior officials to give evidence like this. There had never been anything like it. It was due to conclude in October. Lord Hutton finally published the report at the end of January 2004. It went over the dossier, its compilation, the role of Alastair, the activities of each minute section of the Ministry of Defence and Downing Street, what Dr. Kelly did, and went over it all exhaustively. This was part of the conclusion:

> The dossier was prepared and drafted by a small team of the assessment staff of the JIC. Mr. John Scarlett, the chairman of the JIC, had the overall responsibility for the drafting of the dossier.
>
> The 45-minutes claim was based on a report which was received by the SIS from a source which that Service regarded as reliable. Therefore, whether or not at some time in the future the report on which the 45-minutes claim was based is shown to be unreliable, the allegation reported by Mr. Gilligan on 29 May 2003 that the government probably knew that the 45-minutes claim was wrong before the government decided to put it in the dossier was an allegation which was unfounded.
>
> As the dossier was one to be presented to, and read by, Parliament and the public, and was not an intelligence assessment to be considered only by the government, I do not consider that it was improper for Mr. Scarlett and the JIC to take into account suggestions as to drafting made by 10 Downing Street and to adopt those suggestions if they were consistent with the intelligence available to the JIC.
>
> The BBC management was at fault in the following respects in failing to investigate properly the government's complaints that the report in the 6.07 a.m. broadcast was false that the government probably knew that the 45-minutes claim was wrong even before it decided to put it in the dossier.
>
> There was no dishonourable or underhand or duplicitous strategy by the government covertly to leak Dr. Kelly's name to the media.

What the judge found was all he could find, really, on the evidence. But it was a seminal moment in the way the media behaved.

The judge, of course, had come under the most intense media pressure. He had stood up to it well, but in the days preceding publication I was worried, not about the facts, but about whether he really would feel able to judge on them. Up to that point, the media had been egging him on: he was a man of Ulster granite; he would put the government spin doctors in their place; he would be unafraid to call a lie a lie, etc.

When I was his pupil, Derry used to tell me that there were two types of judges: those who made up their mind, but left loose ends, something for the losing side to cling to, something that expressed the judge's own inner hesitation about making a clear decision; and those who made up their mind, and once of that view, delivered the decision complete, unadulterated and unvarnished, with every allegation covered and every doubt answered. Lord Hutton was of the latter kind.

It was a comprehensive judgment, comprehensively delivered. Michael Howard, responding to it in the House, stupidly tried to carry on as if the judge hadn't found as he had, a bad mistake and one which heightened the sense of him as an opportunist who supported the war and, now it was tough, wanted to access some of the anti-war sentiment.

For us, it was a huge relief, but in our relief, we made our own mistake, a serious one with severe consequences. I had been having private conversations with Gavyn Davies throughout, keeping lines open and ensuring our entire relationship with the BBC was not jeopardised. After all, they were the main news outlet of the nation.

We had agreed in the course of these discussions that in the event of the judgment finding fault, we should try to keep the temperature down on both sides. The last of these conversations took place just before Hutton declared his verdict and I reassured Gavyn that we would not be asking for anyone's head if any in the BBC were criticised.

The day the report was published—28 January—was hugely busy for us. The close team sat in the Cabinet Room with trepidation and anticipation, awaiting copies which Godric Smith, who had been Alastair's number two, brought in. I joined them and we scoured the conclusions hungrily and there was an audible collective sigh of relief as we realised he had found in our favour; and then genuine amazement that he had had the courage not to dress it up for the BBC, but to call it as it was.

I then had to prepare my statement to the Commons. It was only the day after we had narrowly survived the tuition-fee vote (to introduce tuition fees at universities) and both events had taken it out of me. I just wanted to go back to my den and write my statement.

Alastair said he also wanted to do a statement. He had left Downing Street by then, but had come back to receive the report, as one of the main actors in the drama. We were still very close. Reluctantly, I agreed. In fact, I think he would have insisted. He wrote some words out. The statement included a passage about how if he or someone under him had been found guilty of such a thing—the judge had essentially found that the BBC broadcast was not just wrong but they had known it was—heads would have rolled. I took it out, much to his dismay, and he protested vigorously. He couldn't understand why. As I had agreed with Gavyn, I had told no one about our conversations, apart from Anji. So,

Alastair didn't know why I was so vehement that the passage had to come out.

I had, insensitively and foolishly, not quite appreciated the strain Alastair had been under. He is, as I have said, a highly strung character. Believe it or not, I only really understood this to its full extent when I read his diaries. I hadn't realised that the months since he had left had been lived in agony about the verdict. Of course, having left Downing Street he didn't have the all-enveloping nature of the job to distract him. His life had been on hold. Meanwhile, he was still regularly accosted in the street and accused of murdering Dr. Kelly, and receiving hate mail, often with bloodstains attached, at his family home. So, for him, this was a moment of enormous emotional release. But all the anger bottled up inside—and Alastair had a lot of that in him—also erupted. He wasn't thinking, he was lashing out.

When he came to make his statement, which he did with an emotion I could see was inspired by sadness about the whole business, but others would see as revenge on the media he had come to hate, he had put the passage about "heads rolling" back in, in milder form but still there.

Even then, I could have rescued the situation. But I was insufficiently focused on the BBC; rather I was preparing my House of Commons statement, clearing my name and whacking Michael Howard for his opportunism. In any event, I thought Gavyn would call me before doing anything. I made my statement. It went well. I then went on a visit to a college. As I did an impromptu press conference afterwards, I was still unsure exactly what the BBC had decided to do. I should, however, have said there and then that I didn't want anyone dismissed over it. Instead, I just concentrated on saying all I ever wanted was the withdrawal of a wrong story that reflected on my integrity.

It was a mistake. Gavyn, I think, assumed I had rescinded my side of the bargain, given the severity of the judgment. He and Greg both resigned. I really didn't want that. Greg was just Greg and was never really suited to the BBC, but Gavyn was a decent and honourable guy and I felt I had let him down.

It also helped provoke the media into a fightback. For about twelve hours, they were stunned. Then, with the Mail Group and the BBC again in alliance—one of the most sorry aspects of the whole affair—they decided to pit their strength against ours. "WHITEWASH" screamed the *Daily Mail* headline the next day. The others took it up. Suddenly the man of Ulster granite was a Downing Street lackey, the BBC were victims of the most awful conspiracy and cover-up, and actually didn't everyone know we were liars anyway? It was wall-to-wall for several days and then topped off with polls showing the public did indeed believe it was a "whitewash." So what should have been a way of lancing the boil of mistrust simply reinforced it and made it more poisonous.

When allegations that we were a government of "spin" are made and I ask for examples, the dossier is always the one that figures. But, I point out, there was an inquiry (one of four) lasting six months that found the opposite. Yes, but it was a "whitewash," as we all know.

The basic problem is that the manner of conducting the political debate does not lend itself to reasonable disagreement between reasonable people. The Gilligan broadcast led the news because it alleged misconduct, a lie, in effect. He thought he had a source, but an allegation that serious should at least, you would have thought, be put to the people against whom it was made. We were never even contacted before it was broadcast. In any event, a mere mistake was never going to lead the news.

Now, in actual fact, it should do. The intelligence was wrong and we should have, and I have, apologised for it. So the real story is a story and a true one. But in today's environment, it doesn't have that sensational, outrage-provoking "wow" factor of scandal. Hence an error is made into a deception. And it is this relationship between politics and media which then defines the political debate. The Opposition feel obliged to join in, otherwise they look like patsies. Instead of the debate being between one view of the country and another, it becomes a battle as to who is "more honest" or "less deceitful" than the other, a real mug's game for most of the time in politics.

But anyway, there it was. More serious, in the end, was the developing situation inside Iraq itself. A proper study of the aftermath will be necessary for its own sake but also, most importantly, for the future. The truth is that the likelihood of British troops being engaged in the defence of British soil is remote. The more probable endeavour will be engagement with others, usually the Americans, in far-off lands that fall victim to extremism. How we deal with such a situation needs critical analysis. The question, unresolved, but urgently requiring resolution, is: to what extent are the challenges we faced and face in Iraq or Afghanistan avoidable; and to what extent are they inevitable given the scale of the mission?

Let me explain this further. What happened in Iraq after May 2003 was, at first, relatively benign. There was looting and some violence; some attacks on coalition forces, but they were containable. I have described how the UN was brought back into the picture. In early July, with UN help, we convened an Iraqi Governing Council. It was a crucial moment. It had twenty-five members: thirteen Shia, eleven Sunni, one Christian. It came out of a process of consultation. It was the first step to the restoration of Iraqi sovereignty. As Sergio Vieira de Mello put it: Iraq was "moving back to where it rightfully belongs: at peace with itself and as a full participant in the community of nations."

Meanwhile, elsewhere, though there were military operations to deal with any lingering Saddamist elements, things were moving to a new state of rebuilding the country, schools reopening, hospitals functioning and police reporting for duty. Down in Basra at the end of June, 17,000 students at the universities took their exams normally.

This is not to say there was no violence in the south. There was a tragic incident in Maysan province on 24 June in which six Royal Military Police officers were killed in the town of Al Majar Al Kabir, situated to the south of Al Amarah. These were isolated attacks. But, even in early 2004, people could drive around Basra, and when the UK representative down there, Sir Hilary Synnott, came to see me on leaving his post in February 2004, he was relatively upbeat.

As Jack Straw outlined in a Commons statement on 15 July, we made it clear that as soon as Iraq was on its feet, we would be preparing to go.

We were receiving generous pledges of financial support from around the world. The Oil Trust Fund was established. ORHA was starting its work and ramping up significantly. In Baghdad the traffic was busy. Mosul and Kirkuk were generally calm. The Kurdish areas naturally felt liberated.

The point is this: we and the majority of Iraqi people wanted the same thing—Saddam out, the country helped to its feet, then us out. And a new and representative form of government.

Freezing the frame for a moment at July 2003 is absolutely of the essence in understanding what then happened. Yes, 8,000 Iraqi dead was 8,000 too many, but it was a fraction of those killed year on year by Saddam. Our losses were more than we could have wished for, but fewer than we might have had, and, in return, a nation at odds with the international community and which had started two major wars was now able to be a friend, not a foe.

The notion that what then happened was somehow the ineluctable consequence of removing Saddam is just not right. There was no popular uprising to defend Saddam. There was no outpouring of anger at the invasion. There was, in the first instance, relief and hope.

Yes, of course ORHA might have done better on the reconstruction plans, but that wasn't the problem. We had enough money, effort and people to have rebuilt Iraq within a year of the conflict's end.

What happened was that the security situation deteriorated. It did so in part as a result of Iraqi elements acting of their own accord, of tribal, religious and criminal groups deciding to abort the nascent democracy and to try to seize power. But the critical, extra dimension, the one which translated a difficult situation into near chaos, was the linking up of these internal dissident factions with al-Qaeda on the one hand and Iran on the other.

In the course of this, the terrorists discovered two things: if they could cause terror for ordinary Iraqis, particularly by the use of suicide bombs, the blame would fall on the coalition and the Iraqi government, not on them; and, in respect of the coalition, the pain threshold of the con-tributing nations losing soldiers was very, very low, and if it could be breached, then the coalition would lose heart—not the troops them-selves, but the public back home. In other words, if terrorists could cause chaos, the resulting fear and security clampdown would become a signal that the mission had failed, that the democratic experiment was mis-guided, and that a return to the old ways was the only path open to Iraq.

Instead of outrage at the evil acts of terror, the reaction was dismay and disillusion about the undertaking. At one level people might understand that the terrorists were the ones we should be fighting; but at another, as car bomb succeeded car bomb and soldiers died not in battle but in the wretched IED attacks, the fact of the carnage obliter-ated analyses of why we were there and why it mattered. The bloodshed eliminated the hope and brought, in its place, despair.

It may be that it was here that the absence of a broader coalition and the divisions in the international community played their part. But as we watch the same thing happen in Afghanistan, I am not sure that is wholly correct.

The defining moment came on 19 August in Baghdad. A lorry bomb at the UN HQ killed over twenty UN staff, including, tragically, Sergio. It was a ghastly and unforgettable day. I heard the news on holi-day. I spoke to Kofi; he was in shock. I later wrote to Sergio's partner. I felt and feel still a deep sense of personal responsibility. I had been anx-ious for his appointment and had pressed it on Kofi.

At the time I did not quite appreciate the full significance of the attack. It was utterly wicked. The people were defenceless civilians. They were there to help Iraq. They were there with the full backing of the international community; indeed, they *were* the international community. But it was a defining moment for other reasons. That was the point at which we should have realised that the conflict had metamorphosed into something different. It was pretty likely the work of al-Qaeda, whose chief in Iraq, al-Zarqawi, a Jordanian, had entered Iraq just before the invasion. It was the moment we should have rallied international support and said: "We take our stand, we will not have the UN pushed out; however it began, this is now a fight against the same enemy we are fighting elsewhere and we stand together."

Instead, the UN immediately withdrew its staff, and they didn't return in numbers for several years. For al-Qaeda it had worked. They had eliminated the UN presence. They had sown fear rather than defiance. The bloodshed told the story of our failure to protect, not their propensity to kill the innocent.

Even then, however, in the first half of 2004, there were only thirty suicide attacks. The political progress continued. By the first half of 2005, the number had risen to two hundred. By mid-2005, the Sunni insurgency had linked up with al-Qaeda; the Iranian-backed militia started their work destabilising the south. Then they started sectarian attacks on the Sunni. Most of those who died were, of course, Iraqis, but Spain and Italy also suffered the loss of soldiers and civilians, and calls for withdrawal of their forces from their home populations grew instantly and in the end carried the day. Dutch, Danish, Japanese and soldiers of other nations were also among the victims, as were diplomats and journalists.

As U.S. forces retaliated, so naturally people were detained, some rightly, some wrongly. In April 2004, pictures were released from Abu Ghraib prison showing American soldiers brutalising Iraqi prisoners. No doubt they were exceptional incidents, and the offenders were prosecuted. But the damage was colossal. For those always opposed to the action, the photographs were a heaven-sent opportunity to blacken the name of the U.S., while Al Jazeera, and others in the Arab world, used the pictures as a symbol of American attitudes to Muslims.

Similar allegations were made against British soldiers. I did my best to protect soldiers from a witch-hunt but it was hard, and the law officers felt under huge pressure to prosecute. It was a sickening time. Of course such treatment of prisoners was totally unjustifiable and required punishment; but it was so monstrously unfair that these isolated acts of misconduct completely overwhelmed the wonderful work most of the British soldiers were doing to help Iraq and its people.

However, all of this was used to fuel anti-Western feeling on jihadist websites and even in much of the mainstream media. I don't think there was ever a single protest anywhere outside Iraq about the suicide attacks, or the fact that the insurgency was aimed at stopping Iraqi people deciding their own government.

The paradigm was: you invaded; it was your choice; so it's your mess, go and clean it up. It was entirely understandable and, you might feel, justified. But it did ignore one important dimension: the mess was also visited on Iraq by external forces—al-Qaeda and militant Islam—which we were fighting everywhere. Fighting them in Iraq was not therefore a diversion from the real battle. It had become part of it.

It is this that we failed to convey. I realised very early on that we had to widen the campaign and link it up with the overall struggle. It was also where the combination of soft power and hard power mattered so much; why pushing forward on the Middle East peace process, reaching out to the moderate and modernising parts of Islam, was so critical.

The al-Qaeda leader in Iraq estimated that between 2003 and 2006 there were thousands of suicide bombs that they successfully detonated. My point is very simple: take those out of the equation and the security task would have been enormously different: tough but manageable.

In particular, as the political development of Iraq proceeded with the establishment of a proper Iraqi sovereign government in June 2004 under Ayad Allawi, a very capable and non-sectarian politician, al-Qaeda realised that the bombing campaign targeting civilians was insufficient. Then after the first proper Iraqi election, a new government was formed and al-Qaeda immediately tried to destabilise it. However, through 2005, despite it all, the majority of Iraqis came out, voted and showed that they wanted their country to stabilise. Very slowly their own capacity began to grow.

So, to deepen the conflict, in February 2006, al-Qaeda bombed the Samarra mosque, the most holy Shia site in Iraq. It was a devastating new development. It meant that now the al-Qaeda desire was to provoke sectarian violence. With courage and difficulty, senior Shia clerics called for calm. But a pattern was established: soon Shia militia groups formed inside and outside of the official forces, and carried out brutal reprisals against Sunnis. Of course, this was exactly the al-Qaeda intention. Some of the suicide bombers were Iraqis, but many weren't, having come in over the border from outside. Some were women; one even a pregnant woman.

Up until early 2004, the south had remained relatively quiet. There were isolated incidents, and sabotage of infrastructure was an increasing problem, but the situation was more or less under control. However, Muqtada al-Sadr, a radical Shia cleric with strong links to Iran, was leading Shia opposition to the British "occupation," and rallying support. He began openly to incite violence.

In January 2004, I visited Basra and the new police academy we established at Az Zubayr. It was a good facility and, at that point, we were reasonably confident of the loyalty of the police we were training. Basra continued to get better. But as 2004 wore on, it became clear that some Shia forces inside Iraq, and more importantly in Iran, were viewing the political progress in the south with alarm and anger. Despite al-Qaeda, despite Baathist elements in the insurgency, the truth was Iraq was going forward. There were parliamentary and provincial elections. It was tough for the people to exercise their democratic rights, but exercise them they did, and in large numbers. At that time, the voting was on pretty predictable religious and tribal lines, but there were signs of a crossover in some quarters and there was an increasing disposition to vote for people they thought would do the job. Also, the oil money, despite the terrorist attacks on the production facilities, was beginning to flow. All in all, given the total debauching of the country's politics over three decades, and given the absence of real democracy in the region, this was a remarkable achievement.

But of course it was a huge threat and menace to all the elements that opposed the idea of a free, democratic Iraq. Curiously, they had a far clearer and more stark analysis of what was at stake than we did. If Iraq were to settle down as a reasonably well-functioning democracy, Iran would not last long in its present state. Iraqi prosperity would grow—as indeed it is now growing—and the link between living standards and systems of government would be clear. It is true that with the Shia majority in government in Iraq, Iranian influence would be easier to peddle—Saddam was indeed an obstacle to that influence—but as time has gone on (and as I always thought would happen), Iraqi Shias nonetheless regard themselves as Iraqi. When al-Sadr went away, he quickly lost support and his Iranian-backed militia were disbanded in 2007, under threat of force.

However, back in 2004, gradually at first, Basra became increasingly unstable. The first really sophisticated IEDs were used against British forces in March 2004. The first fatality from an IED was in June 2004. These deadly devices became the preferred method of the rogue militia elements attacking British forces. The more we armoured the vehicles, the more explosives they used. The view was that, in all probability, as the devices grew in sophistication and power, they were made in Iran.

Certainly Iran was behind the training and arming of the militia, who, as the time went on, became more determined to take over the south, and Basra, in particular. But many of the factions were just corrupt and criminal.

In her recent book *The Surge*, the American military historian Kimberly Kagan describes how over time al-Qaeda and Iran began to work together to unhinge the fragile democratic structures of Iraq. According to her account, by the middle of 2007, Iran was both funding and training al-Qaeda operatives. On several occasions from April through to July 2007, the Americans tried to reach out to Iran to get an accommodation. The Iranians talked happily. But their actions didn't change.

That year saw the highest number of fatalities among the UK forces, most through IEDs. Of course, the British troops were keeping up a constant fight with the militia and hitting back hard each time they were attacked. As parts of the south were handed back to full Iraqi control, operations became more and more focused on Basra. Troops would stay in reserve in other provinces like Maysan, but in essence they were trying to deal with complex political and military challenges in the main city itself.

Back in late 2006, there was a pretty acute sense among the senior command in the army that we had done all we could in Basra. We had, in effect, entered into a modus vivendi with the governor and the militia there. The economic conditions of the people had improved, but the security situation hadn't. The question was: were we a provocation or a support? There was an increasing opinion that it might be the former.

I confess I was always very doubtful about this. Though the conventional wisdom was that Basra had to be managed this way because that was just the reality of it, I was deeply sceptical about the notion Iraqis or indeed anyone else preferred to live like this. But I could understand why people felt it. For some time, our civilian people in Basra had been able to do little, their HQ often locked down for fear of bombs and violence.

In October 2006, while I was at St. Andrews for the Northern Ireland negotiation with Ian Paisley and Sinn Fein, General Sir Richard Dannatt, the new Chief of General Staff, gave an interview to the *Daily Mail* essentially saying that we had reached the end in Iraq, we were as much a risk to security as keeping it and we should transfer our attention to Afghanistan where, in effect, we had a better chance. As you can imagine, I wasn't best pleased, my humour not improved by Martin McGuinness and Gerry Adams telling me the IRA would never have had one of their generals behaving like that.

I visited Basra again in December 2006 and of course, as ever, found the troops in good heart and determined to take on the enemy. The major general there, Richard Shirreff, seemed to have the required mettle. The soldiers told me of an operation they were going to mount against a rogue police unit, which greatly cheered me, and which they carried out on Christmas Day, arresting the whole lot and disbanding the unit.

We then offered to mount a major offensive to take Basra from the militia. We were losing soldiers but that was, in part, because the militia forces controlling the Basra streets knew that as long as we remained, they were in jeopardy. The attacks, unlike those in the centre of the country, were now almost exclusively on British forces, not civilians.

However, for reasons I understood, the new Iraqi government under Prime Minister Maliki did not want the offensive carried out by coalition forces but rather led by Iraqi ones. The British had done a good job with the Iraqi 10 Division and it was clear that in the not too distant future they would be capable of mounting such an operation, albeit with coalition support.

Eventually, in March 2008, Iraqi and U.S. forces, with British support, mounted the biggest and most successful security operation in Basra since 2003, which the Iraqis called Charge of the Knights, and effectively ousted the Iranian-backed and criminal militia from the city. It was an important moment, but I was left with the feeling that had we believed in our mission more and not despaired so easily—as indeed the soldiers on the ground showed—we would have had a far greater part in the final battle. Our relatively small role in cleaning up Basra in 2008 left a bad aftertaste for our forces.

However, when all is said and done, the truth is the British forces were heroic, they played an absolutely vital and irreplaceable role in stabilising the south and in staying there until the Iraqi force capability was such that Charge of the Knights could be mounted.

It should also be pointed out that from May 2003 the forces of the UK and the U.S. were in Iraq with full and indisputable UN backing. It made no difference to those attacking them. It should have made a difference, however, to those criticising their presence from the outside. But those British Army actions in 2007 were vital in laying the ground for the clearing up of the city in 2008.

In the rest of Iraq, the story was even more bloody. As suicide bomb attacks increased, the security situation grew so bad that it became impossible for foreign civilians to help Iraq. They had to have bodyguards if they went out and they too were targets. Criminal elements started to kidnap people for ransom. Religious fanatics began to persecute anyone who disagreed with them. Christians were singled out and intimidated.

The U.S. Army performed absolutely magnificently; they were tough, dedicated and with raw and rare courage. Our special forces together with theirs, in Baghdad, went on one of the little-known missions of the conflict, but one of immense significance for the future. I visited them a few times. Truly incredible people. Brave beyond imagining. And smart, not gung-ho or macho, just intelligent soldiers doing their job and with an utterly clear-sighted view of what was at stake. Essentially they went out after al-Qaeda. Over time, they beat them down. The surge counted, of course, as did the scaling up in capacity of the Iraqi Security Forces (ISF). But what the special forces did in Iraq was one of the most remarkable stories of the whole campaign and deserves a special chapter in their history. For sure, they badly damaged al-Qaeda's capability and set them back not just in Iraq but worldwide.

I also agreed to put the Black Watch, an elite military regiment of the British army, into a mission to help the U.S. forces in Operation Dogwood, in north Babil, in November 2004. I was criticised for agreeing to it and there was the usual nonsense about Brits taking risks for Americans, ignoring the fact that the opposite was also true; but, as usual, the troops themselves were totally up for it and performed with distinction.

By mid-2006, however, it was clear that the Iraq campaign was not succeeding. We hadn't lost control, although we were being fought to a stalemate, and ordinary Iraqis were, unsurprisingly, complaining and saying we had failed to provide security. Articles were appearing comparing the situation unfavourably to that under Saddam. In 2006, according to the Iraq Body Count, almost 28,000 Iraqis died and almost as many were to die in 2007. Most were dying in terror attacks and reprisals, killed not by U.S. or UK soldiers but in sectarian violence. But we, as the coalition forces, got the blame.

In November 2006, George Bush replaced Donald Rumsfeld with Bob Gates. In early 2007, George took the decision to surge U.S. troops. It was a huge decision that I don't think anyone else would have taken. He took it. The surge began in late 2007. It worked. There were many other factors: one was the Sunni outreach and the bringing on board of former Sunni insurgents, an effort led in part by Major General Graeme Lamb, a Brit. Also, the Iraqi government was ramping up the ISF.

In 2008 the Iraqi deaths fell to just over 9,000. By 2009, the figure had come down to under 4,000. By May 2010, it was 850.

So the aftermath was more bloody, more awful, more terrifying than anyone could have imagined. The perils we anticipated did not materialise. The peril we didn't materialised with a ferocity and evil that even now shocks the senses.

So: could it have been prevented? And was it worth it?

The shortcomings on the reconstruction and essentially civilian side can, as I have indicated, be blamed in part; but only in part. Done more quickly, it might have created a more benign atmosphere and this undoubtedly would have helped. But it is essential to remember one thing: the terrorist activity did not arise from frustration at the lack of progress on reconstruction. It was rather aimed at preventing such progress. Frequently in the south, the British would repair vital infrastructure only for terrorists to blow it up again. The pattern of al-Qaeda operations in the centre and north of the country was directed at intimidating and inhibiting Iraqis from rebuilding their country. These weren't, therefore, expressions of frustration about the pace of change; they were deliberate attempts to sabotage it.

Now it is correct, as I shall say, that a bigger pre-planned effort and a massive civilian reconstruction programme would have filled an early vacuum. It would have been an immediate jobs programme for unemployed Iraqis. But my personal view is that it would be naive in the extreme to believe that this in itself would have stopped the violence, the origins of which were profound and political.

With a manageable security situation, any shortcomings could quickly have been overcome (and the same is true in Afghanistan). Security was the issue—not one among many, but *the* issue.

The disbandment of the army and the de-Baathification are more open to dispute, since they impacted on the security situation. There is a case that both contributed to the anarchy. But it is a case with limits. The truth is the army more or less melted away. The visibility and blanket nature of the initial de-Baathification policy was quickly altered, partly under UK prompting. And it must be remembered that for large numbers of Iraqis, the Baath Party was the embodiment of the Saddam regime, detested, feared, and its continuing existence in any form an obstacle to liberation.

Of the two million Baath Party members, only around 25,000 were excluded from office. It was a far less drastic programme than, say, the denazification programme in Germany after the Second World War. When the British in the south initially used a former Saddam general—highly competent—to keep order, there was an outcry from the people in Basra, who saw him as a hated symbol of the old regime.

With hindsight, both the de-Baathification and the disbanding of the army could and should have been done differently. Possibly if that had happened then, as General Petraeus has suggested, part of the Sunni insurgency would have been tamed. But this is, as I say, a judgement with the benefit of hindsight, and it is fair to record it would be hotly disputed by those taking the decisions at the time, who would tell you that they were actually under pressure to do more.

It is crucial that the right and not the easy lessons are learned from the aftermath. Of course, there will be a natural desire to draw simple, bureaucratic conclusions—to say with different ministers at differently constituted meetings, the outcome would have been different. At least so far as the British effort was concerned, I really think that would be glib and mistaken.

Even on the U.S. side, for all the errors undoubtedly made—which the U.S. now accepts—to blame those for the chaos and carnage that followed is a leap that has to be very carefully analysed. Rereading the accounts of all the meetings, assessments and reassessments, the impression is not that of feckless or reckless people taking foolish or rash decisions; but is rather one of people straining to get policy right in a situation that was evolving, twisting and turning constantly, with highly unpredictable consequences for all.

So what lessons would I draw? This matters because we may well be in similar situations in the future.

First, assume the worst. We believed that Iraq had a functioning Civil Service, that the basic infrastructure of government was intact and capable. It wasn't. Saddam had wrecked the country completely. Without the control exercised by sheer fear and force, there was nothing. Iraq was a total basket case. That will be the likelihood in such situations. Failed states are just that: failed. In every conceivable way, including security. In future we should be prepared for a shadow government to be in formation, ready for deployment—as we have provided for, through creating in 2004 what is now known as the Stabilisation Unit, an inter-departmental body that aims to support nations coming out of conflict.

Similarly, the troops needed for the military campaign may well be different from those required for the aftermath, and there was certainly a case for more troops, though it is also fair to point out that in certain parts of the country—in the south, for example—a greater foreign presence would have been resisted and resented. The point is, however, we should be in a position with sufficient flexibility for us to call on more troops and to have that call answered.

We are going to be in the position of nation-builders. We must accept that responsibility and acknowledge it and plan for it from the outset. That was clearly a failing in respect of Iraq.

Second, we need to build the indigenous local capacity on security as soon as possible. Tough stuff is plainly easier to do, and, politically, infinitely more sellable for local politicians under pressure, if done by local forces.

To be fair, in Iraq, this began almost immediately and, as has been recounted earlier, police academies and training facilities were being established in mid-2003. But creating a new Iraqi Army was a challenge of a wholly different order of magnitude. This took time. As my notes to President Bush in May and June 2004 indicate, General Petraeus, put in charge of the process of "Iraqi-isation" of security, was excellent, and by then had in place a plan for the Iraqi forces. Also, partly because this theme of "Iraqi-isation" had very much been my concept, we got the British deputy in beneath General Petraeus. But it was an immense logistical, technical and political effort. An army was being built from scratch. It needed training, an officer class, support units, equipment, legitimacy—and it needed all of this in circumstances where we had to be on constant watch for disloyalty or infiltration.

In June 2004, a further UN resolution gave the ISF the authority they needed and envisaged a timetable of handover. By November 2004, I was able to send a note saying that it looked like the Petraeus plan was working; but by the end of the year, as the terrorist attacks intensified, I returned time and again to the theme that we needed to improve the plan for "Iraqi-isation" and somehow hasten its implementation.

The elections in January 2005 were obviously a critical moment. The insurgency was diverted towards stopping them. Allawi, prime minister up to the election, was deeply frustrated that he couldn't provide the security his people wanted. I signed off an additional $120 million for Iraqi forces in the south. As I said: "Can I be sure it is essential? No. But I'll take the risk rather than find six months later that it was."

From then on through 2005, as Ayad Allawi was succeeded by Ibrahim Jaafari and then Jaafari by Nouri Maliki, I was in a constant dialogue with the U.S. and my own people about how we could speedily improve the efficacy of the Iraqi forces. But the truth is, it was always going to take time. By 2007 they were ready, or at least in the first stages of proper capability, and in a sense maybe the surge was only going to work if it coincided with such a minimum capability. Going back over 2006, in particular, I am struck by the continual and detailed pushing for a better, faster, more effective plan.

The other recurrent theme of the notes of meetings was the requirement for Sunni outreach. This is the third lesson. The politics must accompany the security and the reconstruction. The Sunnis were bound to be destabilised through losing their position of total power, though they were only a minority of the population. It took time for them to understand that we did not wish to replace a Sunni dictatorship with a Shia one. From the beginning, we made outreach a priority. But Saddam remnants and al-Qaeda cleverly exploited Sunni anxieties. Throughout the political process, in spite of all our efforts, there was a persistent sense of alienation among them. We knew, too, that some of the terrorism was being financed from outside Iraq by wealthy people afraid of Shia power. Then as the Shia started to retaliate, so their sense of being in a sectarian war increased. During 2006, people really did see Iraq as in a civil war. Some even suggested partition of Iraq was the only solution.

In the end, however, as Sunni areas tired of the constant fighting brought about by al-Qaeda activity, they started to look for a way out. During 2007 and 2008, with the strong participation of Major General Lamb, slowly but surely they struck deals with the multinational force and the Iraqi government and turned on the al-Qaeda terrorists who were causing them so much hardship and grief. Once that happened, in conjunction with the surge, the tide turned. Sporadic eruptions continued, but the ISF activity had weakened al-Qaeda badly and they began to lose heart.

Then Maliki showed in his actions against followers of al-Sadr that he was prepared to take on Shia as well as Sunni rejectionists. The progress of the constitution through 2009, with all its attendant problems, shows how fragile it all remains. But whereas even those Iraqis who supported the war were increasingly pessimistic during 2006, by 2008 they had recovered their optimism. "It will take time," one remarked to me, "but it will be done." I pray he's right.

My last meeting with Maliki was in late 2006. He still generates a lot of internal dislike (some described him as a sectarian underneath it all, and he was plainly struggling with the scale of the challenge); but as we sat in his room, one to one, we had a frank and friendly conversation. As ever, I had flown in by helicopter from the military airbase, circling around the danger areas and landing in the Green Zone, the fortified and isolated part of Baghdad housing the international community and the government. I visited the embassy where the day before mortars had fallen.

The government building was a former Saddam palace. Security was heavy. It was hard to believe real government could be conducted from there. As Maliki and I talked and I pressed him on the utter necessity of not just saying but demonstrating he was governing for all Iraq, not just Shia Iraq, he responded in very simple language. He told me he would show comprehensively that he would deal with anyone who took on the legitimate government. He said that some of the insurgents were former Saddam people who would never be reconciled and would be crushed; but also that he had had enough of the radical cleric Muqtada al-Sadr. "He will learn I will not tolerate this," he said. I wasn't sure I believed him.

But I was wrong. He did indeed take him on and disarm him. In the 2010 election, Maliki and Allawi both headed units that crossed sectarian lines. President Talabani continues to play a pivotal, unifying role.

So: could we have had more troops sooner? Done more to build up Iraqi forces faster? Made more effort to reach out to Sunni groups earlier? No doubt there were failings in all these areas. But in truth, in all of them we worked as hard as we could to make it work. Our troops fought valiantly. We built an Iraqi Army in under three years. We tried perpetually to involve even the outermost limits of Sunni opinion.

In all of those areas—security, reconstruction, politics—we could have done more and done it better, that is for sure, but I have a feeling that this will always be so. There never has been, there never will be, a campaign of any nature that does not turn out differently from what is anticipated.

Our assessments of what to expect in Iraq were not casually made.

The full array of experts were consulted. There were Iraqi exiles who added their knowledge, and though some had very clear personal agendas, others didn't. We were told there would be a functioning Iraqi Civil Service. There wasn't. We were told there would be a humanitarian disaster. It was averted. We were warned that Saddam might fight to the bitter end. He collapsed.

We were told that Shia/Sunni sectarian violence would be a factor. Actually, to begin with, it was much less than feared.

Above all, most people saw no connection between Iraq and al-Qaeda; and little risk of Iran interfering except at the margins. And in this lies the biggest lesson of all.

Towards the end of my time as prime minister, I asked our military and intelligence people at a meeting in Downing Street: Suppose we had not had al-Qaeda and Iran as players in this drama, would it have been manageable? Without hesitation, the answer was yes.

It was this external threat linking up with internal dissidents that very nearly wrecked the prospects for Iraq. They conducted this attempt at destroying a nation with a wickedness and vicious indifference to human life and human suffering that almost defies belief. Suicide bombers sent into markets. Worshippers targeted at their place of prayer. Soldiers and police, there to help put the country on its feet, assassinated. UN officials, NGOs, civilian workers trying to assist the Iraqi people to a better life, gunned down, blown up, kidnapped and killed.

Yet after saying all this, my conclusion does not concern the bombers' attitude to this carnage and misery inflicted with brutal deliberation, but ours.

When was there a single protest in any Western nation about such evil? Where was the moral indignation? And where were the Iraqis' Muslim brothers and sisters at their hour of need? Who came to their aid? Where was the focus of criticism?

It was on the forces of the U.S. and the UK who were trying to stop the carnage; not on those conducting it. Yet these agents of al-Qaeda and Iran are not confined to Iraq. Iraq became for them, and by their choice, the field of battle. Their influence is the same menace we face in Pakistan, in parts of Lebanon, in parts of Palestine, all over the Middle East and beyond it in Somalia, and even in parts of the Far East. It is what we face on our own streets, on our airways, in the meeting places of our own nations, each country now obliged to spend billions each year in protecting ourselves against terror.

So, my final conclusion is this. Whatever the planning, be prepared for this: to stand up and fight, if necessary in a long, protracted and bloody battle. Be prepared not just to build a nation that has failed, but to do so in the face of an enemy doing as much wrong as it can to prevent us from doing what is right.

Are we up for this? Does our determination match theirs? That is the real question.

Had we foreseen what Iraq was going to be like following the removal of Saddam, would we have still done it? Should we have still done it? Many would say no. The cost in money and blood has been enormous.

My response, however, is very clear. Had this money and bloodshed been expended in removing Saddam, I would agree. But it wasn't. It was largely expended in dealing with the consequences of extremism whose aim was not to implement the will of the Iraqi people, but to defy it.

What are we saying when we ask: Look at the bloodshed, how can it be worth it? First, consider who is responsible. It wasn't UK or U.S. soldiers. There was no inevitability about the violence. These were deliberate acts of sabotage. Had we conceded to them, we would have strengthened the wider ideology they represented. By refusing to concede and by supporting Iraqi democracy, we struck a blow against that ideology everywhere.

Perhaps, as Zhou Enlai said when asked for his assessment of the French Revolution, "It's too early to say." All I know is that I did what I thought was right. I stood by America when it needed standing by. Together we rid the world of a tyrant. Together we fought to uphold the Iraqis' right to a democratic government.

I still keep in my desk a letter from an Iraqi woman who came to see me before the war began. She told me of the appalling torture and death her family had experienced having fallen foul of Saddam's son. She begged me to act. After the fall of Saddam she returned to Iraq. She was murdered by sectarians a few months later. What would she say to me now?

SIXTEEN

DOMESTIC REFORM

I t is easy to look back on the early years of Iraq and think they were dominated by that event alone. In reality, it was precisely during this time when the domestic agenda moved forward most radically and most satisfactorily.

Through 2003–4 and the beginning of 2005, there were critical battles over foundation hospitals (trying to devolve decision-making from the central government) and NHS reform; tuition fees; the beginnings of the city academies programme for children of all abilities; ID cards for legal UK residents; and antisocial behaviour. The closest I came to losing my job, ironically, was not over Iraq but over tuition fees. The nearest I got to giving up my job voluntarily was during 2004, when I thought I had had enough and would yield to Gordon, since I felt he might continue the reform agenda. And the clearest I became that I should stay despite it all was when I realised he wouldn't, and that I should therefore fight a third term.

So though the headlines were often dominated by the travails of war, the battle inside the government was over the issues of reform, which went to the heart of the New Labour project.

I have described a journey. At first we govern with a clear radical instinct but without the knowledge and experience of where that instinct should take us in specific policy terms. In particular, we think it plausible to separate structures from standards, i.e. we believe that you can keep the given parameters of the existing public service system but still make fundamental change to the outcomes the system produces. In time, we realise this is wrong; unless you change structures, you can't raise standards more than incrementally. By the beginning of the second term, we have fashioned a template of the reform: changing the mono-lithic nature of the service; introducing competition; blurring distinctions between public and private sector; taking on traditional professional and union demarcations of work and vested interests; and in general trying to free the system up, letting it innovate, differentiate, breathe and stretch its limbs. Each aspect was subject to the most detailed searching enquiry and scrutiny. Each reform was painfully iterated and reiterated. Each was amended and adjusted; and occasionally—and each time to my cha-grin—watered down. But together they added up to a substantial cor-pus of change and set the system in a new direction. They will form the essential basis of any future reform and where departed from, will, over time, be returned to.

For sure, however, each was harshly attacked, criticised and opposed. Perhaps the most fiercely contested was the change to university funding i.e., tuition fees. The whole debate provided a fascinating glimpse into the difficulties of making change in the modern world, and almost led to my resignation. It aroused unbelievably tenacious dissent. It cost us several seats at the 2005 election, and what appeared like a poor result even with a majority of over sixty might well have appeared differently with those extra seats and a majority of over eighty. It split the govern-ment; but by the time the reforms were actually introduced in late 2005, they caused very little stir and the debate today is as much how to fur-ther them as how to dismantle them.

It is an object lesson in the progress of reform: the change is proposed; it is denounced as a disaster; it proceeds with vast chipping away and opposition; it is unpopular; it comes about; within a short space of time, it is as if it had always been so.

The lesson is also instructive: if you think a change is right, go with it. The opposition is inevitable, but rarely is it unbeatable. There will be many silent supporters among the many vocal detractors. And leader-ship is all about the decisions that change. If you can't handle that, don't become a leader.

And the lesson goes wider: it is about rising above the fray, learning how to speak above the din and clatter, and about always, always, keep-ing focused on the big picture. Rereading the daily news about the changes, I am struck by how fevered each story was at the time, and how forgotten each story is today. Tuition fees in particular had an extraordi-nary series of mini-crises, debacles and revolts attending its every step. Yet all that matters now is that a necessary reform was made; and having been made, it is the structure upon which future reforms will be built.

It began with the usual fraught exchanges with Gordon and the Treasury.

I had allowed David Blunkett to put in our 2001 manifesto that we would not allow top-up fees. This was somewhat against my better judgement, but there were sound political reasons: worries that we were planning this had been circulating among the Parliamentary Labour Party and National Executive Committee, and David felt we had to kill the story. It was one of the few compromises I allowed with the 2001 programme.

But shortly after the election the challenge for our universities became clear. I had come to the view then—and believe this even more strongly today—that the future of developed nations such as ours, relying heavily on our human capital (as we must), depends on having a vibrant, dynamic and world-class higher education system. In addition, a country like Britain with its traditions and its language is ideally suited for such a challenge. However, like so much else in this country, we can't rest on our laurels. I looked at the top fifty universities in the world and saw only a handful in the UK, and barely any in mainland Europe. America was winning this particular race, with China and India coming up fast behind. The point about the U.S. was especially telling. Their domination of the top fifty—and top hundred, for that matter—was not by chance or by dint of size; it was plainly and inescapably due to their system of fees. They were more entrepreneurial; they went after their alumni and built up big endowments; their bursary system allowed them to help poorer students; and their financial flexibility meant that they could attract the best academics. Those who paid top dollar got the best. Simple as that.

We had also got ourselves into a typical egalitarian muddle over the universities that were lower ranked. The previous Tory government had converted the so-called polytechnics (which usually focused on vocational education) into universities, which was fine except that it fuelled the myth that all universities were of the same academic standing, which manifestly they weren't. And even the universities that had been polytechnics, some of which were offering outstanding service, needed flexibility in funding.

In late 2001, the key heads of the Russell Group—the twenty leading British universities—came to see me in Downing Street. Their message was stark: they needed significantly more funding. Roy Jenkins, then Chancellor of Oxford, was strongly in favour of tuition fees, urging them to me privately. Ivor Crewe, at that time president of Universities UK (the university principals' and vice chancellors' committee), was equally emphatic. As an old SDP hand—and so someone with knowledge of progressive politics—Ivor got the politics completely, and he was unequivocal that there had to be change.

I had promoted Estelle Morris to be Secretary of State for Education in June 2001, following on from David Blunkett who became Home Secretary. Estelle was an interesting example of what you see rarely in politics. She eventually resigned in October 2002, and said simply, "If I am really honest with myself I was not enjoying the job . . . I could not accept being second best. I am hard at judging my own performance. I was not good at setting the priorities. I had to know I was making a difference, and I do not think I was giving the prime minister enough." I wasn't sure if she was serious; and came to the conclusion she was. It had just got too much for her, and she was unhappy. She was by no means emotionally frail—on the contrary, she had held her seat against a fierce and, as ever with the Lib Dems (her main opponents), pretty vicious local campaign. She was by all accounts exactly as she seemed: decent and hard-working; but the top flight in politics is extremely rough, and she just felt overwhelmed.

So she went, and was replaced by Charles Clarke who, having lived through the Kinnock years, was sufficiently tough and could be rough himself. He gave the whole area a big push forward. However, he also had to inherit what had become a very tricky piece of politics with Gordon.

Once the university chiefs had laid out the problem, I knew we had to act. We had the manifesto commitment not to allow top-up fees, it was true, but frankly it would have been absurd to postpone the decisions necessary for the country because of it. So I began what turned out to be a process of internal debate and discussion, essentially with the Treasury, that lasted almost two years. From the outset it was clear that Gordon intended to resist. It was only afterwards I understood his problem. Essentially he thought he was going to fight the third election and he didn't want anything that cramped his programme or was unpopular, and this was plainly going to be so. Therefore he approached the thing, as ever, not with outright dissent but with the tactic of postponement.

In late 2001, we first broached the subject. Not unreasonably at that point, he asked for a lot more work to be done. The work was duly done, and at further meetings during the first half of 2002 we started to get down to the decision. It was here that Estelle felt caught between the two of us, and her own instincts were insufficiently powerful for her to take a stand. So it more or less developed into a battle of wills between myself and Gordon. I would say that it was at this time that the creative tension, which up until then had been on balance positive, became on balance negative. I'm not saying there weren't still enormous positives in having him there—he was, as I always repeat, a big figure, a credible one and without question an asset to the government in broad terms and therefore it was right that he remained as chancellor—but the problem was that because of his expectation and desire, he wanted to freeze progress until he took over. I was never totally sure where his own proclivity lay in terms of policy, but the desire to freeze-frame the government—evidently impossible—became overlaid with an agenda that defined itself subtly but actually very clearly to the left as time went on. This was almost personified in our advisers: Ed Balls for his part (then chief economic adviser to the Treasury), Andrew Adonis for mine.

Andrew and I were both close to Roy Jenkins. I missed Roy hugely after he passed away in early January 2003. When Andrew phoned to tell me the news, I was desperately sorry. Roy was, to the soul of his being, someone of genuine integrity. He had been a friend and mentor. He would have opposed Iraq, I am sure; but he would have understood why I did it. He had passed on to Andrew not just his politics but his political character: a rational, reasoning seeker after truth. To him, as to Andrew, the first question was: is this right? Only after that question was answered would he ask: is it politic? It was and is the correct approach to politics and, incidentally, is certainly consonant with the public's approach. But it is rare.

Ed Balls was and is immensely capable intellectually, and also has some of the essential prerequisites for leadership: he has guts, and he can take decisions. But he suffers from the bane of all left-leaning intellectuals. As I have remarked elsewhere, these guys never "get" aspiration. They would deny it of course, but they see the middle class—apart from the intellectual part of it—as an unnatural constituency for them. Not that they see them as the enemy or anything—that would be to exaggerate grossly—but they would think that a person worried about their tax rates was essentially selfish, and therefore by implication morally a little lost. They could "get" that it might not be smart to penalise them; but not that it might be wrong to do so.

Ed had worked out a strategy for Gordon that sort of went like this: there is a trade-off between equity and markets; Blair is pushing us too far towards "marketisation" and thus away from equity. So all of this language around choice, competition, diversity, flexibility; all of it is in the end an attempt to move us to a system that is intrinsically inequitable; and what's more poorly motivated, since it's all part of an obsession with the middle class—historically a small part of Labour's support—at the expense of our "core" voters.

To this intellectual critique he added a truly muddled and ultimately very damaging party critique. This was the view—I fear tutored by Gordon's inclination in dealing with the party—that I deliberately chose confrontations with the party in order to demonstrate my independent credentials with the public, i.e. I sacrificed the party to woo the public. This was a very common opinion.

Mostly he was pretty respectful. Over time and the innumerable meetings with Ed and Gordon, I gradually got Ed to lose his reserve—after all, I was prime minister—and provoked him into his true opinions. His basic sense was that this whole assault on traditional party thinking was to prove I was "exceptional." "Exceptionalism," he called it. What he meant was that I believed only I could win, and that all these rows—over tuition fees, schools reform, health reform, ID cards, asylum, law and order, welfare—were almost manufactured, in order to create the sense of a leader above the party. He believed, and I think persuaded Gordon, that you could be a traditional Labour leader and still win.

I used to tell him this was fundamentally and dangerously to misunderstand both the intellectual and the political basis for New Labour. Intellectually, it was perfectly straightforward: all governments round the world, certainly those getting re-elected, were refashioning their state and public services to make them more accountable to consumers and users, who in the other domains of their lives were habitually making their own choices and decisions. In other words, my argument was that these reforms were cutting with the grain of where "the people" were heading.

Politically, I tried to explain that the whole purpose of my period as leader was to create a permanence in New Labour that meant precisely that I was not the exception. Even back in 2002, it was plain that we were a stronger, more enduring, more stable Labour government than any before us. It was true that I believed a Labour leader could not be a traditional Labour politician to win, but only because I believed we had to change the tradition. Once New Labour became integral to the way the Labour Party thought and operated, we would have a different tradition, one more sustainable, more credible and more electable. I didn't choose to have rows with the party; I chose to reform. But if the reform was resisted, then you couldn't avoid the row.

Anyway, as 2002 went on, it became apparent that we were stuck. In early 2003 and with Charles Clarke now pressing, we held further meetings. This time I insisted that the Treasury come forward with a specific alternative, rather than continually raising objections to the tuition-fee proposal we had outlined.

In summary, we were proposing that rather than pay tuition fees of £1,150 per annum upfront, while the student was at university, there should be a variable fee of up to £3,000 per annum—the variation to be at the discretion of the university—to be repaid after graduation on a means-tested basis, depending on the income of the graduate. There would be maintenance grants for the poorer students and bursaries (fees paid by the university that did not have to be repaid) would be encouraged. The whole package would boost the income of the universities considerably, by over 30 per cent per annum. It was plainly a fairer system. It was true there would be more debt, but we would only recover the money from graduates as they started earning. And poor students would get real and significant help. As ever in these situations, there were tactical compromises along the way to sweeten the pill—some of which I was reluctant to make and all of which added to the cost—but there was no doubt it would be enormously advantagous to our universities, separate them out from those struggling in mainland Europe and bring us back into contention with those of the U.S. Indeed, after the measures passed, several vice chancellors told me the change literally saved their universities from financial collapse. Also, as our opponents knew, once introduced as a concept, there was no looking back.

The Treasury kept demanding that more work and analysis be done. They pointed to the fact that our proposals had drawbacks. I responded that all systems have drawbacks. They produced polling that said our scheme was unpopular. I said that all changes were unpopular, except funding universities better through higher general taxation, and the moment it stopped being a question about funding and became a question of tax, that of course was unpopular too. In truth, therefore, this was a classic case of a change that was necessary and right and would never prove popular. On the other hand, as I always reasoned, people expected governments to take unpopular decisions, expected to complain about them and expected leadership to overcome complaint. However, if ever you stopped leading, it would cease to be a complaint and become a notice of dismissal; because, in their heart of hearts, people know governments are there to lead.

Eventually, we flushed out of the Treasury a kind of alternative, which was to all intents and purposes a graduate tax, pure and simple. This, naturally, was equally unpopular according to the polling, but more than that, it suffered from what I thought was a serious and irremediable defect: it meant that instead of a graduate paying back their own fees, there would be a general tax on graduates, dependent on their income and not on the education they had personally received. In other words, it amounted not to a personal repayment of a personal debt, but a general graduate repayment of the collective student debt. I didn't like this at all. It broke the essential link between what a student got and what they gave back; and it changed the nature of our taxation system radically, but not sensibly or sensitively.

Being plainly Ed's idea, it was never pushed very hard by Gordon, and so it kind of fell away. That meant it was our proposal or nothing. Eventually in mid-2003 I just said: we will meet again in a month's time; the final decision will be taken; at that point you put up or we proceed. We proceeded, but we had wasted valuable time.

Throughout, Andrew Adonis had been a complete star, producing endless analyses and counter-analyses, marshalling the arguments with his customary clarity, patiently and politely urging it all forward. Andrew was in stark contrast to Ed. In a political scrap, Ed would win. And Ed, as I say, was generally a clever guy. But in terms of public appeal and sense, Andrew was just in a different league. He understood entirely why it was so crucial that we reach out beyond Labour's traditional base; he was himself a representative of aspiration, his father having been a Greek Cypriot immigrant postman; and he knew that if Labour was to govern for significant periods, it had to be as a party of the future-orientated centre ground.

Andrew carefully put together the facts and arguments. Charles Clarke was strongly in support. For the first time, I felt with Charles, Alan Milburn and David Blunkett I had people alongside me fully in tune with what I wanted to do and why. They had the same instincts and each had the political skill to mount the Labour case for modernisation and change. All of them had honed those skills in umpteen interactions with recalcitrant union leaders, bolshie MPs, lefty activists and assorted intellectuals whose main contribution was to explain why nothing should change in the name of being real radicals.

Whereas I had a tendency to think I could persuade anyone of anything provided I truly believed it (not even experience ever quite eliminated this trait of mine), they were more realistic and more effective. They knew the difference between tactics and strategy and how and when they had to be synchronised.

We held back the Queen's Speech (announcing our legislative programme) until late that year—almost the end of November. Of course the news continued to be dominated by Iraq, by the continuing attempts to stop terrorism threatening that country's fragile condition, and by the Hutton Inquiry. But the real reason for the delay was sorting out what was going to be a major domestic agenda around the NHS, schools, antisocial behaviour and tuition fees. After much prevarication and again a lot of opposition from Gordon, I had also got agreement in principle from him to identity cards. All of these issues—at various stages of legislation—were going on apace.

The saga on tuition fees came to a head around the time of the House of Commons debate about it, which was scheduled for the end of January 2004. It was truly knife-edge stuff. It seems strange to relate that now, but it really was.

Michael Howard had just become leader of the Tories, and had made his first mistake. He had inherited opposition to tuition fees from Iain Duncan Smith. Of course, the Tories knew perfectly well that they should support the measure, and the reason why they didn't do so is an interesting reflection on the art of good Opposition.

Leave aside principle for the moment—i.e. the rights or wrongs of the policy—and let us focus on the naked politics. The conventional view of Opposition is: pick up votes where you can. All the polls say tuition fees are unpopular. There is a public bandwagon of opposition. Clamber on board.

In many cases, that is the right thing politically. Take the rows over MPs' expenses. The truth is MPs are underpaid and the expenses were used to top up income; but you can't say that. The public is whipped into outrage. The bandwagon rolls. It is completely unreasonable to expect the Opposition to resist it. Not wise long term, by the way; I frequently rued such moves made in Opposition which boomeranged in government. But fair enough. It's what happens, and the Opposition, eager for votes, benefits in the short term.

But such bandwagons are dangerous if they are heading in a direction with which serious, elite cross-party opinion disagrees. Then it's a mistake, and never worth it, because even though that opinion is elite and held by only a few, its quality is high and it marks you down sharply.

Every key Tory who had been in government and who had wished they had made such a reform was onside with us. Elite opinion was clear: the change was necessary and right. By allying himself with the opposition—unions, the left, etc.—Michael Howard didn't win many votes and lost a lot of credibility. It tied in with his attempt to exploit the Hutton Inquiry when he had been vigorously in favour of Iraq, and it all contributed to our development of a telling counter-attack on him, namely that he was opportunist and therefore unreliable.

The charge of being an opportunist may seem a bit of a low-key attack. And in that also lies a lesson. With each successive Tory leader, I would develop a line of attack, but I only did so after a lot of thought. Usually I did it based on close observation at PMQs. I never made it overly harsh. I always tried to make it telling. The aim was to get the non-politician nodding. I would wonder not what appealed to a Labour Party Conference in full throttle, but what would appeal to my old mates at the Bar, who wanted a reasonable case to be made; and who, if it were made, would rally.

So I defined Major as weak; Hague as better at jokes than judgement; Howard as an opportunist; Cameron as a flip-flop, not knowing where he wanted to go. (The Tories did my work for me in undermining Iain Duncan Smith.) Expressed like that, these attacks seem flat, rather mundane almost, and not exactly inspiring—but that's their appeal. Any one of those charges, if it comes to be believed, is actually fatal. Yes, it's not like calling your opponent a liar, or a fraud, or a villain or a hypocrite, but the middle-ground floating voter kind of shrugs their shoulders at those claims. They don't chime. They're too over the top, too heavy, and they represent an insult, not an argument. Whereas the lesser charge, because it's more accurate and precisely because it's more low-key, can stick. And if it does, that's that. Because in each case, it means they're not a good leader. So game over.

In fact, if Michael had backed me over tuition fees, it would have done me real damage with my own side; done him a power of good with sensible, informed opinion; and not changed the result. But he didn't. And that helped me.

The rebellion on my side was not small, however. And it was led by Nick Brown and George Mudie, both close to Gordon and both supremely good organisers. I had my political team working overtime. Sally Morgan was at her best, performing to the highest level. She was New Labour but had the benefit of the 1980s student union training, and could reach the women in the PLP in a way others couldn't. Some women, by the way, are the last people best placed to canvas other women. Others do it superbly. Sally could reach outside of that New Labour circle, could talk more than one political language and was relentlessly realistic about the challenge. Charles and I were a bit of the "let's just go and do this damn thing" school, which was fine, but doing the damn thing did also entail getting the damn votes. And we were way short. Sally and Hilary Armstrong—who was a great chief whip and also skilled in the highways and byways of PLP politics—told me in no uncertain terms that the vote hung in the balance.

At a meeting before Christmas, we sat in Downing Street: me, Charles, Sally and Andrew, together with David Hill who had become press secretary after Alastair's departure. Much to my delight, David had agreed to come back and serve after some years in the private sector, having been the Labour Party's chief press officer for the 1997 election.

"I feel very confident," Charles said in typical Charles fashion.

"I really don't see why," Sally remarked a little sourly. "Is it a calculation of the votes that leads you to think that, or just your natural good spirits? Because I'm looking at the votes and you don't yet have them."

It was an ugly period. We were to have the Commons vote on 27 January 2004, and the Hutton Inquiry reporting the next day. January was going to be uncomfortable. A bad result in either could mean curtains.

I always used to think, though, that if you go out on a point of principle, well, there are worse ways of exiting. As I have stated many times, I wasn't obsessed with staying. I explained this to Sally as we sat having a cup of coffee after the others had departed. "Well, that's very big of you, I'm sure," she said tartly with a smile, "but if you don't mind, I think we should concentrate on winning the vote."

"How do we win then?" I asked.

"You can't win," she replied, "without your Chancellor fully and unequivocally on board."

And that was the nub of it.

Early in the new year I restarted my conversation with Gordon about leaving. This was probably unwise in all aspects, but I was feeling genuinely worn down. At every major passing point in every major path of policy, there were barriers being thrown across the road ahead.

The first foundation hospitals would shortly be coming into being. Carefully chosen from those already getting the highest ranking, these hospitals were to have greater freedom, power and discretion. They were the first big step to creating self-governing entities capable of making the changes in medical care in the way they wanted, in order to meet the changing challenge of modern health care.

The problem with the NHS was quintessentially that of the monolithic, outdated public health service: it was rigid, and had no incentives to innovate. Bad practice and good were equally rewarded. Powerful professional interests, with widespread but ultimately ill-informed public support, held sway. Foundation hospitals were the breach in the wall of the monolith. In time they were to be followed by choice, by the introduction of the private sector and by far-reaching changes to the working practices of staff.

We had begun, with Alan Milburn, the task of introducing them in January 2002. They had provoked a furious row with the Treasury, however. Gordon felt Alan was hostile to him. As ever, he met the argument not head-on but by a Treasury-related argument: by having the power to borrow against their assets, foundation hospitals were a threat to the public finances. The debate was endless, rancorous and destabilising. By the time we finally got the legislation agreed—again with a major rebellion, and again with many taking their cue from apparent Treasury disagreement with the policy—Alan had left the government.

In May 2003, a month before the vote, he had come to see me. He knew it would be a bad blow, but he had had enough. I was very sorry to lose him. He was a quite exceptional minister. I don't blame his fight with Gordon for his departure; there were many reasons for his standing down. One of them is something that British politics really needs to watch.

Being at the top now in British politics is like taking your political life in your hands each day. OK, politics is a hard business, not for the faint-hearted—that has always been so—but in today's politics, the pressures are so intense, the criticism so brutal and the targeting so arbitrary, that we are in serious danger of creating a situation where "normal" people feel inclined to walk away, leaving the manically ambitious and the weird in their stead. Of course, people don't always walk away, but there is an inclination to do so that is directly attributable to the sheer force of the storm that is in an almost perpetual swirl of scandal and intrigue, breaking around their heads. Someone with a life, a family, interests beyond politics, the ability to do other things, can feel deeply inclined to do them and leave the storm to itself.

Alan was the first person (though maybe Estelle fitted the same mould somewhat) who, in my time, just left because they wanted to. He was relatively young, under fifty, at the height of his talent; but he chose to leave. Needless to say the Westminster rumour mill refused to believe someone could make such a rational decision and tried hard to invent all sorts of "real" reasons why he left, but he left for the reason he gave: he no longer enjoyed it and wanted out.

John Reid was asked to pick up the baton. At first he was reluctant. He was a Scot, and under devolution, authority for the NHS in Scotland had been passed to the Scottish Executive. I think he may have felt it also a poisoned chalice since it was going to be so hot politically; and of course he had followed the Alan/Gordon row. He had also been moved several times and probably wanted to stay in one place for a while, but I was sure he was right for it. For once, the judgement was undoubtedly correct: he completely understood the rationale for the reforms; understood their politics; understood how to make the case both in the party and to the public; and was determined to take it all further. He was a perfect fit, and was also absolutely capable of standing up to Gordon—and what's more, enjoying it. John believed—I have no idea whether rightly—that Gordon had tried to ignite a scandal under him some time back; and John was not a character to forget such an assault. He would work with him, but not buckle.

At the same time, David Blunkett was motoring on the law and order agenda and to great effect. The 2002 Queen's Speech had had antisocial behaviour legislation at its heart. We had also published the first consultation paper on identity cards, presenting all views. Both measures were right in themselves but also played to an important political game plan.

For many communities, especially those in poorer parts of town and city, antisocial behaviour and low-level crime and disorder was the number-one concern. The graffiti, petty drug dealing, violence and abuse could turn a nice neighbourhood into a nasty one within months. In terms of quality of life, there was no bigger issue. Live in such a place and you will know exactly what I mean. The Americans had come up with a "zero tolerance" idea to tackle it, and our antisocial behaviour laws were based on the same notion. The concept is this: if you tolerate the low-level stuff, you pretty soon find the lawbreakers graduate to the high-level stuff. So cut it out at source; tolerate nothing, not even painting a street wall or dropping litter. It fitted completely with my belief in cohesive communities based on a combination of improved opportunity and greater responsibility. We were investing billions in inner-city renewal, but it would count for nothing if life on the street degenerated as a result of lawlessness and disorder.

The reason for special laws to deal with antisocial behaviour was simple: the individual crimes were sufficiently small in themselves not to warrant either major police effort or serious punishment. As a result, treated conventionally as specific criminal offences, no one did much. The purpose of the new laws was to get them put under a rubric of antisocial behaviour, simplify the procedures and impose real restrictions on the offenders.

Naturally they aroused deep opposition—and in some ways reasonably so, since the laws did involve short-cutting traditional procedures—though never, it may be said, in the communities in which they operated, which loved them and only wanted more of them. The Tories got confused. They felt they should oppose because their lawyer friends rather despised or disagreed with the whole notion. Their constituents, however, agreed with the measures; and after all they were supposed to be the party of law and order. So they faced both ways, with much discomfort.

Identity cards were another thing altogether. In this case, there was a substantial body of opinion opposed, including many on practical grounds. I was convinced that they were necessary for two reasons: firstly, I could see no other alternative to dealing with illegal immigration. I was worried about immigration both in itself and because I thought, unless tackled, it had the capacity greatly to undermine good race relations. Secondly, I thought that over time ID cards would help simplify transactions in both the public and the private sectors, which are nowadays the warp and woof of ordinary living. Mortgage transactions, bank withdrawals, credit cards, underage drinking, dealing with a myriad of public services, welfare—all of these interactions frequently require some form of proof of identity.

I could see all the practical problems. I could envisage that it might take time. The civil liberties argument I thought a little absurd, I confess—many well-functioning democracies have identity cards, and the information stored is less than most supermarkets have. However, the clincher for me is and was a technical one. Due to new technology, it is now possible through fingerprint and iris scans to create a card that is extremely difficult to replicate, so the chance of fraud or identity abuse is therefore hugely diminished. It was the combination of changing ways of living and changing technology that convinced me that this was correct.

After a bit of toing and froing, the Tories came out against it—once more, in my view, mistakenly.

Gordon had multiple good arguments against ID cards, since practicality and cost were genuine issues. His argument against antisocial behaviour legislation was one which once again he was given by the people advising him. He had his own pollsters and unfortunately they used to give him unbelievably duff advice on occasions. Their argument here was that immigration and law and order issues were only of great salience because we insisted on talking about them. David, in particular, was accused of inciting the issues rather than responding to them.

I treated this with some wonderment. You only had to travel the country for half an hour to realise these issues were very real and very live, and the idea that they would melt away if we only stopped focusing on them was utterly crazy. On the contrary, the only thing that prevented them from capsizing us was that we were talking and acting on them. Of course, nothing we did was enough; but doing nothing as a response was plainly a thousand times worse.

In this area, though, there was less of a Treasury locus and so the opposition was, if not muted, unable to obstruct much.

But I'm afraid you get the general picture: I was pressing forward; Gordon was resisting. The whole thing was enervating and depressing. So not for the first or last time, I came back to the central dilemma: how to deal with it?

By then, even more so than 2001, removing Gordon would have brought the entire building tumbling down around our ears. He had massive support in the party and had backing among powerful people in the media. As I fell out with Paul Dacre of the *Daily Mail*, he had fallen in with him. Rupert Murdoch liked Gordon. As Iraq divided me from the left papers, his own relationship with them blossomed. Serious people rated him, and for perfectly good reasons: he was an excellent Chancellor, he had a towering intellect, he had immense, even incredible energy and drive. He was a problem for me; but he wasn't a significant problem to anyone else—well, some of the other Cabinet ministers maybe, but none were at that point powerful enough to take him on, even with me. He was also careful enough, as always, to put resistance on a Treasury and not an anti-reform footing.

Besides, for all the resistance, the effect was to slow down and sometimes water down the process, but not to stop it. Each reform—painful though it was—got through. Manifestly it would have been easier and less painful if it had been done with his support; but he was a brake, not a brick wall.

The alternative to removing him was the one I chose: to try to reach one last understanding with him; to try to reassure him that if he and I cooperated, if we truly shared the same agenda, I would go before the election and hand over to him.

It was unwise because it was never going to work. It was almost certainly unwise also to use John Prescott as the go-between. I say this not because John was badly intentioned—on the contrary, he was only motivated by what he believed was good for the Labour Party—but the trouble was he thought the policy differences between us were immaterial. He thought it was essentially personal. Because John had his own deep reservations about New Labour, they blinded him to the fact that the differences went to the heart of what New Labour was about.

To me, at least, though I was of course at points angry and dismayed at Gordon's behaviour, it really wasn't personal. The thing that mattered most was getting the New Labour programme through, proving that the Labour Party was indeed the party that could, because it had changed, change the public services and welfare state it had helped create; change them radically, make them secure because we had made them modern, right for the twenty-first century, right for a world that was an era away from 1945 in its thinking. I saw this as the supreme fulfilment of my mission: to show how progressive politics, itself modernised, could modernise the nation; to escape from Labour's hide-bound and time-bound fixation with its past, and in doing so help the country escape from theirs. I thought I could see where Thatcherism was right and where it was severely and dangerously limited. I also believed—and this belief increased over time—that a new politics was opening up in which traditional distinctions between left and right were not so much blurred as often profoundly unhelpful in analysing either the past or the future.

Was it reasonable for him to block measures simply because I would not yield to him the position of prime minister? Of course not. But then look at it from his point of view: constantly waiting; constantly fretting that I might sacrifice all political goodwill before the crown was his; constantly fearing the passage of time.

Look at it from my point of view: by late 2004, I would have done more than seven years. The job had taken its toll. Iraq and 11 September had taken their toll. The fight with him had taken its toll. Peter gone, Alastair gone, Anji gone. The shadows had grown larger and darker.

Suppose I am the block to his assumption not just of the position but also of his destiny? Suppose once he gets it, he changes, he relaxes, he breaks open the shell and takes wing? Surely what matters is the programme. Surely if he completes it after I have begun it, that is to the credit of us both. So if he will only agree to carry it through, why not put the burden down, get out, escape? Imagine the relief. Imagine the freedom. Contemplate a new life without that strain, stress and struggle.

One that allows me to think; allows me to build; to study the religious philosophy that fascinates me, and then perhaps to build something even more important than what I was able to build in politics.

It was a delusion, of course. Worse, it was an act of cowardice. I was worn down. Simple as that. Prosaic as that. Nothing grand about it. Nothing elevated. Not really to do with destiny, his or mine. Just born of the normal weakness of a normal person.

In November 2003 we had agreed to meet at John's flat in Admiralty House. A previous meeting down at Dorneywood had been pretty stormy and inconclusive. The vote on tuition fees was only weeks away and it remained very tight. My office were adamantly opposed to me having the dinner with John and Gordon. They guessed where it would lead. It wasn't so much that they didn't trust John or think he was against me; they just thought that he thought we were interchangeable when we weren't, and therefore they didn't trust his instincts.

I walked across Horse Guards Parade in Whitehall. It was a cold evening and the square was just about empty. I went in the side door and made my way up to the flat in the lift. It was a good-size apartment and well furnished, but as with all these grace-and-favour places, always to my mind a little anaemic. John and Pauline's home in Hull—the old Salvation Army hostel—had much more character. But the flat was comfortable and convenient.

I had a drink with John and we waited for Gordon, who came a little late. We sat down to dinner immediately. It was a rough conversation. After a time I asked John to leave to let us talk. I told Gordon bluntly of my concern: I was prepared to go—as I had often said, I had only wanted to do two terms—but the constant obstruction and wilful blocking of the reform programme had to stop. He denied, as ever, that he was obstructing, only really raising legitimate financial points. I said I needed to know that he would be one hundred per cent committed to the reform programme and would carry it through after I left. He said of course he would. John came back in. I said: I have made it clear I won't serve a third term and will go before an election, but I need Gordon's full and unconditional support. John said he thought that was sensible. We parted.

I have put it down baldly. He would say: I received an assurance Tony would go. I would say: I received an assurance Gordon would cooperate and carry through the agenda. You can then debate who kept his word and who didn't.

Unfortunately, I have come in time to a different view. It was an assurance that should never have been asked or given. It was not our right to apportion power like that. Not our right. Not wise. Not sensible politically, let alone democratically.

But more than that, there was an obvious flaw at the heart of it. To demand I give up the office in order to agree the programme is, if you think about it, a disqualification for the office. Whatever leadership is, that is the opposite of it. Likewise, to yield to the demand is an act of deep expedience. Now, I didn't know what else to do. But the feelings on his part of entitlement—which should never enter into a discussion of the office of prime minister because no one is "entitled"—burgeoned still further from that moment on. Maybe he would have got there anyway. Maybe he should have. But never through entitlement bestowed on one holder of the office to another.

I don't mean to make any grandiose point about democracy. There are frequent occasions in which a prime minister has a chosen successor. The point I make is more a political one; it's just a thoroughly bad method to make the choice.

Of course the obvious question, and one repeatedly put by friends and occasionally even by foes, is why I didn't sack Gordon. A perfectly legitimate question with no very obvious answer.

Sometimes my close staff would say to me: You don't owe him what you think you owe him; your past friendship shouldn't stand in the way.

But it was neither obligation nor friendship that stopped me. It was that I still disagreed with the premise that his absence from government was better than his presence within it. Given the nature of some of his behaviour, especially towards the end, that might seem an extraordinary thing to say. The answer to the question "Would life have been easier if he was removed?" seems so clear; however, the answer assumes that had he been sacked, everything else would have remained the same, i.e. it would have been the same world, minus Gordon.

That's not how politics works.

In the end, a political leader has both to manage complex situations and to judge them. Gordon might be said to be such a complex situation, and he had to be managed. And there is a crucial difference between political management and running, say, a company or a football team. A humorous conversation I used to have with Alex Ferguson pinpointed this. "What would you do if you had a really difficult but brilliant player causing you problems?" I would ask. "Get rid of them," he would reply. "And supposing after you got rid of them they were still in the dressing room, and in the squad?" I would say. "That would be a different matter," he would reply, laughing.

Gordon had enormous support within the party and the media. He was regarded by many as a great chancellor, and by nearly all as a strong one. When it's said that I should have sacked him, or demoted him, this takes no account of the fact that had I done so, the party and the government would have been severely and immediately destabilised, and his ascent to the office of prime minister would probably have been even faster. By 2004, but possibly well before then, the media—left and right—would have insisted that I had acted spitefully and wrongly. It is easy to say now, in the light of his tenure as prime minister, that I should have stopped it; at the time that would have been well nigh impossible. I would have had barely any support in any influential quarter for doing so; and some of those most critical of Gordon now, were singing a quite different tune then.

However, that is not the reason I didn't do it. The leader has to manage but also to judge. If I had decided he really was unfit to remain as chancellor I would have dismissed him, even if it had hastened my own dismissal. My failure to do so was not a lack of courage. Nor was it simply about managing a complex situation. It was because I believed, despite it all, despite my own feelings at times, that he was the best chancellor for the country.

I formed this judgement for two reasons. First, just as during the time when Gordon sheltered beneath my umbrella as prime minister the benign view of him was misguided in his favour, so now it is misguided to underestimate his huge strengths. The truth is that every time I considered who might replace him, I concluded he was still the best for the job. He gave the government ballast, solidity and strength. Many of his interventions were excellent, especially at an international level. At his best, his intellect and energy were vast and beneficial to the country. When, sometime in 2001, I think, there was talk of him taking an international job of some description, I reflected and decided the government would be weaker and not stronger without him. Later, when I ran through possible replacements, I still bumped up against the same uncomfortable but—I thought—incontrovertible reality. He was head and shoulders above the others. Only towards the very end did the thoroughgoing New Labour people start to emerge who had sufficient seniority and experience to have taken his place.

The second reason was that, though Gordon resisted many of the reforms and slowed some of them down, he didn't prevent them. We did them. By the time I left, choice and competition were embedded in the NHS; academies were powering ahead; the crime bills had passed;

Right: once I was prime minister, the boundaries between work and life became increasingly blurred. On the phone in the middle of the Pyrenees, August 1999

Below: carrying baby Leo as we arrived at Florence airport, August 2000

Below right: finding time to strum my beloved guitar in Italy

Left: Leo George Blair was the first child born to a serving prime minister in 150 years

Below: Bill Clinton after a swim at Chequers, pushing Leo in his buggy

Above: Robin Cook meets Fatoun Korumain, who was injured by the rebel fighters, 8 June 2000

Above: the Chief of the Defence Staff, Sir Charles Guthrie, arrives in Freetown, Sierra Leone, to assess the situation on the ground, 14 May 2000

Right: a British soldier meets a young local boy during a patrol through a western suburb of Freetown, 10 May 2000

Left: inspecting the troops, Sierra Leone, 9 February 2002. I am immensely proud of what we achieved there

Above right: the fuel crisis of November 2000 was rapidly followed by the foot-and-mouth outbreak the following February, *right*

Above left: visiting Scotland with the army during foot-and-mouth, March 2001

Left: celebrating Labour's second election victory with Cherie, 8 June 2001

Right: my dad was so proud that we had won a second term

Far right: Leo's first appearance on the steps of No. 10 with me and Cherie later that day

Above: my first meeting with George W. Bush following his election as president, at Camp David, 23 February 2001

Left: George and Laura Bush visited the UK in July 2001. On the terrace at Chequers, 19 July 2001

Right: at Chequers with Cherie, Leo and George W. Bush, 19 July 2001

Above: I was about to address the TUC conference in Brighton on 11 September 2001, when the devastating news of the attacks on the Twin Towers, *main picture*, started to come through. I made a brief statement and returned immediately to Downing Street to convene emergency meetings, *right*

Below left: in New York with Mayor Rudolph Giuliani, left, and Governor George Pataki, right, after a memorial service for the British victims of the 9/11 attacks, 20 September 2001

Below right: at a press conference with George W. Bush at the White House, before he addressed a joint session of Congress, 20 September 2001

Left: with Hamid Karzai in Kabul, Afghanistan, 2002

Below: meeting British troops at Camp Bastion in Helmand Province, November 2006

Above: months of negotiations on Iraq came to a head during the Azores summit. With, left to right, Spanish prime minister José Maria Aznar, George W. Bush and Portuguese prime minister José Manuel Barroso, 16 March 2003

Right: with Kofi Annan at the United Nations headquarters in New York, March 2003

Top left: working on my Commons speech for the Iraq debate, 15 March 2003
Top right: gathering my thoughts before a Downing Street press conference on the Middle East peace process, 14 March 2003. *Above left and right*: last-minute thoughts and preparations with the inner team moments before I stepped into the chamber
Below: the crucial debate in the House of Commons, 18 March 2003

Above: the war cabinet meets in Downing Street, 20 March 2003
Right: with Jacques Chirac at the European Council, 24 March 2003
Far right: with the Chief of the Defence Staff, Sir Mike Boyce, in the den in Downing Street, 23 March 2003

Above left: at Camp David with Alastair Campbell, George W. Bush, Tom Kelly, Matthew Rycroft, David Manning and Jonathan Powell, 27 March 2003
Above right: security briefing at Hillsborough during George W. Bush's visit, with Condoleezza Rice, White House spokesman Ari Fleischer, Jack Straw, Colin Powell and Alastair Campbell, April 2003

Left: addressing the joint session of the U.S. Congress, 18 July 2003. It was one of my most important speeches

Main picture: as the Iraq War continued, there were protests outside the Royal Courts of Justice where the Hutton Inquiry was being held, 28 August 2003

Top right: returning from the Green Zone after a visit to troops in Baghdad, 2003

Centre right: leaving Downing Street to give evidence to the Hutton Inquiry, 28 August 2003

Bottom right: the statue of Saddam Hussein being toppled in Baghdad after the arrival of U.S. troops, 9 April 2003

Above: the loyal and dedicated Alastair Campbell left Downing Street, 29 August 2003

Top: Bono addressed the Labour Party Conference on world poverty in 2004

Above: with David Blunkett at the 2005 conference

Left: ice creams with Gordon on the campaign trail, 2 May 2005

Below left: with youngsters on the way to a drop-in centre in the North-East

Below: receiving the Queen's invitation to form a new government following our historic re-election on 5 May 2005 for a third term

Above left: the Middle East peace process continued. A press conference with Ariel Sharon in Jerusalem, 22 December 2004

Above: Shimon Peres in front of a picture of Yitzhak Rabin, two key figures in the peace process. Jerusalem, 19 July 2004

Left: with Yasser Arafat for talks in the Gaza Strip, Palestine, 1 November 2001

Above left: under the media spotlight, Angela Merkel, Jacques Chirac and I talk during the G8 in St. Petersburg, 17 July 2006

Above right: TV cameras crowded in as I visited the floods in Gloucester in November 2000

Right: walking along the beach with the leaders of the G8 at the Sea Island summit, Georgia in June 2004

Above: Bob Geldof, the force behind the worldwide Live 8 concerts of 2 July 2005

Above right: Denise Lewis leapt for joy alongside mayor of London Ken Livingstone and Tessa Jowell in Singapore as London won the bid to stage the 2012 Olympic Games, 6 July 2005

Right: Londoners celebrating the same moment in Trafalgar Square

Below: the following day, three bombs were detonated on the London Underground and one on a bus in Tavistock Square. Fifty-two people lost their lives. 7 July 2005

Left: my statement on the atrocity of 7/7, at the G8 summit in Gleneagles, 8 July 2005, on behalf of the assembled leaders

Left: speaking on world poverty at the Old Vic theatre in London, with Gordon listening

Below: celebrating the day on which power sharing was finally restored to Northern Ireland, with, left to right, Martin McGuinness, Bertie Ahern, Peter Hain and Ian Paisley. Stormont, Belfast, 8 May 2007

Below left: on 10 May 2007, I announced at the Trimdon Labour Club that I would step down as prime minister the following month

Below right: in my last months, I undertook a wide range of visits. With British troops in Basra, Iraq, 19 May 2007

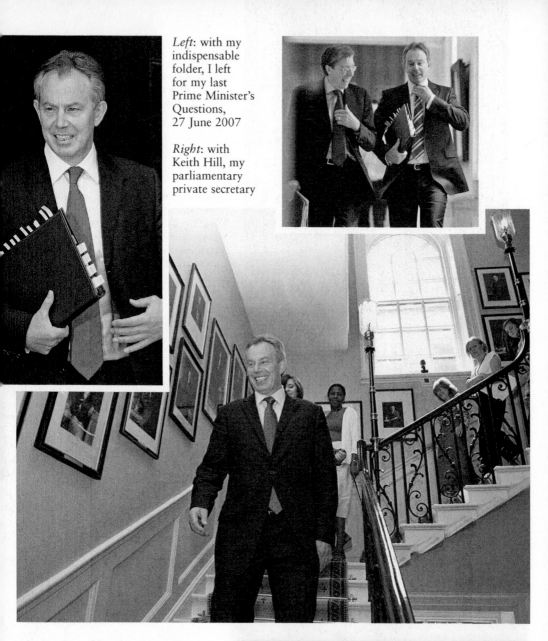

Left: with my indispensable folder, I left for my last Prime Minister's Questions, 27 June 2007

Right: with Keith Hill, my parliamentary private secretary

Above: after addressing the staff, I walked down the stairs at Downing Street for the last time, 27 June 2007

Right: boarding the train to take me back up to the North-East

Above: the final photocall on the steps of Number 10 with the family, 27 June 2007

Left: with Barack Obama, 28 July 2008

Below: with Mahmoud Abbas, 9 March 2010

Above left: as part of my Africa Governance Initiative, meeting officials of the Sierra Leone tourist board, Freetown, April 2009

Above right: in my role as the Quartet representative, meeting Palestinian Maj Ibrahim Attallal in Beit Skarya near Bethlehem, 19 March 2009

Left: as part of my Faith Foundation, speaking to students at Winchester School in Dubai, 6 January 2010

Below: with pupils from Barnes School, Sunderland, at the sports complex at Northumbria University, Newcastle-upon-Tyne, which is being run in cooperation with my Sports Foundation, 25 June 2010

tuition fees were in place; and welfare and pension reforms were formulated, if not introduced. These weren't small items. They were major changes. In the final analysis he supported them. He wouldn't have initiated them; but when it came to the crunch, he went along. They got through. And herein lies a lesson. There is a reason, apart from the principal one of New Labour, why the government I led was the first Labour government to win even two successive full terms, let alone three; and why it governed for more than double the length of the previous longest-serving Labour government. This is the part that even my closest advisers never understood; but as I used to tease them, these judgments are why I'm the leader and you're not!

Ultimately, though the relentless personal pressure from Gordon was wearing, it actually troubled me far less than they (or perhaps he) ever realised. And it was in many ways a far less toxic and deadly opposition than might have been the case.

Because Gordon was the standard-bearer for dissent, his banner the one to which the internal critics naturally gathered, the natural opposition that progressive politics always contains was kept within bounds. Put him out and one of two things would have happened: either he would have been in a position, and long before ten years, to mount a successful challenge (or at least a challenge that would have been terminal in its consequences); or another banner, probably more to the left, possibly more destructive to the party's long-term health, would have arisen. I came to the conclusion that having him inside and constrained was better than outside and let loose, or, worse, becoming the figurehead of a far more damaging force well to the left.

So was he difficult, at times maddening? Yes. But he was also strong, capable and brilliant, and those were qualities for which I never lost respect.

There was another interesting factor that occurred to me. I had always taken the view that Margaret Thatcher, great prime minister though she was, should never have stood in the way of Michael Heseltine becoming leader. It was her determination to stop him that made her withdraw from the leadership contest following the challenge to her, and allow John Major to win. Heseltine had many flaws, but he was a big figure and would have been a far more potent force to deal with. He may also have stopped the Eurosceptic virus from taking over the Tories. So I always took the view that she allowed personal preference to stand in the way of her party's true interests.

I was set upon not repeating that mistake. I would be big enough to put aside personal bitterness and not stand in Gordon's way. In so doing, I just made the same mistake differently. I too tried to choose my successor, and by the time I realised the choice was mistaken, it was too late.

However, it did buy me peace. After the dinner, Gordon and I began talking again properly. Though it came about rather tortuously, by degrees he got George Mudie of the Treasury Select Committee and Nick Brown to stand down their opposition. We won the tuition-fee vote. The Hutton Report concluded favourably.

In my own mind, I became more settled. I told no one in the office that I had agreed to stand down if Gordon cooperated, but naturally they guessed. Rather sensibly, instead of pushing back they just let matters take their course. Jonathan and Sally in particular were confident it wouldn't happen. They understood my desire to leave, but thought it inconceivable that I would conclude that Gordon shared the same agenda. They were completely sure he didn't.

Meanwhile, events crowded in on us as thick and fast as ever. In March 2004, there were the terror attacks in Madrid, timed for the Spanish general election. Almost two hundred people died and over 2,000 were injured. It was a stark reminder that the terrorist movement remained alive and kicking. The memories of 11 September had dimmed, despite events such as the 2002 Bali bombings. The anti-terror laws passed in the first flush of fear after the attack in New York were now subject to a steady drumbeat of opposition from those who felt them inconsistent with Britain's liberties. I was continually conscious of the fact that the terrorists would love to strike at Britain. We had more or less regular updates and briefings and were watching numerous cells of activity.

In May, ten countries entered the EU. We had been staunch advocates of enlargement. It was a big moment. The Constitution for the EU had been agreed. With deep misgivings, I accepted we had to promise a referendum on it. We wouldn't get the Constitution through the House of Lords without it, and even the Commons vote would have been in doubt. My statement met with predictably and justifiably raucous cheering from Tories, who knew my heart wasn't in it.

Jacques Chirac was also aggrieved as he felt it presented him with a real problem. In this, he was right. If Britain promised a referendum, it put enormous pressure on France to do the same. But truthfully, I couldn't avoid it, and as Jack Straw insistently advocated, better to do it apparently willingly than be forced to do it by a vote. However, it reminded me how far I had to go to persuade British opinion of the merits of being in the mainstream of Europe. As ever, the difficulty was that the Eurosceptics were organised and had savage media backing; those in favour of a constructive attitude were disorganised and had the usual progressive media "backing," i.e. spending more time criticising their own side than rebutting the propaganda of the other.

For all that, though, we remained reasonably strong in Europe. We chose our battles carefully. I went out of my way to construct alliances that protected us against any potential French/German stitch-up, and, despite a profound disagreement over Iraq, kept lines open to Chirac and Schroeder.

Gerhard Schroeder was a really tough cookie. Despite falling out over foreign policy, I generally admired his radicalism in domestic policy reform, sympathised with his problems with Oskar Lafontaine, his former Finance Minister who was now parked strongly on his left and soon to start a new party, and I thought Gerhard had real leadership qualities.

As I say elsewhere, my motivation for bringing Britain into the centre of Europe is nothing to do with starry-eyed idealism, though I happen to share the European ideal; it is about naked national self-interest. In time, and a time fast approaching, no European nation, not even Germany, will be large enough to withstand pressure from the really big nations unless we bond together. United, we are strong. Divided, we are not only weak, but we also unbalance the geopolitical power game. Europe can play a role positioned not between but alongside the U.S. and China, India, Russia, Brazil and the other emerging powers. In that role it can do a lot, not only for itself but also for the equilibrium of international politics. But if Europe's countries are played off against each other—and major powers are swift to spot that opportunity—the downside is felt not just by us but by the international community as a whole.

So all this was going on, along with the usual flotsam and jetsam: the campaign group Fathers 4 Justice, a fathers' rights organisation, threw a condom filled with purple flour at me during Prime Minister's Questions (it was the shortest PMQs I ever did, and much was I grateful); Ken Livingstone was re-elected as mayor of London, and England got knocked out of the Euro 2004 football competition on penalties. For a moment, the eye of the media beast was distracted and some semblance of normality reigned. I appointed Peter Mandelson as the new EU commissioner, despite intense internal opposition from parts of the PLP and Cabinet. We lost one seat to the Lib Dems and narrowly held on to another against them in two by-elections. We had a heavy but not utterly disastrous defeat in the local elections. The by-election in Peter's seat was won.

Our political position seemed fragile, but in reality we remained strong. The Tories never won a by-election from us during my time as leader. I should have taken more heart from all of that than I did. As Peter used to say to me, but I never quite accepted, "You are far stronger than you think."

In the course of the first part of 2004, we had proceeded with the next stage of the reform plans. We now had on the books a schools programme that included greater freedom for schools but also the first embryonic academies; variable tuition fees, modelled on the U.S. system; NHS hospital trusts and the first foundation hospitals and again the beginnings of private sector competition; asylum reform; antisocial behaviour legislation; a new system of early-years learning in childcare; and work under way on pensions, welfare and ID cards.

The aim now was to construct a clear forward agenda to take all these changes to a new, sustained and pervasive level. The changes so far had shown clearly that the greater the autonomy for schools and hospitals, the greater the innovation; the more choice and competition, the higher the quality of outcomes; and especially with the NHS, cuts in waiting times were all coming from the combination of the system being open to private sector investment and money increasingly following the patient; and the only problem with the law and order changes was that people wanted them to go faster and further.

In summary, extra money plus system change delivered results. Through 2004 and after seven years in power, we were finally getting real and substantial improvements. The Delivery Unit set up by Michael Barber after the 2001 election was producing big dividends. Along with the Strategy Unit, it had been a major innovation. It had been harshly criticised and remained subject to fairly continual sniping from the traditional Civil Service, but Michael and his relatively small team of around thirty were making a quantitative and qualitative difference to the performance of government.

As Michael explains in his book *Instruction to Deliver*—which has become something of a public sector hallowed text round the world—for the first time we were tracking priority commitments, receiving real-time data on how they were proceeding and following up so that obstacles were removed and policies adjusted as necessary. Most of all, those charged with delivering knew they were being monitored. It was not a heavy process. Michael's consummate skill was to make performance management seem, and indeed be, a partnership. It was highly effective.

By this time, I felt things were really moving but, as I say, we now needed to take it all to the next stage. So we began work on a series of five-year plans, to be published at the end of the summer session. The aim was to give the party a solid, radical New Labour platform on which to win a third term. Of course, critical to this was to ensure that Number 10 and Gordon's office were working closely on it, so we began the sessions to try to take it forward.

Meanwhile, I prepared for the likely departure. Cherie and I had been out of the London housing market since 1997, during which time prices had rocketed. With the help of Martha Greene, a friend, we began discreetly to look for a house. It's not an easy thing to do without being discovered, but Martha handled it all with great skill and we identified a house in Connaught Square which would allow us to keep Leo at the Westminster primary school where he was very happy.

I was reasonably settled in my own mind that two terms was enough. I had, as I explained, taken the decision over Iraq in good faith. Right or wrong, I tried to do what I thought was in the best interests of the country. But the coming together of a right-wing media that wanted me out because I could win for Labour and a left-wing media that was genuinely outraged by war led to a campaign that tested even my resilience and fortitude. You should get used to being criticised as prime minister. Being vilified was a little different. I am not by nature a whiner; but inside I was starting to whine.

Worn down is, again, how I would describe it. It's hard to express what it's like. Naturally, it is a great privilege and honour to do the job—and by the way, it really is!—but here's where my greatest strength was my greatest weakness: I am normal. Faced with a choice between a thriller with plenty of action and special effects, where in the end the hero triumphs, and a psychological drama about a dying wife who discovers her husband has been having a passionate affair with her best friend, her only child commits suicide and who then dies in solitude and penury, I go for the first. Ask me whether I would prefer to eat out at a good restaurant with friends talking about anything other than politics or sit through Wagner's *Götterdämmerung* and you would find me in the restaurant. Like most of humanity I prefer laughing to crying, enjoyment to mourning, feeling up to feeling down. My natural disposition is to wake up looking forward to the day ahead.

And I found I wasn't. Of course, sometimes life is more like a psycho-logical drama than a thriller; Wagner's opera can provoke more reflection than a casual night out with friends; and tears are more appropriate than laughter. There were many tears being shed as a result of my decisions, so why should I not share them? Indeed, how could I not share them?

The euphoria, the boundless optimism of the early years had long dissipated. Instead, each day, each meeting, occasionally each hour seemed a struggle, an endless pushing up against forces, seen or unseen, that pushed back sometimes steadily, sometimes violently, but always with what seemed like inexhaustible energy and often malice.

So when does fatigue turn to self-pity, and to surrender? I was very aware that these feelings were gripping me. I accepted the first, despised the other two, but could feel my will ebbing and my resistance falter-ing. And I had told Gordon I would go if he carried through the same agenda. So that gave me my reason (or was it excuse?) to go. Whatever, I wanted out.

I talked about it with Cherie. She thought I was wrong to go, but made it clear she would support my decision. But, as she could be at critical moments, she forced me to be honest about why I wanted to go. She told me bluntly I was kidding myself if I thought Gordon shared the same programme. "You just want out," she said. "I understand why. In many ways, so do I. But let's be honest about it."

I wasn't sure she was right about Gordon. I had thought it possible he might go with the agenda once he owned it. And there was another reason motivating me, concerning the Labour Party. In modern politics, to go two terms is a big achievement; I did ten years, which must be the maximum nowadays. In earlier times, when the pace of politics was slower and the leader was far less visible, less scrutinised and criticised, you could go for three or four. Today, a new prime minister or presi-dent becomes almost boringly familiar to people even after a year. By year eight, they've had enough. Actually, you've had enough.

We had put in an offer on the house. It had been accepted. My feel-ing at that point was to announce around conference time that I would go, and be out by Christmas. That would leave a good six-month run-in for the election for Gordon.

However, the work on the five-year plans was now running into seri-ous difficulties. The trouble is that once you declare an intention that you are going to go, even if only to yourself in your own mind, it seeps out as if by osmosis.

Also, one stipulation I had made with John Prescott and Gordon was that neither should mention my departure, not even to their closest staff. In particular, I had said to Gordon he must not on any account discuss this with the two Eds, Balls and Miliband. I permitted him to tell Sue Nye and I told Anji (who was of course no longer working for me), but that was it. In spite of this, he had actually told his inner circle as a whole.

This was a real problem. I had set up the possibility of my going by saying to the *Guardian* that if I felt I was a liability to the Labour Party then I would leave. That was as far as I wanted to go—if my leaving became current and imminent, then self-evidently all authority would evaporate. But articles were now appearing discussing the possibility of my departure, with some even saying it was all agreed.

I resented this, but in the end I suppose it was inevitable he would talk to his people, and he would say he needed to plan. Actually, the reason for my change of mind was not to do with that.

The reason I started to draw back was to do with the ongoing discussions with the Treasury. Matthew Taylor and Jeremy Heywood, who were conducting them on behalf of Number 10, were saying in effect that it was completely clear there was no way that Ed Balls, in particular, was supportive of this programme. Other Treasury officials were talking of me and describing how—as one put it—"It's all a bit pointless anyway as he's not going to be there."

This had been filtering back to me in dribs and drabs, and then one day in May, Matthew had a quiet word with me. "You do know there is not the slightest possibility of them running with these five-year plans, don't you?" He also told me they were contemplating significant alterations to the tuition-fees reforms.

I decided to have it out with Gordon, and we met later that month. I told him that we were having serious worries that this agenda wasn't in line with his thinking. It was then that he miscalculated.

I'm sure I never quite handled him right in tense situations. Maybe we knew each other too well, and like some quarrelling, married couple we let emotion run out on the pitch before thinking. But on this occasion he made a grievous error: he should have reassured me, and instead he tried to bully me. He snarled when he should have charmed.

In effect, he said: you've promised to go and that's that. That was completely the wrong tactic, and I became very tough in response. He then altered and said of course we agreed the agenda, refuting that Ed Balls was anything other than one hundred per cent in favour of it, and also denying that he had told Ed anything about my going. I knew both things were wrong.

The meeting ended badly. But worse, the hostility started up again almost immediately. They had decided to force the issue. It was the stupidest thing—it forced me to confront or yield. And if I yielded, what word could I utter when I looked in the mirror except "coward"?

At the end of June I went to a NATO meeting in Istanbul, where I recall getting the first headlines from the British papers from David Hill. Normally, and mercifully, David showed me little of the media. As he put it, "I show you this stuff on a 'need to know' basis." He was a consummate operator with really excellent political judgement, calm, assured and as good a suffocator of a febrile story as there was. And there were plenty to suffocate, as you can imagine. The papers were full of what was obviously, and almost openly, a GB press operation arising out of critical comments which Derek Scott, my former economic adviser, had made about Gordon. Derek had by then left Downing Street. Although a really good and freethinking adviser, he had been "independent" (i.e. uncontrollable) enough when he worked in Number 10; outside it, there was no hope of keeping him "on message." Anyone knew that. Gordon knew that. But Derek's comments were hyped and presented as an attack on Gordon as if authorised by me, which was absurd. It saw the start of a "Gordon as victim" line which ran pretty constantly from then until I left.

"What do we do?" said David.

"Nothing," I replied, "except make it clear we are fully supportive of Gordon and don't share Derek's views."

I left Istanbul, went on to the Special EU Council, and came back to London on 30 June to make a statement on both the NATO and the EU meetings. It had been an incredibly busy month. The week before we had had the ordinary EU Council. The week before that, we had had the G8 summit at Sea Island in Georgia. I had been more or less continually on the go, with barely time to think on Gordon. But I could feel the pressure building and getting uglier by the day.

I did the usual Thursday Cabinet, held various other meetings and then went to Chequers on the Friday. I used to entertain there sporadically, and had leaders there when it was unavoidable, or when discretion and secrecy were paramount (as in some of the Irish talks); but on the whole Chequers was a place for relaxation and reflection. I've always found the two go together.

In the summer I could sit out on the terrace, ploughing through the box papers, stopping every so often for a mug of tea or to take a call. I used to have a light lunch with nothing to drink, watch *Football Focus* if it was a Saturday and pretend I was a pundit, or a live game if it was on at midday, work a little more and then go to the gym. In the early days I might go off to RAF Halton and play tennis.

On this weekend, I sat and thought long and hard. I came to one inescapable conclusion, and then another. The first was that I didn't really believe Gordon would carry on the agenda. The truth is: if he believed in it, he would have supported it. And you can tell a lot from the people around someone; those around Gordon didn't agree with it. OK, they might be cajoled into it, even pressed into it, but once I was gone there was no earthly hope of the fledgling programme being pursued.

The second conclusion was that the only reason I wanted to go was cowardice, pure and simple. I could try to dress it up in grand gestures of selflessness, pretend that I would be going for the good of the party or country, or even family; but it wouldn't wash. That motive was not selfless but selfish. I would be going because I couldn't take it any more, the abuse, the pressure, the hounding, the misrepresentation of my motives, the denigration. The kitchen temperature had become too high; I was sweating.

Also, I now knew what would be coming after me. It would not exactly be Old Labour, but it wouldn't be authentic New Labour either. Very soon we would be back to conventional Labour versus conventional Tory. And there would be only one winner from that.

A couple of weeks before, in a rare break from the helter-skelter, John Reid had come to see me. John is a very wise man. Once he broke the grip the demon drink had on him, he flourished into one of the most shrewd and profound politicians in any party. Had he come through earlier, he could have played a huge part in keeping Labour as New Labour.

We had sat out on the wicker chairs in the Downing Street garden. As was his wont, he was very direct.

"You must not go," he said. I began to protest but he waved me silent. "I know you're thinking about it. It would be the most terrible mistake not only for you but for the party and the country. You must not do it. You know as well as I do what Gordon will be like. He may become leader some day, he may not; but to hand over now would be irresponsible. What is more, you need to fight the election even after Iraq, even with its burden, and you need to win it. And if you don't, however you may present it, you are running away."

As I sat in the gentle July sunshine at Chequers in 2004, I realised not that John had persuaded me—Tessa Jowell, Alan Milburn, Peter Mandelson and others had made the same argument—but rather that he had brought my own thoughts out from under the cover of my fantasy and illuminated them. It would be tough to stay, even at points horrible; but it would be a failure of simple, basic courage to go.

The British people, whom I genuinely adored and with whom the political relationship, at least on my part, was on occasions almost like a love affair, had ceased loving and were not going to start again. Support remained, but many were sullen, even resentful. The enjoyment that remained was the joy of doing what I believed in wholeheartedly, winning a third term, forcing the Tories therefore to change, and seeing through a programme of domestic reform that I was sure was right. Iraq would be a severe headwind; but I was again sure that whatever the wisdom of doing it, the folly of retreat was unthinkable and precipitate withdrawal a disaster. I looked as dispassionately as I could at our programme, and at that of the Tories under Michael Howard, and I didn't really have any doubt as to what was sensible for Britain. But our winning depended vitally on us remaining clearly and unashamedly New Labour. If we shifted from it, even deviated from it at the margins, I knew we would be finished.

My mind was made up. I could not hand over to Gordon, at least not at this time and quite possibly never. The following week I informed him. You can guess the reaction. I took back the management of the five-year plans. We just worked with departments, and worked round and despite the Treasury. We got the plans in proper radical shape, and they became the basis of the third-term manifesto. After a good two weeks' holiday, I came back fully refreshed.

In my conference address, I set out our stall for the third term. Previously, Alastair and Peter Hyman would supply a draft speech, something they excelled at. I would then amend and re-amend, usually over ten or fifteen drafts. They would tend to pull one way ideologically, Anji and Jonathan the other. Over time, starting with the 2001 speech, I would do the draft myself. Peter and Alastair would write certain key passages or be commissioned to give the speech colour. The others would give a view. Meanwhile, David Hill would point out pitfalls or unintended headlines. Matthew Taylor and Andrew Adonis would look after policy. Sally Morgan would comment.

I made the case for what we had done, and what we still had to do. As always, I tried to unite traditional values with an analysis of the future world in which they had to be applied. I also attempted to settle the party with their new status, not as the underdog allowed to govern only occasionally, but as a party able to govern for a substantial period.

At the end of the conference I had another situation to handle. The previous year I had suffered arrhythmia for the first time, a heart condition that means that the top part of the heart can start to beat out of sync with the bottom part. It then causes an irregular heartbeat, breathlessness and a feeling of being tired. If untreated, it can cause a stroke (yes a stroke, strangely enough, rather than a heart attack). It had been treated by a process which essentially jump-starts the heart back into rhythm.

In the summer of 2004 I had noticed that the arrhythmia had come back. The recurrence had left me short of breath (it was most apparent in the gym and I realised something was wrong). This time the doctors said I should have a surgical procedure known as an ablation, which effectively burns off the bit of the heart that is short-circuiting. Anyway, don't ask me to debate the medical details; I just asked for the advice, got it and took it. The date for the operation was set for straight after party conference.

Gordon was still in a highly dangerous mood. In his conference speech he had gone out of his way to extol the merits of "Real Labour." It was, of course, a mistake, but it was also an ominous signal to the party. I felt I had to deal with the leadership issue.

Against much advice, I resolved to say I would fight the next election but not the one after. Many people thought it fatal ever to say when you may stand down. I pointed out that this was the view Margaret Thatcher took, and a fat lot of good it did her. Past a certain point, you're damned either way. Say you are going, and they say: Why stay? Say you will carry on without limit, and they say: You intend to go on forever. There is no easy way.

I decided to throw so much at the media that they wouldn't quite know what to make of it all, and I gave them three stories at once: I would fight the third election but not the fourth; I had bought a house; I was having a heart operation. It was the only way to do it and I was highly amused by the spluttering and reeling as they tried to work out the "true" significance of the stories being released simultaneously, since of course it wouldn't do simply to report the three things as they were. David Hill handled it brilliantly. I had my operation. The house was bought. And so was some time.

SEVENTEEN

2005: TB/GB

The 2005 election was ugly: fraught in its build-up; marred in its running by internal disputes; vicious in the nature of the campaign; and precarious in its aftermath. I didn't look forward to it. I didn't enjoy doing it. But we won. Looking back on a majority of more than sixty over all the other parties combined, it seems like a minor miracle. Which, in one sense, it was.

I had taken the country into an unpopular war with a very unpopular Republican American president. The war had finally allowed right and left opposition to find a point of unity. In terms of my personal political position, it gave the party a reason to think if we could only lose that albatross, we could renew with Gordon as leader.

All of it obscured what was actually a more fundamental and important truth: the basic position of New Labour was still the dominant and determining centre of gravity for British politics. We had won despite all the drawbacks, despite the war, the length of time I had been prime minister, tuition fees (which cost us dear), the internal wrangle with Gordon, and a fairly incessant drumbeat of negative and destructive criticism from right and left. This was an election we were never destined to win with enthusiasm, but as I tried to point out in the post-election dissection and analysis, the crucial thing was: we were never going to lose.

The Queen's Speech of November 2004 had gone surprisingly well. The legislative programme—always a bit of a weird vehicle to describe what the government wants to do—had vigour and lift. We had a strong agenda in the election. The platform was indisputably New Labour and

there were detailed plans in all main areas of policy: on schools, especially academies; on the next stages of NHS reform; on welfare, crime,
ID cards; on housing and planning; on local government; and even on a
new industrial strategy. Frankly, with the media climate as it was—and
by then the BBC were more or less in a monotheme on Iraq—there was
never going to be much coverage of policy, especially domestic policy.
But here's a curious thing about the public. Even without knowledge of
the policy detail, they sensed that we were a government with a programme, a party that still retained a sense of mission, with a leader who
could still lead. The ministers and party had something to carry with
them, that kept them focused even as they struggled with the onslaught
around Iraq, "Blair the liar," "time for a change" and the general static
of a raw and nasty campaign. Though the Tories had a set of policies,
they seemed more like a set of talking points designed to provoke anger
or grievance, but not reflection or the mobilisation of a plan for the
nation's future.

George Bush had been re-elected U.S. president. I am, of course, a
Democrat, and I liked John Kerry and thought he would have made a
good president. But the issue, whatever my own political tribe, was—in
terms of perception—completely obvious: a defeat for Bush was a defeat
for Blair.

Also, as I have said, I had come to like and admire George. I was asked
recently which of the political leaders I had met had most integrity. I
listed George near the top. In what was a fairly liberal audience, some
people were aghast. Others even tittered, thinking I was joking. But I
meant it. He had genuine integrity and as much political courage as any
leader I ever met. I said to my audience: You can disagree with him on
Iraq (which I didn't) or on other issues (which I did), and still accept he
sincerely believed in spreading freedom and democracy.

He was, in a bizarre sense (bizarre because it appears counter-
intuitive), a true idealist. I remember at the time of the Palestinian elections in January 2005 when many people thought they should be
postponed, George was all for them going ahead. He didn't ignore or
fail to comprehend the advice that this might give Hamas a victory; he
simply said: "If that's what people think, let's find it out."

It's one of the oddest things about modern politics. The paradigm
imposed, usually by a particular media view, completely disorients the
proper analysis. I used to smile at the way the Obama/McCain election
of 2008 was framed: Barack was the man of vision, John the old politi-

cal hack. One seemed to call America to a new future, the other seemed a stale relic of the past. This was a paradigm that determined the mood and defined the election.

Actually, it was John who was articulating a foreign policy that could be called wildly idealistic for the cause of freedom. Barack was the supreme master of communicating a brilliant vision, but he was a practitioner of realism, advocating a cautious approach based on reaching out, arriving at compromises and striking deals to reduce tension. For these purposes, leave alone who is right. It's just a really interesting feature of modern politics that the mood trumps the policy every time.

So it was with George. He was basically considered a right-wing Republican bastard for getting rid of hostile brutal dictatorships and insisting they be replaced not with friendly brutal dictatorships but with an attempt at liberal democracy. Of course, part of this feeling was an entirely natural dislike of war. Part was also the Republicans' fault for allowing this ridiculous notion of "neoconservatives" to take hold. I often warned George of this.

It meant that the war was presented as ideological in a right/left sense, instead of being presented in a manner that could unify, something which so easily and correctly could have been done. Even Guantánamo, a policy that was both understandable and, done in a different way, justifiable, came to be seen as a poke in the eye for all those who believed in the rule of law.

The truth is that the prisoners picked up in the war zone of Afghanistan were, in a sense, prisoners of war. In normal circumstances, the war ends, they are returned; we all live peacefully ever after. Except in this case, the war hadn't ended and wasn't a conventional war. There was no way of proving, as in a proper court of law, that they were "guilty." On the other hand, many of them would undoubtedly be a threat if released. But the whole way it was handled was done almost in the most provocative way possible, as if we deliberately sought to alienate liberal opinion rather than try to face up to the reality of the dilemma for our security.

But in any event, George's re-election had deprived those inside and outside the party of another hammer to hit me with, and their profound disappointment was evident.

Other events came and went: the Queen opened the new and controversial (because expensive) Scottish Parliament building in Edinburgh in October 2004; Yasser Arafat died in November; in December I lost David Blunkett as Home Secretary, over accusations that he had fast-tracked a visa application for the nanny of his ex-partner.

I was really sorry for him. He had allowed himself to fall for someone who was wholly unsuitable and married, and who had also conceived their child. David had told me about it some months before, very honestly and with deep regret. He was long divorced himself, his boys were grown up, he got lonely; simple as that. However, this particular relationship was never going to work—he was devoted to the baby, but the mother was not going to leave her husband, and the situation was plainly destabilising for him and impossible either to maintain or to keep secret. When it came out, I stuck by him but the media were going to invent something to get him out. There was going to be a conflict of interest. One was duly found in the visa application. It didn't actually amount to anything, but by then it no longer mattered. The pain and stress were making it hard for him to do his job. So he went.

We had an emotional farewell. I determined to try to bring him back after the election. I adored and deeply admired David, and also found his whole attitude over his child—he wouldn't give up on access, despite the threat of publicity if he proceeded—very principled. He was a truly decent guy, a great political talent. He picked the wrong woman. Easy to do. Fatal in politics.

I was due to take a break in Sharm el-Sheikh in Egypt over the new year. As I prepared to leave Chequers, I took a phone call about a tsunami in Asia on Boxing Day. I hesitated about leaving. There were going to be thousands killed, with British casualties bound to be among them.

I decided to go. I had been working flat out. Leo had barely seen me recently. I had just returned from yet another fairly gruelling European Council. I had an election coming. The fallout from the tsunami would in any event be handled on the phone. Sharm was nearer the relevant time zone. However, I knew I would be criticised for going. And I was.

The days in Sharm were divided between calls from early morning until late lunch and then relaxation later. We arranged for all the help we could. We got our foreign and consular services, and our forensics and police, to help the authorities in Indonesia and Thailand; and to look after the administrative challenge of helping families who were grieving or still forlornly searching for their loved ones. As it turned out, I knew the families of some of the victims, including Dickie and

Sheila Attenborough, who had lost their daughter, granddaughter and their daughter's mother-in-law.

As ever in these situations, I was desperately sorry for the bereaved. When I spoke to Dickie—who is just a superlative human being—he was crying. I thought of how I would feel to lose Euan or Nicky or Kathryn—his granddaughter was fourteen—and realised the sense of devastation. My heart ached for him.

When I returned home, I had plenty to occupy me. One piece of excellent news was the defection of Robert Jackson, the Conservative MP for Wantage. Robert had been a don at All Souls College, Oxford, and an education minister in the previous Tory government, and was totally onside with tuition fees, recognising them as an essential step forward for higher education. He had a rather upper-class air to him that hid what was, in fact, a warm and delightful personality. I put Alastair (with whom I remained in close contact) on handling duty, and it all went pretty well.

Interestingly, in the light of what I did later, I organised a conference in London to support capacity-building for the Palestinian Authority and its new leader President Mahmoud Abbas, or Abu Mazen as he was known.

The truth is, I was still absolutely set on a strategy that had a twin track—hard and soft. Hard: we see through Iraq and Afghanistan. Soft: we deliver Palestinian statehood. Whereas the international community, in its usual purblind way, saw disengagement from Gaza as a "unilateral" Israeli act and therefore wrong, I was emphatic that it could be presented as lifting the occupation and removing settlements. For all the problems, therefore, we had no serious option but to go with it.

Ariel Sharon was an extraordinary man. He would drive you mad at meetings, just sitting there telling you about terrorism as if we in Britain had never heard of it; lecturing; hectoring; and above all, even when you agreed with him, continuing to talk as if you had just contradicted him. I used to walk out of meetings, saying to my officials, "Does he think I'm French?"

But at the same time as being utterly maddening, he was a real leader. A big man in every sense. Really tough, uncompromising, and if he didn't want to be moved, unmovable. Someone who took no nonsense from anyone, including his own supporters. Someone who made the s*** go back up the bull's bottom. He made it as hard as possible to support his disengagement policy in Gaza. He did it in as alienating a way as could be imagined for international opinion. But as I pointed out in arguments with other leaders, so what? He has Israeli opinion to worry about, I used to say, and they've had four years of terrorism. They aren't going to do it in a way that looks as if it is helping Palestine or appeasing Western sensibilities. There's no disputing one simple fact: Israel has left Gaza, so let's make the most of it.

The London conference was a success, but I wasn't sure George's heart was yet fully in it, and Condoleezza Rice, newly appointed as Secretary of State, was feeling her way. With everything else and the election, I scarcely had time to focus on Palestine anything other than intermittently. (Later, Condi came to focus on the Middle East and did so with vigour and an effect that, had it not been for the convulsions of 2008 in Israeli politics, may well have succeeded. She is a remarkable human being, extraordinarily clever and committed and, if she has a fault, probably too decent for the world of politics. She is also a classic example of the absurdity of people with experience and capacity at the highest level not being given big political jobs after retirement from office. But that's another point!)

The early months of 2005 were peppered with my internal notes, setting out election plans, going back over in minute detail the upcoming grid of statements, tearing my hair out at announcements from government departments at the most inconvenient moments. The Civil Service had really got into the groove of "transparency" with the coming into effect, after several years' legislating, of the Freedom of Information Act on 1 January 2005.

Freedom of Information. Three harmless words. I look at those words as I write them, and feel like shaking my head till it drops off my shoulders. You idiot. You naive, foolish, irresponsible nincompoop. There is really no description of stupidity, no matter how vivid, that is adequate. I quake at the imbecility of it.

Once I appreciated the full enormity of the blunder, I used to say—more than a little unfairly—to any civil servant who would listen: Where was Sir Humphrey when I needed him? We had legislated in the first throes of power. How could you, knowing what you know, have allowed us to do such a thing so utterly undermining of sensible government?

Some people might find this shocking. Oh, he wants secret government; he wants to hide the foul misdeeds of the politicians and keep from "the people" their right to know what is being done in their name.

The truth is that the FOI Act isn't used, for the most part, by "the people." It's used by journalists. For political leaders, it's like saying to someone who is hitting you over the head with a stick, "Hey, try this instead," and handing them a mallet. The information is neither sought because the journalist is curious to know, nor given to bestow knowledge on "the people." It's used as a weapon.

But another and much more important reason why it is a dangerous Act is that governments, like any other organisations, need to be able to debate, discuss and decide issues with a reasonable level of confidentiality. This is not mildly important. It is of the essence. Without the confidentiality, people are inhibited and the consideration of options is limited in a way that isn't conducive to good decision-making. In every system that goes down this path, what happens is that people watch what they put in writing and talk without committing to paper. It's a thoroughly bad way of analysing complex issues.

At that time, the consequences were still taking shape and it didn't impact much in 2005. It was only later, far too late in the day, when the full folly of the legislation had become apparent, that I realised we had crossed a series of what should have been red lines, and strayed far beyond what it was sensible to disclose.

Meanwhile, we were busy getting the words right for the election. I decided eventually on the strapline "forward not back." I knew our strength was that, despite it all, we had a future agenda. I knew the Tory weakness was that under Michael Howard they hadn't really changed. "Forward not back" was prosaic to the point of boring, but it was clear and a good banner under which to congregate the wide array of policy. All the way through, we were on a dual line: Iraq and the domestic agenda. Our opponents would try to focus it all on Iraq. We had to broaden it. I knew Iraq would make the public resentful and begrudging; but I also knew that they would be discomfited by an attempt to exploit Iraq as a reason for changing government. They knew the Tories had supported the war, and for the same reason as me. Michael's attempt to use Iraq showed that, deep down, he lacked a true political instinct.

We had the usual Gordon problem about the election. I had asked Alan Milburn to come back to help coordinate the election. This had caused a flurry of briefings against him and an attempt to unnerve Ian McCartney, who was doing a valiant job as party chairman. Ian was a great party man, a good organiser and loyal, but he wasn't a strategist. I tried to create a structure that enabled Alan to put together the right campaign, without undermining Ian. Alastair came back to help. Naturally Philip Gould was central. But it caused no end of bother with GB. Through Alastair and Philip we just about kept the show together, but I emphasise the "just about."

There was one other somewhat difficult and dangerous consequence. Alastair and Philip both thought it should be very much a dual TB/GB campaign. I was unpopular in many quarters; Gordon was a successful Chancellor; it made sense. But Peter Mandelson and Alan were strongly opposed, with Peter repeating to me that I was stronger than I thought and didn't need this. The disagreement between Peter on the one hand and Alastair and Philip on the other was at times very sharp.

For once, I wasn't totally sure what I thought. At one level, I knew the agenda was mine and felt really confident on policy. At another, I felt oppressed, and if I'm honest a touch demoralised by the sheer weight of the opposition and its very personal nature. As I said earlier, the term "Bliar" had first been used in the 2001 election, but the saga of WMD had given the concept booster rockets. Despite the conclusions of the Hutton Report, despite the fact that anyone who wanted to could see the intelligence on the government website and judge for themselves, it was too good an opportunity for those who by then hated me; and I think for some "hate" wasn't too strong a word.

It was partly that they felt angry at their own impotence. Tories in particular could see a third defeat on the horizon—and they had never lost three times in a row before. Of course, just as with Labour in the 1980s, they lost for a reason and that reason was their own fault; but again just as with the Labour Opposition and Thatcher, the frustration boiled over into savagery. ("She's a dictator," I remember people screaming at me once. "No she's not," I rather unwisely replied, "she won an election.") Whereas Mrs. Thatcher always had the main papers on board and rooting for her, I had key papers effectively licensing the very personal campaign against me. The *Daily Mail*, in particular, was vicious. As I say, Gordon was close to Paul Dacre, the editor-in-chief of the Mail Group. The combination of the two factors made it fairly toxic.

In the course of the ridiculous so-called "Cheriegate" affair of 2002—in which Carole Caplin's partner Peter Foster became involved with Cherie's purchase of two flats in Bristol—I crossed a threshold with Dacre. Usually, I let what the media said wash over me, irrespective of what it was. Sometimes I met journalists who had written something foul about me or even Cherie and I just said "Hello" cheerily, without being overconcerned. Also, it's amazing how quickly people can forget the publicity, whether good or bad, that accumulates around a public figure—unless it is sustained and driven by an agenda, in which case it can be an irritation and occasionally it can do lasting damage. But often I would meet someone else in public life and say, "How are you?" and they would look at me as if to say: "You mean you don't know?" They would still be smarting from some wretched story that put them on the rack, but for me, as a person just watching it disinterestedly as it were, I would perhaps have permitted myself a "tut" or a smile but in any event I would have moved swiftly on. I knew it would be the same when I was attacked, so I was neither paranoid about the media nor did I obsessively follow it. The stories would prick me, but my recovery time was relatively fast.

In this particular story, Carole made a poor judgement in allowing Peter Foster into her life, as she has both honestly admitted and apologised for. Cherie should probably never have tried to buy the Bristol flats, but Euan was at university there and she thought they might be useful. The trouble is you can't really do that as the prime minister's wife, for no better reason than you just can't. There was nothing the least wrong in the purchase itself, or the manner of it. Peter Foster's role was pretty minimal. Cherie had met him for five minutes; I never met or talked to him. And by the way, you can't blame the *Mail* for running the story; it was almost too good to be true. But as a result of one of those classic Saturday-afternoon calls in which a Sunday newspaper phones to get a response to a story at the last moment, so as to give the subject the least time to respond, I, by phone, got the wrong end of the stick from her, said Foster had had nothing to do with the purchase, passed it on to Alastair and days later we were in the perennial media firestorm. Then, as more and more came out about Foster and his history, it turned into something really ugly. The *Mail* was leading the way. That was its modus operandi, so there was no point getting upset about it.

To counter the campaign against me, I decided in the election to deliberately face my critics. It wasn't easy and had to be carefully calibrated. There is a thin line between "brave enough to face the music" and "everyone hates him," but on balance it worked as a strategy, unpleasant though it was.

During the run-up to the election, we nearly had a vast panic over the approaching "flu pandemic." There is a whole PhD thesis to be written about the "pandemics" that never arise. In this case, the WHO had issued a report claiming there would be 500,000 to 700,000 deaths across the world. The old First World War flu statistics were rolled out, everyone went into general panic and any particular cases drew astonishing headlines of impending doom. Anyone who caught a cold thought they were part of a worldwide disaster.

I'm afraid I tried to do the minimum we could with the minimum expenditure. I understood the risk, but it just didn't seem to me that the "panpanic" was quite justified. And in those situations, everyone is so risk-averse that, unless you take care, you end up spending a fortune to thwart a crisis that never actually materialises.

However, the reaction of the system is perfectly understandable. The first time you don't bother is the time when the wolf is actually in the village, so you have to steer a path, taking precautions and be ready to ramp it up if it looks like this time it's really happening. But oh, the endless meetings and hype of it all!

Anyway, we got over that. We were just about to start the campaign when Pope John Paul II died in early April. He had been a remarkable and hugely popular leader of the Catholic Church. We had celebrated Mass with him two years before in his own private chapel. He had been so solicitous, kind and concerned. He didn't agree with Iraq, but he understood the perils and pressure of leadership, and when he spoke to me about it, he did so not to make a point but to give spiritual counsel. He was, of course, a theological conservative but with the true common touch.

When he died, literally millions took to the streets. World leaders went to St. Peter's in Rome for the funeral. The Vatican is an amazing place. As you drive in, you are suddenly in another world. The Swiss Guards—a tradition there since the early sixteenth century—greet you and usher you in. It is grand beyond grand. The king of Saudi Arabia once told me it was the most palatial building he had ever entered (and he would have known a few). If you visited the Pope, in order to get to the audience room you would go through a series of antechambers, each grander than the last, until you finally greeted His Holiness. If the purpose was to impress, it succeeded. From Pope Gregory in the fifth century onwards, there had always been that curious mixture of the political and spiritual in the Vatican, and the same sense still resides there—it is the headquarters of a religious organisation, yes, but also a power, to be engaged with and certainly not to be trifled with.

The funeral service was held on the steps of the cathedral. On high were the leaders. In the square the people were amassed. Everyone came. There was an amusing moment in the seating of the dignitaries. The Vatican decided to sit us all by alphabetical order. Unfortunately this put me next to Robert Mugabe, the UK being next to Zimbabwe. I was literally just about to take my seat when, in the nick of time, I spotted who was in the next chair, luckily at that moment talking to his neighbour on the other side. He hadn't seen me. I was on the point of starting the election campaign, and this would not have been the ideal launch picture. It was too ghastly to contemplate.

I capered off to the back steps, where the ambassadors and security people and so on were assembled. This provided consternation among the priests doing the seating, who kept trying to drag me to the front row to take my seat. As the service was about to get under way, to my horror I saw Prince Charles enter and of course get ushered to the UK seat. I rushed forward, but it was too late, and he sat down bang next to Mugabe. At least royalty don't need to get elected.

A couple of days later, we launched the bid for the historic third term. We started as favourites, the polls showing us with a five-point lead or thereabouts, despite having had a difficult few months. There had been the continued rumblings and fallout from my decision to fight the election. Robert Peston—a close journalist associate of Gordon—had recently published a biography of him which basically put up in lights the "victim/betrayal" thesis, and this had reverberated for weeks. To be fair, I think the book had been supposed to coincide with his assumption of the leadership and it then took on a different context, but it meant that the TB/GB divide was now common currency.

However, I felt very sure of our manifesto, our record and our ability to expose the frailty and thinness of the Tory campaign. The first visit was down to Weymouth, right in the heart of former true-blue Tory country, where we had won Dorset South for the first time in 2001.

The eventual result was actually less remarkable for its outcome or even the size of the majority, as for the lack of uniformity in the swing. In our two most marginal seats, of which Dorset South was one, the majority increased, an extraordinary result. In some places, we had a swing towards us. In others, we lost traditional Labour seats to the Lib Dems who campaigned rigorously against the war and on opposition to tuition fees.

At the core, the New Labour vote held firm. It was intact. But as it became clear that we would indeed be re-elected, so votes were peeled off from people who felt that they could safely vote Lib Dem in the secure knowledge they weren't going to get a Tory government.

Nonetheless, in what was a serious misreading of the result, the party became convinced that with a different leader, i.e. Gordon, we would have done better. The truth is with a different New Labour leader we may have done, certainly with one who could have made Iraq someone else's decision. But the real difference between 2001 and 2005 was in the 4 per cent loss to the Lib Dems, not in any significant swing to the Tories. This was, in other words, a classic protest vote, easily recoverable in a third term in time for a fourth-term bid, provided we did not lose the core New Labour support that had stuck with us. The very lack of uniformity in the swing, therefore, was not a quirk—it held, on analysis, a profoundly important political lesson.

So we got under way. The mood was OK, but soured by the decision of some to make Iraq the only issue—which included a disproportionately large part of the media—while for most of the electorate, Iraq played differently.

This was not because people didn't care about the war or its consequences—they manifestly did, and by then we were losing soldiers with horrible regularity in the terror campaign being waged around Basra. It was rather that most people felt Iraq was a difficult decision. In other words, they had a keener appreciation of how tough it was to decide the issue than the black-and-white predilection of the media. Even if they disagreed, they understood the dilemma. They sympathised with the fact the leader had to take the decision. During the campaign, many people said to me they were glad they did not have to take it themselves. Also, as I said before, they distrusted the way my opponents used it, especially the Tories.

Other issues abounded, such as the Longbridge factory in the Midlands, right in the heart of swing territory, where the owners of the major and historic car plant were on the verge of bankruptcy. It all kicked off just as the campaign got under way. Here Gordon and I worked well and with visible impact, immediately getting up there, speaking to people, trying to sort it, clearly in charge and in gear, as it were.

My programme revolved around visits to schools and hospitals, to children's centres, to the whole infrastructure of public services in which we had invested massively and where the results were coming through. You could see the bricks-and-mortar effect of the money. The statistics on school results, hospital waiting times and crime figures told of the benefits of reform. Ten-year-old pupils ranked third best in the world in literacy and the fastest improving in numeracy, with three-quarters of eleven-year-olds reaching high standards in reading, writing and maths. Less than four-hour waits in accident and emergency for 97 per cent of patients, and virtually no one waiting more than nine months for an operation. Overall crime as measured by the authoritative British Crime Survey down 30 per cent—the equivalent of almost five million fewer crimes a year. Record numbers of police—almost 13,000 more than in 1997—working with 4,600 new community support officers.

The fresh programme in the manifesto no longer seemed like a politician's wish list, but the next stage of an already fructifying and coherent plan. The people who worked in the public services felt we were on their side and felt, instinctively, the Tories weren't. So on the domestic agenda, we were strong.

The Tories had one good issue to beat us with: immigration. In our early years, we had had a real problem with asylum claims made by people who were really economic immigrants. The system to deal with such claims was, as I described earlier, hopelessly out of date. Eventually and after much bureaucratic agony, we had battered it into shape, but illegal immigration persisted as an issue. Britain was not the only country facing such a problem, of course, but I watched with dismay as progressive parties around Europe, one after another, got the immigration issue wrong and lost.

People on the left are, on the whole, people with immensely decent instincts on migrants. They loathe racism and know the issue of immigration is often a carrier for the racist virus. When people in Britain used to say they were against immigration, a goodly proportion would really be against a particular type of immigrant, i.e. a black or brown face. It was unspoken, but everyone knew it was there.

So the tendency for those on the left was to equate concern about immigration with underlying racism. This was a mistake. The truth is that immigration, unless properly controlled, can cause genuine tensions, put a strain on limited resources and provide a sense in the areas into which migrants come in large numbers that the community has lost control of its own future. In our case this concern was natural, given the numbers involved. It was not inspired by racism. And it was widespread. What's more, there were certain categories of immigrant flow, from certain often highly troubled parts of the world, who imported their own internal issues, from those troubled parts of the world, into the towns and villages in Britain. Unsurprisingly, this caused real anxiety.

Every time we regulated and tightened the asylum laws, I would get grief from well-intentioned progressives who thought I was "conceding" to racism. I used to explain that it was precisely to avoid racism that we had to do it. The laws were a mess. The political challenge was to prevent subjective racism building up into a coalition that was mainstream. But time and again across Europe, right-wing parties would propose tough controls on immigration. Left-wing parties would cry: Racist. The people would say: You don't get it.

The Tories were desperate to push us into the same bind, so they began a high-profile assault on illegal immigration, claiming that it was not racist to be worried about it and hoping that we would say that it was. Of course, I insisted we did no such thing.

Instead, some way into the campaign I visited Dover, where unfounded asylum claimants were often lodged, and made a speech that directly took on the issue. Gwyn Prosser, the MP for Dover, was someone on the left himself, and canny enough to understand that if he wasn't armed with an argument that conceded there was a problem, he was not going to be re-elected. I praised the contribution of immigration to Britain, but also acknowledged the problem of illegal immigration. I described how we were going to tackle it. I attacked the Tories for raising the issue without having a policy to deal with it, i.e. they were exploiting the issue, not solving the problem. Rather to their surprise, I put ID cards at the centre of the argument, reasoning that some system of identity check was the only serious way of meeting the challenge. Essentially, after that speech we shut down that Tory attack, and for once the media actually allowed an issue to be aired and debated. Because our position was sophisticated enough—a sort of "confess and avoid," as the lawyers say—we won out.

However, all this did was leave our opponents, especially those in the media, with nothing to go on except Iraq.

The campaign had to be very carefully managed. Well, obviously, you say. But in this instance, we had to be more than usually careful. Wherever we went in the 2005 campaign, anyone who shouted or made a scene captured the news. Of course, the campaign then reacts by trying to ensure it doesn't get disrupted. Result: media and politics in a standoff. We feel unfairly treated; they feel unfairly shut out or manipulated.

It was a nightmare for the party organisers, but they were a brilliant and deeply loyal bunch who were prepared to throw themselves in front of a passing train in a heartbeat if it was of help. I had taken care to build a strong party machine. Although it was always going to be harder raising money for this campaign than in 2001, it wasn't that much harder, and Michael Levy, our chief party fund-raiser, had done superbly well, as ever. Our basic, centre-ground, reasonable, middle-opinion coalition remained solid, and the business community instinctively distrusted the Tories and didn't like the slightly nasty edge of their policies on Europe, and immigration or the personal attacks on me. The Tories were well funded from Eurosceptic sources, but the modern, sensible money stayed with us.

Kate Garvey and the campaign managers also did a great job of pre-serving our energy, carefully ensuring that we didn't become exhausted. The TV inquisitions were bound to be challenging. And, self-evidently, the whole thing was really about me—my record, my personality, my decisions. I was on the perch. I was the target. I was the one to knock off. All very obvious and natural, but it meant we had to be extremely careful. And we were.

I was also in a good deal of pain. As I found out later, I fought the entire campaign with a slipped disc. I alternated between trying to appear young and dynamic, bounding up onstage, moving fast, pacing with purpose—all the usual rubbish—and frequently suffering the most agonising twinges as I did so. If that happened, above all, I couldn't let my expression change. I was more or less continually aware that of the score of photographers who picketed my every move, at least four or five were only there for the bad picture. And, as Diana used to say, the picture is what counts. If you've ever suffered back pain, you know what I mean. There's nothing worse. Actually, there is for a public figure. Back pain is awful, but it is invisible. Visible illness is at all costs to be avoided, especially with our media. Broken limbs are OK, but anything disfigur-ing and, before you know it, Quasimodo is running for office. Not good.

So I would go from meeting to meeting, each event a risk, each encounter potentially explosive, each remark liable to be scrutinised, each facial expression a cause for either serenity or alarm, each smile a grimace if too small, cheesy if too large . . . And they say political cam-paigns are overly manufactured. Well, they need to be.

The relations with Gordon were, believe it or not, rather good dur-ing the campaign. This was partly because we were together a lot, and I think this calmed him. We had an interesting debate, not quite a contretemps, about tax and spending. My view was that we had reached the limit of spending. We had increased National Insurance to pay for the NHS, yet even with the economy still growing I could sense that enough was enough. We had stayed within New Labour boundaries, but we were bumping up against the fence at points; or so I thought. The third term had to be about making the money work. After all, we had increased investment in health, education and public services by amounts unprecedented outside of wartime. It was always one of the ridiculous things about the charge that we were not really a progressive government. The truth is we made a radical increase in public spending to cure the underinvestment of the Thatcher years; but it was not an end in itself.

Ed Balls was of the opinion that the public wanted even more spending and was prepared for the extra tax, by reference to polls that the Treasury had—which I said was nonsense. On these issues, the public fib. They say they want increased spending, and in theory they do—but in practice they think someone else should pay for it. However, there it is. As I used to say, the public aren't always logical, but that's their prerogative. They do expect their government to be, nonetheless.

During the campaign, I slowly but surely started to posture, to be in a position of saying: there are no big increases in tax to pay for more spending coming this time. After all, in 2001, we had fought on keeping income tax constant. We had kept the promise, but a little disingenuously since we had increased National Insurance to pay for the NHS. This was justified. But there was no way we could pull the same trick twice; nor should we try to do so.

Gordon was more inclined to keep all options open, but as the campaign progressed, he found, as I said would happen, that by doing so everyone assumed he was planning a fresh National Insurance hike, which he wasn't. So over time, perforce, he more or less assumed the same posture as me.

All in all, though, we got on fine and by the end of the second week the poll lead was extending. The strength of our forward agenda, its New Labour nature, the fact we were so manifestly on top of the policy debate—all these were moving people towards us. By contrast, the Tory campaign looked a little paltry, shamefaced even. The Lib Dems were eschewing a highly personal campaign at a leadership level—because Charles Kennedy was essentially a decent bloke—even though locally they basically plastered areas with leaflets of me and George Bush with words that the Socialist Workers would have been proud of.

Two-thirds into the campaign, it was clear we were going to win and win comfortably. As we hit the last days, the media, deprived of a close fight, decided to go on the offensive. People at the BBC were genuinely outraged by Iraq. As the campaign had gone on, they also became outraged that it wasn't dragging us down in the way they felt it should. It was of course a big part of the campaign, but it didn't dominate. They thought that was because we were so damned clever. In fact, as I say, it was because while people understood its importance, they also understood its complexity. They didn't ignore it, but they were wary of it determining the outcome.

The *Mail* had been given a secret copy of the Attorney General's advice. Like all lawyers' advice—especially where plainly there are arguments on both sides—it was nuanced, explaining the pros and the cons and coming to a conclusion. We had published the conclusion that on balance the war was lawful, but in accordance with hallowed practice— in this instance, for a very sensible reason—the advice itself remained confidential to all except senior members of the government and the Butler Inquiry, which had been shown it on Privy Council terms.

The *Mail* published excerpts essentially suggesting he had advised the war was unlawful. The BBC took it up. Although we released the entire thirteen-page document the next day, 28 April, they had the opportunity they wanted. Tragically, we lost another soldier shortly before the election day. The result was that the final ten days of the campaign were virtually submerged in Iraq. In desperation, the Lib Dems and Tories returned to the "liar" attack. We lost 3 to 4 per cent in that final period as votes went to the Lib Dems. The *Mail* didn't really try to say: Vote them out. Instead it cleverly concentrated, as did the BBC, on effectively saying: Curb the majority. It chimed with the mood—another huge, three-figure majority would have been considered too much. So I suppose the public got what they more or less wanted.

However, as a result, election night felt more like a setback than a victory. I sat in Myrobella waiting for the exit polls. Gordon phoned to tell me Andy Marr, the BBC political editor, had told him that they thought it would be a hung Parliament. I really doubted this. Even with the huge focus they had given Iraq, I was sure Britain wanted the government to survive intact with a proper working majority. Also, I was sure that although in north London and elsewhere a certain type of

Labour voter was going to defect, the more aspiring lower–middle–class voter—the core of New Labour—were sticking with us.

Philip Gould phoned to say he thought we could get a majority of eighty. If we had, it would have been fine. Funny that. The difference between sixty-six—what we got—and eighty is only fourteen seats. In fact, if seven were changed, that would be the difference; and we had lost seven at least on the student vote over tuition fees. But the vote at just below 36 per cent was very low for a winning party, and it dampened my spirits.

As ever, I had the count to go through. In my constituency, one of the candidates was Reg Keys, the father of Lance Corporal Tom Keys who was among the six Red Caps killed by a mob in Iraq in June 2003. I felt profoundly sorry for him, sorry that he felt his son had died in vain, convinced that it was all for nothing. I wanted to reach out and talk to him about it; but I knew too that the cameras were ever-watchful for the scene that could define the election in the way they wanted.

We made our way down to the party headquarters to "celebrate" the victory. Quite rightly, the party staff thought: Historic third term, majority of over sixty, what's the problem? So there began a rather curious disjunction between my mood (deflated) and theirs (elated).

However, I had another reason to be down. In the course of the night, as the result became clear, so the relationship with Gordon deteriorated sharply. I couldn't fathom why. Ostensibly, it was because he thought I was refusing to consult him over the new Cabinet, whereas actually I was—only I was refusing some of his choices in the positions he wanted them. He made a huge thing of Geoff Hoon becoming chief whip, a post I thought Geoff was completely unsuitable for; he wanted Ed Balls, freshly elected, to go straight into government, which I thought inappropriate; and we had the usual rigmarole over Michael Wills, Dawn Primarolo and others whom I really didn't think right for government for various reasons, but whom I did try to accommodate because they were strong supporters of his.

The consequence of all of this was that as I reshuffled over the coming days—by and large it was going fine—I found that the PLP was becoming distinctly ungenerous in its thoughts. On the one hand I was taking congratulatory calls from the outside world, who naturally thought a third term a cause for general rejoicing, and on the other hand there was an increasingly fractious reaction from the PLP who had ended up persuading themselves it was all a bit grim.

Gordon's people—and at this time it included those like Clare Short—were out in the media more or less perpetually dissing me and saying we could have done better with another leader, and my people were on the defensive. Looking back it was ludicrous of course, but it was in part, as Peter had always warned, a result of the fact that we had run a dual TB/GB campaign. It allowed his folk to interpret the result as: we won because of our guy, but our guy had the albatross of the other person to deal with. In fact, while I had repelled some voters, I had also recruited others. It didn't necessarily follow that someone else could have done the recruiting, even if it was true they might not have done the repelling—i.e. I was divisive. And though the media treated me as if I had lost, the fact is I hadn't. However, I allowed myself to be caught up in this mood, which was all a little crazy.

Then Michael Howard did me a good turn by announcing that he was quitting as leader of the Conservatives. It changed the mood; not entirely, but just enough. Suddenly people remembered the Tories had lost and we had won. The madness ebbed, and by the time I addressed the PLP on the Wednesday, things had quietened down somewhat, although a lot of static remained and again Gordon's people were hard at it. I realised that from then on, every day I remained was going to be a struggle.

Although the campaign was horrible, I had hardened during the course of it and it was also clear to me that I had grown up as a leader. The weakness, the fear, the desire to run away all remained, but crucially I had acknowledged these feelings. They were now my avowed companions, and because they were avowed, they were contained, no longer demons; there to be suffered, and there to be argued with and faced down too; the ordinary, natural feelings that any human being would feel in the same situation. Nothing to be ashamed or frightened of. Nothing beyond my capacity to control.

Now I was prepared to manage what I knew would be a continual fight with Gordon. I had to get the reform programme embedded (and whatever his manoeuvres, I judged Gordon wouldn't dare be in outright opposition); do all I could to settle Iraq, and if possible get our troops on their way out before I left; conduct successful presidencies of the G8 and the EU; if at all possible—though I doubted it—deliver the Olympic bid. And set out a programme that would serve as an agenda for a fourth term if Gordon was sensible enough to take it; and if he wasn't, my alibi for the defeat that I'm afraid I thought would be inevitable if he took over and moved a millimetre from New Labour.

There was also one other major event looming. The EU Constitution—fatally named from our point of view, and leading inexorably to our commitment to hold a referendum on it—was going to be a dominant part of the first months of the third term. France and the Netherlands were due to hold their own referenda in May. The polls were unclear but I assumed France would still say yes; and if they did, the Netherlands might well follow suit. Our polls were resolutely against success and not many people believed we could shift them. As ever, I was more sanguine. I thought we might just turn it into a referendum that was effectively: in or out. If France voted yes, Britain might just follow. My advisers disagreed, but I rather fancied mounting a really big public argument on an issue I felt strongly about and on which I was right. I could also see how, in the course of such a campaign, the progressive alliance—fractured over Iraq—might heal. So although plainly a tough challenge, I somewhat relished the fight.

As things settled down a little, I took a break in Tuscany in late May, staying with our friends the Strozzis at Cusona. I had a great time with Leo, able to spend proper moments with him. At five years old, he was getting to that fascinating age where you can almost see the brain sprouting forth. Except to the doting parents, babies are frankly pretty boring—sweet and cuddly, but still a bit inanimate, if you see what I mean. From about age three onwards, they get interesting and remain like that up to around twelve, when the dark mists of hell envelop them. Unbelievably, they emerge again as semi-civilised human beings around the age of twenty, you stop thinking you are a bad parent or there is genetic delinquency in the family, and realise they are still your children and you love them. There are exceptions, of course, but that's my experience.

Anyway, I digress. Cusona was lovely. There was sunshine and privacy, and since all the news focused on France and its vote, the eye of the beast was temporarily diverted, and I relaxed. Nicolas Sarkozy came over, at that time still a minister in the French government. It was clear that there was a battle royal going on over the future of the centre-right UMP party which he led, but it was also clear that he was certain he would win it.

Nicolas and I had certain things in common: energy and determination; impatience with the traditional categories of right and left; a deep dislike of doctrine and rigidity; we both liked to analyse problems by instinct rather than ideology; and we had both learned that the twenty-first century could not conform to the politics of the previous hundred years. However, we differed in one respect: he had superabundant self-confidence. There was not a glimmer of self-doubt. As we walked through an avenue of trees that led down from the villa where the Strozzis lived, he talked frankly and with complete conviction about his own victory: "I will win. I will become president."

From anyone else it would have sounded vain or even slightly mad, but he said it with a combination of charm and clarity that made it seem entirely factual. The British would have wanted to cut someone who talked like that down to size, but I could see that the French would go for it. It was an attitude which had passion, elan and also that touch of arrogance which in some small way defines France, and which in some small way I admire. I could see them looking at Nicolas and thinking: Now that's a president.

Towards the end of our stay, the news came through during dinner: France had voted no to the Constitution. I knew at once I was off the hook. It was true I fancied the fight, but it was also true that had I lost, it would have been *au revoir*. You could almost feel the waves of relief coming over the English Channel and making their way down to Italy. I spoke to Jack Straw, who was absolutely undivided in his feelings. "Great news," he said.

"I was rather looking forward to a referendum," I said.

"Then you're dafter than I thought," he replied.

The referendum result was significant to us for another reason. On 1 July, we took over the six-month presidency of the European Union, which we had last held in 1998.

During my previous spell as president of the EU all of seven years before, I had been in the first flush of enthusiasm as a novice prime minister, new on the European scene, something of an unknown quantity to them and to myself. It was not one of the highlights of the first term. I was more interested in proving Britain had changed than in changing Europe. We were full of stunts but not strategy, and I rightly wince at some of the "initiatives." One bright soul had the idea that our presidency tie (each successive country had its own tie and logo to mark the presidency) should be a compilation done by schoolchildren of their images of the individual nations. I had no knowledge of this idea until I got a call from Romano Prodi, then in one of his periodic bouts as Italian prime minister. Romano could often be a little hard to follow, but on this occasion he was as clear as a bell. "Hey, Tony, you insult my country. We are more than a pizza, you know. We have Rome, Florence, Venice, Michelangelo, Leonardo da Vinci, Galileo, Verdi, Garibaldi, and now my nation think the world see us as a *quattro stagioni* pizza. It is not right. It must be changed or relations between Britain and Italy suffer very bad," etc. If I tell you that's about all I can recall from that spell as president, you will understand that it was not one of my more distinguished periods.

Now, just after a third election victory with eight years of being prime minister under my belt, I was a different type of leader, and the challenges Europe faced had also transformed, qualitatively and quantitively. For a start—and partly due to strong British insistence—the EU had enlarged to twenty-five member states, soon to be twenty-seven. It had been through an immensely divisive period over Iraq, where it had more or less split evenly in favour and against, but since France and Germany had been in the "no" camp, that had been particularly painful. After years of internal wrangling, a consultation exercise had resulted in a Constitution for Europe which now had been rejected. So: quo vadis? And to cap it all, there was a battle over the EU budget, then up for renewal.

In this last area, Britain had been in the thick of the debate and the disagreement. Essentially, the old British rebate was up for grabs, along with consideration of the common agricultural policy. The rebate system was negotiated by Margaret Thatcher whereby the UK received back money it had paid to the EU, as it was at the time a less well-off member of the EU Community, but paid most to the budget. The agricultural policy had been set up throughout Europe in response to food shortages and rationing following World War II. The rebate was as highly politically sensitive for the UK as the CAP was for France.

All in all, this presidency, especially under this country, was going to be interesting, not to say explosive. As if to stir it all up even further, just before I took over we rejected the attempt by Luxembourg and its prime minister Jean-Claude Juncker to get a budget compromise. Jean-Claude was someone steeped in EU Councils, having been a finance minister since the 1980s. Although a small country, Luxembourg was a founding member state, and Jean-Claude was very well respected as an experienced and wise Council member. He had worked hard to put an agreement together, and had been sensitive to the British issue on the rebate. But I felt I couldn't pull the thing off. It was just the wrong side of the line. He was bitterly and justifiably disappointed. I was the party-pooper and he would have been quite within his rights to consider me a real pain in the neck.

I had two problems over the rebate, both significant for how our relationship with Europe under my leadership could develop. The first was the near-hysterical—sorry, correct that—truly hysterical behaviour of the Eurosceptic media. Papers with a combined daily circulation of around eight million—a situation unique in Europe in terms of pervasion—were totally, wildly and irredeemably hostile to Europe, misrepresented what Europe was doing and generally regarded it as a zero-sum game: anything that pleased Brussels was bad for Britain. The Murdoch papers were especially virulent. Much of the media had become like that under Mrs. Thatcher, and in time I came to see the sentiment she engendered as the single worst legacy that she bequeathed Britain (though on the whole she was undoubtedly a great prime minister).

The myth developed and abounds today that she was always like this. She wasn't. In 1979 and 1983 particularly, she had been the pro-Europe candidate for prime minister. At the time the *Mail* was in favour, as was the *Telegraph*. But when Mrs. Thatcher turned sceptic, she infected her media supporters and by 2005 it had become a leitmotif of a large part of British journalism.

In general terms, for me, Europe was a simple issue. It was to do with the modern world. I supported the Europe ideal, but even if I hadn't, it was utterly straightforward: in a world of new emerging powers, Britain needed Europe in order to exert influence and advance its interests. It wasn't complicated. It wasn't a psychiatric issue. It was a practical question of realpolitik.

I regarded anti-European feeling as hopelessly, absurdly out of date and unrealistic. It was also the product of a dangerous insularity, a myopia about the world that I thought affected adversely the whole psychology of the country. It was a kind of post-empire delusion.

It was bolstered over a time when the American right—who rather despised European feebleness on foreign policy (and the Brussels bureaucracy was of course a byword)—got together with the British right and constructed an argument that was a plaything for the U.S. but a dangerous cul-de-sac for the British. This was the idea that somehow we should remain close allies of the U.S. in contradistinction to being key partners in the EU.

Of course, this was a delusion as well. The U.S. was so much more powerful in terms of economics and politics than the UK that such a dependence suited them but not us. It was also absolutely apparent to me that if we had reach in Europe, we were treated more seriously in Washington.

Moreover, in the rest of the world a Britain semi-detached from Europe was regarded as odd, part of British eccentricity, something to be amused by, a "good old Brits" type of thing which I really detested. I recall visiting Lee Kuan Yew—the smartest leader I think I ever met—in Singapore in 1995 when I was Leader of the Opposition. He was something of a bête noire for the left. Rather to his surprise, I didn't ask him about democracy in Singapore. Since I had heard tell of how clever he was and any fool could see what he had achieved in Singapore was one of the greatest creations of modern political imagination, I asked him simply: Tell me how to win and how to govern.

He grunted, paused for a moment and then basically laid it out for me. His advice on governing was: keep the Thatcher reforms but get rid of this madness on Europe. "I've told Margaret she's crazy on this," he said. "Britain can't afford to be out of Europe in the world as it is today. It's just not realistic." Much later, the wonderful Indian prime minister Manmohan Singh told me the same thing. The Chinese were too polite and formal to say it quite so plainly, but it was obvious that's what they thought too.

Quite why Britain had taken this Eurosceptic attitude so much to heart was a curious question. My theory—but this may be total nonsense—is that our problem with Europe is that we didn't invent it; or at least weren't a founding member. Then when Harold Macmillan sensibly decided we should join, de Gaulle said, "*Non.*" This, combined with the strong imperial feelings that still lurked beneath the surface of the British psyche—part superiority complex, part insecurity complex—gave us a national narrative about the EU that was deeply unhelpful.

Of course, Europe had its own delusion: that the way to make Europe stronger was simply to integrate its decision-making processes. In other words, "pro-European" opinion was in favour of more qualified majority voting, more powers to the European Parliament, more areas for European legislation, etc. It was a focus that was essentially constitutional, and this didn't help either. It became, in time, a way of avoiding the real issue affecting European strength: how to make strong policy decisions that took Europe in the right direction. People wanted endless debates about the technical framework, tending to shy away from the core political questions: to liberalise our economy or not; to be strong players in defence or not; what sort of foreign policy, and so on.

What all this meant was that the British delusion—a prejudice—was sustained by objective material it found in the European delusion. There were criticisms of Europe that were entirely valid, but none of them should have resulted in our separating ourselves from Europe. They gave the Eurosceptics solid and well-founded points to make about Europe's direction, and their negativity more or less dominated the British debate.

Also, by this time the British rebate had assumed a mythical, almost cult status in the 2005 budget negotiation. To challenge it was like introducing Darwin to an ardent creationist. In the early years, Britain had paid a disproportionate amount under the then basis for calculating contributions to the EU budget. In 1983, Mrs. Thatcher secured a rebate on a complicated formula, but with a simple purpose: to reduce the UK contribution and make it more proportionate. She had dug in hard; and this had become part of hallowed mythology.

As Europe enlarged, the formula—which at that time had barely compensated Britain for the unfairness—worked in such a way that it then became unfair to the others. This was not hard to see. The figures were there. Agreed. Clear. In pounds, shillings and pence. Or euros.

But none of this mattered in the UK debate. The rebate was untouchable. To question it was to betray the nation. To analyse the figures was itself to push Britain down the slippery slope. The Spanish Inquisition would have afforded more leeway to an apostate.

I said there were two problems with the rebate issue. The other was Gordon. He was taking a very hard line and I knew he would have to be carefully managed. There were already numerous reports suggesting he was having to "stop" me giving it all away. Needless to say, Rupert Murdoch's papers were in full flow. So I thought it was going to be a darn sight easier to navigate my way through if I were the pilot. The Luxembourg deal was not a bad one; it wasn't quite good enough; I could do better. And I could do it with much greater facility if I were in charge of the negotiations. It was a real gamble of course, and it raised the stakes of my own presidency hugely. If I failed it would be very damning, but if I succeeded it would be a big achievement.

On 22 June, just after the Luxembourg summit had ended without agreement, Jean-Claude addressed the European Parliament as the outgoing president. I was due to address them next day as the incoming president. Jean-Claude, who the MEPs thought had been very badly treated, got a rousing reception. He was a true European. He had been let down by Perfidious Albion. He had fought the good fight, and the

European Parliament, a bit like the Labour Party, likes nothing more than a valiant loser. He got a standing ovation, gave a very federalist address and basically accused those who didn't agree of undermining Europe.

It wasn't a great scene-setter for my visit the following day. Having heard from the shocked and outraged father of the kidnapped maiden, so cruelly violated, they were now going to listen to the person what did it.

It was a very significant occasion for me. I was a three-time election winner (which made some admire me, and some resent me—especially on the left, since they took the view that a progressive leader who won elections was therefore almost certainly unprincipled); I was, after Iraq, a divisive figure; I had not got Britain to join the euro. Though my general posture was pro-European, I took care not to go beyond what was reasonable for British opinion. This meant I was slagged off by the right for being pro-European and by the left for being insufficiently so. But it allowed me to govern and to move things forward where I could.

And so I did, and with Jacques Chirac launched Europe's common defence policy. As president in 1998 I had actually chaired the Council which brought the euro into being (I was being a trifle facetious a few pages ago), and managed to negotiate the appointment of Wim Duisenberg as president of the European Central Bank—a mess of a negotiation, by the way, where French pride ran into Dutch obstinacy and collided with German interests, represented by the great (but by then somewhat fading) Helmut Kohl. I had been instrumental in the Lisbon process, the first serious attempt to put European economic reform within a coherent framework of action, with limited but still real success. I had weaved my way through three major European treaties—Amsterdam, Nice and the Rome Constitutional Treaty—all of which could easily have pushed Britain back to the margins of Europe where we had languished from 1992 to 1997. Instead, Britain remained pretty much at the heart of things.

Most of all, in June 2004 I had organised opposition to the French/German demand that the Belgian prime minister Guy Verhofstadt become president of the Commission, and instead got José Manuel Barroso appointed. This was the first time that the twin-engine motor of Europe had been stalled in respect of such a big issue. My relationship with Gerhard Schroeder never recovered. Jacques Chirac took it more philosophically. But Barroso was plainly the better choice if you wanted

Europe to reform in a non-federalist direction. However, the point is that without that relationship with other leaders, without Britain being mainstream and not marginalised, it would never have happened. It was, in fact, a real object lesson on why it is important to stay at the centre of things. As a result of being in the middle, we could achieve. On the periphery, counting for nothing, we achieve nothing.

Of course, there was also the fact that I was criticised by the pro-Europe lobby for not being sufficiently "courageous" in taking Britain into the euro. In truth, this was nothing whatever to do with courage or the lack of it. Nor was it to do with Gordon's opposition. At first, indeed in 1997, he had been the one wanting a more pro-single-currency position and I was resisting. My problem with the euro was very simple. In principle, I was in favour and for me the politics were clear: better to join and be full players in Europe's economic decision-making. But I also knew that the politics were also very clear in another direction. It is, after all, as I used to say to my folk, an economic proposition. It is called economic and monetary union. Unless it was economically plain that it would be good for Britain, it was simply not politically sellable, i.e. the political problem was the economics. The trouble was that the economic case was at best ambiguous and certainly not beyond doubt. At the time of the 2001 election, I thought it conceivable the economics would shift decisively in favour, and I was absolutely determined that, if they did, I would chance it all on a referendum. My disagreement with Gordon was that he was expressing himself negatively on the euro. I was always saying, Even if we don't join—and maybe especially if we don't—for reasons of diplomacy, always sound positive. If the economics had changed, I would have gone for it. They didn't. And for me, that was that. (Just for the record, it is also completely untrue that I offered to stand down if Gordon agreed to try to take us into the single currency.)

So, in summary, I had a record which gave me supporters and detractors, but right at that moment on 23 June 2005, the latter outnumbered the former.

The speech ended up as one of my more important ones. I wrote it myself, sat at my desk early in the morning in my Brussels hotel. It was one of those that just flowed. I picked up my pen, and wrote until it was finished.

As I stood up in front of the EU Parliament, they were ready to jeer. Mind you, after the House of Commons at PMQs, it was like being in a girls' school playground after serving a long stretch in a high-security prison.

I knew what I wanted to say. I had thought about it for years, and this was my chance. For me, Europe was ripe for a debate over classic third-way politics. It was pinned between those who talked of social Europe, which basically meant more regulation, and those who wanted Europe to be only a market and nothing else. So: sceptics versus federalists. Essentially I said that the purpose of social Europe and economic Europe should be to sustain each other, and that "the purpose of political Europe should be to promote the democratic and effective institutions to develop policy in these two spheres and across the board where we want and need to cooperate in our mutual interest. But the purpose of political leadership is to get the policies right for today's world."

I then went on to set out Europe's challenge: how to change in a changing world in which not just the U.S. but China, India and the emerging powers would play an ever bigger role, as nations far outweighing individual European nations in size, population and thus, in time, influence.

I praised Europe. I also mocked the pretensions of the endless constitutional focus, pointing out that each time we said that the purpose of such an obsession was to bring us "closer to the people" we lost even more of their support. I then set out an agenda for change, based on big policy decisions and direction.

Of course, I was hugely assisted by the fact that due to the French and Dutch rejections of the Constitution in the referenda, it could hardly be argued that the present politics of Europe was working. That Europe was in crisis couldn't really be disputed, and this fuelled my argument for change.

The speech made a big impact, and resulted in the first decent publicity I had had in Britain for years (though that was for bad reasons as well as good, since Eurosceptics also liked it). It reverberated around Europe and became the talking point.

In the questions in the Parliament that followed the speech, I also gave them a bit of PMQs showmanship, slapping a few of them around a bit (their colleagues always like that), putting down the UK Independence Party mavericks, whose main message is for the UK to be withdrawn from the EU (demonstrating you could take on the British sceptics), and generally making jokes and delivering put-downs that entertained the crowd. Danny Cohn-Bendit, the 1968 Paris revolutionary, was due to speak after me. I told him I used to listen to his speeches in the old days, and now he had to listen to mine, which was progress. They all liked that and it flattered him.

In time the effect wore off, naturally, but it set the stage well for the presidency. What could have begun very inauspiciously ended up with people intrigued and willing to give it a go.

Of course, the hard fact remained we had no budget deal. Europe's politics were also about to undergo a big change in leadership with the September election in Germany. Gerhard and the SDP fought back really hard from being way down in the polls and very nearly did it, but Angela Merkel just came through to become the new Chancellor.

As I say, my friendship with Gerhard had dimmed. He got over Iraq, but he was furious over Guy and the presidency of the Commission. At the dinner where Guy's appointment was blocked, he rounded on me in a very personal way. I tried to explain that Guy was not someone whose direction for Europe I could agree with. It wasn't personal on my part. Gerhard made it clear: it was on his, and that was that. It was a pity. He had many really significant leadership qualities, which I admired.

I had spent time with Angela before the election. The truth is—and I fear this was becoming increasingly the case in my relations with the European centre right—there was more in common with her than with the German SDP. The SDP were very close to Russia, and although Gerhard was a reformer, his party wasn't. Their view of the European social model was very traditional. Angela would see the need for change. I liked her as a person also. She seemed at first rather shy, even aloof, but she had a twinkle that swiftly came through. I thought she was honest and instinctively a kindred spirit, and we got on well.

Her arrival—made somewhat ungainly by the protracted German coalition negotiation after her narrow victory—was a major new factor in the budget deal. It also bore on another critical challenge: relations with Turkey. Under its new government, Turkey had been making significant strides towards Europe. The government was controlled by the Islamist AK Party, contrary to the secular mould of Turkish politics. The prime minister Tayyip Erdogan, however, and the then foreign minister, Abdullah Gül, were sensible, forward-looking men who, frankly, were, at least at that time, the easiest Turkish politicians I had met. They were smart, knew what they wanted, were anxious to come into Europe and, what's more, reasonable on Cyprus.

Europe had worked out a position that was in favour of Turkish EU membership in the long term, but it was going to take time. There were criteria for accession; they should be met. This latter point allayed the nervousness of Europe with large Turkish migrant populations like Germany; and it gave Turkey's modernisers something to aim at. So, in principle, yes; in practice, very much in the future. But that was OK. It just about held together.

The reason for the reluctance was partly that EU membership had only recently enlarged and people wanted time to digest, and partly that Turkey, a nation of over 70 million Muslims, was clearly something else again. The point was not that EU leaders were anti-Muslim, though among the population no doubt that sentiment was present. But, plainly and actually reasonably, this would be a major change in the nature of Europe and had to be got right.

I was and am in favour of Turkey's accession. I want Turkey looking west and Europe looking east, and, handled correctly, Turkey's membership would do us all good. It is very dangerous—for us and for them—to push Turkey away, because it would appear to underscore the fact that Judaeo-Christian and Muslim civilisations cannot coexist. The implications of estrangement are very large. After I left office, Turkey was politely but firmly pushed back in the direction of something less than full membership. It is a perilous mistake for both parties.

At the end of October, I held an informal EU summit at Hampton Court Palace. Unusually for such meetings, it produced an agenda on issues like universities, research and development, energy and innovation, on which a new European budget should sensibly concentrate. Europe was at risk of falling behind, and I attempted to lay out a programme that focused on areas that would be vital to Europe's competitiveness in the future.

But the budget remained as the only real issue, and the UK rebate was the point most talked about. The more it was discussed the harder it was for me since, as I say, even talking about it was tantamount to political blasphemy. The French would raise it in a real "pulling your nose" way, and did so constantly. I sparred back with some anti-CAP rhetoric.

As the budget of course also spanned the whole of EU expenditure, here's where the complexity set in. This really was a zero-sum game. It was a fixed budget, so someone's gain meant someone else's loss. In this arena every country had an active interest, with the new members wanting EU money to develop, and the old members looking to hang on to whatever concessions history had tossed them.

It was a nightmare of detail, political cross-currents, national pride, presidential and prime ministerial ego, all played out in vivid public technicolor. After the December summit, which would be the final negotiation, each participant would have to go back home to cheers or tears. They would all spin like crazy to get the cheers, but each nation's media was prepared to believe the outcome should merit tears. I was stuck in the middle and very obviously, because of Britain's position on the rebate, *parti pris*.

The negotiations involved hours, days and, in the later part of the year, weeks of painstaking discussion. I became a veritable expert on the intricacies of structural and cohesion funding, on the Spanish preoccupation with Ceuta and Melilla, on the Swedish and Dutch formulae for their rebate on the rebate, on what the average French farmer might earn, on what the German *Länder* might tolerate, and of course on the details of the appropriations in respect of each crucial policy area of EU spending.

I was blessed with a great team led by my EU adviser in Number 10, Kim Darroch, and the UK Brussels representative, Sir John Grant. They were utterly brilliant, the British Civil Service at its best, immensely creative, willing to think outside the box (and there was a legion of boxes) and with a deep network of contacts in member states.

The final negotiations were set for 15–16 December. It was clearly going to be an all-nighter. Like a giant jigsaw with myriad pieces, if the contours of one piece were changed, suddenly another five wouldn't fit. Around a third of the total budget had to be reallocated in favour of the new members. That meant all the old members, including Britain, had to pay more.

European councils meet on the fifth floor of the Justus Lipsius building in Brussels. The meeting rooms are so ghastly that you always have an incentive to agree and get out. The country holding the presidency has a suite of rooms just off the main corridor, where you sit and see nation after nation, listen to their leaders complain, cajole and threaten as you assess what is bluster and what is real, what can be conceded and what has to be confounded, and when it is right for the president to turn menacing.

No nation likes to be taken advantage of, but no nation likes to be fingered as the cause of failure. So throughout every successive wretched meeting in that boring and soulless room, you are calculating when to advance, when to retreat and when to defer.

My strategy was this: make an ally of Angela and share credit for success with her—that could settle down her Chancellorship and make her well disposed; sort the Spanish and the Italians; champion the Poles; deal with the French. And then slip in our own piece of the jigsaw right at the end, when everyone wanted an agreement and wanted to go home.

We got a deal which actually left Britain paying roughly the same as France for the first time. The UK media called it a betrayal, but frankly they would have done that even if I had led Jacques Chirac in chains through the streets of London. And by then I was past caring. We preserved the rebate, tied its demise to the CAP and agreed a break in the budget period where both could be reformed. Though I shouldn't say it, it was close to a minor miracle.

I had had the most frightful time with Gordon throughout, however. He was essentially insisting that France accept the demise of the CAP, and in public statements was asserting this in terms that enraged the French. Actually, he didn't merely want them to disown the CAP, but also sort of apologise for ever having supported it. In a funny way it helped me, because I was able to say: see my problems? Now are you going to be reasonable? So we did a kind of unintentional good cop/bad cop on them.

But as the negotiations went into the early hours, it became more serious. He was refusing to agree the deal. Jon Cunliffe, an exemplary and bright Treasury official who was go-between, was getting annoyed, poor bloke. Gordon was content to let the thing go down and fight on in the next presidency. I knew that would be absolutely appalling for the reputation of the country, the government and me; and once we were out of the driving seat, there could be no guarantee that Britain would get a better deal. In fact, the deal would almost certainly be worse.

Finally, I'm afraid I just stopped taking his calls. Poor Jon would come into the presidency room and say: "The Chancellor really wants to speak to you." I would say: "I'm really busy, Jon." And he would say: "He really is demanding it." Then I would say: "I'll call him soon." And Jon would say: "Do you really mean that, Prime Minister?" And I would say: "No, Jon."

It more or less worked out. We got a good deal. Gordon was able to distance himself. And soon there were plenty of other things to think about.

EIGHTEEN

TRIUMPH AND TRAGEDY

T he schedule of today's political leader gets ever crazier. The convenience of modern travel; the emergence of foreign affairs as a
dominant part of the job; the range and scope of the events you
are called upon to deal with; all this means that you can travel to four or
five countries in the space of as many days. Because it's possible, sooner
or later you are expected to do so. The schedule is much more punish-
ing than just twenty years ago.

I got used to it and have a huge advantage: I don't suffer from jet lag.
For me, if the sun is shining, it's day; if it's dark, it's night. I also take a
melatonin pill. Pop one of those and you get six hours' sleep wherever
you are, and in whatever time zone.

The one problem is that travel does play havoc with the digestive system. You need to eat healthily and with discipline. I am very typically
British. I like to have time and comfort in the loo. The bathroom is an
important room, and I couldn't live in a culture that doesn't respect it.
Anyway, that's probably more than you ever wanted to know. But
politicians, as I frequently say, need to be seen and understood as human
beings. Have a bad night's sleep or feel lousy because your system is shot
to pieces, and you perform badly. And the difference with us is that each
performance is on film or reported, and there are no second takes.

I always knew the seven days starting on 2 July 2005 were going to be
challenging: fly out to Singapore for the Olympics bid and spend a hec-
tic two days there, then fly back to Gleneagles in Scotland for the G8,
which that year was chaired by Britain, and so by me. Two very big
challenges; two very big risks; if they failed, two very big failures.

When the Olympics open in London in 2012, many people will be remembered as having brought them to Britain, but it all started with Tessa Jowell, who at that time was the Secretary of State for Culture, Media and Sport. When the bid was first raised as a possibility, most of the Cabinet were dubious and the Treasury was hostile. I liked the boldness of the notion, but it didn't seem likely we could get it—the French were runaway favourites, with other powerful bids from Madrid and New York—and after the Dome we were all a trifle nervous of anything so immense, costly and liable to turn out tricky. The athletics community, however, immediately understood its significance, came out strongly in support of a bid, advocated it intelligently and showed admirable firmness for it all the way through. Tessa was equally emphatic.

She is a great person, Tessa, just a gem. She represents the best of political loyalty, which at its best isn't blind, but thoroughly considered. She understood that to be successful, a political party needs to be led strongly and a strong leader needs loyal supporters. If you think the leadership is wrong or fundamentally misguided, then change leaders; but don't have a leader and not support their leadership. That way lies political debilitation. Tessa was the ultimate sensible loyalist and was with me to the end, however bitter, because she believed in my leadership. And if she hadn't, she would have told me.

On the Olympics she was telling me it was an enormous opportunity. Think of the impact on our young people, on fitness, on sport, on the country's self-belief. I would say, "Yes, but suppose we get beaten, and what's worse, we get beaten by the French and I end up humiliated?" One day when I had finished saying this to her in graphic terms, sitting in the Downing Street garden where, if the sun was shining, I would sit and have one-to-one meetings, she looked at me reproachfully and said, "I really didn't think that was your attitude to leadership. I thought you were prepared to take a risk. And it is a big risk. Of course we may not win but at least we will have had the courage to try." When Tessa says this, you feel a complete wimp and rather ashamed. You know she is manipulating you, but you also know it's a successful manipulation. "Oh, OK, we'll go for it."

The Cabinet came round, but only because I was then really going for it and JP as ever waded in manfully with support, chiding and generally prodding in a JP-like way that made everyone think that they might as well go with the flow.

In the middle of 2003 we had established a bid team under Barbara Cassani who were thoroughly professional and competent. Craig Reedie from the IOC was an adept and skilful committee politician. In May 2004, Seb Coe took over. I had only ever really seen him on telly running his famous races against Steve Ovett. He was a great athlete; on the other hand, he had later been William Hague's chief of staff—and that hadn't been great. I didn't mind in the least that he had been a Tory—he obviously wasn't someone who was hopelessly tribal, and anyway it would help to keep everyone together politically for the bid—but to be frank I wasn't sure of him. However, I trusted Tessa, and she was certain. It turned out to be an inspired choice. Being the athlete he was, he could instantly enlist anyone in the athletics world. Being the person he is, he did so in an intelligent, decent and persuasive way. He had none of the worst Tory traits and most of the best ones.

But it was clearly an uphill task. We weren't even second in the running, and personally I doubted we would ever win. There was a fierce debate over whether I should go to Singapore. In the end I did, but as much because this was a crime scene I had to be present at in order to have an alibi, to avoid being criticised for not trying hard enough. By the time I got there, the bid team had been ensconced for several days. It was the usual ridiculous pantomime in these situations: we could talk about the bid, but we weren't supposed to canvass. Try to work out the difference if you can. I couldn't.

The bid strategy had two parts to it: there was a ceremony and a party at the British High Commission to show off our wares and to give the team a sense of unison and solidarity; then we would see the various members of the committee, of whom I was deputed to meet around forty on a one-to-one basis. Out of a total electorate of 115, it was a fair proportion. I sat in the hotel suite, and just before they were ushered in I was handed slips of paper with their details on, so I would know roughly what their likes, worries and dislikes might be. In the course of two days of meetings, I learned again the lesson that, at a profound level, electorates are the same everywhere: each member has one vote. In small electorates, this is crucial.

When I ran for the Sedgefield nomination, John Burton taught me this. There were lots of big mouths, movers and shakers on the General Management Committee (the selection body at the time) who would take the floor, but John identified the little old ladies, the not very assiduous attendees, the shy, the diffident, the uncertain and the unaligned, and together we went after them. When all was said and done, they had the same number of votes as the movers and shakers: one.

Because the Olympic electorate are globally dispersed, the adage was even more true. The person who spotted this first was Cherie. Ever since we had launched the bid, she had been going to different parts of the world and meeting the less significant members. There are several people without whom we would not have won the bid, and she is one of them. She can be difficult, my wife, but when determined, she is determined. She can also work a room better than anyone I've seen.

She and her mum and the wonderful Jackie, our nanny, are all passionate about athletics (truthfully I'm not) and so she enjoyed it. But enjoy it or not, by the time we all converged in Singapore, she had met, followed up and kept in touch with a large part of the committee. At the IOC party we were continually bumping into her "old friends" who were usually on their own as they weren't considered important, but each of them of course had the same vote as those over whom a lot of fuss was being made. So, hidden from sight, we had been building up a lot of quiet support. Seb too had been travelling the world and was very effective.

As I discovered quite quickly, the people seeing me hadn't the slightest interest in talking to me about athletics, rightly figuring me as an ignoramus on that score; but they were fascinated about politics and meeting a famous political figure. I found that my recent speech to the European Parliament was a huge talking point. Bizarre, I know, but it struck a chord, and though some agreed and some disagreed with Iraq, they all had a strange respect for the fact that I took a deeply unpopular decision.

Because we shouldn't exaggerate the pulling power of politics, we also put David Beckham into the mix. David is a complete pro—he did what he was asked to do with no messing about, and generally sent Singapore into a twitter, which is exactly what was required.

In the course of the meetings, I learned yet again how important it is to listen as well as talk. Knowing when to shut up is one of the most vital rules in life, never mind politics. Basically, most people are psychological itinerants in search of someone who wants to hear about them, who is interested in what they have to say, and who will regard what they say as both sage and stimulating. This applies at any level. In fact, the more elevated the level, the truer it is. In most of my meetings with other leaders—less so those whom I knew really well, or when there was real immediate business to transact—I would listen or ask them questions to get them talking, so that I could listen. A good meeting is one where you have listened more than you have spoken.

Also, know when to disagree and when to let a comment pass. If it matters and there will be a frightful misunderstanding, you have to step in and contradict; but frequently, even if your interlocutor makes some completely ludicrous assertion, contradiction will only lead to a futile, sterile disagreement which it is then embarrassing to move on from. Unless it is germane to the real issue at hand, let it pass.

So, anyway, I met endless members of the IOC and paid as much attention as I could in the time allotted. Occasionally, they came in too thick and fast. I would get the slips of paper out of order and the people muddled up. One chap came in who my paper said was a champion javelin thrower. I thought it odd that he seemed so small—about five feet eight. I thought they were supposed to be big, though truth be told my knowledge of javelin throwers was limited. I asked him what was the most important factor in his sport. His reply completely threw me. "The quality of the ice."

God, I thought, I really don't know anything about javelin throwing. "I see," I said. "Is that very important to you?"

"Yes, the most important thing," he replied. "It determines how high you can go," he went on. I could see Seb gesticulating wildly but not very articulately behind him.

"How high do you go?" I asked.

"About three feet," he said.

Seb intervened. "He knows all this because for years he was the champion ice skater. Very famous for his skating on ice."

Another moment of drama was when the Russian delegation came in to see us, led by the mayor of Moscow. Ken Livingstone told me mysteriously that they were close, and that they had an understanding. He didn't give details and I thought it better not to ask.

They trooped in looking very Russian. There is something about a group of Russian men that makes you want them on your side. You feel that in the wrong context, or any context, they could become excessive; that the boundaries which circumscribe our conduct and character don't apply; that you fully realise why Napoleon failed and why Hitler was daft to try.

They sat down heavily, and looked at me. I looked at them. Then they smiled knowingly and nodded. Ken, who had joined me for this one, looked at me and we both nodded at them. The nodding went on for some time until a conversation began that was, for me at least, entirely elliptical. The gist of it was that we all understood each other very well, that they were very true to their word and so were we, and they didn't like people who weren't (I got a bit uneasy at that). But since they were and we were, there was no need to say any more. After another round of knowing smiles and nodding, they trooped out.

"What the hell was all that about, Ken?" I asked when they had left.

"Don't you worry your pretty head about it," he said. "I think it went well."

In between all the "non-lobbying," there were formal meetings and receptions. The Queen of Spain—very gracious and a real asset for them—turned up with the newish Spanish prime minister, José Luis Rodríguez Zapatero, who, despite my friendship with Aznar, always behaved very well towards me, and was obviously a smart leader. Big politicians mixed with small royals. At the reception, given by Singapore's prime minister in the wonderful old colonial General House, we all mingled uncomfortably, talking to one person, watching with snake-like intensity the moves everyone else was making, acutely aware that an inadvertent word or snub could lose a precious vote. Really horrible stuff: being competitive without appearing to be and trying to maintain dignity while begging.

Princess Anne was also touring the meetings, and doing so carefully because she was an IOC member. She was genuinely respected because genuinely knowledgeable and, of course, an Olympian herself. She does a huge amount of largely unnoticed charity work and is a tremendous ambassador for the country. I always liked her. I doubt the feeling was mutual, or perhaps more accurately she was indifferent, except on the hunting ban, which I'm sure she would have hated. She is a chip right off the old man's block. People think Prince Philip doesn't give a damn about what people think of him, and they are right: he doesn't. Anne is exactly the same. She is what she is, and if you don't like it you can clear off. It's not a quality I have, but I admire those who do. The unfortunate thing is, it stops people seeing the other side of their character.

During our first time at Balmoral, Princess Anne called Cherie "Mrs. Blair," and Cherie (being Cherie) said, "Please call me Cherie."

"Actually, I prefer Mrs. Blair," Anne replied. At one level, it is stunningly rude and discordant in our democratic age. At another, it shows an admirable determination not to be concordant with our democratic age but to tell that to clear off as well.

I remember, early on in government, Buckingham Palace thought they should have a reception for a few Labour MPs. Since we had a rather large majority, perhaps they thought they should do so in case there were any latent republican tendencies that might erupt. It was going fine until Prince Philip wandered up to Joan Walley, a very sincere leftish feminist MP. "Hello," he said, "where do you represent?"

"Stoke," she said.

"Ghastly place, isn't it?" he replied.

On the evening I was due to leave Singapore we had the grand ceremony, the opening speeches and the IOC drinks party. I met the Spanish footballer Raul, and tried, unsuccessfully, to persuade him of the merits of moving to Newcastle United over Real Madrid. By the time of the drinks party I was desperate to get away. I was exhausted, and frankly wanted to kill the next person who gave me their opinion of the present geopolitical challenges facing the world today. I had had just about enough of the Olympic movement, its members and its ceremonies. My brain was switching on to the G8 preparations, about which I had had continual and not always positive reports throughout the stay. I was more and more conscious of the double-whammy possibilities of failure: lose the Olympics, screw up the G8.

Jacques Chirac arrived, swinging into the party like he owned the Olympics and everything in it. I noticed in a rather jaundiced way—but it may have been my mood—that everyone fluttered around him. Maybe I had stayed too long, become too familiar, been too modest, not grand enough. I started to exhibit signs of whining, signs my staff recognise.

This is when it is important to have people around you who don't respect or revere you too much. Jo Gibbons from Number 10, in charge of events, was sympathetic to my exhaustion but utterly unsympathetic to my leaving. There were many people to see. Seb was very kind, but completely firm: stay. Cherie seemed inexhaustible. I was going to miss the big presentation the next day because I had to get back to prepare for the G8. Jacques could do his in person, I could only be in a video. So stay it was.

Finally, when I had just about given up the will to live, and when all the drinks waiters had had their picture taken with me in turn, it was time to go, get on the plane and head back, a twelve-hour flight.

In fact, the difference between me and Jacques at the drinks party kind of summed up and symbolised the difference in approach of the Paris and London bids.

In 1948, London had to be persuaded to host the games. Then the Cold War somewhat distorted the bidding process. But by the 1990s, the Olympics had come of age. It was no longer a case of a country doing the Games a favour by hosting them, but rather the hosting of the Games became a prize to be desired devoutly. Nowadays, the IOC assume that countries can get the infrastructure built and physically put on the games. What used to be the end point is now only the starting point. The real value added is what the host city can contribute to what might loosely be described as the Olympic spirit—the intangible but deeply felt soul of the Olympic movement.

During the IOC preliminary visit to London to assess our bid, Buckingham Palace put on a dinner for the assessment team, whose chief I sat next to. It was only in the course of talking with her that I realised London's bid had to be about them, not us; or more accurately what we could do to advance the ethos, the spirit, the inner emotions of the Olympic movement, rather than being simply about London, infra-structure, and so on. The IOC were a curious mixture of athletes, busi-ness people, royals and the general great and good; but whatever their origins, they were immensely sensitive to the charges that the whole thing had become commercialised and had lost touch with its inner self. They wanted the Olympics to mean something again, a higher and bet-ter thing, not just a great moneymaking celebrity fest.

People talked about the Games needing a legacy, which normally meant facilities that didn't close as soon as the Games were over. I took it to mean something that would make a positive difference to the world. I found Seb and the others in a similar mood, so we set about presenting London as modern, dynamic, multicultural, multiracial and proud of it. London on its contemporary merits—modernity as much as tradition.

Rather like at the drinks party, the French affected an attitude of "we are going to win and aren't you lucky when we do" and tried to sweep people along as if invincible—very French. We affected an attitude of "we humbly beg to offer our services to your great movement" and paddled and conspired like crazy underneath the surface—very British. The French way can in many cases be the right way, but they overdid it just a fraction. It undoubtedly made a difference; our presentation just had a better feel.

There was one final person without whom we may not have won:

Silvio Berlusconi. The previous August I had gone to visit him at his home in Sardinia to seek his help with the bid. Italy was a key player. He asked me how much it mattered to get the Olympics. "It matters," I said.

"Greatly?" he asked.

"Greatly," I said.

He said, "You are my friend. I promise nothing but I see if I can help." Typical Silvio, which is why I like him. Most politicians say "I promise" but then do nothing. He said, "I promise nothing," but then delivered.

Personal relationships matter—this is obvious, of course, but is also completely ignored by people who think it's florid stratagems and mathematical calculations that drive negotiations and compromise. At all levels, but especially at the top, politics is about people. If you like a leader, you try to help them, even if it stretches your own interests. If you don't, you don't. And if you distance yourself on political grounds—for example because, like Silvio, there's controversy around them—then fine, but don't kid yourself: your own country's the loser. That leader is not a fool, and knows you are not prepared to pay a price to have a relationship. You think they don't harbour a grudge about it? I have no idea how the Italians voted, but . . .

We left Singapore not daring to hope and yet still hoping, which I put down to the exhilaration of it all and the fact that people are always nice to your face. But somehow it didn't feel like a done deal for France any more.

We landed at Edinburgh airport after flying overnight, and drove up to the grand Gleneagles hotel. I'd chosen Gleneagles not because it was grand, but because we needed somewhere that could be secured. The 1998 G8 in Birmingham—my first—had been right in the city centre, but the world of summitry had changed in the seven years since then, even before 11 September and certainly after it. We live in an era of publicity through protest. Because the modern media works essentially through impact, protesters know that if they protest in a sufficiently disruptive way, they lift the agenda from the democratically elected politicians. Hordes can descend on a summit and wreck it, dominate the news coverage, diminish its salience; in short, devalue it. In turn, this forces politicians to try to insulate themselves from the protest, and after the Genoa summit in 2001 they tended to be held in faraway or remote places not so susceptible to disruption: Evian in France, Heiligendamm in Germany and Sea Island in the U.S.

As we drove into Gleneagles we could hear the shouts of the anti-globalisation protesters who were against us meeting, who were against the G8, who were against the whole system. My thoughts towards them were not charitable. Why shouldn't we meet and talk? After all, it is about Africa and climate change. What is your problem? In other words, I felt about them roughly what they felt about me.

I then had to meet Jack McConnell, the Scottish First Minister. It was important for him to be seen as part of the "happening" as the security arrangements had all been really tough to carry out. He had had to meet local residents, sort out the policing of the huge pre-G8 rally held a few days before in Edinburgh and, as usual, everyone wanted the G8 but at the same time wanted to complain about the disruption.

Amazingly I had slept on the way back from Singapore, thanks in part to my pill. Once I had bathed and sorted myself out I felt fine, except of course for the sick feeling waiting for the Olympic result. Clearly there was nothing else I could do about that now, so I concentrated on the G8.

I had decided to do it differently this year. I was in a weaker position internally following the election. Gordon and his folk were agitating. The media were kicking my backside more or less incessantly. I had been forced into talking about the transition to a new leader when doing so was both a little humiliating and weakening.

By then, however, I had reached a new stage of development within myself. I was not happy—the pressure was really tough—but I was mentally very strong. I would give it two years minimum. That was at least the most consistent I could be with my pledge to serve a full term—not a fulfilment of it, obviously, but not so flagrant a breach as to be a real betrayal of trust. If Gordon and I had been working in tandem on an agreed agenda, I might have gone before that, as I have said; but on the assumption it was still difficult, I would continue at least two years.

If those in the party or the media were to go for me and get me out forcibly before then, there would be a bloodbath. And prior to that point, I was going to do what I thought was right. I had been operating on that principle for the past few years and it was going to continue like that. I wasn't going to back down. Simple as that. I was going to take the risks of failure rather than let fear of failure diminish the scale of ambition. And I wasn't going to waste a moment or set my sights low. Hence the different G8 agenda.

Usually, the G8 focused on the issue of the day and, traditionally, was always about the world economy. Its membership represented historical rather than present economic and political power. Gradually we started to involve others informally, something we began at the G8 in Birmingham in 1998.

This time I took it on to a whole new level. First, I invited five nations—China, India, Brazil, South Africa and Mexico—for more or less the whole summit, supplemented by various African and Arab leaders. G8+5 became a new format that enabled the largest global players—or most of them—to gather, albeit informally, at the only non-regional global political meeting outside a formal UN or WTO structure.

Second, I decided to go for an ambitious set of outcomes. I defined the objectives as twofold: get a comprehensive package of support and partnership agreed for Africa; and at least establish the principle of a new global deal on climate change—to include the U.S. and China—to follow the expiration of the Kyoto Protocol in 2012. The Africa package was based on the Commission for Africa that I had set up back in 2004 at the instigation of Bob Geldof.

Bob. What can I say about Bob? He can drive you completely nuts. He can talk forever. He can speak to world leaders like they were errant schoolkids. Personally I didn't mind that—but I was the exception, believe me. Bob can be rather unreasonable in his persistence, actually manic about it. However, he has two enormous saving graces: he is smart, and he is brave. He is smart enough to know when to stop short of provoking catastrophe or making an unreasonable demand non-negotiable. He is brave because he isn't one of your fair weather, "don't sully me with compromise," "now you're not popular I don't want to associate with you" types of which the arts world is inordinately full. He and Bono are both genuinely committed, properly knowledgeable and ultimately care more about getting things done than protecting their egos.

The Africa Commission was staffed by high-quality people. The make-up was balanced but serious, the African members in particular being savvy, clear-minded and determined to demonstrate the central thesis of the report: in the end Africa should sort out Africa. They were in the classic "hand up, not handout" mode. Yes, we needed increased aid, but the purpose was to help get Africa on its own feet, with no rubbish about not being able to govern because of the wicked colonial past. My view on Africa had always been essential third-way stuff: we need a partnership between the developed and undeveloped world, not a donor–recipient relationship. Governance and corruption were as big a problem as debt and aid. Conflict resolution was central. In other words, the hard and the soft. Though the Western citizen felt genuinely sorry for the plight of the Africans, they had also somewhat come to fear it was a hopeless situation. Giving money was a moral imperative, but there was little real belief in it delivering the outcome, which in turn led to "donor fatigue." This was something Bob and Bono knew instinctively, and if they hadn't, their first meeting with George Bush would have put them right.

I knew Bono would be an important person to get to see George. Bono could have been a president or prime minister standing on his head. He had an absolutely natural gift for politicking, was great with people, very smart and an inspirational speaker. I spent a long time wondering what made him so good at what he did. I finally decided that, apart from hard work, he had that characteristic I saw in every truly successful person I ever met: he is motivated by an abundant desire to carry on improving, never really content or relaxed. In the right way and under control, that motivation also imparts a certain humility. I knew he would work George well, and with none of the prissy disdain of most of his ilk.

George was, truth be told, anxious about my G8 agenda. He never loved summits, even in fact distrusted them. He felt their pressure, disliked the inevitable focus on America "not doing enough" and resented the hypocrisy that marked and occasionally defined them. I had to use a lot of my capital with him—which was nonetheless considerable—to get him to agree the agenda and go with it.

He was very tough on Africa and governance, rightly, and he had after all doubled aid to Africa and was sceptical about climate change. George is a real conservative, and has the qualities I admire in conservatives and also those, politically, that make me not one myself. One of these qualities is that if a great public lather is whipped up over something, the first instinct of conservatives is to resist it—and they are often right to do so. They don't come to a viewpoint because everyone tells them they should.

This attitude is the reason that while people might say they don't like conservative politicians, they still vote for them. People tend to go with the crowd; but in an odd sort of way, they respect a leader who is prepared to defy the crowd. Indeed, if he or she is not prepared to do so, the public suspect he or she is not a proper leader. It's weird the way it works, but there it is. Progressive politicians often don't get this. They prefer to be with the tide of thinking, and get confused when the public say in an opinion poll that they believe X, only to vote Y at the ballot box.

I always remember in the 1983 election fighting on the then Labour policy of withdrawal from the European Economic Community. I didn't support it myself and had told my selection committee as much; but out on the campaign trail as a new candidate, trying to keep my nose clean, I stood on the party platform. The opinion polls showed big majorities in favour of withdrawal, especially among Labour supporters. In a strong Labour seat, it should have been a sure-fire vote winner. It wasn't. Much to my consternation, I was advocating a policy that not only was one I did not believe in, but neither did my natural supporters. In the end they accepted the Conservative argument that it was just not practical to get out of Europe. Interestingly, the party positions later reversed; but the public reaction was the same. No party in Britain will win an outright majority on an anti-EU platform today unless the public go daft, and by and large they don't.

Anyway, that is to digress. The point is that when all the world says climate change threatens the planet, the natural reaction for people like George is to reply: "So you say, but I'm not convinced." The more strident the claim, the more resistant they become.

At the Genoa G8 in 2001—his first—we had a discussion on climate change. The Belgians at that time had the EU presidency, and so they were also at the G8 table. The then Belgian prime minister, Guy Verhofstadt, is a nice guy and bright, but very Brussels. Kyoto had been agreed and Bill Clinton had signed it, but the U.S. Senate had voted 98–0 against ratification. On assuming office, George had flatly dissed the whole thing. Later, I think he knew he had made a tactical error. The truth is that whatever he said, at that moment and in those circumstances there was no way Congress was going to pass it. He could have taken a low-key position. Instead, as is his wont, he said what he thought, which was that he wasn't convinced, either by Kyoto or actually by the basic argument about the changing of the climate. He added that there was no way America could possibly meet the Kyoto targets without doing immense damage to its economy, and he was just not going to do that.

After George had finished, Guy said he understood what George was saying, but really the American problem had a very simple solution, one that would be good for the world, but also immensely beneficial for the inner well-being of the American people: they could cut their emissions significantly if they doubled gasoline prices by raising the taxes on it. Such an action would be bold, it would help wean the American people off their obsession with the motor car, and earn George the high approval of international political opinion, not least in Belgium.

George had arrived bang on time for this first discussion and had not fully said hello to all the participants. He didn't know or recognise Guy, whose advice he listened to with considerable astonishment.

He then turned to me and whispered, "Who is this guy?"

"He is the prime minister of Belgium," I said.

"Belgium?" George said, clearly aghast at the possible full extent of his stupidity. "Belgium is not part of the G8."

"No," I said, "but he is here as the president of Europe."

"You got the Belgians running Europe?" He shook his head, now aghast at our stupidity.

So to describe George as a sceptic on climate change would be an understatement. As time progressed he shifted his thinking, but did so too slowly—a quality of conservatives I don't admire—and as much because he could see American dependence on carbon was putting their future into the hands of unstable and treacherous parts of the world. Once he had moved, he spent more on developing clean fuel than any previous administration. Actually, he also trebled aid to Africa. But as ever, because the world had come to have a fixed view of him, he got no credit.

I once asked one of my backbench MPs why he hated George so much. This had been one of those embarrassing occasions that even cropped up with some of my close friends, who would ask in private what I really thought of George Bush. I would say I really liked him. It never failed to produce complete incomprehension. Having asked my backbencher why he hated him so much, he said, "Just do. Can't explain it fully, but just do." I then asked if it would make any difference if he turned out to be right. "In that case I think I would hate him even more," he replied.

So that was how it was with George. He had moved some way by the time of the July 2005 G8, but not as far as I wanted. He had constantly refused to say he would commit the U.S. to being part of a deal on climate change. And although he had been really forward on Africa and had a really impressive record on funding action on HIV/Aids, we

were asking big numbers—$50 billion extra over the coming years—
and filling in details of how it would be spent. Instead of an agreeable
but general set of discussions, we were putting real figures, real commitments and real deliverables on the table. George was nervous and I was
absolutely aware that although others were going along, they were
doing so in the belief that George would save them by volunteering to
be the party-pooper. I also knew that if he agreed, no one else would
dare disagree.

I was putting real pressure on, to be honest quite a bit above and
beyond what the other leaders thought was desirable or necessary.
Without George's backing, indeed, it would have been impossible.
Even with it, there were limits, and I was significantly outside them.

The U.S. style of summit negotiation is to be really difficult, be prepared to crash it, argue over every last word, then come in at the end
and make everyone feel grateful they've even shown up. It doesn't win
many friends but they know everyone hides in their slipstream. If they
cave, no one will do their fighting for them, so they fight for themselves. It's fair enough, but it causes anxious moments for any summit
host, including me. I knew if push really came to shove I could probably bring George into agreement, but we were going for both climate
change and Africa and he might just think one was enough, whereas I
wanted both.

Also, once inside a process, people find it really hard to extricate
themselves. George knew that from the moment he conceded, he was
on a travelator that would take him a long way—as indeed he went, two
years later in Germany. He knew that if he agreed this process now with
a statement that acknowledged the seriousness of the challenge and the
fact that it was essentially man-made, he was locking in the U.S. And he
never hid behind Congress. If he said he would do it, he would actually
try to do it rather than just agree in the knowledge that others would
block and save him from delivering.

The G8+5 was a crucial forum in which debate and discussion
between the main emitters could happen reasonably informally. As I
never tired of pointing out to people, it was a fat lot of good over a hundred nations coming together under the UN to agree a climate deal if
the U.S. wasn't part of it, and India and China weren't willing to accept
any forward obligations to reduce emissions. This is why to this day, no
matter how many countries have ratified Kyoto, very few—Britain
being an exception—have met their targets.

On Africa, I knew that without real figures it was going to be another "poor Africa, we care so much about you" load of old rubbish in a communiqué that wasn't going to fool anyone. Bob, Bono and the NGO alliance had mounted an effective campaign, essentially going to each main nation in turn and trying to frighten the pants off the leadership by demonstrating the breadth of public support for action on Africa. It was done cleverly, with them always giving enough praise to the leaders to encourage them. With Bob and Bono at the helm, there would be a sensible debate. If we delivered, they'd say we'd delivered. If not, they would condemn us. Fair enough. The Greens would be opportunist even if George came dressed in sackcloth and ashes, pleading forgiveness for his neocon past and said henceforth all Americans would give up the cars and drive wind-powered scooters.

Over time, I'm afraid I came to dislike part of the NGO culture, especially the Green groups. NGOs do a great job, don't misunderstand me; but the trouble with some of them is that while they are treated by the media as concerned citizens, which of course they are, they are also organisations, raising money, marketing themselves and competing with other NGOs in a similar field. Because their entire *raison d'être* is to get policy changed, they can hardly say yes, we've done it, without putting themselves out of business. And they've learned to play the modern media game perfectly. As it's all about impact, they shout louder and louder to get heard. Balance is not in the vocabulary. It's all "outrage," "betrayal," "crisis." They also have their own tightly defined dogma and conventional wisdom which, if you challenge them, they defend fiercely—not usually on their merits, but by abusing your motives for challenging them. On Africa, I tried constantly to get them to see free trade, with aid for trade, as an essential African interest, but it was virtually impossible. Part of their coalition basically took the position that "globalisation is a rich-country conspiracy," and challenging that was to fracture their support. So they resisted.

It's like the Greens over nuclear power. The case for nuclear power is now so overwhelming that frankly it is almost irresponsible—faced with an energy crunch and climate change—to oppose its development. I bet many of them know that privately, but it would be such heresy to say so and would divide the movement.

The point I am making is that there's as much politics in NGOs as in politics—sometimes more—and they are treated as objective observers when they simply aren't. Partly they campaign for a cause, and partly for vested interests. However, this doesn't mean that everything they say is wrong, and they are part of a healthy democracy (this time I mean it).

At Gleneagles we were lucky to have some bright, warm weather, and would sit out in the sunshine—or at least the others did. I would get up in constant agitation, flitting from the detail of the G8 to the perpetual speculation about the Olympic decision eagerly awaited by crowds in Trafalgar Square and the Champs-Elysées. The first intimation of the result came through: Moscow was out, then New York.

The tension was now very thick, and my staff gave up trying to talk to me about Africa and climate change since I was talking gibberish back to them. It was obvious from my many conversations with Latin American members of the IOC that if it came down to a contest between London and Madrid, they would back Madrid (Spanish speakers sticking together), whereas if it was London and Paris, they might well back us. It was plainly close. Like all electorates as small as this, there were naturally more votes pledged to the key contenders than there were voters. Every time Seb told me how many firm pledges he had, I would give a hollow laugh—as would anyone who had ever been through a Labour Party selection process.

Around 10 a.m. the news came through that Madrid were out. It was us and Paris. It wouldn't be long now. Jo and the team went off to watch the announcement on television, but I couldn't bear to. I was outside when Jonathan Powell, who was irritatingly calm, joined me. I don't think he cared greatly. When the talk in the office turned to football, as it usually did at least once a day, Jonathan would put his fingers in his ears as if to say please talk about this elsewhere, some of us have work to do. His phone rang, and he took the call with much indifference; then somewhat conversationally, as though he had just been told that the 4 p.m. appointment had moved to 4:15, he said, "Oh, we won, did we? Good, OK."

I, of course, shot up like a rocketing pheasant on one of the nearby moors. Oddly enough, at that moment I remembered the time when, aged twelve, I found out I had won an exhibition to Fettes, running round our garden in Durham in sheer delight and of course relief, the draining anxiety replaced by joy. I think I danced a little around Jonathan and then hugged him. Jonathan is not a natural hugger; but he was there, and he got hugged. Then the others came running through, and of course were very willing to be hugged.

It was a great victory, a stellar victory indeed. To be honest, I knew also that although the G8 would naturally still be a big hurdle to leap, this was going to relieve the pressure on me. The phone calls of celebration were made, interviews given, the crowds in Trafalgar Square addressed. I could turn back to thinking about the G8 in an optimistic, confident frame of mind.

One of the first to arrive for the summit was Jacques Chirac. I felt genuinely sorry for him—no, I really did. He had lost the referendum on the EU treaty, a terrible blow and I am sure a deeply felt, personal rebuff from his own people. Now this. And because I had been so high-profile in spearheading our bid and he had led his, it would be doubly humiliating. I would have felt gutted in his place, really low—beyond low, actually.

But whatever else you may say about Jacques, he has courage and he is a pro. He turned up and was immensely gracious, congratulating me personally as well as the country, wishing me all the best and doing so with dignity and sincerity. I don't know whether in the privacy of his room he chewed the carpet and beat his fists on the floor, but I suspect not.

He had been a minister in the 1960s, and had been prime minister when I was a barman in Paris thirty years earlier. He has seen it all—in fact, he's probably seen it too much, but one advantage is he's not fazed. In defeat, he was rather magnificent. He also always had one great attribute, I thought: he looked like a president, spoke like one and carried himself like one. His policies—in my view—were another thing, but as a personality he was the part. When he fought Lionel Jospin for the presidency in 2002, Jospin being the socialist prime minister in the nonsensical cohabitational arrangement that the French system can give rise to, the polls were close. But I was always sure Jacques would win, and when people would ask me why, I could only say: because he looks like a French president, whereas Lionel looks like a French professor; and the French want their presidents to be, well, presidential. Like Mitterrand.

The summit was to begin with a sumptuous dinner hosted by the Queen. Beforehand, George and I had a drink together with Cherie and Laura. I could see he was going to help and, of course, Cherie and Laura always got on really well. Our mutual friend Bill Gammell dropped by. Bill was becoming richer by the minute, having bought some oil concession off Bangladesh that no one else wanted and which turned out to be far better in deposits than anyone anticipated. "We made the wrong career choice, George," I said after Bill left. He agreed, but neither of us meant it. Politics is voluntary.

As if Jacques didn't have enough problems, a few days earlier he had reportedly joked about British food in some unguarded remarks to Vladimir Putin and Gerhard Schroeder, effectively saying that you can't trust people whose cooking is so bad. For good measure he had also put the Finns in the same bracket. Personally I didn't give a damn and thought it was quite funny, but of course everyone had to pretend to be thoroughly outraged and get very pompous. The fact that Jacques denied the remarks mattered not a bit, and various celebrity chefs, assorted cooks and general French-haters were wheeled out to condemn this monstrous attack; and the Finns, I think, really did take umbrage. The Finnish prime minister later told me solemnly that this had been a very big issue in Finland (I thought, blimey, get a life).

As we sat down to dinner with the Queen, the Japanese prime minister Junichiro Koizumi hit on a great line of banter. Koizumi is one of the most interesting people I have ever met in politics, and certainly unlike any other Japanese politician I had met till then: a great leader, very lively, with an unusual personality. As he tucked into the first course, he said loudly in his halting English across the table to Jacques: "Hey, Jacques, excellent British food, do you think?" followed by peals of laughter. Jacques looked at him a trifle acidly, forced to join in the joke, while protesting to the Queen that he had never actually said what it was alleged he had said. "Said what?" she asked, being the only one not to have heard the story, thus necessitating the whole thing being explained again, much to everyone's amusement—especially Koizumi's, who realised he was on to a rich vein and exploited it mercilessly, punctuating each course, and at times virtually each mouthful, with raucous comments about the brilliance of the cooking, until I thought Jacques was going to take out his aide-de-camp's gun and shoot him.

These G8 dinners are always weird affairs. The leaders are usually a little jet-lagged, they have to keep an eye on the agenda and at Gleneagles especially so. The surroundings are invariably grand, but the publicity is always about how grand, and inevitably the question is raised about the cost of staging the summits. Of course the big cost is security, yet somehow this is the leaders' fault for having the temerity to meet and talk about world affairs, rather than that of the motley variegated protesters who, unrestrained, could run amok. It's kind of a mixture of a very fancy busman's holiday, a workshop conference and a big political deal. And you are never sure how it will work out.

The opening dinners tend to be fairly convivial—give leaders a drink or two and they are almost human—but as the crunch comes in the following days, they can get more guarded. This dinner was good. The Queen handled them all well, though some guests didn't always quite know how to handle her. Some got matey with her. Now let me tell you something: you don't get matey with the Queen. Occasionally she can be matey with you, but don't try to reciprocate or you get The Look. I watched with some amusement those who understood the difference between a queen and a president and those who didn't. Both are heads of state, but the Queen is the Queen. That's royalty, not some jumped-up elected pleb. And don't you forget it.

After dinner I went back to the suite to work on the agenda. There was still a lot to do—people were apart on numbers on Africa and there was still stiff resistance on climate change. I slept not long but well, was up early preparing, still elated, but now really starting to focus.

The first meeting was a bilateral with George. Pretty quickly we threw out everyone else and had breakfast together. I needed to get the feel for whether he would cross the line and agree to be part of a dialogue with the express objective of reaching a new post-Kyoto deal. He wouldn't commit to a target now, that was understood, but would he be part of a process where eventually that would be on the agenda? He was more or less there on Africa.

In handling the whole G8 agenda, I was supremely blessed by having a fresh and really capable team around me, including Sir Michael Jay, who had been ambassador in Paris and was now head of the Diplomatic Service. To my surprise and delight, he agreed to take on the role of G8 sherpa (i.e. the government point person for the preparation of the summit). This was way below his pay grade, as it were, but it demonstrated our commitment and the importance we attached to the summit. He had the right blend of experience, weight and conviction.

He was supported by Justin Forsyth, who had joined from Oxfam. In other words, he was from the bête noire NGO movement. He turned out to be fantastic; he knew them all, was one of them, could spot their tactics, identified accurately their foibles and fault lines and was a really sharp non-political politician. He did the politics of the NGOs, Michael did those of the governments. And Sir Nigel Sheinwald, my foreign policy adviser at Number 10, kept his beady eye on it all and followed through notably with the Americans in the way only he could.

George and I did a short press conference together. He had to explain why he had knocked over a policeman while he was on a bike ride in the grounds the evening before. It could only happen to George. Typically, he spoke to the policeman in hospital and was very self-deprecating about it, but naturally the whole thing had been treated in the media as if George had come to Gleneagles with the express intention of finding a Scottish bobby to knock over and probably that afternoon would be lining up a few more and mowing them down.

Nothing seemed set to disturb the mood of buoyancy. A bit of pushing and the G8 would come together, which would be a landmark in summitry. I knew the risks on making it about what the big and powerful nations could do for the world and abandoning its traditional economic role. I knew it was the right gamble to take. I felt confidence surging back through me, in my own judgement, in my self-belief and in my destiny.

I walked the few steps to the little press briefing room, where I was to meet President Hu of China. He tended to be very formal, but very much on top of his brief and, I think, quintessentially decent. We began our session with my asking him to appoint someone we could liaise with more informally so that UK/China relations, radically improved since the return of Hong Kong, could move to a new level. He made a suggestion, we agreed and started to move on to the G8 agenda.

China was very reluctant to move on climate change because it was wary of being bound into obligations inappropriate to its stage of economic development. The Chinese were terrified of being pushed to accept something that was inimical to their number-one priority: growth. They had over 60 per cent of the population still earning a living from agriculture (the U.S. and the EU had around 3 per cent) and wanted to move vast millions of people from the land to cities. Without strong economic and industrial growth—and hence greater energy consumption—it was an impossible task. The Chinese doubled their coal consumption between 2000 and 2006. They knew that consenting to be part of a dialogue with the aim of an agreement at the end was a lot less innocuous than it appeared, so they were understandably cautious, yet were also feeling their power; sensing the responsibilities that went with it; recognising that they couldn't be outside and inside the power club at the same time. I thought I could get them to come on board, provided I didn't overdo it or ascribe to them positions they weren't ready for.

Fifteen minutes in, Jonathan passed me a note. It simply said that there had been an incident on the Tube. Possible casualties. Might be an accident, might not. Instinct said it wasn't.

Suddenly Jonathan left the room and then came back in looking agitated. I apologised to President Hu, explained the note and asked Jonathan if we knew anything further.

"There is more than one explosion," he said.

Oh God, don't let it be a terrorist attack, not that, not here. What I always feared, so obvious for them, so divisive for us. Right now, at this moment, there are people I don't know whose lives have just changed forever, perhaps ended forever, the world forgotten in the extinction of one human being's hopes, dreams and ambitions, all ended for reasons they will never know, nor understand, nor can ever argue about. Terrorism is the ultimate injustice: the targeting of the innocent precisely because they are innocent.

I got up and asked the president's indulgence but I had to go and check it all out. On the way up to my room, clutching the mobile Jonathan gave me and getting the barest details, I bumped into George. He had heard already, of course. "Terrorist attack?" he queried.

"Could be an accident," I said. But we looked at each other and knew that it wasn't.

By now it was clear there had been three attacks, all on the London Underground, all at peak rush hour. I spoke to Charles Clarke, who was as I expected: focused, not panicking, and trying to think through the logistics of the response. Shut the networks, train stations of course, but what other precautions? What help would the emergency services want?

"How many casualties?" I asked.

"I can't tell," he said.

"Deaths?"

"Bound to be, I'm afraid."

"How many?"

"Don't know."

Pointless questions and pointless answers; no one knew.

At first, we thought it might be a handful of people, each one a tragedy but less than the worst case. The worst case would be very bad at that time of day, between Aldgate and Liverpool Street, Russell Square and King's Cross, Edgware Road and Paddington—all very busy commuter journeys.

Around 10 a.m., news came through of a fourth explosion. This time it was on a bus at Tavistock Square just south of Upper Woburn Place, somewhere I used to go regularly as a barrister, where the old industrial tribunal having to do with employment matters used to be. I thought inconsequentially of all the times I had been there, and pictured it now in my mind, the bus with the roof blown off, limbs, bones and blood strewn everywhere. And for what? In the name of God?

Anger, pity and determination jostled like queue-jumpers barging into each other. I took a deep breath. Cut out the emotion, just think. Get a sense of the magnitude, work out the emotions of the country but do so in a way that leaves you free to describe them, but not to share them except for the purpose of description, so as to leave your mind clear. Do I leave the G8? Do we cancel it? How can I chair it waiting for news? Do we hand the enemy a victory by altering our arrangements? Do we show insensitivity to the victims by carrying on?

I know it sounds callous but calculations have to be made. There will be a time for me to weep later. Now you are the leader, so lead.

Slowly, by the odd Socratic process that takes place in a crisis, we put a plan together. The magnitude was plain: not the worst case, but fifty-two dead and many more injured, and heaven only knows how many more traumatised. Fifty-two dead people. Fifty-two people with families, friends, girlfriends, boyfriends, children. Fifty-two people who used to engage in all of life's fullness and variety. Fifty-two people who had got up that morning not knowing it was the last time they would ever wake up or kiss someone goodbye.

I called the other leaders together and explained the situation. I was in a genuine quandary as to whether to leave the summit. In hindsight it was obvious; I should return to London. It didn't seem like it then. It was Jacques who was most emphatic: you have to go back, the British people will expect it. What about the summit? I asked. We agreed it would be chaired by Sir Michael Jay.

I did some very brief media, after telling them I would do a statement later in Downing Street once I knew the facts. Charles would take care of the House. I boarded an RAF helicopter, and from Dundee airport we flew to Northolt and thence to Downing Street.

Even at moments of the highest tragedy, there can be moments of absurdity. The French ambassador Gerard Errera asked if he could come back with us on the plane. We naturally assented. As we flew down, the steward asked us if we wanted anything to eat as we had all missed lunch and were hungry. Having no time to prepare anything, lunch consisted of a bowl of stale crisps, some forlorn old salted peanuts and a few sandwiches which would have been rejected by British Rail in its heyday. Errera momentarily caught my eye and his face twitched. Had we brought a libel case against Jacques for his attack on British cuisine, Errera would have been the first witness for the defence.

Back in Downing Street we assembled the facts as best we could, and convened the emergency COBR meeting. The worst thing was not knowing what else was out there. Was that it? Who and why? It was obviously part of the al-Qaeda network, but who was it specifically, here or abroad? It was some time before all these answers could be given.

In the aftermath, we had several weeks in which there were calls threatening new attacks, or intelligence of such an intent. It was a nightmare. Each call could be a reason for shutting down the airport or transport infrastructure, or closing down city centres. We had the tragic killing of the Brazilian student Jean Charles de Menezes on 22 July, which turned out to be a terrible error but where I also felt desperately sorry for the officers involved who were acting in good faith trying to keep the country safe. On one occasion we had a COBR meeting about the latest threat that had been made, although the intelligence seemed flimsy. Ignoring it was hard. Acting on it was also hard. Yet again we would have to shut down the Underground. So: act or ignore? I looked round the table and finally asked Ian Blair, the Metropolitan Police commissioner who had done an excellent job through the attacks and after, what to do. "I'm afraid this is your call," he said. I decided not to act, but I passed a very restless and anxious night when the time of the threatened attack came.

All the way down in the plane from Scotland, I had thought carefully about how we should respond as a nation. Jonathan, Charles and others could take care of the detailed, immediate response; what I had to focus on was how to express our thoughts as a country. This wasn't about "emoting" or "empathising," as people often stupidly and cynically say. At times like these, it is about defining the feeling so the reaction could be shaped and the consequences managed. Because there would be consequences from fifty-two totally innocent people dying, the worst ever terrorist attack in the UK, worse than any Irish Republican attack in forty years of the Troubles.

People could react in any number of ways: there would be the anti-Muslim brigade; and there would be a response that said it's really all the fault of Blair and Bush (I could see this coming the moment parts of the media thought it safe); but most of all there would be the sense of despair and tragedy. How could this be done, and in London, the embodiment of a multicultural city, the place just lauded by the award of the Olympic Games, no less; and precisely because of its open, friendly and unprejudiced character? Unbelievable. First triumph, then tragedy.

I formed the view that the first good instinct of the British people—Muslims, Christians, all of us—would be to unite and close ranks against the extremists, to reject prejudice in favour of solidarity. I knew that after a while there would be a second emotion: anger and a demand for action to prevent the possibility of this happening again, by tough measures, including legislation. By this point of my premiership, the iron had entered my soul on the issue of liberty versus anti-terror laws. When Lord Hoffmann had described the anti-terror laws as more of a threat to the country than the terrorists, I just couldn't believe it, couldn't credit how a sensible person could say anything quite so grossly stupid. So I knew there would be a battle to come.

But I knew the first thing was to unify, so I gave the Downing Street statement which tried to do that and I think by and large did do it. Specifically, I paid tribute to the Muslim population of Britain. I had real doubts about some of the leaders of the community and how they were confronting—or rather not confronting—this extremism, but it wasn't the time to entertain such doubts. It was the time to let the Olympic spirit flow, through the tragedy as well as the triumph.

Late that night, I went back to Gleneagles. We had done what was necessary to show proper sensitivity to the victims of the appalling act of terror. Now we had to show that the G8 was our way of doing politics, and that also mattered. The contrast between our way and the terrorists' way was essential. We had to fight terror not just through police, intelligence and security services, but as I constantly reiterated, it was a battle of ideas. I didn't know if they had timed the attack for the G8, but that's when it happened; so we had to paint the contrast in the boldest letters imaginable. Good politics and evil. Stark. Simple. Undeniable to all but the deranged.

By the time I got back, it was clear that the consequence of the terrorism on the leaders was to bring out the best in them. They had reacted brilliantly, and with total solidarity. There was an implicit collective decision to support the G8 agenda and get a result. The African numbers came together. The G8+5 dialogue was agreed. Michael Jay was performing with great skill, but they were getting there through political instinct and a genuine revulsion at the horror. We weren't going to get everything we wanted, but as Michael said, it's eight or nine out of ten. And believe me, for a summit, any summit but particularly G8, that is a real result. In the end, it set a new standard for such summits and rightly was regarded as historic.

We assembled the next day for the final session and communiqué. I had the idea of doing a statement setting out our achievements and contrasting that with terror, doing it all together, leaders of the world united, and symbolically signing the communiqué to give it added resonance and credibility. That's what we did, forty-eight hours after I had heard the Olympic result, two days of the most extraordinary turbulence I had lived through in my time in politics.

On Africa, we agreed a comprehensive plan of action, based on the Africa Commission. We got the $50 billion uplift in aid, debt cancellation, commitments on Aids treatment, on malaria, on governance and corruption.

On climate change, we agreed to begin the G8+5 dialogue with the express aim of reaching a new global deal that would first slow down emissions and then cut them.

For good measure, we also agreed a package of support for the Palestinian Authority.

But most of all we stood up for proper politics. Even with all the suits, the paraphernalia of summitry, the flat words of the communiqué, the grand surroundings all looking like politics as usual, there was something felt by us all—hardbitten and inured to most political emotions though we were—that was true and real about what we were doing.

I did the press conference in the garden of the hotel. There was the usual nonsense from some NGO bloke about how we had all let Africa down, and the unusual riposte from Bob who basically tore the bloke's head off for being so negative and followed him down the path from the press area, shouting abuse as only an irate Irishman can.

I recorded an interview with Jim Naughtie for the *Today* programme. I like Jim, but I knew already where it was heading: if we hadn't gone to Iraq, we might have been spared this. It's a nightmare of an argument to deal with because, of course, at one level, if you don't fight these people, it's possible you don't feature so much on their hate list. But what does that say about how your foreign policy is determined? And you know that if you give even a sliver of credence to the argument, then suddenly it's our fault, not theirs, which is, naturally, the very thing they want.

At that moment I was content simply to walk around it and not confront it. However angry it made me feel, at this point there was no point. But I could feel this whole debate moving to a new place, one where I was going to be very isolated, falling out not with the party but with the people. I felt it at a profound level, about us as a country, about our character. I felt it not with any fear of political mortality—though I could sense that coming—but in a way that was both less frantic and more painful.

I had a vision for Britain. All the way I had believed I could and would persuade the country it was the right choice, the modern way, New Britain going along with New Labour. It was about something bigger than Iraq, bigger than the American alliance, bigger than any one thing; a complete vision of where we should be in the early twenty-first century; about how we finally overcome the greatness of our history to discover the full potential of our future.

But now I wasn't sure I could do it. I wasn't sure people were really persuadable any more. The forces aligned against me were so many. If I fought back too hard, there would be so much division and bitterness—and yes, be honest, personal pain—when I could so easily be released.

All of this I felt, but put to one side. There would be a later reckoning. For now, I was just relieved that the week had finally come to a close. It had begun in triumph, was enveloped in tragedy and ended in some sort of truth about the best politics could be.

I thought of how the week would be viewed in retrospect. For some families as a moment of supreme bereavement. For others in Africa, unconscious of the efforts made to free them from poverty, hunger, conflict and disease, maybe life instead of death measured not in tens of people, but in millions.

As I staggered through the flat door that Friday night, I looked in on Leo sleeping up in his room, poured myself a drink, decided on a movie—something utterly escapist—tried to focus on the family things Cherie was asking me about, and tried to put it all out of my mind; tried to free myself of the worry of what comes next, of the next call, the next slip of paper, the next confrontation, the next frisson of fear.

I reflected on the awesome nature of the weight on my shoulders; the pain and the excitement. Politics: noble causes, ignoble means; the plans you make and the events that turn them upside down; the untold misery and the imperfect attempts to alleviate it.

I went back upstairs and looked in on Leo again, still sound asleep. A life ahead of him.

How much triumph, how much tragedy, how much happiness and sorrow would he accumulate? How many tears, and to what purpose? I remembered my mum. At fifty-two, I had just passed the age she had been when she died. So young, I thought now. When she was already ill and knew she might die soon, I once asked whether she would go back to being my age, then twenty, and live it all again if she could. "No," she said, "no, too much pain. Wouldn't like to go through it all again."

"But you were happy, Mum, in life, weren't you?"

"Yes, of course. But no, I wouldn't repeat it all, no, definitely not."

I knew what she meant now: not that it's better to be dead—of course it isn't—but going through it all again, the anxiety, the ambitions that have to be fulfilled, the dreams you know will be dashed, so much striving . . . That's the purpose of life: to strive.

Leo could have been on that Tube train, on that bus. Oh God, don't let my children die before me. I think of the grief of it, of the fathers and mothers of the soldiers who died in Iraq, in Afghanistan, of the other people, buried in the rubble of Baghdad or Kandahar.

Think of the horror. My responsibility.

I quietly closed the door to Leo's room and paused for a moment to throw it all off me. Let me forget for a while. Till the time comes to put it back on.

NINETEEN

TOUGHING IT OUT

The last two years in office were, in many ways, the best of years and the worst of years. The best because by this time I felt liberated, strong and up for anything. The worst because it was just as well I felt like that. For these two years, the party was revolting; Gordon was in a perpetual state of machination; the anti-Blair media (i.e. most of it) had given up any pretence at objectivity; Iraq teetered on the brink; and when all else failed, there was a police inquiry into me and my staff that very nearly toppled the government without a charge ever being laid. I look back on it now and think: How did you survive it?

In this time, I was trying to wear what was effectively a kind of psychological armour which the arrows simply bounced off, and to achieve a kind of weightlessness that allowed me, somehow, to float above the demonic rabble tearing at my limbs.

There was courage in it and I look back at it now with pride. I was cornered, so it was either go down or fight. I remember years ago a friend of mine in the constituency, who was used to rough neighbourhoods, told me: if you ever get in a street fight, stay upright, never go down. People always think if you're on the ground they will let you be; they won't, they will kick you in the head and most likely kill you. So stay on your feet, he warned. They'll rearrange your face, but you'll live.

While my face was certainly rearranged, I stayed on my feet and got a lot done.

I had more or less set in my mind a date of mid-2007—the halfway point of the Parliament—as the right time to leave, but I was open to going sooner if Gordon cooperated, and later if he didn't. As it happened, he didn't really, or not in any way that gave me confidence he would continue the programme properly; but I was pushed out regardless after the September 2006 uprising, of which more later.

Despite all the difficulties, I felt enormously confident of what I was doing. Of course, it would have been better to have stayed an extra year or eighteen months and embedded the reform programme still further, better for the party and for the country. Nonetheless, what was done was significant and will last.

The reason for the confidence was that I was now completely on top of the policy agenda. I had ministers in key positions who understood what I was trying to do and why. Although the programme was subject to continual frustration from next door, I could tell Gordon was worried about pushing it too far for fear of Murdoch people and others concluding—as opposed to merely suspecting—that he was against reform.

Each step was a battle; but by then I was inured to it all, ready to get up each day and gird my loins, to go out and fight whatever might be barring the path, not unafraid exactly, but near to being reckless about my own political safety.

It wasn't that I didn't do all the normal political body swerves to find a way through, I made the odd tactical compromise, here and there. But by and large, for the first time since I became prime minister, I was guided simply by what I genuinely thought was right on domestic as well as foreign policies. I was prepared at any point to be defeated and walk away, but I was not going to budge on the essential strategic objectives.

In February 2006, I wrote a paper for the meetings that Philip, Alastair and I were having with Gordon, Ed Balls, Ed Miliband and Sue Nye. I was consciously involving them, putting ideas before them, trying actually to persuade them. Several times I offered on sensible terms to go, if there was a proper relationship in the meantime. But by then I was adamant: there would be no voluntary departure unless it was clear the reform programme was going to be continued.

In the February paper I set out a basic template for how we could work and then went through a potential future agenda on each individual item. In addition, I had launched an internal exercise, after much Treasury dissent, called the Fundamental Savings Review. The purpose of the FSR was to get to the point where we could move beyond the catch-up in investment in public services, and instead focus on a smaller, more strategic government. This was, in my mind, right in itself but also critical to dealing with the "big state" and "tax and spend" arguments that I was sure, in time, would pull apart our coalition in the country, and therefore our ability to win. It went back to the argument, already described, during the 2005 election.

Unfortunately, the FSR was fought every inch of the way and was the one element I was unable to put in place prior to departure, it being the one that really did depend on Gordon's cooperation.

However, the rest of the programme proceeded apace. In the domain of schools reform, in particular with Andrew Adonis now a minister and Conor Ryan my special adviser, we were able to forge ahead with what was a very ambitious programme that finally got me to where I needed to be.

The months before Christmas 2005 had been especially busy. On 25 October, we published a new schools White Paper in which we advocated the idea of independent non-fee-paying state schools. We did not revive the principle of selection, which had so riven the country between grammar schools and comprehensives; but in every other respect we broke with the traditional comprehensive state school. We made it clear that, in time, all schools could and should become self-governing trusts, either foundation schools or academies, with far greater flexibility in staffing and pay, with partners from whatever sector they wished, and as extended schools be part of the community in which they were situated, able to be used by the adult and youth population for learning, sport, leisure and community services.

In a speech in the summer of 2005 to the National Policy Forum, a body which was the product of an earlier reform of the party to make policymaking more rational and less confrontational, I had set out the rationale for reform.

Although by now I was writing most of the crucial speeches myself, Phil Collins, who had joined the team, was by far the best speech-writer I ever had and was helping greatly. Under pressure of time, the speeches would often be written in the early morning in the Downing Street flat. I would get up at about five, slipping quietly downstairs so as not to wake the children, make myself a mug of tea and take it into the sitting room. There, perched on a chair by a round leather-topped table, I would write in longhand, occasionally looking out of the window at the back of the house, watching as people went jogging in St. James's Park or scurried to work in the early-morning light, sometimes stealing a glance at Britain's most famous home. I wondered about them, what lives they led, what mood they were in that day, what thoughts occupied them, each life a web of friendships, anxieties, ambitions and fears.

In the speech I said:

If it is a system that is keeping people back, the system should change. Not to change it is to say we care more about the system than the people. That is totally unacceptable.

And, of course, the reforms must be the right ones, the changes able to achieve their purpose. But far too often people claim the change is a breach of principle whereas in reality, they're not protecting a principle but a practice and often an outdated one at that.

The good news, however, is that there are real examples of progress, driven by our willingness to overcome resistance to change but also by the willingness, indeed enthusiasm, of many public servants to let their own creativity and innovation loose. So this is a time to push forward, faster and on all fronts: open up the system, break down its monoliths, put the parent and pupil and patient and law-abiding citizen at the centre of the system. Yes, we've made great progress. Let us learn the lessons of it not so as to rest on present achievements but to take them to a new and higher level in the future.

Eight years in, there is a body of empirical evidence to draw on. The conclusion of it is plain: money alone doesn't do it. It is where money has been combined with modernisation of systems, working practices and incentives that the best results have come.

All these reforms are, in the final analysis, simply means to an end. The end is not choice. The end is quality services irrespective of wealth. The end is opportunity to make the most of your ability whatever your start in life. The end is utterly progressive in its values. But the only progressive means are those that deliver the progressive ends.

The first academies had been massively oversubscribed. It was plain this was not solely because of the new buildings. It was precisely because the academy school seemed to belong not to some remote bureaucracy, not to the rulers of government, local or national, but to itself, for itself. The school would be in charge of its own destiny. This immediately gave it pride and purpose. Because the sponsors were determined and successful individuals, they brought that determination and drive for success into the school. And most of all, freed from the extraordinarily debilitating and often, in the worst sense, politically correct interference from state or municipality, the academies just had one thing in mind, something shaped not by political prejudice but by common sense: what will make the school excellent.

So, even in areas like Hackney, where I visited the new Mossbourne Community Academy at Hackney Downs on the site of a previously failed comprehensive, and where you might have expected the local middle class to be a bit sniffy and precious, the emphasis on rigorous discipline, a proper dress code and good manners was like a dream to parents, poor and comfortably off alike. When the *Dispatches* programme on Channel 4 did a covert programme on the new Doncaster Academy, with footage of some parents complaining that their kid had been threatened with expulsion if he didn't turn up to school on time, I knew we were really getting somewhere. Of course, the programme-makers thought people would be outraged by such draconian discipline, whereas naturally the other parents were delighted.

Though the academy idea was watered down after I left, it had an unstoppable momentum and will easily recuperate and get back to full strength. In late 2006, I announced—again I'm afraid to shrieking and barking from next door—that we would double the existing programme to four hundred schools, and was satisfied then that if we attained that and combined it with foundation schools, we would be on a transformative path.

Gordon will protest that he never opposed the programme, and to be fair he never did so head-on; but it was obvious his people weren't in favour, and getting anything out of the Treasury required a machete constantly slicing through the thick foliage of their objections day by day. I recall an event at Downing Street where we welcomed head teachers who were going to apply for foundation-school status. One of them blithely told me he had come up against the express advice of his local MP. "Oh," I said, irritated, "who's that?"

"Ed Balls," he replied, unaware he had confirmed my sense of where the GB team sympathies really lay.

The initial assessment of academies was often described negatively, but the whole tenor even of the negative coverage was, in a sense, a mark of their success. People compared academies to the best schools, conveniently forgetting that they had, in every case, replaced state schools that were failing chronically—i.e. we had chosen the toughest nuts to crack. The very fact people made such a comparison was a measure of the highly heightened expectations around them. It was assumed they would be good, a cut above, fit to sit alongside the best. And that was precisely the measure we wanted.

Today, of course, the results are clear: academies are improving three times faster than other schools. But, back then, some were bound to struggle, some even fell by the wayside and had to be recovered; yet taken as a whole, they succeeded—not beyond my imagination, but in line with it.

The party opposition was fairly steady and consistent. To my sadness, even Estelle Morris questioned academies, going back to the old saying "standards not structures" and bemoaning the fact we had ditched the mantra. But the whole point was that without the different structure, there was no possibility of achieving the higher standards. Neil Kinnock weighed in, by now pretty much routinely offside and agitating for my replacement by Gordon. His take on academies was that they were elitist, though on closer examination it was less that they were elitist in the sense of being for the wealthy—plainly they weren't—and more that they were better than other local schools. For me, this was the point. However well motivated, it was classic levelling down. It was an argument that went to the heart of what New Labour was about and its championing of aspiration. Equity could not and should never be at the expense of excellence. My abiding insistence was never give up on excellence, wherever it might be. Attacking it—irrespective of what we felt about grammar schools, private schools, special schools, any schools—was to commit a fatal solecism. It meant that, in the ultimate analysis, we were prepared to get rid of something that was excellent on the basis that it represented the wrong ideology.

Now, by the way, it can be true that such a school might represent the wrong ideology. I am opposed to selection aged eleven. It's too crude, too final, and therefore too determinative at a ridiculously young age of a child's life chances, or, to put it less emotionally, their academic ability. I used to reflect on the experience of my brother Bill. He is a wise, sensible, level-headed and thoroughly decent man. It was and is a privilege to have him as a brother. He is also very clever, now a High Court judge, after being a top QC and author of academic works on banking law.

When Bill came to take his entrance exam for Fettes back in the 1960s at the age of thirteen, he only just passed and was put in a lower academic stream. He really had not shone at all. By the time he sat the

Oxford exam five years later, however, he had developed and got to Balliol.

Kids change, and therefore separating them out at an early age is not right or fair. But the way comprehensives were introduced and grammar schools abandoned was pretty close to academic vandalism. And not a great reflection on the Secretaries of State—mainly Labour but also Tory—who, of course, continued to send their own children to private school. Not experiencing through their own children the reality of the change, and hugely egged on by the teaching establishment, they legislated so that grammar schools (selective but also excellent) were changed into comprehensives (non-selective and frequently non-excellent, and on occasions truly dire).

This was done because the assumption was that the only reason grammar schools were better was because they were selective. This is to make the same mistake as when people say that private schools are good just because the parents are middle class, better off and the facilities are better; i.e. they are better only through privilege and class.

The truth is that both types of school are good for other reasons too. They are independent. They have an acute sense of ethos and identity. They have strong leadership, and are allowed to lead. They are more flexible. They innovate because no one tells them they can't. They pursue excellence. And—here is a major factor—they assume excellence is attainable. In other words, they believe failure is not inevitable, it is avoidable; and it is their fault if they don't avoid it, not the fault of "the system," "the background of the children" or "the inadequacy of the parents."

Now, of course, these characteristics—attitudes of thought, if you will—are easier if your parents are middle class or you select. Easier to think; easier to do. But the whole basis of my schools reform was that they weren't impossible or unattainable in state schools that were non-selective, provided we were a) prepared to acknowledge the reasons why grammar and private schools worked, b) prepared to let state schools have the same freedoms and encourage new ways of working with new partners, and c) prepared to fund them better.

I used to have fierce internal arguments all about this, even with my closest staff. In the end, the trouble often came down to this: if you introduced a really good school in an area full of really average ones, lo and behold the parents all clamoured to get their children into the really good one. And, yes, of course that caused consternation among all the parents that failed to get in, and the local councillors, teachers and so on. But as I used to argue: that simply cannot be a reason not to have the really good school; that must be a reason for analysing why the others are average or worse and changing them.

I remember visiting a school in London just before the 1997 election. As the head teacher welcomed us in, there was a fight going on in the foyer. We stood talking for a time until—the noise of the scuffling being distracting—he said, "We'd better move elsewhere."

"Shouldn't we stop that?" I said, pointing to the scrapping students.

"Not really," he said as he led us down to his study. He then explained how the families in that neighbourhood were problematic, drugs were a real issue, kids were badly brought up and not interested in studying. It was a credible—and to him absolutely persuasive—explanation of why the school was bound to fail. He was, by the way, a nice guy and committed. He also said that since the school had "not a great" reputation—i.e. everyone locally thought it was a dump—they ended up taking the excluded pupils from other schools.

The point was that we accepted failure, and not just the individual failure of certain of the pupils, but a collective failure for all of them. I knew two things were clear: I would never accept such a thing for my own children; and it would never be true that all the pupils and/or all the parents shared the same attitude or problems. What we were permitting was a disaffected and alienated minority to sour it all for the majority. Of course, we shouldn't accept failure even for the disaffected and alienated. But to accept it for the entire school—and there were hundreds like this when we took office—was gross, an unbelievable social injustice; and what's more, one which our mistaken ideology had helped perpetrate.

Prior to 1997, the Conservatives had partially tackled the issue with grant-maintained schools, whose status gave greater freedom and independence. The trouble was it was partial, and basically freed those schools already doing better. This was not wrong, and I fought hard to ensure that though we altered the status—the party hated grant-maintained schools—we tried to keep the basic freedoms. But the journey from 1 May 1997 to 27 June 2007 was really about first correcting the partiality of that programme—focusing on the poorest schools instead—and then, second, creating through the academy programme a whole new type of school that could fulfil the purpose both the grant-maintained and our reforms aimed for: quality state schooling. Whereas the Tories paid most attention to middle-class schools, I knew that in order to gain universal or at least widespread acceptance, the programme had to be for the worst of the system as well as the best.

But what a fight it all was. And even in the latter months of 2005 when I was battling away, now with a trusted inner group of ministers who shared the same vision and knew this was where Labour had to be, we were still very much in a struggle with a large part of the party. However, I felt we were winning the argument.

We were battling on other fronts too. Just before Christmas, the Civil Partnership Act came into force, granting the same rights and responsibilities to same-sex partners as enjoyed by married couples. I was really proud of that. On this one, the PLP were largely supportive, of course, but I reflected on how absolutely vituperative the debate had been in days gone by, when the Tories had savaged us over our position on gay rights. In the 1980s it had been a real problem for us as we feared losing votes in by-elections, and yet here we were with the Act coming into force, and a general air of celebration.

The first couples to use the ceremony were in Belfast. I must say I expected a bit of a backlash, but it passed with barely a murmur. We received messages from round the world and I appreciated just how much it meant to so many people, more than I had ever thought when passing the legislation. It must be a horrible thing to feel you are consigned to second-class status as a result of something that is natural to you. So I shouldn't have been surprised by the extent of the outpouring. But I was.

In a way, the best part was that by then the Tories had also come to support it, meaning that the issue would not be used again as a dividing line in British politics. This was an important gain for the health of our political debate, I thought, and the way the issue played revealed something of the changing nature of politics. I always felt progressive politics had to create a different set of paradigms about politics in order to achieve a greater and deeper spread of support. I evolved over time a position—again, similar to that of Bill Clinton—of what I would call "tough on crime, pro-gay rights" politics.

This might seem the correlation of two completely separate questions, but to me they indicate a significant shift in progressive social attitudes. In the old days, a Conservative was hard line on law and order and on "political correctness" issues like immigration and gays. The left-winger was liberal, the right-winger illiberal. My generation had defined a different paradigm: what you did in your personal life was your choice, but what you did to others was not. So a distinction came about between attitudes to human beings (non-discriminatory in race, gender or sexuality) and attitudes to social order (we need to impose it). It is still possible to find on both right and left the old attitudes and divisions prevailing, but much less so, and politicians who don't understand these changing currents are likely to flounder.

Less happy was the episode over the new anti-terror laws which we were seeking to pass following the House of Lords ruling in December 2004 that our existing power to detain suspects was unlawful under the European Convention on Human Rights, which was now incorporated into UK law. Here, there was simply a fundamental disagreement between myself and the judiciary and media, or at least a large part of it, about the threat we faced.

Although these decisions are supposed to be a strict matter of law, inevitably in the human rights field there is a lot of subjective judgement around the politics. I doubt such a ruling would have been reached in September 2001 or July 2005—i.e. in the wake of terrorist attacks in the U.S. and London—but as time passes, the sense of urgency goes with it. And it was true: we were asking for draconian powers, unacceptable in principle except in the most rare circumstances.

Essentially, the problem was straightforward, at least to describe: the terrorist suspects being watched were, we believed ("we" being the security services, police, political leadership), a danger. But proving a charge beyond reasonable doubt was often very difficult. We were spending a large amount of time and manpower watching such groups, in more or less constant surveillance and assessment. Frequently we would want to wait until evidence of terrorism was collected, but were also afraid of waiting too long in case something unexpected happened, the plot came to fruition and we missed it. With suspects who were foreign nationals, and most were, I conceived of offering them a choice: leave the country, or stay in custody. This both fell foul of the usual principles of habeas corpus and also discriminated between foreign and UK nationals, so it was a problem legally but born of a real-life security conundrum.

Once the House of Lords made the ruling, we had to amend the law. The issue was over the power we sought to allow the police to detain terror suspects for up to ninety days without charge. Of course, there was a stack of safeguards, including the fact that every seven days they had to come before a court. But the police were clear the power would help and after the July bombings I just felt we had to err on the side of toughness. We tried before the 2005 election. The Tories opposed any further detention without trial. David Davis, who was at that time the Shadow Home Secretary, had moved the Tories to a liberal position on many law and order issues, opposing not just the international terror laws but measures on fraud trials by jury, antisocial behaviour and proceeds of crime. I liked David and thought him an unusual and principled politician. But I also thought it a crazy mistake for the Tories.

However, in the run-up to the election, traditional Tory support rallied to an untraditional Tory position. Right-wing papers like the *Mail* and *Telegraph* that, had I been a Tory prime minister, would have been tearing the Opposition apart, instead tore us apart. It all got very ugly.

After the election we were able to take it more calmly, but the Tories remained opposed. The Lib Dems were naturally against it, and a hefty group of the PLP rebelled. I knew that at the time, and for all I know the position is the same today, we were watching a score or more of cells of radical groups and potential terrorists, and I wanted the power both in its own right but also to send a strong signal out that Britain was going to be a severely inhospitable place for terror groups to operate. As I used to say to people: you may not like Bush's methods, but since 11 September 2001 no serious terror attack has occurred in the U.S. Don't ignore the possibility that it may not be luck.

Although the public were with me, the majority of the House of Commons wasn't. In November 2005, we lost a vote for the first time since we came to office. However, I was easy enough with it. By then, I had calculated that my only chance of survival for the two years I had set myself as a minimum time necessary to put in place the reform programme was to govern in a way that kept people constantly surprised by the seeming indifference to party or even public opinion, provided I thought what I was doing was right and would work for the long-term benefit of both party and public. In other words, I believed that the only way to keep power was to be prepared to lose it, but always to lose it on a point of principle.

I had complete clarity about what it was I had to do. I really did feel absolutely at the height of my ability and at the top of my game. I appreciated the bitter irony that this had happened when my popularity was at its lowest, but I also knew that in May 2005 I had won, not lost, and that there was a residual respect for and attachment to strong and decisive leadership. I might be bloodied but I would definitely also be unbowed.

Contrary to conventional political wisdom, when it came to the vote I decided not to compromise on the essentials, but to lose without having yielded. Of course, when we lost there were all sorts of articles about the prime minister's vanishing authority, etc.; but I could sense that the very recklessness of it, on something I believed was right, got me traction among the public. Now, to have done that on schools or the NHS might have been different. But on this—a simple, almost pristine issue of national security—I felt instinctively more comfortable losing than winning through compromise.

A couple of weeks later, the storm already behind us, we introduced another controversial measure: allowing UK drinking laws to come into line with those in Europe. I thought the insistence on a strict closing time was irrational and in many respects counterproductive. I also had an inbuilt resistance to the idea that because a small minority misbehaved, the overwhelming majority should be restricted in their freedom to enjoy a drink when they wanted. The answer, I reasoned, was to come down hard on the lawless minority, not penalise the law-abiding majority. There was the usual *Mail* campaign, supported by some of the others, but we held our nerve. Tessa Jowell was adamant and saw it through (though from that moment she became a target).

I was pushing hard on all fronts. At the end of 2002 I had appointed British businessman Adair Turner to do a review of pensions policy. This had provoked strong opposition from Gordon, as had the appointment of David Freud, an independent consultant, to do a similar review on welfare. I knew Adair and David would give me radical proposals. Both issues had to be confronted.

Both also had to do with my concern over the future pattern of public spending. The FSR, as I say, had been created to try to shift the debate from the amount of investment to the value added by it, which is why the pace of reform had to be quickened. I had no precise percentage of public spending in my mind that corresponded to the right figure for the economy's equilibrium between public and private sector, but I knew there was a limit. So I thought, post-2005, this was the time to shift focus and to drop the notion that it was all about who would spend most.

I thought this right for the country, and also smart politics. It would have been tougher if the Tories had carried into effect their initial instinct, which was to back the reforms. It is always uncomfortable to be cheered on by the Opposition. Although David Cameron did take this view to begin with, and in education they more or less kept to it, else-where in public service reform they started allying themselves with vested interests, especially on health. In a political sense, this was far more congenial and allowed us to secure our basic coalition, who distrusted the Tories on litmus-test questions and felt they were changing position too often.

However, it wasn't just about the amount of public spending, it was also crucially about its composition. This is where the pensions and welfare reforms were so critical. Like every other developed nation, we were going to face major problems from the pensions bill in time to come. A growing elderly population; a declining younger generation; expectations of increased living standards; and increased health care costs as people live longer: there was inevitably going to be a crunch at some stage. Better to confront it now and set in place a framework that over time would make costs manageable and tilt the responsibility for provision from state to individual. The state would still be there as an enabler and, in case of hardship, guarantor; but it made sense for people to provide more for themselves; and also to do it in a way that reflected something else: that today they choose far greater flexibility in how they provide for their retirement—in working part-time, in the equity in their home, in various savings investment vehicles, instead of conventional pension arrangements.

We had tried once before with the ill-fated reforms of Labour's Harriet Harman and Frank Field, but the trouble with "stakeholder" pensions, as they were called (low-cost pensions that people can take out to boost their income later in life), is that they were never quite one thing or another, sitting uneasily between state and private provision. During the course of that attempt at reform, I had learned one rather larger lesson: be clear that if someone isn't screaming somewhere, it probably isn't going to work. Consensus is great, but in modern politics, where debate unfortunately works through disagreement, it is like the philosopher stone sought by alchemists: if it sounds too good to be true that you can turn base metal into gold, that's probably because it is. So consensus is wonderful, but not if it is part of a delusion that making real change with real impact is going to please everyone. It isn't. And in these circumstances the "consensus" can be a sign that the reform isn't really biting, in which case it probably isn't going to fulfil its purpose.

Stakeholder pensions hadn't aroused much opposition; but nothing much had flowed from them. We needed to think far more radically and devise both a more realistic package for state support, including raising the retirement age, and a far more comprehensive method for middle-income earners to save.

I asked Adair to lead on the reform. He had two sensible wing players with him in John Hills and Jeannie Drake. What they produced in two reports of October 2004 and November 2005 will, in the end, form the basis of the next generation's pension provision. The reform protected the basic state pension, but used it as a platform upon which the individual could choose to enhance the pension by his or her own efforts and decisions, and it did so within a framework that meant spending on pensions would not rise as a percentage of GDP.

As a team they conducted a hugely wide-ranging consultation, and actually, *pace* what I said earlier, got as close to consensus as it was possible to get without yielding on the essential principles of reform. But bits of support peeled off on various different aspects. The Tories were not fully behind it, and the Treasury reaction was fierce. On this occasion, to be fair, Gordon's disagreement was genuine. It wasn't simply to frustrate progress—he felt that by protecting the basic state pension we were making an unnecessary commitment. He was in favour of rebalancing rich and poor in provision of the basic state pension.

I was totally opposed to that. I felt that the public at large would consider the basic state pension as their "dividend" or "entitlement" for their National Insurance contributions. Start tampering with that, and especially on the basis of some drive for redistribution, and we were going to be ensnared in a really damaging debate.

This touched on another highly sensitive political issue. I had opposed the 50 per cent top-rate-tax idea before the 1997 election. I had always wanted to keep the option of tax cuts open, on the basic rate. But I had allowed some really significant measure of redistribution. National Insurance ceilings had changed; personal allowances altered; and above all, as the economy grew we had spent billions on the poorest families and pensioners. It was and is the purest moonshine to suggest the 1997–2007 government wasn't redistributive. It was, and massively so.

Now it is also true that because the economy grew strongly, the middle class and highest earners did well, and the very highest did best. So you could always take the income gap—very top to very bottom—and say it's widened. In reality, this was a function of the very top doing well. The bottom deciles had had their income changed really substantially. I might have done it differently, not being a fan of tax credits, but I would have done it anyway. The poorest pensioners had a huge rise in income, something that the better-off pensioners came to resent (as my mother-in-law used to express to me with consistent persistence).

Emotionally I shared the view that some of the top earnings were unjustified, but rationally I thought this was the way of the world in a globalised economy, and there was more harm than good in trying to stop it. Should a soccer star like Wayne Rooney earn more than a nurse? Or actors or best-selling authors? Or market traders of stocks or derivatives? Or people who sell businesses at the right time and pocket hundreds of millions with a low capital gains tax? In a sense none of it is rational, but it's irrational to stop it in a world in which, like it or not, certain people have transferable, global skills in high demand and short supply.

And, ultimately, you could tax every Premier League footballer double and it wouldn't bring in much money. What you inevitably end up doing is pushing the higher taxes down the income chain, until the people you are hitting are those who work hard, don't have global transferable skills and aren't really what we might call the "undeserving rich" at all.

So I also thought post-2005 that we needed to take care. Some might say we hadn't been redistributive enough. I was sure we had done plenty of redistribution and needed to give some TLC to our middle-class and lower-middle-class aspirants as well. Therefore I backed and encouraged Adair to come up with a policy that eschewed any notion of redistributing the basic state pension.

And, on this account, the left were also happy since they feared undermining the basic state pension from the other perspective, i.e. leading to a diminution of the principle of universal provision. What's more, we did it on the basis of changing back the uprating of pensions to be done in line with earnings, not prices. This had long been a demand of the unions. But by conceding this—which I thought right in any event, given the link between pensions and National Insurance contributions on earnings—we managed to achieve a package that seemed fair and balanced.

The debate on welfare was always going to be much tougher, but it was just as necessary and there were good and sound people on the progressive side of politics who could see the need to change. The *raison d'être* for reform was set out earlier: incapacity benefit was abused; too many people were in long-term benefit dependency; too little was done by way of active support to shift them into the labour market.

John Hutton had been a great minister in health, giving a sharp boost to reform. He was in his element in welfare. John was a thoroughly nice guy, loyal, hard-working and bright. To people whose ambitions were unlimited (me, I'm afraid), he seemed consciously lacking in the final thrust of determination; but in his own skin, he felt comfortable with the level of ambition he had. What this gave him, among other things, was courage—he wanted to do the right thing in his job or he wanted nothing to do with the job. It was a great attitude and served him well. He didn't so much argue with Gordon as cheerfully work around him, like a postman delivering a letter to a house with a large barking hound straining at the leash. He wouldn't ignore him, or refuse to pay careful attention. He might even chuck a biscuit at him. But in the end, he would deliver the letter.

David Freud's review of welfare spending, with emphasis on incapacity benefit, also produced a sensible report that was radical and would allow us in time to redesign the welfare budget.

Both the Turner proposals and those of Freud gave us a huge opportunity to characterise, define and implement reforms of a vital nature not just for the country but for the survival of the government. I kept saying to Gordon, Quite apart from the fact that both sets of proposals are manifestly right in themselves, if we don't do them, a future Tory government will, but in a Tory way. So let us own them and do them. They will also give you a great platform to prove continuity and commitment to reform.

Both, in essence, redrew again the boundaries between individual and state responsibility. This I saw as the proper way to express the relationship between society and citizen for the twenty-first century. People have to—and what's more will want to—take more of the burden on themselves, rather than paying ever higher general taxation; and though they are perfectly prepared to fund those who can't look after themselves, that generosity doesn't extend to those who they believe, with some justification, are simply playing the system. Unfortunately I couldn't get Gordon to see it.

As all this serious and important work to determine the future nature of the British welfare state was going on, there were the usual scandals—real, less real and surreal—that occupied the headlines. Around this time, I did come to see the interaction with the media in a different light. They could drive down the poll numbers by the most colossal onslaught. But you know what? It would then pass. The key was to survive. And the key to surviving was to keep your head when all around were losing theirs.

During the first months of 2006 we lived a dual existence. Underneath the surface, major changes in the NHS, schools, crime, pensions and welfare were either being made or being planned. The basic design of a modern set of services was being debated repeatedly in the government, but this was at points so hidden from view that the public had no idea about it and therefore, sadly, no real chance to participate in the debate. Growing over the previous two decades, this was now the established media culture. Scandal mattered. Policy didn't (unless combined with controversy, in which case it might).

This trend was multiplied in intensity by the fact that after nine years, the media had decided there should be change. If, for whatever reason—genuine disagreement, boredom, the yearning for something and someone new to report on—a significant part of the media decide they want change, they create a prism of reportage that makes change seem right, inevitable, inarguable. In the final resort, they just excise policy in favour of scandal, and then to the public it seems as if a government mired is all there is. From there, it's a short walk to a perception that the government can no longer deliver for the people.

In my last two years, they would constantly say that we were running out of steam, when on any objective basis we were full steam ahead, at least on domestic reform. What was really meant was that they were running out of patience and interest.

It was as well that by then I had David Hill in charge of communications in place of Alastair. I think the latter would have been tipped over the edge completely in that last period and would have rampaged through the media like a mad axeman! It was an extraordinary time.

In January, we had Ruth Kelly and the sex offenders list. Oh, the days and weeks of howling outrage and frenzied commentary over a fault discovered that meant someone had been missed off a list as part of a wider systemic failure (but with no evidence anyone had actually suffered as a result) and which was really the result of a new system being put in place.

In March, the so-called "cash for honours" scandal broke, of which more later.

Then, in April, there was Charles Clarke and the foreign offenders who on completion of their sentence should have been deported and removed from the country and weren't. This was serious, but Charles made the mistake of trying to be too open too early, when the full facts could not be known—the problem, as with many such things, had existed for a long time, well before we came to power—and he suffered a mauling with bad consequences for me, him and the government.

As with any such issue, what happens is that the spotlight suddenly shines in a corner that has lain dark for ages. That's fair enough; but what then occurs is that a complete *ex post facto* attitude is imposed on it, so that you end up with a ludicrously exaggerated sense of wrongdoing. So when the foreign offenders "scandal" is uncovered, it leads the news and this is perfectly sensible; but then because the media focus is so intense, every detail becomes another headline as if the politician in charge, in this case Charles, has literally been doing nothing else for months on end and is therefore incompetent in not having sorted it all. Then, for sure, someone pops up and says: Ooh, I warned them all about this (usually an oblique reference in paragraph 193 of some memo), and then the frenzy develops into hysteria.

Anyway, you have to go through it, and by the end I became quite deft at dealing with these types of furore. Basically you have to get on top of the detail quick, and then grind people down with fact, context, rebuttal, explanation and the art of blinding with science.

And if all that wasn't enough, then came John Prescott and news of an affair with his diary secretary, Tracey Temple.

It's a strange thing, politics and sex. People have often said to me that power is a kind of aphrodisiac, and so women—politics still being male-dominated—would come on to politicians in a way they would never dream of with anyone else. I suppose it must be true since, let's face it, most politicians are definitely on the debit side of the good-looks ledger. You could say the same about ugly billionaires with gorgeous women. What do they see in them? It's pretty obvious.

What is interesting is why politicians take the risk. My theory is that it's precisely because of the supreme self-control you have to exercise to be at the top. Politicians live with pressure. They have to be immensely controlled to get anywhere, watch what they say and do; and behave. And your free-bird instincts want to spring you from that prison of self-control. Then there is the moment of encounter, so exciting, so naughty, so lacking in self-control. Suddenly you are transported out of your world of intrigue and issues and endless machinations and the serious piled on the serious, and just put on a remote desert island of pleasure, out of it all, released, carefree. You become a different person, if only for an instant, until returned back to reality.

Which is not by way of an excuse, incidentally. It's very stupid to put yourself in that position; and irresponsible; and on discovery it can cause immense hurt to those around you. Here is where the politician becomes extraordinarily, incomprehensibly naive. He could choose a range of safe options. No, hang on, there are no safe options. But he could choose safer options. He doesn't. He is open to the first person who appears to take an interest, to fancy him genuinely (vanity), to like him as a human being, and to anyone who, above all, doesn't think, act or talk like a fellow politician.

The thing about politics is that it is at a certain level very, very boring. The issues are self-evidently not—they are huge and are usually the reason for entering the political world—but somehow the hugeness can get so easily lost in the habitat in which those issues live. Day by day, meeting by meeting, it can be tedious. Occasionally you meet quite exceptional and inspirational people and I was lucky beyond any reasonable expectation in the people I had working near me, who were on the whole really fun people, as well as being good at what they did. Relations in my office and my close associations among MPs and ministers were always marked with laughter, a certain amused disdain for the absurdities of political life and a definite *joie de vivre*. To the extent I could choose, I would choose the optimistic and upbeat variety of our species to be around me.

But out in the jungle, quite apart from the man-eating beasts, there was the prospect of the swamp, of frustrating bureaucracy, weird and argumentative types, manic media and groundhog-day meetings.

For lots of my fellow politicians, the *joie de vivre* part was distinctly lacking, and the swamp was mostly what they experienced. I totally understood the desire to escape. And it's nothing really to do with how happy or otherwise your marriage is. It's an explosion of irresponsibility in an otherwise responsible life. Unfortunately, like all such explosions, it has consequences.

I was in a meeting with a foreign visitor when Gus O'Donnell, who had taken over from Andrew Turnbull as Cabinet Secretary, asked to see me urgently with Jonathan Powell. This was never going to be good news. I must say, however, I anticipated something more run-of-the-mill than to be told about John Prescott and Tracey.

At first, and I fear this was an error, I was inclined to treat it less gravely than I should. I was principally sorry for him, for his wife Pauline above all, and also for Tracey. What those who are the "telling" party in any such scandal never realise is that they are about to define themselves forever. The politician can recover, at least partially; the telling party can't. They are a one-story footnote. Their only choice is either to make a living from it or to perish with it. The first is demeaning and transient; the second is at least quieter, but nonetheless the fact remains it's all anyone ever recognises them for. No amount of money can adequately compensate for that. In any event, it was clear Tracey didn't do it for money and the story had emerged as much by mishap as malice.

From then on, it was a torrid time, complicated by the fact that since she was an employee, there was a further genuine point of criticism other than the obvious. I was determined not to have John go, however. He was a stalwart in the party, and had, on the whole, been loyal and supportive and at times very brave. I knew that for him to have become deputy prime minister was an achievement of which he was inordinately and rightly proud. To have dismissed him over what was, in the end, a silly sex scandal would have been to have finished his career in a manner that was brutally ungrateful for all the service he had given.

The media finally had him full square within their sights, sat on the wall like a watermelon in target practice. John had never hidden his loathing for them. They had never hidden their contempt for him. Now, and pretty much until the day he left, they kept up a barrage, sometimes with the bazooka of outrage, sometimes with the blowpipe of ridicule, but always with a merciless delight in destruction.

The battering had one other unfortunate consequence for me. In purely selfish terms it would have been better to fire him, I knew that. It would have given the media their scalp. It would have allowed some change at the top, and even if that had turned into a TB/GB contest, it would have served to flush people out. But I just couldn't bring myself to do it. Pauline was determined that he stay, in my view rightly (she always had far more about her than anyone ever thought). She wasn't going to have him defined by the affair, if you can call it that. Also, sensible as she was, she knew what it meant and what it didn't. She felt betrayed but not abandoned; and therefore angry rather than distraught. I felt that I should do right by her as well. So he stayed.

But the unpleasantness of the onslaught got to John. From that moment on, there was no pleasure in staying. There was defiance; but no joy. He wanted out; but it was hard for him to go without me going too. Slowly, and then more insistently, his desire to leave became his belief it was time to change leadership. There were many other factors of course. This one was not insignificant.

It was the oddest of periods. The reform programme was buzzing along, I felt on top form on the issues, but around me was a kind of sustained mayhem of scandal and controversy. In my eyrie high in the trees, with my soulmates, we could replenish mind and body before venturing back out into the undergrowth below; and we cleared our way through it with as good a temper and will as we could muster. But if it felt like we were under siege, that's because we were.

It tripped me into error at times as well. Following the local elections of May 2006, which were bad but frankly could have been much worse, I decided to reshuffle the Cabinet. There's a kind of convention that it should be done every year. It's clear that governments need refreshing and there is a need to let new blood through. Also, a prime minister or president is always engaged in a kind of negotiation over the state of their party that requires people's ambitions to be assuaged. Some ambitions are reasonable, some are not, but they are wholly reasonable to those who have them. If you don't promote someone, after a time they resent you. If you promote them, you put someone else out, and then that person resents you. You look for an elaborate index of methods to keep the offloaded onside, but let me tell you from experience: it never works. The only thing that determines their loyalty from that moment on is their character. The good behave; the bad don't. Unless you give them something that really is spectacular as an alternative to being a minister, then they aren't fooled; and, naturally, it's all played out in the media, and the impression is they've been sacked. The good characters in these circumstances tend to be a small and distinguished minority.

So, you have to reshuffle. But here's some advice: you should always promote or demote for a purpose, not for effect. With this one, I determined that we should make a splash, show we still had vigour, show I was still governing for the future. I had thought of making Charles Clarke Foreign Secretary. He would have done a great job, and probably in retrospect I should have done it, but he was mired in the wretched "foreign offenders" business. There was also a case for keeping Jack Straw. He had done really well and was admired by his fellow foreign ministers. There was no compelling reason to move him, other than that he had been doing it for five years; but when I think about it, moving him for that reason was plain stupid. I even toyed with the idea of

David Miliband, but thought that for his own sake he should remain domesticated, since that allowed him a better profile in the party.

In the end, I made a sort of "worst of all worlds" set of decisions. Having put David in Environment, I moved Margaret Beckett from there to be Foreign Secretary. She was stunned rather than elated with the promotion. Unsurprisingly, Jack was upset at being replaced. I offered Charles Defence, which he refused—foolishly, in my view—and he returned to the back benches. All in all, a mess at the wrong time and with the wrong people, who I needed onside. The rest of it in fact allowed some good promotions of younger people like Douglas Alexander, James Purnell, Andy Burnham and Jim Murphy. But overall, it did little for the government and harm to me.

As if that wasn't enough, in the summer of 2006 came the Israel/Lebanon war. That event, and my reaction to it, probably did me more damage than anything since Iraq. It showed how far I had swung from the mainstream of conventional Western media wisdom and from my own people; but also how set (stuck?) in my own mode of thinking I had become.

The whole episode demonstrated the difficulty in fighting the modern, asymmetrical struggle in which we are engaged. Hezbollah launched an attack on Israel, low-level but killing several Israeli soldiers. Gaza was by this time locked down, following the Hamas takeover and expulsion of the Palestinian Authority. As the Israelis stepped up their siege of Gaza and the peace process went nowhere, Hamas fired rockets into Israeli towns. Then Hezbollah opened up a new front.

It was a quite deliberate provocation. Israel had withdrawn from Lebanon. True, the Shebaa Farms issue—land taken by Israel in the 1980s and still occupied, and the theoretical reason why Hezbollah said they had to remain armed—was unresolved, but the amount of land was tiny. The issue wasn't really troubling anyone and the real challenges inside Lebanon were to do with the slow and steady accretion of control by Hezbollah over the political and military structures of the country. Lebanon was a democracy. Beirut had been rebuilt since the disasters of the early 1980s. But, as all over the region, the essential underlying tensions, born of the much wider struggle, remained extant, not extinct. The country was at peace, but it was fragile, its democratic politicians under threat, several of them like Rafiq Hariri assassinated, and the influence of Syria pervasive. Such a land of beauty, history and promise; but a land that attracted to itself all the poisonous gases of a region that at its core was decaying.

Israel reacted to the provocation in the way it does. Israelis believe one thing and they believe it from their perception of experience: if provoked, do not turn the other cheek; strike back and hard. You take one eye; we will take out both. They believe any sign of weakness and their short history of nationhood, sixty years, will end.

There was no doubt who started the war. There is a familiar pattern to its unfolding. Israel is attacked. Israel strikes back. Here lies the problem. At the outset, people are with them. Behind the scenes, many even in the Middle East, anxious about Hezbollah's links to Iran and seeing them like Hamas as proxies of Iranian power, urged privately that Israel destroy Hezbollah. Western leaders who could see the same thing queued up, at the beginning, to advise Israel to stand firm and hit hard.

As the conflict began, the G8 summit at St. Petersburg got under way. It was memorable for two things. There was a great "George" moment when, not knowing the microphones were on in the meeting room, he greeted me in George-like fashion with "Yo, Blair." We proceeded to have a conversation that was recorded for posterity until I realised we were being listened to, but it was all light-hearted stuff and could have been a thousand times worse. People went nuts back home, for some reason finding it an insult to Britain. We have become something we really never used to be: chippy. Personally I didn't have the chip, so I thought the "Yo, Blair" greeting funny. In fact, it indicated total intimacy. Of anyone I ever met at a high level in politics, he was the person least likely to be rude or offensive. He would talk to Alastair or Jonathan in a way and with an informality that most presidents of most countries would never have begun to tolerate. Alastair in particular used to josh him in a manner that probably nobody did, not even those in his inner circle, and I think George kind of liked it. After I left office, a group of my friends visited the White House with Leo in tow, but without me or Cherie. George happened to be there at his desk and heard they were there. He came out, showed them round, took each one into the Oval Office, had a picture and was thoroughly and completely charming. Didn't need to do it. Wasn't pushed to do it. Just did it.

So "Yo, Blair" was a joke; but unfortunately only I got it!

Anyway, that was a pinprick. The other thing was the discussion of Lebanon. What was interesting was that, behind all the usual statements and resolutions and press conferences, there was a common belief that Hezbollah had it coming, and if Israel took them out, so much the better.

Of course, what then happened is also familiar. After Israel retaliated with force, Hezbollah hit back with rockets. The inevitable visual paradigm of such a battle is: superior "Western" force, with superior weaponry, causes devastation. Within days, the international angst transfers from the provocation to the retaliation. Suddenly Israel is the aggressor. The damage done is truly shocking. But then force employed in that way always is. The alternative is not clear. Do too little and the provokers are emboldened. In Israel, the worry was that it was all too little. In Britain, as elsewhere with the exception of the U.S., the reaction was: it's far too much.

By its nature, such action is not effective, if by "effective" one means the enemy is defeated. That's the point about this modern warfare. Hezbollah were and are an urban guerrilla movement. They target civilians deliberately. Their weapons are poorer, so they kill relatively few. They assume the posture of the plucky underdogs. Israel is a government with a well-armed and well-trained army and air force. They do not target civilians. But their only ultimate weapon, in a civilian setting where the guerrilla movement is located, is deterrence. Therefore they use their force to try to deter further attacks. Inevitably, large numbers of civilians are killed. They quickly assume the mantle of oppressors.

International opinion, at first understanding the provocation, rapidly became dismayed at the nightly scenes of carnage of innocent Lebanese casualties. Dismay pretty sharply then turned to condemnation.

There then came about a choice in politics which did me real and lasting damage. European opinion quickly solidified around the demand that the Israelis should stop. Unilaterally. Even if Hezbollah continued with their rockets. U.S. opinion was in a totally different place, with over 60 per cent of Americans supporting the Israeli action.

I felt it was wrong that there should be a unilateral cessation. It should be on both sides, and we couldn't expect Israel to stop unless the rockets stopped. But that was not how it seemed to most people. They felt we were simply indifferent to the bloodshed. I thought the Israeli prime minister, Ehud Olmert, was in a really tricky position. I knew if I were him I would regard it as impossible to stop unless Hezbollah did too; or unless they were beaten; or, which is what finally occurred, Lebanon took enough pain that Hezbollah would not feel they could do it again. It was a ghastly method of deterrence and horrible for Lebanon. But I could see it from his and Israel's position.

Underneath it all, of course, was the state of the Israel/Palestine peace process. With that stalled, all manner of bad things were going to happen. With that moving, each tunnel—in a region full of dark tunnels—suddenly acquired some light at the end of it. In my mind, it all came back to the same problem, of which the Israel/Arab conflict was the manifestation, not the cause. Israel/Palestine is used as a potent source of friction and war because of religious difference.

The occupation of Palestinian land may be an injustice, depending on your viewpoint, but this is a region with plenty of injustices. What transformed it into a threat to global security was that Jerusalem is sacred for Islam, the third most holy site because according to Islam the Prophet was transported there in a dream; the occupation of that land by Jews was an affront, an indignity and most of all a symbol of Islamic weakness. It invoked every dimension of Muslim victimhood from the Crusades onwards. It spoke of a religion disrespected and people oppressed because of it.

Gradually, but too gradually, with tentative steps when strong strides were required, there came to be the outline of a solution, which was really a compromise. Israel has its state; the state of Palestine comes into being. Jerusalem is divided, at least territorially. The holy sites are shared.

It would do as a solution—there isn't another—but getting to it has begotten all sorts of other obstacles. So a really quite simple answer has come to have a quite horrendously complex process to achieve it. The result is occasional breakthroughs, punctuated by long periods of regression or drift. When it moves forward, everything else looks better; when it doesn't, as I say, bad things happen. The conflict in Lebanon was just another example.

The war went on longer than it should. The alienation of Israel from the international community—and this time international opinion, not governments—became worse. As one of the few people ready to understand their point of view, I suffered accordingly.

In September 2006 I visited Beirut. I had talked constantly to the Lebanese prime minister, Fouad Siniora, throughout. He was a thoroughly decent man, but absolutely caught between dislike of Hezbollah and the impossibility of doing anything other than verbally lacerating the Israeli action. I landed at the airport in a military plane and drove in from the airport with as heavy a security detail as I had ever had. Unsurprisingly, I was not popular with many Lebanese people. But, as ever, the key political leaders understood the complexity of the situation and understood, above all, that for Hezbollah to have emerged victorious would have been disastrous for Lebanon's future. We met in his office in the old part of town and, even being preoccupied as I was with the politics, I thought how beautiful it was, how rich in the history of the region, of its religions, art and culture.

He was dignified and friendly. He had one straightforward message: there will never be peace unless Israel/Palestine is resolved. "With it, everything is possible; without it, nothing is," he said. I pledged again to do what I could to get the U.S. president to refocus our efforts on it.

I met several members of the government, some Muslim, some Christian, some Druze. All were grateful that someone had come to see them. Their message was extraordinarily poignant: their country was on the brink, it had to be saved; but its fate depended on resolving the power struggle of the region as a whole. A couple of them said that their colleagues had been assassinated over the past years, almost picked off one by one, and they said, without a hint of self-pity, that this might be their fate too, but nonetheless the spirit of the people was good and would prevail in time. At our press conference there was an organised disruption, and as always, of course, that took the news.

As I sat with Siniora, I realised that my own political problem was now very acute; terminal, in fact. At points I had wondered why I didn't just cave in and condemn Israel and call for them to stop unilaterally. The Israelis would have understood it, and it would have been the proverbial safety valve for the fierce political criticism.

But I had by now come to see the entire conventional approach in dealing with this problem as itself part of the problem. And by the way, what was the problem? That was a good first question. To most people, in July 2006, looking at the news it was the Israel/Lebanon conflict. I didn't see it like that. I defined the problem as the wider struggle between the strain of religious extremism in Islam and the rest of us. To me, Lebanon was embroiled in something far bigger and more portentous than a temporary fight with Israel. Indeed, I thought the whole issue of Israel part of the broader picture.

Of course, I could see that Israel's action was at one level disproportionate. I could see the unreasonableness of certain Israeli positions. I could see the manifest injustice suffered by the Palestinians. But I had concluded that none of this got to the root of the matter, which was in this deeper, wider struggle that affected the whole of the Middle East and the religion of Islam. So what was holding peace back? The

Shebaa Farms? Not seriously. A dispute about the 1967 borders or land swaps between Israelis and Palestinians? Come off it. Halfway reasonable people could find a way through these issues in a day if they wanted to—if the elements operating on this wider struggle permitted them to.

To me, you can't understand Hezbollah unless you understand the role of Iran; or understand Lebanon unless you understand Syria; or understand Hamas unless you understand the role of both; or understand either country in its present state unless you understand the history not just of the region but of the religion, how it saw itself, how it had developed its own narrative, how it saw its own predicament. And here, just as in Iraq or Afghanistan, there were competing strains of modernity and atavism. As a result, the solution to me lay in neither the sole use of hard power nor the sole use of soft power but in the combination of the two.

As I explained earlier, this had been my recurrent theme from September 2001 onwards. I supported the tough military stance of the U.S.: what else could we have done after thousands of innocent people died on 11 September? When terror became the weapon of choice of al-Qaeda and Iranian-backed elements in Iraq, or of the Taliban in Afghanistan, I believed strongly we had to fight it, not yield to it.

However, I always argued that force alone could not win the struggle for us. Alongside it, there had to be an equally vigorous and determined push for peace, notably between Israel and Palestine and, for reconciliation, a reaching out across the religious and cultural divide to unite people of goodwill, whatever their faith, in an embrace of a modern, coexistent world.

The harshness of the military struggle, its inevitable mistakes and mishaps, had driven a wedge in world opinion. There were those who basically believed Bush himself was the problem, and those who thought soft power a naive distraction. Over time, the latter became distinctly overtaken by the former. An entire school of thought—with consequences that reverberate, and in my view in a damaging way—evolved a position that essentially said: to succeed, be the "not Bush." Do the opposite to him and we'll do fine. It's a dangerous and diverting myth.

I was, therefore, in a word, squeezed. But by then I felt truly uneasy compromising on it. If I had condemned Israel, it would have been more than dishonest; it would have undermined the world view I had come to hold passionately. So I didn't, but I could feel the PLP move more or less en masse to a querulous position. People were getting it in the ear on the doorstep and were feeling they should be agreeing with the complainant, not the leader. But I had my determination to comfort me, and by and large it did (which is, I suppose, what always happens to leaders when the final hubris overwhelms them).

Once Parliament stopped sitting, there were usually a few days before we were due to begin the summer holiday. Normally I spent them down at Chequers, enjoying some thinking time and being with the family. I would sit out in my jeans and T-shirt, doing papers, strumming my guitar, sloping off for a run in the woods, taking my wine outside after dinner and breathing in the night air. The staff down there were friendly, and—I know it sounds a bit pathetic—also unchallenging, there just to help. Of course prime ministers should be challenged, but sometimes you just feel that for one evening nobody is going to bend your ear, nobody is strategising with you, nobody is making you rise to the occasion; nobody is doing anything very much, except asking what you'd like for dinner.

Somehow the human spirit always finds ways to adapt. I don't mean that having a tough time as prime minister ever remotely compares with the truly tough times many people suffer, and suffer heroically. I just mean that in a position of leadership, normal human being though you are, you discover under pressure that extraordinary inner instinct to survive. It may be unpleasant, but you still have to get up in the morning, dress, eat, drink, breathe. You have to go on living. You have to find meaning in doing so. To me, by then, the only meaning was in being true to myself. I might be in a minority of one, but it would be a one I believed in.

That summer, just before we were due to go abroad, with Lebanon still in full nightmarish violence, I realised I should delay the holiday. I was mainly in Downing Street as we tried to put together the UN resolution that would end the conflict. I had been in two minds as to whether to delay. I was very reluctant ever to do so, knowing that if you weren't careful the holiday just didn't happen, and after all there were modern means of communication. In the end, I stayed in London until it was clear the resolution was going through.

By the time I boarded the plane for St. Lucia I was exhausted, and looking forward to being out on a boat in the middle of a warm sea, with a warm wind at my back. It was my last summer holiday as prime minister.

TWENTY

ENDGAME

On the flight I reflected deeply on the politics of what happened in Lebanon and on my own reaction to it. Ruth Turner, head of government relations, had been seeing members of the PLP. These were not necessarily the uber-loyalists but the people it would be risky to lose, people like Peter Hain, John Denham and Karen Buck. They were mainstream PLP people with links to the left as well as the right of the party, and they certainly had their finger on the party pulse.

They were more frank with her than they would have been with me. They disagreed with the position on Lebanon, but that wasn't their real point. They thought my reaction indicated a profound loss of touch, a failure of instinct, a decoupling of me and public opinion that they thought dangerous, and more than that, out of character.

I had always been known as the politician with the sure touch, the one who could express the public's thoughts and therefore shape them, the one who would sniff the scent of popular opinion and follow it with a certain intuition. They felt I had lost this ability; and with it, what made me who I was. At one level, they considered the loss a disaster politically. At another level, they just couldn't comprehend it.

The difficulty I had in response gave me much pause for thought as I settled into the eight-hour flight. It wasn't that I didn't get public opinion on Lebanon, nor that I couldn't have articulated it. My difficulty was I didn't agree with it. I agreed totally that the deaths of so many innocent civilians, especially children, were completely wrong and unacceptable. The human tragedy of such action appalled me. I thought of how many families would mourn, how much bitterness would be generated, and how if you were an ordinary Lebanese caught up in this nightmare, you would just want to rage against the world.

But I also worried about the risk of a Hezbollah "victory," of a situation where they could calculate the provocation, pull Israel into retaliation and emerge as winners. I felt a unilateral cessation gave them that. I felt anything which left them in any doubt as to the calculation of risk next time round was a real and possible future threat. They had to understand that if they tried doing it again, there was a price to be paid that the people of Lebanon would not allow them to pay, at least not with the lives of their civilians.

For me, the analysis could not be confined to the conflict itself, but it had to encompass the potential for future conflict. Ending the conflict on terms that deterred Hezbollah in the future could save lives. It only gave us some political time and space, and here again I wanted to step in with a major soft-power initiative to resolve the Shebaa Farms question, and of course to revive the Israel/Palestine peace process. My isolated "third-way" position had few buyers, but I believed strongly that just because we were shocked at the TV footage of the consequences of war, this could not blind us to the consequences of peace on the wrong terms.

So it wasn't that I couldn't guess which way the wind was blowing; it was that I distrusted a policy of following the prevailing wind. Ten years before, new to office, alive as if wired up to every current of popular imagination, I would have made a different choice. Now, seized as I was of an analysis born not of Opposition's need to connect, but of government's duty to govern, I had evolved. I was not a changed person, but I was a changed leader. I could see as plain as a pikestaff the problem this gave me, but I had come to a view that, above all on this issue of security, I should do what I intuitively thought right, not what I intuitively guessed was popular.

As we came in to land at St. Lucia, I reflected: had I changed, or was I just obstinate? Was it leadership, or just vanity? Having got us into Iraq, was it belief that sustained me, or just the fact I had nowhere else to go? How honest are we ever with ourselves? How hard it is to disentangle our motives from our anxieties, our convictions from our pride.

On the third day of our holiday there was a major security scare when a plot to blow up a number of airliners flying between the UK and the U.S. was foiled at an advanced stage. The plotters had intended to detonate peroxide-based liquid explosives, which is the reason why there are still restrictions on taking liquids onto planes. Naturally it sparked a massive tightening of airport security arrangements.

That day and for the next days, there was a series of conference calls between me, Transport Minister Douglas Alexander and John Reid, the Home Secretary. After the initial panic, my strong desire was to minimise disruption. There then followed a routine set of exchanges between us all, with me, as ever, being on the passenger-convenience side and them very much on the risk-averse side. To be fair, John got it absolutely, but to begin with thought we had to be extremely cautious. Douglas could see awful headlines about us ignoring "expert" advice. I believed that once the panic died down we would do real damage to Heathrow if we went over the top; and the tendency of the system always was to go over the top. So they insisted that business people couldn't carry suit carriers, everything had to go in the hold, perfume was a risk, everything was a risk. After much expostulating by me and much earache for the others, which they endured patiently, we came to a sort of modus vivendi, though it was months before common sense returned to its proper place.

Despite the continual interruption and the usual calls for me to go back to England, I managed to get a break. The job never leaves you, nor the weight of responsibility. It sits there with you all the time, lighter or heavier depending on mood and news; but somehow, away from it all in a different setting, the weight is easier to bear. I had needed a holiday, and I came back at the end of August feeling reasonably upbeat and well rested.

That feeling lasted about ten minutes. The mood in the PLP had, if anything, hardened. The GB crew were agitating more or less openly for me to set a date for departure. His allies were mainly to the left of my supporters, but he was also picking off a few of the younger, more Blairite ones, who for various reasons were drifting offside and, as I discovered later, were being made rather attractive promises of future promotion should they switch.

I knew I was hemmed in. The PLP was divided, and perhaps for the first time the majority were for change. But change to what? To Gordon, for sure, but in order to do what? That they didn't know, and in what I thought was an extraordinary and weird self-inflicted myopia, most of them didn't appear to want to ask.

Along with Ed Balls, and with Nick Brown doing the numbers, Gordon had constructed a coalition that essentially said to the PLP: we can retain the New Labour support while being a different sort of New Labour, i.e. without, on analysis, the "New" elements. But it didn't seem like that, and the analysis never went deep enough for most of them to understand it. Some, to be sure, did ask what sort of change, and concluded that it was either to something that wasn't New Labour or to something that was too ambiguous a version of it to be effective; but they were a minority.

I had by then concluded that what we would get if I left would be a kind of uneasy and ultimately muddled compromise, with, basically, Old Labour organisational politics, and bits of New Labour policy, together with trade-offs to the left. The party would go Old Labour and the government would be New-ish Labour. I thought that how much of New Labour survived depended on how much I could get done before I left; and of course whether anyone would step forward to claim the New Labour mantle and, if necessary, challenge Gordon.

My meetings with Gordon and his close team had continued through-out 2006, but they had never grown into sincere or shared attempts to construct a new policy agenda; and in any event our relationship had changed following the police investigation which had begun in March.

You must beware of resentment in politics even more than in life outside it. First, it is a bad and distorting emotion. Second, it is an unhealthy emotion in a leader. Third, you usually have little overall cause for complaint given the overwhelming privileges leadership bestows. By and large, I never felt resentment during my time in office. Anger in bursts, yes. Despair, very occasionally. But not resentment, which is an ongoing emotion, one that eats away at you rather than breaking out sporadically.

If I ever came close to resentment, it was over the so-called "cash for honours" business. The resentment was less over the fact of it as over the time it took, its totally destabilising nature, and most of all the truly and horribly unfair manner in which members of my staff were tar-geted. It was an attempt to end my premiership in a way that would have been reputationally ghastly.

Funnily enough, I never criticised the police over it. I had got to know and really like the police who worked with me as protection, and I had an innate respect for the officers as a group and the job they did. I got on well with those who helped fashion the law and order policy. I could see their flaws, as with any profession, but I felt they were on the same agenda most of the time, and I thought their frustrations with the courts and the bureaucracy were more or less justified. And I had been at enough memorials to fallen officers—organised so well by the Police Memorial Trust, founded by Michael Winner as one of the lesser-known things he does—to appreciate they really did put their lives on the line.

In this instance, I could see their problem. They were going to be beaten up badly by the media if they didn't pursue it; and the longer it went on, the more they were in a "lose–lose" situation. Close it down and they would be accused of a whitewash; continue it and they would be under intense pressure to get something (or more accurately, someone). The consequence of it all was that the government was rocked more or less monthly by a scandal which could lead the news with the twitch of an eyebrow, but to which there was always very much less than met the eye.

By then I was tough enough for anything, but for those who worked for me, especially Ruth Turner and Jonathan Powell, it was mind-bogglingly awful. Weaker characters frankly would have collapsed. Fortunately they were strong, but by the close of it they had needed every ounce of their strength.

The story was broken by the *Sunday Times* on 15 March 2006. Essentially, they alleged that Michael Levy, as party fund-raiser, had offered peerages to those nominated for the House of Lords in our 2006 list, in return for donations which were disguised as loans. I didn't believe this, by the way. For one thing, as a result of the setting up of the new Appointments Committee to vet peerages, no such expectation could ever have been given. But what had happened was that, since we had taken out loans—and loans did not require the identities of lenders to be made known—there could be perceived an obvious, if mistaken, implication that these loans might then be turned into donations if the peerage was granted.

Part of the problem arose from the fact that donors were now, especially prior to an election, stuck out there, huge and easy meat for the media to tear apart. For some reason, giving to a political party was considered prima facie evidence of corruption. So a donation meant the donor's name was declared. Not so for a loan.

Now it is true that there were many large donors from both Tories and Labour (and Lib Dems I might add) who were subsequently put in the House of Lords as "working peers." But as I used to say, there is no reason why they shouldn't be put there, provided there isn't a sale or trade and there are other good reasons for their appointment. There are lots of folk who give to charity and may anticipate that they will get an honour of some sort, and they probably will. But you can't stipulate it; and they cannot then donate on a promise they will get it.

Anyway, it is a murky business, but it is the system as it has operated for a long, long time. The only difference was that we had introduced rules of transparency and insisted on declarations for political donations. In times gone by, no one had any idea who gave to the Tory Party, not even all the way through the 1970s, 80s and 90s, and no one ever asked. But with us, it was always going to be different. And, of course, we had now changed the law. So once more, ironically, a move to greater transparency ended up backfiring spectacularly.

I was quite sure the individual donors or lenders were not under any such promise. There were very good reasons for all of them being on the list, and each would have made an important contribution to the Lords. People also overlooked the fact that party leaders had within their gift certain party nominations. In other words, there was an assumption on the part of the public—unsurprising really—that there was an objective judgement on a non-party basis for nomination to the Lords. But this was not the way the system worked for working peers. In fact, I was the first prime minister to give away what had, up to then, been the absolute power of nomination over all appointments, although we had retained party nominations for a limited number of party-reserved slots. So, in a way, what was odd was that a trade union leader whose union had donated generously could go in the Lords and no one would bat an eyelid, but private sector entrepreneurs, who might be (and in these cases were) highly successful businessmen, were somehow regarded as illegitimate.

When the *Sunday Times* broke the story, it was a medium-size scandal that got the party all het up (conveniently forgetting where the money to fight the election had come from) and the media excited. But what shifted it from the containable to the eruptive and uncontainable was the party treasurer Jack Dromey's statement on 15 March that he had never been told about any of it and that there should be an inquiry. The next day a Scottish National Party MP called for a police inquiry, and the police felt they had no option but to launch one. From 21 March 2006 to the day I left, it was a running sore of the most poisonous and debilitating kind. A few weeks after my departure, the file was closed without any charges being brought, but it had been nearly eighteen months of absolute hell for all concerned.

Gordon's involvement came about in this way. I have considered at length whether or not to include this episode. It is in the book written by Andrew Rawnsley about the two of us, and written there in certain respects inaccurately. So I have decided to put the record straight. We had been having a huge set-to about Adair Turner's pension proposals. The Pensions Secretary John Hutton and I both thought them right, but Gordon disagreed. We had fixed the crucial meeting to decide it on 15 March. It was going to be a very tough meeting, I was in no doubt about that. I agreed to meet Gordon in the morning, before the trilateral with John Hutton later at 4 p.m. When Gordon came in, he was in venomous mood. I can truthfully say it was the ugliest meeting we ever had. To be fair to him, for some reason he thought this whole donations business had been a way of my leaving him with some frightful scandal, a sort of ticking bomb that would then wreck his leadership in the same way, as he put it to me, Jean Chrétien had done to Paul Martin in Canada (there had been a funding row in the Liberal Party that Paul Martin had inherited from the time Jean was prime minister).

It was all nonsense, of course, but I think Gordon may have genuinely believed it. Or it may have been an elaborate excuse. I can't tell. But what he proceeded to say in the meeting stunned me. He began the conversation not by talking of pensions, but by saying how damaging the loans thing was; that there might have to be an NEC inquiry; and he might have to call for one. I naturally said that would be incredibly damaging and inflammatory and on no account must he do it.

The temperature, already well below freezing point, went arctic when he then said: Well, it depends on this afternoon's meeting. If I would agree to shelve the Turner proposals, he would not do it. But if I persisted, he would.

I remember there was a piece of paper on my desk which bizarrely was a translation of the Royal Irish Regiment's motto *Faugh a ballagh,* which means "Clear the way." I had seen them in Downing Street as they prepared to amalgamate and leave duty in Northern Ireland following the peace process. We had had a joke about whether I would use their motto at PMQs. In the event, I had not had the opportunity.

Suddenly seeing it, Gordon poked at it with his finger. "That's what you should do—clear the way!"

Anyway, it was not pleasant and there were things said that should remain in the privacy of that room and our recollection. Suffice to say, he felt I was ruining his inheritance and I felt he was ruining my legacy.

He believed the policy was wrong; I thought it was right. He made a threat; I disdained it.

We then had the pensions meeting with John Hutton at four, in which I insisted the Turner proposals proceed. It ended around five. At six Jack Dromey made his statement calling for an inquiry. I really don't know for a fact that Gordon put Jack up to it. Gordon denied ever speaking to him. And, as I say, I really don't believe he would have wanted the dire consequences that it unleashed. It did the party immense damage. It pulled our ratings down and mine personally every time it was reactivated. The irony was that the policy agenda was moving forward, so each moment we started to come up for air and get going again, we would be dragged back below the waterline.

Since that event, our relations were on a different footing: formal, at points even friendly, but I couldn't forget it and found it hard to forgive. I was also sad about it; not simply for the obvious reasons, but because it showed the truly nasty side of politics. Somehow it can make people do things that really shouldn't be done, like dirt that won't wash off. Also, he was, and is, a far better man than that.

So, by September 2006, when this had gone on for some months, erupting every few weeks with some fresh "revelation" or leak from the inquiry, combined with Lebanon, combined with rebelliousness over the reform programme, combined with nine years in office, it was not astonishing that the PLP mood had hardened. They could be pardoned for thinking their leader was not exactly their number-one asset.

Although during the investigation we had fallen behind in the polls for only the second time since 1997 (the first being during the fuel crisis)—itself pretty remarkable—the polls were not that bad. We were a few points adrift but I was beginning to get the measure of David Cameron. I could sense he was uncertain not only of how much he could change his own party, but also of how much he wanted to. I thought their policy positions were vulnerable, especially on law and order and Europe, and therefore my strategy was to drive forward fast, constantly challenging them to keep up or fall behind, or divert to a different route. David Cameron was clever and people-friendly, and I thought he had some real steel to him, but he had not gone through the arduous but ultimately highly educative apprenticeship I had gone through in the 1980s and early 90s. I had honed my leadership skills and instincts. His were still pretty unhoned. They existed, but with rough edges.

However, my party could just see one thing: problems if we stick with Blair; comfort if we don't.

After I had come back from the summer holiday, I went to Balmoral for the usual weekend with the Queen. During the weekend, there was a dreadful Nimrod crash in Afghanistan in which fourteen military personnel died. The operation in which the plane crashed—Operation Medusa—had been a blow to the Taliban leadership, giving us a strong psychological victory. They had suffered a lot of casualties.

There had been renewed attention given to Afghanistan during 2005 and 2006. When it is said that people took their eye off Afghanistan because of Iraq, it isn't so, at least not for the British. During the toughest time in Iraq, we were still resolutely set on making Afghanistan work. The elections in 2004 had been successful. As the security situation got tougher, so in the summer of 2005 we started to prepare for taking on the leadership in the south of the country, where the Taliban were still strong and where narcotics formed the main basis of Afghan income. Indeed the military chiefs, dismayed at the limits of what we could do in Iraq, were increasingly wanting to switch emphasis from Iraq to Afghanistan.

In September 2005, John Reid had sent me a note giving a nine-month preparation time for the deployment of British troops to Helmand province. The exchange of notes and correspondence, meetings and conferences continued throughout the latter part of 2005 into 2006. It was agreed that in principle we should deploy. But as John made very clear, it would be a tough and dangerous mission. The Taliban would fight hard to keep hold of the territory that we had never been able satisfactorily to wrest from them. There would be suicide attacks on our forces.

We held a conference on Afghanistan in London in February, which Kofi Annan co-chaired with me. At the conference, the scale of the challenge was plain, in terms of civilian and military capacity, in nation-building and giving Afghans solid hope they would have a stable functioning democracy for the future.

What was apparent in both Iraq and Afghanistan was that the enemy had a very stark picture in their mind of the importance of the struggle we were engaged in. It was, naturally, all masked as their fight against occupying forces of the West, but this ignored the facts that a) there was a UN resolution authorising the presence of such forces, b) there had been elections in both countries resulting in governments who wanted the presence of such forces, and c) above all, the only reason for our presence was their terrorist campaign. If they had stopped that, we would have gone instantly.

Of course, they knew this perfectly well. Their real fear was precisely that of leaving the people to determine the outcome, since it was obvious that outcome, freely determined, would have stood against fanaticism and for modernisation. When Zahir Shah, the last king of Afghanistan (who had made a state visit to the UK in 1971), died at the ripe old age of ninety-two in July 2007, we were reminded of the fact that back in the 1960s and 70s, Afghanistan had been a nation on its way up, with a GDP per head equal to that of South Korea.

While they had a clear view of the importance of the fight to their ideology, public opinion in the West was becoming more and more fuzzy as to the reasons for our presence, asking whether it could possibly be worth it. Once again, people drew analogies with conventional warfare of the symmetrical kind, when what was self-evident was that this was unconventional warfare of the asymmetrical kind. We were engaged in long-term nation-building the purpose of which was as much our security as their nation. That's the way the world is in the early twenty-first century. The wars, the ideologies, the power structures of the twentieth century seem less part of another century as part of another epoch. Unsurprisingly, people's minds are slow to adapt.

So a constant and recurrent theme of 2006 was the increase of endeavour in Afghanistan. I was alarmed about it, uncertain we had the right civilian leadership there and concerned that though our military had a good plan for our contribution, it was unclear our enthusiasm was shared, at least outside of the U.S.

My mind was full of this as well as of the domestic challenge. At the end of August, just before I was due to go to Balmoral, and with carefully orchestrated debate rife as to when I would finally set a date for departure, I decided to give an interview. You would think I would have learned by then. One rule about giving interviews: never do it without knowing the answer to the obvious question. Sounds simple, but it's amazing how many times even the seasoned pro can walk in full of thoughts, full of great things to say, concentrating hard on what they want the story to be, without ever focusing on the answer to the one question they are bound to be asked.

The inevitable question was: Are you prepared to set a date for leaving? Now, in truth, I had decided that in all probability the 2006 conference would be my last. As I have already intimated, if I could have got more time I would have taken it, but I could see it all closing in and Gordon's folk were becoming bolder by the day. If I announced my departure at party conference at the end of September, it would be a surprise and have the necessary elan such things should have. I was reluctant to do it before-hand, so I shouldn't have given the interview, at least not without care-fully working out how I could walk round the question.

However, my mind was full of thoughts about how we had to keep to the New Labour way, how I would flush out opponents on the issues, how I would face the party up to the straightforward task of asking "change to what?" before deciding on change. Maybe, at the back of my mind, I thought if I could squeeze out more freedom of manoeuvre, then who knows what might happen. Politics is a fast-changing busi-ness. But actually I think my mind was really made up. I just wanted to control the announcement.

I did the interview with *The Times* at Chequers in late August. Phil Webster, someone I had always liked and thought was straight, did the questioning and was perfectly fair. Naturally, he asked the obvious question.

Now there had been this rather ludicrous formula worked out after the 2005 election of there being "a stable and orderly transition," which was of course code for "handing over to Gordon." It was, in fact, as a formula, flawed. There should have been no assumption. There should have been a debate and an election. But few wanted a debate, and even fewer an election, so it sort of stuck as an agreed formula.

Part of the so-called "orderly transition" was that I would set a date. Now clearly at some point I would have to. Gordon, naturally suspi-cious of my motives and actions—and by this time in a sense rightly, from his own perspective—was pushing hard for a date and was assum-ing it would be at party conference.

When I came to answer the question Phil put, rather than walking round it which I should have, I more or less said: No, I'm not setting a date.

I had also been hugely influenced by a typically brilliant note from Andrew Adonis that he had written over the summer break. It is so good it's worth quoting in full.

Personal note for Prime Minister from AA—Monday 21 August

I thought I ought to contribute to your thinking on the Big Issue, though only really to say two unsurprising things—*viz.* a) that once you "name the date," your authority will drain away rapidly and will soon be followed by growing calls for you to bring the date forward to "end the lame duckery"; and b) that in my view it is strongly in the public interest that you continue in office until conference 2007, and possibly beyond into 2008 depending on the position next summer.

Your political authority appears to me more than sufficient for this, provided you set out an energetic forward agenda on your return and at conference. By contrast, GB's succession will now inevitably involve (whatever his efforts to claw things back when he succeeds) a shift to the "compromise everything Left," given his associates and the forces he has nurtured. He looks set to be a weak—if extended—interlude between you and Cameron.

Two more extensive thoughts—on the chimera of the "dignified exit" and "orderly transition"; and how to recapture the initiative.

I spent a solitary holiday walk reflecting on changes of prime ministers over the past century, and for what it's worth these are my three conclusions:

1. There are no "dignified exits" and "orderly transitions"—just exits and transitions, all more or less ragged and unsatisfactory. That's life, I suppose.
2. The more successful prime ministers all left No. 10 with the least "dignified" and most "disorderly" transitions. Gladstone, Lloyd George, Churchill, Macmillan and Thatcher all possessed a will to power for a purpose until the very end. If they had been planning their "dignified exits" they would have been lesser leaders and lesser achievers. By contrast, the three long-serving prime ministers to execute "dignified" and "orderly" transitions are Wilson, Baldwin and Salisbury—all drained of energy and purpose, their reputations and uniformly disastrous legacies not enhanced by the warm retirement tributes. (Attlee as ever the enigma.)
3. The closest analogy to your current position is that of Harold Macmillan in the summer of 1963. In fact the larger parallel between you and Macmillan is uncanny. Macmillan too was a long-term largely successful prime minister; a Middle England moderniser with a fine sense of the "wind of change" sweeping his party, country and international affairs, whose domestic success soon came to be taken for granted. By summer 1963, an election looming, he was engulfed in Profumo, the animosity of the sacked and disgruntled, and a media clamour for the "new man" to defeat Wilson. After months of uncharacteristic dithering, brought about by Profumo and other forgotten minor events, and poor advice from

friends, he finally decided to stay and fight the coming election. Indeed, at precisely this point he pulled off the brilliant Test Ban Treaty with JFK after years of foreign policy frustration (apartheid in South Africa and Rhodesia; de Gaulle's first "non," etc.). The Cabinet rallied to him with relief once he declared—but then, on the eve of the Tory Conference, he was laid low with what he briefly feared might be a fatal prostate condition. The rest is history: hasty resignation under pressure; the "new man"—Sir Alec Douglas-Home (!); Wilson winning a year later by only a whisker . . . and Macmillan in regret for the next twenty-three years.

How to take the initiative decisively?

On the domestic front, you need I think to herald a next-phase reform process which you will lead. The best way I can see of doing this is to put yourself at the head of a semi-public "next steps" reform process to run alongside the CSR—and announce next month that you are doing so, to culminate in renewed Five-Year Plans to be published alongside the CSR next year. This doesn't involve the impossible at your phase of leadership—a "new agenda"—but rather the relentless renewal and intensification of an agenda (choice and quality in the public services; rights and responsibilities in welfare and public order) which in fact has been largely successful, and which is regarded by middle opinion and the sensible commentariat as authentically yours and the continuing national imperative—on a par with privatisation and trade union and labour market reform in the 1980s, and the "one nation" economic liberalism of Macmillan. It is precisely this continuing vital reform agenda which will stall if you stand down in the next year, as middle opinion senses strongly whatever the gripes about other matters.

I could quickly sketch out such a "plan of reform" in more detail, on the basis of what is already in the pipeline or ought to be so. But to produce something worthwhile I would suggest bringing together a small group of trusted people who have done the business for you across education, health, welfare and the Home Office over recent years, and get a plan worked up asap for internal strategising.

Hope all this helps a bit.

Andrew

So perhaps subconsciously I was more definitive in my reply to Phil Webster than I meant to be. But the headline was "BLAIR DEFIES HIS PARTY OVER DEPARTURE DATE," i.e. it appeared defiant, as if I had changed my mind and decided to stay after all. Period. The moment the story came out, I immediately called Gordon to reassure him I did not mean to carry on to the end of the term. However, I could tell he, and possibly more particularly his team, had decided they were going to be "robbed" again and had better start the battle.

So began the "coup." Essentially, they decided to organise waves of resignation letters and round robins calling for me to go. Somewhat bizarrely, the first we heard of such a letter was when we were on a visit to a care home for problem kids and teenagers in York on 4 September. I always reflected, going on such visits, how lucky I was as a child and then as a parent. Some of the stories are truly horrendous. The father leaves, for example; the mother takes up with someone else; the new man doesn't get on with the teenager and eventually they throw him or her out on the street. Unbelievable, really. Of course, some of the youngsters have deep behavioural problems and can be virtually impossible to parent; but it is all shocking, nonetheless.

This was a new type of care home, helping them, giving them training and education and teaching them personal skills and manners. It was challenging work, and as always on such visits, I felt an enormous respect for the patient and committed service of those running the place. I wouldn't like to do it, that's for sure. It requires a very special and dedicated sort of person. We took some of the kids back with us to the headquarters of the Joseph Rowntree Foundation, where we held a seminar and had a meeting with some of the foundation's staff in preparation for a lecture on social exclusion that I was to give at the New Earswick Folk Hall in York the next day.

You've always got to see the amusing side of such things. I'm doing this visit, talking to the youngsters about finding a job, getting a purpose in life, etc. Suddenly I am pulled aside by Hilary Coffman, accompanying me as the press officer for what was supposed to be a routine low-level regional trip, and I'm told that there is some letter circulating from thirty or forty MPs calling for me to resign. From then on the visit is interspersed with updates from my staff about the precariousness of my own job. There's me popping out to be told the latest about this quite serious news, then popping back in to talk with Charlene or Robert about job-seeking possibilities.

Eventually, rather to the bemusement of the people in the meeting, I had to take some real time out to assess the situation. The letter had been leaked to the media. What's more, a minister, Tom Watson, was a signatory. I didn't feel angry at the letter, by the way. I understood it was a reaction to the *Times* interview and an indication that the GB team had had enough.

In a curious way, I felt sorry for the party and I more or less remained like that up to the point of departure. By then, I had come to the clear and settled view that unless Gordon spelt out whether he was New Labour or something different—and defined the "something different"—it was going to be a disaster. I knew it. But to be fair, I had taken a long time to come to know it. Even really smart people who knew us both well, like Philip and Alastair, thought it could be OK, so ordinary members of the PLP were bound to be unsure. Of course there were some, like John Reid and Alan Milburn in the party and Jonathan and Sally in my office, who were absolutely clear from the outset that unless Gordon was unambiguously New Labour—which they doubted—we were going to be at the mercy of the Tories. If the Tories didn't square up to the challenge, we might survive. If they did, we wouldn't.

And yet I could see Gordon's enormous ability, extraordinary grasp and unyielding energy, and realised those were all big qualities in a leader. Unfortunately, what I had also come to realise was that those qualities needed to be combined with a sure political instinct in order to be fully effective. And that instinct comes from knowing what you truly believe, not vaguely or at a high level of generality or "values," but practical, on the ground, everyday-life conviction. And at this utterly crucial epicentre of political destiny, I discovered there was a lacuna— not the wrong instinct, but no instinct at the human, gut level. Political calculation, yes. Political feelings, no. Analytical intelligence, absolutely. Emotional intelligence, zero.

Gordon is a strange guy. But by the end I had to come to see that this was not the fundamental problem. (He had and has a sort of endearing charm in the strangeness.) The fundamental problem was that he simply did not understand the appeal of New Labour, in anything other than a polling, "strategy," election-winning sort of way. He could see that it worked, but not why it worked. He could understand its detailed policies, but not its emotional appeal.

So in all the meetings and constant interactions we had after the 2005 election, I could tell he thought these attempts by me to discuss policy were all tricks or devices to buy more time. On each occasion, he would agitate for a date; and I would say: well, what policy direction are you going to pursue? And he would treat that as if it were me being disingenuous or seeking an excuse to prevaricate. Or he would say to me: you're doing this for your legacy, but not my interests; and I would say: but if the policies are right—say on academies or NHS reform or ID cards—it is in your interests that we do them. Anyway, there it is and no doubt he has a different take on it all.

I could see where it was all leading. The party, or a significant part of it, was hell-bent on change. I couldn't realistically survive past mid-2007, not without a fight that would be potentially terminal for the government. I did toy with it, by the way. I had a feeling that my going and being succeeded by Gordon was also terminal for the government. But in the end, I considered it more important for the survival of the New Labour project that if it was to be terminal, it should be clear that it was his departure from New Labour, not my insistence on staying, that had done the damage. Clear to whom, though? And how clear? These were good questions and I was not fully capable of answering them.

However, by this time, I could tell it would be impossible to stay to 2008. The media—*Mail, Telegraph, Guardian, Independent, Mirror*, plus, in effect, the BBC—were emphatic: they wanted me out and him in, pretty much for the same reasons as the party, at least so far as the left media were concerned. The right wanted me out for other reasons too. Rupert Murdoch's media were still broadly supportive, but even he, though not pushing for me to go, thought it was sensible I make way for Gordon.

So I knew that there were very good objective reasons for the party and, more important, the country, that I stay. I genuinely thought I had the right policy agenda for Britain's future, and thought that Gordon didn't. But, in a way that happens sometimes in politics, all this had been more or less swept away in the Gadarene rush for change.

When I got back to London from the lecture in York on 5 September, I brought together the key people and also took soundings from Alastair, Anji, Peter and other long-time close associates. The next day I met Gordon. We sat out on the terrace of Number 10, my favourite meeting place when the weather was good. We had one of those conversations that we had begun to have in the past couple of years, one that takes place on two levels. One is spoken; the other unspoken. Both are equally clear.

He said, in effect, there were other letters on the way. Spoken (him): I know nothing of the details and have had no part in them. Unspoken: You have left me with no choice, I just don't trust you to go.

He had me trapped, and he knew it. But also, in a curious way, he would then need me. And I knew that. It was impossible for me to stay, but it was essential to him that he was not the obvious organiser of my leaving.

Spoken (me): I will make it clear that this conference will be my last. Unspoken: Push me too hard and I will finger you for the coup.

He did argue about the date and I was vague; but I was also determined not to set a precise time right there and then. If I did so, I knew I would be out within weeks. It was going to be a struggle to stay in any event.

I was very calm. Some in my inner circle still tried to argue I should fight him, but I said it was not possible to do it. We would have to allow this to happen with good grace. We would have to use the time to put in place the remaining reforms and to set out a clear and intelligent future programme. Above all, we had to keep the New Labour flame alive. I considered it 90 per cent inevitable he would take over. I agreed it would not work. It was crucial, however, our disloyalty to him could not be blamed.

Tom Watson had been told by the chief whip either to remove his name from the letter calling for me to resign, or to resign from the government himself. News of his resignation was in the media already. I smacked him very hard in my response.

I have heard from the media that Tom Watson has resigned. I had been intending to dismiss him but wanted to extend to him the courtesy of speaking to him first. Had he come to me privately and expressed his view about the leadership that would have been one thing. But to sign a round robin letter, that was then leaked to the press, was disloyal, discourteous and wrong. It would therefore have been impossible for him to remain in government.

It was unusually brutal, but at the time I felt he deserved it. Actually, later I felt sorry for him and regretted I had done it. The trouble with a lot of the younger ones who should have been supportive—Chris Bryant, Siôn Simon and others—is that they just hadn't thought it all through. They got a little intoxicated with the excitement of changing leader and playing a part in it all. They didn't mean it maliciously really. They genuinely thought it was right that I be changed—and so it was, sometime before the fourth election. But, as I say, change to what? That bit was just never, deep down, explained in the way it should have been and had to be, for the purpose of serious political decision-making.

The next day, 7 September, I alighted on an easy enough way of taking the sting out of it all. I had a visit to Quintin Kynaston School in St. John's Wood. I had been there earlier in my premiership, and had watched it develop and succeed. The headmistress, Jo Shuter, was a thoroughly sensible sort and she wouldn't mind me using the visit to make a statement. I went with Alan Johnson, who had always been loyal and in whose company I felt it easier to speak.

The events of the past days had been, naturally, very big news and there was a definite sense of a party in rebellion, a government in disarray and a prime minister at bay. Some in the party blamed me for not going. Some were outraged at the disloyalty. Most were kind of bewildered and wanted it all to be stopped, and with as much dignity as we could muster.

I began by apologising on behalf of the party, which I thought appropriate. I made it clear I wasn't going to set a precise date now, but I said that the upcoming party conference would be my last. I also gave a warning shot across the bows of those who thought an assumed succession for Gordon was a good thing. One really bad aspect of the whole business was the notion of his entitlement to the job. I was sure the public would not see it like that, and though it was almost certainly going to be him, they would resent any idea that it was somehow per se legitimate. It would have to be managed carefully. "I also say one other thing after last week: I think it is important for the Labour Party to understand, and I think the majority of people in the party do understand, that it's the public that come first and it's the country that matters and we can't treat the public as irrelevant bystanders in a subject as important as who is their prime minister. So we should just bear that in mind in the way that we conduct ourselves in the time to come."

The statement took the heat out of it all. The next day, a group of middle-ground people—i.e. those who didn't consider themselves really either Brownites or Blairites—sent a statement to Ann Clwyd as chair of the PLP, welcoming my statement and, in effect, making it clear I should determine the precise date of departure.

At the weekend, the *Sunday Times* had the story that Gordon and Tom Watson had met at Gordon's house before the letter was sent. I reined back my folk who wanted to go into "kill" mode on it. Of course, I never had any doubt that Gordon did not merely know of it all but had organised it; however, I had taken my decision to try to leave on terms that no one could say had caused this disunity, and if that meant an orderly transition to Gordon, so be it.

If someone came forward to challenge him, that might be a different matter. But if it was inevitable, then let it happen decently and without rancour. As with all TB/GB decisions from first to last, I can't be sure I did the right thing in taking such a view, but I did take it and for the reasons given.

A few days later, I spoke at a conference in London for the Progress organisation, which I had high hopes of transforming into a serious New Labour policy think tank. It had good young people who were onside with what we were trying to achieve. The left had its own group in Compass, which basically wanted an Ed Balls/GB type of leadership. They were active and smart but hopelessly wedded to a politics that simply had no prospect of ever winning an election. They had plenty of energy, however, and they were organised. My folk tended to be great with the middle-ground electorate and resounded with a sense of the intellectual future of the party, but in organising, caballing, scheming and plotting, they were, like me, in the introduction class for primary school.

Part of the worst aspect of the GB modus operandi was the rehab-ilitation of old-style trade union fixing and activist stitch-ups. All great fun for those who like that sort of thing—and this was very much part of the Nick Brown/Tom Watson/Charlie Whelan psyche—but com-pletely hopeless in terms of where a modern political party had to be to get anywhere with the right policies and have a hope of winning.

Progress were decent people, but they fast got tricked into this beguiling notion that they had to be a force for unity at a political and organisational level, whereas actually all they needed to do was to strike out with a sound, future-oriented policy agenda and leave political organising alone. The result, as GB's team intended, was that at the very moment they should have been seeking to define the next leader's programme, they became neutered under the pretence of being for "unity."

Of course, to be fair, as some of those closest to me pointed out, this was to a large extent my own fault and born of my insistence that I could not be seen to disrupt Gordon's ascent to the pinnacle. I would constantly stress that New Labour was a joint project with Gordon, which was somewhat beyond what the facts would bear. But I was still trying to co-opt him to the programme and hoping he might accept it, if only *faute de mieux*. Not unnaturally, this left people much confused.

Once I had cast the die, so to speak, it brought a type of relief to the situation; and it reignited an intense sense of urgency in myself. The GB folk calmed down. They had won, though they remained distrustful and I knew would look for a way to bring the date forward. My people were sad, but not as demoralised as they might be. I had to work hard at keeping their energy levels up; but I was thoroughly motivated myself and passed some of that on to them.

After what had been a pretty astonishing week I then went on a trip to Beirut and the Middle East. When I returned to Chequers on 14 September, to lick my wounds and work out my strategy for the remaining time in office, I had much to contemplate. Chequers in September is always a good place to be. The weather tends to be rather benign at that time of year, so there was plenty of sitting out in the grounds.

I had more or less settled into a pattern of living there at weekends. I would work hard in the morning, exercise in the afternoon. A stiff drink and a good supper. Early to bed.

The relationship between alcohol and prime ministers is a subject for a book all on its own. By the standards of days gone by I was not even remotely a toper, and I couldn't do lunchtime drinking except on Christmas Day, but if you took the thing everyone always lies about— units per week—I was definitely at the outer limit. Stiff whisky or G & T before dinner, couple of glasses of wine or even half a bottle with it. So not excessively excessive. I had a limit. But I was aware it had become a prop.

As you grow older, your relationship with alcohol needs to be carefully defined. When young, you do drink to excess at points, but you go days without it. As you get on in life, it easily becomes a daily or nightly demand that your body makes on you for relaxation purposes. It is a relief to pressure. It is a stimulant. It can make a boring evening tolerable. But it plays a part in your life.

I could never work out whether for me it was, on balance, a) good, because it did relax me, or b) bad, because I could have been working rather than relaxing. I came to the conclusion—conveniently you might think—that a) beat b). I thought that escaping the pressure and relaxing was a vital part of keeping the job in proportion, a function rather like my holidays. But I was never sure. I believed I was in control of the alcohol. However, you have to be honest: it's a drug, there's no getting away from it. So use it with care, maybe; but never misunderstand its nature and be honest about its relationship to your life.

I took a few days to prepare my conference speech—the very last I would give to the Labour Party, which I had led for over twelve years by then—and also to reflect and work out my game plan. There could be no easing up, for sure. There were multiple challenges. The media would want me to go earlier, partly because they were impatient for change, partly because it was a sport to them to see if they could score a victory and push me out before my due time. OK, they knew that in one sense I was going involuntarily, but in another, it was too close to being my call, not theirs, for their comfort. We could circle each other, clash with each other, but that was on equal terms. They thought it would be great to get the better of me one last time and force the departure.

Then there was the party. They would accept my ruling as to when the exact date would be, but there would be a constant underlying accusation of selfishness, that I was staying for my own good, not theirs.

There would be a genuine problem of authority. Gordon was the almost appointed successor. He was the future. He would draw people to him. If he disagreed on matters, even Labour ministers would think twice about siding with me over him. And though, to be fair, once I made the decision he did his best to get on with me, his people remained resistant, prone to resentment and straining at the leash.

The unions, who sensed that they were about to come back into the centre of things, certainly in respect of the party, were dismissive. When I addressed the TUC for the last time, they were polite but not much more than that. We both knew what we thought of each other, though there were genuine and really good union leaders—like those in USDAW (the shop workers' union) and Community (the old iron and steelworkers' union)—who were sad and worried about my leaving, but the big unions were never reconciled. We ended our time as we began: in mutual incomprehension. They couldn't understand why I was doing what I was doing; and I couldn't understand why they couldn't see it was the way of the future. Funnily enough, as people I rather liked them and I was a lot more loyal to the basic union and Labour case than many ever realised. But they thought I was a Conservative in Labour clothing; and I thought they were conservatives in labour clothing. So there you are. But if you look back on the history of Labour governments, they were a lot less trouble to me than they were to Attlee, Wilson or Callaghan. Mind you, they had a lot less power by then.

Also, I had to focus on my own closest folk, in keeping their spirits up and maintaining their sense of purpose. They were an incredibly good bunch. There were those who had endured all the way through: Jonathan Powell, Jonathan Pearse and Liz Lloyd. Liz had come on immensely over the years, became deputy chief of staff and brought an order and discipline that Jonathan and I naturally lacked. She had an excellent temperament too: lovely to work with, honest and, underneath all the English feminine charm, quite steely. Above all, capable.

One of the most depressing dimensions of the return of Old Labour politics to the party organisation was that really good young people like Liz were going for nominations for Labour seats and being rejected in favour of those who had the GB machine behind them but who were much less competent. Something I was able to do in the early years of my leadership was to encourage smart, young professionals to join us and to stand for Parliament: David Miliband, James Purnell, Ruth Kelly, Liam Byrne, and, to be fair, the GB equivalents, Ed Miliband, Ed Balls, Yvette Cooper. The mood was for a younger generation of really good talent. Even though I knew GB's lot might be trouble for me, I had an unbending belief that you always promote talent. I've had some harsh things to say about Ed Balls—I thought he behaved badly at points, and was wrong on policy—but I also thought he was really able, and a talent that any political party should be grateful to have. So I was very clear in my instructions to the folk at grass roots: don't organise against these guys. Whatever we think, their ability gives them a right to come and be part of it all, and we have a duty to let them in.

But I could see towards the end that this was not reciprocated. And much more important than it being unfair, it is foolish for the long-term health of the party and will be a serious problem for the future. The very problem I had faced trying to be selected in the early 1980s, and the problem the party then had in attracting talent, had been because of old-fashioned fixing in "smoke-filled rooms." By the end of the 1990s we had overcome it—if you were good, you stood a chance.

In that last period, I could feel it going backwards. Not to have someone like Liz in Parliament, if you could have her, was our loss, not hers. And a serious, indicative one. A party that turns away its talent corrodes its capacity. But she was too close to me and it told against her.

Others in the team had joined more recently. Matthew Taylor had a great combination of intellect and political nous. He could reach across the party in a way that didn't desert New Labour ground, but expanded out from it. David Bennett, head of the policy directorate, had joined from McKinsey. He was a total outsider, and I think at points found the whole political experience alarming, but he was really clever and, as I had wanted, brought an outsider's expertise and different perception analysis to bear. He was very helpful in writing the last policy chapter of the government.

Then the political team, Ruth Turner, John McTernan and Nita Clarke, and in the Labour Party the General Secretary Peter Watt, were of a quality far beyond what I could have hoped for at that stage of the game: dedicated, utterly loyal and fiercely determined on my behalf. But it was a tough hand: a leader on his way out; an alternative power base ruthlessly flexing its muscles; and in respect of all but Nita, a police inquiry into their integrity. When I think of how they managed and performed with distinction during that period, I am overcome with admiration.

Media, party, GB, unions, private office—the moment I declared I was going, all of them were going to take a lot of handling.

I had retreated to Chequers to think. I decided the only way through was to give them a defined and clear reason for believing I should stay until the summer of 2007. "What is the point of you?"— that's the question, as Matthew Taylor and Peter Mandelson both said. So I determined on the point. The point would be: I would go out having taken core, fundamental decisions on policy which embedded completely the New Labour programme on which we were engaged; and then I would create a process whereby the Cabinet and party participated in setting out a future programme. GB could be a full partner, he could agree to take part or stand aside from it, but he wouldn't be able to say I hadn't set it out for him, or that he hadn't had the chance to shape it. If there were disagreements in the course of it, let them be had. At least at the end of it we would have a clear platform. If he took it, great. If he didn't, no one could say he hadn't had the opportunity, and any alternative leadership would be able to grasp it and run with it.

By and large, in the face of much cynicism from many quarters, that's what we did. Despite having said I would leave, I was, after all, still prime minister, and had much nominal and much residual actual power. I could still reshuffle, still promote; even with a hostile media I still had the platform from which to speak, to argue, to persuade. The last nine months could have been a vanity valedictory—lots of media voices tried to make it so—but actually we pinned down crucial parts of the change programme and we left a perfectly sensible set of future policy directions if people want to take them up—on pensions, welfare, the NHS, schools and law and order.

No political leader had ever left like this before. But then, in this regard, like so many others, politics was changing. As leaders get younger and the place of Britain shifts in the world, I may be the first, but I doubt I will be the last.

TWENTY-ONE

DEPARTURE

Those months were a huge strain, especially on the family, a cloud of uncertainty and insecurity hanging over them. Though intimately involved, a family, particularly a young one, is oddly detached from the prime minister's job. They witness the events, they participate in the moments of joy and sadness, but they always feel like bystanders, because, inevitably, in the end they are.

They are relieved of the intense pain and pressure that is the prime minister's alone, but they are not relieved of the scrutiny. And the fact that they can see what you are going through, but at a certain level remain shut out, can give them a strange feeling of being lost, a little betwixt and between, never wholly involved in the prime minister's life but still integral to it.

When we first went into Downing Street, we were the youngest family to have lived there since Lord Russell's time in the 1850s and 60s, when the house was the family home. There were no official functions and it was not really a place of work. Today Downing Street is a busy, bustling thoroughfare of government, with adjoining buildings and hundreds of staff. The iconic nature of the most famous address in Britain means that it is very much the seat of power. It is therefore first and foremost now a working office, and only a family home a distant second.

The introduction of children was at one level lovely; at another, the place was completely unprepared for it. Once Leo arrived, we then had a baby in the building, which was immense fun for everyone and the staff adored him, but it wasn't exactly geared up as an institution to crèche-style working. But we managed, and though I never appreciated how weird it must have been for the kids to have grown up in Downing Street, we coped on the whole pretty well. Also, Chequers was a blessed relief from the Downing Street swirl. Without it, the prime minister's life would have been very different, and worse.

We lived in the flat above Number 11. We redid the kitchen, which badly needed it, but every refurbishment always brought its tales of expense—the contractors had to work to special rules—and "living it up." People used to be amazed that we had no staff in the flat to cook and so on, but in fact we preferred it like that. It was quieter and more private, though of course there would be a constant stream of duty clerks, civil servants and messengers passing through. However, the people who worked in Downing Street were, by and large, friendly, helpful and, in an understated but nonetheless obvious way, supportive of the burden you bore as prime minister. They never talked about it much; but you could feel the emotional succour being gently and kindly offered.

The flat above Number 11 was bigger than was commonly thought and had a clutch of spare rooms above the two main floors, where the living and sleeping quarters were. There at the top, from where you could look out over Downing Street, Horse Guards Parade and St. James's Park, I had a gym with a running machine, rowing machine and weights. Nicky had a room where he used to keep his drum kit along with my guitars and occasionally we would sneak up to the top and jam together, making the most frightful noise, no doubt.

Somehow, and probably mainly due to the extraordinary Jackie, who had been with the family since 1998, we got through the adolescence of three youngsters, the birth of Leo and his first years at primary school. You are at your most real in a family—at your most angry, at your most loving, at your most suffocated, at your most motivated. You can't be fully selfish in a family. You want to be, often, but in the end it drags you back to your need for and your commitment to the company of others. In the family there are few hidden spaces, few facets of character, good or bad, that lie undiscovered, few delusions and even fewer fantasies. There are many glimpses of the best and the worst of the human being. In the end, most important of all, you have to forgive the trespasses in order that yours too can be forgiven. And just occasionally, you espy the essential strength that the family represents, and realise it is a marvel of human achievement and for all its shortcomings, anxieties and tensions, greatly to be cherished.

We survived Number 10 intact and pretty strong. But the strain of living there told on us all in different ways.

The position of the spouse needs careful reflection. In the old days, men worked, women didn't. Nowadays women do. For a working woman, it is always going to be very hard. It was hard enough for Cherie. She chose, rightly in my view, to remain a person with a career rather than become a political wife. I am not sure in retrospect that it's possible, given the degree of scrutiny today.

Cherie kept up her practice but it was difficult. There were lots of cases she couldn't do because they were politically sensitive. She had no support in Number 10 as the "official" wife. Fiona, Alastair's partner, and an old friend Ros Preston actually did brilliantly for her, but it all had to be done in a somewhat concealed way. When Gordon came in and his wife Sarah got a proper office and staff, that was absolutely right and should now be the norm.

Cherie didn't always help herself, and as I have remarked before she had this incredible instinct for offending the powerful, especially in the media, who were unfortunately far too well placed in taking revenge; but she did a superlative job. She used Downing Street, really for the first time, as a proper place to recognise charities, having one function or other virtually every night. And she was a rock to me, strong when I was weak, determined when I was tempted to falter, and fierce in her defence of the family. Her media profile became such a caricature of the reality that it really was a bit of an outrage, but she put up with it and most of the time didn't let it get to her. Mutual cordial loathing about best sums up her relationship with a large part of the press! Some of the criticism she would accept was valid. It was the lack of balance that wasn't.

And the truth is that the media attack is often arbitrary; or, perhaps better, selective. As far as I am aware both my predecessors took holidays in homes provided by friends. Denis, certainly, had to carry on working even while Mrs. Thatcher was in Number 10, but no one persecuted him over it. She was really attacked over her children, but on the whole, more slack was cut in those days. Now people want to know everything, and anything that is known can always have a negative construction put on it. Whether the attack becomes immensely personal or not depends on whether an editor decides to go for it. If a paper like the *Daily Mail* decides to do it, others soon join in, not wanting to be left out of the pack.

Of course, in the end, it is such an exciting and enormous thrill to be there and to do the job that none of the downside should ever blind you to the ineluctable honour of the upside. But after all, you're only human, so you think: Yes, it's a great honour; and simultaneously: You bastards!

People deal with the pressure in all kinds of different ways, both prime ministers and spouses. Some drink, some have a wild side, some crack, some find religion, some find special friendship. I do not believe anyone doesn't have to deal with it, however. The pressure is too great. You always imagine the person of extraordinary character, strong, resolute, without fear and without doubt, willing to be alone and to stand alone, supremely confident astride the muddle of human affairs. Such a person doesn't exist. To be human is to be frail. At points of supreme challenge, such confidence and courage can be summoned forth, as can acts of incredible selflessness and sacrifice, but no person is ever such a character all the time.

Then again, everyone needs to relax, to let their hair down, to be rid of the paraphernalia and pomp of power, if only for a fleeting moment. And if you ever get a person in charge who doesn't need to do this, watch out. There will be trouble.

There is also a certain sadness that settles on you that never leaves. As will be apparent from this memoir, I am basically an optimistic and upbeat person. I think life is a gift from God and should be lived to the full and with purpose. Someone has to do the prime minister's job and someone has to take the decisions, and how many times have I said what a privilege it is to do it?

But privilege though it is, you become aware over time of the consequences of each decision, good and bad. This is especially so when the decisions lead directly to life or death. I remember during Kosovo, when by mistake the allied forces bombed a civilian convoy in which children died. From that moment, I think, the sadness settled on me. I thought of the life those children might have had—the grief of the parents, the feeling I would have if it were my child. Now it's true you have to reflect on those who would have died if you had refused to act. If we had acted as we should have in Bosnia or Rwanda, many lives would have been saved. But there would have been lives lost also. In Iraq, we forget the children that died under Saddam and would have continued to die had he remained in power. But it doesn't remove the thought that there are those who would have lived had we not taken the military action to be rid of him. That thought never leaves you; and in the quiet watches of the night, it comes back insistently and with force.

I dealt with the pressure as well as most, if not better. But I had to deal with it. It may have appeared to slide off me, but that was an act. Underneath, it was there. However, I continuously tried to overcome my own demons by confronting them.

Those last months took a very special kind of immersion mixed with detachment. I had to be totally focused, but I knew it was coming to an end. So I operated at two levels: I was completely up for it and making policy decisions every day as normal; and I was mentally preparing to go, thinking about what I wanted to do, wondering what the future would bring.

The Queen's Speech of November 2006 had law and order as its theme. We put up in lights the changes to the Home Office and the Department for Constitutional Affairs—now to be the Ministry of Justice—ID cards, plus another heavy dose of antisocial behaviour measures.

The reform programme of the ten years of government is known most for the constitutional changes and education and health reforms. Tuition fees, specialist schools, academies and trust schools; choice, competition, foundation hospitals, cancer and cardiac programmes: all these, and of course devolution, are obvious.

The motivation for the law and order changes and, in particular, the antisocial behaviour campaign, I have described before. Same with ID cards. But the completeness of these reforms never really took hold, in terms of popular analysis and imagination, in the same way as the other programmes. I believe this is a mistake. Law and order—and to an extent immigration—were to me utterly mainstream and vital points of what the government was about, as crucial to New Labour as academies or choice in the NHS.

The Queen's Speech, and the actions over the subsequent months, took this agenda to a new point in policy. It was controversial, hotly contested in many parts of the media, opposed by Tories, Lib Dems and significant parts of the Labour Party. I knew Gordon would let it drop when he took over, but I wanted the agenda clear because I felt sure, and still do, it will come back.

I had begun the reorganisation of the Home Office and Lord Chancellor's Department straight after the 2003 reshuffle. It had been the hardest of all, since it meant losing Derry Irvine, my idol and mentor, but we had been trying to get some modernity into the very old-fashioned way the criminal justice system worked. Having David Blunkett at the Home Office helped enormously because his instincts on crime were so good. Charlie Falconer and Peter Goldsmith were both fully onside. We made changes to the Civil Service leaders, and that had an impact, but it couldn't all be done ad hominem. There had to be structural and institutional change.

My problem with the set-up was simple: it led to priorities that didn't coincide with those of the government. The Lord Chancellor's office was an amalgamation of three distinct roles: he was Speaker of the House of Lords, head of the judiciary and administrator-in-chief of the courts. For me it was obvious the roles were qualitatively different. What came last in the pecking order—the courts—was what mattered first to me, since that was where the effectiveness of the criminal justice system lay.

Likewise, the Home Office used to love all the constitutional stuff it handled—exercising the royal prerogative, the monarchy, titles, ceremonial matters, human rights, the Royal Charter, appointments, ecclesiastical matters, marriage and access to information—but what mattered to me was crime and immigration. I could feel its intellectual and political energy sucked into areas that were interesting to an elite class but left the lives of normal folk untouched. And they needed their lives touched by an effective "crime-fighting" and "immigration control-enforcing" machine.

Painful though moving Derry was, and as bumpy and chaotic as the aftermath of the constitutional reform to the office of Lord Chancellor became, the result was absolutely right. The House of Lords got an elected Speaker and sensibly chose a woman, Helene Hayman; judges were appointed by an independent commission; and the Lord Chancellor's Department became the Department of Constitutional Affairs, focused on driving forward the reform and improvement of the justice system, and to reform and safeguard the constitution. In 2007, we then added prisons and probation to their remit, which again makes sense since fighting crime was one thing and dealing with the court process and offenders was another, best dealt with in the same department, as was the norm in most ministries of justice abroad.

So we moved the constitutional affairs brief out of the Home Office, changed the Lord Chancellor's Department and beefed up the immigration, passport and citizenship part of the Home Office. We also needed to put them within a framework of laws that made sense of the modern world. Hence the antisocial behaviour legislation; the attempts to reform the terror laws; the tightening of the rules on asylum and immigration, the elimination of juries in complex fraud trials (which often collapsed after months due to their complexity, and tied up jurors' time for periods that excluded professional working people from jury service). The DNA measures were a hugely important advance, fiercely resisted on civil liberty grounds that I thought completely spurious. Due to new DNA technology we could match the DNA of suspects against that of previous criminals and from crime scenes, and build a DNA database. The results have been dramatic. Old crimes have been solved and innocent people have been freed. If extended—and around half of crimes leave a DNA trace—the change to the whole criminal justice system would be immense. Of course, the information must be handled carefully and protected, but the possibility is there to make it very hard to commit murder without detection, almost impossible to commit rape, and dangerous for a criminal to assault someone.

We had another major row over the Proceeds of Crime Act. This was a reform of enormous purport, which in time will tip the balance of law enforcement in respect of organised crime towards the enforcers, not the criminals. We had begun this legislation in April 2005 with the introduction of the Serious Organised Crime and Police Act. It led to the creation of the Serious Organised Crime Agency (SOCA) in April 2006. It had been, as ever, strongly opposed. The Tories and the Home Affairs Committee criticised the 2005 Act for the absence of a single UK border police force within the legislation, the Lib Dems were cautious over how well financed the agency would be, the Police Federation opposed the agency as they had concerns that they could lose the traditional independence officers enjoy and that their pay and conditions could be at risk, and the media questioned the overall value of the organisation. But it had given us, for the first time, the power to seize assets of suspected or convicted criminals on a basis that really did operate as a deterrent.

The whole business arose out of face-to-face meetings I had with police officers and residents in estates plagued by drugs and prostitution. Often the dealers or pimps would carry around thousands of pounds on them, or drive fancy cars. It was of course impossible to prove these amounts of money were the proceeds of crime, but allowing them to do this had two deleterious consequences. First and obviously, they could conduct their affairs more easily. Second and less obviously but to my mind very importantly, it gave them a cachet and status within the neighbourhood. Young men looked up to them. People feared them; and worse, some admired them. They were top dogs. The effect on the local community was awful. The Act gave the police the power to seize assets—money or property—after which there was an inquiry into whether they had been come by lawfully. Of course, it was a reversal of the normal rules of proof and evidence—that was the reason for the opposition, and understandably so—but I felt it absolutely necessary in the circumstances of modern life on those estates.

Having legislated, we then built on the foundation. Over time, we increased the powers and gave the police an incentive by allowing them to keep a certain per cent of the assets seized from suspected criminal activity. This policy offended virtually every Treasury sensibility, but in the end they agreed, and though we always fought over how much went to the Treasury and how much to the government, the principle was accepted.

The 2006 Queen's Speech extended these powers still further: to establish a new Serious Crime Prevention Order preventing organised crime by individuals, or organisations, by imposing restrictions on them; to introduce new offences of encouraging or assisting a criminal act with intent, or encouraging or assisting a criminal act believing that an offence may be committed; and to strengthen the recovery of criminal assets by extending powers of investigation and seizure to all accredited financial investigators. Given my own way, I would probably have taken it a good deal further still, but we had broken new ground, as we had with the antisocial behaviour legislation; and once different people in government reflect and try to assuage the public demand, they will go back to this agenda and fulfil it.

Fear and personal insecurity are terrible factors in everyday life for too many people. Reduce them and the quality of living improves dramatically. Seizing this agenda, especially on antisocial behaviour, was one of my proudest achievements. There is a trade-off with civil liberties—there's no point denying it—and though it was sometimes felt I was indifferent or dismissive of them, I truly wasn't. I was very conscious of the need to protect the innocent falsely accused of being guilty.

Twice in my career I had good reason to thank God for the independence of the British judiciary and Bar: once in the Hutton Inquiry; and then when the ruling on the "cash for honours" business was made. On both occasions, the lawyer came under intense and at points wholly improper pressure to do what a large part of the media wanted; and on both occasions, they made decisions according to the evidence. So I can bear witness to the value of the independent and impartial authority that keeps power in check, that protects the innocent and judges without fear or favour.

However, I could also see that ordinary people living without any protection in some parts of towns and cities were acutely vulnerable in ways the outdated system did not acknowledge. I've seen lawless places and places where people behave because they know they must. There is always a certain harshness in the latter. But believe me, put it to the vote and people know in which sort of society they would choose to bring up a family.

So we charged ahead on the law and order agenda, and even in the last days of office brought into effect some of the reforms.

We were less successful on the casino legislation. What a saga that one was! An interesting example, though, of how a public mood can be shaped.

We had, and still have, a problem with some of the old British seaside towns. In the nineteenth century and the first half of the twentieth century people would flock to them, not minding the spasmodic evidence of summer, enjoying the arcades, sampling the entertainment, the end-of-pier shows, the carnival atmosphere. They were brash and bulging with good old-fashioned entertainment. Then in the 1960s came the package holiday and air travel. I remember going to Benidorm as it was taking off in the 1960s. I loved it. It was the first time I had ever flown. After a taste of Spain—tapas, Ducados and Rioja (bit underage, but never mind)—staying in the UK seemed tame and unfashionable. Gradually the seaside towns declined, and as the new millennium dawned they faced an unpredictable future; or perhaps all too predictably, no future. Blackpool was the classic example.

Another problem was the explosion in different types of gambling—especially online—alongside traditional betting shops. For years we and these towns had been approached by major leisure companies, often American, wanting to build vast leisure complexes that would have casinos but also a huge array of other entertainments, cinemas, sports outlets and facilities and so on.

I thought we should let them. It would be a big injection of private sector cash. There was realistically no alternative. Seaside towns were queuing up for them. Manchester also wanted one and had advanced plans to redevelop the city centre on that basis. They would be governed by strict rules, and the top operators were well used to complying with them responsibly.

So I gave the go-ahead. There was an enormous backlash. Religious groups protested it would increase gambling, the *Daily Mail* did its usual thing and in the course of it suggested it was all some corrupt deal, targeting various of the civil servants involved. No one had seemed to notice that anything you could do in a casino you could do in an arcade, betting shop or online but with far fewer protections.

Tessa Jowell womanfully supported it and we got it moving, but spurred on by Church and press, it ran into the ground, we lost a vote in the Lords and we were faced with the ludicrous choice of either Blackpool or Manchester, and had to cut down the number of proposed so-called super casinos, those that would get most by way of investment. After I left, Gordon ditched even the Manchester one. It is a real shame for the places for which no very obvious alternative form of investment will be available. It was the worst form of puritanism—partisan as well as ineffectual. So people can gamble to their hearts' content and their wallets' limit—but not in a brand-new town complex with a casino, entertainment centre, sports facilities and shops.

However, even with this, I took a kind of perverse pleasure in just ploughing on, doing what I thought was sensible and catering very little for the waves of public opinion that ebbed and flowed unless I thought they had a permanent case that should be listened to.

In February 2007, we had the avian flu scare. This was potentially serious. The H5N1 virus was confirmed on a turkey farm in Holton in Suffolk. There were constant meetings and preparations in case it should turn into a fully-fledged crisis. As with the flu pandemic, you had to steer an ever-so-careful line between overreacting and underreacting. There is always a torrid deluge of bureaucracy for those caught up in an overreaction.

We agreed to the renewal of the independent nuclear deterrent. You might think I would have been certain of that decision, but I hesitated over it. I could see clearly the force of the common sense and practical argument against Trident, yet in the final analysis I thought giving it up too big a downgrading of our status as a nation, and in an uncertain world, too big a risk for our defence. I did not think this was a "tough on defence" versus "weak or pacifist" issue at all. On simple, pragmatic grounds, there was a case either way. The expense is huge, and the utility in a post–Cold War world is less in terms of deterrence, and nonexistent in terms of military use. Spend the money on more helicopters, airlift and anti-terror equipment? Not a daft notion. In the situations in which British forces would likely be called upon to fight, it was pretty clear what mattered most. It is true that it is frankly inconceivable we would use our nuclear deterrent alone, without the U.S.—and let us hope a situation in which the U.S. is even threatening use never arises—but it's a big step to put that beyond your capability as a country.

So, after some genuine consideration and reconsideration, I opted to renew it. But the contrary decision would not have been stupid. I had a perfectly good and sensible discussion about it with Gordon, who was similarly torn. In the end, we both agreed, as I said to him: imagine standing up in the House of Commons and saying I've decided to scrap it. We're not going to say that, are we? In this instance, caution, costly as it was, won the day.

We had agreed the forward policy process shortly after conference at Cabinet in late October. Rather grandiosely it was called "Pathways to the Future." The purpose was to use the remaining nine months to give a sense of unity, to meld together the Blair and Brown teams, and to allow Gordon's assumption of leadership to be defined as continuity as well as change, and above all as New Labour.

Naturally I suppose he always thought it was designed to constrain and corral him; but by putting Pat McFadden, my person, and Ed Miliband, his, to handle it in tandem right at the outset, I sought to reassure him. The truth was I still hoped it might be possible to convince him. I understood that at least some of the opposition to the reform programme had been for political reasons; but once in office, once he actually had to deal with the issues, I thought it might be different, that he might see I wasn't pushing the programme for effect but because experience as well as intuition had persuaded me that there were no better solutions to the challenges the country faced. As opposed to 2004, we now had clear empirical evidence that the reforms worked: the longest period of economic growth for over two hundred years, with over 2.5 million more in work; in health, no one waiting over six months for treatment; in schools, standards up across the board and spending on education per pupil doubled; and in criminal justice, crime down by 35 per cent.

Also, there was now no longer a competition between us: he had won, he would take over. The only thing that mattered, and it should matter to both of us, was that he succeeded and the New Labour project was established in an enduring way, so that the party never went back to its old routine of short bursts of power and long periods of Opposition; so that Britain escaped the curse of twentieth-century politics; and so that progressive thinking should claim equal if not superior purchase on popular opinion as conservative thinking.

I knew, with every fibre of political instinct, that only through holding to the New Labour course, and with passionate not tactical engagement, could we hope to succeed. As I said earlier, I believed that if he deviated, he would be lost.

But I'm afraid he couldn't see it. He played along with the policy part of "Pathways to the Future" and intermittently he switched on, yet I knew that behind the scenes his folk—with the exception of Ed Miliband—were denigrating it as a vanity project and treating it with scorn. The problem was I also knew that they didn't have an alternative. Frequently I would say to him and to them: OK, I understand you don't agree with my analysis; give me yours. What I got was, on the one hand, a confusion of attempts to avoid the hard choices and questions which lay, like it or not, at the heart of the policy issues; and on the other, a resistance to disclosing their thoughts. They ended up convincing themselves that the reason for this was that they should unfurl their radical ideas at the moment of the takeover. As I began to say to him, that's fine as a concept so long as you know what it is you wish to unfurl, but why not at least discuss it with me and test the propositions out?

As for the party reforms, again with much justification, he wanted to keep those to himself. I had, for my part, two goals. The first was simply to put the party funding business to bed. I thought it possible to reach an agreement with the Tories that would allow us to make sensible reforms. The former senior civil servant Sir Hayden Phillips had been appointed to chair a committee on the subject in 2006, and had approached it in a typically pragmatic and intelligent way. His 2007 report proposed caps on personal donations and campaign spends, together with an increase in the amount and reach of state funding. I thought it was a good compromise package.

Jack Straw was the minister in charge of it. We took the discussions quite a long way but I couldn't really get Gordon to agree a compromise. I think he thought he could get a better deal when he was prime minister, but he lost the opportunity to limit Tory spending and I had a hunch that for election number four, and without Michael Levy's and my participation, we were going to raise a lot less money. This was ultimately a housekeeping issue, but one with clear implications for fighting the election.

The second party issue was for me far more fundamental. For some time I had believed Labour faced a choice in its conduct of politics, in the way the party worked, interacted with the public and campaigned. Essentially, I had come to the view that the traditional method of politics was out of date, i.e. parties with defined members, activists, general committees, executive committees and all the infrastructure of twentieth-century political campaigns. There are some obvious truths about mainstream political parties in Britain and elsewhere that are worth analysing. We have fewer members than grass-roots, single-issue NGOs like those for protection of birds, aid, conservation and environmental groups. The ways in which we communicate with the public who support us would be regarded by the average supermarket chain as antediluvian. Our use of new technology is lamentable—the Obama campaign was an obvious breakthrough, but actually even in the Kerry campaign in 2004, the Democrats were streets ahead of most progressive parties in Europe. The Bush campaign, the infrastructure of which I used to discuss with George and which was devised by his key politicos like Karl Rove, broke new ground in reaching out to sympathisers.

All successful modern campaigns, including the Sarkozy campaign in France in 2007, utilised modern methods and—this to me being the crucial point—blurred the distinction between the inner core—the activists—and the broader public support.

I used to say to my people: after ten years in government, we are now at our lowest point politically. We've lost a certain amount of support—it's inevitable. Some of those who rushed to us in enthusiasm in the run-up to May 1997 have fallen away. But think of 2005: a really tough campaign, a huge onslaught on us, yet many New Labour voters stuck with us and in some seats we increased our majority. What this means is that out there, yes there are those who hate us, but we also have our adherents. What's more, this latter group have not come to us in a rush of enthusiasm, quickly swelling but just as quickly subsiding; they are believers. They're not unaware of all the problems and mistakes, but they have taken a decision to stick with us nonetheless.

Let's say some voters, perhaps many, backed us because they didn't want the Tories. Fair enough. But even supposing only one in ten are true believers (and it's probably more like four or five in ten), that's over a million people. Now that's a political base.

We can identify them. Some of these people are the new stakeholders in New Labour. They may be from entirely new categories of people who, due to our policies, are in jobs—sports coordinators, teaching assistants, small business and professional people in the new industries who buy into the vision of a new economy—people who are pro-Europe, those who support the interventionist foreign policy (and there are a few . . .), people involved in local community campaigns on antisocial behaviour, and so on.

In other words, along with the detractors, I could see a potentially enormous body of supporters, people not there on the bandwagon but with us due to a belief in a modern and different type of progressive politics. These were the people we needed inside our tent, not for their sake but for ours. Long-term, the health of party policymaking, the selection of good candidates, pressures for change coming from below—all depend on the quality, the sentiment, the instinct and the attitude of those involved in the party. In Opposition, even more so. Restrict ourselves to the old-fashioned or the union base and you've got one sort of party; open it up and let it breathe the fresh air provided by real believers and you have a different sort of party, one capable of governing for long periods of time, one with a coalition of support that would sustain a government, one that would prevent any recrudescence of the errors that had given us eighteen years of Tory rule and only nineteen years of Labour government up to 1997 in the whole of our history (for five of which we had to survive in a rickety alliance with the Liberals).

In a way, such a party had always been what I was groping towards all those years ago when I expanded the membership of my constituency party and when we made the reforms to the way candidates and leader were selected. New technology and new forms of campaigning now gave us tools to do it. My vision was to discard the conventional notions of party membership and structure, to treat supporters as members for key decisions and to use the new technology not merely to build out into new support but also to interact with supporters and to campaign in a different manner.

It was clear to me that, today, people in the party would not be supporters for the same reason, or have the same interests or be as passionate about the same subjects. Someone might support us because of aid to Africa, another because of health service changes and another because of antisocial behaviour policies. Young people would have different interests from old people. The fact they lived in the same geographical area was important come the election or in very specific local campaigns, but otherwise geography meant little.

We had a huge opportunity to rebuild the party along modern lines. Also, some change was surely inevitable. Unions were merging. In particular, the amalgamation of the Transport and General Workers Union with Amicus in May 2007 created a new behemoth called Unite. On present going, they would have half the votes at party conference along with Unison, the public service union. The union structures remained deeply in the past. They were still activist-dominated. There was no way it would be healthy for the party to become dependent on them again. So for a multitude of reasons—some external, some internal, but all to do with the consequences of a changing world—reform was not just sensible, it was essential if we were to preserve the enormous gains the New Labour project had delivered.

I could see where the current party debate was heading. Both Jon Cruddas and Douglas Alexander had written pamphlets. Jon made quite a name for himself. It was clever political positioning. To his overall political analysis—New Labour had deserted the working class and thus our base—he had added a programme for the party. It was clothed in some modernist language, but was ultimately an attempt to build a left coalition out of *Guardian* intellectuals and trade union activists. However beguiling—and he was smart enough to make it beguiling—it was, in effect, reheated and updated Bennism from the 1980s. It was not without its public appeal, by the way, but had no serious prospect of reaching the aspiring middle ground once the policy implications were exposed.

Douglas was and is a very clever guy indeed. I had tried to wean him off membership of Gordon's inner circle; but to no avail. It was a real shame. He and his sister Wendy, who is a lovely and also very smart person with great integrity, were a classic product of a decent Scottish Presbyterian background. Their father was a vicar and himself very accomplished. Douglas came to Gordon's attention before Douglas was an MP and had been rightly snapped up. He had a great way with words, a really first-class intellect and could have been (and maybe still can be) an outstanding leader.

But the Gordon curse was to make these people co-conspirators, not free-range thinkers. He and Ed Balls and others were like I had been back in the 1980s, until slowly the scales fell from my eyes and I realised it was more like a cult than a church.

Douglas had written this pamphlet that had a brilliant analysis of what was wrong, but the solutions all seemed to me to avoid the hard questions and lapse into wooliness.

I put Hazel Blears, as party chair, in charge of a commission for renewal of the party. I knew Hazel was a strong supporter of mine. She was a great campaigner, an activist with an understanding of the limits of activism. However, though she struggled with great application, the truth is Gordon was strongly opposed to the outgoing leadership deciding the future of the incoming one. This was all totally understandable except for the fact, as I kept saying to him, there was no alternative vision; and in the absence of a clear vision, the party organisation will just go backwards.

All those years ago we thought we had precisely the same perspectives on politics, party and life, whereas in fact we had somewhat different perspectives, shared at points but not an indivisible confluence. There was sufficient cohesion to allow us both to indulge; and by the time we realised it was an indulgence, it had become part of the party's unique selling point and it was too damaging to ditch it. But indulgence it was.

The policy process fared better and, in the end, produced some not bad conclusions and analysis. On security, crime and justice, "Pathways to the Future" outlined the progress in tackling crime and its causes, but highlighted the rapid changes affecting society which impact on crime, security and cohesion. The paper argued that the continued reform needed was based on three main elements: more effective prevention; better detection and enforcement; and reform of the criminal justice system by applying the principles of public service reform.

The paper also set out the challenges that Britain faces in a rapidly globalised world, and how Britain's interests can be best served working together with shared progressive values and in a world where governments work peacefully within international law. It set out how Britain still has influence and power, but now has to use both hard and soft power. Be prepared to intervene where necessary—using military action where appropriate—but also take global action on issues such as poverty and climate change; recognise that Britain's foreign policy is driven by values—justice and democracy—in a world which is increasingly interdependent. Ensure that everyone has access to an equal standard of life and has certain shared global values, and recognise that climate change is increasingly important and tackling it will only be successful by working on a wider global level.

On families, the paper recognised the important role they have to play in society, whatever their structure. The government also recognised that the success of families is not about their make-up but about the commitment of those who live within them, and that the government still has a role to play in ensuring all families are treated fairly and have access to the same choices others do. The vision that was set out was to: support families to exercise their rights to manage their own affairs while living up to the responsibilities they have; enable a work–family balance, by helping people move from welfare to work, improving childcare and supporting family commitments; and address the hardest to reach families, by tackling the causes and consequences of deep-seated social exclusion.

On the role of the state, the paper introduced the idea of the strategic and enabling state, as a response to the continuing evolution of global and domestic trends. The paper set out the six key features of this state: a strong focus on outcomes; tackling insecurity; empowering citizens; rights and responsibilities; building trust; and a smaller strategic centre.

Finally, the paper drew together the twin challenges of energy security and climate change, outlining a comprehensive policy framework for achieving our goals, including: promoting competitive energy markets; working towards a robust post-2012 international framework; putting a price on carbon that reflects its damage costs; driving the transition to new technologies through standards, incentives and support; removing the barriers to change in behaviours, choice and investment; and ensuring that the UK and others are able to adapt to the impacts of climate change.

Indeed, had we simply taken all these elements and pushed them forward, I think they would have evolved to a pretty strong future agenda, in policy and in legislation.

I also decided to make a series of speeches called "Our Nation's Future," trying to summarise the philosophy behind the New Labour project, what we had done well, what we hadn't and the underlying rationale for it all. There had always been this notion that it was all a bit of clever marketing and I wanted to set it out as a piece of political thinking. I have to say that, unsurprisingly really, the media were disinclined to report them much, except the one on defence. Their problem was not simply that I was leaving; it was unclear whether my departure was solely a change of personnel, or whether it was also a change of policy.

So a series of policy speeches was of insufficient interest unless pitched against someone or something. Of course, you might think it was their job to discover this, but the GB crew had hit on a brilliant device for not exposing any flanks, which was to say that it would plainly be wrong and disrespectful to set out their views while I was still prime minister. To my amusement, this was generally bought hook, line and sinker.

Rereading them now, I think they have contemporary relevance so let me summarise them briefly. The purpose, in each case, was not simply to state a policy but to describe an evolution of my own thinking based on my experience in government.

This comes back to something I said in the opening chapters. In 1997 I had boundless vision but no political experience of policymaking in government. People sometimes analyse politics as if a new government arrives, it has a programme, it works at getting it done, and succeeds or fails in that endeavour.

However, real-life governing, like anything else in life, isn't like that. There is nothing mysterious, still less mystical, about "government." It is indeed like any other activity. You learn as you go. You learn facts; and of course events can change them. You learn processes. You learn the art and science of your profession. But because political power is the outcome of a political fight—"our" ideas, platform policies, against "theirs"—the inclination is to treat the business of government as the closing of the door on the old home and moving to somewhere new. Actually you don't change ownership; you change tenant.

It is therefore quite sensible to try to understand why the previous tenant did this or that, what they learned and what they found when living there. Unfortunately that education is inconsistent with the way politics is conducted. In an age in which objectives are often shared and it is policy that is crucial, where the issue is often not right or left but, as I have said earlier, right or wrong, this is a significant democratic disadvantage. You spend several years relearning what the last occupant could have told you from experience.

So in these late speeches I chose policy areas where I thought there was a lesson to impart.

The first was on law and order. It concentrated on what I discovered in the course of trying to deal with crime, a huge issue for the public which always looms larger for the people than the politicians. I had started with the good old mantra "tough on crime, tough on the causes of crime." Good as far as it goes. What I learned was that the real problem was that in a world of very sophisticated crime—gangs, drugs, people-trafficking, money-laundering, to say nothing of terrorism—and deep social issues giving rise to a type of criminal underclass, traditional law and order didn't work. I understand the traditional view: prove guilt conventionally, according to the normal judicial processes. Sorry, but with these people, it doesn't work. If you want to beat them, you need draconian powers that can be wielded administratively and with instant effect. Hence the antisocial behaviour laws, DNA database, proceeds of crime legislation, anti-terror laws and so on. Now you may decide that this is too high a price to pay, in terms of traditional liberties. Fine, but—and this is what I learned—it is the price. If you don't pay it, you don't get the result.

The trouble is you can identify those who will say—sometimes with justification—we the accused have been denied our rights. But you can never identify adequately the lives lost or buried by criminality unchecked. They are victims; and the criminality could be stopped, but not by conventional means. So choose, but don't delude yourself that it is not a choice.

Linked to this was a speech on social exclusion. Here I was referring specifically to my own education from the time of the Bulger speech back in 1993. I used to think that the shocking behaviour of some young people—violence, knives, drug abuse—was a symptom of a society that had lost its way. In that sense, I presaged David Cameron's later claim of a "broken society."

Over time, I came to the conclusion I was making a dangerous error in eliding the behaviour of what is actually a tiny minority with society as a whole. The truth is most young people are fine—good, even—actually better than I remember many of my generation being. It really isn't true that the shocking behaviour is definitive of society. In fact, it is the opposite: it is wholly exceptional, of a different character. Therefore rather than policy being analysed and then prescribed in the context of general "society," it should instead be absolutely, specifically focused on the exception. When you examine the data, this is not about "young people" or even "poverty." It is about families that are utterly dysfunctional. And neither is this about "family life." Most families, despite all the stresses of modern living, are not dysfunctional. They function. Even those that are marked by divorce or separation. A tiny minority don't. So concentrate on them.

For these families, we need special intervention that, again, can't be done by normal social services procedures. For them, the absence of state interference is not a liberty, it is encouraging them to destructive behaviour that damages them and all around them. There is no earthly point in making periodic visits or checking up on them from time to time. They require gripping and seizing. To do that effectively their "rights" need to be put into suspense, including the right to be a parent. These families are not hard to identify. Neither are their children. I'm not suggesting every such situation means children are taken into care and so on; I'm merely making the point that any policy needs to be formed out of the box. Otherwise it won't work.

Where there is a wider lesson for society, is in the field of personal responsibility for health. In this speech, I set out why, over time, I had come to the conclusion that a modern health care policy had to encompass strong intervention on diet and fitness.

Normally, I am highly suspicious of regulation, but not in this arena, because the cost of poor diet and lack of fitness is borne by the nation as well as the individual. So I made the case for the smoking ban, for food labelling, and above all for sport. In respect of sport, I tried, not with complete success I fear, to persuade the system that sport was part of the day job, i.e. it should be part of mainstream policymaking. We had increased massively the investment in and priority given to sport in schools. I set out the case for going further but also for making that part of an infrastructure in which we opened up fitness opportunities and dietary advice to everyone, going well beyond the elite. My theory was that there was plenty of focus on healthy lifestyles, and much more advice, but the problem was organising, coordinating and widening access to it. I supported Jamie Oliver's school dinner programme for the same reason. These issues are no longer an afterthought, a bit of fun at the end of the ministerial day. They are of the essence.

The fourth speech again concerned a quiet passion of mine that was partly the result of missed opportunities at school: science. I had been a woeful student. Failed my physics, gave up on chemistry, scraped through in maths, never bothered with biology and spent the rest of my life regretting it! For some reason or other, I just couldn't grasp it. I felt a deep stupidity about it, unable to glimpse let alone see fully its principles and elements, in any shape that bestowed understanding. So my early life in regard to it passed in a slough of frustration, incomprehension and indifference.

Now I am fascinated by science and by its possibilities; in awe of how its progress is changing our world and the lives we lead.

The purpose of the speech was threefold: to explain why science was important (and why we had doubled investment in it under the very able guidance of David Sainsbury) and why we should not let its critics undermine its ability to break new ground. I had been having a ferocious argument with critics of GM food, led as ever by the baleful siren of the *Daily Mail*, who invented all sorts of nonsense to suggest it was a health hazard.

I had also battled with the same people over Leo and whether he had had the MMR vaccine. There was an attempt by a Dr. Wakefield—later discredited—to suggest it was linked with autism. The *Mail* took it up. The issue was then framed as to whether Leo had had it—if the government is saying it's safe, has the prime minister's son had it?

It was not actually an unreasonable question and frankly it would have been better if we had just answered it upfront at the outset. But for private reasons the family was sensitive about issues to do with Leo, and so we argued on the ground of saying that the issue of Leo's vaccination is not for the public domain. However, very soon we realised we couldn't sustain it. We then said, off the record, Look, we believe vaccination is best for children, including Leo, and we wouldn't ask others to do what we would not do for Leo so draw your own conclusions; and of course that was an effective admission. So the journalists knew perfectly well that Leo had been vaccinated. But part of the media contrived to write that it was unclear and so public concern continued.

The speech set out a strong defence of science and drew the distinction between the right of science to tell us the facts, and the right to decide to act on them or not. What should not happen in the public debate is that, for reasons of prejudice or because we wish the facts were different, anti-science or bogus science suppresses the truth. From Galileo through Darwin to the modern day, that has always been the consequence of such an attitude; and today a nation like Britain cannot afford to be governed by it.

The next speech was on "multiculturalism." Again it was an attempt to move policy on from a sterile debate about whether diversity is a strength or weakness. To me, it was clearly a strength. But, with citizenship should come certain clear duties as well as rights. This was a common space, which all British citizens should inhabit together. This space included support for basic British values, for our language, culture and way of life. In that regard, we should not be diverse; but unified. Outside of that space, diversity should be free to roam; and then it was indeed a strength.

I gave another speech on defence which set out my basic philosophy but also made one very practical point. We need a new deal for the armed forces today. We are asking them to go back into combat and sustain casualties. For almost fifty years, the Falklands and Northern Ireland duties apart, that wasn't the case. So we need to equip and reward them properly. However, if we fail to participate in the battles ahead, usually with our American allies, then we will lose the armed forces as a significant part of what gives Britain influence, reach and power.

The seventh speech was about the workplace. Rereading it, it strikes me as a little intellectually incoherent, but it had one germ of an idea. Essentially, I was trying to articulate that the modern workplace is today all about utilising human capital and developing it. In this regard a "management/workers" mentality was completely out of date. So rather than concentrating on a zero-sum game with management or capital, government and unions should be demanding the ability for their creativity and skill to be used to maximum effect, and should be active participants in the concept as well as the delivery of wealth creation. Hence government policy should be oriented towards lifetime upgrading of skills, not to labour market regulation.

The subject of the final speech was irresistible after ten years of being prime minister: the media! Naturally I knew they would dismiss it, caricature it and generally ridicule it. In one sense I was worst placed to speak about it. No one has sympathy for politicians and the media, and politicians (and me especially) have to spend much time cultivating them. So the charges of being self-serving, hypocritical and disingenuous are easy to make. I was still determined to make the speech, because, in another sense, only someone with that experience of dealing with them, and with the position and office of prime minister, can dare articulate the criticism.

I wrote it having got up at 4:30 a.m. and just set it down in one draft. I confess as I read it later, live on TV, before an audience of journalists, I somewhat quailed. It was written as felt, and the feeling was strong.

However, the argument was right: the fact that the media now works by impact, which leads to sensation, crowds out a sensible debate about policy or ideas. What's more, the media is 24/7, incredibly powerful and yet without any proper accountability. When they decide to go for someone, they are, as I said, like "feral beasts." But more than that, they are also, partly through the presence of competition, highly partisan in order either to get maximum impact or to put across the views of their proprietors or editors.

Anyway, you can imagine how it went down! Though even today, people both at home and abroad mention the speech to me. Despite the best efforts to distort or discard it, it had cut through.

The last weeks were dominated by the Scottish elections and then the final preparations for leaving. I had now pencilled in the date of 27 June, after the G8 and European Council summits. During that time we hoped to bring the Northern Ireland peace process to final fruition and restore the power-sharing executive, and I was working flat out on that.

We had an interesting contretemps with Iran when they arrested fifteen Royal Navy personnel on 23 March. The Iranians said they were trespassing in Iranian waters, which we were sure was wrong, but it created some anxious days. Though I was outraged by the Iranian action, I played it very cool. The only thing that mattered was getting them back, and soon, so we went the diplomatic rather than confrontational route, despite criticisms for doing so. Unfortunately, some of the personnel were paraded on camera looking as if they were being overly friendly to their captors; and when they were released twelve days later—a "gift" to Britain, as President Ahmadinejad called it—some gave accounts to the papers. This caused much synthetic fury, especially among those papers who hadn't got the story. I just felt sorry for all of them. They were in a totally unexpected situation with little or no experience in dealing with anything like that, so I was inclined to overlook any lapse of judgement. But it occupied the nation's mind for days.

We put forward proposals for reforming the House of Lords. Gordon was signalling he wanted an elected house. Jack Straw had become an advocate for partial election and proposed options. I went along with his recommendation, but personally, as I cheerfully told the Liaison Committee at my last appearance before them in June, I thought it mad. There's a huge head of steam behind it now, though I still somehow doubt it will actually happen.

The House of Lords is a funny old place, a uniquely British institution. Though I'm naturally attracted by iconoclasm, in this instance I think the uniqueness is worth preserving. Hereditary peers are a nonsense and really can't be justified, but the argument between electing and appointing members is far more balanced than the proponents of election ever allow. The danger with appointment is cronyism, place-menship, patronage and so on, but that can be countered by a different system of nomination, as indeed the House of Lords Commission introduced in May 2000 now ensures.

The danger with election is that you end up with a replica of the House of Commons, the only difference being that you elect those who for one reason or another can't get into—or don't want to get into—the Lower House. The whole benefit of the existing House of Lords is that you are able to put in people who have not spent life as a full-time politico, who aren't replicas or ersatz versions of MPs, but who have a different and deeper experience or expertise. For example, to have had someone like Ara Darzi as a lord and a health minister—someone who is a surgeon and knows all about the new frontiers of medical care—is a huge bonus for the political talent pool. Indeed, the ministers in the Lords often turn out to be among the most able, but I doubt many, if any, would want to put in the political apprenticeship necessary to stand for election and become an MP.

Also, it depends on the function you want the House of Lords to perform. If it is a revising chamber, even better to have a different type of member in it. If you want a competing chamber, then I accept that the case for an elected house is stronger. But look around the world at the examples of such bicameral competitiveness, and there aren't many working well; or, at least, not many that don't lead to significant grid-lock. So all in all I was against it.

The election campaign for the Scottish Parliament got under way in April. We had won twice before, but this time would be much harder. We were also coming up to the ten-year anniversary of the government. This was a huge achievement for the party, the first time it had ever got near such a milestone and I thought there was a real chance to focus on some of the successes of that decade.

The truth is, whatever anyone might say, and whatever has happened subsequently, between 1997 and 2007, Britain had ten years of unin-terrupted economic growth. (I deal later with the causes of the 2008 crisis.) The living standards of the poorest 20 per cent improved sig-nificantly compared with the Tory years. Pensioners stopped dying for lack of heating every winter. The NHS was taken out of the news as a crisis case, and waiting lists and times improved, in some cases by leaps and bounds (where was it as an issue in the 2010 election?). In 1997, there were nearly a hundred London schools with fewer than a quarter of pupils getting five good GCSEs. By 2007, it was way down to two. The academy programme was now roaring ahead. It was the only government since the war under which crime had fallen rather than risen. We had introduced a plethora of individual items of change, from the first statutory minimum wage through to vastly expanded maternity and paternity leave through to gay rights and Sure Start for children. Inner cities in Birmingham, Bristol, Leeds, Liverpool, Manchester, Newcastle, Nottingham and Sheffield were regenerated. There was a huge new constitutional settlement and reform. And while many disagreed with the decisions on Iraq and Afghanistan, in 2007 Britain counted in the world, had a strong alliance with America and was a key player in Europe. There was also Northern Ireland. Taking a step back and examining it, the decade had been reasonably successful.

As 1 May approached, we started, unbelievably, to get that message out, and by the time of the anniversary itself, we had narrowed the polls almost to evens. Given we were now absolutely midterm, and given the wretched "cash for honours" inquiry, it was quite something.

I decided to go and campaign vigorously in Scotland. There was a feeling I shouldn't, but I was equally clear I should go and put real credibility on the line. The Scottish local elections were also being held, all of which gave me an opportunity to get out there and remind people what I could do.

The Scottish Labour Party responded brilliantly, whatever they might have felt privately. Lesley Quinn, the organiser and General Secretary, was a real trouper, tirelessly flogging them all on. I did a mixture of visits, speeches and Q & A sessions, some planned—as with a well-prepared speech on devolution—and others more of the stump variety. The audiences had to be fairly carefully selected, however. By then it was clear that anyone who disrupted anything could wipe off any other news, and the media were in a state of constant vigilance to get such a moment of destruction. I also did some more light-hearted media, which involved fairly quick-fire repartee rather than gravitas; but it was all pretty good-natured.

I even got to visit the street in the Govan district of Glasgow where my dad used to live. It was odd to think of him in that poor part of the city all those years ago, collecting his lemonade bottles for cinema money, living in a corporation tenement, a wee Glasgow laddie whose son would one day become prime minister.

The election result came and we nearly won it, losing by only one seat. As the count drifted into recounts and the whole thing hung in the balance, I thought for a short while that Jack McConnell might pull it off. But no; by the narrowest of margins, the Scottish National Party and their leader Alex Salmond were in. Had we had greater belief in ourselves—the assumption being we couldn't win—I think we might have done it.

I was concerned about my own position in respect of both the Scottish and the Welsh campaigns. I wanted to complete Northern Ireland and set out the forward policy agenda, but I knew some people, with understandable feeling, thought I was being selfish in staying on through these campaigns. With a new leader we could have done better, and in particular it is possible with Gordon we would have won in Scotland. Jack McConnell was loyal and decent enough to deny this to me, but I wasn't sure he meant it. On the other hand, people knew change was happening, so it was hardly sensible to vote against someone who wasn't going to be there in a few weeks anyway. It was very frustrating. I knew once Alex Salmond got his feet under the table he could play off against the Westminster government and embed himself. It would be far harder to remove him than to stop him in the first place.

The speeches were going well—not in the sense that they were getting big coverage, but they were well received by those who received them, as it were, and they did amount to a serious corpus of argument about what we had done and why in the ten years in power. Throughout those final months, I was still charging forward with decisions.

I visited Wales a few times also. I could tell the Welsh First Minister Rhodri Morgan, who was a Gordon supporter, was not wildly enthusiastic about my participation in his election, but he handled the visits with good grace.

The news from Iraq continued to be worrying, but as a result of the decision to surge it was clear it could be turned. I made a visit to Baghdad and Basra, thanking the troops for what they had done. Down in Basra they were continuing to be mortared almost daily. As we sat in the compound, one landed nearby, and I knew it must be hellish to be living with the constant fear. Amazingly, the troops themselves stayed in good heart; but I could tell that the senior officers thought our utility in Iraq had ended and they chafed at the bit to get stuck into Afghanistan, which was just beginning to be a bigger problem.

Late in April, I met the family of one of the soldiers who had died on a very difficult and risky mission. I brought them into the den in Downing Street. These are emotional, highly charged meetings. Families deal with grief in different ways. Some grieve as if what has happened is an

inevitable risk, especially in the life of a combat soldier. They are honest enough with themselves to know that we have a volunteer not a
conscripted army, and that their loved ones died doing what they
wanted to do. Others feel the injustice of a young life ended and want
someone to blame. Others still are a mixture of sentiments, some of
grieving, some of grievance.

On this occasion, the wife of the soldier had her two young children
with her, both toddlers, neither of whom would ever know their father
except from snatches of their mother's memory. The parents and
parents-in-law both had military backgrounds and so understood, but it
was uneasy nonetheless. I didn't justify any decisions or make a case. I
just let them ask questions and then I asked them about him, and they
painted a picture of him with pride.

After about forty minutes, I asked to spend some time alone with the
widow. We talked for a bit and suddenly I was overcome with tears.
When you meet such people and realise what effect your decision has
had on someone's life, and by extension the life of a whole family,
something changes within you. You have to have the sensibility to feel
it; and then, without ever losing that sensibility, the courage to overcome it, take the decision and move on despite it.

Of course, much of this reflects the impact made by the person
before you, the real-life reminder, the physical manifestation of a decision. In more objective and detached moments, you can reflect on other
decisions where you may never meet or even appreciate the real-life
consequences of a decision because those affected never stand before
you: the millions helped in Africa, including, incidentally, those helped
by the Bush PEPFAR (President's Emergency Plan for Aids Relief)
programme; those walking the streets in Northern Ireland; even those
saved by the NHS. Or those who have been casualties of decisions
delayed or mistaken, whom you never hear about and can never know.

Whether the decisions' consequences are before our eyes or not, ultimately you have to go on living, go on working, go on striving. But you
do so conscious of the duty born of the impact your decisions have had;
and with an imperative urgency that in my case I know will not leave
me until the day I die.

In the run-up to the European Council, I was also visiting capitals—
Paris, Berlin, Warsaw and elsewhere—trying to drum up support for a
strong resolution on climate change. I saw Nicolas Sarkozy in early May
straight after his election victory. He was in great form, vitality in every

sinew, ambition and determination in lockstep, full of enthusiasm for the challenge ahead.

I recalled seeing him at Downing Street just before the campaign began and he was as bouncy and confident as ever. He had vast plans for France, for Europe, for the world. "God," I said to him after twenty minutes of this, "you sound like Napoleon."

"Thank you," he replied straight-faced; then I looked closely, and saw with relief that twinkle in his eye.

This time in Paris, first over drinks and then over dinner in a restaurant near the Elysée Palace which he walked to greeting startled onlookers as if he were still fighting for every last vote, he repeated his desire for me to be president of Europe when the Lisbon Treaty was agreed. I, a little self-consciously, went along with it and could see its attractions; but I also knew (as it turned out indeed) that it was going to be incredibly difficult to get someone like me into that job. I had respect in Europe; I had a lot of enemies too, people I had crossed, people to whom I had paid insufficient attention. I was a big figure, not someone easy to have around if you were worried about your share of the limelight. I thought Nicolas himself had a relaxed view of big figures around him because of his self-confidence. Others would not see my presence as European president in that way.

He was fascinating company—engaging, energetic and with that captivating French bravado around women, life and laughter that I loved. I liked too the fact that he was a "my way or no way" person. He had the spirit certainly to demand change, and to get it or go. And I was very sure that was the only way to get the necessary reforms fast. But, as ever, it is one thing to propose in theory; another to execute in practice. In that first flush of limitless possibility which characterises the new incumbent, I saw something of my own feeling ten years before. "It will get tougher," I warned him.

"Of course, I know that," he replied, in exactly the way I would have done, when you think you know; but until you have the experience, knowledge is deeply imperfect.

I saw Angela Merkel around the same time, and was rather chagrined to be leaving just as she and Nicolas were arriving. She had been Chancellor for almost two years, but it was clear she was only now establishing herself fully. By this time I was getting on with her really well and liked her immensely.

On 8 May, Northern Ireland came good, with power-sharing

restored. On 9 May, I told the Queen I would announce the next day when I was to stand down. On 10 May, I travelled to Sedgefield as prime minister and as their MP for the last time. It was there that the journey started, and there that it should end. I gave my valedictory speech and announced that I would leave on 27 June, just after the European Council. That left six weeks for a leadership contest or process and then handover for the summer break so that Gordon could play himself in.

Finally, I did a bit of a farewell tour to highlight things we had done and try to bolt it all down. I went to Sierra Leone; to Libya; to South Africa, to emphasise the importance of governance as well as aid to Africa's future. We held the first government-sponsored, high-level interfaith conference. There was the G8 at Heiligendamm in June; a NATO session at Rostock; and then of course the EU Council. I had seen George for the last time in May. I saw the Pope at the Vatican in the middle of June. And, as it sounds, it all passed in a bit of a blur.

The policy documents from the "Pathways to the Future" pro-gramme were coming out, but Gordon had rather lost interest and the country was looking forward to the new man. The deputy leadership contest for the party had several contenders. It was clear that the GB camp was backing Harriet Harman, who went on to win. Alan Johnson never quite got lift-off, though he made it to the last round and by rights he should have won. Jon Cruddas did well. As the out-and-out moderniser, Hazel Blears scored only moderately, but fought a good campaign.

There was no contest for the leadership. John Reid could have stood, but the Murdoch papers, I fear at Rupert's instigation, just wrote him off, though John was obviously more in tune with *Sun* readers than Gordon. This was where Gordon's strategy of tying up Rupert and Dacre really paid off—any likely contenders didn't get a look-in; they got squashed.

David Miliband came to see me. Two years later he would be a dif-ferent calibre of politician, with clear leadership qualities; back then in May 2007, as he sought my advice, he was hesitant and I felt fundamen-tally uncertain as to whether he wanted it. And that is not a job to be half-hearted about. He asked me if I thought he should stand and I said I couldn't make that decision for him. "What would happen if I did?" he asked.

"I think you might win, not obviously but very possibly," I replied.

David thought, with good cause, that Gordon had it sewn up. I didn't think so actually, and I also thought the moment there is a campaign and people start to flush him out, the ambiguities in his position, the gaps in hard thinking and also the trading off to the left, would become apparent. Played correctly, it would put full square the choice of New Labour or not.

But David was unconvinced. Some then and later criticised him for being too cautious. Personally, I really sympathised. This wasn't like me in 1994. This was a wholly different order of calculation of risk. I didn't blame him at all, but I did say he should be prepared in case the issue arose again, sooner than we might think. I thought by then that a) it was going to be a mess, not quite New Labour, not quite not; and b) as a result, Gordon's self-evident personal drawbacks would very quickly turn into a pretty brutal attack for which he was not psychologically wired. With a strong clear programme he could have come through. Without it, he would be running on his personality and that was never going to work.

Man to man, as it were, we got on fine; I just totally disagreed with what I knew he was going to do. But I had realised the impossibility of changing it. I wrote him one last memo in February 2007, though not with any confidence it would persuade. I can't say I can hold it against him. From his point of view, he had waited ten years for the damn job. He could be forgiven for thinking: Why doesn't he just clear off and let me get on with it? So we talked through some issues, gauged our thinking on the up-and-comers for promotion and it was all perfectly amicable.

In the memo I explained that there were only two ways that Labour could win the election. One was a decisive rupture with my time in office, what I called "Clean Break." But that would require a new and credible agenda. The other was "Continuity New Labour," i.e. keeping to New Labour but using it to address the new challenges. I told him, however, that he could only win on the second, as he was part of the previous ten years. Any distancing and he would drift off slightly to the left, just enough to destroy the New Labour coalition. I laid out a plan for us to coordinate and cooperate in the months before I left so that he was seen as authentic New Labour, and not a traditional Labour leader.

In conversation after conversation, I tried to explain that he didn't need to worry about separating out from me. That was obvious; he was a completely different personality. The contrast in character would be sharp. But if he attempted to switch the basic track of policy, he would end up shunted off in a siding that led nowhere.

I reread the note now and I'm afraid it is precisely what he should have done and didn't. The Budget was a great chance to bind in a joint legacy, and to consolidate the fiscal position, but the people he felt closest to didn't really agree. He could talk to me and at one level respect me, as I did him, but the intimacy was broken. As with me, so with Alastair. And Peter. And Philip. He could absorb what we said and see its force, but deep down he didn't feel the same in the guts, as it were; and those with whom he was intimate actually disagreed with it in their guts. It was never going to work.

It's really hard to say all this, and I have thought long about it. There's nothing worse than "oh if only he had listened to me" rubbish, and so, after trying valiantly not to fall into self-justifying mode—a bane of political memoirs, I fear—it's a pity I have. Yet I look at those policy papers now—the work on social exclusion, on the use of social security budgets, on structural financial savings, on tax reform, on the next phases of crime, health and education reform—and I do think how different it would have been if we had done it. If we had struck out to a new level of New Labour and not wandered into a cul-de-sac of mixed messages and indecision, we would have been so much better placed for the economic crisis; and so far ahead of the Conservatives in thinking. But there it is. It didn't happen, and that is that. The milk was spilt. The weeping and gnashing of teeth is pointless.

So we come to the final few days.

It was strange to be bowing out. I was at the height of my powers, if not my power. I knew I was a much better prime minister in May 2007 than in May 1997. I still felt highly motivated and energised. I was convinced that the policy agenda I had been working on was the only viable one for Britain's future. It probably had support in the country too, if explained effectively. Yet I was leaving.

My constituency in the media had evaporated. They admired the showmanship and political skills, but they had ceased listening to the political argument. They were bored. They were cynical. Iraq still caused too much bitterness and obstructed sensible analysis of the broader picture. They had bought the GB package, though I felt their motives were very mixed in doing so. Some on the left genuinely thought he would deliver a leftist programme. I had a hunch those on the right principally thought he would deliver a Tory government.

For my part, I thought I had gone as far as I could at that moment in time with that constellation of political circumstances. Gordon had me hemmed in. Many senior members of the Cabinet had no real sense of the policy divide between us, with notable exceptions like John Reid and Tessa Jowell. Many of the others could see which way the wind was blowing and thought: Let's get on with it.

I had toyed with the idea of staying in Parliament. I knew pretty soon the problems with Gordon would emerge and the party would not know what to do; but I also knew that although there would be a clamour for me to return from some, fiercely rejected by others, there would be the most frightful falling-out and the pitch would be queered for anyone else. Neither could I engage in the political debate while he was leader. If I did and said even one word that was a millimetre out of place, there would be accusations of disloyalty and disunity. So I decided I had little option but to leave the UK political scene, at least for now.

As for the country, they too, or at least a large proportion of them, had stopped listening and were irritated with the manner in which I continued to press policies they had decided they didn't agree with. They didn't buy the foreign policy, which they thought far too close to the U.S. They didn't like Europe and I seemed to. They were persuaded there were easier, less confrontational ways to reform public services. They were confused over the law and order agenda, supporting its basic message but unconvinced we were actually enforcing it.

Most of all, they were being bombarded, deluged even, with stories about "cash for honours," "lies" over Iraq, this corruption, that scandal, the other shortcomings of government. We were like two people standing either side of a thick pane of glass trying to have a conversation. I thought, and still think, that they could be persuaded, but when I spoke they couldn't hear me; and after a time they stopped trying to.

When I ventured out and met people, which in those last months I did very frequently, the people I met would not have the pane of glass in the way. We would converse very well and both found the experience interesting. Right up to the last moment, I was really learning from those encounters, but they can never be with more than a tiny fraction of the people. The rest can only engage indirectly, and for them, the pane of glass swiftly becomes a pain in the neck.

For me and for the people, this was sad. My relationship with them had always been more intense, more emotional, if that's the right word, than the normal relationship between leader and nation. It was partly the sensation of the 1997 victory; partly New Labour; partly that I communicated and felt normal at the beginning, and then over time seemed to become distant, aloof, presidential, and therefore full of my own importance but not of theirs. Of course, part of the media worked hard to construct this image and then make it stick.

However, it was more than that. In 2005, I had an unusual polling presentation by Charles Trevail of Promise Corporation. Their theory, which at the time I found amusing and diverting but far-fetched, was that my relationship with the British people was more like a love match or marriage. At first, the people felt an abnormally close bond. They trusted and liked me. Then in the second term, I suddenly left and went off on a foreign adventure, almost on an affair. I stopped caring about them. I became arrogant. I seemed to think I had grown bigger than them; or to put it another way, we grew apart and I found Britain too small for my egotistical ambition. I used to make them feel good; now I just sounded irritated that they wouldn't go along with me.

Charles said they had never conducted research on a person and seen such strong feelings aroused. Indifference was virtually non-existent. Now, Mrs. Thatcher aroused that strength of feeling, but that was about her policies; this was about me as a person. Some hated, some loved; but they talked about me as someone they knew not just as a leader but as an individual. The predominant view, however, was that I had lost that common touch which had defined the earlier time in office and which had created the bond.

I was certain part of this derived from the nature of the job. People see you on the news every night—serious face, serious issues, laying down the line, other people saying nasty things, PMQs and its confrontation, all messy, all off-putting. Occasionally I would step into an arena that was different, as I had done with the Des O'Connor interview in 1996. In March 2006, just before the "cash for honours" imbroglio began, I appeared on the chat show *Parkinson*. Again it showed the other side and really worked. Kevin Spacey was the other guest and got it just right, chafing me about George Bush but in a funny way that had no malice in it. It was to be part of a major effort to reconnect on a personal level, but once the "scandal" broke, it was stillborn.

However, I came to realise that this almost inevitable distancing over time was not at the core of the problem. The problem was that I was doing things, not just in foreign policy but more broadly, that were generating opposition and disagreement; and I wasn't budging. The left hated the support for America and public service reform; the right hated the support for Europe, the style of the government and, most of all of course, the fact we were still in power and they were still marginalised.

The difference between the TB of 1997 and the TB of 2007 was this: faced with this opposition across such a broad spectrum in 1997, I would have tacked to get the wind back behind me. Now I was not doing it. I was prepared to go full into it if I thought it was the only way to get to my destination. "Being in touch" with opinion was no longer the lodestar. "Doing what was right" had replaced it.

I knew this was causing upset in the matrimonial home in which I and the nation had lived happily together. It seemed arrogant; conceited even. But it wasn't that I had run off with another woman. I had reached the conclusion that the family wouldn't prosper and be taken care of unless we lived life differently. I wanted to move location. I could see the world changing rapidly. I could see our place in it needing fundamental and quick adjustment. The comfort zone was not where we needed to be. This time, the feeling was not about the party. It was about the country.

I looked at the G8—and this was before the economic crisis in 2008—and I realised that there was no way it could survive. China, India, Brazil and others would demand a seat at the table; and if they didn't get one, they would get their own table. I saw the danger for Europe of a G2: U.S. and China. And then, if we weren't careful, a G3: U.S., China and India. Or a G4: U.S., China, India, Brazil. And so on. In other words, we had to face the fact that Britain is a small island of 60 million people off the continent of Europe, in a world where two nations alone would each have populations twenty times ours and, in time to come, economies to match. How absurd and futile to believe we could be Little Englanders in such a scenario, or ignore the vast importance of our U.S. relationship.

As the new economies emerge, we have to compete. How? By brains and skill, by moving up the value-added chain. By working harder. By competing on merit, on ability. To do that, our education system and welfare state have to be reformed not more cautiously but more boldly. I could see the twentieth century left/right debate of Western politics dying on its feet, still swinging the odd punch but essentially just getting in the way of the practical debate about what needed to be done, and done urgently.

I looked at the NHS and was proud of the change we had made, but I was in no doubt: as technology advances and people live longer, there is no way that health care systems of developed nations can survive at reasonable cost and with a minimum level of equity in provision, without putting individual responsibility and public health policy at the centre of the debate. I have described already how I saw the problems of nineteenth-century criminal justice procedures trying to cope with twenty-first-century crime and social dysfunction.

The point is that it wasn't dissatisfaction with the relationship that was driving me; it was a sense that unless I spelt out the necessity to seek a different context in which to nurture that relationship, I was not being honest or trustworthy. The irony was, right at the moment when, to my detriment, I was being most open about what needed to be done and why, my integrity was most under question.

I had taken the fourth step, the incalculable risk, and imbibed its lesson. I was now embarked on the fifth: doing what I thought was right, even though the people disagreed. I had started by buying the notion, and then selling the notion, that to be in touch with opinion was the definition of good leadership. I was ending by counting such a notion of little value and defining leadership not as knowing what people wanted and trying to satisfy them, but knowing what I thought was in their best interests and trying to do it. Pleasing all of the people all of the time was not possible; but even if it had been, it was a worthless ambition. In the name of leadership, it devalued leadership.

None of this meant or means that the leader should not seek to persuade, and in doing so use all the powers of charm, argument and persuasion at their command. That's tactics, and they should be deployed effectively and competently. The strategy should be to point to where the best future lies and get people to move in that direction.

As I have said, in those last weeks, we were going full pace, both at home and abroad. Inside the Downing Street flat we were packing up. I don't suppose there has been a period when the prime minister has had so much time to prepare the leaving. There were vast boxes full of the accumulated detritus of ten years. It was the longest time I had ever lived in one place. Leo had never known anywhere else. However, I am not sentimental about houses. When I left Downing Street and Chequers, I was sad to leave the people, but I didn't mope over the physical structures. It's lovely to live in historic and beautiful places, but it's not of the essence. Home is where the family is.

I got back from my last European Council on the Saturday, and then went up to Manchester on the Sunday for a special party conference to announce the leadership results and the handover to Gordon. I made my speech, shortly and without emotion—I had done all that at the last party conference. I could see they were eager to get on with welcoming the new era. Also, I was now, in my own mind, anxious to quit the stage. The farewells had to be gone through, with dignity and if possible with elan, but without mawkishness.

I made a statement to the House on the European Council on Monday 25 June. On Tuesday I did my last visit as prime minister. It was to a primary school and was, in a surreal touch, with Arnold Schwarzenegger, the governor of California, who had come to Downing Street for a meeting on climate change. As he walked down the line of children who had been sent out to greet him, one infant piped up—in a slightly halting rehearsed tone, obviously having been tutored by one of the teachers who must have been ignorant of Arnold's films—"Hello, Mr. Governor. I did like watching your film *The Terminator.*" I hastened to tell him we might have misheard. Anyway, he was great and the schoolkids were delighted.

Next day, the Wednesday, was my last PMQs. I knew it would be weird. There was no point in me trying to advance things; no point in the Opposition trying to criticise things; no point in anything other than try to take one's leave decently. The first thing, however, was to send condolences from the House to the families of fallen soldiers. Having done so, I also said the following:

> Since this is the last time that this, the saddest of duties, falls to me, I hope the House will permit me to say something about our armed forces, and not just about the three individuals who have fallen in the last week. I have never come across people of such sustained dedication, courage and commitment. I am truly sorry about the dangers that they face today in Iraq and Afghanistan. I know some may think that they face these dangers in vain. I don't, and I never will. I believe they are fighting for the security of this country and the wider world against people who would destroy our way of life. But whatever view people take of my decisions, I think there is only one view to take of them: they are the bravest and the best.

At the end, I gave some words in support of politics and politicians, which I also felt strongly about and knew the House would welcome:

> Some may belittle politics but we who are engaged in it know that it is where people stand tall. Although I know that it has many harsh con-

tentions, it is still the arena that sets the heart beating a little faster. If it is, on occasions, the place of low skulduggery, it is more often the place for the pursuit of noble causes. I wish everyone, friend or foe, well. That is that. The end.

David Cameron kindly got them to give me a standing ovation; and there it was. I went back to say farewell to the staff at Downing Street, and unlike in 1997, they were now crying at my leaving, not my arrival. The family posed with me one last time on the steps of Number 10. I went to the Palace, said goodbye to the Queen who was, as ever, very gracious; and got on the train to Sedgefield to say goodbye to my constituency too.

I felt calm and at peace. I felt there was unfinished business; but then I consoled myself with the thought that the business is never finished. I was on to my new life. I had always been fortunate in having a passion bigger than politics, which is religion. I had, have, new ambitions now. I have come a long way on the journey, but I am painfully aware I have much further to go. There are greater steps and larger lessons that lie ahead. Maybe in time a more complete assessment of the ten years will come. Maybe not. But my own assessment of it no longer depends on whether it does or does not.

In any event, the knowledge that the journey continues, the excitement at the new challenges to be explored, the sense of purpose that is as great as ever, make me a very fortunate human being. There is so much frailty still to overcome, but in overcoming it lies the meaning of life. That, at least, I have learned.

TWENTY-TWO

POSTSCRIPT

The term "the West" is a bit of an old-fashioned throwback to the days when the world was split by Communism, but it serves as shorthand for "our" type of nation: open, democratic, committed to a market economy, confident militarily (certainly since the fall of the Berlin Wall), and led by the world's only superpower, the U.S. For almost twenty years after 1989, the West set the agenda to which others reacted. Some supported us and some opposed us, but the direction of the globe, the destination to which history appeared to march, seemed chosen by us.

True, certain cracks in the edifice had begun to appear. There was even the odd hole punched in the outbuildings. New forces were busy building something different, not far from where we were. But it was our model that still imposed itself and commanded most attention. So it looked in June 2007, when I left office.

The three years since then have seen something of a revolution in that apparently unassailable order. The economic crisis of 2008 ruptured our confidence in the rationality of the market economy. The war in Afghanistan hangs in the balance. The Obama orgy of expectation, despite the brilliance of the president himself, has settled into something more recognisable and routine. The rise of China is there in real life, visible and pulsating, a fact, no longer an interesting intellectual conjecture. Power is shifting east. Other nations such as Brazil and Turkey grow assertive, no longer seeking permission to play a role, but simply playing it. The European Union is in trouble, and for once the word "crisis" is not an exaggeration but a description. We in the West remain democracies, but we have never had less respect for those we elect.

We thought the ultimate triumph of our way of life was inevitable. Now it is in shadow. Our confidence is low and our self-belief is shaken. Most of all, we feel weak, at points almost listless. The future, once so firmly in our grip, seems to have broken loose in search of new masters. Read much of our media, and that's how it is: malaise, decline, impotence, challenges unmet, promises unfulfilled.

Personally, I have never felt a greater sense of frustration or indeed a greater urge to leadership. I enjoy my new life much more than my old one, and find in it huge purpose. I am fighting for my world view, but in a different manner from that of being in conventional office. I have tried to gain a bigger and deeper understanding of the world. China is no longer such a mystery, though that is only a relative sentiment. The Middle East is endlessly fascinating and frightening. I see the economy from a broader and different perspective in business. In my two major charitable areas—Africa and faith—I find complete spiritual as well as political satisfaction.

I'm living life full tilt, but I find my old world in a state of despair and feel both shocked and galvanised by this. Perhaps that is because I am removed from it and so think I see it more clearly. (This could be an illusion.) Perhaps it is because some of the *bouleversement* is directed at precisely what I represented in office: liberal economic policies, market reforms in welfare and public services, and engagement and intervention abroad. For whatever reason, a chapter that I intended to write as a postscript now resembles more of a credo.

To summarise: I profoundly disagree with the statist, so-called Keynesian response to the economic crisis; I believe we should be projecting strength and determination abroad, not weakness or uncertainty; I think now is the moment for more government reform, not less; and I am convinced we have a huge opportunity for engagement with the new emerging and emerged powers in the world, particularly China, if we approach that task with confidence, not fear. In short, we have become too apologetic, too feeble, too inhibited, too imbued with doubt and too lacking in mission. Our way of life, our values, the things that made us great, remain not simply as a testament to us as nations but as harbingers of human progress. They are not relics of a once powerful politics; they are the living spirit of the optimistic view of human history. All we need to do is to understand that they have to be reapplied to changing circumstances, not relinquished as redundant.

The dramatic and far-reaching impact of the financial crisis of 2008 is still being played out. It will probably register in history as the most significant economic event since the 1930s. The facts of what happened are well known and don't require repetition, but the interpretation of them is and should be a matter of enormous debate.

Almost at once, as occurs now in virtually any such drama, a conventional wisdom arose that was extremely resistant to challenge. It has gone roughly as follows: there was a catastrophic failure of "the market," necessitating a rescue by "government" and a Keynesian reflation to counter the deflation. In late 2008, banks were stabilised by the injection of government support; regulatory systems began to be overhauled in order to bring the rogue financial sector into line; deficit spending became economic policy.

Politically, all of a sudden, the state was back in vogue. The market-led reforms of the 1980s and '90s appeared wrong. The economic growth was said to be a delusion based on debt. Above all, government was in the ascendant. You could almost touch the *Schadenfreude* of large parts of political and academic opinion as "the market" was exposed as having been bereft of clothes after all.

This led progressive politicians, on the left especially, to assert that politics was going to undergo a radical shift of direction towards a more interventionist and statist position. This seemed to accord with the change in mood in the U.S. (though I was never sure President Obama really shared this line). It signalled the end of an era that began over thirty years ago with the Thatcher/Reagan economic and political philosophy.

Disentangling all of this and putting it in some order is a hugely difficult task, made much more difficult by the fact that challenging any part brings a fair amount of criticism, since it is a conventional wisdom that is so entrenched. But we do need urgently to unravel it and come to a better and more considered view.

First, "the market" did not fail. One part of one sector did. The way sub-prime debt was securitised, spliced and diced and sold on with no real appreciation of underlying risk or value was wrong, irresponsible and immensely damaging. Some of the rewards, the huge payouts for shuffling around securities, the bonuses, are not just presentationally awful; they can't be justified and, at worst, have helped create a propensity to "do the deal" whatever the long-term merits for short-term gain, in a way that significantly contributed to the crisis. All this is correct and should be acted on. However, such practice should not define or represent the whole of the banking sector, let alone the whole financial sector, let alone "the market."

Second, government also failed. Regulations failed. Politicians failed. Monetary policy failed. Debt became way too cheap. But that wasn't a conspiracy of the banks; it was a consequence of the apparently benign confluence of loose money policy and low inflation. The responsibility for the crisis should be shared, not borne by the market alone or even by the banks alone.

Third, the failure was one of understanding. We didn't spot it. You can argue we should have, but we didn't. Furthermore—and this is vital for where we go now on regulation—it wasn't that we were powerless to prevent it even if we had seen it coming; it wasn't a failure of regulation in the sense that we lacked the power to intervene. Had regulators said to the leaders that a huge crisis was about to break, we wouldn't have said: There's nothing we can do about it until we get more regulation through. We would have acted. But they didn't say that.

Fourth, financial innovation is not bad per se. Actually, very often it is good: it increases liquidity and boosts economic activity. The danger lies in innovation that has consequences we don't understand, and effects which we therefore can't track.

Fifth, when a crisis occurs—and I suspect this may be true of any significant economic crisis today—its consequences are magnified beyond any comparison with days of old by the supremely interconnected and interdependent nature of the modern global economy. It impacts in its own right; and then the impact is multiplied through that elusive but profoundly powerful force called "confidence."

I am not suggesting confidence is just some airy sentiment unconnected to the facts. The arithmetic, naturally, determines the fundamentals of the confidence. But the swings in confidence derive, in part, from the psychology of how the arithmetic is being handled, and that depends crucially on the politics. The equation revolves around the interplay between arithmetic, psychology and politics. So the arithmetic remains uncertain, the politics unclear, the psychology therefore troubled, and confidence therefore erratic.

When I say we have to disentangle the conventional wisdom, I mean this: it is absolutely right that the state intervened at the outset of the crisis—not to have done so would have been ideologically blind and practically stupid; the problem, I would say error, was in buying a package which combined deficit spending, heavy regulation, identifying banks as the malfeasants, and jettisoning the reinvention of government in favour of the rehabilitation of government.

Funnily enough (or perhaps predictably enough), the public has got this more than many politicians and commentators, which is why the great lurch leftwards has not materialised. The public understands completely the difference between the state being forced to intervene to stabilise the market and government back in fashion as a major actor in the general economy. The role of government is to stabilise and then get out of the way as quickly as is economically sensible. Ultimately the recovery will be led not by governments but by industry, business, and the creativity, ingenuity and enterprise of people. If the measures you take in responding to the crisis diminish their incentives, curb their entrepreneurship, make them feel unsure about the climate in which they are working, the recovery becomes uncertain.

This is even true of the financial sector, however heretical it sounds to say it. Of course there should be a regulatory overhaul, but most of all there should be systems of national and global supervision that enable us to understand this new financial world and to track it, so that we can intervene where the risk of systemic failure demands it. What there should not be is a wholesale attempt to predict every potential crisis and construct rigid rules in advance to prevent it. That way we risk flattening our financial system, squeezing the innovation out of it, trying to return it to the world of yesteryear, which is neither sensible nor economically productive. One result will be that as the banks do less, the state will have to do more. At present, we have gone from irresponsible lending to the other extreme whereby even worthy businesses and customers are refused credit. Indifference to risk should not be and need not be replaced by aversion to risk. For example, credit default swaps and derivatives are not in themselves a bad thing. On the contrary, properly used and understood, they can be immensely helpful. So understand them, supervise and regulate them when necessary, but don't treat them as a consequence of greed. Treat them for what they are: new financial instruments to be used with care.

My preference is to approach regulation with caution, not to deny the financial sector a say in putting it right since it was the author of the wrong, but to deal with it as a partner in trying to achieve the correct balance between supervision and regulation, global and national action, and diminishing risk while allowing innovation.

As for the state itself, and the role of government, that also should be regarded as suitable material for reform, as part of the problem and not just part of the solution. For one thing, the fact that anxiety over the economy has shifted from banking practices to sovereign debt should illustrate how foolish it is to ignore government and state responsibility for what happened.

The eurozone crisis has not created the sovereign debt issue; it has merely exposed it. The truth is that over an extended period of time, the developed world has been moving—but with far too much hesitation—towards reform of their welfare, public service and governmental organisations. Ageing populations, declining birth rates, greater expectations and changing social conditions have been confronting us, ever more insistently, for decades. The economic crisis should have been (and indeed still can be) the moment when, instead of lazily succumbing to the idea that more state spending dressed up as fiscal stimulus is the sole answer, we used the crisis as an opportunity to accelerate and sharpen reform. Getting value for money in services like health care, opening up competition in areas like education, radically altering welfare so that it becomes a genuine safety net for those who need it and a leg up for those who can and should stand on their own feet, and at every point questioning, reassessing, changing, not so as to abandon social solidarity but to make it effective in a changed world; that is what we ought to be advocating as progressives and embracing as nations.

Take two examples: procurement and pensions. With the first, there is no doubt we could get far better value if we adopted practices the private sector has long regarded as axiomatic. But we still confuse the aspects of public services that are genuinely different in scope and purpose from private services, with means of doing things common to both, and where they are done either efficiently or inefficiently. Procurement during my ten years came a long way, but it is nowhere near where it should be and could be.

In respect of pensions, I favour the link between earnings and pensions because of National Insurance contributions. But as a society we need to ask ourselves what we really mean by retirement now. In our developed world, people expect to be still energetic in their late sixties and beyond. Maybe I am an exception, but I would regard the idea of stopping work at sixty as absurd; horrifying, in fact. Now we can change gear, even change job, so it makes no sense to analyse the world of 2010 through the eyes of my grandfather.

Step by step we have been feeling our way towards a new paradigm of the state and the services it provides, how technology can save money through new ways of working; flexibility in professional demarcation; outsourcing, and so on. But the crisis simply brings home to us the need to speed it up.

Which brings me to the related issue of deficit spending. Again, there is no doubt that in the event of the sharp contraction and credit crunch of 2009, governments needed to stimulate domestic demand. However, there are two important qualifications on such action. The first is that when a historical analysis of stimulus packages is conducted, I think we will find that the specific and targeted measures, e.g. for the car industry, were the most effective.

The second is that the operation of such deficit spending needs to be calibrated with immense care in the circumstances of the global economy of 2010.

Keynes was a great man, a revolutionary thinker, a rare example of an outstanding intellectual who could give practical advice. I bet he would be surprised at how his theory is being applied today.

In the 1930s, the amount of public spending relative to GDP in the UK was 26 per cent, in the U.S. 19 per cent. In 1950, after a world war, it was 34 per cent and 24 per cent. Today, it is 47 per cent and 45 per cent.

Of course there was a need to have a fiscal stimulus as demand dropped sharply in 2009. Keynes' insight was that the state should act to lift demand if the consequence of contraction was a spiral downwards of shrinking growth, cuts to spending, resulting in even less growth and so more cuts. But it was never clear that the effect of 2008 was going to be a savage fall in growth that continued over years. The savage fall was itself partly due to the psychological collapse of the markets after the Lehman Brothers failure, leading to a collapse in confidence, leading to people deserting the market, cancelling investment and retreating to the bunker. What I noticed in 2008–9 was that even those with money were hanging back. Once the market stabilised, they came out of the bunker and recommenced activity.

The danger now is this: if governments don't tackle deficits, the bill is footed by taxpayers, who fear that big deficits now mean big taxes in the future, the prospect of which reduces confidence, investment and purchasing power. This then increases the risk of prolonged slump. So yes, fiscal consolidation has to proceed with care. There is a need to balance the opposite impacts of deficit reduction: less overall demand, because of a contraction of government spending on the one hand; more confidence among consumers and businesses due to reining in the deficits on the other. There is a judgement to be made. But if we fail to offer a convincing path out of debt, that failure in the global economy of 2010, as opposed to that of the 1930s, will itself plunge us into stagnation.

The other vast difference today is the position of the emerging economies. They are a wholly new dimension and have their own fragility, but essentially they will keep on pushing forward. Ironically, they will continue to embrace liberalisation at the very point we seem to lose faith in it. Their risk is either failure to implement their own government reform (e.g. India) and/or that through policies that stagnate growth we curtail the market for their goods (e.g. China).

So, if we take Europe, what Europe needs is a package of measures: a carefully calibrated deficit reduction plan; the fundamental reform of the European social model, the need for which the crisis has highlighted, not created; regulation that tracks systematic risk but does not suppress innovation and enterprise; and, for the eurozone, the fiscal coordination that a single monetary policy was always going to require.

But it is a package. Do one part and not another and we risk a worse crisis. In particular, cut the deficit and reduce incentives, or fall short on true structural reform, and the imbalance in measures will cause the package to fail, or at least significantly reduce its effect.

Consider the issue of Greece or Spain. If they have, as I hope they do, credible policies to sort out, in the former case the deficit, and in the latter the financial health of their banks linked to the deficit, the euro will stabilise if accompanied by far-reaching reforms. The market will recover and the reforms, necessary in any event, will make both countries more competitive. The result will not be to change the fundamentals of the economy the West has been developing over many decades, but to provide adjustment and reform to make them work more effectively.

What should strengthen this belief is that the new economies now rising up in the rankings are doing so precisely by following more open economic policies, and faltering when they don't. China is opening up, and thrives as it does so. India needs less bureaucracy and less state power, not more. President Lula's success in Brazil is partly because he continued the anti-inflationary macroeconomic policy of his predecessor Fernando Cardoso. The economies in the Middle East, like Saudi Arabia, are focusing today on competitiveness and removing barriers to enterprise, not erecting them. It would be odd if we moved in the opposite direction. And foolish.

However, we may recover our confidence faster on the economy than on security. I have set out my explanation for Iraq, how it happened, what went wrong and why I still believe the decision was nonetheless right. Now Afghanistan hangs in the balance in a similar way. As in Iraq, we remove a regime that is hated, and do so with good intentions. The citizens of the country seem to intend the same, but we are thwarted by those with the opposite intentions. Over time, the issue ceases to be who is well intentioned and who is not, and becomes the apparent inability to overcome the forces against us and secure a definitive "victory." So our allies lose heart, our public loses faith, and we ask: When and how will it end?

This is a picture moving fast; and with each evolution of political or military struggle, things can look different month to month, even week to week. So trying to stand back and see the picture clearly is hideously difficult. I will go right back to the first principles and try to put it in simple, even crude terms.

What is the nature of the threat? It does not derive from something we have done; there was no sense in which the West sought a confrontation. This is essential to the argument. The attacks of 11 September came to most of our citizens as a shock that was utterly unforeseen. Countries like America and Britain were not singling out Muslims for unfair treatment; and in so far as Muslims were caught up in generalised racism towards those of a different race or colour, such attitudes were on the way out, not the way in.

The extremism we fear is a strain within Islam. It is wholly contrary to the proper teaching of Islam, but it can't be denied that its practitioners act with reference to their religion. I feel we too often shy away from this assertion, as if it stigmatises all Muslims. But if it is true—and it is—it has to be faced, not just because it is true, but because otherwise we don't analyse the problem or attain the solution properly. If it is a strain within Islam, the answer lies, in part at the very least, also within Islam. The eradication of that strain can be affected by what we outside Islam do; but it can only be actually eliminated by those within Islam.

Most problematically, there is a (natural) tendency for us to believe that the best way to empower those within Islam to take on the extremists is to reach out and meet people halfway. Let me explain what I mean by this, because it is at the root of our present policy dilemma.

The conventional wisdom is that the Bush/Blair position was wrong because it confronted when we should have reached out. It is accepted by many that Afghanistan was a justifiable conflict; Iraq was not. Iraq then "caused" a schism between the West and Islam, it is said, that made it harder for our allies to get traction within Islam to take on the extremists. Our policy towards Israel is likewise seen as one-sided and that fuels the view of the West as inherently inimical to Islam. Turkey's rebuff from the European Union is seen similarly.

President Obama's speech in Cairo in June 2009, which was a brilliant exposition of the case for peaceful co-existence, marked a new approach, and if he is given the support and partnership he needs, it is an approach that can combine hard and soft power effectively. While hanging tough in Afghanistan, he has reached out. The speech was carefully calibrated. The hand of friendship would be offered, even to Syria and Iran. It was in part an apology, and taken as such. The implicit message was: We have been disrespectful and arrogant; we will now be, if not humble, deeply respectful. But join us, if you will.

The trouble is: respectful of what, exactly? Respectful of the religion of Islam, President Obama would say, and that is obviously right; but that should not mean respectful of much of the underlying narrative which many within Islam articulate in its policies today.

Here is where the root of the problem lies. The extremists are small in number, but their narrative—which sees Islam as the victim of a scornful West externally, and an insufficiently religious leadership internally—has a far bigger hold. Indeed, such is the hold that much of the current political leadership feels impelled to go along with this narrative for fear of losing support.

This is a situation with practical consequences. Iraq and Afghanistan are seen as the West's battles. With a few notable distinctions, this is not perceived as a struggle for the heart and soul of Islam. Yet the outcome is surely vastly determinative of such a struggle.

I have my criticisms of Israel and my ideas of to how to make progress, set out in earlier chapters. But leave aside for a moment the details of the peace process. As I started to spend more time in Palestine, I was surprised to find it is often easier to raise money for the "resistance" than to fund the patient but essential process of Palestinian state-building. Israel can and should do more to push forward the necessary changes on the ground—the West Bank and Gaza—that can underpin the peace process. However, it is also true that if the Palestinian cause gave up violence emphatically and without ambiguity, there would be a peace agreement within the year. Not enough voices in the Muslim world are asking them to.

It is America today that leads the challenge to Iran and its nuclear ambitions. But let us be frank: Iran is a far more immediate threat to its Arab neighbours than it is to America. It is of course a threat to us, too, but this is partly because of what a nuclear-armed Iran would mean for the Middle East, rather than as a direct threat.

The problem is this: defeating the visible and terrifying manifestations of religious extremism is not enough. Indeed I would go further: this extremism won't be defeated simply by focusing on the extremists alone. It is the narrative that has to be assailed. It has to be avowed, acknowledged; then taken on, inside and outside Islam. It should not be respected. It should be confronted, disagreed with, argued against on grounds of politics, security and religion.

If we argue this case confidently and persuasively, it will give strength to those within Islam who know this argument has to be had and yet hesitate. They hesitate because they are afraid of being left out there alone, because we in the West, who are their allies, tacit or overt, find it all too hard, too wretched and above all too long a battle to contemplate.

Which brings me back to Afghanistan, though I would make the same point about Iraq. What is happening in Afghanistan is really very simple: our enemies think they can outlast us. Our enemies aren't alone in thinking that. Our friends do, too. Therefore the ordinary folk think: I should make my peace with those who are staying, not those who are going.

And our people say, "How long are you seriously saying we should hold out?" If, in the 1950s, when faced with the threat of revolutionary Communism, I had asked you how long you expected us to fight it, you would have answered: As long as the threat exists. If I had said it may be for decades, you would have raised an eyebrow, as if to say: Well, if the threat remains for decades, what choice have we? In other words, you would have seen this as a clearly defined threat to our security that left us no alternative but to take it on and beat it. Of course, there were those who said "Better red than dead," but that was surely one of the least appealing slogans to the human spirit ever devised, and only a minority bought it. Most people realised the threat was real and had to be confronted, however long it took.

The difficulty with this present battle lies in defining what "it" is.

After 11 September the phrase "the war on terror" was used. People distrusted this, partly for its directness, partly because it seemed too limited. So we dropped it. Yet if what we are fighting is not a war, what is it?

The threat is obvious enough: weapons of mass destruction in the hands of those who would wage mass destruction. If they could get a dirty nuclear device, they would use it. But the threat is more than this. The movement also has the capacity to destabilise governments and take over countries, some of which are immensely important to our security and strategic interests, not simply in a selfish sense but to those of the global community. That's why Iran matters. Iran with a nuclear bomb would mean others in the region acquiring the same capability; it would dramatically alter the balance of power in the region, but also within Islam. Then there is the actual war in Afghanistan.

However, the threat is more than that, too. Like revolutionary Communism, it is an extremist movement, not just a series of extreme acts. It doesn't begin on the battlefield, it begins in the school. It starts not with talk of military weapons, but with talk of religion. You have to take on the clerics who foment the extremism, not just the people who engage actively in terrorism; and empower those clerics who will stand up for what is right. The ideology is not born of a desire for military domination; it is born of a world view based on belief in God's will. Not only its narrative but also its ideology has to be systematically dismantled, just as it has been systematically constructed.

We need to link what happens as the latest car bomb detonates in Kabul or Baghdad to what is taught in the madrasas of Pakistan, or about the rights of women in Yemen. We need a religious counter-attack, not just a political or military one. Iraq is just one part of this picture, as is Afghanistan; and so are the deaths in the Philippines, Bombay, Kashmir, Chechnya and Karachi—anywhere this ideology has a connection, however remote.

So the answer to the question "How long should we hold out?" is: "As long as is necessary to defeat the extremism." Sometimes it will mean fighting. Sometimes it will mean preaching. Sometimes—as with the Israel/Palestine question (not the cause of the extremism but a powerful tool in the hands of extremists)—it will mean peacemaking. But at every level, in every respect, in each and every one of its locations, among different peoples and political contexts, it has to be confronted and beaten.

We need to mobilise and support the modernising forces within

Islam, those who embrace peaceful coexistence. But most of all, they need us to be strong, to show determination, to show this is a fight in which we have our heart and soul. What they fear, much more than us being overbearing, is us being weak.

We need the suasion in argument of Obama (or Clinton) and the simplicity in approach of Bush (or Reagan). We need an intellectual case, brilliantly marshalled, combined with a hard-headed ability to confront. Now is the time to do it. From the years since 11 September we have learned we haven't beaten the threat, and we can't beat it fast. It still threatens us. The question is: have we learned that we have no choice but to beat it and so the only issue is how?

In doing this, we should renew confidence in our way of life and the values it represents. This is no more a simple issue about our national security than the battle against Communism or fascism was. In those battles, we knew what we were fighting for: not just our nations' freedom but the freedom of humanity, the idea that tyranny and extremism are the enemies of the human race, not of individual countries. In conducting those battles, we were inspired by more than a desire to win: but also by belief, by a passion originating in the interests of progress, to consign the forces of darkness back into the darkness in which they belong.

We need some of that inspiration and passion now. When we read of car bombs driven into crowded streets, in whatever part of the world, our response should not be one of resignation or despair, but of outrage, indignation and, above all, resolve.

In this, America and Europe should stand together. Together we should take it on; together we should reach out and persuade the new powers to join us. There is no challenge facing the world today that would be met more easily if the U.S. and the European Union stood apart. Not the challenge of the economy, and certainly not the security threat. Of course the geopolitical power structure is changing. China, India, Brazil, Russia and, in time, Indonesia, Mexico and others demand, rightly, to be treated as equals and partners. But, to state the obvious, they do not all share the same interests or views. Alliances in each case will be different, but none of those alliances will work better with Europe and America at odds. None of the opportunities will be easier to grasp; none of the challenges easier to handle.

I find the insouciance towards the decline of the transatlantic relationship, on both sides of the ocean, a little shocking. There's a feeling that it belongs to an era that has passed. This is to misunderstand the way the world is changing; or perhaps better put it is to look at the issue upside down.

It is said: new powers are emerging, therefore we should seek deeper relationships with them and there is less need for the old relationship. Yet it is precisely because the relative power of Europe and America is changing as new powers come on the stage that it is sensible for the two to combine. Just as the European Union is necessary to increase the power of the individual nations, so the U.S. and the European Union should work together.

Possibly we have not yet internalised the true significance of China's rise (or indeed that of India). I now travel to China frequently. There are many riddles to be solved about how it will be in the future, and even those most intimately connected with the decisions live in a state of uncertainty, but some things we do know: the country is opening up at an extraordinary rate. Its economic and political power, already vast, is only a fraction of what it will be. Its people are smart, determined and fiercely proud of their nation. The varieties of ethnic and racial group-ings, the diversity in different parts of the country, the almost unimag-inable scale of the challenge of development—all of these things are understood, though their full consequences are still tricky to divine. But the will to overcome the challenges, the desire never again to let China slip into unfathomable obscurity, are sentiments that define the character of the country and its leadership.

We need to offer China the partnership that it is in both our interests to have. And strong partners are always better than weak. A divided West, competing for favours with the new powers, is sensible for no one.

For Europe, the starkness of the choice and the challenge is greatest. After all the debate over the Lisbon Treaty, it now has to make some very straightforward decisions. These are not about more process, which Europe loves to debate endlessly. They are about policy direc-tion. If Europe wants to be strong, capable of partnering the U.S., China and others, and also attractive as a partner, it has to focus on cer-tain fundamental decisions.

First, it should make full use of the economic crisis to redefine its social model, coordinate fiscal and monetary policy, liberalise the single market and therefore get the benefits of European cohesion. It should match the budget to the priorities, not fit the priorities to the budget.

Second, it should create a genuine European defence policy which concentrates on combat capability. Europe needs to be able to field significant numbers of troops, plus logistical and technological backup, with the will, the desire and the ability to engage in fighting the new type of insurgency and terror campaigns. This requires not only organisation and cooperation, but also a debate within our societies about how we approach the military engagement, and in particular the casualties we will inevitably face if we engage. There is no place for this other than with the men and women prepared for the risks and willing to undertake them, who need to be rewarded accordingly.

Third, Europe would gain enormously, economically and in terms of leadership, by adopting a common energy policy. A unified grid is not a physical impossibility, and the savings would be huge. The differences in policy over nuclear power, for example, can be overcome by accepting there will be such differences, but there will be many areas of cooperation. It would reduce costs to business and consumers dramatically.

Fourth, Europe has common borders and faces a common menace in illegal immigration and organised crime. This is not just about Schengen rules concerning asylum and immigration. It is about practical legislative and policing cooperation. Most of all, it is about an agreed approach: that we remain open societies free of racism but determined to impose rules and order on a system that otherwise, by its disorderly system for deciding and enforcing who comes in, fuels xenophobia.

Fifth, Europe has universities that used to be global leaders. The number of European universities in the top fifty or hundred today is an extraordinary rebuke to our capacity to modernise. Each nation will want to decide its own policy; but Europe could benefit greatly by agreeing certain key principles for reform, research and collaboration, at least among the elite group, and using such agreement to build the intellectual capital Europe needs to compete. Successful economies today depend on successful entrepreneurial institutions of higher education. Go to California and you will see how and why Silicon Valley came into being.

These are just five policy directions, but think how much difference they would make to Europe, not just to its economy but to its standing, its self-belief, its confidence about the future. It needs to stop thinking like a small country and start acting like a big one. This is not a point about big and small European states—actually, in today's Europe, all states are small compared to the emerging powers. That's why we need Europe to get bigger and stronger, and therefore more able to exert influence and shape events. This isn't an analysis born of a complex les-son of politics; it is a clear-cut, unvarnished lesson, self-evident since the first committee meeting of Neanderthals in a cave. Those with the power, count. Those without it, don't. But the stupidest thing is to have it but not know you do; or to be able to get it yet to be too timid to make the effort.

Where does the UK sit in all this? I don't want to repeat what I learned from 1997–2007. Let me concentrate on 2007–10. First, why did Labour lose the 2010 election?

The answer to that, I'm afraid, is obvious. Labour won when it was New Labour. It lost because it stopped being New Labour. This is not about Gordon Brown as an individual. It is true he is unsuited to the modern type of political scrutiny in which characters are minutely dis-sected. He was never comfortable as the "normal bloke" sort of politi-cian. As I say elsewhere, he didn't need to be. He had strengths: he was regarded as hard-working, with his heart in the right place, intelligent, and definitely committed to the country.

Had he pursued New Labour policy, the personal issue would still have made victory tough, but it wouldn't have been impossible. Departing from New Labour made it so. Just as the 2005 election was one we were never going to lose, 2010 was one we were never going to win—once the fateful strategic decision was taken to abandon the New Labour position.

At this point, some will be scratching their head. Did we abandon New Labour? Wasn't Gordon in the New Labour camp, especially after Peter Mandelson came back? The answers are yes and no. And here's why.

The economic crisis, strangely enough, was an opportunity. At first, we took it. It was here Gordon acted at his best, intellectually rigorous, totally driven, sure in his touch. The plan for the banks was right.

But then he decided that a paradigm shift had occurred. He bought completely the so-called Keynesian "state is back in fashion" thesis that appeared dominant. Alistair Darling was an excellent Chancellor but (I would hazard a guess) he was not given the chance to implement policy in the way he wanted. The top rate of tax was put up to 50 per cent; the 2009 Budget signalled a return to tax and spend; in 2010 the hike in National Insurance was the route taken to tackle the deficit; and the decision was made to fight on the grounds of cuts versus investment. Elsewhere, the academies programme was watered down and the thrust of public service reform weakened. Crime and antisocial behaviour were downplayed until too late. ID cards—actually the only answer to the immigration issue—were scaled back.

What should we have done? As I suggested in my analysis of the economy earlier, in my view we should have taken a New Labour way out of the economic crisis: kept direct tax rates competitive, had a gradual rise in VAT and other indirect taxes to close the deficit, and used the crisis to push further and faster on reform.

I believe such a programme is economically right. Its politics are also crystal clear. What happened in 2010 was that we broke up our coalition. We had done enough over thirteen years to avoid a wipeout. In certain areas support solidified, but the core middle ground—which brought us the seats in Hove, Hastings, Crawley and Dorset—deserted. They weren't at all sure of the Tories, as a matter of fact, but they were sure of us: we had become the old Labour Party. Funnily enough, the commentariat didn't always see it like that (the media became obsessed with the debates on TV), and from the news coverage you might think tax and spending weren't huge issues. But underneath, with the public, they were definitive. The voters knew that whoever was elected was going to take tough measures. The taxpayers, the aspiring people, the ones who agree with Labour on social compassion, but who need us to be sensitive to their desire to spend their own money, thought the Tories would go easier on them.

Tellingly, we lost business. This was crucial. When the Tories brought out thirty or so chief executives who were against the National Insurance rise, I knew the game was up. Some commentators waited for Labour to reply with their own group. I phoned Peter and asked if we had any. "No," he said, "they won't come out for us." The important thing politically is this. Labour's case in 2010 was that the Tories would put the recovery at risk. If thirty chief executives, employing thousands of people in companies worth billions of pounds, say it's Labour that will put the economy at risk, who does the voter believe? Answer: the chief executives. Once you lose them, you lose more than a few votes. You lose your economic credibility. And a sprinkling of academic economists, however distinguished, won't make up the difference.

What the public ended up doing, in that remarkable way they have, is electing the government they wanted. They were unsure of the Tories, so they put a strong Lib Dem showing alongside and urged them to get together. They elected a Tory version of New Labour. There's been lots of speculation about the possibility that there could have been a Labour–Lib Dem coalition. In my view, it was never on. The people would have revolted; the votes weren't there. The truth is that, on any objective basis, seven points adrift of the Tories, we were hammered. The fear of a meltdown, unrealised, made the heavy defeat seem a reprieve. But it only means we live to fight another day.

The danger for Labour now is that we drift off, or even move decisively off, to the left. If we do, we will lose even bigger next time. We have to buck the historical trend and face up to the reasons for defeat squarely and honestly.

Of course, you can point to the fatigue after thirteen years, the loss of trust over Iraq, the wear and tear that comes with power, but none of those things is determinative. We won in 2005 after Iraq, and the public were hardly likely to elect Labour under the prime minister who took the country into war, then wait five years to take it out on the person who didn't. The Tories' 1992 victory shows it is possible for a party to win again despite thirteen years in power. It could have been done. The 2010 election was our equivalent of 1992, not 1997.

If Labour wants to come back, it has to realise just how quickly defeat has altered the political landscape. It means the Tories get to clear up the economic deficit and define its nature, and can do so while pointing the finger of blame at the previous government.

If Labour simply defaults to a "Tory cutters, Lib Dem collaborators" mantra, it may well benefit in the short term; however, it will lose any possibility of being chosen as an alternative government. Instead, it has to stand up for its record in the many areas it can do so, but also explain where the criticism of the thirteen years is valid. It should criticise the composition but not the thrust of the Tory deficit reductions. This is incredibly difficult. Of course, the key factor in our economy, as elsewhere, is the global economic crisis and all nations are having to cut back and adjust. However, we should also accept that from 2005 onwards Labour was insufficiently vigorous in limiting or eliminating the potential structural deficit. The failure to embrace the Fundamental Savings Review of 2005–6 was, in retrospect, a much bigger error than I ever thought at the time. An analysis of the pros and cons of putting so much into tax credits is essential. All of this only has to be stated to seem unconscionably hard. Yet unless we do this, we cannot get the correct analysis of what we did right, what we did wrong, and where we go now.

Attacking the nature of the Tory–Lib Dem changes to public spending requires greater intellectual depth and determination, and each detail has to be carefully considered. So, for example, if we attack as we should the cuts to school investment, we have to be prepared to say where we would also make more radical savings than the new government. But it is better than mounting a general attack on macro policy— "putting the recovery at risk"—and ending up betting the shop that the recovery fails to materialise. It is correct that the withdrawal of the stimulus in each country's case is a delicate question of judgement, but if you study the figures for government projections in the UK, by the end of 2014 public spending will still be 42 per cent of GDP.

Such an approach is the reverse of what is easy for Oppositions, who get dragged almost unconsciously, almost unwillingly, into wholesale opposition. It's where the short-term market in votes is. It is where the party feels most comfortable. It's what gets the biggest cheer. The trouble is, it also chains the Opposition to positions that in the longer term look irresponsible, short-sighted or just plain wrong.

The real challenge for the coalition will be simple: the Tories and Lib Dems don't really agree. In many areas of domestic policy, the Tories will be at their best when they are allowed to get on with it—as with reforms in education. They will be at their worst when policy represents an uneasy compromise between the Old Labour instincts of the Lib Dems and the hard decisions the Tories will instinctively want to take; or where, as with the Tory and Lib Dem insistence on being the "civil liberties" proponents, they end up failing to meet genuine and legitimate public concerns about security.

On the other hand, they have a common interest in stability. The Lib Dems desperately desire the game-changer: electoral reform. And there are areas such as Europe where the Lib Dems will have a healthy effect on the Tories.

The Tories are the only party with options: they can work with the Lib Dems, in which case, fine; or they can cut them loose and seek a mandate on the basis that they are governing OK but could do better without the ball and chain. The Lib Dems have to cling on, or the coalition will be seen as a historic mistake.

Labour has no option but to be credible in its own right. That means, as I say, having a coherent position on the deficit. It means remaining flexible enough to attack the government from left and from right. It means being ready at any time to assume the mantle of government. It has to be permanently in contention.

Where the Tories will be vulnerable is where they always are vulnerable: their policies will be skewed towards those at the top, fashioned too much by the preoccupations of the elite (which is why they despised action on antisocial behaviour) and too conservative, particularly in foreign policy.

Labour should also focus attention on renewing the party, and it has to do this in a genuinely radical and modern way. I wish I had had the time to devote to this when prime minister, but the prime minister never does. We should use this period of Opposition to restructure membership, methods of selection, and policymaking. We should resist any notion of letting the now heavily amalgamated and concentrated trade unions get back any dominance in policy. We should link up with other modernising progressives across Europe and beyond, where at present our representation in government is pretty limited.

From this it can be seen that I still favour the third-way progressive politics, still believe it represents the best chance, not just for the centre-left but for the country; and indeed not just for the UK but for others too.

Many people on the progressive wing of politics, however, will read the analysis of the financial crisis and the security threat and say: But there are those on the right who can agree with that, so what's progressive about it?

The answer to that question is vital, decisive even of the fate of progressive politics. First, what makes you a progressive? I would say: belief in social justice, i.e. using the power of society as a whole to bring opportunity, prosperity and hope to those without it; to do so not just within our national boundaries but outside of them; to judge our societies by the condition of the weak as much as the strong; to stand up at all times for the principle that all human beings are of equal worth, irrespective of race, religion, gender (I would add of sexuality) or ability; and never to forget and always to strive for those at the bottom, the poorest, the most disadvantaged, the ones others forget.

Notice these are all values, not policies. They may beget policies. Hence the trebling of aid to Africa and the cancellation of debt during my time as prime minister (an example of great cooperation between myself and Gordon, rightly celebrated for his part in it). Or the investment in health, education and inner cities. Or better maternity rights. Or civil partnerships. Or the minimum wage. Or the winter allowance for pensioners. But we are defined by values that are static, immoveable, not subject to the ravages of time; rather than by policies which necessarily are ravaged and altered.

Second, it is true there are people on the right who might share some or all of these values and some of the policies. Today's Tories are committed to aid and development, and as a party, not simply as individual ministers. George Bush doubled the HIV/Aids programme of the U.S. It is also true that some programmes cross left and right. The Obama administration continues the Bush commitment to charter schools; David Cameron's government continues my commitment to academies. Sarkozy has socialist ministers in a UMP government. In other words, the policy space is now as much shared as in single occupation.

The point is: that's the way it is! And it's not a bad thing—in fact it's rather good, and the public, by the way, understood this ages ago. Defining where you stand by reference to the opposite of where the other person stands is not just childish, it is completely out of touch with where politics is today. Progressives should not fret about or feel threatened by such cohabitation. They should be entirely comfortable with it because, in being at ease, they have more chance to lead it.

In fact, the real risk—right or left—is that at the very moment when the public has lost its enthusiasm for traditional political divisions, the parties and their activists become more obsessed with them. The result will be a dangerous incongruence between "normal" people and "abnormal" political militants, which will only increase public disaffection with politics.

The differences of course between Tories and Labour or Republicans and Democrats may be great, and actually the financial crisis has, to an extent, brought them back in vogue (though I suspect the fashion is more dominant among politicians than people). The point is that these differences aren't necessary for progressive politics to remain progressive. And even where policies are in the same space, progressives will often slant them towards the poorest, whereas conservatives will not. You don't lose your identity as a progressive simply because you share space with conservatives. It is the new world, and we should get used to it.

The genius of Barack Obama was precisely that he reached out and over the partisan divisions. He did so explicitly. The desire of some of his present-day critics to drag him back from the centre is absurd. The espousal of centrist politics is not a betrayal. It was what he promised.

Third, there is a new divide in politics which transcends traditional left and right. It is what I call "open vs. closed." Some right-wingers are free-traders, others aren't. Likewise with the left. On both sides, some are pro-immigration, others anti-. Some favour an interventionist foreign policy; others don't. Some see globalisation and the emergence of China, India and others as a threat; some as an opportunity. There is a common link to the free trade, pro-immigration (controlled, of course) interventionist and pro-globalisation political positions, but it is "open vs. closed," not "left vs. right." I believe progressives should be the champions of the open position, which is not only correct but also a winning position, as Bill Clinton showed conclusively. However, it is a huge and important dividing line in modern politics.

Fourth—and tactically hardest of all for the centre left—progressives have to be proud of policies that lead to efficiency as much as those that lead to justice. Why? Because the lesson learned since 1945 is that driving value for money through public services is not a question of being efficient rather than just—it *is* just. Spend less on bureaucracy and you spend more on front-line care. To me, reform of health care, education, welfare and pensions was based on both efficiency and justice. Better services were also fairer. Likewise I was as keen on Bank of England independence as on a minimum wage; on encouraging business as giving people the right to be union members; on growth as much as tackling poverty. Now it is true some of those policies and even sentiments are sometimes more associated with the right; but that's our fault—and our bane, actually.

This will focus especially around the role of the state, which is why it is so important not to misread the political consequences of the financial crisis. Big-state politics today will fail. In fact if you offer "small state vs. big state," small will win. Even now, after the crisis. Progressives have to transcend that choice, and offer a concept of the state that actively empowers people to make their own choices and does not try to do it for them. So the state will be smaller, more strategic but also active— not a necessary evil, as some on the right would have it, but redesigned for today's world. In that world, the choices technology offers have undergone a revolution. Any political position that doesn't assimilate this is doomed.

So what is crucial is not to leave the people with a dilemma: a right-wing solution that at its worst is nationalistic, socially regressive and economically indifferent to the plight of the disadvantaged; or a left solution that unfortunately, whatever its good intentions, is a different form of regression, where we confuse the state with the interests of the people. Face people with that dilemma and there is a real risk they move right. Third-way politics is the only way out of it, for progressives.

There is also the issue of a general malaise about politics which is a real problem in Britain and elsewhere. This has crystallised around the supposed corruption of our representatives, but the MPs' expenses "scandal" is a metaphor for all that is wrong with the way the current debate about politics is conducted.

Back in the 1980s, there was a perfectly sensible solution to MPs' pay, put forward by an independent commission, the Review Body on Top Salaries, which proposed that rather than MPs voting on their own pay, it should be linked to that of a senior civil servant grade, and expenses would be strictly limited. Parliament should have passed this solution but it baulked at a time of pay restraint in the public sector. Instead, an unspoken pact arose: pay would not rise in line with such a link, but a regime bordering on total self-assessment was allowed on expenses. The abuses were clear and indefensible yet also entirely explicable. But the savaging of MPs as basically a bunch of wasters and fraudsters was unjust and deeply damaging. As ever with such an outpouring of outrage, the innocent or mildly stupid have been executed along with those who really did cross the line. It is a real shame that no one stuck up for the MPs. Instead, everyone competed in condemnation of them.

It is damaging because it also completely misses the point. The problem with the modern generation of MPs has nothing whatsoever to do with their character. On the whole, in my experience, of whatever party, they are a pretty public-spirited lot. The problem is lack of experience of real life, a huge narrowing of the talent pool for political representatives, and the obsessive nature of the activity required to get on the greasy pole of politics today. The very thing that people think is the issue—the absence of full-time dedication to the job of being an MP—is the opposite of the case. The problem is precisely that most MPs now come into politics from university, become researchers or work for political parties, get selected, get into Parliament and, no matter how able, have absolutely no experience of non-political life. As I described earlier, my seven years as a full-time barrister in industrial and commercial law were invaluable. They taught me how real people, real businesses and real life work.

There are exceptions, people who in later life turn their attention to politics and enter Parliament, but they are just that: exceptions. This, in turn, has another consequence: the best ministers are often now those in the House of Lords. The gene pool for ministers and MPs is now worryingly restricted. If this continues, it will not be long before we look at whether ministers really have to be drawn from the stock of MPs or lords. People are woefully underprepared for what running a vast department entails, and it shows. You end up with people who are great at the politics and lousy at the management.

Which brings me to another issue: it is probably less likely to be fatal to a political career to be bad at management than to be bad at politics. That is also a problem. A good politician can survive being a lousy manager, but a good manager will find it hard to survive being a lousy politician.

Each time I tried to bring, for example, a person from the private sector into government, I found that a part of the media would immediately try to find some angle to show they were suspect in some way. People who were prepared to forgo a large salary to devote time to public service ended up being done over as trying to get their feet on the ladder of corruption.

The role of the media in modern democracy is an issue every senior politician I know believes is ripe for debate. Yet it is virtually undebated, because the media on the whole resent the debate and inflict harm on those who attempt to engage in it, and the politicians are scared of the consequences of challenging powerful media interests. In an era of 24/7 media saturation, the absence of a debate about the media's impact, and how its interaction with politics affects the quality of the public discourse about political affairs, is objectively astonishing even if subjectively easily explained.

Every walk of life involving power is now subject to strong rules of disclosure, scrutiny and accountability, except one: the media. Just in the past few years, politicians have seen rules on fund-raising, earning, expenses and information revolutionised. Yet the average member of the public knows little or nothing about those who exercise far greater control over what happens in Britain than the average Cabinet minister, let alone the average MP.

Anyway I've made the point before. I dare say I'll make it again! It is actually part of a far bigger question which is this (and as I write, it seems a slightly curious way to put it, and I am not sure even now I fully see its implications).

Three years out of office have given me time to reflect on our system of government and to study other systems. I have no doubt democracy is the best system. And India remains the shining example of a large nation, still developing, that manages to be genuinely democratic. But I think there is a tendency for those of us in democracies to become smug about the fact that we are democratic, as if universal suffrage and no more were enough to give us good government.

The truth is that in order to function well, democracies need to be more than simply places where universal suffrage decides who governs. They also need to have the capacity, institutions, culture and rules to make it work effectively. Sometimes this will take time, which is why a nation like China, unlike India, will only be ready for simple democracy at a certain point in development. At present what it needs is well-intentioned leadership taking the decisions necessary for it to develop faster. Four hundred million people lifted out of poverty in twenty years is pretty impressive.

But the same also applies to countries that are developed and democratic but whose political systems are not delivering effective government. In other words, democracy itself needs to mature; it needs to adapt and reform as circumstances change. I would say that the way we run Westminster or Whitehall today is just not effective in a twenty-first-century world. Many might say the same about Congress and the U.S. The Civil Service requires a totally different skill set today from thirty years ago, far more akin to that of the private sector. I have already discussed the position and training of MPs.

Yet the debate, though it acknowledges that the public are disillusioned and disquieted, focuses exclusively on the issues of honesty, transparency and accountability as if it were a character problem. It isn't. It's an efficiency problem.

Provided we see the problem as one not of people but of systems, we cease also to be so worried about it. Yet if we lack the people, we really should be fearful. Systems can be changed.

I end on a note of optimism. My new life takes me round the world. There is a common theme to what I do. My theory of the world today is that globalisation, enabled by technology and scientific advance, is creating an interdependent global community, in which, like it or not, people have to live and work together, and share the world's challenges and opportunities. The drivers behind this are not governments, but people, and it is an unstoppable force. Its consequences, however, are a matter of choice. We can choose, in the face of this force, to co-exist peacefully, to be tolerant and respectful towards each other, to rejoice in the opportunities now available to us, and try to share them. Or we can see globalisation as a threat, as displacing our traditional way of life and culture, as undermining our identity. The first leads to a world at peace; the second to conflict. Both choices are on offer.

For us to choose peaceful co-existence, certain things need to happen and some of these I work on: peace between Israelis and Palestinians; respect between the four billion people of different faiths; progress in Africa; and protection of our physical environment. A global community requires values to match, values that are shared. Above all, it requires a world in which justice for the many, not the few, is the guiding light of global government.

In each area I am putting into practice something I learned and reflected upon when prime minister, but which only now I have the time to try and implement. In each case I have an unconventional view, based on my experience.

I do not believe we will see a peace agreement between Israelis and Palestinians based simply on a standard political negotiation. Don't misunderstand me—such a negotiation is necessary; but the real problem is a "reality" problem, not one resolvable merely by negotiation. The Israeli reality is security. The Palestinian reality is occupation. They are linked. Only when and if the Israelis are sure that a Palestinian state will be securely and properly governed will they agree to it, whatever its borders. Only when the Palestinians are sure that if they take measures to ensure proper governance and security, Israel will leave their territory, will they believe any assurances of statehood are credible. We need to build a Palestinian state not just through a process of negotiation but through building the institutions, capacity and economy consistent with a state—not one suitable for an agreement made and then left on the shelf, but one taking shape and root in reality; one achieved bottom up as much as top down.

I have always been more interested in religion than politics, but in the work my Faith Foundation does, the two overlap. To create peaceful co-existence in an era of globalisation, people of different faiths have to learn to understand and respect each other. The Foundation is highly practical. We have a programme that uses new technology to join up schools of different faiths so that from a young age children can learn about each other's culture and faith based on the truth, not on often deeply misguided perceptions. It operates now in twelve countries, and children of Christian, Muslim, Jewish, Buddhist, Hindu and Sikh faiths can take part.

We have a university programme, begun at Yale but now in eight other universities, to teach a course on the issues of faith and globalisation.

We have an action programme, which is to encourage those of different faiths to work together to implement the UN Millennium Development goals, and we have begun with the fight against malaria in Africa.

Africa is, naturally, another major area of work. Here the proposition is that, yes, aid is important; but what Africa really needs is help on capacity and governance. The money may be there for health care or agriculture support, but if the government doesn't have the capacity to deliver, then nothing happens. So we work alongside the presidents—for the moment in three countries, Rwanda, Sierra Leone and Liberia—to help them build basic effective levers of delivery. We hire teams of highly qualified young people (aged 25–35)—it may be from governments, the World Bank, McKinseys or private banks—who work on the ground alongside the president's team and build capacity, so that in time the locals can do it. They also focus on getting in quality private sector investment, which is essential. I work closely with the presidents and political leaders so that what we propose is not only technically sensible but politically doable.

Finally I work on business solutions to climate change, and with the Climate Group have produced reports aimed at practical and business-friendly ways of achieving a low-carbon economy. My idea here is that the only way to achieve political buy-in to reducing emissions is to make business the partner of change, not its victim.

So that's my new life. What makes me optimistic? People. Since leaving office, I have learned one thing above all: the people are the hope.

It is sometimes said that young people have lost their passion to do good; they're all just obsessed with getting on and the latest gadget. My experience is the opposite. The young people working for me in Africa are absolutely committed. All could earn better outside. All do it out of a drive to help bring about change. There are hordes of volunteers who work with my Faith Foundation, incredibly well motivated, fantastic, interesting, dynamic, young people, whose religious commitment is totally without prejudice against those of a different faith.

In Palestine, even when the politics are dark, what lights the situation up is the realisation that young Israelis and Palestinians are not inhabitants of a different world, polarised irredeemably by culture, religion and politics; they are striving for the same fulfilment and chance to do well, and are held back by a situation they would love to change.

In other words, for every bad event, malign conjunction of circumstances or individual act of hate, there are changes for the better, benign possibilities and above all people of good faith, good intentions and worthy actions.

My conclusion, strangely, is not that the power of politics is needed to liberate the people; but that the power of people is needed to liberate the politics. An odd thing for a politician to say; but then, as you will gather from this memoir, it has never been entirely clear whether the journey I have taken is one of triumph of the person over the politics, or of the politics over the person.

INDEX